W9-BSU-642

Degrees of Freedom
Canada and the United States in a Changing World

Unless Recalled Earlier

DATE DUE

DEC – 9 2002

DEMCO, INC. 38-2931

A compar   ses to the
changing i   f social diversity in d   ct of these
pressures o   itical institutions, an

The boo   a and the
United Stat   s have become more   e authors
conclude th   res clearly
constrain na   me areas,
distinctive c   distinctive
national resʲ   century.

KEITH BAN   Studies,
Queen's Un

GEORGE HO   Jniversity
of British Co

RICHARD SI   versity of
Toronto.

Degrees of Freedom

Canada and the United States in a Changing World

EDITED BY
KEITH BANTING,
GEORGE HOBERG,
AND RICHARD SIMEON

RECEIVED

JUL 2 6 1999

MSU - LIBRARY

McGill-Queen's University Press
Montreal & Kingston • London • Buffalo

F
1034.2
.D43
1997

© McGill-Queen's University Press 1997
ISBN 0-7735-1447-3 (cloth)
ISBN 0-7735-1448-1 (paper)

Legal deposit first quarter 1997
Bibliothèque nationale du Québec

Printed in Canada

McGill-Queen's University Press acknowledges the support received for its publishing program from the Canada Council's Block Grants program.

Canadian Cataloguing in Publication Data

Main entry under title:
    Degrees of freedom: Canada and the United States in a changing world
    Includes bibliographical references and index.
    ISBN 0-7735-1447-3 (bound).–
    ISBN 0-7735-1448-1
    1. Political planning – Canada. 2. Political planning – United States.
    3. Canada – Politics and government. 4. United States – Politics and government.
    I. Banting, Keith G., 1947–   II. Hoberg, George, 1958–   III. Simeon, Richard, 1943–
    FC635.D43 1997   320′.6′0971   c96-900973-9
    F1034.2.D43 1997

This book was typeset by Typo Litho Composition Inc.
in 10/12 New Baskerville

Contents

Tables

Figures

Acknowledgments

This book flows from a larger project launched by the School of Policy Studies of Queen's University as part of its mandate to conduct research on the forces that shape the modern policy agenda and the ways in which governments respond to it. Along the way, we have benefited from the support of a substantial number of institutions and individuals. Most importantly, we wish to acknowledge with gratitude the generous financial support of the Donner Canadian Foundation, which demonstrated its faith in the project at an early stage. Along the way, we have also received support from the Canadian Studies Program of the federal government and from Queen's University. In addition, George Hoberg would like to acknowledge a research grant from the Social Sciences and Humanities Research Council.

This book embraces such a wide range of subject matter that we can only acknowledge in general terms the large number of colleagues, students, and others who have helped shape our ideas. However, we would like to express special thanks to the contributors who joined with us and who shared the conviction that assessing the degrees of freedom enjoyed by the contemporary state is a fascinating intellectual challenge. We also wish to thank the two reviewers for McGill-Queen's University Press, whose suggestions helped strengthen the book considerably. The transition from manuscript to book depended on the skills and dedication of a very professional group of people. We would like to express our appreciation to Carlotta Lemieux for her meticulous editorial work, to Marilyn Banting for creating the integrated bibliography and the index, to Mark Howes for the preparation of the figures, and to Sharon Alton for her secretarial and administrative support.

Finally, we would like to thank our families, whose doubts about whether this book would ever be completed have now been laid to rest.

Keith Banting
George Hoberg
Richard Simeon

Degrees of Freedom

1 Introduction

KEITH BANTING, GEORGE HOBERG,
AND RICHARD SIMEON

The late twentieth century is an era of dramatic change. Governments in advanced industrial nations such as Canada and the United States are under powerful pressures from changes that are sweeping through both international and domestic life. A deep restructuring of the global economy is reducing the economic importance of national borders, and new technologies are transforming traditional processes of production. Exciting opportunities are emerging for those on the leading edge of innovation; but many jobs are disappearing, average incomes are stagnating, and the wider sense of security that most citizens enjoyed in the postwar years is eroding. At the same time, more complex domestic societies are emerging on both sides of the border. Greater social diversity, or pluralism, characterizes virtually every aspect of society: occupational and class structures, the racial and ethnic composition of the population, the forms of family life, the nature of religious practice, prevailing patterns of sexual behaviour, and the range of broad lifestyles.

International economic restructuring and increasing social fragmentation have produced a daunting policy agenda to which Canadian and American political leaders must respond. More critically, these changes often press in very different and competing directions, and the state is the point where they collide. On one side, the need to remain competitive in the global economy creates pressures to promote economic adjustment, to reduce detailed regulation of economic activity, to lower taxes on corporate activity, and to tame large budget deficits. On the other side, increasingly diverse social groups demand government action to advance a variety of reform agendas and to cushion the impact of dramatic economic change on workers and communities. In a sense, contemporary governments serve two masters. Each generates distinctive and often contradictory demands. One registers in exchange rates, investment patterns, and international agreements, the other in ballots and organized interests.

In Canada and the United States, as in many other Western nations, there is serious division over how government should manage these contradictory pressures. If government pursues a redistributive agenda, business and financial interests complain that their ability to compete in the global economy is impeded by the apparent incapacity of government to set its house in order; but if government pursues a competitiveness agenda, domestic social groups fear for the future of welfare, labour, and environmental programs. The inability of governments to fashion a consensus of these central issues is fuelling a crisis of confidence in political leaders and institutions. In both Canada and the United States, failure to deliver on public expectations contributes to a widespread disaffection, which shows up in numerous ways: in the intensity of public protests, in the lack of trust in political leaders, in the erosion of faith in existing political processes, and in the sudden emergence of protest parties and movements such as Ross Perot in the United States and the Reform Party in Canada. Not surprisingly, this disaffection further undermines the capacity of governments to build consent for major policy change.

In effect, deep-seated economic and social changes have eroded the social contract – the predominant understandings about core economic and social relationships – that was built up during the postwar era. The challenge for governments in Canada and the United States is to fashion a new accommodation between the economic and social pressures that increasingly define contemporary life. The gnawing concern centres on their capacity to do so.

This book is a comparative study of the responses of Canada and the United States to the changing international economy on one side, and changing patterns of social diversity on the other. It traces the implications of these pressures for the economic and social structure of the two countries, their culture and political institutions, and the policy regimes that each has put in place. Finally, it reflects on the capacity of these two countries to respond to the contemporary condition, and on the prospects for the establishment of a sense of common purpose about the future.

In comparing the responses of Canada and the United States, we seek to identify both their fundamental similarities and their fundamental differences. A common issue in all comparative study is whether to be impressed by and to emphasize differences or to be impressed by and emphasize similarities. One can build a strong case for focusing on either dimension in the case of Canada and the United States.[1] This study, however, seeks to capture both. Moreover, focusing on the ways in which the two countries are adjusting to a new economic and social order adds a dynamic element to the analysis, highlighting patterns of convergence and divergence between the two neighbours. We ask not only how they are similar or different, but also whether they are becoming more or less alike. Which forces promote convergence, and which drive Canada and the United States along different pathways?

Modernization theorists have long debated whether industrial societies in general are converging towards a common social and economic model.[2] In keeping with contributors to that debate, our analysis starts from the assumption that convergence and divergence occur in different dimensions of societies – economic, social, cultural, and political – and that relationships among these dimensions are complex. While related, they develop separately; some dimensions may show considerable convergence, and others may be marked by continued difference or greater divergence. Hence our concern to trace and explain the patterns of convergence and divergence between Canada and the United States in a variety of dimensions and across a number of policy areas.

We ask therefore whether the Canadian and American economies have become more similar as they have become more integrated. Similarly, have social changes made Canadians and Americans more similar in terms of their ethnic and racial backgrounds, their family and gender relations, their religious practices, levels of violence, and so on? Are the attitudes and beliefs that Canadians and Americans bring to their politics more similar than in the past, or do important contrasts remain? Do traditional differences in the political institutions and processes of Canada and the United States remain intact, or do the two systems increasingly resemble each other? And, finally, is there evidence of convergence in the policy agendas and the policy programs which the two governments put in place in earlier decades, or does public policy in these two neighbours reflect distinctive approaches to the problems of contemporary life?

By exploring these multiple dimensions, the book uses the comparison of Canada and the United States to illuminate three larger questions about the role of the state in the late twentieth century. First, are we witnessing a steady harmonization in the policy patterns of modern nations and the consequent fading of the rich diversity of national policy regimes that characterized the postwar world? Second, is the modern state still capable of developing creative responses to new problems, or is the state now so confined by international and domestic constraints that it is no longer an instrument of change and progress? How many degrees of freedom does the modern state retain? And third, in a more evaluative mode, how effectively is the state responding to the major economic and social issues that jostle for priority in the agenda of the modern state? Although the cases of Canada and the United States cannot answer such broad questions for all nations, the experience of these two countries is revealing.

APPROACHES TO THE STUDY OF MODERN STATES

Since the dawn of the state system in the Europe of the seventeenth and eighteen centuries, each state has existed at the point of intersection between the wider international system and its own domestic society. In the words of Theda Skocpol, "The state … is fundamentally Janus-faced, with an intrinsically dual anchorage" in domestic society and the international system (Skocpol 1979, 32). As a result, it must constantly mediate between pressures emanating from these two domains. In part, the role of the state is to protect domestic interests in the wider global environment, seeking where it can to nudge international developments in directions compatible with domestic preferences. In part, the state conveys to domestic society pressures emanating from the wider global context, adapting public policy and affected interests to international conditions that it cannot alter. In periods of relative stability, this process of mediation can seem relatively uncomplicated, as existing accommodations provide a template for responding to new issues. In periods of rapid change, however, new accommodations and new policy balances must be found. The late twentieth century is such a period for Canada and the United States.

The framework that structures the organization of this book flows from this general perspective. It can be summarized briefly. International economic change and new patterns of social diversity constitute powerful forces of change in both Canada and the United States. Not only are these twin forces altering the economic and social configuration of the two countries; they are also reordering the policy agenda that confronts governments. However, the way in which governments respond to these tensions is conditioned by the culture, political institutions, and policy legacies of each country. Cultures, institutions, and legacies are not immune to changes in the economic and social context within which they exist, but they tend to evolve more slowly. As a result, in both Canada and the United States they represent distinctive elements of life which embody long historical traditions and which help shape how problems are defined, the range of policy options that are actively considered, and the design of final policy choices.

Thus, our framework has three distinct components. First, global economic change and domestic social change are the dynamic, causal factors, or the independent variables in the language of formal analysis. Second are culture, institutions, and policy legacies, which we see primarily as mediators between economic and social conditions on one side and contemporary policy responses on the other. Hence, these mediating factors are themselves influenced by the economic and social environment; but they also help shape public policy responses to economic and social changes. In the language of social science, they are both dependent and independent variables. Third is the broad pattern of policy responses, seen as the dependent variable. One of our chief tasks is to analyse the relative weight of the first two components in accounting for policy change. Obviously, this is a much simplified model of the complexities of modern life. In the longer term, policy responses themselves become factors that influence the patterns of international and domestic change. Nevertheless, this simple framework helps to structure the chapters in this book and the assessments that flow from it.

This approach seeks to bridge a number of broad divides in the literature on advanced industrial states. First, we align ourselves with the growing trend to erase the division between international and domestic politics. However, most of the research that reflects this blending of the international and domestic domains has been oriented to increasing our understanding of how domestic politics influences international collaboration or foreign policy (Katzenstein 1978; Gourevitch 1978; Putnam 1988; Evans, Jacobson, and Putnam 1993). Several major works have emphasized, in a general way, the implications of the openness of a country's economy, as measured by its dependence on foreign trade, for its domestic politics and policy (D.R. Cameron 1978, 1986; Katzenstein 1985); others have emphasized how the international economic context affects the interests of different domestic groups and the resulting coalitions that coalesce in domestic politics (Gourevitch 1986). Overall, however, there has been strikingly little attention paid to the mechanisms through which international forces directly or indirectly influence domestic policy outcomes. By analysing the impact of economic globalization and domestic social fragmentation on public policy in a variety of fields, we hope to improve the understanding of this interface between the domestic and international dimensions of modern life.

Our approach is therefore different from the large body of literature that focuses on the dynamics of Canadian-American *relations*. One strand of that literature focuses almost exclusively on foreign policy and diplomatic relations between the two countries (Clarkson 1985;

Granatstein and Hillmer 1991; Hillmer 1989). Another strand emphasizes the asymmetry in the relationship between the two countries, with
Canada seen as the weaker partner ever more closely integrated with
its economically and politically dominant neighbour. Many of the contributions to this literature by Canadians are highly critical, seeking
ways to carve out a greater freedom from the American embrace, and
opposed to closer ties between the two countries. In the 1960s and
1970s, the literature focused on the implications of foreign direct investment in Canada (G. Grant 1965; Levitt 1970; Lumsden 1970; Rotstein and Lax 1974); in the 1980s and early 1990s, critics focused on
the Canada–U.S. Free Trade Agreement and the more recent North
American Free Trade Agreement (D. Cameron 1988; Warnock 1988;
D. Cameron and Watkins 1993; L. Martin 1993; I. Robinson 1993).
Although we give close scrutiny to the economic relations between the
two countries, we place these pressures within the context of other
forces shaping public policy. As will be seen in later chapters, where
students of Canadian-American relations tend to see inexorable pressures for convergence, we also see domestic pressures for divergence,
and greater room for differences in many policy areas. Where they see
convergence primarily as the result of American pressures – both
governmental and economic – we see other, less coercive, sources of
convergence as also being important. In the final analysis, ours is a
study not primarily of bilateral relations but of comparative politics
and policy.

Our approach also seeks to bridge intellectual concerns that often
do not intersect. On one side is the tradition of political economy,
which sees political action as rooted in economic structures and the
class imperatives they create, and tends to pay less attention to other
social forces that are reshaping the world in which we live (Panitch
1977). On the other side is the expanding literature on emerging
forces of social change – new social movements and the politics of diversity (B. Anderson 1983; Bibby 1990; Glendon 1991; Schlesinger
1992; S. Phillips 1994). Except at the most general level, this literature
pays little attention to economic influences and constraints. Our assumption is that fundamental change is occurring in both domains,
that they interact with each other, and that the fundamental challenge
facing all governments is the need to respond to both, a task that is becoming increasingly difficult.

Finally, we seek to incorporate the insights generated by the debate
over institutionalism. This, too, is a contested area in political analysis. A
number of long-standing intellectual traditions have emphasized the
dominant effects of economic and social factors in shaping public policy. The primary impulses that determine what governments do were

seen as emerging from the wider society, in some versions leaving only minor variations in the style, language, or timing to be explained by political or institutional factors. More recently, a new institutionalist literature has stressed the relative autonomy of politics and the state. From this perspective, economic and social conditions may generate stresses and strains in a society, but they do not dictate the way in which these tensions are interpreted in political discourse; nor do they determine final policy outcomes. Therefore they leave more room for the influence of distinctive political and institutional factors (Cairns 1977; Nordlinger 1981; P. Evans, Rueschemeyer, and Skocpol 1985; Weir, Orloff, and Skocpol 1988; March and Olsen 1989; Steinmo 1989). This book draws on both these approaches, finding the roots of changes in policy agendas deep in the economic and social changes that are reshaping both Canada and the United States, but seeing political and institutional dynamics as powerful shapers of policy choices and important sources of policy divergences between the two countries.

The perspective that pervades the book is thus a broad one and deserves somewhat fuller elaboration. The rest of this chapter introduces each of the components of the framework: economic globalization and social fragmentation; culture, political institutions, and policy legacies; and the patterns of policy response.

GLOBALIZATION AND SOCIAL DIVERSITY: FORCES OF CHANGE

The economic forces on which we concentrate have been captured in the concept of "globalization," the growing integration of the international economy.[3] The underlying dynamic here is the internationalization of manufacturing, and increasingly of services as well. Large firms now compete on the basis of global strategies, selling in worldwide markets and spreading production among a variety of nations; the international trading system has become intensely competitive; and financial markets are now linked on a worldwide basis through sophisticated telecommunications systems. The enhanced mobility of goods, services, capital, and information implicit in these developments generates strong pressures for the restructuring of domestic economies and has altered the world of work for countless people. Familiar occupational hierarchies are being shaken as the economic forces of "creative destruction" sweep away many unskilled jobs and expand the ranks of technologically advanced jobs. Moreover, the political balance between business and labour, and the economic equilibrium and links among regions have proved sensitive to international economic pressures.

Closer economic integration on a global level also tends to constrain the room for manoeuvre of individual nations. Not surprisingly, the tightness of these constraints varies from country to country, depending on size, wealth, and reliance on foreign trade. A hegemonic power, by definition, is able to define the international rules and to export the costs of its economic and social polices; a small, open economy is under much greater pressure to adapt. Clearly, there is a large initial difference between Canada and the United States here. Canada is, in the language of economists, a small, open, price-taking economy, whereas the United States for most of its history has been able to manage its domestic policies with relative independence from the rest of the world. But equally clearly, all countries – including the United States – have recently moved farther along the continuum from pure autonomy to constrained agent. As Gill and Law point out, "economic integration and interdependence create constraints for even the most powerful countries" (1988, 12). The decline of American economic hegemony, the shift from creditor to debtor status, and the dependence on foreign borrowing to sustain its trade and government deficits have clearly shifted the balance in that country. As John Agnew opens his book, *The United States in the World Economy*, "America has discovered the rest of the world ... They can no longer take their insulation or their superiority for granted" (1987, 1).

In looking at changes in domestic society, our study focuses on the common theme of increasing diversity, or social pluralism. Although both Canada and the United States have long-standing pluralist traditions, the pattern of cleavages has become much more diverse and variegated in recent years. Both countries have seen changes in traditional social divisions. In Canada, the dominant political divisions have centred on language and region; in the United States, on race. However, the influx of new immigrants and the political mobilization of aboriginal communities have added greater complexity to the politics of language, race, and ethnicity on both sides of the border. In addition, both countries have seen the mobilization of social groups, or new social movements, based on gender, sexual preference, religion, environmental concerns, and so on. These movements have generated a new "politics of difference" and have vigorously forced themselves into the political process, challenging the dominant frame of reference through which economic and social problems have been viewed, and sparking intense debates about diversity, rights, and social integration. This development reflects both domestic realities and an international flow of ideas. Movements for new forms of equality and environmentalism have transnational dimensions, and the relevant policy networks spill across national boundaries. Thus, the reshaping of traditional lines of division and the emergence of new social movements mean that governments in both Canada and the United States must make collective choices in a context of greater social diversity.

As noted at the outset, economic globalization and greater social pluralism are often in deep tension, generating conflicting pressures on the state. Global economic forces create imperatives towards greater competitiveness, efficiency, flexibility, and adjustment in the domestic economy. They constrain government spending and taxation; and by constraining the sovereignty of national governments, they may limit the scope for effective political democracy at that level. Social diversity at the domestic level often pushes us the other way, towards greater intervention in market processes and greater concern for equity, social justice, and redistribution. It pushes for more rather than less government in a wide variety of areas, and for greater concern with citizen participation and an enhanced quality of democracy. The resulting contradictions can be profound.

When globalization and pluralism are in conflict, governments exist at the centre of the tensions and hence must mediate between them. They use varying strategies to manage the pressures: for example, by trying to insulate economic policy making from normal domestic political pressures, or by trying to export the costs of the contradiction onto others, as the United States does through its monetary policy, or as Canada and the United States have done by exporting the costs to future generations in the form of deficits. But it is an increasingly difficult balancing act, and governments ignore it at their peril.

The intensity of the conflict between globalization and social pluralism varies from country to country. In some countries, the pressures for greater harmonization implicit in international relationships may actually imply an expanded role for the state, as the British resistance to the adoption of a mandatory social charter as part of Europe 1992 suggests. The negotiation of side agreements on labour standards and environmental protection as complements to the North American Free Trade Agreement suggests that Mexico may be under similar pressure; and in the final moments of the Uruguay Round of the General Agreement on Tariffs and Trade (GATT), Western nations such as the United States and France served notice that the social dimension will constitute an important element in the next round of world trade talks. In a similar fashion, pressure from consumers in the United States and Europe has forced Canadian governments to tighten environmental restrictions on the forestry industries, especially in British Columbia. In addition, it is important to remember that new forms of social pluralism at the domestic level can also have a conservative face, as witnessed by the social and religious sources of support for the new right in the United States. Clearly, in some contexts and for some interests, globalization and new forms of social diversity can reinforce each other. Moreover, the tension between these economic and social changes is likely to vary across policy sectors. Global economic forces press most directly on macro- and microeconomic policy; social forces are likely to leave their greatest imprint on cultural policy and the definition of rights. It is perhaps in social policy where the two sets of forces interact most powerfully. Our task, therefore, is to assess the nature of the relationship between globalization and social pluralism in Canada and the United States.

Chapter 2 starts to do this by mapping in greater detail the dimensions of economic globalization and social fragmentation as they influence Canada and the United States. As we shall see, economic and social changes are not impelling Canada and the United States towards an identical model. Many traditional differences persist and in some cases are growing greater, as in the case of the relative strength of organized labour. However, convergence does mark many other dimensions of economic and social life, from the narrowing of productivity differentials in the two economies to the impact of immigration on the social composition of the two populations. More important, however, is the powerful convergence in policy agendas. Prime ministers and presidents, members of Parliament and members of Congress, confront a strikingly similar agenda shaped in both cases by the imperatives of economic restructuring and social diversity.

CULTURE, INSTITUTIONS, AND LEGACIES: MEDIATING INFLUENCES

The book next turns its attention to culture, political institutions, and policy legacies, which condition the response to an increasingly common policy agenda. Here, too, we are interested in the impact of economic globalization and social diversity on these elements of Canadian and American life. However, our primary emphasis is on the role of culture, institutions, and legacies as mediating factors that condition each country's policy responses to globalization and social fragmentation, and therefore act as important sources of distinctiveness in national reactions to a changing world.

The political system and beliefs of a society tend to reflect long historical traditions and distinctive national experiences. As a result, they can often accommodate important social and economic changes without serious rupture. The general literature on modernization, for example, suggests that although there has been significant convergence in many aspects of the economic and social organization of industrial societies, their political systems and cultural patterns remain highly diverse (Kerr 1983, ch. 2). This is not to suggest that cultural beliefs and political institutions are immune to the imprint of changes in their context. However, changes in cultures and political institutions come more gradually than changes in economic and social structures, and this lag underlines the importance of the role of culture and political institutions in mediating between globalization and social fragmentation on one side and the policy responses of governments in Canada and the United States on the other. The way in which economic and social trends are defined, the range of policy alternatives that are actively debated, and the capacity to mobilize sufficient consensus for action all depend heavily on the beliefs, institutions, and processes that shape the politics of collective choice in each nation.

The analysis of the cultures of these two countries raises the dilemma noted earlier: whether to be impressed by and to emphasize similarity or difference. Much commentary, including Lipset's *Continental Divide* (1990), highlight the historical differences in the cultures of Canada and the United States. Yet one can also make a strong case for important similarities in the public philosophies of the two countries (Manzer 1985). This tension pervades public debate in Canada. The controversy over free trade was in large part about the cultural differences between the two countries and whether these could be preserved under high levels of economic integration. There is an irony here – the intensity of concern may have arisen precisely because of a sense that the differences are rather small. If they had been much greater, presumably the sense that economic integration would erase them would have been far smaller. This is one reason why Quebec was so much less concerned than the other provinces about free trade: language is a shield against pressures for cultural harmonization, at least to some degree.

To illuminate the cultural patterns of Canada and the United States, chapter 3 traces public attitudes in the two countries. The attitudes that Canadians and Americans bring to their politics – their priorities and policy preferences, as well as their broader orientations towards government and political leaders – condition government responses to economic and social change. The lack of good data over a long period of time makes a discussion of convergence and divergence over the entire postwar period difficult. Nevertheless, an analysis of similarities and differences in the beliefs of the two peoples during the last decade is possible, throwing light on their reactions to key elements of the policy agendas generated by economic restructuring and new forms of social pluralism.

Once again, the pattern that emerges is a fascinating blend of difference and similarity. Not surprisingly, structural differences between the two countries generate strong contrasts in the priority concerns of citizens. Canadians worry more about national unity; Americans, more about international issues and the combination of race, crime, and inner-city problems. At a deeper level, however, there are striking similarities in the broad attitudes of the two peoples towards economic and political life. The major exception is that Canadians hold a more positive and expansive view of the role of government, although there are suggestions of a narrowing even here.

Chapter 4 examines political institutions, starting with the obvious differences between the two countries – the parliamentary system versus the congressional system, fragmented parties in the United States and relatively disciplined ones in Canada, Canada's more decentralized federal system, and so on. Then the chapter compares the ways in which the two systems themselves are being influenced by economic and social forces of change, and the ways in which the institutional frameworks condition the policy responses that emerge. For the most part, core institutional differences have remained intact; the obvious exception is the introduction of the Canadian Charter of Rights and Freedoms in 1982 and the subsequent judicialization of politics. However, we have witnessed greater convergence in the "political styles" of the two countries – the more informal processes of interaction among politicians, organized interests, the media, and citizen participation. Moreover, a widespread concern about the capacity for collective choice permeates both countries. Public and academic commentary in Canada and the United States has reflected on the incapacity of institutions and the disaffection of voters from political elites and the policy process. In each case, a pervasive theme is that divided and fragmented power is a fundamental barrier to the hard choices that must be made if the country is to respond to the policy challenges – domestic and international – that it faces. The institutional forms clearly differ, but the anxiety is the same.

Policy legacies also condition the ways in which countries respond to change. The different program structures that Canadians and Americans have inherited embody the traditions of earlier decades, when the underlying societies formed sharper contrasts than they do today. These different policy legacies project the past into the present, and they condition responses to new challenges in several ways. First, policy change tends to be incremental rather than radical, involving adjustments to established approaches, and convergence in public programs can therefore be considerably slower than convergence in the underlying economic and social structures. Second and more fundamentally, historical choices can lock in particular approaches, especially when the countries have made major investments premised on their chosen approaches and when powerful interests have grown up around them. This "path dependency" means that previously viable alternatives become less so over time and that historical choices narrow the range of options considered as circumstances change (Pierson 1994, 43–4). By implication, one expects greater convergence between Canada and the United States in the newer areas of public policy, such as environmental protection and child care, than in the more established programs such as health care. Overall, however, policy legacies are another source of distinctive national responses to common problems and agendas.

POLICY RESPONSES: CONVERGENCE, CONSTRAINT, AND EFFECTIVENESS

Having explored the key changes in the economic and social structures of Canada and the United States, as well as their cultural and institutional frameworks, we move on in part 2 to look at the patterns of public policy. In what ways do economic globalization and social fragmentation generate new policy agendas? To what extent is there a coherent response to them? And to what extent is there a convergence in the policy stances of Canada and the United States? The answers to these questions are likely to vary across policy sectors, and chapters 5 through 9 explore a broad range of the policy domains in which modern governments act. Given the breadth of the questions that animate the analysis, we emphasize general patterns of policy rather than details of specific programs. The sectors examined are macroeconomic policy and performance (chapter 5), industrial policy and economic restructuring (chapter 6), social programs, especially health care and income security (chapter 7), the legal conception of rights, freedom, and equality (chapter 8), and environmental policy (chapter 9).

Policy Convergence

These chapters seek to establish a stronger empirical base for analyzing the extent of convergence in the policy patterns of the two countries.[4] Is the structure of public policy in the two countries becoming more alike or not? What do we find as we look across policy areas? Is there convergence in some, and divergence in others? And what are the factors that promote one or the other? Although most of the debate over convergence between Canada and the United States takes as its starting point the growing integration of the two economies, convergence in the policy structures of two countries could emerge from a number of very different dynamics:

1 *Convergence as the result of parallel domestic factors.* Convergence in the policies of two countries can be the product of similar domestic pressures, without any necessary influence or pressure being brought to bear by one country or the other. In this case, convergence can result from changes in either country. For example, had President Clinton's proposal for health-care reform been adopted, a traditional difference between Canada and the United States would have narrowed somewhat. However, not even the most ambitious Canadian would have suggested that the outcome had been driven by Canadian pressures on its southern neighbour, notwithstanding the interest of some American politicians in the Canadian model of health care.

2 *Convergence as the result of emulation.* Politics is not simply a process of conflict between powerful groups. As Heclo and others reminded us some time ago, policy making is also a process of "social learning," in which policies are influenced by the perceptions of problems and options held by decision makers and by the information flows that connect them with their environment (Heclo 1974; Deutsch 1963; Vickers 1965; Steinbruner 1974). In this context, governments continually learn from one another, and the policies of two countries can converge if one country adopts the policies of the other because it finds the program and experience of that country attractive. The flow of scientific and other policy data across national boundaries, facilitated by advances in modern communications and by supranational organizations such as the Organization for Economic Cooperation and Development (OECD), is an underestimated source of convergence (Rose 1993; also symposium in *Journal of Public Policy* 11, no. 1 [1991]). While ideas have many sources, in the context of the two countries examined here there is a heavy flow of ideas and data from the United States to Canada and barely a trickle in the opposite direction. Hence, most cases of convergence through emulation involve Canadian adoption of American examples.

3 *Convergence as the result of international constraints.* Policies can also converge because of the constraints inherent in the political and economic relations among countries, which limit the capacity for autonomous action by individual states. These relations are highly complex and can be subdivided in important ways. International constraints can take a *legal* form, such as bilateral or multilateral treaties that mandate similar policy stances on key issues, limit or prohibit the use of certain policy instruments, or create supranational decision-making bodies. Less formal but nonetheless powerful are the *economic* constraints that arise from the mobility of factors of production, especially capital, in an increasingly globalized economy. The competitive pressures for a narrowing of policy differences that raise the costs

of production in one country above those prevailing in its trading partners are almost palpable in the contemporary world. Economic theory may insist that flexibility in exchange rates can compensate for such differential costs of production and can preserve the scope for distinctive national policy choices; nevertheless, governments often act on the assumption that economic integration requires policy convergence on sensitive dimensions. Although both Canada and the United States confront these pressures, Canada is more exposed. Not only is it more open to international economic influences generally, but it is particularly vulnerable to its dependence on the United States economy, a relationship which Pierre Trudeau aptly likened to that of a mouse and an elephant. From the Canadian perspective, there is a danger that globalization can simply mean Americanization.

The contemporary world thus generates a diverse set of forces that work towards narrowing the diversity of public policies of national governments, forces that seem to be growing in strength. Nevertheless, pressures for convergence do not go unchallenged. A powerful set of countervailing forces continue to press for distinctive approaches to policy issues, and it remains an open question what balance will prevail in different policy sectors. In part, policy diversity is sustained by the different positions of individual countries within the global economy and the international order generally. More important, however, are the domestic sources of diversity. Differences in the domestic economy and social cleavages contribute to distinctive political imperatives; and differences in the mediating influences discussed earlier – culture, political institutions, and policy legacies – also remain important sources of divergence in national responses to common economic and social problems.

The question confronted in part 2 is whether, on balance, globalization and new forms of social pluralism are in fact tipping the balance between these contradictory pressures towards greater convergence in the policy patterns of Canada and the United States. The variety of policy areas examined allows us to compare the pressures for harmonization in different policy areas. These comparisons suggest that there has certainly been no comprehensive hamonization of Canadian and US public policies. There is convergence in a number of areas, but there are also persistent and important differences in the ways in which Canada and the United States are adjusting in other areas, including areas fundamental to Canadian identity, such as social policy. Moreover, in some areas where convergence has appeared – for example, the environment and rights policies – it has resulted from parallel pressures arising from common values, interests, or problems in each country. The more troublesome cases, where Canada has been "forced" to converge with American norms because of international constraints, are largely restricted to the domain of economic policy.

The Constrained State

The final chapter shifts the focus. In addition to convergence, we are interested in the extent to which globalization and social pluralism constrain or enhance the autonomy of the state. The central issue here is the extent to which countries retain an ability to make collective choices and to implement them effectively. How many degrees of freedom are there for domestic political choices?

Pressures for convergence rooted in the international context are clearly part of the pattern of constraints on the modern state. However, the constraints on contemporary government go well beyond international ones. Domestic pressures are equally important. Fiscal restraint, for example, is a product not only of international competitive pressures but also of the balance between societal demands and the capacity of governments to generate revenues. It can be argued that in both Canada and the United States the fragmentation of interests has, in Cairns's image of the "embedded state" (Cairns 1986), bound governments down with a thousand threads, like Gulliver in Lilliput. These threads are not unbreakable. However, when governments do act boldly, they must mobilize enormous amounts of political will and risk high levels of political protest.

Moreover, the tension between economic globalization and domestic social forces has implications for the locus of state autonomy and the relative strength of different states. Globalization implies that the state has less autonomy or sovereignty in the international domain, in the sense that its freedom to enact distinctive policies is constrained. However, to the extent that the state must as a result impose tough decisions on a recalcitrant society, successful adaptation to global realities may require a state that is more autonomous from its own domestic society. Put another way, it may take a "strong" state to produce a less expansive state. Conversely, the social forces we describe generally operate in the other way: they often call for a more expansive state, but one that is "weaker" in the sense of being more responsive to, and thus having less autonomy from, domestic pressures. The relative intensity of international and domestic constraints is likely to vary between such countries as Canada and the United States, and our task is to compare the patterns of constraint and autonomy in them.

Overall, however, we conclude that the constraints on the modern state, while palpable, do not constitute a strait-jacket. To change the metaphor, the constraints facing governments are not impenetrable walls; they are costs to be weighed. As a result, states still enjoy important degrees of freedom in charting their course.

The Effectiveness of the State

Chapter 10 summarizes our conclusions about continuity and change, convergence and divergence, constraint and choice, and seeks to assess the relative importance of the explanatory factors we have set out: international economic forces, domestic social change, cultures, institutions, and legacies. It ends with some reflections on how well the two countries have responded to the challenges they face. Have the public authorities in each country been able to develop effective strategies for responding to the policy challenges before them? How successfully have they carried out the balancing act imposed on them by globalization and social pluralism? Such evaluations are inevitably informed in part by the policy preferences of the observer. Nevertheless, it may also be possible to find some more neutral indicators of effective performance. For example, it is possible to compare governmental capability in the two countries. Weaver and Rockman (1993) suggest that governments can be assessed in terms of their capacity to set and maintain priorities, target resources, engage in innovation and risk taking, coordinate conflicting objectives, impose losses on powerful groups where necessary, represent diffuse unorganized groups in the policy process, ensure effective implementation, make and maintain international commitments, and manage social divisions. How have Canada and the United States fared along these dimensions?

We conclude by suggesting that a fundamental determinant of success is the existence of a widely held agreement on a social contract, seen as a set of understandings about the role and purposes of the state. The social and economic foundations of the postwar social contract manifested in the Keynesian welfare state have been deeply shaken by global and domestic change. The question is whether it is possible for these countries to develop new social contracts, attuned to the new environment.

This book clearly tackles an ambitious agenda of broad questions about the nature of modern society and the role of the state at the end of this millennium. Ambitious research agendas inevitably generate problems for devotees of the scientific method. Nevertheless, the citizens of these two countries live in a complex world, and their future is shaped and reshaped by large changes that defy perfect understanding. It is important to shed even partial light on the way ahead.

PART ONE

The Changing World of Canada and the United States

2 Changing Economies, Changing Societies

KEITH BANTING
AND RICHARD SIMEON

The economic confidence and social stability of the postwar era is a fading memory in Canada and the United States. For almost a generation now, Canadians and Americans have struggled to come to terms with a new economic and social world. The sense of economic security enjoyed by the great majority of citizens in both countries during the 1950s and 1960s has waned, as stable economic growth has given way to deep restructuring in many industries, stagnating real wages, and greater inequality in market incomes. Some groups have clearly prospered in recent years. The prospects of many Canadians and Americans, however, seem less secure. New forms of inequality are emerging: many individuals and families are struggling simply to preserve their existing living standards, and today's generation of young people may well be the first not to surpass the standard of living of their parents.

The relative social stability of the immediate postwar years has also given way to pervasive social changes. The striking pattern is greater diversity in the racial and ethnic composition of the two countries, in the structure of family life, in relations between men and women, and in religious practices, sexual behaviour, and lifestyles. Increased social diversity brings increased awareness of difference. New social movements have enlarged the political domain, bringing new issues, new resources, and new identities into the process. This mobilization of a wider range of social differences has unleashed powerful hopes and fears on both sides of the border. For some, a culture of diversity holds the promise of greater freedom and escape from a confining set of social mores. For others, it produces a sense of cultural disorientation.

Such people feel less and less at home in their own society, replicating in the social domain the insecurity that characterizes contemporary economic life.

From the perspective of history, the exceptional nature of the current economic and social transitions can be overstated. The usual comparison is with the affluence and stability of the postwar period, but in the longer view it is that period that is the aberration, not the present. The rate of economic growth in the postwar years was well above the average for the last century, and the relative social harmony of those years did not represent the historical norm. Change has been a hallmark of these two countries throughout most of their history. They have been transformed and retransformed through waves of geographic expansion, immigration from abroad, migration among regions, and economic restructuring. In this sense, the contemporary economic and social turmoil simply reflects and extends the past.

Nevertheless, rapid change remains politically unsettling. Canada and the United States are confronted with twin challenges: to respond effectively to the deep restructuring of the international economy on one hand, and to manage and accommodate the enhanced diversity reshaping domestic society on the other. Either one is demanding; in combination, they are stretching the collective capacities for adaptation in both countries. Signs of the tensions involved abound. For example, in 1988 – a year of rapid economic growth – a *New York Times/* CBS News poll found that for the first time in many years, Americans did not have faith that their country's future would be an improvement over its present or past (cited in Cuomo Commission 1988, xxii). North of the border, a survey of the dreams and aspirations of Canadian children aged five to eighteen found that they were acutely aware of the financial pressures and hardships facing their families: "Children live this. They have absorbed the feelings of insecurity, worry and fear that have come to characterize their parents' and families' world" (Insight Canada Research 1993).

In order to set the context from which these challenges spring, this chapter surveys the patterns of economic and social change in Canada and the United States. It also traces dimensions of convergence in their economic and social structures. Although the transformations of recent years have left many of the historic contrasts between the two countries reasonably intact, other traditional differences have faded, and new economic and social trends have often emerged in a similar form on both sides of the border, enlarging the spheres of experience that are shared by Canadians and Americans. Finally, the chapter highlights the implications of change for the policy agendas of the two countries. Economic globalization and social fragmentation have produced a sharp convergence in policy agendas. Increasingly, the president and the prime minister, Congress and Parliament, struggle with common problems and debate similar alternatives. Undoubtedly, the pattern of pressures on decision makers differs in important ways. As we shall see, there is greater tension between the imperatives of globalization and the imperatives of social pluralism in Canada than in the United States. Nevertheless, at the broadest level, converging policy agendas are a striking legacy of the economic and social change of recent years.

CHANGING ECONOMIES

In the early years of the century, Wilfrid Laurier repeatedly told Canadians that "the twentieth century belongs to Canada"; and in 1941 Henry Luce, the publisher of *Life* magazine, assured his readers that they were living in "the American Century."[1] Such optimism about the future has given way to considerable unease as a new century approaches. The sources of the contemporary sense of economic insecurity are complex, rooted in the first instance in the changing nature of the global economy, the pace of technological change, and productivity trends in both Canada and the United States. Their combined impact has flowed through labour markets quickly and with uneven effects, generating new opportunities for some and hardship for others.

The Global Economy

In part, the turbulence facing Canadians and Americans originates in the speed of change in the global economy. The economic significance of national boundaries is declining dramatically. Successive rounds of trade liberalization under the General Agreement on Tariffs and Trade (GATT), the development of regional trading blocs in Europe and North America, and closer economic ties among the nations of Asia have opened economic borders. Advances in communications and transportation have also linked local and global markets more tightly. Multinational enterprises increasingly organize production on the basis of global strategies, with the result that many corporations and the goods and services they produce no longer have a clear nationality. Modern manufacturing can incorporate the design and engineering skills of nationals of different countries; it can incorporate finance raised on international markets, parts sourced from around the world, assembly operations in different markets, and marketing on a global scale. Globalization is particularly evident in the world of finance. The collapse of the Bretton Woods agreement, the dismantling of many restraints on the flow of capital, and the deregulation of financial

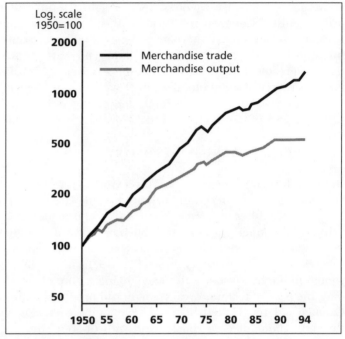

Figure 2.1   Long-term trends of world merchandise trade and output,
1950–1994
Source: World Trade Organization 1995a

institutions in many countries have integrated financial markets
around the world. Every day, billions of dollars are transmitted between countries with a single keystroke; and flows of short-term capital
are now many times bigger than those of direct corporate investment.

The pace of integration can be tracked in the patterns of trade and
investment. The volume of world trade has grown much more rapidly
than world output throughout the postwar era, especially in the manufacturing sector (see figure 2.1). Moreover, a growing proportion of
trade involves cross-flows of similar products, or "intra-industry" trade,
much of which is conducted through multinational corporations. In
1964 intra-industry trade accounted for 46 per cent of total international trade among the ten major countries of the OECD; by the mid-
1980s, the figure had risen to 60 per cent (Economic Council of Canada
1988b). On a world level, intra-firm trade in 1993 was estimated to
present one-third of total trade (United Nations 1995). As figure 2.2
shows, the financial counterpart of this pattern has been the growth in
foreign direct investment, which since the mid-1980s has risen more

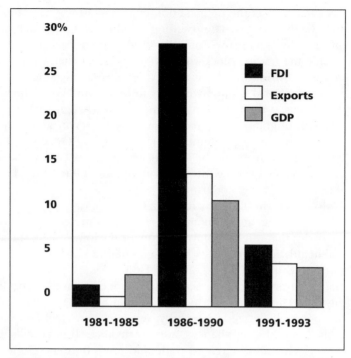

Figure 2.2   Average annual growth in foreign direct investment, world exports, and world GDP, 1981–1993
Source: United Nations 1995

rapidly than either foreign trade or domestic product, as multinational companies position themselves effectively in an increasingly global economy (OECD 1994b).

Movement towards an integrated economic system at the global level has not gone uncontested. Although the Uruguay Round of the GATT has been completed, regional trade arrangements play an increasing role. Trade within the emerging blocs represented by the European Community, North America, and the Asia/Pacific region has been growing more rapidly than trade between them. In part, this regionalization of economic activity reflects a natural tendency for trade and investment to flow most easily to contiguous areas, because proximity and similarity of social systems lower the costs of transportation and information gathering. To some extent, however, the emergence of regional trading blocs also reflects explicit political choices, as neighbours have combined economically in order to build a stronger sense of solidarity, to counter competitive pressures from outside the region, or to gain bargaining leverage vis-à-vis other blocs; and in some cases, regional blocs may reflect the political dominance of a local hegemon (Fishlow and Haggard 1992). The resulting trend towards regionalization is significant. Krugman, for example, predicted in 1990 that world trade outside the trading blocs will grow more slowly than world output and may even shrink in real terms. "At least as far as trade goes," he suggests, "the world economy is likely to be *less* unified in the year 2000" than it was at the beginning of the decade (Krugman 1990, 194; emphasis in original). More recent analyses are sceptical that regionalization will prove so predominant (World Trade Organization 1995b). Whatever the eventual balance between global and regional economies, however, growing interdependence among individual nations is a core feature of the modern world.

Moreover, the modern international economy is intensely competitive, as trade in manufactured products increasingly incorporates countries that offer employers dramatically lower wage, social security, and health and safety costs. Trade competition has placed intense pressures on firms in Canada and the United States, producing economic restructuring on a major scale and the decline of some traditional industries. The sectors in which traditional North American dominance has been challenged is lengthy: automobiles, steel, ships, machine tools, household appliances, and electronics. Traditionally, economic theory celebrates increased trade and open borders. Trade is seen to be advantageous to all parties: production and investment can move to areas with clear comparative advantage, and consumers benefit from a wider choice of less expensive products. While this may be true in the long run and on a global scale, it is more problematic within the particular countries and particular economic sectors that face adjustment. Canadian and American workers, who have for a long period enjoyed their position at the top of the international-league tables of wages, now find their position threatened. Although economic theory can afford to be indifferent to where economic activity is located, that is not the case for workers, communities, and governments, for whom the answer must always be "here."

Concern about competitiveness is compounded by a growing appreciation of the extent to which economic integration constrains the capacity of states to protect domestic society from global change. Competitiveness in the trading system generates pressures for harmonization in regulatory standards to facilitate the free movement of goods, and also pressure for convergence in other policy instruments that affect the costs of production; meanwhile, the international integration of financial markets constrains the scope for a truly independent monetary policy at the national level. The tightness of these constraints is often overstated, and their intensity differs dramatically from one policy sector to another, as the chapters in part 2 of this book will demonstrate. Nevertheless, there has clearly been a shift in the role of the state in modern societies. During the postwar years, the state often sought to insulate domestic society from international sources of instability – especially in smaller nations, which even then were highly dependent on international trade and vulnerable to external shocks (Katzenstein 1984, 1985). In the contemporary period, however, the state is under increasing pressure to adapt domestic society to the forces emerging from international economic change, a dynamic that has contributed immensely to a growing tension between governments and their electorates, and is reducing popular faith in the effectiveness of state action.

In this sense, economic globalization has generated a striking convergence in the policy agenda in Canada and the United States, for both countries must now grapple with the economic implications of international interdependence. In many ways, this represents a more difficult economic and psychological transition for the United States. As Johnson, Tyson, and Zysman note, "For the first twenty-five years of the postwar period, America was indeed a hegemon. It had the capacity to shape the international system, forcing others to play by its rules. Its domestic economy was little affected by economic policy choices abroad ... Interdependence was for others; the United States was at the center of the system" (1989, xv). The United States undoubtedly remains a major economic power. Changes in the performance of its economy still reverberate far beyond its borders; its government still carries considerable influence in multinational negotiations over trade and other economic relations; and it is the dominant component of one of the regional blocs. Nevertheless, the United States is having to adjust to a more constrained role. Its government faces stronger international limits on its discretion in macroeconomic policy; its economy has proved vulnerable to external shocks; domestic groups complain that international trade agencies such as the new World Trade Organization will undermine its sovereignty; the country is focused on trade competition with Japan; and it has moved rapidly from being a major lending nation to a major debtor.

This transformation has generated policy concerns that have long been familiar in Canada. The impact of globalization in narrowing the scope for independent monetary policy is much more novel in the United States, because Canada has always been open to international financial flows and because Canadian and U.S. financial assets have been highly substitutable for many years (Economic Council of Canada 1989b). American political debates about foreign direct investment and the ownership of major companies, or the implications of

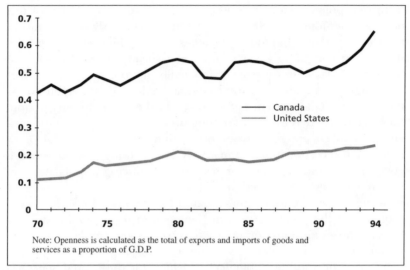

Figure 2.3   Degree of openness of economy, Canada and the United States,
1970–1994
Source: Calculated from data in International Monetary Fund 1995

transfer pricing for taxing multinational corporations, sound haunt-
ingly familiar to Canadian ears. Similarly, the debate in the United
States over the North American Free Trade Agreement paralleled the
intense controversy in Canada over the Canada–U.S. Free Trade
Agreement just five years earlier.

Despite this convergence in policy agendas, many of the traditional
differences between the two economies remain intact, and Canada
clearly remains much more vulnerable to a changing world. Canada
has always been a trading nation, exposed to international economic
shifts. As figure 2.3 indicates, foreign trade represents a much larger
proportion of GDP for Canada than for the United States, a traditional
difference between the two neighbours that is growing. Figure 2.4 provides another measure of the greater penetration of international
flows, demonstrating Canada's marked dependence on imported inputs in its manufacturing industries compared with other major industrial nations, especially the United States. As the smallest of the G7
countries, Canadian policy decisions and economic performance have
little impact beyond its borders, and the country must work hard to
craft strategic alliances in multilateral negotiations. Nor is Canada a
large enough producer to have a significant impact on world prices for
any of the commodities it sells to other nations. In the awkward lexi-
con of international trade economists, Canada is a "small, open, price-

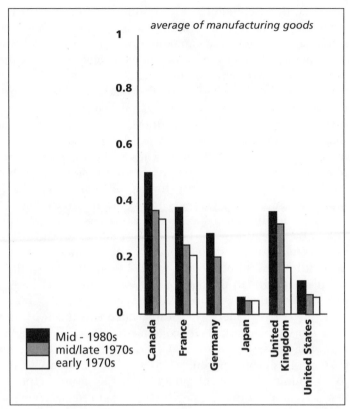

Figure 2.4   Ratio of imported to domestic sourcing of inputs
Source: OECD 1993a

taking economy" and, as such, is locked into a global economy over which it exercises negligible influence.

Canada remains particularly sensitive to shifts in international commodity prices. The country's relative dependence on resources has declined since 1951, when resources represented an overwhelming 86.9 per cent of exports (Canada, Royal Commission on the Economic Union 1985, 2:407). Nevertheless, in 1995 exports by Canadian resource and resource-based manufacturing industries still accounted for more than one-half of the country's total exports, compared with about one-third in both the United States and the European Community (Statistics Canada 1995). This centrality of resources varies across Canada's trading partners. Almost three-fifths of Canadian sales to the United States consist of non-resource-based manufacturing products; however, in some of the world's fastest-growing markets, such as Japan and Asia, the preponderance of resource-based products in Canada's exports is dramatic (Economic Council of Canada 1992, 11). As a result, changes in global commodity prices are quickly felt throughout the Canadian economy and society, especially in regions that are dependent on the resource sectors.

Canadian vulnerability is also accentuated by Canada's extreme dependence on the American market. Although the two countries are each other's largest trading partners, the relationship remains profoundly asymmetrical. Canada's dependence on the U.S. market is dramatic; no other OECD country relies so heavily on a single market. Moreover, this dependence has increased. Despite the efforts of the Canadian government to diversify trading relations during the 1970s, the proportion of Canadian exports bound for the United States rose from two-thirds in the mid-1970s to three-quarters a decade later (OECD 1992). By 1994, the proportion was over 80 per cent (Statistics Canada 1995). During the postwar period, the steady integration of the Canadian and American economies was led by multinational firms and accomplished through the instruments of foreign direct investment and intra-industry trade. As Aitken remarked in the early 1960s, the relatively unrestricted mobility of capital between the two countries has done more to integrate their economies than any other single factor except geography (Aitken 1961). Canada continues to have a higher proportion of its economy controlled by foreign investors than any other OECD country. The role of foreign-controlled firms is especially prominent in manufacturing; a 1987 survey of 711 establishments in this sector found that approximately 75 per cent of manufacturing exports and 88 per cent of manufacturing imports were attributable to foreign-controlled multi-nationals (Economic Council of Canada 1992, 11).

The vulnerability inherent in Canadian dependence on the U.S. market was highlighted in the late 1970s and the 1980s by the threat of American protectionism. As a major Canadian advisory commission warned, "Even where we are not the principal target, we risk being the major victim of a spate of protectionist legislation before Congress. No realistic amount of diversification can offset the degree of Canada's vulnerability to unilateral action by the United States" (Canada, Royal Commission on the Economic Union 1985, 1:247). The response came in the form of the 1989 free trade agreement between Canada and the United States and the subsequent North American Free Trade Agreement (NAFTA), which incorporated Mexico. These moves remain highly controversial, and the Canada–U.S. agreement certainly did not eliminate trade frictions between the two countries, frictions that inevitably pose a much greater risk to Canada than to its giant neighbour.

Canadian critics of the bilateral trade agreements argued that they would unleash pressures for convergence, not simply in policy agendas but in policy responses as well. Canadian governments, they insisted, would be increasingly be forced to harmonize their policies in a wide range of sectors to standards prevailing in the United States. They predicted that Canadian producers would argue persuasively that higher taxes or more exacting regulatory regimes would hamper their ability to compete in the larger American market; and they warned that American producers would launch trade challenges to Canadian government policies that lower the costs of production north of the border by socializing costs borne by the private sector in the United States. In the words of one critic of the free trade agreement, "The parameters of Canadian public policy choice – the range of options open to Canadian policy-makers – will be set increasingly by U.S. politics, and not by our own" (Stairs 1988, 457). Defenders of the trade agreements rejected the more sweeping form of these contentions, insisting that the growing constraints on economic policy instruments such as monetary policy, industrial policy, and regulatory regimes, while real, were inherent in the larger process of global economic interdependence and would not be significantly increased by the bilateral trade agreements themselves. In addition, they insisted that Canadian governments would retain the capacity to mount distinctive responses to the social programs. The exchange rate could compensate for any increased production costs north of the border; and broad social programs, such as medicare, which socialize costs borne by employers south of the border, would not be challengeable under trade legislation (see the various contributions to Crispo 1988). This debate touches on fundamental questions about the future of sovereignty and the role of the nation-state in the contemporary world, and part 2 of this book, which explores the extent of policy convergence between Canada and the United States across a number of policy domains, sheds considerable light on it.

Restructuring in the global economy has thus exposed Canada and the United States to major economic changes, contributing to a deep restructuring of economic activity on the continent and constraining the capacity of governments to insulate their societies from the pain associated with rapid change. Globalization of economic activity has not eliminated traditional structural differences between the two countries; for example, the resources sector remains larger in Canada than in the United States, and the Canadian economy still remains more dependent on trade. Nevertheless, the changing international economy has led to considerable convergence in the two nations' policy agendas and to a tighter set of constraints within which policy responses are crafted.

Technological Change

Economic change and insecurity rooted in international trade and finance is accentuated by changing technology. New technologies are producing sweeping changes in the production and distribution of goods and services. New information systems, robotics, computer-aided design and manufacturing (CAD/CAM), and telecommunication technologies are transforming production processes and rapidly increasing the skill levels required of modern workers. Moreover, these technologies are intimately related to shifts in the nature of product markets. In some sectors, mass markets for highly standardized products are giving way to more fragmented markets and shorter product cycles. For example, the number of distinct underbodies of cars being sold in the United States rose from twenty-four in 1955 to ninety-one in 1986, with annual sales per underbody dropping by more than half over the same period; and according to Kodak, no camera today lasts more than six months before it is redesigned and new features are added (Wein 1991).

To compete effectively in such a world, firms must develop more flexible forms of production that operate efficiently with shorter production runs and are able to shift smoothly from one model or product to another. The character of the workplace is changing. In some sectors, new production techniques have increasingly replaced the assembly-line model pioneered by Henry Ford.[2] Fewer workers are needed, and those who remain require greater skills than before. The world is closing in for the traditional high-school-educated, semi-skilled blue-collar workers. In the 1990s, greater competition combined with technological change also began to affect white-collar managerial workers as one large corporation after another shed employees.

Once again, common challenges have prompted common debates in Canada and the United States. The embrace of technology is regularly advocated in both countries as the secret to sustaining the high-employment, high-wage pattern that characterized the postwar generation. Competition from low-wage workers in low-technology sectors in the newly industrializing world should be met with a North American shift to production of high-technology products. Whether this strategy can be successful is uncertain, given the ability of corporations to combine high technology with low wages in many countries, and the worrying levels of skill and education among North American workers. Nevertheless, a high-technology economy remains at the heart of economic strategy in both countries.

In this race, Canada again faces the larger problem. Many American commentators worry that the United States is no longer the leader in

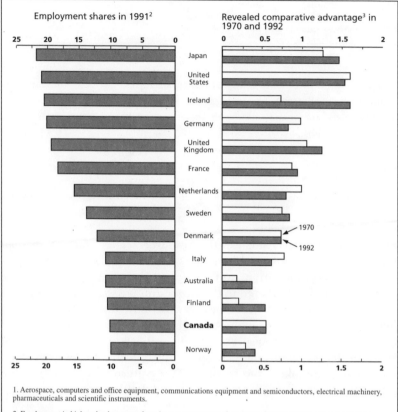

1. Aerospace, computers and office equipment, communications equipment and semiconductors, electrical machinery, pharmaceuticals and scientific instruments.

2. Employment in high-technology manufacturing as a percentage of total manufacturing employment. For Ireland pharmaceuticals are excluded.

3. The share of a country's high-technology exports in total manufacturing exports divided by the same share of all OECD countries taken together. If the indicator is greater than one, the country's share of high-technology exports in total exports is greater than the share for all OECD countries taken together.

Figure 2.5   High-technology manufacturing[1] in selected OECD countries
Source: OECD 1994a

the world of technological innovation. Various advisory bodies have lamented the country's slowness compared with Japan and parts of Europe in the adoption of advanced manufacturing technologies (AMT) such as computer-aided design, robotic manufacturing, and total quality management (Council on Competitiveness 1989, 1991). Nevertheless, as figure 2.5 indicates, high-technology manufacturing represents a more substantial component of the economy of the United States than it does of Canada, both in terms of employment and in terms of the composition of exports. Moreover, technological change has been more rapid in the United States, as table 2.1 attests. Although·this

Table 2.1
Proportion of establishments using advanced manufacturing technologies, by major
industrial group, Canada and the United States, 1989

	Canada	United States
Transportation equipment	12.0	19.4
Electrical/electronic equipment	15.2	21.5
Instruments and related products	13.1	18.7
Machinery	14.0	18.3
Metal fabricating	9.1	13.2
Average	12.7	18.2

Source: Economic Council of Canada 1992

comparison does not include the resource sector, where Canadian
AMT use might be greater, the sectors covered in the table do represent the heart of modern manufacturing in both countries. Part of the
difference can be attributed to the larger average size of U.S. establishments, to differences in the industrial mix of the two countries, and to
the size of the defence sector. According to the Economic Council of
Canada (1992, 40), however, Canada still lags behind the United
States in the use of advanced manufacturing technologies even when
such factors are taken into account. This pattern is replicated in the
proportion of GDP devoted to research and development.

Productivity Trends

A third major factor underpinning the economic prospects of North
Americans has been productivity growth. Productivity in the industrialized world has reflected two powerful trends over the last thirty years:
convergence and slowdown. As figure 2.6 highlights, productivity
growth among the leading trading countries reflected a pattern of convergence as countries with initially lower productivity levels adopted
the best-practice technologies of the most advanced economy, the
United States. Moreover, this convergence in productivity sustained a
parallel convergence in wealth, as measured by GDP per capita (Helliwell 1994a,1994b). For the last twenty years, convergence has coexisted with slowdown as the rapid productivity growth of the postwar
decades declined sharply throughout the industrialized world. Between 1960 and 1973, the average rate of growth in real GDP per capita for the OECD nations as a whole ranged between 3.5 and 4.0 per
cent; between 1973 and 1993, it fell below 2.0 per cent (OECD 1995).

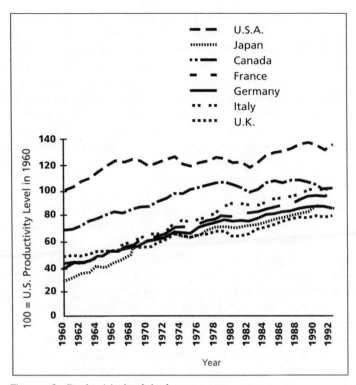

Figure 2.6   Productivity levels in the G7
Source: Helliwell 1994a

The reasons for this stall are not well understood. A variety of suspects have been named: a slower rate of capital accumulation; sectoral shifts, including the slowing of movement out of the low-productivity agricultural sector and the acceleration of movement from manufacturing to the service sector; increases in energy prices; weak demand conditions, which lead to lower capacity utilization; and so on (Council of Economic Advisors 1992; Economic Council of Canada 1992). Although there is no consensus on the relative importance of these factors, or on others that could be named, they clearly have been sufficient to offset productivity-enhancing factors such as growing international trade and technological innovation.

The economies of Canada and the United States have faithfully reflected these international patterns of convergence and slowdown. Over the entire period, Canada benefited from a significant convergence with U.S. productivity levels: in 1950 productivity in the United

States was 32 per cent greater than in Canada, but by 1990 the difference had fallen to 7 per cent (Economic Council of Canada 1992). However, the data for the early 1990s in figure 2.6 raise questions about the durability of this convergence, for U.S. productivity growth began to inch ahead again. This divergence was particularly strong in the manufacturing sector, which suggests that Canadian manufacturing had been slower to adjust to shocks than its U.S. counterpart (Economic Council of Canada 1992; Rao and Lemprière 1992). Over the longer period, however, the historical pattern has been one of convergence on American leadership.

During the 1980s, the particularly sharp slowdown in productivity growth in both the United States and Canada intensified the concern that economic leadership is slipping to other regions of the world. Both countries plunged into a vigorous debate about the determinants of productivity growth and the potential contribution, if any, of industrial policy to economic performance in the contemporary era. The apparent return of more rapid productivity growth in the aftermath of the recession of the mid-1990s has taken some of the steam out of these controversies, at least in the United States. Indeed, a raft of commentary insists that the ruthless restructuring of North American firms has reinstated their global leadership. "Ready to Take On the World," trumpeted the *Economist* (15 January 1994); and the *New York Times* soon confirmed "The American Economy, Back on Top" (27 February 1994). Earlier, Canadian newspapers had announced similar news, albeit in a typically restrained cadence: "Productivity Growth Returns" and "Canada's Factories Catching Up" (*Globe and Mail*, 18 May and 17 June 1994). Whether this optimism is warranted remains to be seen, for some economists are convinced that this productivity burst simply reflects the enhanced utilization that normally occurs after a recession, rather than representing a more significant increase in the underlying trend of productivity growth.[3] Much depends on which of these views is correct. The cumulative effects of long-term productivity trends shape the competitiveness of individual firms in international trade, the economic and political power of different nations, and the well-being of citizens. In the words of Johnson, Tyson, and Zysman, "If [the United States] cannot keep pace at this juncture, we could find ourselves beginning a long, cumulative economic decline that ultimately threatens our national wealth and power" (1989, xiv; see also Competitiveness Policy Council 1993).

The sweeping restructuring triggered by globalization, technological innovation, low productivity growth, and general economic volatility has had a major impact on labour markets and the social well-being of Canadians and Americans. These changes can be seen both at the collective level, in economic organizations such as labour unions, and at the individual level, in the lives of displaced workers and others who are struggling to protect themselves from the forces of "creative destruction" celebrated by champions of market economies. Once again, however, the patterns of adjustment to change in the two countries reveal a complex mix of similarity and difference, convergence and divergence.

Organized Labour

Economic restructuring has generated intense pressures on organized labour. Unions have long been challenged by the relative decline of manufacturing and the expansion of employment in the service sector and in small businesses, both of which are more difficult to organize. Moreover, driven by an increasingly competitive environment, firms in both countries have insisted on a wide range of changes: new technologies and production systems, new forms of workplace organization, enhanced managerial discretion, greater flexibility in job classifications and work schedules, reduced employment levels, and changes in the form of compensation and employment security. In some cases, these pressures have involved reductions in the benefits, protections, and traditions embedded in collective agreements that were developed in a more secure economic climate; in others, firms have sought to create a non-union environment altogether.

These pressures are felt acutely in both countries, and there are many reasons why we would expect the two trade union movements to have followed similar trajectories as they grapple with them. After all, from the 1930s on, the growth of the Canadian labour movement closely tracked that in the United States, just as Canadian labour law was modelled after the American Wagner Act. Most major Canadian unions were part of international unions based in the United States, and Canadian and American workers were often part of the same industries and firms. Increasing economic integration between the two countries might have been expected to usher in a powerful convergence in their union movements and labour-management relations.

In fact, labour relations are a domain of dramatic divergence. This is most evident in the comparative rates of union "density" – the proportion of workers who are members of trade unions. As figure 2.7 indicates, by 1950 unions incorporated almost identical proportions of workers in both countries. However, beginning in the mid-1960s, the two labour movements began to diverge, with Canadian unions expanding to include close to 40 per cent of the workforce in the mid-1980s, then declining moderately to 36.2 per cent in 1990 and stabilizing thereafter. By contrast, American unions began a long decline, which

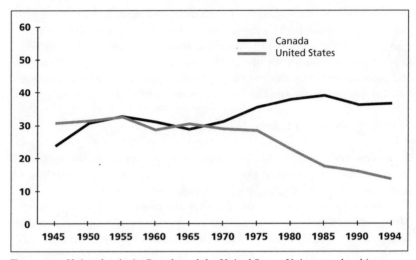

Figure 2.7   Union density in Canada and the United States: Union membership as a
percentage of non-agricultural employment, 1945–1994
Source: Based on data from Kumar 1993, table 1, updated from Labour Canada 1995 and
U.S. Department of Labour 1996

accelerated in the 1980s. By the mid-1990s, only 15 per cent of American workers were unionized, less than half the Canadian rate. While total union membership in the United States has been stagnant since
1968, total membership in Canada has almost doubled in the same period (Kumar 1993). These divergent patterns have been paralleled by
an internal change in the composition of the Canadian labour movement, with a decline in the role of U.S.-based international unions and
the expansion of national unions.

These broad differences show up in other ways as well. In general,
Canadian unions have in recent years been much more active in recruitment and more successful in winning certification votes (Kumar
1993). While the growing service industries have been hard to organize
in both countries, the Canadian unions have been the more successful.
Between 1977 and 1988, U.S. union membership in private service industries declined by 26 per cent, while in Canada it grew by 58.5 per
cent. And in the traditionally highly unionized sectors, such as mining,
manufacturing, and construction, Canadian unions, although threatened, faced a far less damaging decline. During the 1980s at least, Canadian unions also were more successful than American unions in
resisting employer pressure for "concessionary bargaining" – wage
freezes and rollbacks, the establishment of two-tier wage settlements,
and the acceptance of wage settlements based on lump sum or profit

sharing, rather than on wage increases (Chaison and Rose 1988). Indeed, in the automobile sector, disagreements over bargaining strategy split the international union and led to the formation of the Canadian Auto Workers (CAW), which opposed management proposals for partnership and workplace reorganization. As one study of the split concludes, "Paradoxically, while the economies of Canada and the United States have become even more interdependent in recent years with the signing of the free trade agreement in 1989, generating pressures for the creation of a 'level playing field' and harmonization of social and economic policies, a 'continental divide' has emerged in the goals, priorities and strategies of the two unions operating in a highly integrated industry" (Kumar and Holmes 1993, 30).

Whether this pattern of divergence will persist is subject to considerable debate. Some analysts see a "lagged convergence," insisting that the pressures for enhanced flexibility and efficiency will eventually take their toll in Canada as well, and pointing to the decline of unionization in the private sector in Canada as a harbinger of the future (Richards 1993). Others reply that the decline in private-sector unionization is not nearly as precipitous in Canada and that there are deeply rooted reasons for assuming that the Canadian labour movement can maintain its comparative strength (Meltz 1993; I. Robinson 1990).

Interestingly, this divergence is not rooted in broad cultural differences between the two countries or in differences between the two workforces; in both countries, public attitudes towards unions are remarkably similar, and differences such as age, gender, industry, and occupation explain only about 15 per cent of the gap in union density (Riddell 1993; Bruce 1989). The only structural factor that matters is the larger presence of the public sector in Canada, and the very high levels of union organization within it. But this is not a large part of the story. Another explanation lies in the somewhat differing union cultures. While there are many variations within each country, American unions have tended to focus narrowly on "business unionism," aimed at improving wages and working conditions. Canadian unions have embraced a stronger element of "social unionism," giving greater weight to notions of collective solidarity and to the role of organized labour in the larger social and economic setting (Robinson 1990; Kumar 1993; Adams 1988). Compared to American unions, Canadian unions have been more politically active over a wide range of economic and social issues, from free trade to child care and the environment. They have placed greater emphasis on building coalitions with a wide variety of other "progressive" groups, such as those concerned with women's issues, the environment, pensioners, and visible minorities. Moreover, the Canadian movement has had stable political links with a political party, the NDP, although these links have recently come under considerable strain. Thus, in some respects, the Canadian labour movement is more like the European model of social democratic unionism than it is like the American model. This emphasis on the solidarity of social unionism may provide Canadian unions with a stronger reservoir of member support with which to resist current threats, compared with the U.S. model, in which support for the union is predicated primarily on its ability to deliver at the bargaining table.

A final reason for the Canadian-American divergence is public policy. Canada's parliamentary form of government and its disciplined parties, when combined with narrow parliamentary majorities, has facilitated influence by labour and its political allies in shaping labour legislation. The trend in the United States has been to favour the rights of employers over unions, both in the law and in its administration; by contrast, the Canadian legal regime has tended to support collective bargaining and has played an important role in encouraging the union representation of workers (Riddell 1993). In comparison with the United States, Canadian law tends to facilitate certification and make decertification more difficult; twenty-one states in the United States, but no Canadian provinces have right-to-work laws; Canadian laws provide stronger protection for workers whose companies change hands or who are faced with new technologies; and there are significant differences in employment standards in such matters as health and safety, minimum wages, employment equity, and termination of employment. In addition, despite much overlap of firms, Canadian employers tend to have a broader acceptance of the legitimate role of unions and a willingness to work with them to facilitate adjustment and adaptation (Riddell 1993; Kumar 1993).

All this suggests that while workers in both countries face very similar challenges, Americans do so in something close to a pure market model, in which trade unions as organized expressions of workers' interests play a small and declining role. Even though Canadian unions, too, represent only a minority of all workers, they appear to be in a stronger position to mediate between market forces and worker concerns. Their greater organizational strength and legislative protection suggest that they will continue to be able to maintain this role, even as they also are forced to deal with restructuring and as their ability to restrain the mobility of capital under NAFTA and other trade liberalization measures is reduced.

Employment, Incomes, and Inequality

In the early stages, the social aftershocks of the economic earthquakes in recent decades seemed broadly similar for individual Canadians and

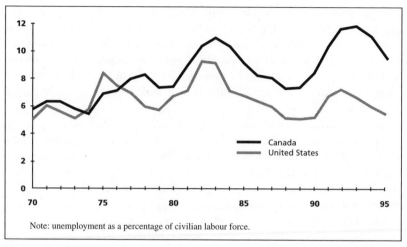

Figure 2.8   Unemployment, Canada and the United States, 1970–1995
Source: OECD 1996

Americans: higher levels of unemployment, including long-term un-employment; extensive churning in the labour market; the growth of non-standard forms of employment, such as part-time and short-term work and self-employment; greater inequality in the income that indi-viduals derive from the operations of the market; and a higher general sense of economic insecurity. However, as the process of economic re-structuring continued, important differences between Canada and the United States began to emerge, especially in the overall pattern of un-employment in the two countries and in the willingness of their gov-ernments to protect the most vulnerable elements of society.

The level of overall employment in Canada and the United States is shown in Figure 2.8. The direction of change has been broadly similar, as the two countries rode the same roller-coaster through recession in the early 1980s, expansion later in the decade, recession again in the early 1990s, and slow growth thereafter. Although the direction of change has been much the same, a major gap in unemployment levels opened up in the 1980s and expanded in the 1990s. Compared to Canada and most other OECD nations, the United States has enjoyed much stronger employment growth in recent years. As will be seen in a moment, this has been accompanied by weak wage growth, a sharp de-cline in the real wages of low-skill workers, and higher levels of social inequality than in other countries (OECD 1994a). Nevertheless, by the mid-1990s, the United States had returned to the unemployment lev-els that prevailed in the early 1970s. In contrast, Canada continued to suffer stubbornly high levels of unemployment. By the mid-1990s, the gap in unemployment rates was enormous. This is clearly the most troubling point of divergence between the economic performance of the two countries, and it has sparked a lively but as yet inconclusive debate among economists who have sought to understand its causes (Ashenfelter and Card 1986; Card and Riddell 1993)

Although the overall patterns of unemployment diverged, the impact of economic restructuring on particular categories of workers has been much more similar. Displaced workers represent an important example. The first wave of large-scale redundancies in the manufacturing sector during the early 1980s has a profound impact on public consciousness in both Canada and the United States. Since then, the waves of restructuring have spread throughout the economy as a whole. The profile and fate of displaced workers was broadly the same in the two countries. Surveys have shown that the largest contingent of workers displaced in the 1980s consisted of men in their primary working years who lost blue-collar jobs in the manufacturing sector. The majority of displaced workers did find new employment within twenty-six weeks, and many did so at wages that were equal to or higher than in the original job. Nevertheless, a substantial minority of displaced workers in the United States and a slight majority of their Canadian counterparts bore a larger cost, being out of work for longer periods, having to accept lower wages when they found work, or dropping out of the labour force altogether. Moreover, additional analysis indicates that these higher costs tended to fall most heavily on certain groups. Unskilled workers, older workers, women, and ethnic minorities were likely to be unemployed longer, were less likely to find another job at all, and were more likely to suffer a fall in wages if they did find one. (For a survey of relevant studies, see OECD 1990a.)

The costs of economic turbulence have not been restricted to the unemployed. Employed workers have also felt the effects of economic restructuring and stagnating productivity. Figure 2.9 confirms that after substantial growth in the postwar period, the real earnings of the average worker have virtually stood still since the late 1970s in both Canada and the United States. Families dependent on the earnings of a single worker have seen no growth in real family earnings, and other families have depended heavily on the contribution of additional earners – especially women – for any economic advance they have enjoyed. Moreover, for many two-earner families, any financial gain has been mitigated by increased work-related costs, child-care expenses, the loss of leisure time, and added stress.

Both Canada and the United States have also seen a polarization in earnings, with the relative loss of middle-wage jobs and the relative

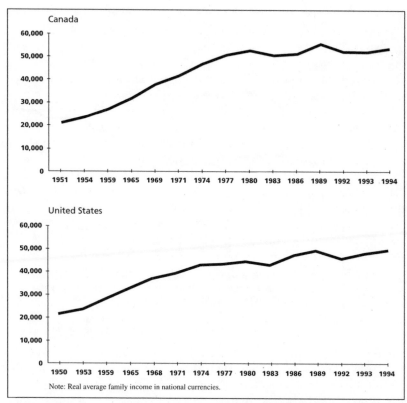

Figure 2.9   Real average family income, Canada and the United States, 1951–1994
(in 1994 dollars)
Sources: Statistics Canada 1995; U.S. Bureau of the Census 1996

growth of jobs paying very low or very high wages. Polarization has been considerably stronger in the United States, but the direction has been similar on both sides of the border.[4] Moreover, in both cases, men have been more affected than women. Despite all the commentary about deindustrialization, the loss of unionized manufacturing jobs to low-wage countries, and an accelerating shift to services – normally accompanied by stories of former steelworkers flipping hamburgers – polarization in the distribution of earnings has not resulted primarily from a shift *between* sectors. In both Canada and the United States, the important shifts have been occurring *within* sectors, including the service sector. Indeed, the pattern of greater wage polarization is common to most industries and occupations. The balance of factors at work, however, does seem to vary in the two countries. The American experience is more consistent with the argument advanced by

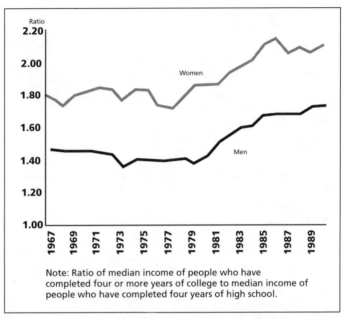

Note: Ratio of median income of people who have
completed four or more years of college to median income of
people who have completed four years of high school.

Figure 2.10   Ratio of median incomes of college-educated to high-school-
educated workers in the United States
Source: Council of Economic Advisors 1994

Reich and others that a global and technological economy favours
highly educated workers (whom Reich [1991] calls "symbolic analysts") but undermines the position of other workers, especially routine production workers. Figure 2.10 provides support for this view in
its examination of the wage gap between workers with a college education and those with only high school. The income premium for
college-educated workers in the United States, which had actually declined marginally during the 1970s, began to grow strongly during the
1980s for both men and women. However, the impact of education
was less discernible north of the border.[5] The burden of economic
change in Canada has fallen most heavily on young workers. The pain
of restructuring and adjustment, as reflected in unemployment, layoffs, churning in the labour market, and lower wages, is being felt most
by new entrants to the labour market. For these workers, wages have
proved quite flexible in a downward direction. This pattern was widespread during the 1980s, occurring across levels of education, industrial sectors, occupational groups, and regions (Myles, Picot, and
Wannell 1988a). In addition, the distribution of working time has
been important, since firms have increasingly preferred to have existing

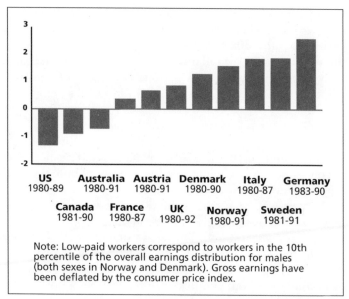

Figure 2.11   Growth in real wages of low-paid workers (annualized percentage change)
Source: OECD 1994a

employees work longer hours rather than taking on new employees (Morrisette, Myles, and Picot 1995) The symptoms of this intergenerational shift are showing up in a variety of dimensions, including a declining incidence of home ownership among young Canadian families (Economic Council of Canada 1989a).

Nevertheless, even when all the subtle differences between the experience of Canada and the United States are noted, the reality has been the common one of growing inequality in the income that families and individuals derive from their involvement in the economy. One sign of this is the comparative erosion of the position of low-income workers, which figure 2.11 places in a comparative context. The fundamental difference between the United States and Canada is in the extent to which each sought to offset these market pressures through the political choice. The role of the state in mitigating the inequality generated by market economies has varied considerably. In the United States the redistributive impulse faded during the decade, and government programs failed to offset the growing inegalitarian pressures inherent in economic restructuring. As a result, the distribution of final income, which measures income derived both from the market and from government transfer programs, also became less equal over the decade. In

Canada, however, the redistributive role of government continued to stabilize the level of income inequality. The larger system of income security programs offset the changing pattern of market pressures, with the result that the overall distribution of final income remained essentially stable throughout this period. This very different response to a common set of economic pressures is addressed at length in chapter 7.

Economic Restructuring and Economic Insecurity

The economic insecurity that many North Americans feel every day is deeply rooted in a changing economic order at both the global and the domestic level. Both countries have changed. Many traditional differences persist, to be sure, but the two economies are more tightly integrated and have converged on several dimensions of economic activity, such as productivity levels. The most striking convergence, however, has been in the policy debates and agendas of the two countries. Despite the continuing contrasts in the size, structure, and global weight of the two economies, both countries are focused on a policy agenda that is dominated by international economics, technological change, productivity failures, and a growing inequality of earnings. The problems and priorities that preoccupy president and prime minister, Congress and Parliament, are much more similar than in past years.

CHANGING SOCIETIES

If the economic circumstances in both Canada and the United States underline the pervasiveness of change, restructuring, and volatility, much the same is true of the domestic social environment. Changes here are generating increased social diversity along many dimensions of social life: language, race, ethnicity, family structure, relations between men and women, religious practice, sexual preferences, and personal lifestyle. Even more than the fact of greater difference is the perception that social differences are increasingly mobilized, politicized and institutionalized.

Undoubtedly, important continuities form strong links with the past. The contemporary developments are laid down on top of the historical divisions (such as race in the United States and language in Canada), and these divisions continue to influence the policy agendas in distinctive and powerful ways. Nevertheless, it is social change that defines the contemporary era. Both countries are having difficulty in coming to terms with what Gillian Peele and her colleagues describe as "fractured pluralism" (1992, 4), and the result has been a powerful convergence in social agendas. On both sides of the border, the postwar understanding

of nationwide citizenship has begun to crumble in the face of newly mobilized demands by collectivities for a "less universalistic understanding
of citizenship, and for categorical equity" (Jenson 1992, 197). The challenge for both countries is how to accommodate this diversity.

As noted earlier, the heightened perception of difference triggers
hopes and fears in both countries. For some, greater social diversity
holds out the promise of a more tolerant, open society; for others,
change generates a sense of cultural insecurity. Moreover, an intensified social pluralism raises questions about the future of the national
community and about the sense of mutual obligation and responsibility for one another. Arthur Schlesinger (1992) worries about the *Disuniting of America* and asks, "Can the centre hold?" He and others
worry about the dangers of "fragmentation" and "balkanization" in the
United States. In the same vein, the Canadian sociologist Reginald
Bibby entitled his 1990 book *Mosaic Madness*.

This section, like the previous one, focuses on the patterns of stability and change in Canada and the United States, though in this case it
concentrates on the dimensions of convergence and divergence in the
social structure of the two countries and the powerful convergence in
their social agendas. It begins with the primordial divisions of language and race, which stand as bedrock differences between the two
societies, and then moves on to sources of growing similarity in their
social structures and agendas: ethnicity, Aboriginal peoples, family and
gender relations, and religion.

Language

In the 1960s, the Canadian Royal Commission on Biculturalism and Bilingualism documented important inequalities between French and
English speakers. Francophones had considerably lower incomes and
lower positions on the occupational ladder than anglophones. They
were grossly underrepresented in the upper levels of the private sector
and of the federal bureaucracy. Federal institutions – and, even more,
provincial institutions – were often unable to respond to francophones
in their own language. By the 1980s, much of this had changed. The
linguistic face of the federal government had been dramatically altered;
francophones no longer suffered income or occupational discrimination (Vaillancourt 1992); and a dynamic new Quebec business class had
emerged. These changes were no doubt partly a function of higher levels of education and other social changes, but they were also a product
of policy. The Quiet Revolution carried out by Quebec governments after 1960 sought to modernize all facets of Quebec life, and successive
language laws opened the private sector to French-speaking workers. At

the federal level, the Official Languages Act promoted minority language rights, official bilingualism, and the aggressive recruitment of French-speaking Canadians to the higher levels of public service.

French-English tensions remain a fundamental issue on the national agenda, but they focus largely on the politics of identity. They are prominent, for instance, in the national debate about constitutional recognition of Quebec as a distinct society within Canada, and in the internal Quebec debate about whether Quebec's future national security is best to be found in a federal Canada or in some form of political sovereignty. Official bilingualism and the rights of the linguistic minorities (English-speaking in Quebec and French-speaking outside the provice) remain contentious: Quebec laws restricting the use of English on commercial signs provoked vigorous opposition across the country and contributed to the demise of a constitutional agreement embodied in the Meech Lake Accord (1987); meanwhile, the Reform Party speaks for those outside Quebec who resent the promotion of bilingualism and minority language rights across the country. The record is thus one of remarkable success on the socio-economic front, combined with continued uncertainty about the future of Canada as a political entity, especially in the aftermath of the 30 October 1995 referendum on sovereignty in Quebec, in which the federalist forces won by a mere few thousand votes.

In the United States, because of the overwhelming predominance of English speakers, black and white, language has not traditionally been an important source of division. The emphasis on assimilation for the early waves of non-English-speaking immigrants left little room for teaching "heritage languages" in the schools. However, the increasing number of Spanish-speaking migrants in recent years and the concentration of Hispanic communities in the Southwest, California, Texas, Florida, New York, and elsewhere have politicized language in the United States. On the one hand have been demands for Spanish-language education and public services; on the other, concern for the preservation of English, and the passage of "English as the official language" ordinances in a number of states and localities (Vaillancourt 1992). These conflicts are likely to increase. There is some parallel here to the language debate in Quebec. Increasing levels of immigration to Quebec and the tendency of immigrants to assimilate to the English-speaking community, along with a drastically lowered birth rate among native-born francophone Quebecers, provided the impetus for the Quebec language legislation which was designed to ensure that Quebec continued to be a predominantly French-speaking society. But although increasing ethnic diversity, and especially the growth of Hispanic communities, has greatly increased the salience of language politics in the

Table 2.2
Selected indicators of black disadvantage in the United States, 1990[1]

	White	Black
Poverty rate	8.8%	31.9%
Unemployment rate	4.1%	11.3%
Income > $50,000	32.5%	14.5%
Income < $15,000	14.2%	37.0%
Four years of college	24.4%	12.7%
Life expectancy (years)	76.0	70.3
Infant mortality (per 1,000)	8.1	16.5
Proportion of all prison inmates	39.6%	45.3%
Families headed by women	17.3%	56.2%

Source: Hacker 1992, 98, 100, 103, 197, 231

[1] Figures exclude Hispanics and Asians. Data on prison inmates are for 1986.

United States, and although this is likely to continue, the parallel is not to the great French-English divide in Canada; rather, it is to the Canadian debate about providing education and services in languages other than French or English for new immigrants in all provinces.

Race

Race dominates the American political landscape much as French-English relations dominate the Canadian one. But the recent American record of race relations has played out very differently. The pattern is summarized in Andrew Hacker's title, *Two Nations: Black and White, Separate, Hostile and Unequal* (1992). Overall, the economic position of African Americans did improve through most of the 1960s and 1970s; there was considerable convergence between whites and blacks in occupational status, levels of education and average incomes. But progress slowed or reversed in the 1980s (G. Thomas 1989). Table 2.2 shows that inequalities between blacks and whites in the United States remain very large, however they are measured. As Hacker and others point out, the United States remains a highly segregated society. Racial separation is still "pervasive and penetrating" in housing and other areas (Hacker 1992, 3). In twenty-five major cities, public schools are as racially segregated as they were in 1954, the year the U.S. Supreme Court declared segregated schooling unconstitutional (Jarvis 1992). Overall in 1991, two-thirds of black students and three-quarters of Hispanic schoolchildren were clustered in predominantly minority schools (*New York Times*, 14 December 1993). However, aggregate data on the relative status of blacks and others conceal considerable shifts within the black community. Most dramatic here is the increasing tendency to "bifurcation" – the simultaneous emergence of a considerable black middle class, many of whom have followed the white migration to the suburbs, and the growth of an increasingly impoverished black underclass, concentrated in inner-city areas. This trend has led William Julius Wilson and others to suggest that there is a "declining significance of race" in the United States (Wilson 1980). Class-related factors such as education, Wilson argues, are becoming a better predictor of life chances and attitudes than racial background, though his thesis has been challenged (Herring 1989). Others have suggested that the chief beneficiaries of antidiscrimination and affirmative action policies have been members of the black middle class, not those in the working class or underclass (Lowi 1988).

The definition, size, composition and causes of the underclass are all highly contested. Most commonly, the term refers to a concatenation of social and economic characteristics that are concentrated in many inner-city gettos: poverty, unemployment (especially among young men), low skill levels, high crime rates, and a high proportion of families headed by poor, single young women. All these dimensions feed off one another to produce what in many respects is a substantially large Third World country within the United States.

Explanations for the persistence of the underclass vary widely. For some, it is a direct result of the pervasive racism of American society and the inadequacies of its welfare state. For writers such as Murray (1984), it is a self-perpetuating and self-destructive culture of poverty, combined with the allegedly perverse effects of a social policy regime that rewards dependency; more recently and more controversially, genetic endowment has been added to the mix (Murray and Herrnstein 1994). Perhaps the most influential explanation is that of William Julius Wilson (1987), who links it to larger changes in the American economy. The biggest losers from economic adjustments have been young and poorly educated minority men (Peterson 1991, 19; Massey and Eggers 1990). As industry and jobs moved out of the city centres to the suburbs, the city centres lost the unskilled and semi-skilled manufacturing jobs that had previously provided relative economic security. Whites and educated middle-class blacks were able to follow industry; the unskilled and uneducated were not. The urban ghettos are thus the result of the pernicious interaction between poverty and segregation and between race, class, and gender. Or, as Wilson puts it, the underclass is a function of the simultaneous presence of economic marginality and extreme social isolation (1991, 462).

The result of all this is that in the United States most whites and blacks continue to live in different economic and social worlds. Racist attitudes among whites appear to have declined over the long term, support for integration is high, and there has been a notable convergence between the attitudes of Southerners and other white Americans. At the same time, there is considerable resistance to affirmative action, bussing, and other such measures (Schaefer 1986; Firebaugh and Davis 1988). Thus, there is a disparity between the positive general attitude towards blacks and the actual support for policies that might achieve greater integration (G. Thomas 1989). Various voting rights acts have removed legal barriers to black participation, and African Americans have enjoyed considerable electoral success, especially at the state and local level. One important device to increase the representation of minority representatives has been the drawing of district boundaries in which African Americans constitute a majority, a form of "principled gerrymandering." These devices have been highly controversial, and their constitutionality has been thrown into question by the United States Supreme Court (*New York Times,* 29 and 30 June 1993). The debate in this and other areas is the classic one between individual and group rights, and over whether to recognize and institutionalize difference in order to overcome the disadvantages of difference (Guinier 1991; Kymlicka 1992).

With regard to the situation in Canada, race – at least in the American sense of the relations between black Canadians and others – is to Canadian politics what language is to American politics. Afro-Canadians constitute a much smaller proportion of the Canadian population than Afro-Americans or even Hispanics do in the United States. With the important exception of such historic black communities as those in Halifax and Windsor, most black Canadians are recent immigrants. Thus, most Canadian analyses include blacks as one group within the larger category of "visible minorities."

Nevertheless, Afro-Canadians seem to face higher barriers and greater discrimination than members of other visible minorities. Caribbean immigrants tend to have lower incomes and less educational attainment. They are also much more likely than other minority groups to perceive themselves – and be perceived by others – as discriminated against, though the figures are also high for East Asians (Goldfarb 1992; Decima Research 1993). The Economic Council of Canada looked at the earnings of immigrants who had Canadian education and experience and were from a variety of countries, and compared them with Canadians of similar socio-economic characteristics. The only groups for which a statistically significant wage discrimination was found were immigrants from the West Indies and East Asia (Economic Council of Canada 1991a).[6] A more impressionistic analysis puts it in starker terms. A report to the Ontario government in the aftermath of tensions in Toronto concluded that racism in the province "fundamentally, is anti-Black racism"; it is "Blacks who are being shot at ... unemployed in excessive numbers ... inappropriately streamed in schools ... disproportionately dropping out ... on whom the doors of upward equity slam shut" (S. Lewis 1992, 2).

Thus, as in the United States, there has been an increase in racial tensions – especially in Toronto and Montreal. Many of these tensions are focused on relations between the police and blacks and, to a lesser extent, the schools. At the same time, there has been a general rise in racial tolerance in the population at large. (For the most careful assessment of the relevant public opinion data, see Economic Council of Canada 1991a, ch. 9; Angus Reid Inc. 1991.) Thus, race has made itself felt on the Canadian policy agenda, but it has none of the pervasive, primordial character of race relations in the United States.

Ethnicity

Language and race, then, remain profoundly divergent influences in the two countries. When the frame of reference is widened to capture the broader pattern of ethnic diversity, however, it becomes clear that the two are converging as both become more complex multicultural societies. Table 2.3 captures the growing complexity of each society, as conventionally defined in each country. In the United States, just one relatively recent immigrant group, the Hispanics from Mexico, Cuba, Puerto Rico, and other Latin American countries, may exceed the number of native-born black Americans by the year 2000. Almost 11 per cent of California's population and 6.6 per cent of New York's arrived in the country in the last decade (*New York Times*, 28 May 1992). By 1990, almost 40 per cent of Los Angeles' population was foreign born, and Hispanics and Asians together constituted half of the city's population (*Washington Post Weekly*, 9 May 1992). In the single decade 1980–90, Los Angeles' Hispanic population grew from 2 million to 3.4 million, and its Asian population more than doubled to almost one million (*New York Times*, 6 June 1993).

In Canada, the dominant position of descendants of the French and British "founding peoples" is eroding rapidly. In 1991, 12.5 per cent of the population reported a mother tongue other than English or French, and more than half of these people lived in Toronto, Montreal, or Vancouver. Almost one-third of Torontonians spoke a mother tongue that was not one of the official languages; the figures were 24 per cent in Vancouver, 21 per cent in Winnipeg, and 17 per cent in Montreal. It is predicted that by the year 2000, "visible minorities" will

Table 2.3
Ethnic composition, Canada and the United States, 1981 and 1991

	1981	1991
CANADA		
British	40	28
French	27	23
British and French	6	4
British or French and other[1]	na	14
Other European	19	15
Asian	3	6
Other	4	6
Aboriginal[1]	na	4
UNITED STATES		
White	79	75
Black	12	12
Hispanic	7	9
Aboriginal	0.6	0.7
Asian	2	2.3

Sources: Canada: Kalbach 1990, table 2.4; Vanier Institute of the Family 1994, 22. United States: U.S. Bureau of the Census 1994, 19

[1]   This category was not used in the 1981 census.

constitute 18 per cent of Canada's population (Gusella 1992). The concentration of recent immigrants in a few large urban areas has brought about enormous changes in these cities' economic, cultural, and social life within a relatively short period of time. As in the United States, there is a sharp bifurcation between the ethnically diverse large cities on the one hand and, on the other, the smaller cities, rural areas, and some provinces and states that have been little touched by these changes. For example, in Canada, just over 1 per cent of New Brunswick's population has a non-official mother tongue; the figure is about 2 per cent in Nova Scotia, but more than 17 per cent in Ontario and British Columbia.

The changing ethnic make-up of the two countries reflects important parallel changes in their immigration and refugee policies (Reimers and Troper 1992; Zolberg 1992; Sullivan 1992; Li 1990). In both countries, immigration rates slowed greatly in the depression and wartime periods, then picked up in recent decades (see table 2.4). Relative to the total population, Canadian immigration levels, while fluctuating, have remained higher than those of the United States, though

Table 2.4
Immigration levels, Canada and the United States, 1960–1992

	Canada	United States
1960	104,111	365,398
1970	147,713	373,326
1980	143,117	530,639
1990	212,166	1,536,483
1992	252,842	973,977

Sources: To 1980, calculated from Reimers and Troper 1992, tables 2.1 and 2.2; later data from U.S. Bureau of the Census 1994 and Thompson Educational Publishing 1994

the numbers would likely be closer if the higher rate of illegal immigration to the United States, especially from Mexico and other countries in Latin America, were taken into account. Officially, immigrants constituted 16 per cent of the Canadian population in 1991, in contrast to 8 per cent of the population of the United States in 1990 (Reitz and Breton 1994).

Beginning in the 1960s, both countries liberalized their practices, increasing the number of immigrants and reducing the bias against those from the Third World. The mix of migrants shifted from Europeans to Asians, Latin Americans, West Indians, and Africans. In 1957, 91.4 per cent of immigrants to Canada were drawn from Britain and Europe; between 1955 and 1964, 50 per cent of all immigrants to the United States were Europeans and another 26.4 per cent were Canadians. As table 2.5 indicates, the mix had changed dramatically by the 1980s. Asia, the Caribbean, and Central and South America predominated, with powerful implications for the social composition of both countries (Reimers and Troper 1992.)

The changing immigration policy is making the United States and Canada more similar societies. The new waves of immigration also challenge older divisions in both countries. There have been important tensions between blacks and some of the newer immigrant groups, especially Cuban Hispanics in Miami, Hasidic Jews in Brooklyn, and Korean shopkeepers in New York, Los Angeles, and elsewhere. In part, this may reflect black frustration at the continual pattern of "leap-frogging," whereby new ethnic groups rapidly move ahead of native-born black Americans. It also reflects black fears that the new immigrant groups diminish job opportunities for blacks, although there is little evidence of this. In Canada, the politics of ethnicity challenges the centrality of politics based on French-English and regional interests – for example, by broadening the constitutional

Table 2.5
Region of origin of immigrants: Canada 1980–1989; United States 1975–1988

Region	Canada (%)	United States (%)
Asia	46	43.6
Europe	27	11.0
Americas	20	41.9
Africa	5	2.8
Oceania	1	0.7

Sources: Canada: Thompson Educational Publishing 1994, 32. United States: Reimers and Troper 1992, table 2.4

agenda and by challenging the "hierarchy of rights" that is alleged to privilege French and English groups (Kallen 1990). It has also challenged Quebec nationalists to reshape the basis of Québécois identity from ethnicity and language to a more pluralist conception of identity based on civic citizenship (Breton 1988; Kymlicka 1992, 39–40), a challenge that became acute in the aftermath of the October 1995 referendum on Quebec separation. Thus, the changing ethnic make-up has considerable potential for "altering the relationships between the original founding groups" (Kalbach 1990, 19).

The similarities in the everyday life of immigrants in both countries deny the divergent symbols of the American "melting pot" and the Canadian "mosaic." In contrast to the traditional image that minority groups in Canada are encouraged to maintain their distinctive cultures whereas their counterparts in the United States are encouraged to melt into the cultural mainstream, public attitudes – as measured by public opinion polls – are more supportive of cultural retention by minorities in the United States than they are in Canada (Reitz and Breton 1994; see also Decima Research 1993). Moreover, the differences in the actual experience of immigrants tend to be small. The broad rates of cultural assimilation are similar, as are the overall levels of occupational mobility (Reitz and Breton 1994). In both countries, there are differences between the various immigrant groups. Many Asian immigrant groups have education levels well above the national average, median family incomes above the average, and unemployment rates that are lower than the average; other immigrant groups do less well, for example, many Hispanics and Pacific Islanders in the United States and Caribbeans in Canada (U.S. Bureau of the Census 1994, 38; Economic Council of Canada 1991a). In both countries, immigrant women appear to face greater hurdles in the workforce than immigrant men (Economic Council of Canada 1991a). And in both, racial discrimination in such areas as employment and housing remains a reality (Reitz and Breton 1994). Overall, the similarities in the experiences of immigrants in the two societies far outweigh the differences.

Nevertheless, the traditional symbols of melting pot and mosaic retain potency in official ideologies and cultural policy. On both sides of the border, the political mobilization of ethnic groups has increased the salience of multiculturalism in political and social life. The term has become not only an empirical description of the composition of society but also a movement, seeking formal recognition within institutions and policies. However, Canada has moved further in this regard. From the beginning, official culture in Canada has been predicated on the recognition and coexistence of distinct cultural groups (Lipset 1990a). The historic conception of Canada as a coming together of two founding peoples, English and French, legitimated an ethnically based policy regime and created an opportunity for newer immigrant groups to demand inclusion in the cultural policies of the country. In 1971 Parliament formally endorsed a policy of multiculturalism. The next year, the federal government established a multicultural directorate within the Ministry of the Secretary of State and provided financial support to minority groups. Several provinces officially embraced multiculturalism. The multicultural character of the country was given explicit constitutional recognition in the 1982 Canadian Charter of Rights and Freedoms, and in 1988 the federal government passed the Multiculturalism Act, whose goal is the "preservation and enhancement of Canadian multiculturalism" (Elliott and Fleras 1990). Multicultural groups also sought equal recognition with other groups in a proposed "Canada clause" defining the fundamental characteristics of the country in the ill-fated constitutional proposals of 1992. Canadian multiculturalism policy still has its critics, who insist that it remains a weak instrument (Kallen 1990; Stasiulis and Abu-Laban 1990; Simard et al. 1991). Nevertheless, it can be argued that the historical experience of recognizing linguistic duality and regional difference has facilitated the growth of today's "accommodative pluralism" in Canada (W.L. Morton 1981).

Multiculturalism has received less formal recognition in the United States, especially at the level of constitutional symbolism. It is played out primarily in specific arenas, such as the schools. Indeed, the term itself is controversial, often carrying a pejorative connotation. While many Americans celebrate American ethnic and social diversity, and while ethnicity continues to play an important role in American politics, the ideology of *e pluribus unum* contributes to a reluctance to institutionalize difference. Many American commentators fear that multiculturalism could quickly shade into "cultural separatism" (Hughes 1993), promoted by the "ideologues of ethnicity" (Schlesinger 1992, 131). Although the bitter ideological debates about such matters as the nature of "the canon" in literary and cultural studies in American universities do have Canadian parallels, the Canadian debates appear to be far less intense and divisive. Some Canadians argue that state recognition of cultural differences can exacerbate intergroup competition for status, power, and economic benefits (Breton 1992; also Moodley 1984) and that in emphasizing the parts, the common strengths of the whole are lost: the mosaic becomes no more than a collection of scattered shards of glass (Bibby 1990; Bissoondath 1994). However, so far at least, such critiques have greater political resonance south of the border.

Despite different levels of institutionalization, both countries are engaged in remarkably similar controversies about policy responses. Each debates alternative models of expressing ethnic pluralism: the classic liberal model of nondiscrimination and equality of opportunity versus the "corporate" model of cultural diversity, group benefits, equality of condition, "enhanced structural separation," and multilingualism (M.M. Gordon 1981). The debate has affected the policy agenda, both at the national level, where immigration and refugee policy is of growing concern, and at the local level, where increased numbers of visible minorities, most speaking English as a second language, intensify pressures on such services as the police, schools, medical care, and social welfare. The growing salience of ethnic diversity and the debates about how to manage it are a powerful element of convergence between the two countries.

Aboriginal Peoples

Convergence in the broader patterns of ethnicity is reinforced by the mobilization of Aboriginal peoples: Indian, Metis, and Inuit in Canada, and Indian, Aleut, and Eskimo in the United States. In both countries, these peoples still bear the legacy of conquest and of subsequent policies. In both countries, their socio-economic status – in income, unemployment, levels of education, and health – remains far behind that of all other ethnic groups, including most recent immigrants. In both countries, native communities face enormous stress, a result both of poverty and of the social disorganization engendered by the loss of traditional values and cultures. Moreover, the underdevelopment of Indian reservations has produced an accelerating urbanization of the Aboriginal population, again with serious social consequences (Jarvenpa 1985). While there were important differences between Canada and the United States in the pattern of white settlement and the occupation of native lands, there have also been important parallels. In both countries, especially in regions where Aboriginal peoples are concentrated, there are many points of friction between the Aboriginal peoples and the dominant society – on the ownership of land, on hunting and fishing rights, on the rights of Aboriginal peoples to set up their own regimes in such areas as gambling, and so on.

There has been a similar pattern in the recent mobilization of Aboriginal peoples, centred on the concept of Aboriginal self-government and a reaffirmation of native identities and cultures. In both cases, white attitudes have shifted – from a celebration of conquest, a marginalization of Aboriginal peoples, and an emphasis on eventual assimilation, to a greater recognition of past injustice and of the need for Aboriginal peoples to gain more control over their lives. Both countries have had to reinterpret their history.

The political dynamics generated by the politics of self-government have differed in the two countries. American Indian peoples have long had greater control over their own affairs. Since the middle of the nineteenth century, American law has recognized a degree of sovereign authority for the Indian nations, expressed in Chief Justice Marshall's term "domestic dependent nations." The Indian nations have been "legally free to exercise inherent jurisdiction over internal affairs, subject to an overriding federal power and duty of protection" (Macklem 1993, 1317). This has traditionally meant that they have had more latitude than Canadian Indians to design tribal governments and to exercise power in a wide variety of areas. It has also meant that state governments have had less room than Canadian provinces to exercise authority in matters affecting Aboriginal peoples. Given this history, native Americans have continued to rely on the courts to reinforce their traditional right of self-government. As a result, the struggle has tended to be defensive in nature and not to be a major issue on the national political agenda (Brock 1993).

The Canadian political experience has been very different. Traditionally, Canadian law saw all authority, including that over Indians, as emanating from the Crown, and treated any Indian government as exercising delegated authority (Macklem 1993). A right to self-government was denied at the outset, and the Canadian government took extensive control of the internal life of the tribes (Brock 1993). The struggle for self-government has therefore had to be waged in political as well as judicial terms. As in the case of multiculturalism, the efforts at broad constitutional reform in Canada created an opening for Aboriginal communities. Effective political mobilization led to constitutional recognition of Aboriginal and treaty rights, and a guarantee that the new

Charter of Rights and Freedoms would not derogate from any such rights in the Constitution Act, 1982 (Frideres 1990). Efforts to provide a more precise constitutional statement of native rights led to a series of first ministers' conferences on the issue in the mid-1980s, and eventually to the full participation by representatives of the leading Aboriginal groups in the constitutional negotiations of 1992. The resulting Charlottetown Accord embraced the concept of Aboriginal self-government and set out procedures for the establishment of a "third order of government" in Canada. Although it, too, was rejected in the 1992 referendum, the idea of the empowerment of Aboriginal peoples through self-government, land claims, and recognition of historic treaty rights is now well established. Indeed, the issue came to be defined as an "inherent right to self-government." The Royal Commission on Aboriginal Peoples concluded in 1993 that the right to self-government already exists within constitutional law and does not require any new constitutional amendment (Canada, Royal Commission on Aboriginal Peoples 1993).

Although the (re)discovery of the rights of members of the First Nations clearly is a point of convergence between the two countries, the issue has recently had much greater political salience in Canada.

Family and Gender Relations

Another fundamental element of convergence with major consequences for politics and policy is the changing nature of relationships between women and men, and the associated transformations in the family. The most obvious indicator change is the position of women in the workforce. In 1960 less than one-third of women with children in the United States were employed; by 1988 the figure had risen to 65 per cent. In Canada, the proportion moved from 35.4 to 57.4 per cent, with three-quarters of all women aged twenty-five to fifty-four in the workforce. More than half of all women with children under six were working (compared with less than one in five in 1960). In both countries, women still took primary responsibility for child care and housekeeping. At the same time the postwar baby boom ended, and both countries experienced dramatically lower birth rates. This in turn altered the age distribution of the population, with the proportion of children under fourteen declining and the proportion of persons over sixty-five increasing. Between 1970 and 1990 the proportion of those sixty-five and older increased from 8 to 11.4 per cent in Canada, and from 9.8 to 12.2 per cent in the United States (Sorrentino 1990, 43, table 2).

Family structures were changing dramatically. Divorce rates rose in both countries. Canadian divorce rates jumped rapidly after liberalization of the divorce laws in 1968 and again in 1985 (O. Adams 1990),

Table 2.6
Divorce and remarriage, Canada and the United States, 1991

	Canada (%)	United States (%)
Divorce rate	28	44
Remarriage rate	70	81

Source: Vanier Institute of the Family 1994, table 27

but they remain somewhat lower than in the United States, as table 2.6 indicates. In both countries marriage was occurring later, and more couples were living together outside marriage (Turcotte 1990; Caplow et al. 1991), though common-law marriage was more frequent in Canada and more acceptable in the eyes of the public, especially in Quebec (Eichler 1990; M. Adams 1993b). In recent years, the number of children born to or living with a single parent has almost doubled (Eichler 1990). This suggests that the traditional link between family and child rearing has been weakened. Marriage continues to be a popular institution in both countries, but on both sides of the border an increasing proportion of marriages involve remarriage for at least one partner; this is the case for about one-third of all marriages in Canada and more than one-half in the United States (Eichler 1990, 8). Kinship structures in "blended families" have become more complex, and the traditional model of the nuclear family is growing less and less common (Glick 1990; Ontario Law Reform Commission 1993).

For some observers, these changes constitute a "crisis" in family life involving huge social costs, both for the individuals involved, especially women and children, and for society as a whole (Glenn 1987; Furstenberg 1990; Beaujot 1988, 1990). Conservatives tend to emphasize measures to strengthen the responsibility of family members and to discourage perceived threats to the traditional family, such as gay and lesbian rights or abortion. Liberals, on the other hand, tend to argue that what both countries have been seeing is less a decline of family than a shift in the nature and meaning of family, and a broadening of the kinds of relationship it denotes to include blended families, gay and lesbian relationships, cohabitation arrangements, and the like – a "mosaic of family forms and functions" (Bibby 1990, 64). In this view, change in family structure does not herald a breakdown of social order. In the United States, these changes have fuelled the debate on "family values," which was prominent in the 1992 election campaign, and have placed the future of the family on the political agenda. Perhaps because the changes have not been as dramatic in Canada – and

Table 2.7
Ratio of female to male earnings, Canada and the United States, 1960–1990

		United States		
	Canada	All	White	Black
1960	54.2	60.7	–	–
1970	52.2	59.4	58.7	69.8
1980	52.6	60.2	58.9	78.8
1990	60.3	71.6	69.4	85.4

Sources: Canada: Rashid 1993, table 1. United States: U.S. Bureau of the Census 1992

have not been focused so much on a single racial group – the debate has not been so strong or divisive.

Although increased participation in the paid workforce has transformed family life, it has not brought about economic or political equality between men and women. Table 2.7 documents that women earn considerably less on average than men in both countries, and this proportion has begun to change only recently. Women have moved into a number of professional occupations that were formerly male bastions, such as law, medicine, and management, but have made little progress in others, such as engineering (Fox and Fox 1987; Wharton 1989; Parliament 1990; Caplow et al. 1991). Numerous studies suggest that where women have entered formerly male professions, they face barriers to advancement, and many occupations remain "pink-collar ghettos." In this context, divorce can have devastating financial consequences for women and children; single-parent families headed by women have the lowest median income of all family forms in both countries (Mossman and MacLean 1986; Abowitz 1986; Eichler 1990). Moreover, despite some recent advances, including a record number of female members in both Congress and Parliament following the most recent national elections, women remain underrepresented in political life (Megyery 1991; Brodie 1991).

These realities have fuelled the political mobilization of the women's movement. The modern manifestation of women in politics began in the United States in the 1960s, in part a product of the movements for civil rights and expressive freedom in that period. These ideas quickly spilled over the border, strengthening a parallel women's movement in Canada which had indigenous roots in the peace movement and the New Democratic Party (Vickers 1992). This cross-fertilization and the similarity of the issues that concern them mean that the American and Canadian movements have much in common. In both, the women's movement has itself become diverse, embracing different ideological and tactical strands, including liberal, socialist, and radical and both heterosexual and lesbian (Burt 1990; Peele et al. 1992). Both originated among white middle-class women, and both have recently been challenged by women of colour and poor women, who are calling for greater sensitivity to the interaction of gender, race, and class (Valverde 1992; Mukherjee 1992; Stasiulis 1990). "Totalizing feminisms" and an undifferentiated concept of gender are being replaced by multiple and shifting conceptions, "complicating the idea of gender" (O'Barr 1992:146). Finally, both movements have relied heavily on the courts in addition to grass-roots direct action and traditional lobbying. In Canada, this has especially been the case since the advent of the Charter of Rights and Freedoms.

At the same time, different cultural and institutional settings have sustained differences in the two movements. Some commentators argue that accommodating the various strands of feminism has been more successful in Canada than in the United States (Hamilton and Barrett 1986). In particular, Canada's national umbrella organization, the National Action Committee on the Status of Women, has been more successful at integrating the various streams within the movement than has its closest American counterpart, the National Organization of Women (Peele et al. 1992). The former is a coalition of a large number of groups (including churches) and the three major political parties, while the latter relies on individual membership. On the other hand, the Canadian movement has been divided between the Quebec and English-Canadian women's movement. The two sides differ not so much over their feminism but in their perception of the national context in which it takes place – Canada or Quebec (De Seve 1992).

Moreover, as in the case of multiculturalism, state-sponsored institutions have played a central role in energizing women's concerns in Canada. The Royal Commission on the Status of Women (1970) and the Royal Commission on Employment Equity (1982) defined much of the agenda for years afterwards. The first federal "Minister Responsible for the Status of Women" was appointed in 1971, and an Advisory Council on the Status of Women was created in 1973. As well, public funding has played an important role in supporting women's organizations and their activities, even though it has been reduced in recent years. These differences reflect a larger difference between the two women's movements. Jill Vickers (1992) argues that the movement in the United States has been strongly shaped by its origins in the new left, and the movement in Canada by its roots in the NDP. She sees in the Canadian movement a greater commitment to electoral politics, a stronger belief in the efficacy of state action, and a greater optimism that change is possible. Others note strong linkages between the women's movement and other "progressive" interests on broad issues of social, trade, and economic policy (M.G. Cohen 1992). The American movement, Vickers argues, is more populist, more libertarian and antistatist, and more focused on radical change through changing consciousness. In addition, it appears that militant opposition to the women's agenda in the United States, such as Phyllis Schafly's successful "Stop ERA" and the many "pro-life" movements in the abortion debate, have been stronger and more vocal than parallel groups in Canada, such as REAL Women.

While it is important not to overstate these differences, there is clearly a greater Canadian willingness to institutionalize difference through the structures of the state. American women's groups have recently been involved in a major constitutional issue – the battle for the Equal Rights Amendment. Their failure stands in strong contrast to the successful campaign of the Canadian women's movement to ensure gender equality in the antidiscrimination provisions of the 1982 Charter and in its section 28, which guarantees all rights equally to men and women. This battle was an energizing event in the Canadian women's movement, and women's groups continued to play a role in both the Meech Lake Accord (1987) and the Charlottetown Accord (1992). Both agreements, they argued, seemed to establish a "hierarchy of rights," potentially subordinating women and some other groups to the traditional Canadian preoccupations with Quebec and federal-provincial relations.

Whatever the debates about the "success" of the women's movement or about a perceived growing backlash against feminist goals, there is little doubt that in both countries it has greatly altered the political agenda and has helped pioneer new forms of political action. It has indeed brought "the personal" into the political arena. Despite some differences in organization and strategy, the parallels outweigh the differences. This is another powerful element of convergence in Canadian and American societies.

Religion

If changes in ethnic composition and gender roles are powerful elements of change in Canada and the United States, other spheres combine both continuity and greater social diversity. Religious belief and practice is one such area. Here, some of the older differences between Canada and the United States persist. In both countries, very large majorities express a belief in some form of God and identify with a religious

Table 2.8
Religious identification, Canada and the United States (in per cent)

Canada	1961	1981	1991
Catholic	46.7	47.3	45.7
Protestant	48.9	41.2	36.2
Other	3.9	4.2	5.8
No religion	0.5	7.3	12.4
United States	*1957*	*1980*	*1991*
Protestant	66	61	56
Catholic	26	28	25
Jewish	3	2	2
Other	1	2	6
No religion	3	7	11

Sources: Canada: Vanier Institute of the Family 1994, 26. United States: U.S. Bureau of the Census 1994, 70

denomination. As table 2.8 reveals, those claiming no religious preference have increased in both countries but still remain small minorities. Regular church attendance by Americans has changed little since the 1960s; in 1987, 40 per cent reported attending a church or synagogue in the previous week. Rates were lower in Canada, where only 30 per cent of those with an affiliation reporting attending in the past week (Mori 1990). Two-thirds of Canadians agree that their religious beliefs are important to them, while one-third disagree; in the United States, four-fifths agree (M. Adams 1993a).

Immigration has led to some shifts among denominations: in both countries a small decline in the proportion of Roman Catholics and Protestants, and a rise in the proportion belonging to religions originating in other parts of the world. Both countries have seen a shift among Protestants, with a relative decline in the membership of traditional denominations and a rapid rise in support for more fundamentalist, evangelical, Pentecostal churches (Mori 1990; M. Friedman 1980; Roof 1982). There has also been a growth in various manifestations of "heterodox religiosity" (Robbins and Dick 1979), represented by movements such as Islam among African Americans and New Age spiritualism among other groups (Ahlstrom 1988). Thus, rather than declining, religion and its role in American and Canadian life seems, like the family, to be diversifying. Writers in both countries argue that there has been a privatizing of religious belief and activity; churches are no longer centres of authority. Instead, it is a matter of individual choice in which "selective consumers" choose their religion *à la carte* (Bibby 1990, 85; also S. Hart 1987).

Despite this convergence, there remain some important differences between Canada and the United States. In particular, religion appears to be considerably more politicized in the United States. Based largely in fundamentalist Protestant churches, the "New Christian Right, "involving a multitude of groups of which the Christian Coalition has become the most prominent, has emerged to play a vigorous role on a range of issues, including abortion, and school prayer (Harden and Shupe 1988; Boone 1989; Wills 1990; Hunter 1991; Diamond 1994). The Christian Right has been especially active at the state and local levels, claiming considerable success for its candidates. It constitutes one of the most important factions within the Republican Party, and its members control the party apparatus in a growing number of states. It has campaigned for and against individual candidates in recent elections, claiming considerable success, and has led the fight in many state referenda on issues such as homosexual rights and women's equality (*Economist* 1992, 25). In recent elections, it has also sought with some success to broaden its support among more secular conservatives (Kaufman 1994). By contrast, although the fundamentalist churches have grown in Canada, they have had far less impact. Religious imagery plays little role in the rhetoric of the Reform Party, which espouses some of the same conservative issues. Of the total interest-group spending in the 1988 federal election measured by Janet Hiebert (1991), only one Christian conservative group, Campaign Life Coalition was identified, and it spent only $75,000. Tanguay and Kay (1991, 92–5) found that Christian fundamentalist groups had no measurable effect on the results. This contrast between the two countries suggests both a continuation of the different national religious traditions – "utopian moralism" in the United States versus "Canadian coexistence," identified by Lipset and others (Lipset 1990a, 76–84) – and the greater permeability of the American electoral process to groups of all kinds.

Social Diversity and Integration

The pattern of domestic social change, then, is one of increased diversity. Traditional divisions such as race and language have not been displaced; but they been challenged by a host of more complex cleavages – based on ethnicity, Aboriginal status, gender, religious practice, sexual preference, and others – with which they interact in complex ways. In both countries, social diversity echoes through many spheres of life, sustaining greater variety in lifestyles, music, food, communications, entertainment, and other cultural activities. The basic patterns are remarkably similar. Increasingly, social divisions seem to be rooted less in structurally defined or inherited social characteristics, such as class or religion, than in shifting identities, values, and ideologies. They are less "givens" than they are continually shifting "imagined communities" (Anderson 1983). Identities and interests once linked only loosely to the political domain have become politicized. Politics is as much about status as it is about material interests. Social conflicts are worked out in a wider range of institutions. And new conceptions of equality such as requiring affirmative action for distinctive groups challenge traditional conceptions of equal rights and benefits to all citizens, regardless of race, colour, or creed.

Important differences remain between these two North American societies, to be sure. There is no Canadian parallel to the fissure of race in the United States and the associated crisis of the inner cities; and the United States faces no threat to its territorial integrity that parallels the Quebec independence movement. Differences also persist in the management of social divisions. In Canada, a constitutional culture based on the institutionalization of ethnolinguistic difference has been expanded to incorporate newer divisions. The more state-centred Canadian tradition has meant that differences rooted in multicultural, Aboriginal, and gender experiences may have been more easily incorporated into governmental symbols, structures, and processes.

Given this increased diversity in its many forms, a pervasive theme in commentaries on these two North American societies is, Where is the glue? Where is the basis for social cohesion? Has a collective sense of national community been drowned in a welter of special interests? Thus, Bibby asks: "If what we have in common is diversity, do we really have anything in common at all?" (Bibby 1990, 92). And in the United States, Robert Bellah and his colleagues argue, "What has failed at every level – from the society of nations to the national society to the local community to the family – is integration ... We have put our own good, as individuals, as groups, as a nation, ahead of the common good" (1985, 285). Such fears are characteristic of any period of rapid social change and of any period in which newly mobilized or empowered social groups challenge the existing social order. In some cases, the fear of disintegration and disorder can be exaggerated. For example, in both countries, but especially in the United States, fear of crime is pervasive, and there has been an enormous increase in the rates of imprisonment. But overall there has been little change in the rates of major crimes (U.S. Bureau of the Census 1994, 166, 170).[7]

The challenge for both countries is not to repress or ignore the diversity – which is neither desirable nor possible – but to accommodate and manage it. This challenge, however, emerges as part of an even broader sense of a decline in the "social capital" (J.S. Coleman 1988, 1990; Putnam 1993a) or "civic engagement," which binds disparate individuals into cohesive communities. Such analyses come in many guises. At the macro-level, there is Robert Reich's argument that the American business and knowledge classes have "disengaged" from American life under the pressures of globalization (Reich 1991). At the micro-level, Robert Putnam and others have documented two sets of phenomena in the United States. First is a decline in membership and participation in a wide range of associations, ranging from the Boy Scouts to the Red Cross, to civic and school associations, to trade unions. Not only has voter turnout declined, but so has social and political activity of all kinds (Putnam 1994). Reginald Bibby tracks a similar decline in formal group membership in Canada. Indeed, overall, group membership remains slightly higher in the United States than in Canada (Bibby 1990, 92–7; Inglehart 1994, fig. 14).

Thus, the economic, social, and technological changes explored in this chapter seem to be undermining "the material and even physical basis for civic engagement" (Putnam 1994, 24). This decline in "connectedness," Putnam and others suggest, is both a consequence and a cause of much of the contemporary political malaise.

CHANGE AND THE POLICY AGENDA

Economic restructuring and new forms of social pluralism are reshaping the world in which Canadians and Americans live and work, challenging traditional social norms and sweeping away familiar aspects of their economies. As in earlier waves of modernization, the contemporary forces of change are not impelling Canada and the United States towards an identical social and economic model. Traditional differences persist: the greater weight of the United States in the international economic and political order, the asymmetrical trade relationship between the two countries, the greater role of the resource sector in the Canadian economy, and the contrasting role of race and language in social life. Moreover, new differences, such as the strength of trade unions, have opened up. These fundamental disjunctions inject distinctive dynamics into national life on the two sides of the border.

Nevertheless, Canada and the United States are increasingly similar along many dimensions. Convergence can be seen in the substantial narrowing of productivity levels in the two economies since the Second World War (with all of the similarity in technology and production processes which that entails) and the enhanced diversity or pluralism of contemporary society (with all of the concern about fragmentation which that has generated). The detached observer from another continent could not avoid the sense of deepening similarities in these two North American countries.

Convergence in the policy agendas of the two countries is most palpable. The decline of American economic hegemony in the last two decades has increased the similarities in the economic problems confronting the president and the prime minister as both countries come to terms with growing interdependence in the global economy. Although the psychological adjustment here is probably greater for the United States than for Canada, which has always had to deal with international constraints, the result is a similar litany of concerns about the scope for national independence in macroeconomic management, the adequacy of international trade agreements, the implications of foreign direct investment, and the burden of foreign indebtedness. Canada certainly remains more vulnerable because of its extreme dependence on the American market. However, the agenda of both countries reflects the erosion of the economic sovereignty of nation-states in the late twentieth century. This parallel is reinforced by the common agenda thrown up by economic restructuring – enhancing productivity growth, research and development, and education and training, and responding to the victims of the destructive side of economic change, higher levels of inequality in market incomes, and a pervasive sense of economic insecurity on both sides of the border.

Greater social diversity in both countries has stimulated parallel policy agendas and, in some cases, convergence in what were historically distinctive concerns. New patterns of immigration and multiculturalism, the new politics of Aboriginal communities, the mobilization of the women's movements and other movements not examined in detail here – such as the more forceful assertion of the rights of disabled persons and the emergence of active gay movements – have all combined to spark similar controversies about diversity, rights, and social integration. The issues and language of these debates have proved to be transnational.

· Clearly, the economic and social trajectories of Canada and the United States have generated important similarities in the policy agendas of the two countries. However, common problems do not necessarily mean common responses. The reaction of each country to the policy agendas of the late twentieth century have been defined and constrained by their domestic cultures, politics, institutions, and inherited policy legacies. It is to these dimensions of society that the next two chapters turn, following which the chapters in part 2 will trace their impact on policy responses.

3 The Constraints of Public Opinion: Diverging or Converging Paths?

GEORGE PERLIN

Chapter 2 described various forces of change impelling the policy agendas of governments in Canada and the United States towards a concern with an increasingly common set of new and difficult issues. However, the way in which governments on the two sides of the border respond to economic and social problems is conditioned by the configuration of public opinion in the two societies. Public issue priorities and policy preferences, as well as broader orientations towards government and political leaders, impose constraints on government policy making. It is therefore important to examine the pattern of similarities and differences in the opinions and attitudes that Canadians and Americans bring to their politics.

This examination needs to be seen in the context of a scholarly and popular literature which has argued that there are important differences in the historical experiences, values, and interests of the two countries. As recently as 1990, Seymour Martin Lipset, in a major work comparing them, argued that despite two centuries of social and economic change, Canada and the United States "are like trains that have moved thousands of miles along parallel railway tracks. They are far from where they started, but they are still separated" (1990a, 212). The extent to which the new forces described in chapter 2 are cutting across historical differences and producing a convergence in the opinion environments for policy makers in the two countries is one of the general themes to be explored in this chapter. The second involves an exploration of the ways in which public opinion may constrain the responses of Canadian and American policy makers to the new issue agendas with which they are confronted. These themes are pursued through an inquiry into three questions about the opinion environments of the two countries. First, are there differences in public conceptions of the policy agenda in Canada and the United States? Second, do the opinions of Canadians and Americans reflect differences in values that might affect the range of policy options from which elites may choose in attempting to solve problems? Third, are there differences in the extent to which citizens may be willing to comply with courses of action recommended by elites – particularly courses of action imposing increased costs or reduced benefits?

THE FORCES OF DIVERGENCE AND CONVERGENCE

Comparative analyses asserting the existence of significant differences between the two countries have identified both cultural and structural factors that might be expected to produce differences in their opinion environments. The principal cultural argument centres on the ideological origins of the two countries. The Loyalist migration to Canada following the American Revolution is widely held to have been a critical event that set the political cultures of the two countries on different paths. The outlook of the Loyalists, in this view, was more collectivist and hierarchical than that of other Americans. Thus, on the one hand their departure removed from the United States elements that might have modified the liberal value system which developed there; while on the other, their departure ensured that as liberalism developed in Canada, it was exposed to this modifying influence.

Gad Horowitz argues that the "toryism" of the Loyalists created an ideological pluralism in Canada, in contrast to the monolithic character of ideology in the United States. On the right it produced a distinctive Canadian conservatism, which valued political leadership and the virtue of social order while according wide latitude to the state to intervene in the interests of the collective goal of national development and the collective responsibility of society to protect its weaker members. On the left it helped foster the development of an enduring socialist movement in Canada, because it established the legitimacy of the concept of action by the state on behalf of collective social interests. Horowitz claims also that the presence of toryism in Canada contributed to "the ambivalent centrist character of left-wing liberalism in Canada as contrasted with the unambiguously leftist position of left-wing liberalism in the United States" (G. Horowitz 1968, 9). All of these are among what he describes as "the most important un-American characteristics of English Canada" (ibid.).

Lipset sees the effect of the American Revolution and the Loyalist migration to Canada in more holistic, but clearly similar terms: "The very organizing principles that framed these nations, the central cores around which institutions and events were to accommodate, were different. One was Whig and classically liberal or libertarian – doctrines that emphasize distrust of the state, egalitarianism, and populism ... The other was Tory and conservative in the British and European sense – accepting of the need for a strong state, for respect for authority, for deference" (Lipset 1990a, 2). Lipset believes that these differences have had several long-term consequences: First, there is not in the prevailing ideology and political culture of Canada the same suspicion of the state that characterizes the prevailing ideology and political culture of the United States. This has led to a greater willingness in Canada to use the state both to promote national development (through direct intervention in the form of public ownership, subsidization to business, and the protection of monopolies) and to provide a wide range of social benefits to citizens to protect them from the effects of economic inequality and the depredations of the market. Second, Canadians have placed greater emphasis on achieving equality of condition; Americans have placed greater emphasis on achieving equality of opportunity. Third, there has been a greater emphasis on elitism in the Canadian value system, in contrast to the egalitarianism of the American value system. Fourth, there is a greater emphasis on achievement orientation in the American political culture, which is reflected in greater entrepreneurial drive and a more competitive orientation to economic and social relations.

Lipset also observes that "efforts to distinguish Canada and the United States invariably point to the greater respect for law and those who uphold it north of the border" (1990a, 90). This difference is said in the first instance to be a further manifestation of the collectivism in the ideology of the founders of the Canadian political community. It is argued that the founders set Canada on a course of development that emphasized a respect for social order which contrasted with the self-regulating individualist view of the law that was to develop in the United States. This difference in fundamental outlook is said to have been reflected in the fact that the United States achieved its independence by an act of revolutionary war while Canada became an independent state through a process of evolution under the authority of the Crown. The difference was subsequently reinforced, Lipset argues, by the contrasting frontier experiences of the two countries. The West was brought under American control by individual conquest in which order was established largely through individual action, either without the direct authority of law or through locally developed institutions of authority. By contrast, Canada's expansion into the West was carefully controlled by the central government, which imposed its own regime of law and order as the frontier advanced. The greater respect for law and order in Canada is said to be manifest in a greater willingness by Canadians to accept state actions that limit individual rights (as reflected in the emergency powers provisions of the Constitution Act and in laws limiting harmful speech).

A further cultural argument points to significant differences in the character of religion in the two countries. In Lipset's account, the individualist and democratic values incorporated in the American political culture were "reinforced by a voluntaristic and congregational religious tradition," while the more conservative outlook in Canada received support from the Anglican and Roman Catholic churches, "hierarchically organized religions that supported and were supported by the state" (1990a, 2). After the Revolution, religion followed very different paths of development in the two countries. Religion in the United States has been more pluralist, evangelical, and fundamentalist than in Canada (cf. Lipset 1990a, ch. 5 *passim*). The result is reflected today in differences in the degree of religious commitment among the populations of the two countries. Data on church membership and attendance and from survey research have consistently shown a higher degree of religious commitment among Americans. For example, the Canada and the World Study, in 1992, reported that 53 per cent of the Americans interviewed, compared with only 31 per cent of Canadians, expressed strong agreement with the statement "Religion is a very important part of my day-to-day life" (Reid and Burns 1992). The political relevance of this difference is apparent in the observation by Bellah and his colleagues that "though Americans overwhelmingly accept the doctrine of the separation of church and state, most of them believe, as they always have, that religion has an important role to play in the public realm" (1985, 219).

A factor of critical importance with cultural implications but reflecting a fundamental difference in the social structures of the two countries is the presence in Canada of a separate French linguistic and cultural community, geographically concentrated in the province of Quebec, with distinct social and political institutions. The efforts of French Canada to preserve its language and culture laid the foundation for what Lipset has called the particularism of the Canadian political culture. One result is that while the United States has sought to assimilate all ethnic and cultural groups in a transcendent national political culture, Canada has valued ethnic and cultural diversity. Another is that the concept of group rights has been incorporated in the Canadian political culture. Thus, while in the definition and protection of rights and entitlements the United States accords virtually exclusive emphasis to individual rights, Canada balances individual rights against a wide range of group rights, in particular rights to protect language and culture.

At the same time, the particularism of French Canada contributed to the development and persistence of a regionalist style of political mobilization throughout Canada, a style of political mobilization distinguished not just by the articulation of regional interests but by their articulation in the name of the preservation of regional communities, together with their cultures and institutions. This, in turn, has contributed to recurring conflict over conceptions of the role and responsibilities of the central and provincial governments.

Never far from the centre of these conflicts has been the place of Quebec within Confederation. The issue of national unity, settled for the United States by the Civil War, has not been settled in Canada. Quebec has followed a distinctive path of economic, social, and cultural development which has fostered a strong sense of national community consciousness. Over the past three decades, Quebec nationalism has become a powerful force in both provincial and federal politics. It has provided the separatist Parti Québécois with a base of popular support which has not fallen below 35 per cent in elections since 1976 and which, in the referendum of 1995, brought Quebec to within a single percentage point of supporting a proposal for secession.

Equally important in differentiating the historical experience of the two countries was the role of slavery in the United States and its absence in Canada (except during the early years of settlement). The American political culture has been profoundly influenced by the struggle over the issue of slavery itself, the Civil War, the long history of discrimination against African Americans, and their efforts to achieve equality. While Canada has had its share of racial conflict, this has never been on the same scale or conducted with the same intensity as the conflict between African Americans and whites in the United States. As a result, race has had a much more central place in American politics. Rights and civil liberties issues, the problems of poverty and crime, and issues of equality have been much more race centred there. As chapter 2 pointed out, the structural underpinnings of this point of difference are beginning to break down, reflecting the effects of immigration into Canada, particularly over the past three decades. But Canada remains much more predominantly a white society than the United States, and it is free of the residues of social, economic, and cultural experience that have shaped race relations in the United States.

One of the most important structural differences between Canada and the United States is the immense difference in the size and distribution of their populations. The United States is a country of

260 million people; Canada, a country of 30 million. The United States has many more big cities than Canada, and urbanization occurred there much earlier. As a result, the United States has had to deal with a much more complex set of urban problems. Recurring crises in the delivery of urban services, the physical decay of the inner cities, and high urban crime rates are all more characteristic of American than Canadian cities.

A further important structural difference is the enormous disparity in the international power of the two countries. While Canada is among the more advanced capitalist countries, its economy is less than one-tenth the size of that of the United States, and it exists in a relationship of dependency with the American economy. Canada's military power, as measured by defence expenditures, is less than one-fiftieth that of the United States. Measured by the actual destructive capacity of the weapons systems of the two countries, the disparity is manifestly many times greater. In short, the United States is a superpower and Canada is at best a middle power. Thus, Canadians and Americans are likely to have different conceptions of their national interests and different views of the kinds of action they might take to pursue those interests.

Related to this, there are fundamental differences in the nature of nationalism in the two countries. The development of "the American creed," linking individualist ideology to nationalism, reinforced by the greater strength of fundamentalist Protestantism, has given the United States a more assertive, moralistic, and expansionist view of its place in the world. In contrast, "Canadian nationalism has the opposite tendency. It is the nationalism of a small state struggling to preserve its independence, not the nationalism of an expansionist great power" (Forbes 1978, 310).

Cutting across these differences between the countries is a set of forces that would appear likely to create a growing convergence in public concerns and attitudes. Of these, the most far reaching in their effects or potential effects have been economic. As Banting and Simeon pointed out in chapter 2, decision makers in Canada and the United States face an increasingly common set of economic issues, driven by the processes of globalization, technological change, and restructuring. There is no need to elaborate here on their exposition of these forces. What needs to be underscored is the fact that the changes they describe are occurring in a context in which there has already been considerable economic integration. This is reflected in trade relations and in the high incidence of American direct investment in the Canadian economy. Because Canada and the United States are at essentially the same stage of economic development and because of the extent to which the Canadian economy has been integrated within that of the United States, economic change has produced much the same social effects in the two countries. Official unemployment rates have tended to be higher in Canada, but the general distribution of wealth, the distribution of income by occupational category, and the incidence of poverty today conform to much the same profile. Thus, to the extent that economic factors affect them, there is good reason to expect increasing convergence in the political attitudes of Americans and Canadians.

In chapter 2, Banting and Simeon also pointed to social changes that are impelling policy agendas in the two countries towards convergence. Of these, none has had more impact on elite political discourse than the development of the women's movement. Second-wave feminism became a significant political force in Canada and the United States at approximately the same time. While in the United States feminists tried to secure passage of the Equal Rights Amendament, in Canada they fought successfully to have gender equality included in the Charter of Rights and Freedoms, which was entrenched in the constitution in 1982. The efforts of feminists to achieve gender equality in the workplace and politics, to secure autonomy in decisions about their bodies, and to end sexism and sexual harassment in society, and the reactions to these efforts have created an important new dimension of political cleavage in both countries. In addition, Banting and Simeon noted the potential convergent effects of changes in the ethnic composition of the two countries. As these changes occurred, elite discourse in both was widened to incorporate debates about such issues as multiculturalism and racial balance in hiring and promotion practices. They also provoked debate about immigration policies.

Another force, which is not mentioned in chapter 2, is critically important for understanding public opinion in the two countries; it is the extent to which Canada has become integrated within the mass communications system of the United States. This is true for all forms of communication, but particularly for the most important of them: television. With the development of satellite and cable transmission, there is no corner of Canadian society that remains outside the orbit of American television. Canadian channels are dominated by American entertainment programming and must compete for audience share with up to ten times as many American channels on domestic cable systems. The impact of this American dominance of the Canadian television market is not just confined to the way in which it may influence popular culture in Canada. Of perhaps even greater significance from the perspective of our analysis here is the way in which it influences Canadian views on public affairs. American television news and public affairs programs have large Canadian audiences, and Canadians are routinely exposed to the advertising and coverage of American election campaigns. Thus, Canadian views of the political process and political issues in their own country have continual direct comparative reference points from the United States. The significance of this is reflected in the way political strategists in Canada follow American politics, adopting both techniques and messages from American campaigns in crafting their own appeals to voters.[1]

It is against this background that our analysis of public opinion is set. On the one hand, explanations of the historical development of the two countries and differences in their social structure, size, and power would lead us to expect differences in their opinion environments. On the other hand, there are powerful forces of change that appear to be impelling public opinion in the two countries towards increasingly similar sets of concerns and attitudes.

THE DATA

At the best of times, opinion research is a problematic enterprise. In this case, the normal array of problems is compounded by the fact that there has been very little research designed explicitly for the purpose of comparing public opinion in Canada and the United States. The data used here are drawn from dozens of separate studies designed for differing purposes, using different techniques, and conducted at different times over a period of three decades.[2]

Analysis based on intersurvey comparisons of this kind poses special interpretive problems – for three reasons. First, the reliability of comparisons between surveys is affected by variations in sample characteristics. The most common are differences in sample size, which result in differences in the error parameters from one survey to another. In addition, samples often differ in the accuracy with which they reproduce the social characteristics of the population they are attempting to represent. It is now quite common to weight samples to make them representative of these characteristics, but weighting procedures are not always reported and, in any event, one cannot have the same degree of confidence in the quality of data from a sample that has required weighting. Second, there are problems because of differences in questionnaire design. Responses to questions will vary with differences in question wording, with differences in the location of a question in a questionnaire, with differences in the form in which the question is asked, and with differences in the general context of the survey (whether, for example, it is an omnibus survey dealing with several disparate subjects or a survey focused entirely on one subject). Third, every survey is to some extent a product of its time. Changes in the context of current events are likely to have some effect on how people perceive and respond to questions. For this reason, comparisons of responses to surveys done at different times may not be very meaningful.

It is difficult to control for these problems here because most of the data have come from secondary sources and have not been available in a form that would permit their independent analysis. Thus, there is the need to take a cautious approach in interpreting the data. The interpretive strategy I have adopted incorporates the following guidelines. First, in all comparisons, rather than focusing on numerical differences, I have looked for variations in the *prevailing* view. Thus, if 75 per cent of Americans and 65 per cent of Canadians take the same view on a particular issue, the fact that *most* people in the two countries hold the same opinion is the point to emphasize, rather than the difference of 10 per cent. Second, in making comparisons, rather than focusing on responses to individual questions, I have looked for the general direction of responses across several questions.

There is one other important observation to be made before proceeding to the data. The point was stressed earlier that there is reason to expect significant differences in outlook between anglophone and francophone Canadians. While most published studies present data for Canada as a whole, wherever it has been possible I have gone to the original sources to try to distinguish between francophone and anglophone responses. Where there are significant differences between the two, they are reported in the text and tables.

ISSUE AGENDAS

The setting of the political agenda – the determination of what issues are to be dealt with – is a critically important aspect of the democratic political process. A lack of congruence between elite and public issue priorities poses serious problems. On the one hand, it can prevent governments from taking effective action on vital issues. On the other, if elites ignore public perceptions of what it is important to deal with, there may be a weakening of support both for the elites and for the democratic process itself. Thus, our first question is about the issue agendas of mass publics in the two countries. In this part of the analysis, we are able to avoid some of the difficulties of intersurvey comparisons because, for each country, there are single sources of time-series data based on responses to a similarly worded question. The question asks respondents to identify the political issues they think are currently most important. For the United States, the data are from surveys by the American Institute of Public Opinion (AIPO, the Gallup organization) as reported in its periodic reports and in *Trends in Public Opinion* (Niemi, Mueller, and Smith 1989). For Canada, they are from the quarterly surveys done by Decima Research for its privately distributed *Decima Quarterly Report*.[3] Since the Canadian data do not begin until 1980, that will be the starting point for the comparison.

There are two special problems to be noted in the presentation of these data. The first is that the coding categories for the two countries were not identical. Decima provides an extensive explanation for its coding choices, which facilitates interpretation, but comparable explanations were not available for the American surveys. Second, the coding categories used for the AIPO surveys have varied over time. These variations seem to reflect changes in the importance of issues that were previously unmentioned or were on the margins of the issue agenda, and for this reason they are helpful, but they make it impossible to track every issue over the whole period.

The most striking feature of the data is the extent to which issue agendas in both countries are dominated by a concern with economic problems. Over the fifteen years, economic problems were identified as most important on average by 51 per cent of respondents in the United States and 48 per cent of respondents in Canada. (Percentage distributions discussed in this section are reported in tables 3.A1 to 3.A3 in the appendix to this chapter.) When allowance is made for non-responses, which were reported in Canada but not in the United States, the average number of references to economic problems (inflation, unemployment, interest rates, and the economy in general) was virtually identical in the two countries. And the numbers follow a very similar pattern of rises and falls over the fifteen years.

The one major difference in references to economic issues was the greater frequency with which unemployment was mentioned in Canada. The average number of references to unemployment in Canada was 27.1 per cent, while in the United States it was 15.5 per cent. In part this may be explained by the fact that the rate of unemployment in Canada usually runs 2 to 3 per cent higher than in the United States. Although this is not a large difference in terms of the number of people with personal experience of the problem, one might assume that the higher rate of unemployment would create a higher general degree of awareness of it as a societal problem.

Although economic issues dominate the public's agenda in both countries, there are significant differences in the importance attached to other issues. Most notably, as figure 3.1 shows, the relative importance ascribed to foreign policy issues has been greater in the United States for all but one brief period – 1987 and 1988. The exception is explained, as Decima's coding notes show, by the preoccupation of

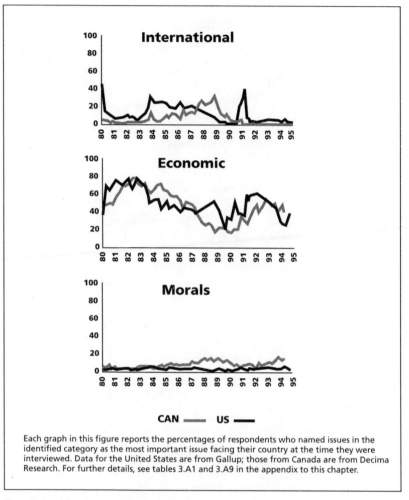

Figure 3.1   Most important issues in Canada and the United States, 1980–1994

Canadians in that period with the issue of free trade with the United States. For most of the rest of the period, in Canada the number of respondents assigning importance to foreign policy issues tracks in a fairly flat plane at less than 5 per cent, while in the United States it moves more unevenly but averages more than 15 per cent and rises as high as 41 per cent, a level never reached in Canada. The exception underscores the fundamental difference in the orientations of Canadians and Americans to the external world. For Canadians, what is most important is their relationship with the United States. The free trade agreement rang the tocsin for Canadian nationalists, evoking deeply

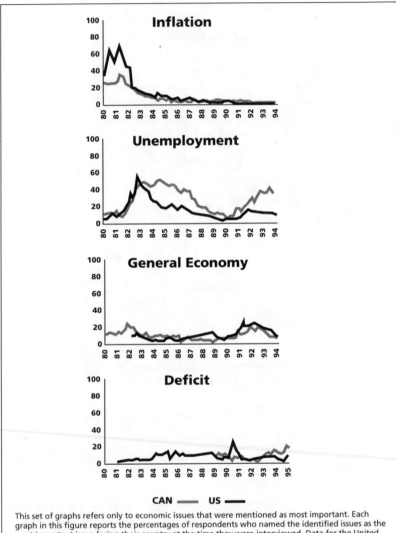

This set of graphs refers only to economic issues that were mentioned as most important. Each graph in this figure reports the percentages of respondents who named the identified issues as the most important issue facing their country at the time they were interviewed. Data for the United States are from Gallup; those for Canada are from Decima Research. For further details, see tables 3.A2 and 3.A3 in the appendix to this chapter. Note that numbers for the deficit do not begin until 1989 because it was not until then that they appeared in the Canadian data.

Figure 3.2   Most important issues in Canada and the United States, 1980–1994

felt concerns about the domination of Canada by the United States. Even during the economic blockade of Iraq and during the Gulf War – the period from September 1990 to March 1991 – events in which Canadian military personnel were directly engaged, the number of Canadians who identified international issues as most important never rose above 6 per cent; in the United States, not surprisingly, international issues were mentioned by an increasingly large number of respondents, and they reached a plurality in February 1991.

The data also show how the national unity issue affects the public's policy agenda in Canada. From the spring of 1980 to the spring of 1981, during the first Quebec referendum on sovereignty and the subsequent debate about new constitutional arrangements, national unity issues were identified as most important by from 14 to 19 per cent of Decima's respondents, numbers exceeded only by those who mentioned inflation (averaging 25 per cent). During the constitutional negotiations in 1990, national unity achieved primacy, being ranked most important by 21 per cent in the spring survey and 30 per cent in the summer survey. From then until the autumn of 1992 it only once fell below 10 per cent and was normally between 15 and 18 per cent.

While these data confirm what we might expect in respect to Canada, the parallel expectation that race issues might have a distinctive effect in shaping the public's agenda in the United States was not fulfilled. During this period, despite the attention they continued to receive in debate among elites, civil rights and race relations issues were rarely ranked first and only once reached as high as 2 per cent. Presumably, this is partly to be explained by the fact that these issues are not of primary concern to whites, who make up 90 per cent (or more) of the U.S. samples.[4] It may also be that many African Americans see these issues in terms of their economic situation and respond by ranking economic issues first.

In another area in which the issue agenda in the United States might be expected to be distinctive, it was. The Gallup data show that crime and the crime-related issue of drug abuse were ranked most important by at least 4 per cent of respondents in every poll reported and that the number of respondents referring to issues of this kind has been rising steadily, running in excess of 12 per cent in every poll, except those during the Gulf War, since 1986. There was no separate set of issues of this kind in the Decima reports. When they appeared, it was at the "trace" level, and they were included in the "miscellaneous" category.[5]

Contrary to what we might expect, moral issues were more consistently on the public agenda in Canada than in the United States during the period of this analysis. They averaged about 7 per cent across the fifty-eight quarters, and for a period of six quarters (beginning in the fall of 1988) they ranged from 12 to 16 per cent. This would appear to be a reflection of the attention given by the media to the issue of abortion: there were two cases before the courts involving a pregnant woman's right to make her own choice about an abortion; and debates in Parliament over the reform of an abortion law struck down by the Supreme Court. Where, in this area, the United States does differ from Canada in a manner more consistent with expectations is in the greater disposition among Americans to articulate a generalized concern about moral issues. That concern is captured in Gallup's coding category of "moral decline." Few Canadians are ever reported to have made references of this kind.

One other notable difference is the greater attention accorded in Canada throughout this period to issues coded by Decima under the heading "government/taxes." The difficulty with this category is that it incorporates issues as widely different as taxes, the qualities of political leaders (their competence and integrity), the size of government deficits, and general frustration with government. Data from Decima's coding notes show that all these issues, at different times and at different levels of intensity, have had an impact on public opinion in Canada over the past decade. However, the big increase in responses coded under this category – which began in the summer of 1989, when it rose to 27 per cent – occurred because of the reaction against the goods and services tax, which the federal government proposed to implement (and subsequently did) in January 1990,[6] and after 1992 because of a growth in concern about the federal deficit.

To sum up, there are two general points to be made about public issue agendas in the two countries over this period. First, these agendas converge in their main focus around economic issues, yet they manifest significant differences. The qualities and actions of particular incumbents of public office and chance occurrences can always be expected to produce some variation in issue concerns from one political arena to another, and variations of this kind are apparent here. But a number of the variations we have seen can also be ascribed to more fundamental and enduring differences in the characteristics of the political environments of the two countries. In particular, the different roles of the United States and Canada in the international community, the persistent effects of Canada's linguistic and regional divisions, and the differences in urban conditions in the two countries (as manifest in concerns in the United States about crime and the crime-related issue of drug abuse) all have had effects on distinguishing the policy agendas of Americans and Canadians.

The second point arises from some things we have not observed. Chapter 2 described forces of social change that have produced increasing pressure on political elites from new social movements and interests. There is little evidence that these have been mobilized in the public's consciousness. For example, despite the growing media attention accorded issues raised by environmentalists and feminists over the past two decades, environmental issues and issues related to gender equality have not succeeded in achieving primacy in the minds of more than a few citizens. References to them were episodic and rarely occurred at more than the 2 or 3 per cent level. (The number of references to environmental issues was slightly higher in Canada, but the difference was marginal.) This is not to say that these issues have failed to evoke a public response. As we shall see later, they have. Rather, it is to point out that they have not succeeded in shifting collective priorities.

The same point needs to be made in respect to the efforts made by economic and political elites to focus the political agenda on their concerns about government deficits. Despite the attention this subject has received in the media, in neither country has it become a priority issue for more than a small minority of citizens. In the United States, concern about the deficit averaged less than 3 per cent between 1980 and the end of 1983, and 10 per cent from 1984 to mid-1990. It peaked at 24 per cent in July 1990 (the only occasion on which it exceeded 20 per cent) and gradually dropped back to an average of 5 per cent between 1991 and 1995. In Canada, from 1980 to the middle of 1992 it never exceeded 3 per cent. It began to rise in 1993 reached 21 per cent at the end of 1994, but then dropped back under 20 per cent. The failure of elites to mobilize public opinion to support deficit cutting as a first priority is among the most striking demonstrations of the potential problems for government when elite and public agendas do not coincide. This, too, is a subject to which we shall return later.

POLITICAL VALUES

The second question we posed was whether there are differences between Canada and the United States in the kinds of policy options that public opinion will accept. At the core of the argument that the range of available policy options in the two countries is different is the claim that there are differences in the fundamental political values of Canadians and Americans. The measurement of attitudes of this kind is not easy, because the central ideas imputed to them are not easily converted to concise, testable statements. Moreover, many respondents feel uncomfortable with abstract questions and therefore choose not to answer them. Nonetheless, there have been attempts to explore political values through survey research, and there are some comparative data to which we can refer. The major work in this area was done by Herbert McClosky (McClosky and Brill 1983; McClosky and Zaller 1984) in the Opinions and Values of Americans study, 1975–77, and the Civil Liberties study, 1978–79. Some direct comparisons can be made with McClosky's findings because two Canadian surveys, the

Charter Project of 1987 (Sniderman et al. 1988) and the National Election Study of 1988 (Johnston et al. 1992) replicated several of McClosky's questions. The long interval between the administration of the surveys in the two countries clearly poses a problem, although it is arguable that attitudes about fundamental values would not be subject to significant variation over the period of a decade. In any event, there are some data from other studies conducted at shorter intervals that provide a partial control.

The central proposition in the argument that there are differences in the fundamental political values of Canadians and Americans is that while the political culture of the United States is predominantly individualist, the Canadian political culture has incorporated elements of both individualism and collectivism. The data permit us to test three specific forms in which the presence of a collectivist strain in the Canadian political culture is said to manifest itself: a weaker commitment to unrestricted capitalism, a greater emphasis on social order, and a stronger commitment to the concept of equality of condition (as opposed to equality of opportunity).

The Capitalist System

In the literature arguing that differences exist, Americans are said to have a stronger commitment than Canadians to capitalist values. Table 3.A4 (in the appendix to this chapter) displays responses to several questions that relate to these values. The data in this table suggest that the level of commitment to the culture of capitalism in the two countries is essentially the same. The prevailing disposition for nearly all the measures shown in the table is in the same direction and in most cases at approximately the same level. Canadians and Americans show approximately the same measure of support for the virtues of competition, individual self-reliance, hard work, and the profit system.

Concepts of Social Order

The differing emphasis on collectivism and individualism is also claimed to manifest itself in attitudes towards order in society. Canadians are held to place greater value on social order, while Americans are held to place greater value on individual rights. There are four pieces of evidence that bear on this claim.

First, the Charter Project in Canada in 1987 repeated a question from the McClosky study of 1976 in which respondents were asked to choose which of two statements better represented their opinion: "Our laws should aim to enforce the community's standards of right and wrong" or "Our laws should aim to protect a citizen's right to live by any moral standard he [*sic*] chooses." Sixty-four per cent of English-speaking Canadians chose the statement emphasizing community standards, while 55 per cent of Americans chose the statement emphasizing individual choice. Among francophone Canadians, 37 per cent chose the collectivist response and 46 per cent chose the individualist response (see table 3.A5). The authors of the Charter Project expressed some caution in interpreting the Canadian responses because the question conflates two ideas: judgment about what is right and wrong, and the community-individual distinction. They noted that in response to a question that asked respondents to choose between the statements "In our society today, too much emphasis is placed on conformity and obedience to the community" and "In our society today, too much emphasis is placed on individual freedom at the expense of the community's interest," anglophones and francophones gave identical answers (Sniderman et al. 1988, 22–3). They also reported that in answering a question which asked whether respondents believed that "too little emphasis is placed on respect for established institutions" or "on the rights of the individual," while a larger number of francophones (49 per cent to 39 per cent) gave the individualist response, there was no significant difference between the two groups in the numbers giving the "established institutions" response (18 per cent and 20 per cent). There is a further reason to be cautious in interpreting the responses to these questions. For both the second and third questions, the number of respondents who said that neither statement reflected their opinions was very high – for the sample as a whole in both cases in excess of 40 per cent.

Second, the Charter Project also replicated two questions from McClosky's research which tested the value of social order against that of free speech. In one, respondents were asked whether they agreed or disagreed with the statement "It is better to live in an orderly society than to allow people so much freedom they can become disruptive." In the other, they were asked whether they agreed or disagreed with the statement "Free speech is just not worth it if it means we have to put up with the danger to society of radical and extremist views." The number giving the social order response to the first question was 77 per cent of francophone Canadians, 61 per cent of anglophones, and 51 per cent of Americans, while to the second it was 38 per cent of francophones, 35 per cent of anglophones, and 28 per cent of Americans. Thus, in answers to both questions more Canadians than Americans gave "social order" responses, although the balance of opinion in both countries was the same – towards social order in response to the first statement and towards free speech in response to the second. Note that among Canadians, in both cases, it was the francophones who were more likely to give social order responses.

The third piece of evidence is from parallel surveys in Canada and the United States conducted by Decima Research in 1989. Respondents were asked, "In times of crisis, do you believe government should have the power to declare a national emergency and remove all civil rights?" Fifty-two per cent of English Canadians said yes, compared with 37 per cent of French Canadians and 41 per cent of Americans. But the relevance of this, too, is contestable. For Canadians, the question evoked a particular episode, the use of emergency powers legislation by the government of Pierre Trudeau to deal with two kidnappings by a radical Quebec separatist group in the fall of 1970. Trudeau's action created a strong negative reaction among francophones, particularly francophone nationalists, whereas English Canadians, fearing the consequences of separatism, were much more supportive of it. One would expect the Decima question at least in some measure to reflect these attitudes.[7]

Fourth, if Canadians place greater value on social order, one would expect them to take tougher stances than Americans in their views on the handling of crime. In fact, the responses to questions on this subject are remarkably alike in both countries. Majorities in both, in the order of 70 per cent, favoured tougher sentencing by the courts, the use of capital punishment, and tougher regulation of parole. And on subjects for which there are extended time-series data, these opinions have shown no significant variation for twenty years.

In summary, the data about attitudes towards social order do not fall into a consistent pattern. On the general questions, Canadians as a whole seem to be slightly more collectivist than Americans, but the differences are small and their meaning is confused by the inconsistencies in the responses of anglophones and francophones. Most importantly, the general direction of attitudes in both countries is the same, predominantly individualist.

Equality

Perhaps the most important question for this analysis is whether there are differences in the ways in which Canadians and Americans think about economic equality. The claim is that economic equality to Americans means equality of opportunity while to Canadians it means equality of condition (cf. Lipset 1990a, 136). Manifestly, if this is true, we would expect differences in public attitudes across a wide range of policy choices.

The evidence, shown in table 3.A6 of the appendix, is mixed. In response to a question that asked for judgments on the fairness of the existing distribution of income for unskilled workers, the opinions of Americans and anglophone Canadians were about equally divided; 43 per cent of the Americans and 42 per cent of the anglophone Canadians said that these workers "usually receive wages that are about right considering the amount of skill required," while 38 per cent of the Americans and 39 per cent of the anglophone Canadians said that the wages were "much too low for the dirty work they do." In contrast, a majority (57 per cent) of francophone Canadians gave the second response – that is, they said that unskilled workers are not paid adequately.

When respondents were asked about how income ought to be distributed, there was a larger measure of agreement – both among Canadians and across the groups. There was little support in either country for positions consistent with the concept of equality of condition. Only about one in five said "A person's wages should depend on how much he or she needs to live decently," while less than one in ten Americans and anglophone Canadians and only three in ten francophone Canadians said that in "a fair economic system all people should earn about the same."

However, the responses to another question conveyed a different impression. The question asked whether respondents believed the government "should see to it that everyone has a job and a decent standard of living" or whether each person should "be left to get ahead on his [sic] own." While the number of Americans who said that government should be responsible was still only 24 per cent, among anglophone Canadians it was 44 per cent and among francophones it was 73 per cent. This is a striking difference and clearly gives strong support to the thesis that Canadians and Americans view economic equality in different ways. But it is not necessarily a demonstration that equality of condition is more prized by Canadians, since the provision of "a job and a decent standard of living" is perfectly consistent with the concept of equality of opportunity. Rather, what this piece of data shows is that substantially more Canadians than Americans are prepared to countenance an active role for the state in providing for the welfare of its citizens.

That, in and of itself, of course, is a significant finding. It is reinforced by data from parallel studies conducted in 1986 by Decima Research in Canada and by Cambridge Research in the United States, which asked respondents whether they agreed or disagreed with the statement "The best government is the one that governs least." The number taking the statist position – that is, disagreement – once again was largest among francophone Canadians (50 per cent). Majorities of both anglophone Canadians and Americans took the antistatist position although there were somewhat more statist responses among anglophone Canadians (39 per cent) than among Americans (32 per cent).

The table also contains a piece of evidence that may appear to conflict with these data. In the World Values Study of 1990, in response to a question asking whether "individuals should take more responsibility for themselves" or whether "the state should do more to see that everyone is provided for," substantial majorities in approximately the same proportions among all three groups rejected the statist position. It is arguable that this question tests a different issue – the willingness of respondents to expand the role of the state. But the fact that the general direction of dispositions was antistatist does suggest that this difference between Americans and Canadians is not very strong.

In summary, these data do not appear to show a significant difference between Canadian and American concepts of economic equality. The prevailing view among Canadians, as among Americans, accepts the individualist idea of equality of opportunity. However, among Canadians there is a greater willingness to use the state, in contrast to the antistatism that is so centrally a part of the American political culture.

In making this observation it is important to note the distinctiveness of the opinions of francophone Canadians. As we have seen, substantially more francophones take a position consistent with equality of condition – more believe that unskilled workers are not fairly paid, substantially more believe that the state has a responsibility to ensure that citizens have jobs and a decent standard of living, and a much larger number of francophones believe that in a fair economic system all people should earn about the same.

Why would this be so? One explanation is that there has been a more vigorous class-based politics in Quebec. In particular Quebec's trade union movement has been more ideologically militant than the union movement in the other provinces. Another explanation is that ideas from the left were closely linked to the nationalist renaissance that began in Quebec in the 1960s. There was a significant group in Quebec that was influenced by the anticolonial national liberation movements that developed in Third World countries after the Second World War. A third explanation is to be found in the thesis that Quebec's political culture contains a stronger element of collectivism than that of English Canada – because of the distinctive origins of Quebec as a society more deeply imprinted by the legacy of feudalism (cf. McRoberts 1988).

OPINIONS ABOUT PUBLIC POLICY

The direct evidence about political values should be viewed with some caution. There are good theoretical reasons for taking this approach.

They are well documented in the literature, which questions the extent to which mass publics think of politics in the abstract terms of generalized statements about values (cf. Converse 1964). To explore this matter further, we need to look at how people in the two countries respond to questions in specific areas of public policy.

In doing this, I shall focus on the issues that were highlighted in the discussions of chapters 1 and 2. I shall look first at opinion about state-market relations, discussing the economy in general, labour relations, fiscal policy, and social policy. I shall then briefly examine opinion about some of the new issues that have been placed on the agendas of political elites as a result of the social changes described in chapter 2.

The Economy

The shared commitment of Canadians and Americans to the principles of private enterprise is reflected in the fact that business in both countries is held in higher esteem than government (see table 3.A7 in appendix). More people on both sides of the border are prepared to trust the leaders of business, over whom they have no direct control, than the leaders of government, whom they have chosen and can remove from office! This remained true throughout the 1980s, even though it was a decade in which confidence in both business and government steadily declined. The data from the *Decima Quarterly*'s assessments of levels of confidence in major institutions shows this particularly clearly. The space between the net confidence ratings for the two remains more or less the same, even though both are tracking downward (Gregg and Posner 1990, 55–65).

The higher regard in which business is held has limitations. In both countries there has been a growing disposition to mistrust big business (majorities in both countries say that they do not trust it). In addition, undoubtedly reflecting the impact of events reported in the news media (as Gregg and Posner point out [1990, 58]), certain industries are held in lower esteem than others (for example, at various times the energy and pharmaceutical industries). While these patterns are common, the larger number of people with antistatist attitudes in the United States is reflected in the fact that Americans have been more supportive than Canadians of the deregulatory policies of the past decade and a half. While support for deregulation, as a general policy, rose in the United States to as high as 60 per cent (Page and Shapiro 1992, 157), in Canada it peaked at 54 per cent and by the mid-1980s had dropped below 45 per cent. Page and Shapiro have pointed out, however, that even in the United States "the deregulatory 'right turn' was small and, at least in respect to certain areas of business activity, did not persist. At the beginning of the 1990s it was clear that the overwhelming majority of Americans was committed to government protection of consumers and the environment" (ibid., 159).

There is one area of economic policy in which differences in attitudes towards the role of the state is clearly manifest. As Page and Shapiro point out, government ownership in the economy has been so completely rejected in the United States that researchers do not even ask about it in their surveys. In Canada, attitudes towards the issue of public ownership were a continuing focus for inquiry in the 1980s as governments sought to divest themselves of their ownership role. But the data show that Canadians collectively have mixed views on privatization. There remains a strong undercurrent of support for continued public ownership. These views are closely linked to the opinion that the resources of the state are needed to promote an independent Canadian presence in certain vital sectors of the economy and to perform important functions of national integration and national development.

Labour Relations

There is little difference in attitudes towards trade unions in the two countries. In both, most people (in the range of 70 per cent) say they support unions, but it is qualified support. Gregg and Posner report that in Decima surveys in Canada at the end of the 1980s, "half of all respondents continued to believe that organized labour was too powerful" (1990, 59). And throughout the decade, the number of Canadians who said they had almost no confidence in unions exceeded the number who said they had a great deal of confidence in them, by from 30 to 40 per cent. The gap between the positive and negative answers given in response to the same question in the United States was not always as large, but the general direction was the same, negative, and since 1983 in a range from 25 to 30 per cent.

Different questions asked in the two countries suggest that majorities would support regulatory curbs on unions. This is most clearly apparent in the responses to questions about public-sector strikes. Majorities in both countries would outlaw strikes by public employees.

Social Policy

There are strong levels of commitment to the social programs of the welfare state in both countries, and these have persisted over many years, despite some short-term fluctuations. This is reflected both in the answers to questions about specific programs and in the answers to questions about spending priorities (table 3.A8). Negative stereotypes about people on welfare appear to influence responses to questions about spending on welfare (cf. T. Smith 1987), but large majorities in both countries affirm government's responsibility to provide for the poor. Even the negative connotation evoked by the use of the word "welfare," instead of the word "poor," does not shift the balance of opinion on this principle from support to opposition. Consistent with the greater statism in the attitudes of Canadians, the level of support for help to the poor is higher in Canada (about four in five respondents) than in the United States (about three in five).

A significant difference in attitudes towards social policy is apparent in the responses to questions about health care. Support for a government role in the funding of health care is widespread in the United States, but Americans are divided about the extent of that role. In contrast, the vast majority of Canadians consistently express support for the comprehensive state plan that is now in effect. This difference is reflected in responses to a question asked by Decima in parallel surveys in Canada and the United States in 1989. Respondents were asked whether they thought certain programs were an "absolute right" or a "limited right"; 71 per cent of Canadians, compared with 52 per cent of Americans, said that "a publicly funded health-care system available to all, regardless of financial situation," should be an absolute right. It seems reasonable to suppose that this difference at least in part reflects the effect of Canada's twenty-five-year experience with a universal, state-financed medicare program. While this is a substantial difference, it is striking – given the failure of President Clinton's proposals for a wider government role in health care in the United States – that a majority of Americans supported this principle even when the Clinton plan was being rejected by Congress.

It is particularly noteworthy that this is the only piece of evidence that supports the hypothesis that Canadians would be more disposed than Americans towards the principle of universality in social programs. Questions by Decima in 1990 and 1991 show that less than half of all Canadians would support universality in a government-funded day-care program, while questions from several surveys show that a substantial majority of Canadians support needs-based old age pensions and child support benefits. The commitment of Canadians to universality has also been held to be manifest in their persistent rejection, by very large majorities, of proposals for user fees for doctor and hospital services. But in the latest research there is evidence of a shift in these attitudes.

Fiscal Policy

In both Canada and the United States, one of the most difficult issues on the agenda of political elites in the 1990s is the management of government deficits. As we have seen, this issue has not yet become a first priority for more than a small percentage of voters in either country. However, when they have been asked about it explicitly in direct questions, most people in both countries have said that they are concerned about the size of government deficits and, as the Canadian data in table 3.A9 of the appendix show, the number identifying the size of deficits as a very serious problem has been growing steadily.

By the early 1990s, majorities in both countries were prepared to accept the need for deficit reduction, but this should not be construed to mean that public opinion in either country is as yet willing to endorse rigorous regimes of fiscal conservatism. There is certainly little support for further measures on the revenue side. It is no surprise to learn that surveys have always reported that most people think taxes are too high, but there is clearly a toughening resistance to further tax increases. In part this is manifest in the fact that in both countries the number of people mentioning taxes as a "most important" problem, although still small, has been growing. In addition, when asked directly if they would approve tax increases to reduce deficits, most respondents say no – except for increases that clearly would not affect them personally. Thus, it is on the expenditure side that public opinion sees the solution to the problem.

In both countries there are two areas in which there is widespread agreement that cuts can be made. First, substantial majorities believe that large savings can be effected through administrative reforms. Although one might expect Canadians to have a more trusting view of the administrative efficiency of government, they do not. Majorities in both countries say they think that people in government waste a lot of money, and they look to reductions in "government waste" as a means of reducing spending. Second, in both countries there is a widespread belief that significant amounts of money are lost because of the abuse of welfare programs. Beyond these areas of relative consensus, there is little to encourage those who would like to bring deficits down quickly.

For one thing, to the extent that majorities in both countries support specific program cuts, the programs they focus on account for a relatively small share of total public expenditures. In addition, most voters in both countries say explicitly that they would not support cuts in areas that absorb such large shares of program spending as education and health care. In fact, in some of these areas, majorities say they think spending should be increased.

Attitudes towards reductions in spending on social policy are more complex. The widespread belief in abuse of the welfare system affords some latitude for cuts to social spending, but the way in which elites frame proposals for cuts in this area is critical to their chance of success.

This is because while majorities believe that spending on "welfare" can be reduced, equally large numbers say there should be no reductions in support to "the poor" (see table 3.A9). The distinction between deserving and undeserving beneficiaries of social policy is further manifest in the fact, already noted, that in both countries there is acceptance of capacity to pay as a criterion for determining eligibility.

Another constraint on elite action to cut spending is the fact that few voters appear to accept the notion that giving priority to deficit reduction is likely to help stimulate job creation, and if they are asked to choose between increasing spending to create jobs and cutting spending to reduce the deficit, most voters say they would prefer to increase spending. In sum, there is little evidence that elites in either country can expect public support for dramatic change in fiscal policies – either in the form of increased taxes with wide application or through substantial cuts in major areas of program spending.

New Issue Areas

There are three developments in particular among those described in chapter 2 which have brought important new issues onto the policy agendas of political elites over the past three decades: "second wave" feminism, environmentalism, and the assertion by ethnic and racial minorities of claims for measures to effect their right to equality. What has been the response of public opinion in the two countries to the pressures for change produced by the emergence of these movements?

Gender issues. Opinions about gender issues suggest a persistent ambivalence in the public mind in both countries. On the one hand, there has been a marked change in attitudes reflecting the impact of the women's movement. This is manifest first in perceptions of the roles of men and women within the family. Thus, for example, the number of Americans who agreed with the statement "It is much better for everyone involved if the man is the achiever outside the home and the woman takes care of the home and family" dropped from 65 per cent in 1977 to 41 per cent in 1988, while the number who disagreed with the statement "It is more important for a wife to help her husband's career than to have one herself" increased from 41 per cent in 1977 to 67 per cent in 1988. In addition, the change is expressed in attitudes towards the right of women to equal opportunity and equal treatment in the workplace. In Canada, for example, the number saying married women should have equal opportunity with men to compete for jobs increased from 23 per cent in 1960 to 77 per cent in 1985 (see table 3.A10).

On the other hand, there is evidence that many people feel that women ought to emphasize their family role. For example, majorities of Canadians in Decima surveys over the period from 1983 to 1991 repeatedly agreed with the statement "It's much better for children if mothers stay home rather than going out to work," while opinion among Americans was relatively equally divided in surveys in 1985, 1986, and 1988 in responses to the statement "A preschool child is likely to suffer if his or her mother works." This collective ambivalence seems to be shared across the gender cleavage. There are few significant differences between men and women in their responses to the questions referred to here, and even in cases where there are such differences they are small.

In sum, the available data suggest that at the level of general attitudes, the women's movement has had success, but it is limited. This point is underscored by the fact that in surveys in the two countries in 1992, only 29 per cent of American women and only 32 per cent of Canadian women said they thought of themselves as feminists.

Family values. The development of the feminist movement has of course involved a broader set of issues related to changes in the nature of the family. The issue that most centrally reflects these is abortion. Anti-abortion advocates have been among the most active interest groups in the politics of both countries for the better part of two decades.

The religious differences between Canada and the United States might be expected to figure significantly in public opinion around this issue. As we have seen, survey data support Lipset's claim that fundamentalist Christianity has a much deeper vein of support in the United States than in Canada. Politically this has been manifest in the electoral activism of the Moral Majority movement, the widespread politicization of "televangelism," and the explicit appeal of the Republican Party to "family values," none of which has had any parallel in federal politics in Canada.[8] Yet at the popular level, attitudes to the abortion issue do not differ significantly between the two countries and they have remained remarkably stable over time. About 25 per cent consistently say that abortion should be legal in all circumstances, about 16 per cent say that it should be illegal in all circumstances, and 55 to 60 per cent say that it should be legal in some circumstances (see table 3.A11).

Nor is there any evidence that the difference between the two countries in the degree of political activism by groups advocating moral conservatism has had any significant effect on the distribution of opinion on other "family values" issues. For example, the preponderance of opinion in both countries supports doctor-assisted suicide. Whenever questions have been asked about gay rights, majorities in the range of 55 to 60 per cent in both countries say they believe that gays deserve equal treatment in job opportunities, access to public employment, and in other areas related to civil liberties. Finally, substantial majorities in both countries oppose the legalization of marijuana.

This is not to say that there are no significant minorities in Canada who can be mobilized around some of these issues, just as in the United States. The attempt by the NDP government in Ontario in 1994 to afford gay couples the same rights to government benefits as heterosexual couples was opposed not only by the Conservative and Liberal parties but also by some members of its own caucus, particularly from rural ridings, apparently because they feared its potential electoral harm. And there has been a consistent minority in the range of 30 per cent in national surveys who oppose equal treatment for gays. The point is that the number of people hostile to the extension of gay rights is about the same on both sides of the border.

Environmentalism. This has not achieved the degree of political mobilization in either Canada or the United States that it has in Europe, where Green parties have become a significant force in electoral politics, but in both countries environmentalism has succeeded in winning widespread public support at least for the principle of its general goals. Substantial majorities of Canadians and Americans – in the order of 60 to 70 per cent – have consistently expressed their support for increased environmental protection, even at the cost of losses of jobs or increased government spending and attendant increases in taxation. The level of support has persisted in this range over a period of nearly two decades.

Whether this support would hold up if tested against less abstract measures of costs is doubtful. For example, in 1990 Decima asked samples in the two countries whether they believed they "should have the right to drive an automobile anytime or anywhere you want as long as it is within existing laws" or whether they believed that "driving an automobile should and can be restricted further to protect the environment and reduce congestion." Only 50 per cent of the Canadians interviewed and 34 per cent of the Americans said they would support further restrictions (see table 3.A12). The difference in responses between the two countries is suggestive, but there is no evidence from other sources to corroborate it.

Racial diversity and multiculturalism. As pointed out in chapter 2, both Canada and the United States are becoming increasingly diverse in their ethnic composition. Canada might be assumed to be better equipped to respond to this change, since it has long been argued that

in contrast to the American political culture's stress on ethnic assimilation within a transcendent national identity, the Canadian political culture values ethnic and cultural diversity. This difference is widely held
to be reflected in the fact that Canada has had a national policy to promote multiculturalism since 1971.

But in fact Canadians do not express the same degree of commitment
to ethnic diversity as Americans. This is reflected in surveys that put the
same questions to samples in both countries in 1989 and 1992. In the
first, which was conducted by Decima Research for *Maclean's magazine*,
61 per cent of Canadians, compared with 51 per cent of Americans,
said that immigrants should be encouraged "to change their distinct
culture and ways to blend with the larger society"; and in the other, the
Canada and the World study by Angus Reid, 52 per cent of Canadians,
compared with 41 per cent of Americans agreed with the statement
"People from different racial and cultural backgrounds would be better
off if they became more like the majority instead of keeping their own
cultures." Despite this difference, Canadians remain more open to immigration than Americans. In the Decima survey, for example, 58 per
cent of Americans, compared with 39 per cent of Canadians, said there
should be a reduction in the numbers of immigrants allowed into their
country (see table 3.A13).

There is little survey evidence to compare the depth of racist sentiment in the two countries. There have, of course, been extensive studies on this subject in the United States, but it has only recently begun
to attract the attention of researchers in Canada. Canada has an ample
record of mistreatment of racial minorities, and there is some evidence that racism is becoming a more serious problem, with recent
outbreaks of racial conflict in major Canadian cities. None of these episodes has been on the scale or had the consequences in deaths, inju-
ries, and property damage of those in the inner cities of the United
States, but their occurrence clearly points to increasing strain in race
relations in Canada.

POLITICAL CONFIDENCE

The ability of political elites to manage the complex new agenda of issues they face, particularly those related to the economic and fiscal
constraints imposed by structural change in the economy and uncon-
trolled government deficits, depends not just on the issue priorities
and policy preferences of citizens. To be successful in dealing with
these issues, the political elites must also be able to command the confidence of the voters, because they must be able to persuade citizens to
accept policies that impose personal costs in the form of reductions in

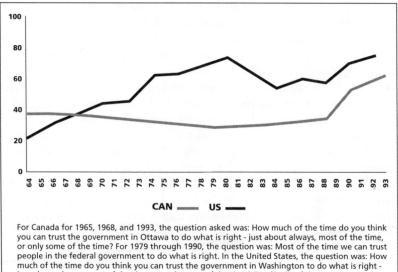

For Canada for 1965, 1968, and 1993, the question asked was: How much of the time do you think you can trust the government in Ottawa to do what is right - just about always, most of the time, or only some of the time? For 1979 through 1990, the question was: Most of the time we can trust people in the federal government to do what is right. In the United States, the question was: How much of the time do you think you can trust the government in Washington to do what is right - just about always, most of the time, or only some of the time? For details of the responses and sources, see table 3.A14 in the appendix to this chapter.

Figure 3.3   Number of respondents giving negative answers to questions about their level of trust in their national government: Canada and the United States, from 1964/65 to 1993/94

benefits from the state or the payment of higher taxes. The premise in this proposition is that citizens must believe in the competence and public-serving commitment of their leaders if they are to be persuaded to comply with policies that are personally painful.

Attitudes on this dimension have been tracked regularly in the United States since 1958. The results of this tracking first began to attract the attention of researchers in the late 1960s when there were significant shifts in responses to questions asking voters about the extent to which they believed in the responsiveness, integrity, competence, and trustworthiness of political elites. Between 1958 and 1970 there was a sharp drop in the number of respondents who gave positive responses to these questions. The question that seemed best to capture this change asked voters, "How much of the time do you think you can trust the government in Washington to do what is right?" The number of people saying "just about always" or "most of the time" fell from 75 per cent in 1966 to 56 per cent in 1970, and it continued to fall through the 1970s, dropping to less than 30 per cent in 1980. (Percentage distributions are shown in table 3.A14 of the appendix.) While the number moved up again during the early years of the Reagan presidency, it remained below

50 per cent and slid downward again during Reagan's second term (cf. Dalton 1988, 230–1). By the end of the Bush presidency, it had fallen to 23 per cent, and has not moved significantly since then.

Levels of political trust, as measured by similar questions, have also dropped dramatically in Canada, though the drop did not occur until twenty years after it was first observed in the United States. When the general trust question was first asked in Canada in 1965, the number saying elites could be trusted almost all of the time or most of the time was 57 per cent. It remained around this level until 1988; but when the question was next asked, in 1990, the number who gave a positive response was found to have fallen to 41 per cent. This shift is apparent across a wide range of measures. For example, Decima data show that between 1980 and 1990 the number of Canadians who believed politicians to be competent fell from 57 to 33 per cent, and the number who believed them to be principled fell from 63 to 28 per cent (see table 3.A15).

Some commentators have argued that lack of trust in political leaders in Canada reflects a short-term response to the person and policies of Conservative Prime Minister Brian Mulroney who, when he announced his retirement in February 1993, had the lowest approval ratings ever given a Canadian prime minister. But there is evidence that this analysis is too simple. *Decima Quarterly* polls from 1980 to 1993 show a steady decline in the number of respondents who said they had a great deal of confidence in the people who ran both the federal and the provincial governments, and they show a steady growth in the number who said they had almost no confidence in them at all. Since 1979, few federal or provincial leaders have been able to sustain high approval ratings for more than a very brief period, even after substantial election victories. Between 1990 and 1995, there were two changes of government in Ontario and the incumbent parties were defeated in three other provinces. In the 1993 federal election, the core vote for the Conservatives completely collapsed. Although they had been one of the two dominant parties since Confederation, they were reduced from 169 seats in Parliament to just two seats, and won only 15 per cent of the popular vote. In the previous ten elections they had never won less than 30 per cent of the popular vote, and their normal share was 36 per cent. Also in 1993, the New Democratic Party, which had been a significant force in federal politics since 1962, saw its share of the popular vote fall from 20 to 7 per cent.

What is most significant about the 1993 election is that the shift in voter preferences was towards new parties, which in different ways challenged the established political order. In Quebec, 49 per cent of those who voted turned to the Bloc Québécois, which campaigned on a platform of separatism, giving the Bloc fifty-four of Quebec's seventy-five seats. In the country as a whole, 19 per cent of the popular vote went to the Reform Party, which advocated a radical agenda of populist reforms.

When the decline in trust was first noted in the United States, it prompted some political scientists to warn of a threat to the underlying legitimacy of the American regime (Miller 1974). Others saw the decline as a response to specific policies and specific office holders (Citrin 1974). In the event, as we have seen, the decline has persisted in the United States, despite changes in administration and policy.

The debate about what these data imply for regime legitimacy goes on. Dalton, for example, argues that "a gradual accumulation of evidence suggests that the decline in public confidence is broader than just dissatisfaction with present political elites" (1988, 235). Whatever the deeper meaning one attaches to the decline, it has a bearing on the question that concerns us here. If large numbers of citizens accord only limited trust to their political leaders, it will be difficult for those leaders to mobilize support for policies that reduce the benefits government provides or that impose higher taxes.

Moreover, while it can be argued that a number of different factors and different specific events have figured in the decline in the public's trust in elites in the two countries, in both there is a direct connection between measures of confidence in elites and perceptions of their performance in dealing with economic issues. For example, Alan Kornberg and Harold Clarke have shown that in Canada, during the 1980s, "judgements about the government's ability to manage the economy were particularly powerful predictors of support for the incumbent political authorities and the regime" (Kornberg and Clarke 1992, 141), and Robert Burge has shown that government economic performance was closely related to shifts in the *Decima Quarterly*'s measure of confidence in the federal government from 1980 to 1989 (Burge 1993). Similarly, in the United States there is a substantial body of research that suggests, as Miller and Borelli observe, that citizens "attribute credit or blame for economic conditions to the government, thus making government economic performance evaluations a likely factor influencing trust in the national government" (Miller and Borelli 1991, 162). Thus, in both countries, the low levels of confidence in elites is tied to perceptions of the way in which they are managing the very issues on which they most need public support.

The Issue of Community Support

Compounding the problem of political support for elites in Canada is the problem of support for the national political community. The broad dimensions of this problem as it has played itself out in the arena of elite-level politics were sketched earlier in this chapter and in chapter 2. The point in raising it here is to observe that this is not just an elite issue; it is paralleled by strong currents in public opinion.

The contrast between Canada and the United States on this dimension is illustrated by data which test the degree of commitment to an overarching national community. Eighty-seven per cent of a sample of Americans interviewed in 1985 said they were "very proud to be Americans" (Dalton 1988, 237). In comparison, Kornberg and Clarke report that among samples of Canadians asked in a series of surveys from 1974 to 1988 to express their feelings of commitment to Canada, the number giving very strong support (scores of 75 or higher on a scale from zero to 100) was as low as 52 per cent (Kornberg and Clarke 1992, 107).

The best measure of the deep-rooted nature of Quebec ambivalence towards the national political community is the fact that whenever Québécois have been asked the extent to which their loyalties lie first – with their provincial community or with the national community – the majority, including many who identify themselves as being committed to the existing system, have always expressed a stronger sense of commitment to their provincial community. This commitment is a powerful emotional force that has both led to and been sustained by the separatist movement.

The lack of clarity in the wording of the referendum question in 1995 has been blamed by federalist leaders for the high level of support for the separatist option. But the reality is that a majority of Quebec francophones have such a strong sense of their distinctive national identity that they are prepared to support some concept of a separate Quebec state. Analysis of one set of polls in 1990 found, for example, that 44 per cent could be identified as supporting "separatism," 50 per cent "independence," 50 per cent "sovereignty," and 55 per cent "sovereignty-association" (Cloutier, Gay, and Latouche, cited in Dion 1992, 87). What is most important is not the level of support for any specific formula for change, but the fact that as many as 55 per cent were prepared to endorse a position that implied at least a semi-autonomous status.

The effect of the threat of separatism on the ability of political elites to govern effectively lies not just in the possibility of Quebec's secession. Outside Quebec there has been a growing impatience with the preoccupation of the country's leaders with issues of constitutional reform. Both private and public polls in the months leading up to and following the Meech Lake crisis found that most Canadians rejected the premise that constitutional problems required the attention they were being given by elites. They wanted politicians to put aside the constitution and get on with other matters.[9] This impatience was further demonstrated in surveys following the Quebec referendum in 1995. Although a majority of voters outside Quebec expressed concern about the possibility of Quebec's separation, at the same time they wanted the political leaders to turn their attention to other issues.

CONCLUSION

The story recounted here consists more of fragments of a tale than a closely interwoven narrative. In large part this is a function of the kind of data available which are not well suited to explanatory analysis. Yet there are discernible patterns in these fragments. Many scholars and popular commentators have attempted to explain differences in the political systems of Canada and the United States in terms of differences in their political values. These cultural explanations have had to rely largely on interpretations of inferences drawn from the conduct of governments and political leaders and, in the case of propositions about mass publics, from a variety of behavioural data. In the absence of more direct evidence, these explanations of the past can never be conclusively tested. But we do have data from public opinion research which permit us to test the extent to which such value differences may be manifest in the attitudes of Canadians and Americans today. In our investigation of this research here, we have seen little evidence of differences either in underlying values or in approaches to public policy – with one significant exception. Canadians, collectively, seem more willing than Americans to use government in an active role to pursue both economic and social objectives. This difference persists, even though there is evidence that a majority of Canadians have been willing to support some curtailment of government's role.

Some of the forces of change described in chapter 2 may be adding to the pressure towards value convergence between the two societies. Some scholars argue that as a result of these changes, there has been a wider and more fundamental shift in values in all advanced industrial societies. Ronald Inglehart, who first set out this thesis, sees movements such as environmentalism as the reflection of a shift from an emphasis on material concerns to a concern with the "quality of life" (cf. Inglehart 1990). Inglehart and his collaborators have developed measures to distinguish between material and post-material values which they applied to a comparison of Canada and the United States in the World Values Study of 1990. They found that 23 per cent of Americans and 26 per cent of Canadians could be classified as having a "post-materialist" outlook, a significant shift from ten years earlier

(Inglehart, Nevitte, and Basanez 1991). A particularly important part of their analysis showed that post-materialism is significantly stronger among young people. Neil Nevitte, in writing about this research, concluded that, "to the extent that the value trajectories identified in the 1981–1990 decade are uninterrupted, and to the extent that the qualities indicated are effectively passed on to the offspring of the generations analysed here, there are reasons for expecting further value convergence" (Nevitte 1991a, 11).

Although these data and the data discussed earlier in this chapter point to a convergence of values between the two countries, there are structural differences between them which have had significant effects in differentiating political attitudes, in particular in respect to the issue priorities of citizens. Most strikingly, Americans are more concerned about international issues, reflecting their country's status as the only superpower, which places it at the centre of world politics. In the period for which we have data, few Canadians ever ranked international issues as a first priority, except when it touched on their relations with the United States, a fact that reflects Canada's status as a small power whose economy is dominated by that of the United States. Another effect of structural differences on the political agenda in Canada results from the fact that Canadian society is divided into distinctive language-based communities. The issue of national integration, resolved for the United States by the Civil War, continues to be a concern of Canadians. Finally, the political agendas of the two countries appear to be differentiated by the effects of different patterns of urban concentration. The problems of the inner cities in the United States have so far been unparalleled in Canada. This difference is clearly reflected in the rates of violent crime in the two countries, which in turn is reflected in the fact Americans have been consistently more likely to identify concern about crime as a first priority.

When the structural differences are controlled, the political agendas of the mass publics in the two countries are strikingly alike – both in what they express and in what they do not express. Economic issues are the principal ongoing concern of citizens in both countries, and the specific nature of these issues at any given time is more or less the same, which reflects the close linkages between the Canadian and American economies. But in neither country have the public's issue agendas been responsive to certain issues that have deeply concerned political elites, notably the problem of government deficits and issues related to race and to the inequality of women.

The disjunction between the political agendas of the elites and the mass publics over the problem of government deficits presents a particular difficulty. This disjunction poses a much larger question about the ability of governments in Canada and the United States to govern effectively in a political environment of uncertainty and change. While it is widely accepted in both countries that persistently high government deficits are a problem, and while the number viewing these deficits as a matter of serious concern is growing, only a small minority of citizens have accepted that deficits should have priority on the policy agenda. Even more important, not very many Americans and Canadians appear to have accepted that deficit cutting has to be personally costly. Few are willing to pay higher taxes and most reject proposals for cuts to spending on the programs that account for the largest share of government program spending.

This is not to suggest governments have no room to manoeuvre. Some state and provincial governments in the two countries have been able to maintain support while making substantial spending cuts. But the fact remains that mass opinion still does not accord the same priority to deficit reduction as elite opinion does. Indeed, even after three years of federal and provincial government insistence on the urgency of the need to reduce deficits, only 19 per cent of a national sample of Canadians in June 1996 was prepared to say that deficit reduction must be a government priority (Southam News/Angus Reid 1996).

Arguably, this is a reflection of the problem that most citizens have grown sceptical about what they are told by their political leaders. The mistrust of political elites, which has persisted in the United States over more than two decades, now pervades Canadian society as well. The close linkage between levels of confidence in political elites and public evaluations of the effectiveness of government in dealing with economic problems reinforces the difficulties governments in both countries will have in trying to deal with the current array of economic and fiscal problems.

In Canada these difficulties are made worse by the very real possibility of the secession of Quebec. The election of a Parti Québécois government in Quebec and the close result in the referendum of 1995 have been helped along by the ineffectiveness of government in dealing with the country's economic and fiscal problems. The arguments made by federalists in the Quebec referendum of 1980 that federalism serves Quebec's economic interests was clearly less convincing in the economic and fiscal climate of 1995. Ottawa's deficit-reduction policies, involving cuts in transfers both to individuals and to provincial governments, give separatist leaders a new focus for their claims that membership in the Canadian federation is not profitable for Quebec. At the same time, in the rest of the country, if the political elites become distracted once again by the issue of national unity, this will almost certainly further anger those who believe that the country's economic problems are not being dealt with.

The situation in Quebec makes the potential for a crisis in political support dramatically immediate in Canada. But this unique aspect of the Canadian situation should not obscure the fact that elites in the United States also face a serious problem in trying to win public support for policies to deal with the difficult economic and fiscal issues the two countries commonly face. As we have already seen, American commentators have been warning for two decades of the potential for a crisis of political support in the United States. The breakdown in enduring loyalties to the established parties (cf. Dalton 1988, ch. 9 *passim*) and the widespread support for Ross Perot in the 1992 election are two of the more obvious pieces of evidence of change related to dissatisfaction with existing political elites.

Another phenomenon, which may be even more meaningful, although it has not attracted much attention from researchers on public opinion, is the dramatic decline in turnout in American elections over the past three decades. Even though turnout was up in the 1992 presidential election, it remains much lower than in Canada and most other advanced industrial democracies (Teixeira 1992). Since 1960 in presidential elections, on average more than 45 per cent of Americans have failed to vote; and in off-year congressional elections, the average number of non-voters has exceeded 50 per cent. For methodological reasons (most notably, getting to the non-voters) researchers are hard pressed to explain why this is so, but it seems reasonable to assume that there is some connection between this behavioural response and the widespread decline in confidence in political leaders and the equally widespread expression of feelings of political inefficacy. Some commentators warn that low turnout could have damaging consequences if it results in the separation of the policy agenda of the political elite from that of the mass public (Teixeira 1992, 101–3, *passim*). This, it can be argued, is precisely what happened in the 1994 congressional election when the Republicans won a majority in both houses of Congress on the basis of a turnout of only 39 per cent. Post-election surveys showed that a majority of Americans did not agree with much of what the Republicans proposed in their "Contract with America."

Political elites in North America are not alone in confronting a majority of citizens who are increasingly sceptical about the competence, integrity, and credibility of their leaders, and the signs of political instability we observe in North America are apparent elsewhere. In all the advanced democracies, there is evidence of a breakdown in loyalties to established parties, a growing "anti-party" sentiment, the rise of new populist and more radical political groups, and demands for more direct popular participation in political decisions (Kaase and Newton

1995, 169). Manifestly, there are worldwide strains on democratic governments.

An exploration of the causes of these strains is beyond the scope of this chapter. But one points bears noting. North American data suggest that anxiety created by economic dislocation has become a significant factor in rising levels of political discontent. And widespread feelings of economic insecurity have been found in studies in both Canada and the United States (cf. Reporters of the *New York Times* 1996). Since economic dislocation is closely related to fundamental technological change, there would appear to be no immediate or purely "political" solutions to the problem of low levels of political confidence that governments in Canada and the United States now face. Thus, while it may be argued that there is no imminent "crisis of democracy" in these two countries, the general disposition of public opinion is likely to create a difficult policy-making environment for leaders in both countries for some considerable time.

APPENDIX

Table 3.A1
Most important issue: United States[1]

	a	b	c	d	e	f	g	h	i	j	k	l
Jan 1980	45	38	1	3	–	11	–	2	–	–	2	100
Mar 1980	15	70	2	4	–	7	–	2	–	–	1	101
Sep 1980	13	65	2	8	–	3	–	3	–	6	2	100
J/F 1981	5	77	2	2	–	–	–	2	–	9	3	100
Oct 1981	6	71	4	2	–	–	–	4	–	13	2	100
Jan 1982	9	78	4	1	–	2	–	4	–	4	–	102
Apr 1982	7	72	2	–	–	–	–	2	–	15	2	100
Jun 1982	10	67	2	–	–	–	–	2	–	17	2	100
Aug 1982	7	71	2	2	–	–	–	3	–	13	2	100
Oct 1982	4	79	2	2	–	–	–	2	–	8	2	100
Apr 1983	11	73	2	2	–	–	–	3	–	8	2	100
Jul 1983	14	70	2	2	–	–	–	4	–	6	3	100
Oct 1983	19	58	5	2	–	–	–	5	–	8	4	100
Nov 1983	32	50	2	3	–	–	–	6	–	6	3	100
Feb 1984	24	54	3	2	–	1	–	6	–	7	3	100
Jun 1984	25	54	3	2	2	–	1	5	–	7	2	100
Sep 1984	26	46	3	3	–	–	–	3	–	19	–	100
Jan 1985	23	52	3	–	2	–	–	2	–	16	3	101
May 1985	19	44	3	–	5	–	–	5	–	21	3	100

Table 3.A1
Most important issue: United States[1] *(Cont'd)*

	a	b	c	d	e	f	g	h	i	j	k	l
Oct 1985	18	48	3	–	3	–	–	4	–	22	4	100
Jan 1986	25	40	3	–	2	–	–	3	–	24	3	100
Jul 1986	19	47	3	2	7	–	–	3	–	17	3	100
Jan 1987	20	42	3	4	9	–	–	3	1	17	2	100
Apr 1987	19	39	3	4	9	–	–	4	1	18	3	100
May 1987	19	39	3	4	9	–	–	4	–	18	3	100
Sep 1988[2]	9	52	2	–	11	–	–	1	–	13	12	100
May 1989	2	41	5	2	24	–	4	5	–	11	6	100
Sep 1989	2	20	3	–	61	–	1	1	–	9	4	100
Nov 1989	1	35	3	1	37	–	3	3	–	11	6	100
Apr 1990	1	33	2	1	30	–	8	1	–	13	9	98
Jul 1990	1	51	1	1	21	–	6	2	–	11	6	100
Oct 1990	20	39	2	4	10	2	2	4	–	10	5	98
Nov 1990	21	39	2	3	8	2	2	6	–	11	5	99
Jan 1991	30	37	1	3	9	–	1	5	–	8	6	100
Feb 1991	40	38	–	2	5	1	1	3	–	5	5	100
Mar 1991	7	60	2	–	11	–	2	2	–	7	6	97
Apr 1991	5	54	2	1	10	–	3	4	–	14	7	100
May 1991	3	58	3	2	10	–	2	4	–	13	6	101
Nov 1991	3	60	4	3	6	–	2	3	4	14	2	101
Mar 1992	2	61	3	4	4	–	2	3	7	13	1	100
A/S 1992	5	54	4	4	3	–	2	3	7	16	2	101
Jan 1993	4	51	5	3	3	–	2	4	10	18	1	101
Sep 1993	3	46	9	3	3	–	1	3	16	15	2	101
Jan 1994	2	30	26	2	4	–	1	3	16	14	2	100
Jul 1994	5	29	18	5	4	–	1	7	13	16	1	99
Aug 1994	2	21	32	3	6	–	1	4	17	12	1	99
Jan 1995	1	38	17	3	4	–	1	4	7	23	1	99

[1] The issues are identified as follows: (a) international, (b) economic, (c) crime, (d) government, (e) drugs/drug abuse, (f) energy, (g) environment, (h) moral decline, (i) health care, (j) other, (k) no opinion, (l) total.

Since Gallup accepted more than one response in most of the surveys, the total number of responses sometimes exceeded 100 per cent. When this occurred, to provide more accurate intersurvey comparisons, the responses were weighted assuming a base of 100 per cent. The number of excess responses was normally in the order of 5 per cent and was never larger than 15 per cent.

[2] Sample included only registered voters.

Table 3.A2
Most important issue: Canada[1]

No.	Season	a	b	c	d	e	f[2]	g	h	i	j	k
Q1	Spring/80	26	10	2	10	10	10	14	6	6	1	5
Q2	Summer/80	24	12	1	12	7	6	14	4	5	3	12
Q3	Fall/80	25	13	1	11	6	8	17	2	7	4	6
Q4	Winter/80	26	11	2	10	7	8	19	3	4	3	6
Q5	Spring/81	28	14	2	13	6	6	15	2	5	4	5
Q6	Summer/81	36	9	7	11	6	9	7	2	4	3	5
Q7	Fall/81	34	8	14	17	4	8	6	1	4	2	2
Q8	Winter/81	23	12	13	22	1	7	9	1	4	4	3
Q9	Spring/82	21	23	9	19	2	11	4	2	4	3	2
Q10	Summer/82	20	27	13	19	1	10	1	2	4	2	2
Q11	Fall/82	17	40	9	13	1	8	2	2	4	2	2
Q12	Winter/82	12	46	3	12	1	10	2	2	5	4	3
Q13	Spring/83	11	48	2	9	1	12	2	2	6	4	2
Q14	Summer/83	10	49	2	12	1	9	2	3	6	3	4
Q15	Fall/83	10	47	1	8	1	11	1	6	6	4	4
Q16	Winter/83	9	43	2	7	0	11	2	13	5	4	5
Q17	Spring/84	8	46	2	9	0	12	3	6	4	4	4
Q18	Summer/84	6	52	4	9	0	9	3	5	5	3	4
Q19	Fall/84	7	53	2	10	0	9	1	5	8	3	2
Q20	Winter/84	7	50	1	8	0	12	1	7	7	2	4
Q21	Spring/85	6	46	2	9	0	9	1	10	8	4	5
Q22	Summer/85	8	44	0	7	0	12	1	8	10	3	6
Q23	Fall/85	4	46	0	8	0	13	1	12	8	3	4
Q24	Winter/85	6	45	0	7	0	12	1	11	9	3	5
Q25	Spring/86	4	39	1	9	2	20	0	6	8	5	4
Q26	Summer/86	4	36	0	3	1	13	1	17	9	8	7
Q27	Fall/86	6	40	1	5	1	15	0	11	9	6	6
Q28	Winter/86	4	38	0	7	0	13	2	12	9	8	6
Q29	Spring/87	4	38	0	4	0	16	1	13	12	6	5
Q30	Summer/87	7	27	0	4	0	19	2	12	11	10	8
Q31	Fall/87	6	26	0	4	0	13	3	22	11	9	6
Q32	Winter/87	3	20	0	5	0	12	2	27	14	7	9
Q33	Spring/88	4	19	0	3	0	17	4	21	16	7	8
Q34	Summer/88	5	19	1	3	0	13	4	24	15	9	7
Q35	Fall/88	4	14	1	3	0	10	2	25	16	18	7
Q36	Winter/88	4	11	0	2	0	11	4	32	13	12	9

Table 3.A2
Most important issue: Canada[1] *(Cont'd)*

No.	Season	a	b	c	d	e	f[2]	g	h	i	j	k
Q37	Spring/89	6	10	3	3	0	15	6	17	16	17	6
Q38	Summer/89	6	11	1	4	0	27	4	11	14	18	5
Q39	Fall/89	5	10	1	5	0	30	3	9	11	19	6
Q40	Winter/89	3	10	0	5	0	32	4	11	14	15	6
Q41	Spring/90	4	6	2	5	0	30	21	5	10	12	6
Q42	Summer/90	3	8	4	5	0	20	30	4	8	13	5
Q43	Fall/90	4	8	2	6	0	35	10	4	9	16	5
Q44	Winter/90	3	17	2	14	0	31	9	6	6	10	4
Q45	Spring/91	4	17	0	10	0	30	18	0	8	9	4
Q46	Summer/91	3	14	0	11	0	33	15	0	9	11	4
Q47	Fall/91	3	19	0	13	0	26	18	1	10	8	4
Q48	Winter/91	3	22	0	19	0	23	14	0	9	6	3
Q49	Spring/92	2	28	0	17	0	19	15	0	5	10	3
Q50	Summer/92	1	24	0	15	0	20	14	0	11	12	3
Q51	Fall/92	1	28	0	19	0	16	20	0	8	5	4
Q52	Winter/92	1	38	0	17	0	22	4	0	9	6	3
Q53	Spring/93	2	36	0	13	0	23	3	0	12	8	4
Q54	Summer/93	1	36	0	10	0	31	2	0	10	8	3
Q55	Fall/93	1	42	0	7	0	27	2	0	13	7	2
Q56	Winter/93	1	32	0	7	0	27	1	0	17	7	2
Q57	Spring/94	1	41	0	6	0	29	3	0	14	4	3
Q58	Summer/94	1	33	0	6	0	23	12	0	16	7	2
Q59	Fall/94	1	30	0	6	0	24	12	0	17	7	4
Q60	Winter/94	1	23	0	7	0	36	9	0	18	4	3
Q61	Spring/95	1	29	0	5	0	32	5	0	20	4	4

[1] The issues are identified as follows: (a) inflation, (b) unemployment, (c) interest rates, (d) economy, general, (e) energy, (f) government/taxes, (g) national unity, (h) international affairs, (i) social/moral, (j) other, (k) no response.

[2] The deficit was not coded as a separate item until 1989. It had previously been included in the "government/taxes" category. To maintain consistency, it has not been broken into a separate category in this table but is shown as part of the "government/taxes" category. The numbers for the deficit as a separate item are shown in figure 3.2.

Table 3.A3
Breakdown of economic category for most important issue, United States, Gallup[1]

	a	b	c	d	e	f	g	h	i	j	k
Jan 1980	34	4	–	–	–	–	–	–	–	–	38
Mar 1980	66	4	–	–	–	–	–	–	–	–	70
Sep 1980	51	13	–	–	–	–	–	–	–	–	65
J/F 1981	69	8	–	1	–	–	–	–	–	–	77
Oct 1981	46	15	–	4	–	5	–	–	–	–	71
Jan 1982	44	25	–	3	–	6	–	–	–	–	78
Apr 1982	20	34	9	3	–	6	–	–	–	–	72
Jun 1982	20	30	9	4	–	4	–	–	–	–	67
Aug 1982	17	34	12	4	–	4	–	–	–	–	71
Oct 1982	15	50	9	3	–	2	–	–	–	–	79
Apr 1983	15	45	7	4	–	3	–	–	–	–	73
Jul 1983	12	42	6	4	–	4	–	–	–	–	70
Oct 1983	11	37	4	4	–	3	–	–	–	–	58
Nov 1983	10	28	3	5	–	4	–	–	–	–	50
Feb 1984	9	25	4	11	–	6	–	1	1	–	54
Jun 1984	13	24	3	10	–	4	–	–	–	–	54
Sep 1984	10	19	3	10	–	–	–	–	–	–	43
Jan 1985	10	17	5	14	–	–	–	–	–	5	52
May 1985	9	18	7	5	–	–	–	–	–	5	44
Oct 1985	6	21	4	14	–	–	–	–	–	3	48
Jan 1986	7	15	3	9	–	–	–	–	–	6	40
Jul 1986	4	20	6	11	–	–	–	–	–	5	46
Jan 1987	5	14	7	9	3	–	–	–	–	5	42
Apr 1987	4	13	8	9	3	–	–	–	–	4	41
May 1987	4	11	8	9	3	–	–	–	–	4	39
Sep 1988[2]	2	9	12	12	3	–	–	–	7	7	52
May 1989	3	6	7	6	3	–	–	–	7	9	41
Sep 1989	1	2	4	5	1	–	–	–	3	5	20
Nov 1989	2	3	7	7	2	–	–	–	5	10	35
Apr 1990	1	3	7	6	2	–	–	–	3	11	34
Jul 1990	1	3	8	24	1	–	1	–	3	8	51
Oct 1990	1	3	10	16	1	–	–	1	2	5	39
Nov 1990	2	3	11	11	1	–	3	1	1	6	39
Jan 1991	2	4	15	4	0	–	2	3	1	6	37
Feb 1991	1	5	16	6	0	–	1	2	0	6	37

Table 3.A3
Breakdown of economic category for most important issue, United States, Gallup[1] *(Cont'd)*

	a	b	c	d	e	f	g	h	i	j	k
Mar 1991	2	8	24	8	1	–	2	4	1	10	60
Apr 1991	2	8	20	6	1	–	2	2	0	13	54
May 1991	2	9·	21	6	1	–	2	4	1	12	58
Nov 1991	0	15	20	3	3	–	2	3	4	10	59
Mar 1992	0	14	23	4	2	–	3	2	3	8	61
A/S 1992	0	15	21	5	1	–	2	1	3	7	54
Jan 1993	0	12	18	7	2	–	2	0	4	8	51
Sep 1993	1	11	15	8	2	–	3	1	2	4	46
Jan 1994	1	9	9	4	1	–	1	0	1	5	30
Jul 1994	1	8	8	3	1	–	2	0	1	6	29
Aug 1994	1	4	10	2	0	–	1	1	1	3	21
Jan 1995	1	10	6	9	0	–	3	0	2	6	38

[1] The breakdown is as follows: (a) inflation, (b) unemployment, (c) economy, general, (d) federal
budget deficit, (e) trade deficit, (f) social budget cuts, (g) taxes, (h) recession, (i) other economic,
(j) poverty/homeless, (k) economic total.
The data in this table are based on the weighting for multiple responses reported in table 3.A1.

[2] The sample included only registered voters.

Table 3.A4
Attitudes related to the values of capitalism

Competition, whether in school, work or business:

	USA[1] (1976–77)	Canada[2] (1987)		
		All	*Eng.*	*Fr.*
– leads to better performance and a desire for excellence	81	76	79	66
– is often wasteful and destructive	8	13	10	22
– neither/undecided	11	11	11	12
	(938)	(1,222)	(947)	(274)

The profit system:

	USA[3] (1976–77)	Canada[4] (1988)			Canada[5] (1993)		
		All	*Eng.*	*Fr.*	*All*	*Eng.*	*Fr.*
– often brings out the worst in human nature	16	9	10	6	17	15	25
– usually teaches people the value of hard work and personal achievement	54	66	64	73	71	73	64
– neither/undecided	29	25	26	22	12	13	10
	(938)	(2,077)	(1,571)	(506)	(2,223)	(1,708)	(520)

When businesses are allowed to make as much money as they can:

	USA[6] (1978–79)	Canada[7] (1988)		
		All	*Eng.*	*Fr.*
– workers and the poor are bound to get less	24	32	30	38
– everyone profits in the long run	42	37	38	22
– no opinion	34	31	32	30
	(938)	(2,100)	(1,592)	(508)

Table 3.A4
Attitudes related to the values of capitalism *(Cont'd)*

If the private enterprise system were abolished:

	USA.[8] (1976–77)	Canada[9] (1988)			Canada[10] (1993)		
		All	Eng.	Fr.	All	Eng.	Fr.
– most people would work hard anyway	21	18	16	20	22	22	23
– very few people would do their best	48	54	57	46	55	55	53
– no opinion	31	29	27	34	23	23	24
	(938)	(2,097)	(1,589)	(508)	(2,223)	(1,703)	(520)

Which statement closer: "Competition is good, it stimulates people to work." *or* "Competition is bad, it brings out the worst in people."[11]

	USA (1990)	Canada (1990)		
		All	Eng.	Fr.
Percent saying competition is good:	74	75	74	76

Which statement closer: "Hard work usually brings about a better life." *or* "Hard work does not bring success, it is more a matter of luck and connections."[11]

	USA (1990)	Canada (1990)		
		All	Eng.	Fr.
Percent saying that hard work brings a better life:	68	65	68	58

1 McClosky and Zaller 1984, table 4.6
2 Charter Project, 1987
3 McClosky and Zaller 1984, table 4.5
4 Canadian National Election Study, 1988
5 Canadian National Election Study, 1993

6 McClosky and Zaller 1984, table 4.5
7 Canadian National Election Study, 1988
8 McClosky and Zaller 1984, table 5.1
9 Canadian National Election Study, 1988
10 Canadian National Election Study, 1993

11 These questions are from the World Values Study surveys in Canada and the United States in 1990. The data were provided by Neil Nevitte, principal investigator for the Canadian survey. Respondents were asked to express their degree of agreement along a five-point scale with one statement or the other. The responses have been added across the scale, excluding the weakest measure of agreement.

Table 3.A5
Attitudes related to social order

Our laws should aim to:

	USA[1] (1976–77)	Canada[2] (1987)		
		All	Eng.	Fr.
– enforce the community's standards of right and wrong	23	58	64	37
– protect a citizen's right to live by any moral standard he chooses	55	24	17	46
– neither/undecided	23	19	17	17
	(938)	(1,227)	(953)	(274)

Per cent saying that in times of crisis the government should have the power to declare a national emergency and remove all civil rights:[3]

	USA (1989)	Canada (1989)	
		Eng.	Fr.
	41	52	37

Per cent who agree or disagree with the following two statements about free speech:

"It is better to live in an orderly society than to allow people so much freedom that they become disruptive."

	USA[4] (1976–77)	Canada[5] (1987)	
		Eng.	Fr.
Agree	51	61	77
Disagree	49	38	21
		(1,562)	(521)

Table 3.A5
Attitudes related to social order *(Cont'd)*

"Free speech is just not worth it if it means we have to put up with the danger to society of radical and extremist views."

	USA[4] (1976–77)	Canada[5] (1987) Eng.	Canada[5] (1987) Fr.
Agree	28	35	38
Disagree	72	62	59
		(1,562)	(521)

In general, do you think the courts in this area deal too harshly or not harshly enough with criminals?

	USA[6] (1972)	Can[7] (1974)	USA (1975)	Can (1975)	USA (1980)	Can (1980)	USA (1983)	Can (1982)	USA (1987)	Can (1986)	USA (1993)	Can (1994)
Too harshly	7	6	4	4	3	4	4	4	3	3	3	1
Not harshly enough	74	66	79	73	88	63	85	79	84	78	86	82
About right (volunteered)	19	16	10	13	8	19	6	11	13	12	6	13
Don't know	–	12	7	10	–	14	4	6	–	7	5	4

In order to reduce crime, the courts should give criminals stiffer punishments.[8]

	USA	Can Eng.	Can Fr.
Agree	84	87	71
Disagree	16	13	29

Table 3.A5
Attitudes related to social order (Cont'd)

Do you favour or oppose the death penalty for murder?

USA[9]

	(1981)	(1984)	(1986)	(1988)	(1994)	(1995)
Favour	66	70	70	71	80	77
Oppose	25	24	22	22	16	13
No opinion	9	6	8	7	4	10

If a national referendum – a public vote – were held today on the question of executing a person for murder, would you vote for reinstating the death penalty in Canada or would you vote against reinstating it?

Canada[10]

	(1982)	(1984)	(1986)	(1987)	(1990)	(1994)
Reinstate	70	71	68	68	60	59
Do not	19	21	20	20	33	26
Can't say	11	8	12	7	12	9

[1] McClosky and Zaller 1984, table 2.11
[2] Charter Project, 1987
[3] Decima Research for *Maclean's*, June 1989
[4] McClosky data cited in Sniderman et al. 1988
[5] Sniderman et al. 1988, figs. 9A–9D; Charter Project, 1987; American source, unidentified
[6] NORC, reprinted in *Public Opinion* 10, no. 3 (1987): 27
[7] Gallup Report
[8] Baer et al. 1990, 90, note that "agree" and "disagree" are aggregates of two responses
[9] Gallup Report
[10] Gallup Report

Table 3.A6
Attitudes related to the principle of equality

Unskilled workers (such as janitors, dishwashers, and so on) usually receive wages that are:

	USA[1] (1976–77)	Canada[2] (1988)		
		All	Eng.	Fr.
– about right considering the amount of skill required	43	38	42	24
– much too low for the dirty work they do	38	43	39	57
– neither/undecided	19	19	19	19
	(938)	(2,107)	(1,593)	(513)

In a fair economic system:

	USA[3] (1976–77)	Canada[2] (1987)		
		All	Eng.	Fr.
– all people should earn about the same	7	12	6	30
– people with more ability should earn higher salaries	78	71	78	47
– neither/undecided	15	17	16	23
	(938)	(2,077)	(1,571)	(275)

A person's wages should depend on:

	USA[3] (1976–77)	Canada[2] (1988)			Canada[4] (1993)		
		All	Eng.	Fr.	All	Eng.	Fr.
– how much he or she needs to live decently	20	20	18	24	22	22	24
– the importance of the job	45	50	50	49	65	65	64
– neither/undecided	35	31	32	27	13	13	12
	(938)	(2,081)	(1,579)	(502)	(2,223)	(1,703)	(520)

Table 3.A6
Attitudes related to the principle of equality *(Cont'd)*

Some people feel that the government[5] should see to it that every person has a job and a good standard of living ... Others think the government should just let each person get ahead on his [*sic*] own ... And, of course, other people have opinions somewhere in between.

	USA[6] (1986)	Canada[7] (1987)		
		All	Eng.	Fr.
– government guarantee jobs	24	50	44	73
– individual on his own	47	24	28	10
– neutral/other	29	26	29	17
		(1,227)	(953)	(274)

Which statement closer: "Individuals should take more responsibility for themselves." *or* "The state should do more to see that everyone is provided for."

	USA (1990)	Canada (1990)		
		All	Eng.	Fr.
Percent giving individualist response.[8]	63	59	56	65

[1] McClosky and Zaller 1984, table 6.5
[2] Canadian National Election Study, 1988
[3] McClosky and Zaller 1984, table 3.10
[4] Canadian National Election Study, 1993
[5] The American question says "the government in Washington"
[6] American National Election Study, 1986
[7] Charter Project, 1987
[8] World Values Study, 1990

Table 3.A7
Attitudes towards business and unions

In the United States, there has been a lot of talk recently about deregulating business – that is, reducing government regulation of how a business must operate. Would you favour or oppose similar action in Canada?[1]

	Canada					
	(1981)	(1982)	(1983)	(1984)	(1985)	(1986)
Favour	44	54	53	54	50	45
Oppose	42	38	39	39	41	44
No opinion	14	8	8	7	10	11

Government regulation of business usually does more harm than good.[2]

	USA					
	(1987)	(1988)	(1990)	(1992)	(1994)	
Agree	55	57	58	61	63	
Disagree	34	35	33	33	33	
Don't know	11	8	9	6	6	

Do you feel that you can count on business to act in the public interest all of the time, most of the time, hardly ever or never?[3]

	USA (1989)	Canada (1989)
Never	7	8
Hardly ever	37	38
Most of the time	54	48
All of the time	3	5
No opinion		1

Table 3.A7
Attitudes towards business and unions (Cont'd)

Big corporations have far too much power in American/Canadian society today.[4]

	USA (1980)	Canada (1982–83)	
		Eng.	Fr.
Agree	81	83	83
Disagree	19	17	17

Who do you feel best serves your personal economic interests – business, government, or unions?

	USA[4] (1980)	Canada[4] (1982–83)	
		Rest of Canada	Quebec
Business	48	52	67
Government	22	20	21
Unions	19	24	9
DK/DNA	12	4	3

Companies owned by government are usually known as crown corporations. The federal Progressive Conservative government has said that it is considering selling some of the crown corporations it owns. Generally speaking, would you strongly favour, favour, oppose, or strongly oppose this action?[5]

	Canada			
	Spring '85	Spring '86	Summer '88	Summer '89
Favour	67	71	57	59
Oppose	33	29	40	38

Table 3.A7
Attitudes towards business and unions (*Cont'd*)

How much confidence do you have in labour unions?[6]

	USA (1980)	Canada (1980)	USA (1982)	Canada (1982)	USA (1984)	Canada (1984)	USA (1986)	Canada (1986)	USA (1988)	Canada (1988)	USA (1990)	Canada (1990)	USA (1993)	Canada (1993)
Great deal	16	11	13	9	9	9	8	10	11	12	11	17	10	8
Only some	53	42	56	37	54	43	50	48	53	48	56	46	56	44
Hardly any	31	46	31	53	37	48	42	42	37	40	33	35	35	48

Labour unions have too much power for the good of the country.[7]

	USA	Canada (1986)
Agree	62	71
Disagree	31	24

Business has too much power for the good of the country.[7]

	USA	Canada (1986)
Agree	58	53
Disagree	35	41

[1] Decima Research
[2] Times Mirror Centre, *The New Political Landscape*, October 1994, 133
[3] Decima Research for *Maclean's*, June 1989
[4] Baer et al. 1990, 90
[5] Decima Research
[6] USA data from GSS; Canadian data from Decima Research
[7] M. Adams 1988

Table 3.A8
Attitudes towards social policy

A proposal has been made to make child care available for all pre-school children as part of the public school system. This program would be supported by taxes. Would you favour or oppose such a program in your school district?

	USA[1] (1987)		
	(1976)	(1981)	(1985)
Oppose	49	47	45
Favour	46	48	43
Don't know	5	7	12

There has been considerable talk recently about the provision of child-care facilities for working mothers. In your opinion, is this primarily the responsibility of the mother and/or family, or should the government share this responsibility?

	Canada[2]		
	(1975)	(1980)	(1982)
Mother/family responsibility	43	45	49
Government should share	44	48	41
Qualified/can't say	13	7	10

I'm going to name some benefits and services which are or could be funded by governments, and I'd like you to tell me for each one whether you believe that all Canadians should be eligible to receive this benefit, or whether only people who have a financial need should be eligible to receive it. How about child day care?

	Canada[2] (1991)
All Canadians	44
Canadians with financial need	54
No opinion	2

Table 3.A8

Attitudes towards social policy (*Cont'd*)

Do you view the following as an absolute right that can never be taken away, or as a limited right, one which in certain circumstances can be limited by government?[4]

i. Job protection for a women on pregnancy leave:

	USA	Canada (1989)
Limited right	27	29
Absolute right	72	71
No opinion	1	0

ii. A publicly funded health-care system available to all, regardless of financial situation:

	USA	Canada (1989)
Limited right	46	29
Absolute right	52	71
No opinion	3	0

iii. A guaranteed minimum income for everyone:

	USA	Canada (1989)
Limited right	47	37
Absolute right	51	62
No opinion	2	0

iv. Child care available to everyone who wants it:

	USA	Canada (1989)
Limited right	53	50
Absolute right	46	50
No opinion	1	0

Table 3.A8
Attitudes towards social policy (Cont'd)

Which of the following approaches would you consider most appropriate to deal with rising health-care costs?

	Canada[5] (1991)
Raise taxes to pay for them	22
Cut back on hospital and medical services	8
Charge fees to use the health-care system	56
Not sure	13

Would you be willing or not to pay higher taxes so that all Americans have health insurance that they can't lose no matter what?

	USA[6] (1993)
Willing	61
Unwilling	33
Not sure	6

How important is it that every American receive health insurance coverage: very important, somewhat important, or not very important?

	USA[7] (1994)
Very important	82
Somewhat important	16
Not very important	2

Some people say that the government should meet certain needs in society. Other people say that individuals and businesses should meet these needs for themselves. How much responsibility – a great deal, a fair amount, not much, or no responsibility at all – should the government take for providing health and medical care?

	USA[8] (1993)
Great deal	56
Fair amount	31
Not much	8
None at all	4
No opinion	1

Table 3.A8
Attitudes towards social policy (Cont'd)

Should the federal government require companies to provide health insurance for all their workers, or should companies be allowed to decide for themselves whether or not to provide health insurance?

	USA[9] (1994)
Require companies	53
Companies decide	40
No opinion	7

Is Bill Clinton's proposed health-care plan fair or unfair to people like you?

	USA[10] (1994)
Fair	44
Unfair	40
Don't know/no answer	16

Do you favour or oppose national health insurance, which would be financed by tax money, paying for most forms of health-care?

	USA[11] (1995)
Favour	53
Oppose	39
DK/DNA	8

We are faced with many problems ... are we spending too much, too little, or about the right amount on assistance to the poor?[12]

	USA										
	(1984)	(1985)	(1986)	(1987)	(1988)	(1989)	(1990)	(1991)	(1993)	(1994)
Too little	62	63	61	66	68	68	68	67	65	59
About right	24	25	27	23	23	23	25	23	23	26
Too much	11	10	9	9	7	9	7	9	12	15

Table 3.A8
Attitudes towards social policy (Cont'd)

Many different individuals and groups receive social services and benefits from government. Would you say the poor should receive more or less social services and benefits from government than they do now?[13]

	Canada					
	(1981)	(1983)	(1984)	(1985)	(1986)	
More	84	78	81	83	81	
Same (vol.)	–	5	3	9	10	
Less	7	7	6	4	5	
No opinion	9	9	9	4	4	

Keeping in mind that increasing services could increase taxes, do you think that the federal government is spending too much, just the right amount, or could be spending more on ... social services for the poor?[14]

	Canada					
	(1987)	(1988)	(1989)	(1990)	(1991)	(1992)
Spend more	49	53	54	55	48	48
Right amount	38	36	33	34	38	36
Too much	8	6	6	7	9	11
DK/NA	6	5	5	5	5	5

[1] Gallup Report
[2] Gallup Report
[3] Decima Research
[4] Decima Research for *Maclean's*, June 1989
[5] CBC-*Globe*, Oct. 1991
[6] CBS/*New York Times*, Sept. 1993
[7] CBS/*New York Times*, March 1994
[8] Gallup Report, March 1993

[9] CBS/*New York Times*, April 1994
[10] CBS/*New York Times*, March 1994
[11] Reporters of the *New York Times*, 1996
[12] Niemi et al. 1989, table 3.24. Data after 1989 directly provided by National Opinion Research Center. No opinion responses omitted after 1989.
[13] Decima Research
[14] Environics Focus Canada

Table 3.A9
Attitudes towards fiscal policy

Let me ask you about the problem of the federal deficit. How serious do you feel the federal deficit is?[1]

	USA (1990)
Very serious	71
Somewhat serious	24
Not very serious	2
Not serious at all	2
Not sure	1

There has been a lot of talk recently about the federal government's deficit. Overall, would you say you are very concerned, somewhat concerned, not very concerned about the federal government's deficit?[2]

	Canada		
	Very concerned	Somewhat concerned	Not very concerned
Aug. 94	50	41	6
Dec. 92	54	35	9
Mar. 91	52	36	8
Dec. 90	56	36	8
Sep. 90	46	38	12
Jun. 90	44	39	12
Mar. 90	48	39	9
Dec. 89	46	38	12
Sep. 89	44	41	11
Jun. 89	40	42	12
Mar. 89	36	45	14

Table 3.A9
Attitudes towards fiscal policy (Cont'd)

Thinking of the reasons why governments have deficits, which one of the following do you think is the primary cause of the federal government's deficit?[2]

	Canada		
	(Dec. 1988)	(Mar. 1989)	(Dec. 1992)
Inefficiency and wasteful spending	80	76	81
Cost of maintaining and delivering useful programs and services	14	17	12
Insufficient tax revenues	5	6	5
No opinion	1	1	2

If there were no other way to cut the deficit while maintaining spending on programs such as Social Security, would you be willing to see:[3]

	USA (1991)		
	Willing	Not willing	Not sure
An increase in the gasoline tax	34	66	1
An increase in the tax on imported oil	55	43	2
A national sales tax	38	61	2
An increase in everyone's federal income tax	34	65	1
An increase in federal income tax rates for married couples with annual incomes of $125,000 or more	74	25	1
An increase in taxes on alcohol, tobacco, and luxury items	75	25	1

Which is more important in the immediate future, creating jobs or reducing the deficit?[4]

	USA (1993)
Jobs	67
Deficit	19
Both equal (volunteered)	12

Table 3.A9
Attitudes towards fiscal policy *(Cont'd)*

In a recession government should be spending money to stimulate growth, even if it means an increase in the deficit.[2]

	Canada	
	(June 1992)	*(Dec. 1992)*
Strongly agree	17	13
Agree	34	37
Disagree	23	31
Strongly disagree	15	21
Depends/No opinion	11	7

Which of the following two statements most accurately reflects your own opinion? The federal government should give top priority to reducing ... (i) the deficit, even if it means maintaining a high level of unemployment, or (ii) unemployment, even if it means maintaining a high deficit?[5]

	Canada		
	(1993)	*(1994)*	*(1995)*
Deficit first	33	35	42
Unemployment first	46	51	42
Both (volunteered)	8	6	4
Neither (volunteered)	6	3	5
No opinion	7	6	7

To reduce the deficit, would you be prepared to see cuts in services like health care and education?

	Canada[6] *(1991)*
Yes	20
No	78
Not sure	2

Table 3.A9
Attitudes towards fiscal policy *(Cont'd)*

In order to cut its deficit the federal government could raise taxes or cut its spending. I am going to read some of the areas where the government spends a great deal of money. For each one I would like you to tell me if you think the government should cut its spending.

	Canada[7] (1990)	
	No	*Yes*
1 Payments made under some programs such as welfare, pensions, and unemployment insurance	60	33
2 Defence	30	66
3 Payments to the provinces for education and health care	88	10
4 Spending on arts and culture	42	51
5 Job training	78	18
6 Subsidies for agriculture	68	24
7 Spending that promotes economic development in the poorer provinces	72	22

I'm going to list some suggestions as to how the federal government might reduce the deficit. For each one, please indicate whether you favour or oppose that particular approach to deficit reduction.

	Canada[8] (1994)		
	Favour	*Oppose*	*Don't know*
Reducing civil service	80	15	5
Reducing foreign aid	75	22	4
Increasing corporate income tax	74	20	6
Reducing defence spending	70	26	4
Reducing welfare spending	59	36	6
Reducing UI spending	51	43	5

Table 3.A9
Attitudes towards fiscal policy (Cont'd)

Reducing or eliminating the tax deductibility of RRSPs	30	61	9
Imposing a tax on the interest generated by RRSP savings	27	65	8
Increasing personal income taxes	23	75	3
Reducing spending on health care	19	79	2
Reducing pension payments to seniors	14	84	3
Increasing sales taxes	14	84	2
Reducing education spending	13	85	3

American attitudes towards different spending areas:

	USA[8] (1988)		
	Spending too little	Spending about right	Too much
Improving and protecting the environment	65	26	5
Improving and protecting the nation's health	66	28	3
Improving the nation's education system	64	24	4
Improving the condition of blacks	35	41	16
Improving the military, armaments, and defence	16	40	38
Improving foreign aid	5	22	68
Improving welfare	23	32	42
Improving assistance to the poor	68	23	7
Improving social security	55	38	6
Improving parks and recreation	29	61	6

Table 3.A9
Attitudes towards fiscal policy *(Cont'd)*

As you know, the President and Congress will be trying to cut federal programs in order to reduce the budget deficit. For the following programs, please tell me whether you think it is more important to reduce the federal budget deficit, or more important to prevent that program from being significantly cut.

	USA[9] (1995)	
	Reduce deficit	*Prevent cut*
Medicare – federal health program for elderly	19	78
Medicaid – federal health program for poor	29	66
Social Security	28	69
Food stamps	60	35
Welfare in general	65	30
School lunch program	28	69
Loans to college students	31	65
Aid to farmers	43	52
Defence spending	52	43
Funding for arts	66	29
Grants to cities to put more police on streets	28	68

We are faced with many problems ... are we spending too much, too little, or about the right amount on improving the nation's education system?

	USA[10]														
	(1980)	*(1981)*	*(1982)*	*(1983)*	*(1984)*	*(1985)*	*(1986)*	*(1987)*	*(1988)*	*(1989)*	*(1990)*	*(1991)*	*(1993)*	*(1994)*
Too little	53	56	56	60	64	60	60	62	64	69	73	69	69	72
About right	33	33	32	31	31	31	33	20	29	28	24	25	25	22
Too much	10	7	8	6	3	5	4	6	4	3	3	5	6	6

Table 3.A9
Attitudes towards fiscal policy (Cont'd)

At present, the federal budget deficit is running at the rate of about 175 billion dollars per year. Basically, there are only a few ways this deficit can be reduced. Please tell me whether you approve or disapprove of each of the following ways to reduce the deficit: cut government spending for social programs such as health and education?

	USA[11]				
	(1983)	(1984)	(1985)	(1986)	(1987)
Approve	41	42	39	41	21
Disapprove	52	52	55	51	76
No opinion	7	7	6	7	3

What is more important, taking steps to reduce the budget deficit or keeping Social Security and Medicare benefits as they are?[12]

	(1995) USA
Taking steps to reduce deficit	24
Keeping benefits as they are	70
Both equally (vol.)	2
Don't know/refused	4

[1] Harris Survey, Jan. 1990, question 1(a)
[2] Decima Research
[3] Harris Survey, Nov. 1991, question 1(f)
[4] CBS/New York Times, Nov. 1993
[5] Gallup Report
[6] CBC-Globe, Oct. 1991

[7] CBC-Globe, Feb. 1990
[8] NORC, GSS, 1988
[9] Gallup Report, Mar. 1995
[10] Niemi et al. 1989, table 3.14. Data after 1989 provided directly by NORC
[11] Gallup Report, August 1987
[12] Times Mirror Report, Feb. 1995

Table 3.A10
Attitudes towards the role of women

Everyone would be better off if more women were satisfied to stay home and raise their children.

	Canada[1] (1990)
Basically agree	25
Basically disagree	71

It is much better for everyone involved if the man is the achiever outside the home and the woman takes care of the home and family.[2]

	USA					
	(1977)			*(1988)*		
	Men	*Women*	*All*	*Men*	*Women*	*All*
Agree	68	62	65	45	39	41
Disagree	31	36	34	53	60	57

It is better for the family if the husband is the principal breadwinner outside the home and the wife has primary responsibility for the home and children.[3]

	USA (1980)	Canada (1982–83)	
		Eng.	*Fr.*
Agree	66	62	55
Disagree	34	38	45

Women should return to their traditional roles in society.[4]

	USA		
	(1987)	*(1990)*	*(1994)*
Agree	30	30	30
Disagree	66	67	67
Don't know	4	3	3

Table 3.A10
Attitudes towards the role of women (Cont'd)

There are not enough women in responsible positions in government and private business.[5]

	USA (1980)	Canada (1982–83)	
		Eng.	Fr.
Agree	78	77	77
Disagree	22	23	23

It is more important for a wife to help her husband's career than to have one herself.[6]

	USA					
	(1977)			(1988)		
	Men	Women	All	Men	Women	All
Agree	51	59	55	33	28	31
Disagree	45	38	41	65	69	67

A preschool child is likely to suffer if his or her mother works.[7]

	USA					
	(1977)			(1988)		
	Men	Women	All	Men	Women	All
Agree	71	62	66	53	43	47
Disagree	26	37	32	43	57	51

Women are going to have to go back to the more traditional roles of wife and mother.

	Canada[8]	
	(Spring '83)	(Spring '89)
Agree	48	47
Disagree	52	52

Table 3.A10
Attitudes towards the role of women (Cont'd)

Do you think married women should be given equal opportunity with men to compete for jobs, or do you think employers should give men the first chance?

	Canada[9]				
	(1950)	(1956)	(1960)	(1966)	(1985)
Equal chance	19	32	23	39	77
Men first	67	59	70	53	18
Qualified	11	7	5	4	3
Can't say	3	2	2	4	2

Do you consider yourself a feminist?

	USA[10] (1992)	Canada[11] (1992)
Yes	29	32
No	63	66

[1] Royal Commission on Electoral Reform 1990
[2] Niemi et al. 1989, table 11.6
[3] Baer et al. 1990, 90
[4] Times Mirror Centre, Oct. 1994, 163.
[5] Baer et al. 1990, 90
[6] Niemi et al. 1989, table 11.4
[7] Niemi et al. 1989, table 11.5
[8] Decima, Spring 1983, 1989
[9] Gallup reports, March 1985 and Feb. 1966
[10] *Time* magazine, *Time*/CNN poll, March 1992
[11] Decima Research for *Canadian Homemaker Magazine*, 1992

Table 3.A11
Attitudes on moral issues

When a person has a disease that cannot be cured, do you think doctors should be allowed by law to end the patient's life by some painless means if the patient and his [sic] family request it?[1]

	USA				
	(1973)	(1978)	(1983)	(1988)	(1991)
Yes	52	58	63	66	65
No	41	38	33	29	31
No opinion	7	4	4	5	4

When a person has an incurable disease that causes great suffering, do you, or do you not think that competent doctors should be allowed by law to end the patient's life through mercy killing, if the patient has made a formal request in writing?[2]

	Canada							
	(1974)	(1979)	(1984)	(1989)	(1990)	(1991)	(1992)	(1994)
Yes	55	68	66	77	78	75	77	76
No	35	23	24	17	14	17	17	16
Qualified/Don't know	10	9	10	6	6	9	6	8

Do you think abortions should be legal under any circumstances, legal only under certain circumstances, or illegal in all circumstances?[3]

	USA	Canada	USA	Canada	USA	Canada	Canada	USA	Canada	USA	Canada
	(1983)	(1983)	(1988)	(1988)	(1990)	(1990)	(1991)	(1993)	(1993)	(1995)	(1995)
Legal under all circumstances	23	23	24	25	31	26	31	32	31	32	35
Under certain conditions	58	59	57	59	53	60	56	51	56	50	49
Illegal	16	17	17	15	12	12	10	13	10	15	13
No opinion	3	1	2	2	4	2	3	2	3	3	3

Table 3.A11
Attitudes on moral issues (Cont'd)

As you know, there has been considerable discussion in the news lately regarding the rights of homosexual men and women: in general, do you think homosexuals should or should not have equal rights in terms of job opportunities?[24]

	USA	
	(1977)	(1993)
Should	56	80
Should not	33	14
No opinion	11	6

In the proposed Canadian Human Rights Act, there has been no provision made for protection of homosexuals from discrimination in employment and in access to public services. In your opinion, should such a provision be included or not?[5]

	Canada (1977)
Should	52
Should not	30
No opinion	18

The Charter prohibits discrimination against women, ethnic and religious minorities, and other groups when it comes to housing, jobs, and education. The Charter does not explicitly extend these rights to homosexuals. In your opinion, should the constitution explicitly prohibit discrimination against homosexuals?[6]

	Canada (1990)
Should	45
Should not	39
Depends	8
No opinion	8

Table 3.A11
Attitudes on moral issues (Cont'd)

Do you think the use of marijuana should be made legal or not?[7]

| | USA | | | | |
	(1977)	(1980)	(1985)	(1990)	(1994)
Legal	28	25	23	17	24
Not legal	66	72	76	83	76

Do you think that possession of small amounts of marijuana should be a criminal offence, or should be an offence subject only to a fine – similar to a traffic violation, or should it be an offence at all?[8]

| | Canada | | |
	(1977)	(1980)	(1985)
Criminal offence	35	36	40
Subject to fine	36	36	34
No offence	23	22	21
Don't know	5	6	5

[1] Gallup poll monthly, Jan. 1991
[2] Gallup Report, Aug. 1990
[3] USA, Gallup poll monthly, Nov. 1990; Canada, Gallup Report, June 1991
[4] Gallup Report, Oct. 1977
[5] Gallup Report, June 1977
[6] Environics Focus Canada
[7] Niemi et al. 1989, table 7.7
[8] Gallup Report

Table 3.A12

Attitudes on environmental issues

CANADA: We should do more to protect the environment even if it means jobs will be lost in the process.
USA: We should protect the environment, even if that means some people will lose their jobs and the government will have to spend a lot of money.

| | Canada[1] | | | | | USA[2] |
	(1980)	(1986)	(1990)	(1991)	(1992)	(1990)
Agree	65	68	71	60	63	71
Disagree	22	22	19	26	26	28
Depends	11	9	10	14	12	

Here are two statements that people sometimes make when discussing the environment and economic growth. Which of these statements comes closer to your point of view? "Protection of the environment should be given priority, even at the risk of curbing economic growth." or "Economic growth should be given priority, even if the environment suffers to some extent."[3]

| | USA | |
	(1991)	(1995)
Environment first	71	62
Economy first	20	32
No opinion	9	6

People should be willing to pay higher prices in order to protect the environment.[4]

| | USA | | |
	(1992)	(1993)	(1994)
Agree	67	57	57
Disagree	32	41	42
Don't know	1	2	1

Table 3.A12
Attitudes on environmental issues (Cont'd)

In general, do you think there is too much, too little, or about the right amount of government regulation and involvement in the area of environmental protection?[5]

	USA			
	(1982)	(1983)	(1984)	(1985)
Too much	11	9	8	10
About right	41	34	27	28
Too little	35	44	56	54
Don't know	12	14	9	8

As you know, business and industry in Canada are regulated by government in a number of different areas. Do you think government is doing too much, about the right amount, or too little in keeping the environment clean and free from pollution?[6]

	Canada		
	(1984)	(1986)	(1988)
Too much	3	3	1
Right amount	31	37	24
Too little	66	60	75

Do you believe you should have the right to drive an automobile anytime or anywhere you want as long as it is within existing laws, or do you feel driving an automobile should and can be restricted further to protect the environment and reduce congestion?[7]

	USA (1990)	Canada (1990)
Drive anytime/anywhere	62	49
Restrict further	34	50

Table 3.A12
Attitudes on environmental issues *(Cont'd)*

Would you oppose or favour shutting down a major company that provided many jobs in your community if it was polluting the environment?[7]

	USA (1989)	Canada (1989)	USA (1990)	Canada (1990)
Oppose	33	37	34	36
Favour	64	60	58	60
DK/DNA	3	3	9	4

[1] Decima Research
[2] *USA Today*
[3] Gallup Report
[4] Times Mirror Center, Oct. 1994, 152.
[5] Gillroy and Shapiro 1986
[6] CBC-*Globe*, Oct. 1989
[7] *Maclean's*, June 1990

Table 3.A13
Attitudes related to race

One of the best things about Canada is the way we welcome people from different races, religions, and cultures into our society.[1]

	Canada		
	(Fall '87)	(Summer '89)	(Winter '91)
Disagree	19	16	19
Depends	7	9	9
Agree	74	75	71

Would you say that race relations in the community you live in have worsened, stayed about the same, or improved in recent years?[2]

	USA (1990)	Canada (1990)
Worsened	17	13
Stayed about the same	56	62
Improved	25	23

When in private, do you never, rarely, sometimes, or often tell ethnic or racial jokes?[2]

	USA (1990)	Canada (1990)
Never	46	38
Rarely	25	28
Sometimes	25	26
Often	4	7

Would you be happy, indifferent, or unhappy if one of your children married someone from a different racial background?[3]

	USA (1989)	Canada (1989)
Unhappy	32	13
Indifferent	51	60
Happy	15	25
No opinion	2	2

Table 3.A13
Attitudes related to race (Cont'd)

Do you think we should encourage more immigration, keep immigration at existing levels, or reduce the number of immigrants allowed into the United States/Canada?

	USA (1990)	Canada (1990)
Encourage more	6	18
Existing levels	33	42
Reduce immigration	58	39

CANADA: If it were your job to plan an immigration policy for Canada at this time, would you be inclined to increase immigration, decrease immigration, or keep the number of immigrants at about the current level?[4]
USA: In your view, should immigration be kept at its present level, increased, or decreased?[5]

	USA (1993)	Canada (1993)
Increase	6	11
Decrease	65	45
Keep same	27	40
Don't know	2	5

What do you think is better for Canada/the United States: that new immigrants be encouraged to maintain their distinct culture and ways, or to change their distinct culture and ways to blend with the larger society?[3]

	USA (1989)	Canada (1989)
Maintain	47	34
Change	51	61
No opinion	2	5

Table 3.A13
Attitudes related to race *(Cont'd)*

The problem with most new immigrants today is that they aren't willing to adapt to our culture and way of doing things.[6]

	Canada	
	(Fall 1987)	*(Summer 1989)*
Agree	53	55
Disagree	36	35
Depends	10	9

I feel uncomfortable with the way Canadian society is changing as a result of all the new people coming to live in Canada.[7]

	Canada
Agree	47
Disagree	42
Depends	9

People from different racial and cultural backgrounds would be better off if they became more like the majority instead of keeping their own cultures.[8]

	USA (1992)	Canada (1992)
Agree	41	52
Disagree	59	48
	(700)	(1,003)

[1] Decima Research
[2] *Maclean's*, 10 June 1990
[3] Decima Research for *Maclean's*, June 1989
[4] Gallup Report

[5] Gallup Report
[6] Decima Research
[7] Decima Research
[8] Angus Reid, March 1992

Table 3.A14
Levels of political trust

CANADA: How much of the time do you think you can trust the government in Ottawa to do what is right – just about always, most of the time, or only some of the time?[1]

	(1965)	(1968)	(1988)	(1993)
Just about always	9	8	3	2
Most of the time	48	50	46	32
Some of the time	37	37	48	63
Don't know	6	4	5	4

CANADA: Most of the time we can trust people in the federal government to do what is right.

	(1979)[1]	(1983)[2]	(1984)[2]	(1988)[1]	(1990)[2]
Agree	69	56	60	59	42
Disagree	31	35	31	35	53
Don't know	0	9	9	6	6

USA: How much of the time do you think you can trust the government in Washington to do what is right – just about always, most of the time, or only some of the time?[3]

	(1966)	(1968)	(1970)	(1972)	(1974)	(1976)	(1978)	(1980)	(1982)	(1984)	(1986)	(1988)	(1990)	(1992)	(1994)
Just about always	17	7	7	5	2	3	2	2	2	4	3	4	3	2	2
Most of the time	58	54	47	48	34	30	27	23	31	40	35	37	25	21	20
Some of the time	28	37	44	44	61	62	64	69	62	53	58	56	68	71	76
Never (volunteered)	3	0	0	1	1	1	4	4	2	1	2	2	2	4	3
No opinion	4	4	2	2	2	4	3	2	3	2	2	1	2	2	–

[1] Canadian National Election Studies
[2] Political Support in Canada survey
[3] American National Election Studies

Table 3.A15
Levels of political confidence

CANADA: How about the people who run the federal government? Would you say that you have a great deal of confidence in them, only some confidence, or hardly any confidence in them?[1]

	(1980)	(1981)	(1982)	(1983)	(1984)	(1985)	(1986)	(1987)	(1988)	(1989)	(1993)
Great deal	19	14	9	11	13	13	9	7	11	7	8
Only some	55	50	48	53	64	68	62	57	61	57	57
Hardly any	25	34	42	36	23	19	29	36	28	35	32
No opinion	1	1	1	1	2	1	1	1	1	0	2

CANADA: How about the people who run the provincial government? Would you say that you have a great deal of confidence in them, only some confidence, or hardly any confidence in them?[1]

	(1980)	(1981)	(1982)	(1983)	(1984)	(1985)	(1986)	(1987)	(1988)	(1989)	(1993)
Great deal	25	23	14	14	13	12	15	17	18	10	6
Only some	55	58	59	61	62	65	62	61	60	56	43
Hardly any	19	18	26	25	25	23	23	23	23	34	38
No opinion	1	1	1	0	0	1	1	0	1	0	1

CANADA: In general, would you say that you have a lot of confidence, some confidence, little confidence, or no confidence at all in governments?[2]

	(1983)	(1985)	(1986)	(1987)	(1988)	(1990)	(1992)
A lot	7	7	6	4	5	2	3
Some	51	52	41	36	50	34	26
Little	31	29	35	37	32	43	42
None at all	10	11	17	20	12	20	30
Don't know	1	1	2	2	2	1	1

Table 3.A15
Levels of political confidence (Cont'd)

USA: As far as the people running these institutions are concerned, would you say you have a great deal of confidence, only some confidence, or hardly any confidence at all in them? Executive branch of the federal government.[3]

	(1973)	(1974)	(1976)	(1978)	(1980)	(1982)	(1984)	(1986)	(1987)	(1988)	(1989)	(1990)	(1991)	(1993)
Great deal	30	14	14	13	13	20	19	21	19	17	21	24	27	10
Only some	51	43	60	61	52	55	52	54	54	55	57	52	52	57
Hardly any	19	43	26	26	35	25	29	24	27	28	23	24	21	33

USA: As far as the people running these institutions are concerned, would say that you have a great deal of confidence, only some confidence, or hardly any confidence at all in them? Congress.[3]

	(1973)	(1974)	(1976)	(1978)	(1980)	(1982)	(1984)	(1986)	(1987)	(1988)	(1989)	(1990)	(1991)	(1993)
Great deal	24	18	14	13	10	14	13	17	17	16	17	16	18	7
Only some	61	61	60	65	55	64	65	63	65	64	61	61	55	55
Hardly any	15	22	26	22	35	23	22	21	18	20	23	24	26	38

[1] Decima Research
[2] Environics Focus Canada
[3] GSS

4 Democracy and Performance: Governance in Canada and the United States

RICHARD SIMEON AND ELAINE WILLIS

A host of commentators and scholars in both Canada and the United States have talked of a crisis of governance. "The government of the United States as a whole has almost lost the capacity to govern" (McDonald 1991, xi). In both countries, there is a widespread sense of policy and institutional failure, a sense that the capacities of the political system and the problems it faces are "out of sync" (Mann 1990, 293). Such observations come from both the right and the left of the political spectrum, and they engage almost every aspect of existing institutions and processes. They address two broad images of failure. The first is the "democratic deficit," a sense that the political systems are unable to respond to citizen concerns for participation, responsiveness, representativeness, and accountability. The second is the "performance," or "managerial" (Mezey 1989, 189), deficit – the sense that public institutions are unable to develop and implement policies that effectively respond to the concrete policy challenges that face both countries, whether these be debts and deficits or child poverty.

The bill of particulars is long and varied. The American system is alleged to promote "divisiveness" and to make it "difficult if not impossible to develop truly national policies" (Dillon, quoted in Sundquist 1986, 9); to be parochial, focused on narrow interests, incapable of asserting a general public interest; and bound by inertia, paralysis, and immobilism, interspersed with brief outbursts of dramatic action (King 1990). It is thought to be incapable of making hard choices among competing interests or of building the stable, long-term coalitions necessary to engage in broad-scale, redistributive policies. Theodore Lowi argues that one of the principal "laws" of the contemporary "Second Republic" is that the risk of policy failure "tends to 100 per cent" (1985, 11). The long-standing budget crisis, argues Forrest McDonald, "is but one symptom of a chronically paralytic condition" (1991, xi).

Many Canadian commentators echo similar sentiments. "Canadians are forced to work within a political system which is dysfunctional when it comes to reaching social consensus" (Canada 21 Council 1994, 21–2). "Canadians have seen the eclipse of faith in both big government and the activist policy-maker … [They] have little faith in their elites' capacity even to define 'just,' let alone give us agreement on how many distinct societies we comprise" (Bliss 1991, 220–1). Most fundamentally, they contemplate the collapse of the Canadian federation (Weaver 1992).

While the specific critiques and proposals for reform differ between Canada and the United States, there is a remarkable similarity in the overall concerns. Surveys from both countries suggest very high levels of disaffection from the political process – what Lipset and Schneider (1983) describe as a massive "confidence gap." Two later soundings of opinion – the Kettering Foundation's study of "main street" Americans (1991) and the Spicer Commission (Canada, Citizen's Forum 1991) – describe anger, alienation, and disconnection from the political system in virtually identical terms.

This chapter has three primary goals. The first is to account for the pervasive sense of institutional failure that is so prominent in both countries. To what extent does the explanation lie in the characteristics of the institutions themselves (such as the "curse of checks and balances" in the United States or the "complexities of federalism" in Canada)? Or is the deterioration in perceptions of performance the result of deeper changes in economic and social forces (McKay 1987, 204) – less a question of declining capacity than of bigger challenges? We argue that two sets of forces interact. On one hand, largely driven by the social forces described in chapter 2, the governing institutions in both countries – though with different starting points and different manifestations – have become increasingly fragmented, divided, and pluralistic. Institutions and processes reflecting social diversity have become more important; institutions reflecting common interests, an overall conception of public purpose, and with the ability to bring integration, order, and coherence to public policy have weakened. "In the United States every major institution that tries to accommodate diverse interests – political parties, trade unions, mainline churches, the bureaucracy – is undergoing severe attack and decline. By contrast, disintegrative movements – single issue special interest groups, charismatic religions, candidate centred political movements, a critical press – are flourishing" (Wildavsky 1990, 270). At the same time, domestic social change, along with profound economic restructuring and the impact of global forces, has made the policy agenda more difficult and intractable. Globalization alters the policy challenges confronting governments and constrains the resources and policy instruments which they can employ to meet them. It places heavy demands on the "performance" side of the equation while leaving governments with "vastly less discretion" (Mann 1990, 298–9). On the domestic side, new social divisions have placed new issues on the public agenda, while old cleavages and issues remain unresolved. Thus, at the very time when these pressures appear to call for more integrated and coherent policy responses, they are harder to achieve. The resulting gap between expectations and performance – between the difficult policy agenda and "political immobilism within" (Mann 1990, 293) – is a primary cause of the sense of failure.

The second purpose of this chapter is to describe and account for recent changes in the structure and functioning of political institutions in the two countries. Institutional patterns have considerable inertia and are resistant to change. In either country a reawakened founder would find much that is familiar. Constitutional change is notoriously difficult to achieve. But institutions are not static: they do indeed respond to changes in their political and social environments. We trace the changes in both countries and show how the responses are themselves heavily dependent on the institutional structure on which they are acting.

Third, as with all chapters, we explore similarity and dissimilarity, convergence and divergence, here focused on institutions and political processes. We find examples of both convergence and divergence; and in other cases the pattern seems more akin to parallel tracks – each is changing in the same direction, but they remain much the same distance apart. Again, our explanation lies in the interaction between the staying power of institutions and changes in the forces operating on them. The primary sources of convergence are found in the similarities among the social forces at work in both countries; continued differences are explained by the powerful influence of their different institutional inheritances.

Thus, we see institutions in two senses: as dependent variables, which are influenced by domestic and global forces; and as independent or mediating variables, which influence how the systems respond. We begin with the inherited institutional structures of the two countries, outlining their different "starting points." We then trace patterns of change across a variety of institutions and conclude with a comparison of the agendas for reform in the two countries. The larger question of institutional capacities will be addressed in chapter 10.

INSTITUTIONAL LEGACIES

Canadian and American political institutions are built on very different principles. Canada has a parliamentary system, or a system of executive-centred cabinet government on the British model at both the federal and the provincial level, while the United States has a presidential-congressional system. The fundamental underlying difference is between a system of checks and balances, with shared and divided powers, and one in which legislative and executive powers are unified. Separated government, in which ambition checks ambition, was a governing principle of the U.S. constitutional design; concentrated authority, responsible government, and majority rule are the fundamental guiding principles of the British and Canadian model.

While both countries are federal, and while the original constitutional documents seem to have suggested that Canada would become a more centralized system than the United States, historical development has proceeded the other way. By most measures, the Canadian provinces are more important political actors than the American states; and the power of the U.S. federal government vis-à-vis the states is much less constrained than that of Canada's federal government. In addition, while the United States has very important elements of intrastate federalism,[1] Canada does not. Before 1982, another basic institutional difference was the absence in Canada of a charter or constitutional bill of rights, and related differences in the role of the judiciary. In 1982, however, Canada added the Charter of Rights and Freedoms as a third "pillar" to Canadian institutions, joining parliamentary government and federalism. This has been the single most important area of institutional convergence between the two countries in recent decades.

THE NEW PLURALISM

Within the continuity of formal structures, change abounds. Since the 1970s, in both countries the dominant tendencies have been centrifugal and decentralizing. Both have become more pluralist; power and influence have become more widely dispersed. These changes have significantly undermined and altered the policy processes characteristic of the New Deal era in the United States and of the postwar Keynesian welfare state period in Canada.

This increased pluralism is more consistent with the American political tradition than with the Canadian; it began earlier in the United States and has proceeded much further. Nevertheless, Canada has been moving in much the same direction. In both countries, but especially in the United States, the dilemmas associated with the increased dispersal of power have generated counter-tendencies designed to restore central authority and the capacity for coordinated action (for example, in the U.S. budget process and in top-down deficit-reduction processes that are now evident in some Canadian jurisdictions). Fundamental to the new pluralism is the diffusion of power and influence. The United States has permanently discarded the "world of establishments" (Heclo 1989, 317). The relatively closed "iron triangles" described by Theodore Lowi as "interest group liberalism" or as closed and autonomous "sub-governments" have been replaced in many areas by more open, fluid "policy or issue networks" (Coleman and Skogstad 1990a).

The new pluralism is sceptical of representative modes of decision making – of delegating power to elected representatives and the bureaucracy – and instead emphasizes "maximum feasible participation" in virtually every political arena. It is hostile to bureaucratic expertise, the role of policy experts, and the delegation of authority to autonomous agencies. It tends to cast policy debates and political discourse in terms of rights and entitlements. Policy issues are more often couched in the language of morality and symbolism in a "politics of principle" and "contested visions" (Pal 1993), challenging a traditional politics that was more focused on bargaining and compromise between material interests. The new pluralism places a high premium on formal conceptions of legal due process, procedural fairness, and direct accountability (Brand 1989). If the typical political style of the New Deal era was relatively closed, consensual, informal, and compromising, the new pluralism is relatively open, conflictual, formal and legalistic, adversarial, and hostile to compromise (Hoberg 1992). Relative to European countries, the United States and Canada have always been "weak states"; the new pluralism fragments authority even further.

These trends are manifested across a wide range of institutions and processes. In the United States, they are found in the fragmented electoral and party systems, in the proliferation of interest groups, in the broadening of citizen access to the policy process, in the politics of divided government, in the enhanced role of the courts in the policy process, and in the blurring of the lines between legislative, executive, and judicial power. All these changes are interrelated and mutually reinforcing. While they respond to social and economic change, they are also a creation of law and policy – pluralism "by design" (Hoberg 1993a).

Canada has traditionally embraced a somewhat stronger state and has accorded more deference and autonomy to political elites. However, all the trends evident in the United States are manifest in Canada as well. Many of them were crystallized in the debate on the Meech Lake and Charlottetown constitutional accords and in the popular rejection of the latter in the 1992 national referendum. These events suggested a fundamental rejection of the politics of "elite accommodation," most emphatically in the critique of the closed, government-dominated process of "executive federalism,"[2] and in the call for more direct citizen and group participation in constitutional reform. Leslie Pal argues that the "post-Meech syndrome" reflects "fragmenting forces" that "threaten to envelop Ottawa and the rest of the country for the foreseeable future" (1993, 272). His prediction was borne out in the 1993 federal elections, in which the governing party, the Progressive Conservatives, were reduced to just two seats, while two new parties – the regionalist, populist-conservative Reform Party and the separatist Bloc Québécois – together took 36 per cent of the seats and 33 per cent of the national vote.

These events reflect larger changes. As in the United States, interest groups have proliferated and developed greater expertise and lobbying skills, and "public interest groups" have come to play a larger role. Multipartite consultation, bringing a wider range of groups into the process, has grown, as has the more conflictual, adversarial pattern of required public hearings. Spurred by the Charter of Rights and Freedoms, political discourse has shifted to a rights orientation, and the courts have come to play a much greater role in the policy process.

In both countries there are limits on the scope and influence of the new politics. It operates much more visibly in social policy than in international relations and economic policy. Even in social policy, fiscal crisis – itself in part a product of the new pluralism – and the consequent "fiscalization" of almost all policy debate put a sharp brake on the kinds of social policy initiatives that might emerge. And while new groups challenge the predominance of business interests, nevertheless business, reinforced by the logic of capital mobility in a global capitalist system, remains a strongly privileged group.

Interest Groups

We begin with interest groups, the most obvious manifestation of the new pluralism. Interest groups have always been more central to U.S. politics than to Canadian. A fundamental ambivalence about the desirability and effects of group politics is a persistent feature of the American political culture. In *Federalist 10*, Madison ponders the dilemma posed by "faction": groups are at once an expression of freedom and essential to democratic politics, and a potential threat to sound governance.

Some of the "advocacy explosion" (the number of interest groups registered in Washington went from 4,000 to 14,000 between 1977 and 1991 [Petracca 1992, 14–15]) is explained by the increase in the size and scope of government, especially since the 1960s. Frequently, government itself promoted the organization of groups; the process was also self-reinforcing, since the mobilization of groups in one sector stimulated competing interests to organize in order to protect their concerns. Developments in other parts of the political system both stimulated and responded to these changes – the decline of parties in the electoral process, the diffusion of power in Congress, and an increased role for public litigation. Technology also had its effect, for example, in the growth of computer-generated mailing lists, and fax machines.

Much of the literature on interest groups suggests that they have hijacked the American political process. Political action committees (PACs) have substituted organization and money for constituency interests. Public opinion has been manipulated by advocacy advertising. Congress is overwhelmed by group pressures on issues such as health care and crime. As Petracca argues, increased group activities can produce "political stalemate at best and ungovernability at worst" (1992, 354). However, these views need to be tempered. The evidence of success in the influence game is far from clear. PAC influence over congressional votes cuts both ways; it is greatest over narrowly focused legislation. Furthermore, PAC influence is subject to countervail by party affiliation, constituency pressures, or presidential intervention (Mahood 1990, 102; Petracca 1992), not to mention the personal convictions of the individual member (Price 1992, 157). Organized interests are most likely to influence policy outcomes when the objective is to block rather than initiate action, when the issue is narrow, technical, and has low public and media visibility, when the organization has sufficient resources to pursue its goal vigorously, and when there is no opposition from the public, from other interest groups, or from public officials (Schlozman and Tierney 1986, 397–8). Hence, there are limits to the influence of interest groups, even in such a group-dominated polity as the United States.

Group politics has never played such a central part in Canadian politics. However, as Canada's leading student of the subject observes, "Interest groups have proliferated in recent years" (Pross 1990, 304). As in the United States, they take many forms: those associated with the new social movements (for instance, Greenpeace and the National Action Committee on the Status of Women),[3] as well as a plethora of business and labour groups, and a large increase in lobbying activity on the part of law firms and consulting groups. The national debates over the constitution and free trade with the United States and Mexico mobilized intense group activity on all sides. The involvement of interest groups in election campaigns "rekindled fears that Canada is contracting the PAC disease" (Pross 1986, 174) and led to measures, struck down by the courts, to limit third-party advertising during elections.

There remain important differences in how group politics is conducted in the two countries. Cabinet dominance and party discipline reduce the vulnerability of MPs to group pressures. Organized interests in Canada traditionally rely far more on bureaucratic contacts, although there is a growing tendency to exploit Parliament by lobbying members. Canada has also developed much more extensive public financing of interest group activities in order to ensure a somewhat more level playing field in the consultative process, though a backlash against "special interest" and fiscal restraint has led to recent reductions in this support (Pal 1993).

Thus, although there is considerable convergence between the two countries in the role of interest groups, Canadian interest groups continue to be far less important than American interest groups in the electoral and legislative processes. Parallel societal developments are pushing both countries in the same direction, but powerful institutional differences perpetuate continuing difference.

Parties and Elections

The same pattern holds with respect to the electoral process and political parties, which, along with interest groups, are the primary mechanisms for linking citizens and government in liberal democratic systems. Both countries have experienced greater volatility at the electoral level, and in both there has been increasing debate about the capacity of political parties to perform their traditional roles of educating voters, providing coherent guides to policy, and aggregating opinion. For some American commentators, "the party is over" (Broder 1971), while some Canadians speak of the "dysfunctions" of parties (Meisel 1991). But the Canadian party system, despite experiencing some of the same pressures as the U.S. system, remains considerably more effective in linking citizens and voters to the broader policy process. Again, this is because of the two countries' differing institutional logic.

Let us begin at the electoral level. In the United States, the most profound indicator of failure is the long-term and apparently irreversible decline in voter turnout – the "turned-off electorate" (Crotty 1984, ch. 1). The largest group in the electorate consists not of Republicans or Democrats, but of non-voters. (6–7) Since the likelihood of non-voting is heavily skewed towards the less educated, the less affluent, and racial minorities, it renders the system less representative and egalitarian (Burns 1984, 162). No such decline has occurred in Canada; nor are turnout rates as variable across class and social groups. This remains a striking difference between the two countries. If Canadians are as disaffected from politics as Americans are, it does not show up in turnout.

The U.S. electorate has also been characterized by a decrease in party identification, an increased willingness of party identifiers to break with their party, and an increased tendency towards "split-ticket" voting – voting for candidates of different parties for different offices. Manifestations of de-alignment "are evident almost everywhere one looks in public attitudes and behaviour" (Wattenberg 1990, 149; Jacobson 1990, 5, 14). One manifestation of the "decay of partisanship" is "the progressive dissociation of electoral outcomes across offices with overlapping constituencies, and the same offices across elections" (Jacobson 1990, 2). The most prominent effect is different partisan control of the presidency and Congress, a pattern repeated in the majority of states (Wattenberg 1990, 148–9). In elections since 1968, the GOP won an average of 55 per cent of the presidential vote, but until 1994 it never won a majority in the House of Representatives and it did so only three times in the Senate. The 1992 federal election brought single-party control over Congress and the presidency, but divided government reappeared only two years later when the GOP gained control of the House. Divided government is thus a product of the American electoral process. As Jacobson argues, the simplest explanation is that voters want it that way. They have different ideas about what they want from Congress – preservation of specific localized benefits – and what they want from the presidency – broader collective goods such as a lower deficit, lower taxes, smaller government, and the like. They can satisfy both sets of demands by splitting the vote (Jacobson 1990, 105, 106–12). Whatever its consequences for policy making, then, divided government may express rather than thwart the popular will (ibid., 133).

In Canada's parliamentary system, divided government in the American sense is not possible. But two analogues have played prominent roles in Canadian politics – minority government at the federal level, and a differing partisan composition of federal and provincial governments. The former has existed for considerable periods in Canadian history and remains a possibility in a multiparty system. Yet despite the fact that the winning party has rarely won a majority of the popular vote, and despite the presence of three or more parties, the first-past-the-post electoral system allied with party discipline has been successful in manufacturing legislative majorities.

As for the latter, during the long period of Liberal dominance prior to 1984, alternative parties came to form the governments of all provinces; and between 1984 and 1988, the Progressive Conservatives lost a succession of provincial governments. After the 1993 Canadian election, the new Liberal government found itself with partisan allies in the five easternmost provinces and faced two Conservative and three New Democratic Party (NDP) governments in the remainder. While it seems unlikely that voters consciously opt for different federal and provincial governments, these outcomes are consistent with a mix of varying expectations of different political arenas, such as those that account for divided government in the United States. At the individual level, the number of "split identifiers" – those who identify themselves with different parties at the federal and provincial levels – has increased considerably over the past twenty years (Pammett 1990, 274). A majority of Canadian voters are now identified as "flexible partisans," more oriented to short-term considerations than long-term affiliations (ibid., 272).

A third manifestation of electoral volatility and "disconnection" from traditional affiliations is common to both countries: the rise of third party movements. This is, of course, not new; both countries have experienced challenges to the dominance of the traditional parties, and in Canada the social democratic NDP is a long-established part of the national (and provincial) electoral scene. In the 1992 U.S. election Ross Perot, running as an independent candidate backed by his "citizens' coalition," tapped a deep vein of discontent and managed to win 19 per cent of the national vote (Lowi 1992; Caesar and Busch 1993, ch. 4). In Canada's 1993 general election, two insurgent parties emerged. The Reform Party, a largely western-based conservative-populist party with several affinities to the Perot program, won 19 per cent of the national popular vote and 52 seats in the House of Commons. The party was able to broaden its regional base, finishing second in the popular vote in Ontario and winning one seat there. (For good analyses, see Laycock 1994; Sigurdson 1994; Archer and Ellis 1994.) In Quebec another new party, the separatist Bloc Québécois, won the largest number of votes and, with fifty-four seats, went on to form the official opposition in Parliament. These two insurgent movements destroyed the inherently unstable coalition of "soft" Quebec nationalists, alienated westerners, and proponents of fiscal conservatism which had elected the Progressive Conservative Party to office in 1984 and 1988 – reducing it to two seats, costing it official party status in the Commons, and raising serious questions about its continuing existence as a national party. The traditional third party, the NDP, also suffered deep losses and was reduced to nine seats in Parliament. In 1993 the major parties won the smallest proportion of the popular vote in history. Only the governing Liberals could claim the status of a national party, able to bridge regional and linguistic differences.

In both countries, these developments were indications of a wide-spread "disconnection" from the traditional parties. The Canadian institutional structure tends to channel this into the formation of regional third parties, while the American structure channels it into non-party challenges to the presidency and a locally oriented Congress.

A final indication of party decline is the increased turnover in legislative membership. In the United States, incumbents retain enormous advantages over challengers. For instance, in the four elections from 1984 through 1990, 97 per cent of members of the House of Representatives who ran for re-election won. However, there are signs that the era of incumbent dominance is eroding. In 1992 a postwar record number of incumbents retired, the rate of re-election of those who did run slipped to 88 per cent (the lowest level since 1974), and those who were re-elected saw much narrower margins of victory than those they had been accustomed to (Jacobson 1993). This trend continued, with dramatic effects, in 1994 when the Republicans gained fifty-one seats in the House and nine in the Senate to form a majority in both houses for the first time since 1954. A record proportion of the members of this Congress were new comers. Turnover has always been higher in the Canadian Parliament, but with the success of Reform and the Bloc, it reached unprecedented levels in 1993, when two-thirds of the elected MPs were new to the job.

All this suggests that political parties have little apparent ability to build and maintain stable electoral coalitions or to organize the electorate around coherent policy programs. Nevertheless, there remain important differences between the two countries. In the United States, the role of parties in critical electoral activities such as candidate recruitment and campaign finance has declined dramatically. Many of these roles have been forfeited to individual candidate initiatives, to the media, and to political action committees. In Gary Orrens's analysis (in Seidle 1991, 163), parties do not educate voters; the media and the candidates do. Parties do not evaluate or appraise candidates; the media do. Parties do not select candidates; they just ratify the choices of voters. And they do not identify and recruit candidates; they are self-selected. Elections have become more candidate- than party-centred. In presidential elections, nomination now depends heavily on the success of individual candidates in primary elections, which account for about three-quarters of national party convention delegates. Similarly, at other levels, nominations have become increasingly a matter of individual contenders mounting independent campaigns, relying little on party ties (Wattenberg 1991a, 88; Price 1992, 73–4). Party organizations play little role in campaign finance – individual candidates tend to rely on their own resources and the support of PACs. Candidates campaign

largely on their own issues and platforms, often paying little or no attention to national party positions and programs.

All these factors contributed in the 1960s and 1970s to the decline
of party unity in Congress and the decline of unity between the president and members of Congress, even those from his own party. As one
congressman put it when explaining his defection from President
Clinton on a recent crime bill, "The basic nature of American politics
has changed. I don't get elected because of what Bill Clinton thinks or
what the House leadership thinks. The electorate makes up its own
mind. That inevitably means that Presidents have a lot less clout with
Congress than they used to have" (Lee Hamilton, quoted in the *New
York Times,* 17 August 1994). Only on rare occasions, such as the 1980
election, can presidential coat-tails bring into Congress members who
are closely identified with the president's program, and even then the
effects are brief.

Developments in the 1980s suggest some important qualifications to
these trends. Rules were modified to give greater weight to elected and
party officials as "superdelegates" to national conventions. Led by the
Republican Party, the national organizations came to play a greater role
in providing campaign finance and other services to congressional candidates. (For a review of these developments, see Caesar 1990 and Sabato 1988.) During the Reagan-Bush years, there was a significant
increase in party unity within Congress (Price 1992, 86–7). About half
the roll-call votes in the House now array the majority of one party
against the majority of the other. This has resulted from the increased
partisanship associated with divided government, and also from a
longer-term trend in which southern Democrats have been replaced by
Republicans, thus rendering both parties more ideologically homogeneous (Rohde 1991). This reassertion of party unity in Congress, especially in the House of Representatives, continued in 1994 as GOP
candidates around the country campaigned on the party's "Contract
with America" and pledged united action to implement it. Leading a disciplined majority, House Leader Newt Gingrich sought to play a role
somewhat akin to that of a Canadian prime minister. Despite these
changes, the U.S. system remains far from the unified party government
of the Canadian model, and it remains to be seen whether the recentral-
ization in the United States can be maintained in the face of continuing
pressure towards fragmentation.

Similar observations about the decline of parties are common in Canada. For example, Tom Kent (1989) argues that Canadian parties have
declined as vehicles for debate about political ideas and as sources of
guidance for voters; that party finance is biased towards business
sources; and that polling and the media have rendered campaigns less

effective as vehicles for public education (see also Canada, Royal Commission on Electoral Reform 1991). Nevertheless, there remains a closer link between voters, parties, and election outcomes in Canada than in the United States. While nominations of candidates for the House of Commons are highly localized, candidates run under party labels and on party platforms. In extreme cases, a party leader has a veto over local nominations. A vote for an individual candidate is simultaneously a vote for a party to govern and a vote for a prime minister. Hence, there is no Canadian equivalent of the candidate-centred campaign, independent of the national party. Candidates who deviate from the party line are quickly reined in. Parties have much more control over election finance and, because of election finance rules, no equivalent to the PACs has emerged. Voters in Canada face a simpler choice than those in the United States, casting a single ballot rather than one for numerous offices at once.

At the electoral level, then, Canada remains a more party-centred system. This in turn translates into far greater party dominance in the national legislature. Even though there has recently been greater party cohesion in Congress, it pales beside the strength of party discipline in Parliament. Yet, again, the pattern is one of both convergence and divergence. In both countries there is disaffection from traditional parties, hostility to incumbents, and increased voter volatility. But in the United States there is a dramatically weaker presence of parties at both the electoral and the governmental level. What accounts for this similarity and difference, this continuity and change?

Various explanations have been advanced to account for changes in the U.S. party system. First, social and economic change has eroded the coalitions that underpinned the party system during the New Deal period, and this has generated greater voter volatility. Issues such as abortion, school prayer, and the war in Vietnam cut across traditional allegiances – for example, increasing blue-collar Catholic support for the Republicans. On these types of issue, the party system has greater difficulty accommodating the increased diversity and multiple cleavages of contemporary American society. This is also true for Canadian parties. They, too, have had increasing difficulty in bridging the major social cleavages of region and language, as well as in responding to new interests which today are more likely to seek expression through interest groups.

Second is changing technology, in particular the growth in the importance of television, which strongly emphasizes leader- and candidate-centred politics, establishing direct links between candidates and voters without having party workers as intermediaries. Television has taken over much of their candidate-screening role, has focused attention on individual leaders rather than parties, has intensified the fragmentation of power in Congress, and has contributed to a political culture that is suspicious of negotiation, compromise, and consensus building (Ranney 1990, 188–90; see also Sabato 1988, 144–6). Former Colorado Senator Timothy Wirth argues that, as a result, it is "nearly impossible ... for public officials to carry on sustained, serious discussions of the fundamental challenges America must understand and, through their government, rise to meet ... Sensation-seeking in the media has trivialized public discourse ... [and] ... attention deficit is the order of the day." The growth of sophisticated campaign techniques, using polling, focus groups, direct mail, and the like has the same effect, reducing the traditional role of parties and party workers. These changes in technology have been enthusiastically embraced by Canadian political campaigners, who have followed U.S. developments closely and often employed American consultants. This in turn has prompted similar Canadian concern about the growth of leader-centred campaigning, the decline of grass-roots activism, the negativism of partisan debate, and so on; but it has not challenged the centralization of the campaign process, and has perhaps strengthened it.

Changes in the rules and institutions governing parties and elections have also been important – another case of "pluralism by design." For example, changes in U.S. campaign finance laws opened the way to the currently massive role of PACs. Changes in the rules for convention delegate selection radically changed the nomination process. (For an analysis of the Democratic reforms and their consequences, see Ranney 1975.) The reforms of the 1970s strengthened individual candidates, the media, and interest groups and movements at the expense of party leaders and their ability to "construct and maintain an effective, large-scale mass organization" (Lowi and Ginsberg 1992, 579; Caesar 1990, 109–10.) Changes in Canada – chiefly in the direction of opening up participation in the nomination process – have been much more modest. Canadian reforms have tended to strengthen, rather than weaken, parties as organizations and to constrain the role of interest groups and private money in elections. As the Canadian Royal Commission on Electoral Reform (1991, 16) pointed out, "We have seen the consequences of U.S. electoral experience with no restraints on election spending and conclude that it is imperative that Canada not travel the same road." More generally, the continuation of major differences in the role of party in government reflects the impact of the difference between the centralizing logic of the parliamentary system and the decentralizing logic of the presidential-congressional system.

What are the consequences of these changes in the party system? On one hand is E.E. Schattschneider's classic observation that democratic government is party government (1942); the decline of party undermines the quality of democracy. In this view, parties remain "the principal institutions for achieving popular control over government" (Ladd 1982, 122). Many critics argue that changes in the U.S. party both reflect and contribute to the fragmentation and rootlessness of the electorate. The changes leave voters "adrift and volatile, lacking the moorings of party or the anchors of ideology" (Burns 1984, 163). The result, according to the Kettering Foundation, is that voters feel they "have lost control of the political agenda" (1991, 13) and that there has been a "hostile takeover" by lobbyists, interest groups, and the media (ibid., 19). There is no vehicle to develop or reflect coherent, integrated policy programs or to reflect the "organic, collective, combined interests" of citizens (Burns 1984, 164). Moreover, the enormous costs of the "capital" rather than "labour-intensive" campaign techniques skews electoral politics to the wealthy.

Party weakness may also help account for failures of performance. If the central role of party in the United States is to "join what the framers had separated" (Mann 1990, 303), to bring some order and coherence into a system explicitly designed to fragment and divide power, the present party system manifestly fails. Again, in the words of James MacGregor Burns, "Team work among office holders, unity across branches of government, collective responsibility and accountability – all these have suffered" (1984, 140). The party system reinforces the dangers of the "personal" or "plebiscitary" presidency (Lowi 1985).

In Canada, there has been no decline of party-in-government. Hence, policy failure cannot be attributed to failure of the party system. Perhaps the greatest concern about Canadian parties today is the fact that only one party, the Liberals, is able to bridge the deep linguistic and regional divisions. Again, we find limited convergence: differences in the basic institutional structures of the two countries exert a profound influence on how parties and party systems respond to parallel pressures.

A final dimension of the electoral process is the role of direct citizen participation through referenda. Many states and localities in the United States provide for voter involvement in policy initiation through referenda. Some of the most contentious contemporary policy issues have been decided in this way; initiatives such as Proposition 13 in California and the common practice of submitting bond issues and tax increases to local votes have greatly constrained legislatures and executives. Such populist mechanisms have traditionally been regarded with much greater scepticism by Canadian elites. However, the 1992 constitutional proposals were submitted to a national referendum, and Quebec has held two referendums on sovereignty, in 1980 and 1995. The convention now appears established that any major constitutional change will be submitted to the people.

The federal character of the party system also mirrors some aspects of divided government. Federal and provincial parties have increasingly gone their separate ways, in terms of program, organization, membership, and financing. The model is less that of a federal party system than one of two parallel and distinct party systems – a confederal rather than integrated model (Smiley 1987, ch. 5). This erodes the ability of the Canadian party system to integrate federal and provincial politics, a parallel to the failure of the American party system to integrate presidential and congressional politics.

Legislatures: Congress and Parliament

No two institutions are as different or have converged as little as the U.S. Congress and the Canadian Parliament. In the United States, power and influence within Congress are highly diffused, while Congress as a whole remains a central part of the policy process. It is equipped with the resources to constitute a powerful rival to the president. Congress has moved in the direction of "functioning as an entire government, alongside or in competition with the executive. Separated institutions compete for shared power" (Jones 1990, 3). In Canada, cabinet government and party discipline ensure that power and influence within Parliament is tightly organized and that its workings are dominated by the prime minister and the executive. Parliament has not emerged as a rival centre of power. The extent of the difference between the two countries is illustrated by the fact that a recent volume on Canadian political institutions and policy could be published without a chapter on Parliament; it is impossible to imagine leaving Congress out of a similar American book (Atkinson 1993).

In the 1970s power in Congress spread "downwards and outwards" (Polsby 1990, 37). The weight of the seniority system and party leadership declined. Staff resources available both to individual members and to congressional committees dramatically expanded – there are now between 25,000 and 30,000 bright, ambitious congressional staffers, "who are not going to be sitting around waiting for a president to tell them what to do" (Jones 1990, 21). These staffers are more policy oriented, entrepreneurial, and technically trained than their predecessors – an important counterweight to the expertise on the executive side (Polsby 1990, 42).[4]

In addition, subcommittees proliferated, leading one writer to observe that Congress actually contained more than two hundred individual legislative units (Burns 1984, 210). Congressional activity became more accessible to lobbyists and constituents (McKay 1987). Decreasing dependence on president and party for political cues contributed to these tendencies and led to a changed "congressional character" (ibid., 68). "A new breed of politicians," born of the more individualistic, candidate-centred electoral process, brought "an ethic of individualism and egalitarianism to the legislative chamber" (Sundquist 1986, 192). In the words of James Reston, "Each of them can and does act as a little president" (quoted in Lowi 1985, 122) or, to use Burns's phrase, as "King of the Rock" (1984). Electoral rationality leads them to cultivate specific constituencies and groups, and to develop specialized policy expertise and initiative. The continual search for policy gaps and opportunities is essential for congressional success (Price 1989, 1992).[5]

These developments involved a paradox. "The various pieces of Congress have enhanced their capacity to delve into the details and micromanage executive branch activities, while Congress as a whole is less able to assemble agreed positions with which to face the president" (Heclo 1989, 306). Dispersion of influence made coordination, leadership, and concerted action more difficult. Thus, the two major changes in Congress – the assertion of power vis-à-vis the president, and the decentralization of its organizational structure – were incompatible: Congress showed a greater inclination to govern, but its structure undermined its capacity to do so. "Congress can act with a collective will ... but it has to be bullied, cajoled or shocked into doing so by external events or by skilled and manipulative Presidents" (McKay 1987, 82). Thus, while conservative critics talk of an "imperial Congress" encroaching on presidential responsibilities and prerogatives – through the war powers resolution, the budget process, the appointment process, and increased congressional oversight of the administration – Congress has not displaced the president as the energizer of the system.[6]

This picture has recently been changing. Congress has sought to cultivate its collective decision-making capacity. The steps towards a "post-reform Congress" (Davidson 1992) include the strengthening of the role of party leadership, enhanced party unity, greater capacity for policy analysis through congressional agencies such as the Congressional Budget Office, and expansion of the Congressional Research Service (Jones 1990, 1994; Polsby 1990, 41), along with changes in the budgetary process in Congress, following passage of the Congressional Budget and Impoundment Control Act in 1974.[7] Flushed with its dramatic victory in the 1994 congressional elections, and armed with its Contract with America, the legislative initiative seemed to swing dramatically from president to Congress in 1995, but by the end of the year the more usual pattern of tug of war along Pennsylvania Avenue was re-established.

The Canadian Parliament and the provincial legislatures share few of these characteristics. Party discipline ensures that the rational behaviour for individual MPs is to toe the party line; there is less opportunity for them to espouse publicly either constituency or interest-group views; and they have far fewer personal and institutional resources at their disposal. There are some qualifications to this observation, however. While MPs must eschew constituency or group advocacy in public, to some extent they do play this role in the privacy of the caucus. There are some indications that parliamentary committees may be coming to play a more important role, either as a vehicle for an entrepreneurial chair or, more notably, as a forum and catalyst for public and group consultation. And while the government has numerous means of controlling the work of Parliament, "parliamentary processes are more flexible and adaptable than simple majority rules would imply," argues C.E.S. Franks. "Parliamentary procedure provides ample opportunities for the expression of dissent and for minorities to delay, demand, persuade, influence, alter and even prevent" (1991, 14). Some proposals now under consideration move further in this direction. Freeing individual MPs from party discipline and linking them more directly to their constituents is a central part of the Reform Party's program. The program of the Liberal government elected in 1993 also called for more authority for parliamentary committees, as well as more opportunities for "free votes" when these would not threaten loss of confidence in and hence defeat the government (Liberal Party of Canada 1993, 92–3). Such proposals, however, seem unlikely to overcome the internal dynamics of parliamentary government.[8]

A more radical proposal for parliamentary reform was a central part of the Charlottetown Accord. Despite having formal powers that are almost equal to those of the House of Commons, the Canadian Senate has been a largely ineffective institution, its legitimacy undermined by the method of appointment and tenure. Senators are chosen by the government in power, and they serve until mandatory retirement at the age of seventy-five. Senate reform emerged as a central issue in the constitutional debate, promoted mainly by western reformers who sought stronger representation in Parliament for the smaller provinces and advocated a measure of "intrastate federalism." Their goal was a triple-E Senate: elected, with equal representation from the provinces, and with effective powers. The debate centred on how equal representation could be reconciled with the enormous differences in population of the various provinces; and how a powerful Senate could be reconciled with the model of cabinet responsibility to the House of Commons. The resulting proposal provided for equal representation and election, along with a complex system for reconciling differences between the House of Commons and the Senate, which would give the Commons overriding weight. (For a summary, see Russell 1993.) With the defeat of the Charlottetown Accord – and the poor prospects for future constitutional change – debate about Senate reform has faded. If the triple-E model were to be adopted, it would be a major step towards the U.S. congressional model, with potentially important implications for the conduct of federalism and the legislative process.

Hence, the Canadian legislature is buffeted by some of the winds of change that have affected the U.S. Congress in recent years, but so far the basic institutional form of parliamentary government has been highly resistant to change. These differences lend a contrasting tone to reform proposals in the two countries. The strengths of the U.S. Congress lie in its openness, accessibility, and transparency; its weaknesses lie in the incapacity for coordinated, coherent action, the building of stable legislative coalitions, and the like. Congress involves a reasonably high degree of individual accountability to constituencies and vocal groups, but it has less collective accountability, or accountability to diffuse interests. Aberbach's assessment of the U.S. congressional oversight system has a wider application: it is "at once highly responsive and accountable in the narrow sense, and not well-coordinated or centrally controlled in the broad sense" (1990, 24). Conversely, the strengths of the Canadian model lie in a greater collective accountability to the broad electorate and in less personal accountability and openness to constituencies and groups. Despite these differences, both legislatures appear to be highly discredited in the eyes of the citizens. In Canada, the citizens' level of distrust of political parties and Parliament exceeds that of any other major institution (Massicotte 1994, 329–31). In the United States, the criticism still focuses on gridlock and on Congress's position as being hostage to special interest groups; in Canada, it focuses on Parliament's lack of responsiveness to citizen interests. Both legislatures are widely seen to be areas for excessive partisanship. Again, this suggests that the fundamental sources of citizen malaise lie deeper than institutional characteristics alone.

Political Executives: President and Prime Minister

The institutions of parliamentary and congressional government underpin differences in the role of executives in the two systems. Legislative and executive power are fused in the prime minister and cabinet in Canada; they are separated in the U.S. constitutional structure. Again, however, changes in the political environment and changes in policy styles have produced similar pressures on executives and have provoked some convergence.

There have been two contending conceptions of presidential power in recent years. One is the image of the "imperial presidency," emphasizing the unconstrained powers of the president, especially in foreign affairs. Triggered notably by the Vietnam War and Watergate, this image tends to be associated with proposals to limit and restrain presidential power and to strengthen Congress's ability to rein in the president. The second is the image of the "fettered presidency" (Crovitz and Rabkin 1989), a president so hemmed in by Congress and the courts that he is incapable of providing the central leadership, direction, and coherence to U.S. policy that is so lacking in other institutions. This perspective tends to be associated with proposals to strengthen the resources and capacities of the president and to limit congressional encroachments on it.

There has been an interesting ideological shift in these perceptions. In the New Deal era, it was liberal Democrats who tended to argue the virtues of a strong president and the need to overcome the localism and parochialism of Congress by vigorous presidential leadership. In the Reagan-Bush years, with Republican presidents and Democratic legislatures, it was the conservative forces that sought to free the president from congressional constraints, and it was the liberals who feared the potential tyranny of powerful presidents (Heatherly 1988). After 1994, the tables were reversed once again.

Theodore Lowi's model of the "personal presidency" captures elements of both conceptions. The decline of parties, evolving communications, and polling technologies, and the associated candidate-centred politics have increasingly detached the president from an organic linkage with Congress. The personal president has a direct, unmediated relationship with voters. Immense expectations are focused on him. But at the same time, the president's powers are limited, and he lacks broad institutional supports in party and Congress. This leads the president to make promises he cannot keep. In no other advanced country is the chief executive so institutionally isolated as the U.S. president (McKay 1987, 117). There is thus a profound gap between the expectations placed on the president and his capacity to deliver on them (Lowi 1985, xii). As a result, Americans have developed an appetite that is seemingly impossible to satisfy: in Ladd's raw imagery, the United States "has been 'chewing up' its presidents" (1982, 123).

Lacking the capacity to mobilize congressional support, the president is led to strengthen his control over the resources he does possess, especially the institutions of the executive branch, and to act unilaterally whenever he can. Hence, we see the strengthening of the agencies of the institutionalized presidency (Office of Management and Budget, etc.), the strengthening of administration control over public-service senior management, the attempt to gain greater control over regulatory agencies, especially through partisan appointments, and the temptation to evade legal and congressional restraints wherever possible – all of which have been characteristic of recent presidencies. The result, argues Lowi, is a built-in tendency towards policy failure and presidential excess. The president is tempted to go on his own wherever and whenever possible (Heclo 1989, 306). This kind of logic leads to incidents such as the Iran-Contra affair and prompts writers such as Donald L. Robinson to argue that the presidency as it has evolved since the Second World War poses "a dire threat to constitutional government in this country" (1991, 212).

The possibilities for acting in this imperial manner are greater in the international arena than in domestic affairs. "The presidency can be as big as the president can make the international threat appear to be" (Lowi 1991, 231). But in most areas, especially in domestic policy, "separated Presidents are indeed captives" (Jones 1990, 21) with limited ability to set and achieve their own agendas, despite media and public expectations (ibid., 23). Only in extraordinary circumstances, and even then only for brief periods, can these constraints be overcome. Thus, King argues, despite Ronald Reagan's successes in lowering taxes, cutting domestic spending, and increasing defence spending in 1981, and despite his continuing popularity in the polls, he too ended his term as a "failed president" (1990, 243–5). Nor is this true only of presidents in divided governments; it seemed equally so in the first two years of the Clinton presidency.

Some Canadian writers have talked of the "presidentialization" of Canadian government; and indeed there are elements of the development of a "prime ministerial government" (Aucoin 1994, 281–2). Campaigning has come to focus on the prime minister and his or her leadership. Like the president, the prime minister is the focus of public expectations and of public opprobrium at governmental failure. Canadian government can still be characterized as cabinet government, but its influence, and that of individual ministers, has declined relative to the prime minister. Like U.S. presidents, prime ministers have sought greater control over their political environment – for instance, by strengthening the Prime Minister's Office and other central agencies. However, they have far stronger institutional supports in party, cabinet, and Parliament than presidents have, and they are not nearly as isolated (Bakvis and Macdonald 1993). In this sense, the prime minister remains a more powerful political actor than the president, though Canada's differing position in world affairs reduces both the temptations and the resources to engage in a global "imperial prime ministership." If governments fail to manage problems effectively in

Canada, this is less a function of the formal or institutional constraints on the prime minister than it is of the range of expectations placed on government, the diverse conflicts to be managed, and the external fiscal constraints on what governments can do.

Divided Government

Many observers agree that the central constraint on coherent policy making in the United States in recent years has lain not so much in the failure either of Congress or the presidency as in the phenomenon of "divided government." Contemporary American government, Jones suggests, consists of "separated institutions competing for shared power," with each institution protecting and promoting itself through a broad interpretation of its constitutional and political status, even usurping the other's powers when the opportunity presents itself (Jones 1990, 23). There is no clear division of labour between Congress and the presidency. "Two systems of government seem to coexist in Washington" (Burns 1984, 117). Weak party discipline, differing constituencies, and institutional rivalries divide president and Congress, regardless of which parties are in control, as Lyndon Johnson in his later years, Jimmy Carter, and recently Bill Clinton all discovered.

For most observers, the consequences of divided government are severe: contradictory and incoherent policies; an inherent tendency to deadlock and indecision (Sundquist 1986, 88); stalemate or makeshift agreements (Mezey 1989, ch. 1); and an incentive to evade responsibility and shift blame (Price 1992, 155, 425). Neither Congress nor president is capable of acting alone, but each is capable of obstructing the other. All these characteristics are illustrated by recurring budget crises, which in 1995 led to two brief periods of shutting down government activities.

In Canada, the closest parallel to divided government is found not in relations between executive and legislature but in federalism itself. Much of the imagery surrounding divided government in the United States is replicated in analyses of federal-provincial relations in Canada. Just as an assertive Congress challenges the president, so do assertive provinces challenge Ottawa. Just as Congress is alleged to have encroached on the president's prime responsibility for foreign and trade policy, blurring lines of authority and making it more difficult for the United States to speak with a clear single voice abroad, provinces have likewise encroached on the federal sphere in these areas. Just as it is alleged that the U.S. system makes it difficult to define and implement a larger public interest, the fragmentation of authority in Canada likewise has the same effect. Just as policy in many areas requires a kind of "codetermination" between the branches in the United States, so it does with federal and provincial governments in Canada. Nevertheless, the analogy cannot be pushed too far. The interdependence and inter-penetration of Congress and president are far more wide-ranging and pervasive than that between Ottawa and the provinces, and the oppor-tunities for each to veto the other are correspondingly greater.

Courts and the Judicial Process [9]

By far the most dramatic convergence in the structure and functioning of the governing institutions in the two countries lies in the role of the courts and the judicial process. The entrenchment in the Canadian con-stitution of the Charter of Rights and Freedoms in 1982 radically en-hanced the role of the courts in policy making and in judicial review of legislative and executive actions (Russell 1994; Mandel 1989; Manfredi 1993). To the more traditional functions of adjudicating the powers of federal and provincial governments was added a greatly expanded role in mediating the relationships between citizens and government. The Canadian courts have thus come to play a role much more akin to the one the American courts have long played.

The adoption of the Charter both reflected and powerfully contrib-uted to the growth of a "legalistic" political style in Canada. But as Hoberg points out (1992), legalism and its associated political values – emphasis on rights, fairness and due process, access, adversarial open processes, and so on – has also increased in the United States. As in Canada, this is a response to changing political values, increasing di-versity, and a growing distrust of elected politicians. Thus, the role of the courts has changed in both countries, but the largest change has been the movement of Canada towards the U.S. model.

In the New Deal policy style, despite many controversial decisions, the U.S. Supreme Court was generally deferential to Congress and the executive. With the advent of the Warren Court in the 1950s, it became a "major domestic policy-maker" (Shapiro 1990, 48) across a wide range of issues: race relations, reapportionment, and criminal justice, to name but a few. It has taken the "policy lead in matters of life and death" with decisions on abortion and the death penalty (ibid., 47). It has extended "property rights" to social entitlements, requiring formal hearings before welfare benefits may be cut off, and so on. Similarly, in regulatory policies and administrative law, it has helped break the dom-inance of iron triangles and bureaucratic discretion by broadening the scope of judicial review, extending the right of standing, imposing higher procedural standards, and expanding the court's ability to re-view the interpretation and implementation of statutes – the "hard-look doctrine" (Hoberg 1993a; Shapiro 1990, 80–1). The "judicialization of the regulatory regime" through the doctrine of "regulatory legalism" shifted the balance of power among societal interests and elevated the judiciary from the periphery of the regime to the status of partnership in the pluralist regulatory state (Hoberg 1992, 324–33).

More generally, Melnick (1989) argues that these changes have expanded the bases of rights in the United States, paying more attention to substantive or programmatic rights, to nondiscrimination rights, and to procedural rights. Equally important – especially given the perception that Americans value individual rights more highly than Canadians do – while being suspicious of collective rights, U.S. legal decisions in areas such as voting rights and access to services such as education and affirmative action have increasingly been expressed in group or collective terms (Melnick 1989, 1994).

Armed with the Charter, Canadian courts have moved in a similar direction. The rights of the accused, abortion, the legality of deviations from "one-person, one-vote" electoral procedures, Aboriginal rights, and procedural requirements for regulatory agencies and environmental assessments – all familiar in the United States – have now engaged the Canadian courts. A stronger tradition of judicial restraint, together with provisions in the Charter such as the "notwithstanding clause"[10] and section 1, which subjects the enumerated rights to "such limitations as are demonstrably justified in a free and democratic society," suggest an intent to minimize judicial policy making or the infringing of parliamentary sovereignty. Even with the Charter, Russell argues, Canadian courts have continued to be somewhat more restrained and more deferential to the legislatures (1994, 352, 353). And they have had less opportunity to take a "hard look" at bureaucratic decisions, because governments have been careful to frame statutory provisions in ways that maintain governmental discretion and "enable" rather than force action (Hoberg 1993a, 327–8, 332). As a result, the Canadian courts have tended to focus on constitutional issues; they have not yet become as enmeshed in the administrative state (Rabkin 1989) as the U.S. courts have.

In both countries there is a complex interaction between the courts and other institutions. Policy issues move back and forth between legislature and courts, each redefining the situation in light of the other's responses. This can be considered exactly the kind of partnership envisioned in systems of shared and overlapping powers, such as the American system and, since the Charter, the Canadian. On the other hand, these interrelationships involve many tensions. In Canada there are basic differences between the logic of democracy embedded in the parliamentary system, which emphasizes majority rule and parliamentary sovereignty; in federalism, which emphasizes community interests and shared sovereignty; and in the Charter, which focuses on individual rights, judicially protected. These tensions are far from fully worked out.

Federalism, the Bill of Rights, and congressional governments have coexisted from the beginning in the United States as well. Yet there, too, there are deep and divisive debates, both academic and political, about the appropriate scope of judicial review, judicial activism versus judicial restraint, procedural rights versus substantive, purposive rights, and the like. Thus, on one side Raoul Berger (1977) castigates "government by judiciary," arguing that the courts are continually rewriting the constitution and have "become a law unto themselves." On the other, Herman Schwartz (1987) points out that the courts have always "been actively and deliberately shaping the social and political structure of the nation." For him, the question is, To what ends? The increased role for the Supreme Court embroils it in political controversy whatever it decides. Consequently, courts become as much a matter for interest-group concern as other political institutions. Judicial appointments, and the appropriate sharing of the political authority to make them, become more and more controversial, with debate focused on the substantive legal theories and policy views espoused by the judges. Ronald Reagan's attorney general, Edwin Meese, was explicit about that administration's objectives: through its appointments, the administration intended to "institutionalize the Reagan revolution so it can't be set aside no matter what happens in future presidential elections" (quoted in O'Brien 1990, 102). In the era of divided government this has meant divisive confrontations between Congress and administration over judicial appointments, which made it clear that the selection of appointees is a policy choice of the first magnitude. In Canada, the closed nature of the appointment process, combined with the tendency of governments to select judges on non-partisan grounds, has avoided such overt controversy. Nevertheless, there are increasing concerns to develop a more open process and to ensure that the judiciary more fully reflects Canadian social diversity (Ontario Law Reform Commission 1991).

Federalism

A survey of the need for institutional reform in the United States does not mention federalism (D.L. Robinson 1990); by contrast, the strains and tensions of federalism are the pre-eminent issues for governance in Canada. Canada and the United States are two of the oldest, most stable, and arguably most effective federal systems in the world. Each was born in the desire to unite pre-existing political communities in different parts of British North America while maintaining some autonomy for the founding communities. Each became a vehicle for building a nation that spanned a continent. Each federal system has evolved in different ways. In the United States, centripetal forces have tended to predominate, leading some observers to wonder if the country is still fully federal. It is a "nation-centred" or "national" federalism (Walker 1985, 2; Beer 1993). In Canada, despite an initially much more centralized constitution, centrifugal forces have tended to predominate – so much so that the very survival of the country as a federation is in question.

By most measures, Canada is a much more decentralized federation; Canadian politics is far more focused on the politics of territory; intergovernmental relations – "executive federalism" and "federal-provincial diplomacy" (Smiley 1970; Simeon 1972) – are much more prominent in Canadian policy making. While federalism, national unity, and the constitution have been the central issues for governance in Canada, they have been of muted significance in the United States recently. The Civil War resolved the fundamental issue of the pre-eminence of the national community, and battles over the New Deal and civil rights established federal dominance over the states. The greater federal authority in the United States takes a number of forms: a virtually unlimited ability to pre-empt state action, especially by means of the trade and commerce power, and the ability to impose regulatory requirements on state and local governments – what has been called "cooptive federalism," or "regulatory conscription" (Conlan 1988, 235).

There are several reasons for these and other differences between Canadian and American federalism. First, Canada is a parliamentary federation, whereas the United States is a congressional one. This institutional difference has profound consequences for the operation of federalism. The centralization of authority within jurisdictions – combined with the smaller number of provinces – powerfully supports the executive-to-executive bargaining process of Canadian federalism. In the United States, summit diplomacy, or the intergovernmental lobby, plays a relatively minor role. This diffusion of power leads to a far more fluid and diverse intergovernmental process, which is played out in a myriad of program-oriented policy networks, involving congressional committees, bureaucratic agencies, and state and local authorities – marble-cake or fruit-cake federalism (Watts 1989, 32–3). This in turn is reflected in intergovernmental fiscal and policy relationships. Canadian provinces command greater proportions of revenue and spending; Canada has far fewer shared-cost, conditional, or grant-in-aid programs, and those it has involve far less detailed federal control and supervision; and a much larger proportion of federal transfers to the provinces take the form of unconditional grants. While, in both countries, local governments are constitutionally creatures of the states and provinces, the more centralized Canadian system means far fewer direct relationships between federal and local governments than in the United States.

The second fundamental impact of the parliamentary versus congressional federal system is that the United States has far stronger elements of intrastate federalism – the representation of regional and state interests within national institutions. The elected Senate, with equal representation from the states, and the loosely disciplined parties in both houses of Congress ensure a high degree of localism in congressional representation. The non-elected Canadian Senate has been unable to play such a role, and party discipline constrains the ability of Canadian MPs to represent provincial or regional interests at all visibly – though this role can be played in party caucuses, and there are strong norms about regional representation in the cabinet (Bakvis and Macdonald 1993). The Canadian pattern greatly inhibits the ability of Parliament to act as the arena for the accommodation and balancing of regional interests, and it powerfully strengthens the role of provincial governments as advocates of provincial interests, even in national policy making.

Indeed, Roger Gibbins (1982) has argued that at root, Canada and the United States are equally regionalized and that the increased salience of regional and intergovernmental conflict is explained by the differential impact of parliamentary and congressional federalism. The exclusion of provincial interests from the centre, he argues, transmutes regional into intergovernmental conflict and vests influence in provincial politicians, who have a direct interest in sustaining the conflict and strengthening provincial powers.

In addition, responsible parliamentary government operates on the principle of majority rule, rather than on the ever-shifting majorities of congress. Hence, it is argued that the interests of the smaller provinces are subordinated in Ottawa to the interests of the largest provinces. Both these concerns underlie the pressure for an elected Senate in Canada, which would temper majority rule by giving greater weight to the smaller provinces. (For an excellent review of this literature, see Smiley and Watts 1986.)

Two other institutional differences help account for the broad differences between American and Canadian federalism. From the start, the United States was a "chartered federation." Canada had no equivalent of the Bill of Rights until 1982. The U.S. Bill of Rights was, from the beginning, a powerful affirmation of the rights of individuals as citizens against governments at all levels. Not only has this been a strong centralizing influence, but it has helped ensure that American political discourse has been more focused on individual rights than on federalism or on the rights and interests of regional collectivities. The adoption of the Canadian Charter was a powerful stimulus to a reorientation of Canadian political debate in the same direction. It, too, was a nationalizing instrument, and it identified and gave status to a range of collective interests – gender, Aboriginal peoples, multicultural groups – that challenged the way in which federalism privileged territorially based identities. The Canadian federal system is in the process of working through the tensions between federalism and the Charter. While similar tensions are not unknown in the United States, they have largely been worked out in favour of the predominance of national norms, whether expressed through Congress or the Supreme Court.

The courts have helped shape the evolution of federalism in the two countries. In general, the U.S. court has placed few limits on the scope of federal power and its ability to impose standards on the states. Despite the fact that the U.S. constitution contains only a short list of exclusive federal powers while reserving all others to the states, the courts have granted almost unlimited scope to congressional authority; there are few legal limits (though there are important political ones) to the reach of federal power. By contrast, the Canadian courts – which until 1949 included the Judicial Committee of the Privy Council in Britain as the final arbiter – took a constitution which on its face was highly centralist and interpreted it to expand provincial powers and constrain the federal government. Nowhere is this more evident than in the differing interpretations of the scope of the trade and commerce power in the two countries. More recently, in a number of crucial decisions, the Supreme Court of Canada has self-consciously sought to balance federal and provincial authority (Russell 1987), though there are some indications of a more sympathetic approach to the scope of federal authority in such matters as trade and commerce, communications, and the environment. In general, however, the Canadian court remains a much more active umpire of the federal system than the U.S. court.

The institutional differences between American and Canadian federalism are reinforced by patterns of political cleavage in the two countries. Provincial identities and loyalties appear to be considerably stronger in Canada, and Canadian political debate revolves much more around issues of province and territory – though, to recall Gibbins, Cairns, and others, there is mutual causation here. Regionalism fosters assertive provinces, and assertive provinces foster regional interests and identities.

More important, federalism in Canada parallels and reinforces the dominant cleavages, whereas in the United States it cuts across them.

Nowhere is this more clear than in the most fundamental division in each country – race in the United States and language in Canada. African Americans are widely dispersed throughout the United States, but the federal lines in Canada largely coincide with the linguistic divisions. This difference has profound consequences for the politics of federalism. The political mobilization of language and region has meant that the same forces of modernization which Beer and others (1973, 1993) see as driving the inexorable movement towards centralization in the United States have had the reverse effect in Canada (Simeon and Robinson 1990, ch. 7).

Despite these initial differences, there are some important parallels, and there have been growing areas of convergence in recent developments in the two federations. First, the mobilization of new social groups, the impact of the Charter, and other forces have mounted a major challenge to the primacy of territorial politics in Canada (Cairns 1991). The interests of the newer groups, and the issues they raise, tend to cut across regional and provincial lines rather than reinforcing them. These groups see federalism as at best unhelpful to their concerns and, at worst, directly hostile to them. Like similar interests in the United States, they tend to look to national institutions – the Charter, the Supreme Court, and the national government – to advance their interests. Some have argued that these developments are "displacing" the older politics of federalism, regionalism, and territory, leading to an increasing disjunction between the institutionalization of territory in the political process and the growing importance of competing definitions of politics. If so, the long-term forces could bring a very strong convergence with the American model; the provinces would remain important administrative and political actors, but in large measure they would be administrative arms of national institutions that defined national standards.

It is, however, important not to exaggerate these trends; it is more likely that the new forces in Canada will add to and interact with the older territorial divisions. Many earlier predictions of the "displacement" of region by class or other divisions have proved premature. In addition, the Charter and the social forces associated with it have had much less impact in Quebec than in the rest of Canada. Thus, the newer developments, rather than transcending or ameliorating the Quebec/Canada difference might actually exacerbate it (Taylor 1991).

The most obvious element of potential convergence between the United States and Canada is in the Canadian proposals for an elected, equal, and effective Senate. Some advocates argue that with an elected Senate providing regional input to the central government, the role of the provincial governments and the premiers as national political actors will be undermined. In the long run, therefore, they hope that it will strengthen the federal government by increasing its representativeness and legitimacy.

There is an interesting dilemma, however, which is illustrated by the American experience. Traditionally, the Canadian model has focused on relations between federal and provincial governments as the chief instrument for accommodating and reconciling national and provincial interests. It has left each level of government considerable autonomy in its own sphere. The American model emphasizes representation and accommodation of state and regional interests within Congress. While this may look attractive to Canadian intrastate reformers, to American critics the cost of importing all the localist influences into Congress is to accentuate the burden of overload on the central government and increase the paralysis, immobilism, and parochialism in federal decision making (Walker 1985, 80–5).

If institutional changes are moving towards Canadian convergence with American federalism, in some other respects the U.S. states are converging with Canadian provinces. Many American observers have commented on the increased activism and innovation that has been occurring at the state level across a wide variety of policy areas (Conlan 1988, 228ff). States and localities have become much more active in promoting economic development and attracting investment. They have also greatly increased their international activities in trade promotion and investment (Fry, 1990b). All fifty states now have economic development departments or their equivalents, almost half of which were created in the 1970s and 1980s. This development of the "entrepreneurial state" is reminiscent of the "province-building" activities of provincial governments in the 1970s, although most U.S. states lack the constitutional power to own state enterprises, as is common in Canada. Meanwhile, fiscal pressures have recently trimmed the entrepreneurial activism of Canadian provinces.

The forces driving these developments are the large-scale economic restructuring that has been occurring in the United States – whether industrialization and growth in the South and West, or the decline of traditional industries in the Northeast. They have also been triggered by the contraction of federal activities and financial support in these areas, opening new policy space for state action. Underlying the pattern is a long-term growth in the administrative capacity of state governments. Thus, although the American states remain more subject to federal controls than the Canadian provinces, they have become more important centres of dynamism. This suggests that in the United States, as well as in Canada, the latest phase of modernization – globalization – is not as unequivocally centralizing as previous stages were. Indeed, as central governments become more constrained by deficits and as they find some of their chief policy instruments constrained by global forces, the result may well be decentralizing. This is a common theme among Canadian scholars of federalism (Courchene 1991, ch. 5); and it is becoming increasingly common in the United States. For example, Alice Rivlin calls for a "restructuring" of federal-state responsibilities, with the states focusing on the "productivity agenda" and the federal government focusing on redistribution. "The best chance of having a successful industrial policy in a country this size is to have a lot of communities, states and regions competing with each other to improve their own economic prospects" (Rivlin 1992, 120).

Finally, both federal systems are affected by fiscal crisis (Leslie et al. 1993; Banting et al. 1994). In both countries, transfers to states and provinces represent a significant share of federal spending, and in both such transfers represent a large proportion of provincial and state revenues. In both, as well, conservative governments at the national level have sought to reduce the size of the federal government and to transfer spending responsibilities to state and local levels. One result is the "cascading" of fiscal problems from one level to another.

Thus, in the 1980s, under the Reagan administration, federal transfers to the states and localities declined quite sharply, falling 33 per cent in real terms and dropping from 26.5 per cent of state-local revenues in 1978 to 18.2 per cent in 1987 (Conlan 1988, 154, 156), thereby reversing a long period of steady growth. The Reagan administration also sought to increase state and local freedom of action by consolidating and simplifying grant-in-aid programs, with their detailed policy and administrative supervision. Congressional opposition, however, sharply limited the achievement of the "new federalism" in the Reagan years; and in the mid-1990s divided government blunted the devolutionist drive of the Republican "Contract with America."

The Canadian federal government elected in 1984 also had a decentralizing thrust, though this had as much to do with its desire to promote cooperation with the provinces as it did with neoconservative hostility to federal power. In its early years, the Mulroney government largely insulated the provinces from its deficit-reducing efforts, but since 1988 there have been significant measures to restrain the rate of growth in federal transfers to the provinces, and a capping of payments to the wealthier provinces in social welfare. Federal transfers represented 21.8 per cent of provincial and local expenditures in 1971 and 17.5 per cent in 1989 (Ip 1991, 190). In its 1995 budget, the federal government announced that its cash transfers to the provinces for health, welfare, and post-secondary education would be rolled into a single Canada Health and Social Transfer, with the total amount dropping 26.8 per cent, to $12.6 billion in one year.

In important respects, the fiscal crisis has been recreated at the state and local level in both countries, for the subnational governments have not only experienced reduced revenues on their own account, but they have received reduced intergovernmental transfers. The problem is especially acute for the U.S. states and localities, since they tend to have less revenue-raising capacity than Canadian provinces, and in most cases there are constitutional limits on their ability to spend more than they raise. In addition, citizen initiatives and referenda on taxation and other matters have limited the states' ability to raise taxes, thus focusing restraint even more on the expenditure side. In both countries we see increasing fiscal pressures on states and localities, but at the same time a broadening of the policy space in which they can act.

Thus, both federal systems face some common pressures in the need to adapt their federal institutions to an increasingly diverse domestic society and to the influence of the global economy. Nevertheless, they have very different starting points. If the Canadian danger remains the slide into "centrifugal disequilibrium," the U.S. danger is "centripetal imbalance" (Walker 1985, 78). The cost for the United States is overload and paralysis at the centre; the cost for Canada is continual uncertainty about the future of the federation. In Canada, as a result, federalism is at the heart of all reform debates, whereas in the United States it evokes far less passion.

REFORM AGENDAS

Not surprisingly, this array of issues has generated a rich and multifaceted set of proposals for reform. These tend to flow in two streams, which largely speak past each other. Each strand is rooted in one of the two sets of concerns identified at the outset. Domestic forces have tended to focus on enhancing the quality of democracy, stressing the empowerment of citizens, the diffusion of authority, increased opportunities for participation, greater institutional responsiveness, and new bases of representation. By contrast, the global forces – or, more precisely, those economic interests most attuned to them – stress the need to free policy makers from domestic constraints and to insulate them from popular pressures in order to achieve greater coherence, consistency, and coordination. These two perspectives generate very different agendas for reform.

This distinction is, of course, not a neat one, for "progressive" reformers need to be concerned with the creation of bureaucratic and administrative machinery to carry out the popular will. This, indeed, was the whole thrust of the New Deal, but there is little doubt that it has faded as a primary concern for such interests, whose suspicion of government authority, even as they call for public redress of injustice, is profound. The emphasis on the courts and on formal, legal procedures is one attempt to reconcile this apparent contradiction.[11] On the other side, conservative reformers – such as the Reform Party in Canada – often place their faith in populist strategies to restrain government.

Reforms to decentralize power and open up government won important victories in the 1960s and 1970s, and they remain prominent on the political agenda. But so do other reforms designed to restore governmental authority in the face of the "excesses of democracy" (Huntington 1975). Proposals such as a four-year term for Congress or limits on the tenure of legislators are all designed to make members less sensitive to the need for re-election and to place them at least somewhat above the political fray. Paradoxically, these proposals are also designed to dispel the advantages of incumbency and to force a turnover that is not accomplished by the electoral process.[12] Another set of proposals reflects pessimism about the very capacity of the system to resolve conflicts and make effective decisions. A notable example is the wave of support for a "balanced budget" constitutional amendment in the United States. Several Canadian jurisdictions have also legislated requirements to avoid deficits.[13]

Perhaps the most important American proposals are those designed to strengthen the capacity of the system to design and implement a broader public interest, in order to counteract the fragmentation at both the societal and the institutional level. The perennial instrument for such proposals is the political party. While few have much faith in the possibility of creating a two-party system within a parliamentary framework on the British or Canadian model, many elements of these proposals continue to circulate – for example, suggestions to permit simultaneous office holding in the executive and the administration, or to require a common ballot. But none have moved onto the active political agenda. (The most complete survey of institutional reform proposals is Sundquist 1986.)

The reform agendas differ substantially in the two countries. In Canada, the absence of divided government and the greater authority of executives generally mean that coordination and decisiveness within the national government have not been central to the agenda. Moreover, all reform efforts have been overshadowed by the constitutional issue, which relates on one hand to the fundamental character of the Canadian political community and on the other to the distribution of authority between governments, including the search for ways to reduce overlapping and entanglement between federal and provincial programs. In addition, given their different starting points, proposals associated with the domestic agenda – with empowering citizens and checking authority – have been relatively more prominent in Canada recently. Americans tend to be more preoccupied with overcoming the consequences of enhanced pluralism; Canadians, with giving greater expression to a pluralism they do not feel is fully reflected in parliamentary institutions. While proposals for institutional reform proliferate in the United States, most are made by scholars, and few have real political currency. In Canada, by contrast, the reform agenda has been shaped by recent populist demands, which have swept over the political elites like a tidal wave.

These differences in emphasis are also evident in the timing of reform. Most of the institutional reforms associated with the new pluralism were developed in the United States in the 1970s, in the aftermath of Vietnam and Watergate. Change since then has tended to seek to restore some coherence to the system – as in the partial resurgence of parties in Congress. In Canada, while there were important echoes of the American events of the 1960s and 1970s, the reform drive did not have significant impact until later. The major reform thrusts then came in two stages: in the introduction of the Charter of Rights and Freedoms – itself initially the project of a visionary politician seeking to build support for national institutions – and then in the rejection of two constitutional agreements, in 1990 and 1992, and the rise of the Reform Party in the 1993 federal election.

CONCLUSIONS

Does the preceding survey of governance and the functioning of institutions suggest a substantial degree of convergence or a substantial and continuing divergence, even perhaps a growing apart? The answers are elusive, not least because there are no objective tests. What to one observer might look like a major convergence may to another be of little note, and vice versa.

Nevertheless, some generalizations are possible. Convergence is least apparent in the structure and operations of formal political institutions. Congress, the presidency, and executive-legislative relationships remain very different from the operations of Parliament and executives in Canada. Here the difference between a parliamentary and a congressional system retains considerable power to shape the behaviour of political actors. The incentives, constraints, and resources available to actors in the two systems vary widely, perpetuating significant differences. The major exception to this is the change in the role of the courts in Canada and their relationship to other elements of the political system. While there remain important differences, courts in Canada now play a role not fundamentally dissimilar from those in the United States. In addition, where there is change in Canadian institutions, the tendency is for them to move in the direction of U.S. institutions. The United States remains by far the most important source of models for Canadian reformers. Thus, there are elements of the "presidentialization" of the prime ministership, and there are proposals significantly to enhance the independence of individual MPs from executive dominance.

Despite the Canadian Charter, the greatest convergence lies not in the formal institutions but in less formal political processes. American policy styles have historically been more participatory, pluralist, adversarial, and legalistic than Canadian ones. In the United States, these characteristics have intensified and, partly through design, have been institutionalized in many aspects of the political process. In Canada, the break with the past appears to be sharper, and the tension between the newer political style and traditional ones greater; and there has, at least so far, been less adjustment of political institutions and processes to the new forces than there has been in the United States.

Why have the formal political institutions converged less than the informal political processes? It is partly because of the power of institutional inertia and the capacity of formal rules to shape political activity. The areas of continuing divergence between Canada and the United States are those where the formal rules are clearest and most distinct. Convergence in informal processes, however, cannot be explained by institutional factors. Rather, the reasons for it must be found in the similarity of the contemporary forces that are acting on these institutions. Here the forces at work tend to be the same in both countries. They are to be found in changed attitudes, including a strong "rights orientation," greater social pluralism, a changed role for the mass media and communications technology, and so on. In so far as these "environmental" changes are similar, so will be the pressures on the governing process. Changes will tend to move in the same direction, but their pace, timing, and extent will vary.

Despite the continuing differences we have stressed, there is a remarkable similarity in both popular and elite assessments of the efficacy of the political process. We began by noting the very similar levels of citizen disaffection: in both countries the people appear to feel that they have lost control of their governors. Perceptions of policy or performance failure, we noted, are also remarkably similar between the two countries. We also saw that in both countries, one of the first responses to such criticisms was to blame the political institutions and to argue for changes to fix them. There is some plausibility to this view. In both countries, the fragmentation of political authority in an already divided society is at the heart of the governance dilemma. It takes somewhat different forms in the two countries: between Congress and president in the United States and between Ottawa and the provinces in Canada. The results are similar. To take two recent examples, social-policy reform in Canada and health-care reform in the United States demonstrate the hurdles that even strongly committed executives must overcome. Nevertheless, there are limits to institutional solutions to popular alienation. After all, the disaffection from government is much the same in both countries despite their very different institutional frameworks. This suggests that the source of the challenges to governance goes well beyond institutions.

Thus we return to the basic argument. The deepest source of disaffection is to be found in the tension between the attitudes and values of citizens in the domestic society and the pressures generated by global economic forces; and by the relation of both of these to the capacities of institutions. Disaffection is explained not so much by the declining capacity of the institutions themselves as by changes in the far more complex environment in which they are embedded. Fundamentally, we believe that the disaffection is driven by the gap between expectation and performance. Performance, in turn, is less a function of institutional structures than of the challenges and constraints, global and domestic, that are facing the system. In this sense, the levels of disaffection and the pervasive sense of failure may be attributable to the sheer range of demands and the often contradictory imperatives which those demands create.

Consensus on institutional reform will be hard to achieve. There will thus remain a disjunction between the perceived need for policy and institutional reform and its occurrence. Moreover, insofar as political institutions do respond, they will be more likely to react to the immediate political pressures of a pluralist domestic society. Calls to reform institutions and practices in order to adapt more effectively to the changed global environment will remain remote and abstract from most citizens. What changes do occur will not be through major institutional changes or constitutional amendments; in both countries the hurdles to constitutional amendment are well nigh insurmountable. This suggests that it may be more realistic to make the existing systems work better than to argue for wholly new ones.[14] However, the past two decades have witnessed a multitude of incremental changes in the United States – in election procedures, congressional organization, the White House, the bureaucracy, and federalism. The same is true for Canada. Many of the changes have had unintended consequences (as in the strengthening of political action committees as a result of changes in campaign finance laws); others have been of limited effectiveness (as in congressional attempts to rationalize the budget process); yet others have pulled in contradictory directions (as in the tug of war between the president and Congress over budgeting, war powers, and trade policy, or as in the mixed consequences of deregulation). Such institutional and procedural changes will continue, but they are unlikely to meet the basic challenge of governance rooted in the global and domestic forces we have outlined. Almost by definition, political institutions crystallize and entrench the past. They are thus a powerful force for continuity – and for the continued difference between Canada and the United States.

This chapter has provided a broad overview of the debates about governance in the two countries. We have noted very high levels of dissatisfaction. But a more nuanced conclusion about the efficacy of these institutions must await the evidence of the chapters to come. As we look at a group of important policy areas, are these broad critiques borne out? Where do we find success, and where failure?

PART TWO

Policy Responses

Chapter 5 is dedicated to the memory of Douglas Purvis, who died before the writing was completed. Doug Purvis was a good friend to me, better than I ever realized before he was gone. Others have written about the important effect he had on the political economy of the country. But on a smaller scale there are many people who, like me, were quietly helped or guided by Doug. I am glad he asked me to work on this paper with him. It was difficult to complete the project without him, since it flowed from the broad view of policy and history that was unique to him. I hope that I have been true to his intentions.

Paul Boothe

5 Macroeconomic Policy in Canada and the United States: Independence, Transmission, and Effectiveness

PAUL BOOTHE AND DOUGLAS PURVIS

INTRODUCTION

This chapter compares Canadian and U.S. macroeconomic performance during the 1970s and 1980s. The comparison of performance will of necessity involve considerable description of key macroeconomic variables. However, it also involves a comparison of policies that must be described and then evaluated. Much of the descriptive material is provided in the first two sections; in subsequent sections we turn to an evaluation of policies. The range of U.S. and Canadian macroeconomic performance and the range of policy responses over this period are so diverse that it provides an almost laboratory-like data set with which to explore a wide variety of policy issues.

Three Key Questions

We are currently in a period of great change in the relations between national economies. Under the general heading of globalization, we see the formation of large trading blocks in Europe and North America, the emergence of newly industrialized countries with powerful economies, and the opening up of Eastern European countries, Russia, and China to business and trade. In addition to these political changes, we are witnessing the effect of technology on economic relations between nations. The close integration of international financial markets and computer and communications technology has given individuals access to world capital markets through the telephone and personal computer.

The growth of trade and the technological changes we are seeing raise critical issues regarding the scope for macroeconomic management. It is legitimate to ask whether nations, especially those with small, open economies, are capable of independent and effective management of their economies. In order to provide some structure to our discussion, and indeed to limit its scope to manageable proportions, in the latter sections we focus on three key questions:

1 *Can Canada and the United States, as open economies (one small and one large) that are increasingly exposed to a globalized international economy, have independent macroeconomic policies?* In particular, we wonder if the process of globalization has reduced the scope for independent policy because of the growth of economic linkages between countries and the access that individuals have to international markets. Further, we ask whether the scope for independent policy is different for small and large economies. In short, how many degrees of freedom do they have?

2 *How and to what extent are policies transmitted between countries?* In particular, we argue that to focus on the traditional transmission of policy effects (for example, the usual export multiplier) is to miss an important aspect of the linkage between countries. Traditionally, domestic policies are thought to be transmitted internationally through their effects on trade. For example, one country's expansionary fiscal policy might increase aggregate demand and therefore the demand for exports from its trading partners, which in turn would stimulate aggregate demand in their economies. This type of linkage, which is the subject of a great deal of international macroeconomic analysis, may be referred to as *outcome dependence*; we argue that this should be distinguished from *policy dependence* – the "transmission of policies themselves." That is, polices adopted in one country are often mimicked in other countries; this pressure to harmonize policies can be fairly direct (as is the case of corporate income taxation), or it can be more indirect, often resulting from a desire to "protect" the exchange rate. [1]

3 *Have macroeconomic policies been "influential"? That is, have policy actions had discernible effects on the macroeconomy?* Here, we wish to distinguish explicitly between policy influence and effectiveness. We say that policies have been "influential" when they have had a discernible impact on macroeconomic policy targets. We say they have been "effective" when they have had the desired effects – insofar as the goals of policy are clear.

The chapter is organized as follows. The next section presents the basic data in the form of time series on the key macroeconomic variables, with only a limited narrative at this stage. We present data on three types of variables: performance variables, such as output, inflation, and unemployment, which might be viewed as the ultimate targets of macroeconomic policy; intermediate variables, such as interest rates and exchange rates, which matter because they influence performance variables but which are not under the direct control of the policy authorities (but may be used by policy authorities in setting their policy instruments); and policy variables, such as monetary aggregates and budget deficits. In the third section we turn to a more detailed discussion of the main historical episodes, focusing on five distinct periods, and in the fourth section we conclude with a brief discussion of the lessons we have learned and with some speculation about the policy challenges facing both countries through the 1990s.

MEASURING THE MACROECONOMIES

In this section we present the basic macroeconomic data for the 1970s and 1980s. Our presentation is divided into four parts. In the first part we review macroeconomic performance, focusing on what economists call "target" variables: real output, unemployment, prices, and international trade in the two economies. The second part presents some of the "intermediate targets" that affect performance, including interest and exchange rates, unit labour costs, and productivity. In the third part we turn to policy "instruments" and examine money growth and government deficits in Canada and the United States. Finally, we assess this experience in the light of our three key questions.

Policy Targets

One of the advantages of looking at twenty years of data is that one is forced, to some extent, to step back from the current economic conditions and take a longer-term perspective. Figures 5.1 and 5.2 show the paths for trend and actual GDP for the two countries.[2] Canada turned in a strong economic performance over the period with an average annual growth rate of about 3.4 per cent – the envy of most of its OECD partners – while the United States grew more slowly, averaging 2.5 per cent. The cyclical patterns in the economy are reflected in the differences between trend and actual output.[3]

Cyclical developments are shown more clearly in figure 5.3, which plots quarterly growth rates for the two economies, and in figure 5.4, which shows their unemployment rates. Given the extensive trade and financial links between the two economies, the relatively close correspondence between their business cycles is not surprising. Focusing first

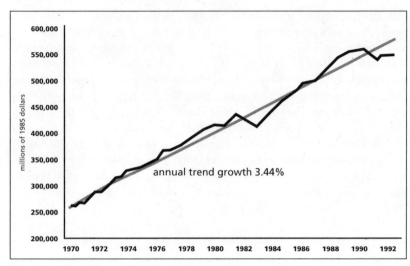

Figure 5.1   Canadian actual and trend real output
Source: Statistics Canada

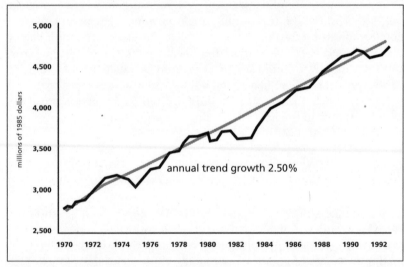

Figure 5.2   U.S. actual and trend real output
Source: CITIBASE

on figure 5.3, we see that the Canadian economy expanded strongly for eleven consecutive years, from 1970 to 1981, while growth in the American economy was interrupted by a significant decline in 1974–75 after OPEC 1 (the first large hike in energy prices). Patterns in the 1980s were identical. Both economies experienced a severe recession in 1981,

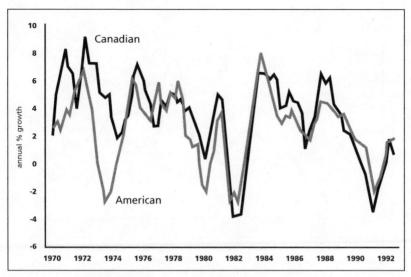

Figure 5.3   Canadian and American growth of real output
Sources: Statistics Canada; CITIBASE

and it took them over three years (until 1985) to return to trend output. Both economies grew strongly for the rest of the decade, although growth slowed after 1988. Then, in 1990, we witnessed the start of the latest recession – which was less severe in the United States.

While the broad picture from the behaviour of unemployment rates shown in figure 5.4 is again one of cyclical coherence, one sees the sharply worse U.S. cyclical experience in 1974, and one sees that the Canadian experience grew worse through the decade as unemployment rose steadily. The sharper severity of the 1982 recession in Canada is also apparent, as is the persistence in Canadian unemployment during the recovery of the mid-1980s.[4] Unlike Canada, prior to the advent of the recent recession the United States was successful in returning unemployment to its previous low near 5 per cent. The increased persistence in unemployment in Canada is generally attributed by economists to the changes in unemployment insurance benefits that took place in the 1970s.

Canadian and U.S. price performance is shown in figures 5.5 and 5.6. Three main features emerge. First, Canadian prices track their U.S. counterparts fairly closely, as shown in figure 5.5. Second, U.S. price performance was marginally superior to Canada's; over the period, Canada's price level grew by more than that of the United States, as can also be seen from figure 5.5. Note, however, that in 1992 Canada's inflation rate was lower. Finally, as shown in figure 5.6, the large and variable price changes that characterized the period up to the

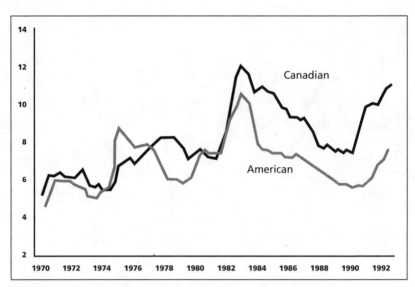

Figure 5.4   Canadian and American unemployment rates
Sources: Statistics Canada; CITIBASE

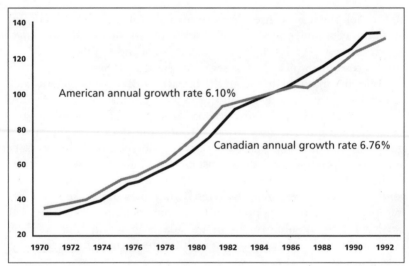

Figure 5.5   Canadian and American consumer price indices
Sources: Statistics Canada; CITIBASE

early 1980s were replaced with a period of relatively small and stable price changes.

For our final performance variable, we consider both countries' external positions. In figure 5.7 we see that the Canadian current account declined substantially over the period. From being near balance

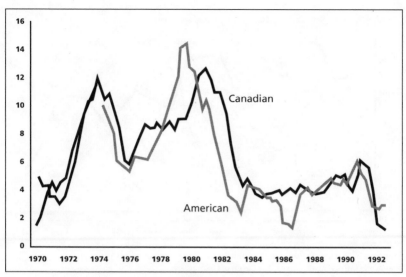

Figure 5.6   Canadian and American inflation rates
Sources: Statistics Canada; CITIBASE

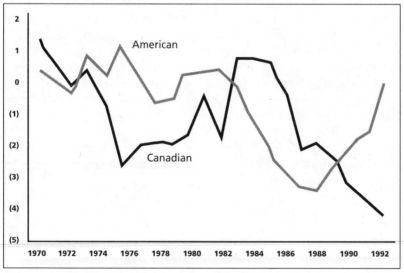

Figure 5.7   Current account as a percentage of output
Sources: Statistics Canada; CITIBASE

in the first four years of the 1970s, the current account declined to a deficit of over $20 billion per year. The sharp downward spike of 1981 (stemming from flows related to the National Energy Program [NEP]) was followed by three years of current account surplus. Thereafter, the

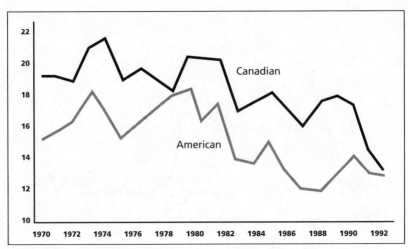

Figure 5.8   Gross national accumulation as a percentage of output
Sources : Statistics Canada; CITIBASE; *Survey of Current Business*

balance began its sharp decline to its current deficit. The U.S. current account remained close to balance until 1982. The balance declined sharply for the next five years, falling to more than $150 billion deficit. Since its 1987 low, the balance has improved substantially, with the current deficit standing at slightly less than $100 billion. Figure 5.8 presents a broad measure of the two countries' external positions, tracking gross national accumulation, which is the sum of investment flows and net exports. No trend is discernible through the 1970s. However, since 1980 both countries have shown a steady deterioration in their external positions. In the case of the United States, this marked the change from being one of the world's leading creditors to being one of its leading debtors.

Intermediate Targets

Intermediate targets such as the exchange rate and unit labour costs are variables that can be used to indicate the stance or direction of policy. While they are not generally under the direct control of policy makers, they are affected by policy variables and in turn affect the ultimate targets discussed above. In figure 5.9 we see that short-term interest rates in both countries exhibited extreme volatility over the period, ranging from below 5 per cent in the early 1970s to almost 20 per cent less than ten years later. Overall, rates in the two countries have moved together, especially in the first decade. However, a large, positive premium of Canadian over U.S. rates has persisted since the mid-1980s.

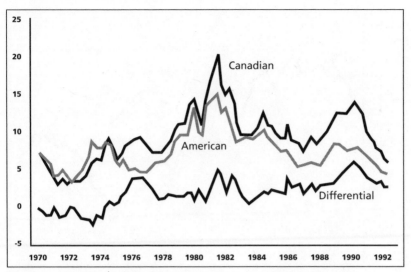

Figure 5.9   Canadian and American short-term interest rates and differential
Sources: Bank of Canada; CITIBASE

Figure 5.9 shows the steady rise from 1983 to 1990 when the differential peaked at over 500 basis points. Since then, the differential has declined to more normal levels, although the real interest differential remains high given Canada's relatively low rate of inflation.

In figure 5.10 we see that the Canada-U.S. exchange rate showed a similarly wide variation over the period. From its fixed parity of 92.5 cents abandoned early in 1970, the exchange rate rose unevenly to a peak in 1976 of about 103. Coincident with the election of the Parti Québécois government in Quebec, the Canadian dollar began a long decline of almost 30 cents over the next ten years. The widening Canada–U.S. interest differential accompanied the subsequent rise to the dollar's level in the 88-cent range in mid-1991. Both the interest differential and the exchange rate subsequently fell, with the Canadian dollar falling through 80 cents in late 1992. In figure 5.11 we see effective exchange rates (based on trade weights) for the two countries from 1976. Both countries were substantially affected by wide swings in commodity prices during the period. On the U.S. side, events were dominated by a substantial rise of the U.S. currency in the mid-1980s and by its subsequent decline. The movement of the dollar in the 1980s vis-à-vis German and Japanese currencies was largely unexplained by existing exchange rate theories, and some economists have turned to theories of speculative bubbles to explain the dollar over this period.

On the production side, Canadian and U.S. unit labour costs (measured in U.S. dollar terms, 1982=100) moved closely together until

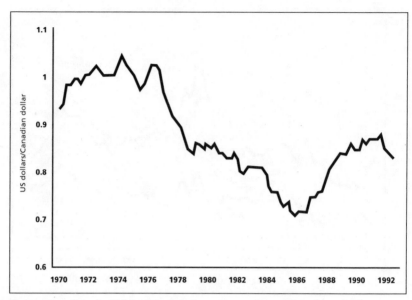

Figure 5.10   Canada–U.S. exchange rate
Source: Bank of Canada

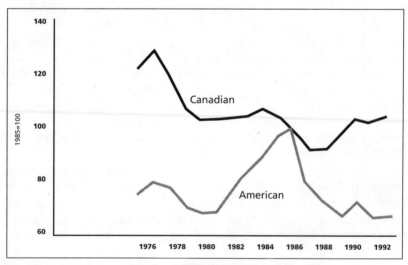

Figure 5.11   Canadian and American trade-weighted exchange rates
Source: IFS

1983. As we see in figure 5.12, Canadian costs declined over the next three years, mostly because of the fall in the Canadian dollar. However, Canadian costs rose sharply relative to their U.S. counterparts in the last five years of the period. Less than one-third of this increase is explained by the dollar's rise; in terms of Canadian dollars, Canadian

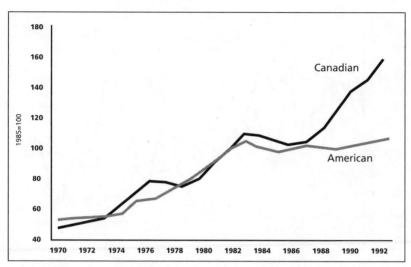

Figure 5.12   Unit labour costs (U.S. dollar basis)
Source: OECD main economic indicators

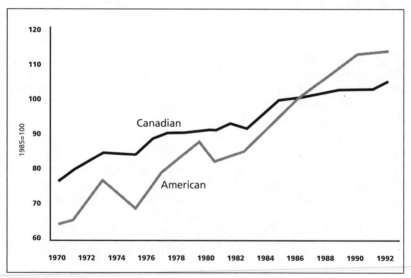

Figure 5.13   Canadian and U.S. productivity
Sources: Economic Reference tables; U.S. *Statistical Abstract*

unit labour costs rose from 100 in 1982 to 120 in 1990. Our second cost measure is productivity. A pattern similar to that of unit labour costs is found in figure 5.13. Using an index of output per employed worker (1982=100), we see that the two countries moved together through much of the period. However, the U.S. developed a substantial competitive advantage over the latter half of the 1980s.

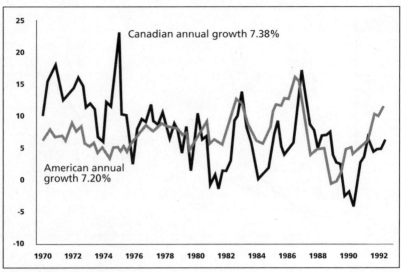

Figure 5.14   Canadian and American M1 growth
Sources: Statistics Canada; CITIBASE

Overall, the data show a close correspondence between both countries' ultimate and intermediate policy targets over much of the period. In large part this reflects both the similarity and integration of the two economies. We shall later examine the data to see whether the two countries were also pursuing similar policies.

Policy Instruments

Our final set of data series are presented to give some notion of the direction of monetary and fiscal policy in Canada and the United States. In figures 5.14 and 5.15 we present annual rates of growth for narrow and broad monetary aggregates, M1 and M2.[5] Focusing first on M1, the most striking feature of the data is the volatility of M1 growth in Canada and, after 1979, in the United States. The rise in volatility in the United States in the second decade may be partly attributable to the change in Federal Reserve Board's operating procedure. Although statistically the average Canadian M1 growth is lower in the 1980s than in the 1970s, visual inspection makes it hard to discern a trend. Further, while prolonged monetary contractions in both countries preceded the current recession, there is no clear relationship between M1 growth and earlier recession in either country. M2 growth in both countries shows similar variability but does not match M1 growth patterns closely – which indicates that a good deal of shifting between M1 and other components of M2 was taking place. It is fair to say that average M2 growth declined

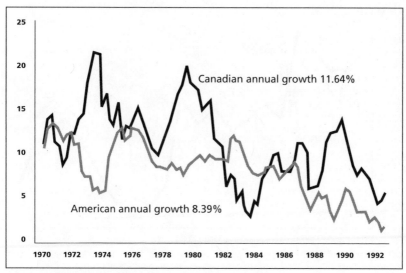

Figure 5.15   Canadian and American M2 growth
Sources: Statistics Canada; CITIBASE

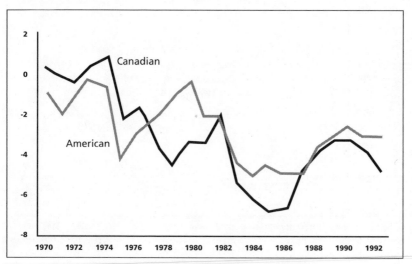

Figure 5.16   Federal government deficit as a percentage of output
Sources: Statistics Canada; *Survey of Current Business*

discernibly from the 1970s to the 1980s, although substantial variability remains.

On the fiscal side, data for federal government deficits as a percentage of national income shown in figures 5.16 and 5.17 confirm that both countries experienced a shift to deep and sustained government

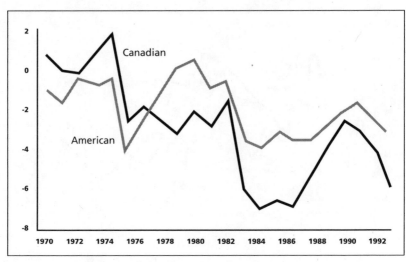

Figure 5.17   Consolidated government deficit as a percentage of output
Sources: Economic Reference tables; *Survey of Current Business*

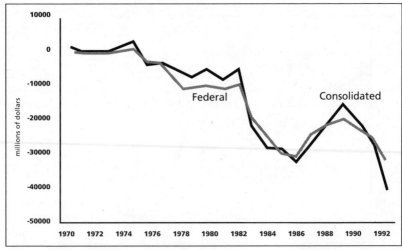

Figure 5.18   Canadian consolidated and federal deficits
Sources: Statistics Canada; Economic Reference tables

deficits as they moved from the mid-1970s to the 1980s. Focusing first on the federal deficits in figure 5.16, we see that after four years near balance, the Canadian federal deficit increased over the 1974–84 period to almost 7 per cent of GDP. The U.S. experience over this period was similar, though less severe; in the early 1970s it was strongly affected by the debt financing of the Vietnam War, but by 1979 the

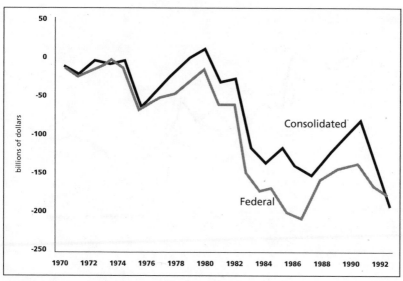

Figure 5.19   U.S. consolidated and federal deficits
Source: Survey of Current Business

budget had returned to near balance. The subsequent deterioration was smaller than in Canada, and the deficit "peaked" in 1983 at about 5 per cent of GDP.[6] After reaching respective peaks in 1983 and 1984, both countries experienced declines in their federal deficits (although neither came even close to balance) until 1989, when the economic slowdown and other developments caused both budget situations to deteriorate once again.

Figure 5.17 shows the data for deficits on a consolidated government basis as a percentage of national income. The role of the other levels of government can be seen better in figures 5.18 and 5.19, which show the Canadian and American experience, respectively, on a federal and consolidated government basis. (These figures are also in terms of billions of dollars rather than as percentages of national income.) As figure 5.18 suggests, the provincial-local-hospital (PLH) sector was in rough balance until 1981, after which it contributed to an increased consolidated government deficit (except in 1988, when the PLH sector briefly returned to balance). In the United States, the state governments (some of which have constitutional prohibitions on deficit financing) balanced their budgets or ran substantial surpluses over the entire twenty-year period – at times in excess of $50 billion. Thus, unlike Canada, the federal deficit is partly offset by significant savings by the state governments. As we moved into the mid-1990s, we see that

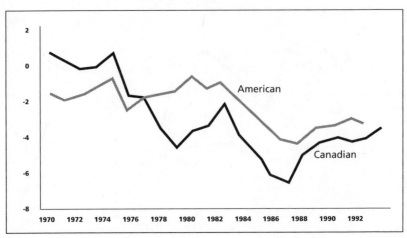

Figure 5.20   Canadian and American deficits cyclically adjusted as a percentage of output
Source: Economic Reference tables; U.S. Bureau of Economic Analysis

the Canadian provincial governments' ballooning deficits opened the gap between the federal and consolidated measures.

An alternative view of government deficits and debt in the two countries is presented in figure 5.20, in which federal deficits have been adjusted to account for the effect of cyclical factors on government spending and revenue. Measures of this kind are sometimes used to examine the underlying "structural" component of government deficits. As can be seen, this component of the deficit increased dramatically through the first half of the 1980s in both countries. The Canadian deficit was relatively large compared to the American, especially when one considers that provincial governments are significantly more important actors in the economy than state governments. Both countries saw some improvement in their structural deficits in the latter half of the 1980s – even as the recession of the early 1990s was causing overall deficits to grow. Canada saw a substantially greater improvement than the United States, although some of this improvement came from offloading a portion of the deficit to provincial governments by cutting transfers that support social programs.

While the federal governments in Canada and the United States may take some encouragement from the improvement in their structural deficits, nevertheless the overall deficit is added to the national debt each year. Figure 5.21 shows the debt implications of these continual deficits. After reaching lows of just under 35 per cent of GDP in the mid-to-early 1970s, the debt-to-national-income ratio in both countries grew rapidly, reaching over 60 per cent by the end of the decade.

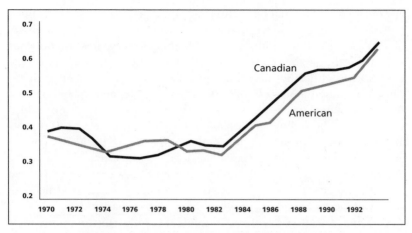

Figure 5.21   Canadian and American central government debt: Output ratio
Source: Statistics Canada; *Survey of Current Business*

While on the U.S. side, adding state government debt would not change the picture substantially, on the Canadian side, the measure would be exacerbated by the growth in provincial deficits and debt that comes partly as a result of federal offloading.

Three Key Questions

At the beginning of this chapter we posed three questions to guide our analysis of this twenty-year period. The first was, Can Canada and the United States run economic policies that are independent of actions in the other country? It is clear from our examination of policy targets that, on occasion, policy *outcomes* have been different in the two countries. Two examples are the 1975 recession in the United States, which was avoided in Canada (figures 5.1 and 5.2), and the divergence of the two countries' unemployment rates beginning in the 1980s (figure 5.4). The first example of divergence of outcomes can be attributed to different macroeconomic policies in the two countries. The second is related to differences in structural policies concerning unemployment benefits. Both countries were significantly affected by important global events such as the OPEC shocks and the breakdown of the system of fixed exchange rates among industrialized countries in the 1970s – although, judging from their current accounts, global events can have significantly different effects in the two countries.

The second question was, How are policies transmitted between the countries? Here, we saw that the traditional linkages remain important.

For example, inflationary pressures in the United States are transmitted to Canada through trade, – that is, for a given exchange rate, the prices of imported goods rise with foreign inflation. However, it is also possible, at least for the smaller partner in a trading relationship, to import poli- cies directly, either because the policies are viewed as desirable or be- cause the consequences of policy divergence are judged to be too costly. A case in point is the rise in U.S. interest rates in the early 1980s, which was directly followed by similar action in Canada (figure 5.9). It is prob- ably not possible to determine whether the cause of the policy conver- gence was fear of a falling Canadian dollar or the attractiveness of the anti-inflation policy itself. In any case, given the divergence of interest rates in the late 1980s, it is clear that Canadian authorities did have some independent choices in the conduct of monetary policy.

The final question was, How influential is policy in the increasingly globalized world economy? The preliminary indication from the data is that policy is generally influential whether it is well constructed or misguided. Monetary policy brought about the severe recession of the early 1980s in both countries very effectively, independent of mone- tary conditions in the rest of the world. The higher Canadian interest rates of the mid- and late 1980s gave Canada a substantially deeper "made-in-Canada" recession in the early 1990s than the one experi- enced in the United States.[7] On the fiscal side, it is more difficult to separate cyclical from trend components of policy. However, the im- pacts of specific measures, such as the National Energy Program in Canada, are clearly reflected in the data from the current account (figure 5.7). Persistent deficits on both sides of the border may have reduced the scope for any short-term fiscal policy action.

MACROECONOMIC PERFORMANCE
1970–1992

This section looks at the events of the last two decades in more detail in order to refine our answers to the three key questions regarding policy independence, channels of policy transmission and the influence of policy. We conduct this analysis by looking at five episodes during this period which capture the major economic events of the two countries.

Episode 1. Inflation and the Fall of Bretton Woods: 1970–1973[8]

Two major shocks hit the U.S. economy in the early 1970s. The first was a change in an important relative price that was beyond the con- trol of policy makers. The second came from the devaluation of the U.S. dollar following the collapse of the Bretton Woods agreement on exchange rate parities. This latter shock was an important signal to the United States that events beyond its borders had important effects on its economy and could not be ignored.

The first shock, which hit in 1972, was a sharp increase in agriculture prices following two consecutive years of bad harvests. The farm price index rose nearly 10 per cent in 1972 and then climbed almost 30 per cent in 1973. A modest increase of about 5 per cent followed in 1974, and then prices remained relatively flat for the next three years. The impact of the bad harvests was to reduce output and increase prices from what they otherwise would have been.

The second shock was connected with the growing overvaluation of the U.S. dollar vis-à-vis other major currencies. In the aftermath of the Second World War, the U.S. dollar had assumed the role of the world's reserve currency. This was formalized by the Bretton Woods agreement, which fixed parities for currencies in terms of the U.S. dollar and in turn tied the U.S. dollar to gold. The United States, which held a large portion of the world's gold stock following the war, pledged to provide gold to foreign central banks at the fixed parity.

At the beginning of the 1970s, the U.S. dollar was substantially overvalued, and foreigners were increasingly coming to the United States to convert their dollars to gold at the fixed parity – thus draining U.S. gold reserves. In 1972 President Nixon abandoned the agreed-upon parity and refused to continue to sell gold to foreigners. The subsequent Smithsonian agreement, which replaced Bretton Woods, lasted less than two years. The U.S. dollar began a dramatic decline against foreign currencies, and the world entered an era of flexible exchange rates. The end of Bretton Woods and the devaluation of the U.S. dollar stemmed the drain on U.S. gold reserves and made American goods more competitive abroad. The impact on the U.S. economy was a dramatic rise in the price of imported intermediate and final goods.

With President Nixon running for re-election in 1972, fiscal and monetary policies were both harnessed to ensure good economic conditions at election time.[9] On the fiscal side, the U.S. deficit almost doubled from $12 to $22 billion between 1970 and 1971, and federal spending rose sharply in 1971 and 1972. On the monetary side, U.S. short-term interest rates fell from 6.4 per cent in 1970 to 4.1 per cent in 1972. The efficacy of these policies was proved by the economy's response. Real GDP in the United States grew at 3.3 per cent in 1972 and a further 7.1 per cent in 1973. Unemployment fell from 5.95 to 5.6 per cent in 1972 and to 4.86 per cent in 1973. With a booming economy, the president easily won re-election. Thus, 1972 witnessed one of the most successful efforts at managing the political business cycle in American history, at least from the perspective of ensuring the re-election of the president. However, as Blinder concluded, "fiscal stimulus transformed 1972 from a year of healthy economic growth into an unsustainable and inflationary boom" (1979, 145).

With the election safely behind him, President Nixon turned his attention to the problem of inflation and to the overheated economy that was partly a result of his pre-election policies. Despite wage and price controls, inflation in the United States almost doubled, from 3.2 per cent in 1972 to 6.2 per cent in 1973, rising to 11 per cent in 1974. Ignoring the important role played by agricultural (and energy) price shocks and the devaluation of the U.S. dollar, the authorities reacted in the traditional manner (appropriate for demand shocks but not for supply shocks) by making monetary and fiscal policy restrictive.

Just as the pre-election policies had proved very effective at stimulating (and even overheating) the U.S. economy, the effects of the post-election policies were felt in very short order. Monetary and fiscal tightening plunged the country into recession, while inflation (which had started with the supply shocks) continued to rise. As we shall see in the next section, "stagflation" appeared on the scene as a new economic virus – one that seemed resistant to traditional economic policy medicine.

Now consider the Canadian experience. While the contractionary policies introduced in the late 1960s had some effect (unemployment rose in 1969 and 1970, and inflation started to fall by mid-1970), they were in basic conflict with the Bank of Canada's commitment to a fixed exchange rate. In the face of a high balance-of-payments surplus, either the economy had to be allowed to expand faster or the exchange rate had to be freed. The latter course was chosen, and the Canadian dollar rose rapidly, almost reaching par with the U.S. dollar. The stage was now set for Canada to carry on its policy of striving for a lower rate of inflation than that in the United States. If Canada was to achieve this goal, the value of the Canadian dollar had to continue to rise at a rate approximately equal to the excess of the U.S. inflation rate over the Canadian inflation rate. However, the Bank of Canada – after adopting a flexible exchange rate in order to be able to pursue its anti-inflation policy – simultaneously adopted a more expansionary posture.[10] This was largely because unemployment had risen, and this was interpreted to be the result of a slowdown in the economy. Expansionary monetary policy was accompanied by expansionary fiscal policy, both federally and in some provinces, and the period ended with sharply increased inflation.

With hindsight, the increase in unemployment can be recognized as the result of an increase in the natural rate of unemployment – the rate at which there is no pressure from labour markets to change the rate of inflation – rather than the emergence of a recessionary gap; indeed, most subsequent analyses of the period indicate that there remained a substantial inflationary gap. Perhaps of as much interest as this "mistake" in the direction of monetary policy is the way in which the policy was developed. In effect, the Bank of Canada adopted a managed, or dirty, float; that is, it regulated the Canadian exchange rate without undertaking an explicit commitment to maintain it at, or near, a publicly announced value. The dirty float was effected not by intervening directly in the foreign-exchange market but by setting domestic monetary conditions (rates of interest and rates of monetary expansion) so that the exchange market would clear at the desired exchange rate without substantial government intervention in the foreign-exchange market. Essentially, this meant adopting the monetary policy that would be consistent with fixed rates; hence, it might better be termed a "dirty fix." This led to a more rapid expansion of the money supply than would have been consistent with the goal of reducing inflation. Indeed it led, predictably, to a rate of inflation roughly equal to that in the United States, and one that was higher than the target rate that had led to the monetary contraction of the late 1960s and the adoption of a flexible exchange rate in 1970.

Indirectly, by maintaining policies consistent with a stable exchange rate, inflation was imported from the United States. Canada thus missed the opportunity to avoid some of the inflation that plagued the world economy in the 1970s. The full benefits of a flexible rate were not realized because the Bank of Canada resisted the appreciation of the Canadian dollar and permitted high rates of growth of the money supply; this experience of "exchange rate protection" arose again in a couple of later episodes, which will be discussed below.

The events of this episode bear directly on all three of our key questions. First, both countries seem to have had scope for independent policy, although some of their policy freedom had to be used to respond to foreign shocks. However, there is little doubt that in the case of the United States, President Nixon was able to harness the policy tools at his disposal to deal with his domestic priorities much of the time. While Canada seemed to have similar scope to use policy, it did so to a lesser extent. The reason for this bears on our second question on policy transmission. Unwilling to accept the fluctuation in the exchange rate needed to stabilize monetary policy and the attending reduction in exports and output, domestic monetary conditions were set to limit fluctuations on the exchange rate. This led to acceptance of the higher rate of inflation that was being run in the United States. Finally, this episode leaves little doubt about the efficacy of policy – especially given

President Nixon's success at managing the political business cycle. In Canada, policy was sometimes based on what we now know to have been mistaken views on the causes of unemployment. The negative medium-term consequences of these policy initiatives in both countries were to be felt in the United States and Canada for some time to come.

Episode 2. Stagflation and Failed Expectations: 1974–1980

By 1974 inflation was at close to double-digit levels in both countries. In the United States fiscal and monetary policy had turned restrictive, while in Canada an expansionary budget (focusing on supply-side measures to stimulate investment and hence augment capacity) had been introduced in May 1974. Then there occurred the sharp increase in energy prices that has come to be known as the OPEC 1 shock. As a result of the actions of the Organization of Petroleum Exporting Countries (OPEC), petroleum prices rose over 15 per cent in 1973, and then almost 30 per cent in 1974.

Stagflation. The effects of OPEC 1 on the U.S. economy were complex. Energy was an important input in almost all U.S. production. Although the United States was an important energy producer, it was also a large net importer of energy. Thus, U.S. costs rose and aggregate supply was reduced. As a net importer of energy, the terms of trade worsened for the United States. Finally, as energy and capital were used in unison, firms began to change their production towards less energy-intensive methods – which often had the effect of reducing the productivity of capital. The United States was again reminded of the importance of foreign events to its economic well-being.

Inflation accelerated as output fell and unemployment grew. This stagflation, which seemed a total mystery then, is now understood to be the expected result of a negative supply shock. Since Canada had essentially balanced trade in oil, the direct aggregate demand effects of the oil shock should have been minimal. However, since OPEC 1 triggered a recession in the United States, it had a contractionary effect in Canada through reduced demand for Canadian exports. The Canadian economy was thus hit by stagflation – recession accompanied by rising prices stemming from the increase in energy costs.

For the first time since governments had accepted responsibility for stabilizing the economy, the direction – not simply the extent – of desirable changes in the stance of stabilization policy was at issue. Reducing the recessionary gap called for an expansionary stance; reducing inflation called for a contractionary stance. As it turned out, the policies in the two countries differed substantially.[11]

As noted above, fiscal policy in the United States had shifted to contraction in 1973. It became even more contractionary in 1974, largely as a result of the surge in tax revenues created by the rapid inflation operating to raise money incomes in the face of a progressive, non-indexed tax system. (Note the different information given by the change in the actual budget surplus and the high employment surplus, as shown in figures 5.18 and 5.20.) Then, in 1975, considerable discretionary fiscal stimulus was introduced in order to offset the severe recession that had developed. Thus, the United States had been put through a sequence of sharp stop-go changes in fiscal policy: increasing stimulus in 1970 and 1972, sharp contraction in 1973 and 1974, and then sharp stimulus again in 1975.

In Canada, primarily motivated by rising unemployment, an expansionary budget was brought down late in 1974. As a result, as figure 5.18 shows, the federal budget moved into deficit in 1975, and the deficit grew steadily through the rest of the decade. In part this reflects discretionary fiscal policy, because the structural balance also moved into substantial deficit. However, the actual deficit also reflects the influence of other factors, including more generous unemployment insurance provisions and a relatively high rate of inflation.[12]

Thus, in effect, the United States chose not to accommodate the OPEC 1 shock in 1974, whereas Canada largely accommodated it. The difference in outcomes is indicated by the paths for national income shown in figure 5.1. The United States experienced a much sharper recession but adjusted to the new higher-cost energy world more quickly. Canada's decision to delay adjustment can be at least partly explained by the strains the adjustment would have put on the federal system – although this, too, was to lead to unintended consequences far into the future.

Sluggish recovery. OPEC 1 seemed to set the tone for the 1970s. Although both economies recovered from the stagflation of 1974–75, the recovery was sluggish. Slow growth (or *slowth*) combined with persistent inflation frustrated most policy makers' expectations for the rest of the decade.

Gerald Ford succeeded Nixon in the aftermath of the Watergate scandal, and he began by attacking inflation with his WIN (whip inflation now) jawboning policy. By mid-1975, with a presidential election looming, Ford was forced to change course and focus his efforts on unemployment. The change in direction was too late to save Republican Ford, who was defeated by Democrat Jimmy Carter in 1976. Carter entered the White House with a mandate to get Americans back to work. Unfortunately, events moved too quickly for him to carry through with his original plans, and new shocks hit the economy hard later in his term. Early in the term, much of what happened could be thought of as simply the medium-term response of the American economy to the shocks and policies of the Nixon-Ford years. Both unemployment and inflation were declining to more normal levels in the early days of the Carter administration. However, further declines in the U.S. dollar began to affect the external balance, raising the price of imported goods and therefore inflation. In 1977, in keeping with the promises made during his campaign, Carter proposed income tax rebates to stimulate the economy, although these were later rescinded. By 1978, with the American economy well into recovery and inflation again rising, he proposed a set of "voluntary" guidelines on prices and wages. In addition, the payroll taxes were raised as a further restraint measure.

Monetary policy reinforced this stop-go nature of fiscal policy. In 1976 and 1977 the Federal Reserve Board pursued a mild expansionary policy, but by 1978 inflation was becoming of increasing concern and monetary policy consequently became more restrictive. International events offset the effects of these restrictive policies, and inflation continued to accelerate; as we shall soon see, this led to even stronger monetary restriction. On the international front, the revolution in Iran resulted in a large cut in oil exports and a jump in the price of oil from $12 to $32 per barrel – OPEC 2. Unfortunately, economists had still not been able to understand the lessons of the first oil shock and thus history was about to repeat itself. Increasingly worried about inflation, Carter supported the Federal Reserve Board's new chairman, Paul Volcker, who changed the Fed's "operating procedure" to one that maintained tight control of the money supply in an effort to contain inflation. The lesson that should have been learned from the Nixon-Ford years was that it is extremely costly to use demand management policies to combat supply-shock-generated inflation. Unfortunately, history did repeat itself, and Carter drove the economy into recession without having much impact on the rate of inflation. Voters judged the president's policies a failure, and Carter was replaced by Ronald Reagan in the next presidential election.

Turning to Canada, the period witnessed steady growth in output and employment, but capacity and labour force participation also grew, so that the unemployment rate and the output gap both steadily increased. While fiscal and monetary stimulus in the previous couple of years had reduced the impact of the OPEC-led recession that was afflicting most other countries, by 1975 inflation had outstripped that in other countries. As a result, Canadian policy was focused on inflation, the two major policy initiatives being the Anti-Inflation Board (AIB) and monetary gradualism.

After a failed attempt at a voluntary incomes policy, the Canadian cabinet decided in the autumn of 1975 to impose wage and price controls. The AIB was set up and given power to control wages and prices for three years. Its targets for wage increases were 10 per cent in 1976, 8 per cent in 1977, and 6 per cent in 1978. The very modest target for reduction in wage inflation in the first year was probably at or above the rate the market would have produced in any case. In 1977–78, however, the targets were reduced on schedule, and there seems little doubt that some restraint on wages was achieved, especially in the public sector. The government had found it increasingly difficult to restrain public-sector wages since the growth of unionization in that sector in the late 1960s. In the private sector, some wage restraint was also achieved, although less than in the public sector and perhaps in part in response to the public-sector slowdown.

In 1975, at about the same time as the AIB came into existence, the Bank of Canada announced a policy of "monetary gradualism," by which it meant that the rate of increase in the money supply (narrowly defined as M1) was to be reduced gradually.[13] The stated objective was to reduce the inflation rate gradually. A target range for money supply growth was to be stated publicly and to be revised downward periodically. This announcement was widely heralded as a dramatic change in practice for several reasons.

First was the emphasis on controlling monetary aggregates. Throughout the 1950s and 1960s, the Bank of Canada had used interest rates as its main intermediate target. Although in some periods there were difficulties in judging the stance of monetary policy by observing interest rates, in others the stance was clear. The so-called monetarist view was that monetary policy would perform better if it were geared to growth in the money supply, and the 1975 announcement was viewed as implicit endorsement of this view by the Bank of Canada. Second, the focus on an inflation objective suggested that the bank was starting to follow policies that made use of the monetary independence created by flexible exchange rates. (While this policy appeared to meet some of the earlier objections to the use of monetary policy under flexible exchange rates, many economists later came to the view that the actual policy was still one of a "dirty float.") Third, there was some hope that the announcement of a target growth rate for the money supply would lead to a favourable response of inflation expectations.

The first target range was set at 10 to 15 per cent growth per year. The first reduction, to a range of 8 to 12 per cent, came in August 1976. Successive steps further reduced the range; in mid-February 1981 the target range was 4 to 8 per cent. The bank was quite successful at keeping actual money growth inside the target range, although there was considerable movement within that range. At first all seemed to go well. The inflation rate measured by the CPI, excluding food, fell in successive years starting in 1975. But after some reduction during the early periods of gradualism, the inflation rate again accelerated, and by the end of the decade it was not far below the rate prevailing in the "crisis" when the policy was introduced in 1975. Had five years of gradual monetary restraint accomplished nothing? The solution to the puzzle turned out to be that changes in the public's demand for money had suddenly become a major source of economic disturbances; in particular, this meant that the restraint sought through money supply control was offset by shifts in the demand for money, many of which were caused by the very inflation the policy was attempting to curb.[14]

A series of spectacular institutional changes showed just how adaptive the financial system can be to shifts in the needs of its users (many of which were noted in Courchene 1983 and Freedman 1983). As a result of such changes, the demand for M1 balances often fell faster than the supply was being restricted. Thus, M1 control did not always create the desired conditions of tight money. Instead of a gradually tightening money supply, money was becoming more plentiful relative to demand.[15] In any event, as a result of the pressure on the Canadian dollar due to the tight monetary policy in the United States, the Bank of Canada eventually gave up on its policy of gradualism.

In summary, this episode provides valuable evidence with respect to two of our key questions. First, the different policies followed in Canada and the United States in the aftermath of OPEC 1 are strong evidence of the possibility of independent policy action. The United States chose to adjust to the energy price shock relatively quickly, whereas Canada chose a slower adjustment path. Second, while policy was undoubtedly effective, it was sometimes based on a faulty or incomplete understanding of the economic events of the day. Supply shocks were still not well understood in Canada or the United States, and this led to calls for expansionary policy, which led to higher inflation rather than real growth. In the United States, President Carter was continually reacting to current conditions rather than anticipating the future, thus demonstrating a lack of understanding of the medium-term consequences of the Nixon-Ford initiatives. In Canada, a misunderstanding of the effects of unemployment insurance reform was leading authorities to expand the economy in response to what we now know was a structural change in it. Finally, the efforts in the latter part of the period by monetary authorities in both countries to control inflation were hampered by their misunderstanding of the effects of shifts in the demand for money.

Episode 3. The Great (Policy-Induced) Recession: 1980–1982[16]

In 1980 the Federal Reserve Board (Fed) continued the Volcker-Carter policy of monetary restraint – indeed, it embarked on a policy of severe monetary restraint aimed at fighting inflation. This caused a sharp rise in interest rates, which helped choke off the recovery that had just started and then fed the downturn, helping to make it the most serious recession since the 1930s.

By January 1981, inflation in the U.S. economy had reached its peak. The CPI had grown 11.7 per cent over the previous twelve months, and the prime rate stood at 21.5 per cent. The newly elected Reagan administration began its monetary policy program with a reaffirmation of Federal Reserve Board independence and called for a steady reduction of money growth rates to one-half of their current levels by 1986. One problem for the administration (shared with fiscal authorities in Canada) was the inconsistency of the assumptions underlying its fiscal plan with its plan for monetary policy. As in Canada, nothing explicit was done to resolve the inconsistency and it was later overtaken by events.

Early on, the administration looked for ways to bind the Fed to a stable price objective. One possibility investigated by Congress was a return to the gold standard, as advocated by strict monetarists. However, after extensive study, the congressional commission recommended against a return to gold, though there was important dissenting argument published by some commission members. After this initial attempt to place constraints on Fed behaviour, a more familiar tension between the fiscal and monetary authorities emerged. As the recession deepened through 1981, the Treasury began to call for an easing of monetary policy in an effort to stimulate economic activity. Indeed, examination of the money growth data showed that the Fed had been restricting money growth even more than was required by the ambitious guidelines set out by the administration.

The debate on the appropriate stance of monetary policy was confused by two events – one institutional, the other external. On the institutional front, notice-of-withdrawal (NOW) accounts for bank deposits, which had been authorized in 1980, were causing a wave of financial innovation whose effects were difficult to predict. This undermined monetary growth rates as reliable targets for the conduct of policy. On the external front, the Mexican debt situation reached a crisis in August 1981 and the stability of the U.S. banking system was becoming a concern.

Overall restraint, and the recession it wrought, was more severe than might have been expected from the intended monetary policy. Once again, the key to the puzzle lay in the relation between the demand for money and national income. As a result of an unanticipated surge in the demand for money, there was a severe money shortage – that is, monetary policy was much tighter than the Fed had expected. This was not because money supply targets were missed; it was because money demand was again misestimated – this time, underestimated.[17]

Forced to choose between its targets and bringing an end to an already deep recession, in October 1982 the Fed formally abandoned its monetary targets. Although this was portrayed by Chairman Volcker as a small technical change without policy significance, many viewed it as the end of the monetarist experiment in the United States. To some, the monetarist experiment had been a failure because strict adherence to monetary growth targets had proved infeasible. However, significant strides had been made towards the ultimate monetarist goal – the achievement of stable prices. Through what some might view as traditional means – a deep recession – the Fed had succeeded in reducing inflation substantially. This success was to endure for the remainder of the decade, and it must be judged as one of the most important accomplishments of the Reagan years.

Of course, the interaction of monetary and fiscal policy continued to be an important factor. Reagan explicitly disavowed any role for fiscal stabilization (this, of course, proved enormously ironic as the huge fiscal deficits that emerged under Reagan clearly had strong fiscal effects) and ushered in "supply-side" economics. Supply-side economics captured the imagination of many Americans; it promised substantial reductions in taxes, which in turn would so stimulate the economy that the deficit would not increase. In the end, tax cuts and military expenditure did lead to some fiscal stimulus (as discussed below in episode 4) but they also led to record and persistent deficits. In the early part of the decade, these fiscal deficits reinforced the high interest rates and strong dollar created by the monetary restraint of the Federal Reserve Board.

Imported monetary stringency. The very tight monetary policy in the United States led to similar monetary restraint in Canada. In part this was because the high degree of integration of capital markets means that there is not very much scope for Canadian interest rates to be held far below U.S. rates. Insofar as the Bank of Canada had some freedom to hold rates below those in the United States, it did not exercise its freedom; in 1980 Canadian interest rates rose, though by less than those in the United States. The resulting interest differential attracted capital to the United States, and as a result the Canadian dollar fell from a peak of U.S. 87.0 cents in July to U.S. 82.5 cents in December. When the next round of American interest rate increases occurred in 1981, the Canadian rates rose virtually as high as their U.S. counterparts, and the dollar remained relatively stable at around U.S. 83.0 cents. While the value of the Canadian dollar fell slowly but steadily from 1982 on, it seems clear that the Bank of Canada acted to "protect the exchange rate" in order to avoid the disruption to trade and the additional inflation that would have arisen. In any case, monetary policy in Canada was tighter than it would have been in the absence of the very tight U.S. monetary policy. It is possible that, discouraged by the failure of gradualism to control inflation, the Bank of Canada welcomed the opportunity to follow the United States in a more severe bout of monetary restraint. By the early 1980s, many commentators felt that the failure of gradualism suggested that a severe jolt of very restrictive monetary policy might be necessary to suppress inflation.

The severe monetary restraint did have powerful effects on the Canadian economy – more powerful, indeed, than many economists predicted at the time. As we have already noted, interest rates soared and a severe recession occurred. Real output growth was negative throughout 1982, and by the end of that year the unemployment rate reached 12.8 per cent, its highest level since the Great Depression of the 1930s. The monetary restraint also reduced inflation – the rate of change of the CPI fell from its peak of 12.7 per cent in the third quarter of 1981 to 4.6 per cent at the end of 1983. The fall in inflation brought with it a fall in nominal interest rates; for example, the ninety-day commercial paper rate fell from a peak of just over 17 per cent in mid-1982 to 9.3 per cent by the end of 1983.[18]

During this period, activist fiscal policy was a minor element in terms of economic stabilization. Nevertheless, some major issues emerged. First, the federal budget deficit had become so large that worries were emerging about its implications. Second, the direction of desirable changes in the stance of fiscal policy was again at issue. Reducing the recessionary gap called for expansion; reducing inflation and concern about the deficit called for contraction. Successive budgets in the 1980s introduced small changes in the overall fiscal stance, being pulled one way and the other by the two competing objectives.

Third, the October 1980 budget introduced the National Energy Program, which was designed to increase the federal government's share of the revenues from petroleum production (mainly at the expense of the industry and the provincial governments) and to provide for made-in-Canada energy pricing in the face of rapidly rising world prices. One macroeconomic implication was that the monetary authorities were forced to deal with a substantial net capital outflow in 1981 and with permanently higher interest payments to foreigners.

In the budget of June 1982, the Canadian government argued that fiscal restraint was not appropriate in the face of the recession, but it tried to contribute to the disinflation process by introducing a package of controls on civil service compensation – the "six and five" program. There remains considerable disagreement over the effects of this program; some economists argue that it stiffened the resistance of private-sector firms to continued inflationary wage increases.

The 1983 budget introduced short-term measures aimed at unemployment and longer-term measures aimed at the deficit. The budget introduced moderate stimulus – about $6 billion phased in over two years – combined with a series of measures, including tax increases, to offset this stimulus later. This tilt – stimulus now, restraint later – was widely viewed as an appropriate way to stimulate the economy without increasing the future high-employment deficit. (It served as a precursor of what President-elect Bill Clinton was proposing for the United States at the end of 1992.) The budget introduced by the newly elected Conservative government in February 1984 maintained a steady course, with very little change in the stance of fiscal policy. However, the National Energy Program was dismantled by the new government in 1984.

In summary, this evidence reinforces what we learned in earlier episodes about the influence of policy. Monetary policy was indeed very effective (perhaps even more than planned) in bringing on a deep recession and thereby dampening inflation. In addition, this episode gives some valuable insights into the channels for policy transmission. While the integrated nature of North American financial markets makes it difficult for Canadian interest rates to diverge substantially from those in the United States, it may be that Canada had an additional motive for importing the high U.S. rates of the early 1980s. The decision to follow a parallel policy may have been as much to help dampen Canadian inflation as to defend the exchange rate. Arguing defence of the dollar probably allowed authorities to pursue a much tougher monetary policy than would otherwise have been politically possible.

Episode 4. Sustained Low-Inflation Recovery: 1983–1989[19]

In early 1983 a sustained recovery began in both countries. The external shocks to the American economy over this period were dwarfed by the effects of policy changes. However, the decline in raw material prices in this period had an important, positive effect on aggregate supply, thus contributing to a low-inflation recovery. The most important of these shocks was OPEC 3, which saw a massive decline in the price of oil in the aftermath of the Iran-Iraq war. However, even this was relatively unimportant when compared to the policy changes brought about by the Reagan administration.

Reagan's economic policy had three main elements: significant tax cuts, government spending reallocations, and tight money. On the tax side, the cuts proceeded in two stages. In 1981 the tax rate on interest and dividends were cut from 70 to 50 per cent. In 1986 the personal tax system was collapsed from fourteen to two brackets, with the top tax bracket falling from 50 to 28 per cent. Spending initiatives resulted in a substantial reallocation within the federal budget. Overall, severe spending cuts in civilian programs were more than offset by increases in defence spending. Attempts to control the overall deficit through legislative limits (the Gramm-Rudman-Hollings bill) proved a dismal failure.[20]

On the monetary side, the key issue was the desirability of accommodating the rapidly rising money demand resulting from growth in national income and the fall in interest rates due to the decline in inflation. This "re-entry issue" played a major role in policy debates at the time. Although the Federal Reserve Board had abandoned its commitment to control monetary aggregates in 1982 when ongoing financial market innovation rendered the targets unreliable, some economists advocated that it stick rigidly to long-range money growth targets even during the recovery period. Instead of doing this, the Fed largely accommodated the major increases in the demand for money that occurred. Most economists now agree that if it had chosen not to accommodate the increased demand for money that arose during the recovery, it would have put contractionary pressure on the economy, thereby slowing the recovery or even stopping it altogether.

Through 1987, the Fed's policies had desirable results and received broad support. National income rose steadily and inflation stayed below 4 per cent. However, concern about rising inflation started to emerge in the latter part of the decade. In 1987 the new Fed chairman, Alan Greenspan, signalled his concern about the potential for a resurgence of inflation and indicated that monetary policy would be tightened as necessary. These words were backed up with a gradual tightening of policy as the rate of growth of monetary aggregates fell, and some increase in interest rates was experienced.

On 19 October 1987 the stock market fell dramatically. While no single factor can be identified as the cause, many commentators have argued that a downward revision of expectations about future economic growth in the face of a tighter monetary policy contributed to it. Many commentators also felt that the reduction in household wealth arising from the market crash, combined with rising interest rates, would serve to slow the economy down. However, throughout 1988 and early in 1989 growth remained strong and inflationary pressures continued to build; the stock market crash had a smaller effect on the economy than expected. In part, this may have been because of the strong infusion of liquidity into the economy by the Fed immediately after the crash.

After the "blip" in response to the stock market crash, monetary policy continued to tighten gradually, but by mid-1989 the question remained whether, in terms of containing inflation, this was a case of "too little, too late." Could sustained growth with steady moderate inflation be maintained, or would inflation continue to grow, eventually evoking stronger monetary restraint which would risk throwing the economy into another policy-induced recession?

The effectiveness of the Reagan policies is still the subject of hot debate. After a deep and prolonged recession, the United States enjoyed unbroken expansion for over eight years. Inflation fell from above 9 per cent to only 2 per cent at its lowest point, and was at only 4 per cent in 1988. While some of the expansion was financed by increased private spending resulting from tax cuts, the other promise of supply-side economics failed to materialize. Federal deficits mounted to unprecedented levels, with the debt-GNP ratio rising from less than 35 per cent to almost 55 per cent. High U.S. interest rates attracted the necessary foreign capital to finance the spending binge, and America went from being the world's largest creditor to its largest debtor.

Tax cuts and spending changes had important effects on the distribution of wealth in the United States. While the economy expanded and inflation remained low, unemployment remained high by historical standards throughout the Reagan years. Critics argue that the distribution of income increasingly favoured the rich. Much of the prosperity came from bond-financed government deficits. At the same time, national infrastructure was allowed to deteriorate so that now the United States faces a massive bill to make up for the deferred spending.

The U.S. tax cuts had an impact in Canada beyond their effect on the macroeconomy. After the U.S. changes, Canada substantially shifted from taxation of a relatively mobile tax base – corporate income – to less mobile bases such as personal income and especially consumption. Some economists argue that these Canadian moves reflected the differing abilities of alternative tax bases to relocate to avoid tax.[21] Canada shared in the U.S. recovery, and by mid-1987 national income had moved back towards its potential. Much of the growth was centred in the export-oriented manufacturing industries in Ontario and Quebec. Although painfully slow for those who remained unemployed, the first four years of the recovery saw a record 890,000 jobs created and cumulative output growth of 15.7 per cent.

The main challenge for monetary policy in this period was to create sufficient liquidity to accommodate the recovery without triggering a return to the high inflation rates that had prevailed at the start of the decade.[22] Thus, the Bank of Canada faced the same re-entry problem as the Fed; the combination of falling nominal interest rates and rising national income led to a sharp increase in the demand for real money balances. Since an increase in real balances can be achieved either by slow growth in the price level or by a rapid increase in the nominal money supply, the Bank of Canada had two options. It could continue its policy of maintaining a low growth rate of the nominal money supply; this would restrain aggregate demand and thus guard against the risk of a resurgence of inflation, but at the cost of slowing the pace of the recovery. Alternatively, the bank could allow a short but rapid burst of growth in the nominal money supply, thus generating the desired increase in real money balances. Once the new level of real balances was achieved, money growth could again be cut back to a rate consistent with low inflation, allowing for the underlying rate of growth in real income. But the trick with this policy was to avoid triggering expectations of renewed inflation. Essentially, the bank had to generate a one-shot increase in the level of the money supply without creating the impression that it was raising the rate of growth of the money supply.[23]

Most economists agreed that the second policy was preferable in principle, but there was wide disagreement over the size and duration of the required monetary expansion and hence whether the bank's actual policy was appropriate. In late 1983 and early 1984, when growth in monetary aggregates first started to surge, many voiced the fear that the Bank of Canada was being overly expansionary and was risking a return to higher inflation. As the re-entry problem came to be more widely understood and as inflation pressures failed to re-emerge, these criticisms subsided and the consensus appeared to be that the bank had done a commendable job of handling the re-entry problem.[24]

Critics have suggested that the bank was too cautious in expanding liquidity during the re-entry problem. Howitt (1986) claims that excessive caution by the bank caused the recovery to be slower than necessary. He argues that the bank erred in focusing almost exclusively on the narrowly defined money supply. The declines in interest rates had caused a substitution of interest-bearing deposits for demand deposits, hence the demand for M1 grew rapidly. The demand for broader money aggregates did not grow nearly as fast since the broader aggregates include both demand deposits (which were growing) and interest-bearing deposits (which were falling). If the bank had focused more on a broader aggregate, the argument goes, it would have seen that the relevant rate of monetary expansion was not excessive.

It is true that Canadian monetary expansion was slower during this period than American monetary expansion, but it is also true that inflation fell more slowly in Canada than in the United States. If the Bank of Canada did err in following a monetary policy that was too tight, it was probably because of a commitment not to relax monetary restraint before inflation had unquestionably fallen to the lower, more acceptable range that the bank was striving for.

Whatever the judgment of monetary policy in that period, many observers began to worry that Canadian policy makers had become too complacent in accepting the 4 per cent range into which Canadian inflation seemed to have settled.[25] In 1987 the question of whether monetary policy should be tightened in order to lower inflation even further was widely debated. Some economists argued that if that was not done, Canada would experience gradually increasing inflation until once again a severe monetary restriction would be necessary.

In summary, both countries had some scope for independent policy in that they diverged substantially from European countries and, as a result, experienced wide variations in their exchange rates vis-à-vis European currencies. Some U.S. policy was transmitted to Canada in that Canada was forced to reduce its reliance on corporate income tax and increase its reliance on personal income and consumption taxes to maintain tax competitiveness with the United States. Canada did not, however, follow the United States in its pursuit of supply-side economics, yet it did not forgo the long expansion of the 1980s – although some of that prosperity undoubtedly came from U.S. demand for Canadian goods. Finally, in contrast to the mistakes of earlier episodes, monetary authorities in both countries seemed to have effectively negotiated the difficult re-entry problem as nominal interest rates fell and the demand for monetary balances grew.

Episode 5. Recession and Global Restructuring: 1990–1992[26]

In the United States, the beginning of the 1990s showed signs that the longest peacetime expansion was coming to an end. However, the threat and then the reality of war with Iraq gave the economy a jolt that kept recession temporarily at bay. Nevertheless, in the aftermath of decisive victory over Iraq, the U.S. economy slid into recession.

American authorities were slow to react to the signs of recession. On the fiscal side, the government was hampered by the size of the federal deficit and debt, and thus had little expansionary room in which to manoeuvre. On the monetary side, the Federal Reserve Board presided over a dramatic decline in short-term interest rates. Without a change in the inflation outlook, this meant a relatively steep yield curve. Pessimism about the economy and the steep yield curve combined to inhibit investment and dash hopes of a quick recovery. The political timing was unfortunate for George Bush and ultimately contributed significantly to his defeat at the polls in 1992.

Through the end of the 1980s, Canadian fiscal authorities had followed a substantially different course from their American counterparts. In attempting to control and ultimately reduce the deficit, Canadian federal authorities had used a two-pronged attack. The first line of attack was to reduce the growth of program spending – including a substantial reduction in transfers to provincial governments. The second was to increase taxation substantially, especially through indirect taxes. The timing of these tax changes was to have a significant effect on the macroeconomy in the early 1990s.

Unfortunately, this attempt to control the deficit was frustrated by the actions of the monetary authorities. In a significant show of independence from U.S. influences, the central bank aggressively began to pursue a restrictive policy in a campaign to achieve price stability. One side effect of this campaign was substantially higher interest rates, which in turn, given the size and maturity structure of the federal debt, translated into large increases in debt-service charges on the federal budget. A second side effect of the Bank of Canada's campaign for price stability was the increase in the differential between Canadian and U.S. short-term interest rates, which led to a sharp rise in the value of the Canadian dollar. Departing from the past, the bank seemed unconcerned about this rise – indeed, it contributed to the fight against inflation. However, it also reduced exports and economic activity in Canada and helped set the stage for a prolonged and deep recession.

The combination of three domestic policy events contributed to the "made-in-Canada" recession of the early 1990s. First, the aggressive pursuit of price stability by the monetary authorities raised interest rates and the value of the Canadian dollar. Second, Canadian manufacturing was in the midst of restructuring to adapt to the new world of free trade with the United States. In this environment, the timing of the rise in the value of the dollar was viewed by many as particularly unfortunate. Finally, as part of its general thrust of increasing taxation, the government introduced the goods and services tax (GST) in 1991 as a replacement for the manufacturers' sales tax (MST). The MST was becoming increasingly difficult to collect, since successive rate increases had given large firms the incentive to find legal means to avoid the tax. The new, more productive consumption tax was essentially a supply shock which further restrained output and raised prices.

By late 1992, the Canadian economy was beginning to show signs of recovery from the recession brought on by these policy decisions. The

Canadian downturn was exacerbated when the United States slid into its considerably milder recession. With the rate of inflation still below target levels, monetary authorities reduced interest rates substantially and the Canadian dollar declined by more than ten cents. Indeed, the speed of the dollar's decline caused a temporary rise in rates to restore some order to the foreign exchange market. However, the rapid decline in the dollar and corresponding relative inaction by authorities confirms the bank's new-found independence in the 1990s.

In summary, this episode gives additional evidence of the scope for independent policy, at least on the monetary side, and its effectiveness. Although growing debts and corresponding interest payments have reduced the ability of the authorities to use fiscal policy to stabilize the economy, monetary policy remains a potent tool. In Canada, this tool was effectively used to reach the Bank of Canada's medium-term inflation target – albeit at the cost of a deep recession. As interest payments have grown as a share of government spending, a new policy interdependence has appeared – the link between monetary and fiscal policy. As we have seen, Canadian monetary authorities frustrated the government's efforts to reduce the deficit by raising interest rates (and therefore public debt charges) as part of its anti-inflation battle. Given the size of public debt in both countries, this new interdependence will likely play a prominent role in the remainder of the 1990s.

LESSONS FROM THE CANADA–U.S. MACROECONOMIES

In this final section we summarize what we have learned about our three key questions from the two decades we have examined. We discuss some of the general lessons to be learned from this period and what they might mean for Canadian and U.S. macroeconomic policy in the second half of the 1990s.

Policy Independence

The first key question of the introduction was whether in an increasingly interdependent global economy it was possible for countries (especially a small country like Canada) to pursue independent macroeconomic policies. The evidence from the two decades we have studied suggests that while Canada and the United States felt substantial effects from foreign shocks (and Canada from U.S. shocks), in general it was possible for them to pursue independent policies. We saw this on the fiscal side with the American attempts to manage the political business cycle and with the Canadian move towards zero inflation in the late 1980s. Policy independence was also demonstrated on the regulatory front, with the different reactions in the two countries to the OPEC price shocks – where the United States chose a fast adjustment path (and corresponding recession) while Canada chose a very gradual adjustment.

The scope for pursuing independent policy, however, is not unlimited. As globalization continues and new economic powers emerge, the need to remain competitive is shaping policy in the United States and Canada. Agricultural subsidies and their effects on government budgets and the macroeconomy are an obvious example. The efforts to reduce trade barriers through negotiation, first of the Canada – U.S. Free Trade Agreement and then of the North American Free Trade Agreement, are further indications of the struggle to protect competitive positions. In our review of the past two decades, we have been reminded repeatedly of the macroeconomic costs of having diverging policies, and governments must be willing to bear them if policy independence is to be exercised. The most telling example of this point comes from Canada throughout much of the period. Despite the opportunities to insulate Canada from American inflationary shocks, the Canadian authorities chose to import monetary ease because they were unwilling to bear the cost of large swings in the exchange rate. In reality, the authorities' efforts to stabilize the exchange rate meant that U.S. monetary policy was imported to Canada. Freedom of action in an interdependent world carries a cost.

Policy Transmission

The second key question we asked was how policies are transmitted between countries. In the course of our examination of this period, we were able to identify four different channels or mechanisms that lead to similar policies across countries. The first channel is the traditional one that stems from the high and increasing degree of integration of the Canadian and U.S. economies, both in trade and financial markets. An obvious example of this link is seen in the transmission of the monetary tightness from the United States to Canada in the early 1980s. Given the high degree of substitutability between Canadian and U.S. government bonds, it would have been very costly (in terms of exchange rate fluctuations) for Canada to try and maintain lower interest rates when the United States was attempting to engineer a sharp recession in order to break inflationary expectations.

A second, related channel comes when countries have similar policy goals. Continuing with the same example of monetary policy in the early 1980s, as we argued above, it was convenient for Canadian monetary authorities to raise interest rates sharply in tandem with the United States, given the failure of monetary gradualism in the late 1970s. Indeed, the rise in U.S. rates and the need to protect the dollar gave Canadian authorities additional latitude to implement a tougher policy than would otherwise have been politically feasible.

A third transmission mechanism concerns the need to maintain international competitiveness. This was clearly shown when Canada followed the U.S. lead in reducing its reliance on corporate tax revenue in the latter part of the 1980s. While it might have been part of the political agenda of the Canadian government of the day, clearly the need to remain attractive to mobile transnational firms was a driving force behind the parallel policy. This occurred at a time when the Canadian government was attempting to reduce its deficit and (unlike the United States) was substantially raising the tax burden on individuals through higher income and consumption taxes.

A final cause of parallel policy which should not be overlooked is the reaction by countries to common external shocks. For example, while fiscal authorities in Canada and the United States reacted differently to the OPEC price shocks, the inflation generated by these shocks later set up similar monetary policy in the two countries through the channels we have discussed. Thus, different countries may run parallel policies simply because they are using similar tools in attempting to counteract a common external shock.

Policy Influence

The final key question of the introduction was whether national macroeconomic policy could be influential in the increasingly integrated global economy. The period we studied gives strong evidence that macroeconomic policy can still have important effects. The management of the political business cycle in the United States, the effectiveness of monetary policy in breaking inflationary expectations in the early 1980s, and the move to zero inflation in Canada at the end of that decade all point to the significant impact that macroeconomic policy can have.

If the impact of policy is not in question, there remains considerable doubt about its effectiveness. We saw that attempts to manage the political business cycle in the United States were often thwarted by imprecise timing – in part perhaps because of the lags and uncertainty involved in the congressional system. In any case, this short-term policy almost always resulted in unintended consequences for the medium term and added significantly to macroeconomic volatility. As we argued above, over a substantial portion of the period, policy was based on a faulty understanding of the workings of the macroeconomy. Examples are found in the responses to supply shocks and the effects of unemployment insurance reform. Indeed, many would argue that the United States' (and, to a less extent, Canada's) prosperity of the 1980s was purchased only at the cost of lower living standards in the 1990s and beyond.

In addition to traditional macroeconomic policy, there were significant changes in regulatory regimes in both countries. While some proved ineffective or had only a temporary impact (for example, the WIN program in the United States and the AIB in Canada), some had a significant impact. An example of an inappropriate regulatory policy that had a significant impact is Canada's National Energy Program.

Institutional factors have sometimes constrained the effectiveness of policy. For example, the demands of the election cycle on governments has sometimes led to inappropriate policy – especially in the United States. In part this may be because the congressional system imposes unacceptable delays on short-run policy so that fiscal initiatives aimed at fine tuning are often too late to be effective. In Canada, it is clear that the federal system with strong provinces and geographically concentrated energy resources caused Canada to delay its adjustment to the OPEC shocks, and it thus became less competitive in the new, higher-cost energy world economy.

Policy is also circumscribed by a relatively new, internal constraint – the growing interdependence of fiscal and monetary policy as public debt grows. The conflict between monetary and fiscal policy in Canada in the late 1980s provides a good example of the problem. Government efforts to reduce deficits were frustrated by the monetary authorities' anti-inflation program. Higher interest rates to reduce inflation raised borrowing costs and thus government deficits. Monetary policy was the clear winner in this contest, while government and the macroeconomy were the obvious losers.

Interestingly, given its demonstrated potency, Canadian monetary policy had been turned away from short-run macroeconomic stabilization. Instead, it focused firmly on the medium-term goal of price stability – even when this had undesirable short-run effects, such as the deep recession that Canada seems at last to be escaping. In contrast, given the debt situation faced by governments on both sides of the border, the scope for fiscal stabilization is probably now limited to dealing with the medium-term issue of debt control and sustainability.

Looking Ahead

With these answers to our three key questions, what can we say about the future of macroeconomic policy in Canada and the United States? First, it is clear that macro policy should be focused on medium-term rather than short-term objectives. Experience shows that while efforts at short-run stabilization have significant effects, these effects are rarely timely or even intended. On the fiscal side, the size of government debt in Canada and the United States means that policy will be focused on the medium-term goal of stabilizing the share of the economy's overall resources going to government. Important fiscal policy in the latter half of the 1990s will be focused on the size and role of government. The removal of fiscal policy (apart from its automatic stabilizers) from the arsenal of short-term policy tools is not a great loss, given how poorly it has worked in this area in the past. In the 1990s we expect fiscal policy to be practised more at the microeconomic level – on such matters as how to enhance competitiveness with other jurisdictions, how to control or reduce the costs of providing government services, and so on.

On the monetary side, we learned from our 1970s experience that gradualism does not work. The 1980s showed that monetary contractions must be severe and prolonged if inflationary expectations are to be altered. Given the costliness of these contractions, measures to prevent the buildup of inflationary pressures seem well worth the effort. Monetary policy, at least in Canada, is already focused on the medium term. The late 1980s saw Canada's first significant assertion of monetary independence in the last twenty years. The 1990s will show whether the benefits of price stability were worth the deep recession needed to achieve it. To date, there has been little pressure from U.S. economic conditions to alter the policy of price stability. However, should the United States choose to stimulate its economy with monetary policy, Canada will again have to calculate whether the costs of an independent policy outweigh the benefits.

Our experience of the 1970s and 1980s has shown us that macroeconomic policy remains a potent tool even as the world economy becomes more integrated. However, we also learned that it is an unwieldy tool for stabilizing national economies in the short run and thus is better aimed at achieving more modest, medium- and long-term objectives. Finally, we saw that although the potential for independent policy exists, the integrated nature of the world economy means that exercising the option for such a policy will sometimes have significant costs – and those costs will have to be calculated and weighed as we develop macroeconomic policy in the future.

APPENDIX

5.1   Canadian real GDP, CANSIM D20463, 1986$ converted to 1985$ using current GDP dollar, CANSIM D20000

5.2   U.S. real GDP, CITIBASE GDPQ, 1987$ converted to 1985$ using current dollar GDP, CITIBASE GDP

5.3   Annual growth rates of GDP, difference/lag

5.4   Canada unemployment rate, CANSIM D767611, all workers 15+; U.S. unemployment rate, CITIBASE LHUR, all workers 16+

5.5   Canada CPI, all items, CANSIM P490000; U.S., CPI, all items, CITIBASE PNUEW

5.6   Annual percentage change of CPI

5.7   Canada, current account, CANSUM D72002; U.S., current account, CITIBASE BPCR

5.8   Gross national accumulation is business investment and current account; current account is same source as figure 5.7; Canada business investment, national income and expenditure accounts, Statistics Canada, from GDP tables "Total Business Investment"; U.S. business investment, *Survey of Current Business,* GDP tables

5.9   Canada treasury bills – 3mo, *Bank of Canada Review;* U.S. treasury bills – 3 mo, CITIBASE FYGN3

5.10 Canadian–U.S. exchange rate, CANSIM B3400

5.11 Canadian and U.S. trade-weighted exchange, international financial statistics rate, nominal effective exchange rate

5.12 Canadian and U.S. unit labour costs, OECD main economic indicators, Canadian observations converted to U.S.$ basis using an exchange index calculated from the exchange rate

5.13 Canada productivity, Economic Reference tables (Aug. 1992), Department of Finance, table 37, "Output per Person-Hour"; U.S. productivity, U.S. *Statistical Abstract* (selected years), output per person hour

5.14 Canada M1, CANSIM B2033; U.S. M1, CITIBASE FZM1

5.15 Canada M2, CANSIM B2031; U.S. M2, CITIBASE FZMS2

5.16 Canada federal government deficit, Economic Reference tables (Aug. 1992), Department of Finance, table 52, "Government Deficit or Surplus"; U.S. Federal Government Deficit, *Survey of Current Business*

5.17 Canada consolidated government deficit, Economic Reference tables (Aug. 1992), Department of Finance, table 64, "Total Government Actual"; U.S. consolidated government deficit, *Survey of Current Business*

5.18 Same source as figure 5.16

5.19 Canada consolidated government deficit, Economic Reference tables (Aug. 1992), Department of Finance, table 64, "Total Government Actual"; U.S. consolidated government deficit, *Survey of Current Business*

5.20 Canada cyclically adjusted deficit, Economic Reference tables (Aug. 1992), Department of Finance, table 64, "Federal Government, Cyclically Adjusted"; U.S. cyclically adjusted deficit, Bureau of Economic Analysis

5.21 Canada central government debt, CANSIM D469409; U.S. central government debt, *Survey of Current Business*

Note: Data in figures 5.16 to 5.21 are normalized by nominal GDP.

6 Industrial Policy in Canada and the United States

ROBERT HOWSE AND
MARSHA CHANDLER

INTRODUCTION

The view that governments should act to encourage economic growth, enhance the living standards of citizens, and protect workers is deeply entrenched in both the United States and Canada. Macroeconomic policy, as discussed in the previous chapter, seeks to influence the economy by setting the broad monetary and fiscal context within which businesses, investors, and workers operate. Industrial policy, by contrast, seeks to shape economic growth and competitiveness more directly. It is the self-conscious effort to use government policy to create or restore the competitive advantage of particular sectors, industries, or firms – or, alternatively, to shelter firms and their workers from threatening economic changes. Traditionally, industrial policy was seen as operating through a narrow range of instruments, such as subsidies or trade restrictions that were clearly targeted towards alteration of comparative advantage in specific industries. However, on both sides of the border, such direct instruments have been receding, and the conception of industrial policy is being expanded to encompass a wide range of policies that effect the economic competitiveness of a nation, including framework policies, research and development, education and training, infrastructure, and quality of life.

Similarly, there is a continuing political struggle in both Canada and the United States to define the basic purposes of industrial policy. All industrial policies, by definition, involve attempts to alter market outcomes. However, there is an important distinction between industrial policies that seek to resist or block changes in comparative advantage or to protect against the impact of market forces, and those that seek to enhance or preserve competitiveness in the light of, or in anticipation of, changing global market conditions. Examples of the former kind of policy are subsidies or trade restrictions aimed at preserving the domestic markets of industries under threat from low-wage competitors in South Asia. Examples of a market-facilitating policy are training and retraining programs to shift human resources from sectors in which a country has lost comparative advantage to other industries where local firms have more potential to be competitive internationally. Understandably, while market-resisting policies focus largely (or, in many cases, exclusively) on protecting the domestic market, market-facilitating policies are also preoccupied with the capture or recapture of export markets.

The discourse of industrial policy in Canada and the United States increasingly shares the language of high technology, human capital, and market facilitiation. The Clinton administration has seized on technology and science as the fundamental building blocks for restoring the United States' competitive position in the international marketplace while maintaining high wage levels. In *Technology for America's Economic Growth: A New Direction to Build Economic Strength*, a report issued in February 1993, the administration identifies three goals as being critical for U.S. success in the new global marketplace: economic growth that creates jobs and protects the environment; more productive and responsive government; and world leadership in basic science, mathematics, and engineering (U.S. Office of the President 1993, 3). Similarly, the Chrétien government's "Red Book," which set out the Liberals' 1993 election platform, speaks of the need to create a technologically advanced and innovative economy by forming technology networks among universities and industry associations, by strengthening research and development, and by expanding assistance for the funding of basic research (Liberal Party 1993).

Both governments emphasize investment in human capital as an integral part of restoring their nation's comparative advantage. Increased training and other labour market reforms, with a view to building a more flexible and responsive workforce, are seen as the primary means by which a high-skill, high-wage economy is to be created. As a result, both the Chrétien and Clinton governments have outlined a number of policy prescriptions designed to move the workforce in this direction. Both have also stressed the need to rebuild and enhance the national infrastructure, especially in communication technologies.

This chapters explores the patterns of convergence and divergence in the broad approach to industrial policy in Canada and the United

States. It argues that, traditionally, Canadian governments at both federal and provincial levels have undertaken more explicit and wide-ranging attempts to shape their economy and have utilized a wider range of policy instruments than American governments. However, in recent years, there has been a strong convergence between the two countries. This convergence has come from two different directions. On the one hand, U.S. policy makers, increasingly concerned with maintaining their competitiveness in a more globally competitive world, have begun to pay somewhat more attention to industrial policy. On the other hand, the faith of Canadian governments' in the efficacy of traditional industrial policies, and in their capacity to achieve these policies, has declined. Industrial policies in the two countries are therefore increasingly alike, both in the objectives they pursue and in the instruments they use. To be sure, different cultural traditions, institutional frameworks, and policy legacies sustain important differences in strategy and detail. Nevertheless, in the industrial policy sector, the most powerful trend has been convergence between these North American nations.

The chapter is organized as follows. The first section explores the implications of globalization for industrial policy, underlining the differences and similarities of the two countries in their location within the global marketplace, and the tightening links between trade policy and industrial policy. The next two sections review the basic instruments of industrial policy, starting with both countries' use of traditional instruments such as public ownership, subsidies, and defence procurement, and then moving on to the more recent emphasis on instruments such as research and technology, framework policies, social programs, human capital, and new forms of partnership. The final section summarizes the extent of convergence and divergence in the industrial policies of Canada and the United States, and looks at some possible explanations for the patterns that have emerged.

INDUSTRIAL POLICY AND THE CHALLENGES OF GLOBALIZATION

Globalization is profoundly reshaping the context within which economic policy is shaped, with powerful implications for the purposes and instruments of industrial policy. Globalization actually has contradictory implications for industrial policy. On one hand, it creates greater incentives to engage in industrial policy; on the other hand, it constrains the instruments through which industrial policy has traditionally been implemented and diverts attention to newer instruments that remain more firmly under the control of nations.

Globalization is also leading to greater convergence in debates over industrial policy in Canada and the United States. Given that industrial policy is essentially concerned with responding to changes in comparative advantage, it is not surprising that interest in industrial policy is often a function of a country's vulnerability to or dependence on global markets. Historically, the contrast between Canada and the United States on this dimension was dramatic, with the Canadian economy characterized by far greater export dependency and import penetration. In 1970, for example, Canada had an import-penetration rate more than five times that of the United States with respect to manufactured goods. This difference, however, is narrowing. By 1985, the flow of imports into the United States had greatly increased, with the result that the Canadian rate was now only three times the U.S. figure (Hatzichronoglou 1991, 191). Indeed, increased competition from third countries has reduced the U.S. share of world manufacturing exports more than that of Canada. Between 1975 and 1987, the U.S. share of total exports by the G7 countries declined from 25.7 to 23.0 per cent, while the Canadian share actually increased from 5.5 to 6.9 per cent.[1] Canada and Japan were the only countries among this group to improve their share of world manufacturing exports significantly during a period of more intense trade competition (ibid., 189). A similar conclusion flows from a wider perspective. For example, the Canadian share of the exports of all countries in the United Nations remained between 4 and 5 per cent from 1950 to 1989, a period during which the U.S. share declined from 18 to 14 per cent (Porter and Monitor Co. 1991). While major differences obviously remain, the United States has begun to feel more strongly the opportunities and challenges of trade dependency long experienced by Canadians.

There has also been some convergence with respect to investment flows. Traditionally, Canada has been a large net recipient of foreign direct investment, largely from the United States (Rugman 1990). By contrast, the United States relied less on foreign direct investment throughout most of this century. However, this has radically changed over the last decade. For example, direct foreign investment in the United States totalled some $56 billion between 1971 and 1981; between 1981 and 1989 the figure was close to $307 billion (OECD 1991a, table 2). Indeed, the U.S. share of total foreign direct investment in OECD countries increased from 13.1 per cent in the 1961–71 period to over 50 per cent in the 1981–88 period, while Canada's share increased from 7.4 to 23.0 per cent (Knubley, Krause, and Sadeque 1991, 26). The outward flow of investment is also more similar than in the past. Canadian firms have significantly increased their foreign direct investment abroad (ibid., 24–32). Between 1975 and 1985,

Canadian outward investment increased from 6.3 to 10.5 per cent of GDP. American outward flows, by contrast, have tended to taper off over the last couple of decades in particular, declining from 8.1 per cent of GNP in 1975 to 6.4 per cent in 1985 (United Nations Centre on Transnational Corporations 1988).

In sum, there has been a significant convergence between Canada and the United States in terms of their dependence on global trade and investment, mostly produced by the increase of U.S. reliance on global markets. This change is the prime mover behind the increased American debate over industrial policy and is a source of growing convergence in the nature of the policy agenda in the two countries.

If globalization has increased the incentives to engage in industrial policy, however, it has also constrained many traditional instruments through which it has been practised, and has shifted much of the pressure to trade policy. Historically, for both countries but especially for Canada, the tariff behind which domestic industry could grow was the most important industrial policy of all. In the postwar period, however, both countries – building on their strengths as the economies most unscathed by the ravages of war – adopted freer international trade as their primary tool for growth. The United States was the major force behind the establishment of an open global trading system through the founding of the General Agreement on Tariffs and Trade (GATT), which succeeded through several rounds of negotiations in achieving significant reductions in tariffs, beginning in the 1950s and culminating with the signing of the Uruguay Round and the establishment of the World Trade Organization (WTO) in 1994. Canada strongly supported multilateral trade liberalization in the GATT. In addition, Canada and the United States joined the trend towards regional trading blocks in Europe, North America, and potentially Asia. The Canada – U.S. Free Trade Agreement (FTA) and the North American Free Trade Agreement (NAFTA) lowered remaining tariffs and locked Canada and the United States into an ever closer trading relationship.

The GATT and NAFTA both contain legal constraints on a variety of industrial policy instruments. Most clearly constrained are new trade protection measures, which are permitted only in very exceptional circumstances, as in the case of temporary withdrawal of tariff concessions where an industry faces serious injury from a sudden upsurge of imports.[2] GATT illegality has, however, not prevented the United States from deploying a variety of unilateral trade restrictions, such as quotas and voluntary export restraints, in a number of sensitive sectors, including automobiles and steel. Domestic subsidies are not explicitly prohibited under the GATT, the FTA, or NAFTA. However, all three agreements permit countervailing duties to be imposed against the subsidies of other countries, provided certain procedural and substantive conditions are met. Although a principal Canadian negotiating objective with respect to the FTA was to discipline the American countervailing of Canadian industrial policies as illegal subsidies under domestic U.S. trade law, no substantive constraints on countervail were achieved in the FTA. A bilateral panel process was entrenched in the FTA whereby decisions of an FTA partner's domestic trade authorities with respect to countervailing duties would be subject to review at the binational level. That review, however, is limited to egregious errors such as bias or the incorrect application of a country's own domestic trade law. This being said, Canada won a number of early challenges to countervail decisions of American trade authorities (Boddez and Trebilcock 1993).

Some industrial policy measures that place limits on foreign investment (for example, domestic sourcing requirements as a condition for approval of investment inflows) have been found in violation of the GATT/WTO accords, and a very wide range of investment measures that discriminate against the interests of other parties are proscribed by the FTA and NAFTA (Trebilcock and Howse 1995; Gestrin and Rugman 1993). As well, these two agreements constrain a range of other potential industrial policy tools, such as domestic ownership requirements for, and some forms of regulatory control over, financial services industries. Some preferential government procurement policies are also proscribed.

Both the ideological left and right in Canada have probably exaggerated the actual impact of these legal constraints on industrial policy. The left has done so in order to claim that the agreements constitute a fundamental surrender of policy sovereignty for Canada; the right has done so in order to argue against activist policies that it opposes anyway, but that it now opposes on grounds that they are, or will soon become, illegal. A more plausible analysis is that of Coyne (1993, 62), who claims that the United States, at least, has always been able to work around constraints in international legal agreements to achieve whatever policies are dictated by domestic interests, and that Canada should do the same with respect to NAFTA. There are, in fact, probably enough loopholes and exceptions in both the FTA and NAFTA to allow the pursuit of a wide variety of industrial policies without effective legal challenge. However, Canada may have less scope to work around the rules than the United States because of its greater vulnerability to retaliation through U.S. trade remedy law and because of its general reliance on the rule of law to protect it from aggressive U.S. unilateralism.

Viewing trade agreements simply as constraints on traditional instruments of industrial policy is, however, a too narrow perspective. It ignores another important dimension of globalization that creates pressures for regulatory harmonization. Market access is conceived not simply in terms of the removal of domestic policies that represent non-tariff barriers, but also in terms of standards for domestic regulation that have implications for trade. Trade policy becomes an industrial policy in the sense that countries press for harmonized standards or rules in areas of traditionally domestic regulation that maximize the competitive advantage of their industries.

Perhaps the clearest example of this use of trade policy as industrial policy is to be found in the U.S.-driven negotiation of agreements in the Uruguay Round on intellectual property and on trade in services. The U.S. insistence on minimum standards for protection of intellectual property rights, with these "minima" closely resembling existing U.S. regulation, came from recognition of the importance of such protection for American access to developing and newly industrialized markets. Similarly, in the negotiations on services, the United States sought to obtain substantial commitments from other countries to change their domestic regulations so as to increase market access for U.S. service industries such as insurance and telecommunications. Likewise, recognition of the importance of investment as a means of access to foreign markets in certain sectors has led the United States to spearhead an initiative to negotiate within the OECD a detailed investment code that would go much farther than the agreement on investment in the Uruguay Round (Trebilcock and Howse 1995).

The much greater negotiating power of the United States in most forums, combined with its greater ability to threaten effective unilateral action as leverage to induce countries to put domestic policies on the negotiating table, means that the United States is much more able than Canada to use trade policy as industrial policy in this way. However, in multilateral forums such as the GATT/WTO, the United States has still had to compromise domestic interests to a certain degree as a price for consensus. This has led to a renewed interest in regional trade pacts, in which the United States can wield more decisive hegemonic power. From this perspective, the embrace of regionalism by Canadian trade policy elites – as well, to some extent, by governments – seems perverse, since in the larger, genuinely multilateral forums there would seem to be a greater chance of diluting U.S. hegemonic power and of forming coalitions with other powers whose domestic interests are similar to Canada's. This is especially so since Canada's strong human capital in technical and negotiating expertise, as well as its credibility as a multilateral player, give it an influence disproportionate to its size in multilateral forums.

Globalization has thus transformed the world of industrial policy. The increased sensitivity of all countries to the international economy has produced considerable convergence in the agenda facing policy makers, including Canada and the United States. But globalization has also altered the relative effectiveness of different instruments of industrial policy. Trade and trade-related policy remain an important tool for promoting, or protecting, the interests of domestic industry in the global environment. But international rules have become an important constraint on many traditional approaches to domestic industrial policy and have helped shift the focus to policies that previously were not considered part of the industrial policy debate.

TRADITIONAL INSTRUMENTS
OF INDUSTRIAL POLICY

To explore this transformation in industrial policy in greater detail, this section turns more directly to domestic policies, beginning with the tried if not necessarily true tools traditionally employed by governments.

Public Enterprise

Traditionally, one of the most striking differences between Canada and the United States has been the extent of reliance on government-owned enterprises. North of the border, Crown corporations played a central role in the economic development of Canada and represented a tool through which federal and provincial governments could influence the nature, extent, and location of economic activity. Historically, public enterprise was most important in such sectors as transportation, energy, and communications. In the 1970s and 1980s, however, the public role expanded to include facilitating private-sector development through equity investment as opposed to direct ownership of productive assets. The Canadian Development Corporation and the Export Development Corporation are the leading exemplars of this new wave of Crown corporations (Laux and Molot 1988). Although Crown corporations never created the kind of links between the public and private sectors often associated with the mixed industrial economies of Western Europe, they have been a significant tool of industrial policy in Canada.

South of the border, by contrast, government ownership of business enterprise has always been marginal to American economic history. This may in large part be attributed to ideological factors, especially the identification of public ownership with socialism and the notion that private ownership of productive assets is one of the clear dividing lines between state and market, necessary to preserve economic and perhaps political liberty (Nedelsky 1991, ch. 6; Lodge 1987). Even under the

New Deal, federal government activism was seldom channelled through direct public ownership of going concerns; more often it was done through intermediate institutions that relied significantly on private companies to achieve public purposes.

The difference in the role of public enterprise in the two countries peaked in the late 1970s. At that point, public enterprises in Canada employed almost 5 per cent of the labour force, and their investments represented 15.7 per cent of total gross capital formation; in contrast, public corporations in the United States employed only 1.6 per cent of American workers and were responsible for only 4.7 per cent of gross capital formation (OECD 1985, tables 20 and 21).

This pronounced difference began to fade in the 1980s and 1990s. In Canada, a wave of privatizations has reduced the role of Crown corporations, as deficit-prone governments have struggled to reduce the cost of subsidies to state enterprises and many corporations have sought freedom from government controls. As a result, many high-profile Crown corporations – Air Canada, Teleglobe, Petro-Canada, the Canadian Development Corporation, Canadian National Railways – as well as a host of smaller enterprises, have been or are in the process of being transferred to the private sector. It is important, however, not to overstate the erosion of the state sector in the Canadian economy. Despite the active privatization program of the Mulroney government, public enterprises still accounted for about 15 per cent of Canadian corporate assets and 11 per cent of GNP at the beginning of the 1990s (D.W. Taylor 1991, 97). A variety of factors slow privatization initiatives: the value of enterprises such as the Canadian Broadcasting Corporation as symbols and agents of national unity; the fear of takeovers by U.S. companies, which would increase Canada's status as a branch-plant economy; and the political unpalatability of possible widespread job losses that can be triggered by privatization (Laux and Molot 1988). Moreover, ambitious provincial privatization schemes in British Columbia, Saskatchewan, and Quebec have not always produced the successful restructuring of public enterprises as private concerns, and this has dampened enthusiasm for privatization as an instrument of positive economic change. Nevertheless, the overall direction of change is clear.

Although the greatest change has been north of the border, the United States has been moving modestly in the opposite direction. Traditional hostility to public enterprise as a vehicle of industrial policy has veered towards an interest in, and some experimentation with, forms of private/public partnerships, such as the Sematech venture, which is described more fully below. At the state level, the last decade has witnessed a proliferation of economic-development corporations, in many instances joint enterprises of the public and private sectors.

Public corporations have been discovered as a means of taking business development programs within a state away from bureaucratic and direct political control, and of involving the private sector in public activities. In effect, they represent less intrusive, more decentralized instruments to achieve industrial policy goals.

Thus, with respect to public enterprise as an instrument of industrial policy, one can see partial or limited convergence from both directions.

Subsidies

Subsidies to industry have been progressively reduced in both countries over the last five or six years, a reflection of the fiscal weakness of governments on both sides of the border and of the constraints inherent in trade agreements. As the OECD notes, this trend extends beyond Canada and the United States: "There has clearly been a move away from defensive policies that were characterised by reliance on subsidies and selective support measures ... This is not to say, of course, that measures geared to alleviate the consequences of economic change on particular industries or areas are being abandoned, but such measures tend to be, today, less frequent, less generous and more limited" (OECD 1990b, 31–2).

With respect to subsidies from the federal governments in both countries, empirical work based on data from the mid- to late 1980s concluded that, outside the defence sector, the average subsidy rate (subsidies as a percentage of the value of industry outputs) was about 0.5 per cent for the United States and 1.0 per cent for Canada (Bence and Smith 1989). All of the relevant studies confirm a significant reduction in these federal subsidies from the mid-1980s to the present. According to Bence and Smith, between 1984 and 1988 the total federal subsidies in Canada declined from $10.8 billion to $8.8 billion. In the case of the United States, the OECD notes a drop in direct federal subsidies of from 0.4 per cent of GNP in 1987 to 0.1 per cent in 1990 (OECD 1991a, 148).

In many ways, state and provincial actions have been more visible in recent years. At the end of the 1980s, the total annual cost of targeted assistance at the subnational level in Canada and the United States was over $20 billion for non-agricultural businesses; tax expenditures and lost revenues for the state approached $200 billion (Fry 1990a, 56–7). Moreover, the form of subnational support seems increasingly similar in the two countries. While Tupper (1986) could remark a decade ago that what was distinctive about Canadian, as opposed to American, aid to industry was the preference for outright grants, more recent empirical evidence shows plenty of direct expenditure in the United States as well (Fry 1990a; M.G. Smith 1990). What is striking is that much of this state aid is highly visible, rather than being hidden in procurement policies, utility rate rebates, and so on. Subnational governments in both countries make extensive use of loans and loan guarantees offered to particular firms. Ironically, such loans, if offered on better than market terms, have been found – with respect to foreign firms exporting to the United States – to be countervailable subsidies.

In sum, as both countries have reduced explicit on-budget subsidies to very low levels, at least at the federal level Canadian policy has converged on the traditional U.S. approach, with the caveat that the United States has always maintained many covert or non-transparent subsidies.

Infrastructure and Industrial Policy

Investment in infrastructure has recently occupied a pre-eminent position in both the Chrétien and Clinton economic agendas. This renewed focus on infrastructure may be attributable in part to the failure of attempts to pick winners in traditional Canadian industrial policy, and to continued ideological resistance to the idea of doing so in the United States. At the same time, the new infrastructure initiatives are being presented as somehow strategic, or at least partly targeted to areas of infrastructure development most closely related to renewed global competitiveness (Eggleton 1995, 14–15). Moreover, the economic return from infrastructure investment is much less controversial in mainstream economic circles than the case for most of the traditional forms of industrial policy, particularly firm- or industry-specific subsidies (D. Lewis 1995).

An infrastructure program was a centrepiece of the federal Liberal Party's campaign in the 1993 election campaign and of the new government's first years in office. The program provided funding for agreed-upon projects undertaken by provincial and municipal governments. It entailed a strong degree of provincial control over the exact form the various projects were to take and over which specific project guidelines were to apply. Similarly, the Clinton administration has endorsed a number of initiatives designed to enhance U.S. competitiveness through investment in sophisticated infrastructure projects. Perhaps the flagship of the administration's infrastructure program is the creation of a national information network. Its policy manifesto outlines a number of initiatives to further this end, including the implantation of the High-Performance Computing and Communications Program, which will create the national high-speed network, and the provision of funding for networking pilot projects designed to enable states, school districts, libraries, and other non-profit entities to purchase the computers and networking connections needed for distance learning (U.S. Office of the President 1993, 29).

Although the language of the infrastructure debates highlights a focus on high technology, in practice such programs are vulnerable to traditional political pressures for a broad array of "public works." The Canadian program is a clear illustration. Some high-technology and communications projects did receive support. A number of communities developed innovative projects fostering high technology. Overall, however, the supposed attempt to use infrastructure spending strategically in order to enhance Canadian competitiveness has fallen victim to regional and provincial pressures to spread spending around geographically. The federal government did not require provincial and municipal authorities to make sophisticated projections about the value to economic development or long-term employment (Andrew and Morrison 1995). Rapid approval of projects as well as provincial distribution of funds were the only true criteria for the spending of the infrastructure money. Kitchen (1995) notes that a large percentage of the money has been spent on traditional works such as roads and sewers, where repair or upgrading would eventually have been undertaken by municipal or provincial authorities in any case, and that the strategic use of such spending to enhance the development of innovative technologies, to reskill the workforce, and to enhance Canadian competitiveness has largely fallen by the wayside.

Defence Procurement

Convergence between Canada and the United States has also been reinforced by the end of the Cold War and a resulting reduction in defence spending, especially in the United States. Its defence commitment as a superpower has been a distinguishing feature of the United States that Canada obviously does not share. While Canadian per capita military spending is the lowest in NATO, the United States' spending has been the highest. On one view, the U.S. defence commitment has required an enormous diversion of productive resources away from the civilian economy, while leading U.S. competitors, such as Japan and West Germany, have been able to focus on intensive investment in the production of sophisticated consumer goods. The opposite view is that defence spending has served as a disguised industrial policy, allowing the commitment of enormous state resources to the development of capital-intensive high technologies with important civilian spinoffs (Kuttner 1991). Markusen et al. (1991) argue that the military-industrial complex has created a culture of research, development, and production that is largely indifferent to consumer applications of technology and to price competition. In addition, they argue, the siting of defence research and production facilities in centres largely outside the traditional U.S. industrial heartland contributed to the decline of this heartland, as people and money shifted to the new centres of defence activity, such as California and the Deep South.

Without attempting here to decide this controversy, it is clear that the existence of an extensive defence commitment permitted large levels of public investment in technology without the kind of intense scrutiny that would have occurred if the state had been seen to be picking winners in the civilian sector. Even if many defence procurement decisions do not have an immediate civilian application, they subsidize the maintenance of vast, highly sophisticated research and development establishments and manufacturing capabilities, with purchasing decisions by government isolating these laboratories and firms, to some extent, from the vicissitudes of normal market forces. In addition, some of the largest spending is in fact in areas where commercial applications are in sight.

Despite the relatively minor importance of its defence role in comparison with the United States, Canada's defence spending has also been used as an explicit, even blatant, technique for industrial policy (or substitute for it), and it constitutes about half of all federal government procurement expenditures. Military bases and production facilities have been regarded as a means to civilian job creation, particularly in disadvantaged regions. Location decisions have been politically charged and politically influenced.

With declining defence expenditures in the contemporary period, however, the traditional difference in the scale of implicit industrial support is narrowing. In both countries, the federal government, struggling to reduce its deficit in the post–Cold War era, has faced politically difficult decisions about base closures. And in the United States, the defence-industrial compex is having to adjust to a more fiscally constrained environment.

NEW INSTRUMENTS OF INDUSTRIAL POLICY

As the discussion so far shows, reliance on traditional instruments of industrial policy has by no means disappeared; they continue to be employed by governments in both countries. However, as we have seen, their use is increasingly constrained by international rules, and faith in their efficacy has declined. Hence, attention has shifted to a range of other policies rooted in different conceptions of the critical factors that make economies grow. Most important is the focus on technology, human capital, and new forms of partnership in the knowledge economy.

Technological Change and Innovation

One of the major structural differences between the Canadian and U.S. economies is the role of technology in production. As chapter 2 noted, Canadian industrial production, particularly production for export, continues to be dominated by resources and low-technology manufacturing. In the United States, by contrast, despite American fears of deindustrialization, high-technology or high-technology-added manufacturing remain a large component of overall production, especially of exports.

The differences between the two countries are startling. For example, a breakdown of total exports shipped by the G-7 countries in 1986 showed that Canada produced only 3.5 per cent of the total in the "high-intensity research and development" category, while the United States generated 22 per cent. In contrast, Canada accounted for 5.5 per cent of "low-intensity research and development" exports, whereas the United States produced only 8.5 per cent of the total. With respect to export receipts from sales of technology itself, the contrast is even more dramatic. Among the same group of countries, the United States accounted for 70.3 per cent of such receipts, while Canada made up a mere 1.9 per cent (Hatzichronoglou 1991, 190). Indeed, production in Canada increasingly relies on imported technology. Davis (1991, 27) reports a drop of over 27 per cent in the employment of domestic Canadian technology by Canadian manufacturers over the 1972–84 period. In sum, Canadians appear increasingly to manufacture and export relatively low-technology products; and when they do employ technology, they increasingly tend to import it. The United States, by contrast, has largely held on to its lead in high-technology manufacturing, including exports, despite persistent fears of being overtaken by Japan and Western Europe.

It is an interesting puzzle how Canada's overall export share has actually increased over a period during which its performance in technology and domestic innovation has experienced a dramatic decline. Niosi suggests that large Canadian companies have become extremely adept at purchasing technology or even undertaking research and development abroad. He argues that "because Canadian multinationals enjoy the advantages of large size, considerable resources and oligopoly control of a substantial market, these multinationals are among the world's fastest 'followers'" (Niosi 1985, 172).

Although a preoccupation with underinvestment in civilian research and development looms large on both sides of the border, Canadian levels lag far behind those of the United States. Even in *government-funded* civilian research and development, Canada trails.[3] Canada does have a relatively high percentage of *government-conducted* research and development, but this is often viewed as distant from or not well integrated with the needs of private firms (Ontario 1988, 97). Various reasons have been offered for the weakness of research and development in Canada. The resource-based nature of much of the economy is part of the explanation; and the branch-plant nature of much of the manufacturing sector means that research and development is often done in the United States and only the basic assembly operations are allocated to Canada (Harris 1985).

Porter and his colleagues warn that Canadian prosperity can no longer depend on the low-technology, resource-based approach of the past, although they also note that such warnings have been around for a long time (Porter and Monitor Co. 1991, 5). Relatively low rates of Canadian investment in research and development may, in fact, be a rational response to the continued success of the older strategy of adeptly acquiring the technology of others. Indeed, stagnation in the growth in expenditures on research and development in the United States may be a more ominous trend, given the much greater dependency of U.S. industrial performance and the U.S. export trade on domestic technology-intensive manufacturing.

Although there are substantial differences between Canada and the United States in the levels of research and development, there has been considerable convergence in the political agendas in this sector. Political rhetoric in both countries sees high technology as the key to economic prosperity, and governments have increasingly been emphasizing the commercial application and transfer of technology through university-government-industry partnerships. In a 1993 report, the Clinton administration called for the devotion of "at least 10–20 per cent of federal lab budgets to R&D partnerships with industry." The new National Economic Council was expected to monitor implementation and provide a forum for matching economic and technology policy. Among the specific initiatives proposed were a permanent research and experimentation tax credit, expanded regional technology alliances and manufacturing extension centres, and promotion of new technology initiatives such as environmentally conscious manufacturing. The administration also called for an increase in the ratio of civilian dual-use research and development to pure military research and development to 50 per cent by 1998. In a 1992 report, the Council on Competitiveness urged the government to devote about $1 billion of the budgets of NASA and the Department of Energy to technology transfer programs, while the National Science Foundation has been directed to work more closely with industry and provide support for commercially viable research. The 1993 Pentagon budget earmarked $1.5 billion for commercial research and development, 20 per cent of which was to be set aside for cooperative projects with industry.

Canadian policy makers have similarly emphasized the need for the commercial application of research. For example, the National Research Council's current five-year plan identifies three primary objectives for Canadian science and technology policy: the promotion of linkages between science, technology, and the economy; the shifting of basic research to more commercial applications in generic technology areas; and the development of national science and technology capacity and infrastructure in Canada. With respect to direct programs to aid industry, the Strategic Technologies Program provides support for industries that are coping with the challenges of technological change. As Guillateri explains, the program was "intended to strengthen [a firm's] capability to develop and apply the new generic technologies of informatics, biotechnology and advanced industrial materials-technologies that are deemed important for Canada's competitiveness" (Guillateri 1994, 313). The program operates on two levels: support for research and development alliances, and support for technology-application alliances. The nature of the research conducted is classified as "pre-competitive" and must involve a university partner (ibid.).

In both countries there is a reluctance to go further and use high-technology industrial policy as an instrument to "pick winners." Such an approach involves attempting to identify sectors or even particular firms that, with an appropriate nudge from government, will have a good chance of developing high-technology production, international competitiveness, and future growth. The idea of picking winners is often linked with the idea that governments should encourage "sunrise" industries while reducing support for industries that are considered to be approaching their "sunset" years. Both Canadian and American efforts at picking winners have been sporadic and not particularly successful (McFetridge 1985; D.W. Taylor 1991). In the Canadian case, most such efforts appear to have failed for a variety of reasons, including the incapacity of public managers to monitor investment decisions properly, the exploitation of public support by fraudulent entrepreneurs, and the intrusion of political patronage and regionalism into key decisions about who should be awarded public backing and where facilities should be located. Examples include the Bricklin sports car, Canadair, Consolidated Computer, the Candu reactor, and Novotel (Borins and Brown 1986; Porter and Monitor Co. 1991, 276–88).

Gertler emphasizes the largely ad hoc nature of industrial assistance targeted at supposedly sunrise industries by the Canadian government. He notes that "the Prime Minister's Office orchestrates the regional location of major federal contracts for defence-related aerospace and shipbuilding manufacturing and servicing, to serve largely political purposes" (Gertler 1991, 386). Politics thus transmutes picking winners into propping up losers.

In the United States, ideological factors have militated against the active pursuit of a "picking winners" strategy. Firm-specific aid, or joint ventures between the public sector and private firms, continues to evoke strong suspicion from business interests, which have strong traditions of interfirm rivalry and a sense of unfairness at the government singling out particular firms for support. Opposition also reflects the conviction that, given the pervasiveness of pork barrelling and special-interest politics in the American system, even a well-intentioned activist industrial policy is likely to turn out in practice to be dominated by handouts and payoffs to politically influential private interests (L. Cohen and Noll 1991).

Where, however, it has been possible to associate high technology with the U.S. national security interest, as with inputs for supercomputers, ideological resistance has proved somewhat less of a problem. The main recent example in the United States is Sematech, a joint venture between the federal government and the private sector aimed at maintaining or recapturing the comparative advantage in semiconductors from Japan. Although Sematech has, in the short run, succeeded in re-establishing U.S. competitiveness in the semi-conductor business, it is unclear whether this will continue to be the case in the longer term. It is also unclear whether Sematech and related initiatives represent a general loosening of the ideological and institutional constraints on an activist industrial policy in the United States. Hawthorne (1991) sees Sematech as a watershed, establishing the legitimacy of a civilian high-technology policy focused on basic processes or components. Such a policy would be clearly distinguished from the still taboo traditional forms of industrial policy that target end-user products. Whether Sematech does prove to be the harbinger of a more general strategy is as yet unclear, but such initiatives have certainly reduced the traditionally wide differences in the role of government in the United States and Canada.

Framework Policies as Industrial Policy

Since picking winners has largely been discredited as a broad strategy of industrial policy, increasing attention is being given to framework policies that create the broad conditions under which winners will be able to emerge by themselves. In both Canada and the United States, policy makers have displayed an increasing awareness of the implications for competitiveness of the framework created by such instruments as competition law, intellectual property law, and corporate and securities law. From the trade policy perspective, as discussed earlier, this has led to scrutiny of the effects of an increasing number of domestic policies on market access through trade and investment. Both Canada and the United States have attempted to adapt these framework policies as a means of increasing national competitiveness and the competitiveness of entire sectors and specific industries. Globalization has created two sometimes conflicting and sometimes complementary pressures: one towards using these policies strategically to improve or support the competitiveness of domestic industries; the other towards harmonizing the policies in order to create a level playing field and thus increase access to global markets. The pressures are complementary if a country is able to ensure that international rules or harmonized standards will reflect the regulatory approach that favours the competitiveness of its own industries. The pressures are conflicting if a country is faced with international constraints on the very policies that it now believes are crucial for the success of its domestic industries. Given their very different weight in the global economy, the United States and Canada are often on different sides of this dilemma.

In Canada, the mandate of the federal industry department has shifted significantly towards providing information and analysis on the relationship between framework policies and competitive capacity, and away from intervening through subsidies to provide direct aid to specific industries and firms (Doern and Tomlin 1995, 12–17; McFetridge 1995). The government has contemplated reform of the Canadian Intellectual Property Office with a new emphasis on the protection of intellectual property rights (Doern and Tomlin 1995, 27–8). It is also undertaking a major review and overhaul of the Canadian standards system (which deals primarily with product standards), with a view to increasing Canadian competitiveness and Canadian influence on the setting of international standards (Trebilcock and Howse 1995).

In the United States, the case of the Sematech venture noted above involved a statutory change to U.S. competition law to permit interfirm cooperation where it was necessary for the global competitiveness of a U.S. industry (Braudo 1995). The Federal Trade Commission's recently revised guidelines on licensing intellectual property reflect an awareness that many kinds of licensing or cross-licensing arrangements that were traditionally proscribed as anticompetitive collusion may, in fact, facilitate innovation that enhances global competitiveness (McFetridge 1995, 9–11).

The growing emphasis on framework policies thus flows from several sources. In part, it is a function of the logic of globalization. In part, it is a function of the erosion of faith in more traditional instruments of industrial policy – for example, the disenchantment with subsidies, and the continuing ideological resistance in the United States to the idea of picking winners (Daniels and Morck 1995). As well, fiscal difficulties on both sides of the border, combined with the dangers to competitiveness of increasing taxes further, point to framework policies that do not rely on spending.

Human Capital, Industrial Policy, and the Labour Market

Globalization and technological change are creating a world in which the comparative advantage of a nation is found less and less in its natural resources or its geographical location, and more and more in its human capital, in the knowledge and skills of its labour force, and in the entrepreneurial talents of business people. The policy agenda in both Canada and the United States has been driven by the perception that, in addition to research and development, the keys to the future are to be found in education and in the effective deployment of human resources. This has generated two related tracks: an emphasis on redesigning labour market and social programs to promote the adjustment of workers displaced by economic change; and greater attention to the role of the educational system in equipping North Americans for a competitive global economy. In effect, social policy and educational policy are becoming instruments of industrial policy.

Social policy as industrial policy. The wrenching restructuring of the Canadian and American economies has generated intense pressures on the labour market. As chapter 2 demonstrated, the consequences have included higher levels of unemployment, displaced workers with few skills and poor prospects, a growth in long-term unemployment, extensive churning in the labour market, and a higher general sense of economic insecurity. All of this has led to contradictory pressures on social programs. On one side are demands to preserve existing programs that protect the incomes of displaced workers and their families; on the other side are demands to reform these programs so as to enhance the flexibility of the labour market and the redeployment of labour to expanding areas of production.

During the 1970s and 1980s, there were significant impediments in both Canada and the United States to policies that focused on positive adjustment, especially the relocation and retraining of workers. In the United States these policies have long proved problematic from the perspective of American values. First, they constitute an apparent admission of defeat, an acceptance that Americans cannot prevail or even effectively compete in the industry in question. Second, they appear to compensate workers for the risks of change and are therefore seen as undermining the values of individual self-reliance, planning, and foresight. Taking care of losers is not a glamorous exercise anywhere, but especially not in America.

In Canada one would expect far less ideological resistance to such policies. Indeed, positive adjustment policies can be understood as a form of social insurance consistent with the risk-adverse individualism that typifies Canadian attitudes. However, to the left in Canada these policies tended to signify defeat, a sell-out to global economic forces and a rejection of nationalism; the preferred alternative often was a strongly protectionist strategy aimed at resisting shifts in comparative advantage. Proposals to transform unemployment insurance into a vehicle of positive adjustment, with benefits linked to retraining and skills development,[4] have failed to gain ideological consensus, largely because they have gone hand in hand with an erosion of the value of insurance entitlements.

By the end of the 1980s, however, interest in positive adjustment measures, whether for training benefits or for mandatory advance notice periods for plant closures, began to attract a new ideological agreement in North America. This emerging consensus – and apparent convergence between the two countries – has been premised on a new-found acceptance that continual shifts in comparative advantage and corresponding worker dislocations are inevitable. The days of lifelong security in high-paid manufacturing jobs are over, and the emphasis is now on ensuring that the workforce is skilled, adaptable, and mobile. Again, social policy becomes an instrument of industrial policy.

Of course, political consensus does not automatically translate directly into expenditures. In both Canada and the United States, the growing emphasis on positive adjustment has encountered a counterweight in the form of public deficits. Overall government expenditures on employment programs, including unemployment insurance, job training, and job creation, represent a considerably higher percentage of GNP in Canada than in the United States: in 1987 the figures were 2.24 per cent as opposed to 0.83 per cent, a disparity much greater than the difference in unemployment rates in the two countries (Advisory Council on Adjustment 1989, 47). However, the two countries are similar in devoting the lion's share of their expenditures to income maintenance as distinct from employment promotion measures, especially when compared with Sweden, Germany, and a number of other European countries. The predominance of income support is marginally higher in Canada (about 75 per cent) than in the United States (about 66 per cent), again presumably in part because of the higher unemployment rates (ibid.).

Indeed, training programs underwent significant cuts during the 1980s. Different commentators measure the depth of the cuts differently. Reich suggests that in the United States public funding for training and retraining was reduced by 50 per cent during the 1980s (1992, 258). With respect to Canada, between 1984 and 1988 "the federal government ... drastically reduced its allocations for training and labour market development nationwide, with funding declining by $600 million over this period" (Labour Market Research Group 1991, 12). The OECD noted a decline in labour market training expenditures in Canada, as a percentage of GNP, from 0.35 per cent in 1986–87 to 0.26 per cent at the end of the decade, but observed a smaller decline in the United States over the same period – from 0.12 per cent to 0.10 per cent. The more dramatic decrease noted by Reich suggests a broader definition of labour market policies, including not only explicit training programs but trade adjustment assistance intended to provide income support during retraining. Whatever the differences in measurement, however, the expenditure decisions clearly did not accord with the rhetoric of positive adjustment.

Towards the end of the decade there were some signs of this trend reversing itself in both countries. In Canada, in the wake of recommendations of the deGrandpré Report (Advisory Council on Adjustment 1989), the federal government undertook a new training initiative in 1989, the Labour Force Development Strategy. No new public funds were actually allocated to training, but $775 million was taken from the existing budget for unemployment insurance (Mahon 1990, 74). In the United States, federal job-training programs were significantly strengthened in 1988–89. Pines and Carnevale (1991, 263) noted that "the almost $1 billion authorized (but not yet fully appropriated) in the new title III of JTPA (Job-Training Partnership Act) should be sufficient to retrain and get new jobs for the approximately 1 million American employees who are dislocated each year." While this may be somewhat overoptimistic, human capital development has been a major theme of the Clinton administration.

Canada continues to lag far behind the United States in private-sector commitment to training and retraining. In 1987 private-sector training expenditures in Canada totalled about $1.5 billion, whereas comparable U.S. expenditures were around $80 billion (Advisory Council on Adjustment 1989, 42). This stunning differential may be significantly related to the fact that the U.S. economy is much more dependent on high-technology, high-valued-added industries, where constant training and retraining are essential to the maintenance of comparative advantage. At play, as well, may be the Canadian legacy of looking to government for training and educational services.

Unfortunately, the evidence drawn from the experience with trade adjustment assistance in the United States and from various forms of adjustment assistance in Canada suggests that these programs have rarely been successful in facilitating positive adjustment. The main example of an adjustment program directly linked to trade-induced dislocation is the U.S. Trade Adjustment Assistance program (TAA). First implemented with the Kennedy Round GATT agreement in 1962, the program offered both supplemental unemployment insurance benefits and re-employment services to workers displaced by import competition. The results were dismal: although $86 million was provided in supplemental unemployment insurance between 1962 and 1975, a mere 125 workers actually took advantage of the retraining benefits (O'Hara 1983: 406–7).

In view of this failure, the program was redesigned and re-enacted under the Trade Act of 1974, with a greater emphasis on positive adjustment benefits. However, an evaluation of the new program by the General Accounting Office found that it too had largely been a failure in facilitating positive adjustment. Two-thirds of the workers who benefited returned to their previous employer after a period of unemployment, and only about 10 per cent participated in retraining or other positive adjustment aspects of the program (O'Hara 1983; Wonnacott and Hill 1987, 42–3). On the theory that supplemental unemployment benefits actually created a disincentive for workers to adjust or relocate, the program was once again revised in 1980, with a provision that allowed termination of a worker's benefits if he or she refused to participate in a training program or to extend the job search beyond his or her own community (O'Hara 1983, 409). Even this change did not seem to make the adjustment aspect of the program more successful; a 1986 study found that the very existence of supplemental unemployment insurance benefits *increased* the labour force in import-affected sectors (Lawrence and Litan 1986, 22).

In 1988 a new positive adjustment program was established in the United States, the Economic Dislocation and Worker Adjustment Assistance program (EDWAA). This program was not limited to trade-displaced workers, and it was designed to function in tandem with the sixty-day required notice period for plant closings or mass layoffs in the Worker Adjustment and Retraining Notification Act. The concept was that of a much more rapid response to worker dislocation than that permitted under the TAA. However, state implementation of the EDWAA has been uneven, and often workers have only been certified as eligible for assistance three to six months after becoming unemployed (U.S. Office of Technology Assessment 1992a, 32–3). As well, training under the EDWAA lasts only from twelve to sixteen weeks, hardly adequate for the acquisition of many of the skills required for re-employability in higher-value-added occupations (ibid.).

Why did targeted trade adjustment assistance largely fail to achieve its broader goal of permitting workers to develop the skills required to move to other sectors of the economy? One reason may be that in the sensitive sectors concerned, the U.S. government was less than unequivocally committed to trade liberalization and worker adjustment. In the steel and auto sectors, for instance, workers were being sent a mixed message: on one hand, the availability of adjustment benefits; on the other hand, renewed efforts to protect these industries from new or intensified import competition, through voluntary export restraints and other measures. Another reason, more directly linked to the consequence of targeting itself, is that the case-by-case determination of whether workers qualified as import-injured resulted in considerable delays in the availability of assistance. Bratt (1982/83, 819) has argued that the Trade Adjustment Assistance program would have been more effective if the U.S. Department of Labour had predetermined (e.g., by sector, region, etc.) those classes of workers most likely to be affected by imports, thereby permitting rapid distribution of benefits without the need for an individualized plant-by-plant or worker-by-worker inquiry into the causes of displacement.

The major initiative of the Mulroney government in the adjustment area was the Canada Jobs Strategy (CJS), which entailed around $1.5 billion in annual expenditures for training and job creation from the mid-1980s onward. The CJS was intended to emphasize private-sector training and job creation. However, critics have seriously questioned whether much of the expenditure has not simply resulted in wage subsidies, without significantly increasing the skill levels of workers or making them more employable in new occupations (Mahon 1990). With respect to training purchased from community colleges and other provincial institutions, the evidence suggests that much of this is for skills that are not in demand or that will not be in demand when the worker completes the training program. In Atlantic Canada, in particular, training benefits have been used primarily as a means of extending income maintenance beyond the limits of unemployment insurance (UI) benefits and not for positive adjustment (Canada, House of Commons, Standing Committee on Labour, Employment, and Immigration 1988, 5–6). An internal evaluation of the CJS conducted by Employment and Immigration Canada found that wage subsidies and in-firm training subsidies were often ineffective in enhancing the employability of the beneficiaries; male workers often gained nothing from these subsidies in terms of employability, though the results for female workers were more positive. Moreover, the review concluded that "the General Projects option [of the CJS] was used as a temporary job creation measure in depressed labour markets and minimal training was provided to participants" (Canada, Employment and Immigration Canada, Strategic Policy and Planning 1992).

Canada has made extensive use of sectorally or regionally targeted adjustment assistance. These programs are probably the closest Canadian equivalent to the targeted, trade-related adjustment assistance in the United States. Particularly in the textile and footwear industries, they have been a prominent aspect of Canadian industrial policy. One feature has been the provision of early retirement benefits for older workers. As the Economic Council of Canada noted, the manner in which these programs were implemented encouraged younger workers to remain in the industry, despite continued declining competitiveness, thereby creating a future adjustment problem for these workers (Economic Council of Canada 1988a, 99–111). Also, older workers, although less likely to find equivalent employment elsewhere, tend to be financially more secure, their children having grown up and their mortgages often having been paid off (Leana and Feldman 1992, 184–5).

Although some sectorally targeted programs, such as the Industry and Labour Adjustment Program (ILAP) and the Canadian Industrial Renewal Board (CIRB), included measures to promote re-employability, such positive adjustment-oriented features were little used. Like the CJS, these programs were primarily used to extend income support beyond what was provided under UI and to facilitate short-term job creation in depressed communities (Economic Council of Canada 1988a, 110–11). An additional problem was that these programs went hand in hand with trade restrictions and with production subsidies to sustain employment in the declining sectors. Thus, as in the United States, conflicting signals were being sent to workers concerning the necessity for positive adjustment (Trebilcock, Chandler, and Howse 1990, 96–7).

In 1991 the government established the Canadian Labour Force Development Board (CLFDB), aimed at coordinating strategies for labour development among governments, business, organized labour, and other affected interests, such as local communities. This initiative emerged through the Canadian Labour Market Productivity Centre (CLMPC), a business-labour consultation mechanism and research facility supported with federal funding (Langille 1991, 609–10). The CLMPC and the CLFDB were plagued by a host of problems: the hostile relationship between the Conservative government and much of the labour movement; the jurisdictional issues surrounding federal involvement in labour policy that were raised by Quebec during the constitutional negotiations; conflict with the senior public service over accountability for public policy; and difficulties in generating a meaningful consensus between business and labour (Haddow 1995). An additional factor affecting union support for these initiatives was the determination of the Conservative government to link reductions in UI benefits to federal funding for the CLMPC and for any sectoral adjustment initiatives undertaken within its mandate.

A model for the kind of adjustment programs to be undertaken under the auspices of the CLFDB is the adjustment program for displaced steelworkers organized by the Canadian Steel Trade and Employment Congress, funded under the CJS. This program has involved a range of positive adjustment measures, including training, search and relocation assistance, job referral services, and structures for exchange of information and experiences among the participating workers. It was financed by a special grant of $20 million from the federal government, allocated to the CJS. An initial study of its effectiveness has suggested a very positive result: many workers have been successfully retrained and relocated outside the steel industry, and the workers themselves indicate a high level of satisfaction with the assistance provided to them (*Quarterly Labour Market and Productivity Review* 1992, 29–30).

Once again, the experience of Canada and the United States shows striking parallels. Despite a common consensus that social programs should be instruments of positive adjustment in labour markets, the financial commitment has often been weak, and the programs have seldom achieved the goals set out for them.

Education, training, and comparative advantage. While part of the reason for the decline of interest in trade adjustment assistance may be the failure of past policies, another reason is that in both countries the problem of adjusting to trade has come to be seen as part of another agenda, that of reorienting general government policies towards the creation of a globally competitive labour force. Training and retraining policies become less a means of helping displaced workers cope with transition costs than a technique for creating a skills base for "sunrise" industries. Education, day care, and social welfare policies are seen as ways of enhancing or preventing the erosion of human capital that is the basis of competitiveness in the contemporary world (Lazar 1990).

This reconceptualization of positive adjustment is attractive precisely for its potential to bridge ideological differences. On the one hand, the agenda is attractive to conservatives and neoconservatives because it promises to reshape the educational and social welfare establishments with a view to enhancing economic growth or efficiency; on the other hand, it may be attractive to liberals (particularly in the United States) who are looking for new ways of defending social policies that have come under persistent attack throughout the neoconservative revolution of the 1980s and 1990s. In Reich's words, "Herein lies the new logic of economic nationalism. The skills of a nation's workforce and the quality of its infrastructure are what makes it unique, and uniquely attractive, in the world economy" (1992, 264).

This perception now pervades policy debate in Canada and the United States. There has been a powerful convergence in the policy agendas of the two countries as the searchlight has focused on training individuals for high-technology, high-skilled occupations.[5] Moreover, both countries face similar constraints in seeking to nurture a training culture. Individual firms setting their internal training budgets know that competing firms may hire away any employees who receive substantial training. This logic can also be extended to public expenditures on the development of highly trained scientific and technical personnel; there is nothing to prevent foreign firms from inducing these people, with offers of attractive financial rewards, to work abroad. Other countries have found ways to internalize the benefits of education and training expenditures more fully. In Japan, for instance, higher spending by firms and worker investment of time on training and retraining seem to be linked to the implicit expectation of a long-term relationship between the worker and the particular firm, an expectation that no longer holds anywhere in the North American context. A key issue is thus whether North America can find ways of compensating for the constraints on training that are inherent in the structure of its labour markets.

As part of his presidential campaign platform, Clinton proposed a special training payroll tax, modelled after the French system, that would be forgiven if industry spent an equivalent amount on employee on-the-job training. Although opposition in Congress has since forced the president to back away from this idea, the Clinton administration has committed resources to long-term training and education initiatives. In *Technology for America's Economic Growth*, the administration outlined four objectives for education and training: a restructuring of primary and secondary schooling; youth apprenticeships to facilitate the transition from school to work for people not headed for college; improvements in the accessibility of training to ensure that all workers who need to upgrade their skills can keep pace with the rapidly changing economy; and development of training programs for workers displaced by declining defence budgets or by increased international trade (U.S. Office of the President 1993, 13–14). The report also emphasizes the need to use technology in education, to enhance skills in mathematics, science, and engineering, and to transfer defence capabilities in training and education to civilian institutions.

In its Red Book, the Liberal government outlined a similar policy prescription for building a flexible and more productive workforce. The objective was to make individuals "job ready" by providing funding for apprenticeship programs and workplace training, by creating a Canadian Youth Services Corps designed to build a "commitment among young workers to labour market activity," and by restoring funds, cut by previous governments, to the Literacy Program (Liberal Party 1993). As well, the government proposed a variation of "workfare" designed to provide training for those on social assistance. Modelled in part on the New Brunswick government's NB Jobs Corp, the proposal requires welfare recipients to undergo training in exchange for their benefits. Under the New Brunswick plan, older unemployed workers are to receive an annual income of $12,000 to work in community-based projects such as silviculture, developing nature trails, and library automation (Yates 1995, 91).

In large measure, both the Clinton and Chrétien proposals for labour market reform and training reflect a similar post-Keynesian supply-side vision of government intervention. On this view, the role of the state is seen primarily as providing inputs into the economy through such measures as investment in research and development and training programs. The assumption is that by providing a highly skilled flexible workplace, jobs will follow through with increased private investment. Job creation is largely left to the private sector. But there are several problems with such a model. First, many nations are pursuing the same policy agenda and some in fact hold a substantial lead in this area. Second and more specific to Canada, such a strategy is likely to exacerbate regional disparities, with areas such as Atlantic Canada receiving less regionally targeted aid than other areas (ibid., 98).

Building Networks and Partnerships

Contemporary debates over industrial policy also focus on the importance of networks and partnerships. Paul Krugman (1993) recently claimed that he and other neoclassical economists considerably underestimated the significance of externalities and the potential, at least in theory, for industrial policy to internalize these externalities. In particular, Krugman was impressed by the evidence presented by Michael Porter, among others, about the importance of geographical clusters in economic growth. This evidence demonstrates the extent to which individual firms do not stand or fall by their own efforts but depend on the mutually reinforcing effects of one another's success. A parallel analysis flows from Robert Putnam's study (1993b) of Italian politics and society. Putnam argues for the importance of "social capital" as a basis for the success of a variety of collective human endeavours. The main form of social capital consists of "networks of civil engagement," which "facilitate flows of information about technological developments, about the creditworthiness of would-be entrepreneurs, about the reliability of individual workers, and so on"; innovation depends on "continual informal interaction in cafés and bars and in the street" (ibid., 161). Putnam further notes: "Like all public goods, social capital tends to be undervalued and undersupplied by private agents" (ibid., 170).

Influenced by this kind of thinking, both the American and Canadian federal governments have announced their intention to facilitate the emergence of strong regional growth centres buoyed by an increase in strategic alliances, consortia, and business clusters, especially among small and medium-sized firms. As Blais explains, "These interfirm strategic alliances can involve contracting out, partial or total ownership, joint ventures or simply buying an intermediate good on a regular basis." The production process itself involves a network of different firms, which might comprise "a venture capitalist, a university research department, a product design company, many parts suppliers, an assembly company and an accounting firm" (Blais 1986, 216). In a knowledge-intensive economy, such regional agglomerations seem to facilitate the innovation process (D. Wolfe 1995).

In Canada, support for regional clusters has permeated policy discourse at all levels of government. For example, in *Creating Opportunity*, the Liberals identified the creation of regional clusters as a fundamental component of their plan for economic renewal (Liberal Party 1993). In practice, however, policy has been less focused on nurturing such relationships than on aiding small and medium-sized businesses in "cutting red tape." In a subsequent policy document, *Building a More Innovative Economy* (Canada, Industry Canada 1994), the government provided a number of measures designed to assist small business: the allocation of public business to small business; an increase in government loan guarantees; assistance to small business to export more; and the provision of better overall infrastructure. Regional development agencies are expected to give priority in loans to small and medium-sized businesses in order to "promote innovation, improved market access and entrepreneurship" (Paquet and Roy 1995, 146–7). Promises have also been made with respect to the further development of business service centres "to provide a single window to provincial and federal programs for small business," as well as the establishment of a National Business Networks Demonstration program, which would "support 30 sectorally and regionally balanced networks" (ibid.).

While support at the federal level for the creation of regional partnerships has been uncertain, the provinces, particularly Ontario, have been much more active. In 1992 the NDP government established the Sector Partnership Fund "to provide assistance to approved cooperative sector projects that lead to higher value-added activities" (D. Wolfe 1995, 23). All sectors are considered to be eligible for support, and since its inception, strategies have been approved in thirteen sectors. As Wolfe notes, one of the major successes of this program, which requires broad-based consultative efforts, is that "most participants have come to recognize that the process itself is one of its most valuable products; new relationships have been developed among business competitors, a greater sense of trust has been generated among all the partners, and the effective identification of common sectoral interests has occurred" (ibid., 25).

In addition to the Sector Partnership Fund, the Ontario government introduced a series of measures designed to assist small innovative companies. For instance, the Ontario Innovation and Productivity Service was established to enable innovative growth firms to overcome barriers to expansion. The program attempts to work with specific firms in an effort to identify challenges and to develop strategic plans to promote growth. The service not only provides funding but also "brokers with the federal government and existing private sector resources" (D. Wolfe 1995, 27). The Ontario Lead Investment Fund was another major initiative introduced by the NDP government to assist small business. The program was created "to develop and increase the financial, management and marketing skills necessary to grow these companies by expanding the number and depth of successful expert investment managers" (ibid.). Whether these initiatives will continue to survive under the current Conservative government in Ontario remains to be seen. But they clearly represent part of the new face of an interventionist industrial policy in North America.

The Clinton administration in its February 1993 policy report also stressed the need to facilitate the development of strong regional centres. Among the vast array of policy prescriptions outlined in the report, it advocated the creation of "regional technology alliances" designed to "promote the commercialization and application of critical technologies in which there are regional clusters of strength, and to encourage firms and research institutions within a particular region to exchange, share and develop technology, and develop new products and markets" (U.S. Office of the President 1993, 9). The report called for the introduction of "agile manufacturing programs" that would support the development and dissemination of information technology to enable "temporary networks of complementary firms to come together quickly to exploit fast-changing market opportunities" (ibid., 10). Finally, the administration contemplated legislation that would "extend the National Cooperative Research Act of 1984 to cover joint production ventures" (ibid., 12).

Although the discourse of the new industrial policy highlights Michael Porter's regional "clusters," such strategies run counter to traditional political imperatives. In Canada, for example, federalism has always pushed industrial policies in the opposite direction, towards geographic diversification rather than towards concentrations of industrial activity. Take any major federal defence procurement contract – given the politics of federalism, Ottawa feels compelled to parcel out various bits and pieces of the contract to different firms in different parts of the country. If anything, this practice discourages the diffusion of technology and know-how throughout geographic linkages and clusters. But consider what the political fallout would be if the federal government announced that it was going to channel all its expenditure on technology into developing a "Silicone Valley" on the outskirts of Toronto. While such a decision would be in keeping with the logic of linkages and external economies that drives the new industrial policy, it would be ruled out by the logic that drives the politics of Canadian federalism.

Even if the Canadian federal government were to undertake a genuine strategy of encouraging geographic linkages, the beggar-thy-neighbour competition for investment that characterizes the industrial policy of most Canadian provinces could easily undermine these gains (Tupper 1982). Provinces would continue to offer large incentives to lure firms away from their "clusters," thereby threatening to destroy any external economies created by the new federal industrial policy. Moreover, provincial policies tend to reproduce internally the same kind of diversification that has plagued federal policies; the political pressures to spread public investment around the province are indifferent to the importance of maintaining and reinforcing provincial clusters. Indeed, if nurturing clusters is the key to a new industrial policy, the best first step in the Canadian context would be to dismantle completely the old policies that impede or counter the natural formation of clusters or local concentrations.

The traditional pattern of business-government relations also impedes the introduction of a new industrial policy in Canada. Traditional industrial policies have been characterized by the very weak monitoring or direction of government-funded projects. Canadian businesses, while open to receiving government assistance, resist forms of assistance that involve direct bureaucratic involvement in or scrutiny of a firm's decision making (Blais, Faucher, and Young 1986). Nor have Canadian governments been successful in translating government aid into leverage on the behaviour of firms, which seems to be a pervasive element in Japanese industrial policy successes. Porter and his colleagues note, "Canadian companies have looked for government assistance in export promotion, investment in specialized infrastructure, government procurement, and other forms of support. They have, however, rarely cooperated with governments in areas that have important impacts on international competitiveness, such as research and development, training and education" (Porter and Monitor Co. 1991, 348). It seems unlikely that a new policy, or more handouts to a different set of sectors, can break this pattern, which seems deeply engrained in the Canadian culture of business-government relations.

SUMMARY AND EXPLANATIONS

Since their inception, Canada and the United States have both engaged in a wide variety of governmental activities designed to shape and promote economic growth. Even in the nineteenth century we would have found important parallels between the two countries – for example, in the waves of railroad and canal building, and in their aggressive policies to promote the settlement of the West. Such policies loom much larger in Canadian political discourse than in the United States, not least because of the desire to create an East-West economy in the face of powerful North-South pulls, and because of the need for government finance to compensate for capital shortages in a capital-short, small, nascent economy.

This tradition extended into the postwar era. Canadian governments remained the more active in embracing explicit, self-conscious industrial policies. As we have seen, at both federal and provincial levels, Canadian governments employed public enterprise as an instrument of economic development far more than American governments did at either level. Canadian governments have made much greater use of industrial subsidies, which have been focused both on building industries in the heartland and on promoting regional economic development. For the most part, "industrial policy" has not been a pejorative word in Canadian government circles.

Industrial policy has had far less legitimacy in the United States. It smacks of excessive governmental intervention into the market. One result is that it is often masked or hidden in American political discourse. For example, the interstate highway system, which was much like the postwar Trans-Canada Highway project, was identified as the National Defense Highway program; similarly, the U.S. government's increased support for graduate education was provided by the National Defense Education Act. Indeed, throughout this period, the single most important instrument of industrial policy in the United States was defence procurement. The difference in rhetoric therefore should not hide the fact that in different degrees and with different emphases, both countries were engaged in broadly similar industrial policy activities. Nevertheless, in the early postwar decades, the Canadian state was clearly more active.

Perhaps most striking in recent years has been the considerable degree of convergence. On the one hand, there has been a disillusionment with the efficacy and cost effectiveness of many Canadian industrial policies. For example, "picking winners" came to be seen as a weak instrument, partly because this strategy was too easily diverted towards supporting weak industries and partly because the ability of governments to make such choices was increasingly in doubt. Similarly, budget constraints and the realization that government aid is seldom likely to overcome the strength of market forces have led to a reduced emphasis on regional development policies. Similar factors have led to a strong move away from public enterprise and towards a wave of privatization in Canada. Both levels of government have recently been trimming a wide range of business subsidies. On the other hand, there has been, especially in the Clinton administration, an increase in American interest in using government to promote international competitiveness. How long this is likely to last, given the vagaries of U.S. politics and the hostility of the Republican Party to targeted industrial policies, remains unclear.

There are other important parallels between the two countries. In both, despite misgivings in many quarters, free trade has been the foundation of their industrial policies, though the economic strength and hegemonic status of the United States allows it to use retaliatory trade sanctions in a much more aggressive way than Canada. The FTA and NAFTA have provided some protection for Canadian industries, although in sectors such as agriculture and softwood lumber this protection has seemed very thin. Nevertheless, trade policy is the foundation of industrial strategy in both countries. Moreover, the discourse and activity in contemporary industrial policies are remarkably similar on both sides of the border, emphasizing research and technology, human resource development and training, positive adjustment policies, and a focus on encouraging networks, partnerships, and alliances. In both, too, sceptics would argue that there are large gaps between the fulsome goals and rhetoric of industrial policies and any measurable impact on growth and competitiveness. In both countries, there is a sense that whatever the stated objectives of market-enhancing and market-facilitating policies, the reality is that most traditional support to industries goes to prop up weaker firms and regions. In general, industrial policy in the two countries appears more alike than it was at the beginning of our period: Canadians are less enthusiastic; Americans a bit more so.

Once again, our explanatory task is to understand both the growing similarity in the industrial policies of the two countries and the lingering differences in approach. To begin with convergence, the most crucial explanation must lie in global economic factors. What generated the increased attention to industrial policy in U.S. policy debates was the dawning realization of its vulnerability to international economic forces, such as the competition from Japan and from low-wage newly industrializing countries. Competitiveness and productivity became the primary concerns in a highly competitive world economy, in which American hegemony, at least in the production of goods, was seen to be threatened. An increased interest in the role of government in securing competitiveness and market access may also have been stimulated in part by the realization that U.S. firms active in the global economy were no longer tied closely to the American flag and therefore would have less interest in ensuring growth in the United States itself. The fundamental difference between business and government in this regard is that, at least in principle, business is indifferent to location. Governments, situated in a particular place on the globe, are centrally concerned with location; they want growth here, not there. Thus, if vulnerability and openness to the global economy account for the historically greater emphasis on industrial policy in Canada, the increasing vulnerability of the United States to the same forces accounts for the increased debate about industrial policy there.

International economic factors also promote convergence in other ways. International trade agreements, especially the GATT/WTO, operate on both countries to constrain the traditional policy instruments available to them. The tariff, to take a notable example, is simply not available any more, nor are such instruments as trade-restrictive agricultural supply-management programs. While these restraints are, as we have shown, by no means complete, they do tend to push industrial policies more to those areas that remain clearly under national control: infrastructure, research and development, education and labour-force training, and the reduction of internal barriers to trade.

Although global forces help account for recent convergence, the nature of domestic cleavages also contributes to similar approaches to industrial policy north and south of the border. Neither Canada nor the United States has the broad industry, labour, and government linkages that are characteristic of countries with more coherent and expansive industrial policies. In both, the business community is diverse, varied, and highly sceptical of government involvement in investment and management decisions. Historically, Canadian business accepted a larger role for the state in economic development, but recent years have seen an apparent convergence with the business orientation south of the border. A recent survey of four hundred Canadian corporate executives, for example, concluded that, "like the general public, corporate executives once saw government as a helpful partner in the building of the national economy. But, today, corporate Canada embraces the radical free market view that government is no longer the solution, but the problem itself" (Compas 1995). In both countries as well, the labour movement is highly decentralized and divided. Although Canada in particular has experimented with various tripartite mechanisms, the cultural and organizational basis for European-style cooperation simply does not exist in either country. These same social and organizational factors help ensure that even when ambitious market-facilitating approaches are attempted, they are likely to degenerate into pork barrelling and protection of existing interests.

There are, of course, continued differences in the industrial policy thrusts of Canada and the United States, differences that are rooted in the factors distinctive to each country – policy legacies, institutional factors, and ideological-cultural influences. Policy legacies certainly account for some of the differences. For example, despite privatization, public enterprises remain far more prominent on the Canadian scene than in the United States. Policy legacies also blend with ideological and cultural factors. The fact that, from the very first days of the Canadian federation, it was believed that governments ought to play a role in nation building and province building accounts for the greater legitimacy of the very idea of industrial policy in Canada. Lipset (1990a, 136–7) argues that Canadian attitudes towards the role of government in the economy are somewhere between American and European attitudes. He also argues that a predominant Canadian attitude is not so much faith in strong government as aversion to risk. But if Canadians seem to be more tolerant of government activism than Americans, the differences are small and are probably getting smaller. Johnston (1985, 181–4) shows that Canadians are not substantially more likely to trust the state to make allocative economic decisions. Chapter 3 in this volume adds to the evidence, finding only minor differences in

Canadian and American attitudes towards the economic role of the state, and showing that Canadians are as sceptical as Americans of the capacity of politicians to manage the economy. Thus, while cultural-ideological differences have been important, contributing to important differences in the policy legacies of the two countries, they seem less so today.

Another broad difference is the Canadian preoccupation with regional equity and regional redistribution. In part, Canada's strong emphasis on policies to sustain and protect economically weak regions may reflect the risk-adverse culture highlighted by Lipset. In part, it reflects a linguistically divided labour market; for francophone workers who are displaced by the forces of economic change, mobility outside French-speaking areas of the country is not an attractive option. Regional equity has often been understood in Canada in terms of the imperative to preserve the economic and social viability of small communities and traditional industries. Short-term employment maintenance has been in tension with long-term economic development goals or the most efficient deployment of Canadian resources. This has placed regional priorities generally in tension with market-facilitating economic strategies, which emphasize the movement of capital and workers to the areas in which they can be employed most productively. In the United States, regional concerns play far less of a role in the nation's policy, except in the defence sector; the general tendency has been to emphasize mobility of people and capital. The centrality of regional imperatives thus remains an important difference between the two countries, even though, as we have noted, the Canadian commitment and ability to sustain regional redistribution is increasingly in doubt.

Institutional differences also play a role in sustaining differences between the two countries. Most obvious is the impact of federalism and of Canada's more decentralized version of it. Federalism has amplified the salience of regional cleavages and has contributed to the greater Canadian tendency to think of industrial policies in regional terms. A more decentralized federation also helps account for the fact that the provinces have historically played a central role in promoting their own economic development, using most of the tools that are also available to the federal government. In some cases, as in the battles over energy pricing and controls in the 1970s, the "province-building" goal has directly challenged both federal power and the well-being of the national economy. An important example is the extent to which these provincial activities have resulted in significant barriers to the freedom of the internal common market in Canada. Here the marked contrast between the two countries may well be declining, since American states have recently begun to play a much more active role in stimulating economic development. Yet most provinces still play a more central role in their economies, deploying powerful Crown corporations and various regulatory instruments that are not as fully developed at the local level south of the border.

It might be expected that with their strong cabinet system, Canadian governments would be better equipped institutionally to engage in a coherent, directed industrial policy than the much more fragmented and divided American system (Weaver and Rockman 1993, 11–16). Indeed, it is true, as Tyson (1993, 193) suggests, that there are no formal, coordinated agencies for developing industrial policy in the United States. Canada, on the other hand, has experimented with a wide array of high-profile ministries and other agencies mandated to pursue industrial policies. But the frequent re-organizations and mergers, along with the resulting alphabet soup of agencies (DRIE, MSERD, ISTC, AOCA, etc.), testify to the myriad of conflicting goals and conceptual uncertainties. This suggests that policy coherence is not a function of institutional structures alone. In fact, in both countries, governments must deal with the enormous diversity of competing interests. Both sets of institutions thus must engage in brokerage and clientelism. The major effect of the institutional difference is that in the Canadian system the accommodations take place largely in secret – in the cabinet room or the Prime Minister's Office, with in the internal party apparatus, or during federal-provincial negotiations – while in the United States they take place more openly, in the wheeling and dealing in Congress.

Thus, the principal theme in the story of industrial policy in Canada and the United States is one of considerable convergence. Globalization, the fiscal weaknesses of governments, disenchantment with the failures of the past, and similarities in the structure of business and labour are increasingly guiding policy makers along similar grooves. Policy variations undoubtedly persist, reflecting historical legacies as well as cultural and institutional differences; but as new approaches to industrial policy emerge, attuned to the realities of a global economy, the policy debates in Congress and Parliament are increasingly following a similar script.

7 The Social Policy Divide: The Welfare State in Canada and the United States

KEITH BANTING

The politics of change are perhaps most intense in the domain of social policy. The globalization of economic life, the fiscal weakness of the state, and the vigorous pluralism of domestic society have placed powerful pressures on the structure of social programs in all Western nations, including Canada and the United States. On both sides of the border, popular social programs have been subject to successive waves of retrenchment and restructuring, prompting increasingly polarized debates about the social role of government.

Social policy represents a critical test of the pressures for convergence or even harmonization implicit in more integrated economies. During the postwar decades, Canadians developed a more expansive welfare state than their neighbours to the south, and the ability of Canadians to maintain distinctive social programs has immense political and theoretical significance. Social programs have become an integral part of Canadians' sense of identity, part of their conviction that they have created something different on the northern half of the continent. Not surprisingly, therefore, the scope for continuing to chart a separate course on social issues sparked intense political debates as the country moved towards closer economic integration with the United States in the 1980s. More generally, however, the case of social policy in Canada and the United States has wider theoretical significance, illuminating in interesting ways the degrees of freedom that nation-states retain in a future framed by global economic forces.

Not everyone is impressed with the differences between the Canadian and U.S. welfare states. Viewed from the perspective of OECD nations

Table 7.1
Public expenditure on social programs in selected OECD countries, 1990
(per cent of GDP)

EC COUNTRIES	
Belgium	25.2
Denmark	27.8
France	26.5
Germany	23.5
Italy	24.5
Netherlands	28.8
United Kingdom	22.3
OUTSIDE THE EC	
Canada	18.8
Japan	11.6
Norway	28.7
New Zealand	19.0
Sweden	33.1
United States	14.6

Source: OECD 1994c, tables 1b and 1c

generally, the differences may seem limited, as table 7.1 suggests. Indeed, some analysts consider both Canada and the United States to be archetypal examples of the liberal model of the welfare state, and contrast their programs with the more extensive benefits provided by the social democratic and corporatist systems of Europe (Esping-Anderson 1990; Myles 1995). However, from the perspective of life on the North American continent, especially for the poor and for marginal social groups, the differences between Canadian and American social programs are important. These differences can be seen along three distinct dimensions:

• *Comprehensiveness.* Public social programs have provided significant support for a broader range of the population in Canada than in the United States. The welfare state in the United States is often described as having two tiers (Wier, Orloff, and Skocpol 1988; Orloff 1991). The upper tier consists of social security programs that provide pensions and health insurance for elderly Americans. Throughout most of its life, social security has been sustained by strong public support, powerful bureaucratic champions, and protective congressional committees; as a result, it provides far richer benefits than other programs. In Michael Harrington's words, "The welfare state in the United States is primarily for people over sixty-five" (1984, 85). As we shall see below, these social security benefits are broadly comparable to those received by the elderly in Canada. The lower tier of the American welfare state, however, affords more meagre protection for children and for persons of working age. This tier consists of unemployment insurance, Medicaid, a variety of means-tested benefits such as Aid to Families with Dependent Children (AFDC) and Food Stamps, and the Earned Income Tax Credit (EITC). These programs offer lower benefits, and they leave many poor and vulnerable individuals without protection. In contrast, the Canadian combination of universal health care, a larger unemployment insurance program, child benefits, and stronger social assistance has provided more comprehensive protection for the non-elderly population. Unlike in the U.S. system, the Canadian welfare state is an important component of the lives of average citizens over their full life cycle.

- *Transfers to the poor.* Canadian mythology suggests that the country is more committed than the United States to universality in social programs, and this has certainly been the case in health care. However, in the field of income security, it is Canada that has the stronger tradition of targeting benefits on the poor through income supplements, refundable tax credits, and social assistance. This difference, which began to emerge in the 1960s, has been reinforced by the recent transformation of several universal income-security programs into selective ones. In the United States, however, the universal components of social security continue to dominate, and targeted transfers to the poor are much weaker. A rich menu of means-tested programs exists, each with its appropriate acronym, and considerable controversy swirls around many of them. Nevertheless, benefits tend to be low, and limited resources are channelled through them.
- *Redistributive impact.* Not surprisingly, the combination of more comprehensive coverage and more strongly targeted programs has reduced the levels of poverty and inequality in Canada more effectively than has been done in the United States. Universal health insurance has a stronger equalizing effect on access to health care, and the tax-transfer system makes a larger dent in the patterns of inequality generated by the market economy. This difference has been particularly noticeable over the last decade, as economic forces generated pressures for greater inequality in both countries.

These differences in the two welfare states lie at the heart of the debate about the scope for distinctive national choices in an integrated North American economy. This chapter explores the issues by analysing the

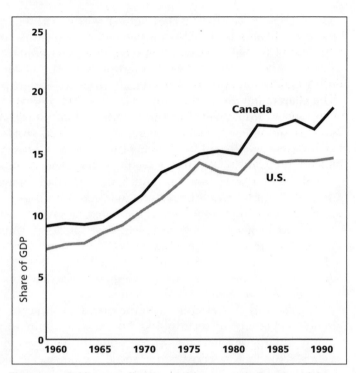

Figure 7.1   Public expenditure on social programs in Canada and the
United States as a proportion of GDP, 1960–1990
Source: OECD 1994c, tables 1a and 1b

roots of their distinctive approaches, comparing their social programs
in greater detail, and examining the extent of convergence in this most
sensitive of policy sectors. As we shall see, the pattern is complex. Many
social programs in both countries have been weakened significantly by
successive rounds of retrenchment and redesign. Yet restructuring is
not driving the two systems towards a single model. There has certainly
been convergence in some programs, but there has also been divergence elsewhere, accentuating traditional differences between the two
countries. Indeed, during the 1980s and early 1990s, the overall gap in
total spending on social policy grew significantly, as figure 7.1 indicates,
in part because of higher unemployment in Canada but also because
cuts in social benefits in this period were more dramatic south of the
border. This expanded difference began to narrow again in the mid-
1990s as governments began to cut more deeply in Canada. Nevertheless, Canada and the United States continue to travel different paths in
social policy, and most components of the two systems are as different in

the mid-1990s as they were in the mid-1970s, the high-water mark of the postwar welfare state. Whether this pattern will prove sustainable in the future remains a compelling question. So far, Canada and the United States have been adjusting to economic and social turmoil according to different inner rhythms.

The chapter is organized in four parts. The first examines the economic, social, and political factors that have traditionally sustained distinctive social policy regimes in the two countries. The second part examines the basic health and income security programs in the two countries in greater detail, traces their evolution in recent years, and assesses their redistributive impact. The next part focuses more directly on the extent of convergence and divergence in the two policy regimes, and examines the reasons for the cases of convergence that have emerged. The final section summarizes the conclusions and reflects on the extent to which differences in social policy are likely to persist.

THE ROOTS OF DISTINCTIVENESS

The different versions of the liberal welfare state that emerged in Canada and the United States are deeply rooted in the economic, social, and political structures of the two societies. The positions of the two countries in the wider global economy, as well as domestic social cleavages such as economic class, language, race, and region, have created distinctive pressures on the social role of the state in each country. These economic and social contrasts have been further sharpened by differences in the political institutions and processes through which Canada and the United States shape and reshape the complex web of programs that constitute the welfare state. Because all the differences point to a stronger social role for government in Canada, it is impossible to weigh the relative contribution of each factor with precision. In combination, however, they have created a firmer foundation for the welfare state in Canada than in the United States.

Position in the Global Economy

Early studies of the welfare state paid relatively little attention to the international context, preferring to search for the determinants of welfare policy in the social and political forces at work within each country. In effect, the welfare state was seen as the creation of national political economies. This approach understated the importance of the wider international economy even during the postwar years, and it is clearly incomplete today. Each country's position in the larger global economy shapes the context within which the domestic politics of welfare are played out, and international constraints provide more autonomy for domestic choices in some periods than in others.

During the postwar decades, the growth of international trade and the expansion of social expenditures seemed mutually reinforcing. The massive support for reconstruction provided by the Marshall Plan, the progressive liberalization of trade and finance under the General Agreement on Tariffs and Trade (GATT), and the improving terms of trade, especially in energy, all contributed to economic prosperity among Western nations, which in turn helped to finance an impressive expansion of social spending (Keohane 1984; Ruggie 1982, 1994). Growth gave nations considerable latitude in designing their domestic social contracts, especially in the case of larger countries that were not heavily dependent on foreign trade. Smaller nations with comparatively open economies were inevitably more sensitive to the international context even in the postwar years, and these countries tended to adopt more expansive social programs as part of a larger attempt to cushion their societies from economic shocks originating outside their borders (D.R. Cameron 1978; Katzenstein 1984).

The United States and Canada reflected this pattern. As a hegemonic state with little dependence on foreign trade, the United States was largely free to design its social programs in the light of its internal economic and political impulses. The country's larger geopolitical role during the Cold War undoubtedly imposed constraints on the government's response to domestic interests (Krasner 1978), and scholars have searched for evidence that military expenditures acted as a significant brake on American social expenditures in this period. The evidence does not point to a strong effect, however, and the social programs appear to have been shaped primarily by domestic pressures and preferences.[1] In contrast, the role of the state in Canada has always been sensitive to the openness of the economy and international influences. The historical dependence on trade in natural resources, the need to create a transcontinental economy in the face of geographic barriers and a sparse population, and the need to counter powerful American influences contributed to a more central role for public initiative in Canada.[2] In the early life of the nation, state action concentrated on transportation, energy, and economic infrastructure; but as the twentieth century unfolded, the tradition also contributed to a broader consensus on the social role of the state. Moreover, the continued vulnerability of employment in Canada to economic shifts in the global economy contributed more directly to growth in public spending during the postwar years (D.R. Cameron 1986).

Since the late 1970s, the postwar symbiosis between the international economy and the welfare state has broken down. Economic integration on a global and regional basis, intense competition in the international trading system, the associated restructuring of domestic economies, and less stable macroeconomic conditions have generated contradictory pressures on the welfare state. On one hand, change creates victims; hence workers, regions of the country, and sectors of the economy that have been hurt create pressures for increased public spending. On the other hand, global economic changes create pressures to limit expenditures and to redesign social programs in ways that reduce rigidities in the labour market, enhance the flexibility of the domestic economy, and reduce the fiscal burdens on the state. This contemporary emphasis on adaptability stands in tension with the concern for security and protection that was embodied in the historical conception of the welfare state. Thus, pressures rooted in the international economy press simultaneously for expanded social security and fundamental restructuring. Both Canada and the United States have been grappling with these contradictions throughout the 1980s and 1990s.

According to many commentators, globalization also generates a second level of constraint, by narrowing the degrees of freedom that each nation-state has to craft its policy response. According to these interpretations, governments are under powerful pressures to harmonize their economic and social policies with those of their trading partners. Even if full standardization is not inevitable, a process of convergence is seen as restricting the rich diversity of policy regimes that characterized Western nations in the postwar era, largely by eroding the levels of social protection achieved in more generous systems.

This issue takes on a special importance in the case of Canada. Although there is no formal harmonization of monetary policy or mobility of labour on the model of the European Community, Canadian financial markets and trade patterns are tightly integrated with the United States. Not surprisingly, therefore, Canada has engaged in an intense debate about whether its more ambitious social programs are sustainable in the context of an ever closer economic embrace with the United States. The most dramatic clash occurred during the 1988 election, which was fought over the free trade agreement with the United States. Apart from a provision in an annex to the chapter on services, the fight was not over the specifics of the trade agreement itself. Rather, the issue was whether the competitive pressures implicit in closer economic integration with the United States would produce greater convergence in the structure of the two welfare states, with the burden of adjustment falling primarily on Canada.

Two basic arguments were advanced by Canadian critics of a closer economic relationship.[3] On one hand, it was argued that if Canada established social programs and related taxes that *raised* the costs of production above those in the United States, investment would drift south, Canadian business would lobby for lower costs, and Canadian governments would have little choice but to reduce their social commitments. On the other hand, it was argued that if Canada established programs and tax policies that *lowered* the costs of production by socializing costs that are borne by employers in the United States, these programs might be interpreted in the United States as subsidies and could be subjected to countervail and other trade action. In either case, the result would be convergence between the two social policy regimes, with the primary burden of adjustment falling on Canada.

Defenders of closer economic links with the United States during the 1980s insisted that economic integration does not necessitate policy harmonization. After all, they insisted, Canada's distinctive social programs were actually developed over a period when the two economies were becoming more deeply entwined, and the country would continue to be free to pursue more ambitious social goals in a closer North American context. Programs financed by taxes that reduce net real incomes rather than increasing the costs of production would present no problem; and programs that do increase business costs would simply trigger a compensating change in the exchange rate. Moreover, social programs that are generally available in Canada would be immune from such actions under existing laws and the prevailing norms of international trade.

This debate was hardly unique to Canada. Broadly similar concerns about labour standards and environmental issues emerged a few years later in the United States during the debate over the North American Free Trade Agreement (NAFTA). Clearly, the world has changed since the early postwar era, and the consequences of globalization for social policy have become a central concern (to which this chapter returns below).

The Pattern of Social Cleavages

While the international economy shapes the general context within which a country develops its welfare state, social divisions within the country have a more direct impact on the politics of social policy. Three cleavages were particularly important to understanding the differences in the welfare states that emerged in Canada and the United States: economic class; social heterogeneity in terms of race, ethnicity, and language; and regional divisions.

The most common interpretation of the politics of the welfare state sees social policy as a reflection of class divisions. Expansive welfare states tend to be found in countries in which the labour force is highly unionized, the union movement is organized in centralized federations, and labour has close links with sympathetic political parties, whether of a social democratic or confessional variety.[4] Viewed from this perspective, the political foundations of the welfare state are weak in both Canada and the United States. In comparison with other Western nations, especially European ones, unionization is low, the two labour movements have often been divided among different federations, and collective bargaining is decentralized.

Within this broad pattern, however, there are important differences between Canada and the United States. As chapter 2 demonstrated, the two labour movements have diverged since the mid-1960s, with union membership declining dramatically in the United States but remaining comparatively stable in Canada. In addition, the two labour movements are animated by different ideological orientations. The predominant tradition in the United States has been an economic unionism that concentrates on the pursuit of the material interests of its members through collective bargaining. While collective bargaining is still the primary function of Canadian unions as well, they espouse a more social unionism, as represented by a social democratic policy agenda and formal links with the New Democratic Party (NDP). The largest labour federation, the Canadian Labour Congress (CLC), places a higher priority on lobbying for social legislation, developing common fronts among unions to fight retrenchment, and establishing coalitions with a wide range of community groups (Haddow 1991). Admittedly, the contrast with the United States can be overstated. The older Congress of Industrial Organizations (CIO) tradition of a wider social agenda continues in the United Auto Workers and other American unions; and in Canada, some unions, such as those within the Canadian Federation of Labour which broke away from the CLC, adopt a more conservative approach. Nevertheless, the different balance within the two labour movements is unmistakable. Organized labour represents a stronger force for comprehensive social protection for the working population north of the border.

Racial and linguistic divisions also shape the politics of social policy. A number of scholars have argued that redistributive policies enjoy greater public support in societies that are relatively homogeneous in terms of language, ethnicity, and race (Wilensky 1975; Gould and Palmer 1988). The differences between Canada and the United States are clear on this dimension as well. The poor are not socially distinctive in Canada; they do not stand out in linguistic, ethnic, or racial terms. The primary fault line in Canadian politics has traditionally been between English- and French-speaking Canadians, but as table 7.2 illustrates, dependence on social benefits is not significantly higher in

Table 7.2
Per capita expenditures on selected social programs in Canada, by province, 1990–1991

	Unemployment insurance	Social assistance[1]	Total federal social security[2]
Newfoundland	1,244	246	3,790
Prince Edward Island	1,011	253	3,796
Nova Scotia	600	273	3,264
New Brunswick	776	351	3,400
Quebec	536	343	2,396
Ontario	319	352	2,527
Manitoba	307	219	2,922
Saskatchewan	258	199	2,806
Alberta	309	278	2,346
British Columbia	438	293	2,808
Canada	429	320	2,627

Source: Human Resources Development Canada, "Social Security Statistics: Canada and the Provinces," tables A7.3, A9.3, and A33.3 (unpublished)

[1] Includes federal and provincial expenditures.

[2] Includes all federal income security and health programs, including transfers to provinces.

Quebec than elsewhere in the country, and it is considerably lower than in the Atlantic provinces. Nor do other ethnic or racial divisions dominate national political discourse over welfare. Certainly, members of certain ethnic and racial minorities are much more likely to be poor; Aboriginal peoples, to take the most striking case, suffer high levels of economic and social distress. Moreover, immigration from the Third World is creating a multiracial society in large urban centres such as Toronto, Montreal, and Vancouver, and is changing the case loads in social assistance and some social housing projects. For example, black families are now significantly overrepresented in the case loads of child-welfare agencies serving Toronto and Montreal.[5] Nevertheless, these changes are not yet powerful enough to give a distinctive ethnic or racial hue to welfare case loads on a nationwide basis, or – more importantly – to the dominant public perception of the poor.

In contrast, race has constituted a core feature of the politics of the American welfare state throughout its history. During the passage of the Social Security Act in 1935, resistance from southern congressmen and other conservatives led to the exclusion of agricultural and domestic labour, denying coverage to three-fifths of black workers. In addition, southern congressmen led a successful campaign in the name of "states'

Table 7.3
AFDC recipients by race, 1973–1992

	1973	1979	1986	1992
White	38.0	40.4	39.7	38.9
Black	45.8	43.1	40.7	37.2
Hispanic	13.4	13.6	14.4	17.8
Native American	1.1	1.4	1.3	1.4
Asian	na	1.0	2.3	2.8
Other/unknown	1.7	0.4	1.4	2.0

Source: U.S. Committee on Ways and Means 1994, 402

rights" against national standards in public assistance, leaving southern blacks at the mercy of the local authorities (Orloff 1988; Quadagno 1988). In the 1960s, controversy swirled around AFDC and the Great Society programs. As welfare rolls expanded and new poverty programs were put in place, the profile of the poor became racially charged. Black families represented close to half of AFDC recipients, and Hispanic groups were also increasingly overrepresented (see table 7.3). These trends generated political resentment. Throughout the 1970s, public opinion polls recorded declining support for programs popularly iden-tified with poor blacks, and Republican electoral campaigns in the 1980s capitalized on these tensions. While blacks continued to support redistributive social programs and the Democratic Party, white union members, urban ethnics, and southerners deserted their traditional political home, especially in presidential elections, in part because of its image on race and welfare issues (Skocpol 1991). In effect, the politics of race drove a wedge into the New Deal coalition and politically isolated the welfare poor, with predictable results. During the retrenchments of the 1980s, programs with predominantly African-American and Hispanic clienteles, such as subsidized housing and AFDC, bore particularly heavy cuts (Slessarev 1988). The issue was so powerful that in the 1990s the Democratic Party sought to insulate itself from race-freighted attacks by embracing hard-edged welfare reforms. During the 1992 presidential campaign, Bill Clinton promised to "end welfare as we know it" by cutting off unconditional welfare support after two years.

Race contributes to the difference between Canadian and American social policy at all levels. It influences the definitions through which social problems such as poverty are interpreted. In the United States the debate centres on the "urban underclass," the African-American and Hispanic inhabitants of inner-city ghettos, and intense scrutiny is focused on the social pathologies and behaviour of the poor themselves.

In contrast, the term "underclass" is virtually unknown in Canada, where the debate centres far less on the characteristics of poor families. Canadian critics of social programs are more likely to emphasize changes in labour markets and the nature of the incentives implicit in the design of social programs (Myles 1991). At the level of program structure, the politics of race also help to explain the less developed coverage for working-aged population and children in the United States, and the less redistributive character of American income transfer programs.

Regionalism represents a third social division with different implications in the two countries. In the United States, resistance from the South represented a barrier to the expansion of welfare. This opposition was rooted not only in race but also in the region's distinctive economic base. In Quadagno's words, "Two distinct economic formations existed within the boundaries of a single nation-state" (1988, 15). In the first half of the twentieth century, the South was distinguished by the system of sharecropping, which was dominated by the power of landlords; and as sharecropping faded, it was replaced by a low-wage economy in which per capita income lagged significantly behind that of the country's North and West. Moreover, potential constituencies of support for social programs remained hobbled in the South during important phases of the history of the American welfare state; labour was relatively unorganized, and most blacks and poor whites were effectively disenfranchised until the 1960s.

The southern states believed that generous welfare programs would jeopardize their labour arrangements and social institutions. They were among the last to adopt mothers' pensions and child-labour laws earlier in the century, and welfare and unemployment benefits in the region remain low today (Peterson and Rom 1990). In addition, southern representatives in Congress fought the establishment of minimum welfare standards by the federal government, not only in the 1930s but in the decades that followed. In 1970 southerners helped defeat Nixon's Family Assistance Plan (FAP); in the late 1970s they fought the welfare reforms presented by Carter; and in 1988 they defeated the proposal to include a national minimum for welfare benefits in the Family Support Act (Quadagno 1990; Pierson 1995).

Canada is also marked by uneven economic development, with Atlantic Canada in particular lagging behind other regions. In contrast with the southern United States, however, Atlantic Canada has embraced national social programs and has come to depend heavily on the large interregional transfers implicit in them. The importance of independent commodity producers in the fishing and lumber industries of Atlantic Canada, and the seasonal nature of much employment there, created a large political constituency in favour of expanded federal income trans-fers. The region welcomed the extension of Unemployment Insurance to fishermen in 1957, as well as a major enrichment of the program and the introduction of regionally extended benefits in areas of high unemployment in 1971. These changes transformed Unemployment Insurance from a traditional social insurance program into a broad in-strument of income supplementation, and its benefits sustain many small communities throughout the region.[6] In contrast to the Ameri-can South, Atlantic Canada has regarded expansive social programs as a mechanism for protecting traditional occupations and communities from the forces of economic modernization (Banting 1995a). As a re-sult, the region has fought vigorously against successive efforts to re-trench the program since the late 1970s. Indeed, the most effective political resistance to cuts in Unemployment Insurance has come from politicians in the poorer provinces rather than from leaders of orga-nized labour (Pal 1988; Smardon 1991). The provincial premiers and MPs from Atlantic Canada have repeatedly fought to protect seasonal workers and to reduce the impact of program changes in their region. The result is that although Unemployment Insurance is a federal pro-gram, its benefits are increasingly differentiated on a regional basis. By 1994, for example, the generosity of the program was about 40 per cent greater in Newfoundland than the national average (Sargent 1995).

Historically, the primary regional obstacle to the expansion of na-tional social programs in Canada flowed from Quebec, which played a role analogous to that of the American South during the first half of the twentieth century. French-Canadian nationalists resisted federal so-cial programs as a form of cultural imperialism that threatened to un-dermine the distinctiveness of their society (Banting 1987a). Like the American South, Quebec was unable to halt the emergence of national social programs, but it slowed the pace and helped to preserve a sub-stantial sphere for provincial discretion. However, this similarity disap-peared rapidly after 1960, when a reformist Liberal Party won power at the provincial level and launched a sweeping program of moderniza-tion which significantly expanded the role of the provincial govern-ment in Quebec life (McRoberts 1988; Simeon and Robinson 1990). Quebec nationalism became imbued with a broadly *étatiste* orientation that produced major reforms to the educational system, the expansion of social services, and the adoption of hospital insurance which the province had hitherto resisted.

This Quiet Revolution was critical to national politics during the 1960s and 1970s, when core elements of the Canadian welfare state were put in place. In the federal Parliament, Quebec ministers and

MPs began to lead rather than resist efforts to expand social programs; and in federal-provincial negotiations, the Quebec government joined the reformist cause on medicare, contributory pensions, and income supplementation. Admittedly, the transformation of Quebec was a double-edged sword. Quebec nationalists were determined to consolidate control over this expanded welfare state in provincial rather than federal hands. The province insisted that it operate new programs such as the contributory pension plan, and it struggled to recapture jurisdictions lost to the federal government during previous decades, thereby contributing to a constitutional struggle that has endured for thirty years (Banting 1995a). Quebec nationalism has lost much of its statist orientation in more recent times. Nevertheless, during the most important period of welfare innovation in Canada, Quebec helped tip the political balance towards expansion.

In contrast to the distinctive social dynamics generated by class, race, and region in Canada and the United States, the emergence of new lines of social division and new social movements represents an element of greater commonality in the politics of social policy. In both countries, the political mobilization of women, ethnic groups, Aboriginal peoples, the gay community, and others has broadened policy discourse and expanded the social agenda. On both sides of the border, these movements have been broadly supportive of governmental activism on social issues and have been committed to modernizing core health and social security programs to reflect a more diverse society. As chapter 2 suggested, this tendency may be more pronounced in Canada, where organizations such as the women's movement have emerged as political bulwarks of the welfare state and have formed alliances with like-minded interests. Moreover, the Canadian movements seem to be less counterbalanced than their American counterparts by conservative organizations rooted in Christian fundamentalism and traditional conceptions of family life. Nevertheless, the contrasts between Canada and the United States are less dramatic here and have therefore been of less account in shaping the different policy regimes of the two countries.

Clearly, differences in the welfare state in Canada and the United States are deeply rooted in the structures of the two societies. Class, race, and region have interwoven to create a less supportive environment for social policy south of the border.

Political Structures

The differences rooted in economic and social structures tend to be amplified by the political structures through which Canadians and Americans make collective choices about social policy. The political institutions themselves and the ideological orientations embedded in the party systems are both important in this respect.

As discussed in chapter 4, political institutions of the United States represent the classic example of fragmented power, combining congressional government, federalism, and decentralized political parties. As a result, policy innovation requires the construction of often fragile and temporary coalitions, a painful process that increases the likelihood that any proposal will be delayed, diluted, or defeated. In contrast, power is more concentrated in Canada by the combination of parliamentary government and cohesive political parties at the national level. Although Canada's federal nature ensures that power is more dispersed than in a unitary state such as Great Britain, its decision making is more concentrated than in the United States, a difference that facilitated the development of social programs.

Institutional complexity in the United States has increased the leverage of conservative political forces. For several critical decades, the congressional and party systems combined to give southern politicians a degree of control over the design of social programs that was much greater than the population or economic importance of their region warranted. One-party dominance ensured that long-serving conservative Democrats from the South chaired the relevant congressional committees and could manage the legislative process. Although this system did accommodate the incremental expansion of social security after its introduction (Derthick 1979), more radical departures were blocked, as the tangled history of proposals for health insurance illustrates. Only exceptional Democratic majorities, as in the 1960s, could break the log-jam. In the 1990s the fate of the health plan developed by President Clinton confirmed once again the paralysing possibilities inherent in the congressional system.

Other more subtle institutional dynamics have also become visible in contemporary struggles, such as that over urban poverty. Equal representation for each state in the Senate significantly overrepresents rural America, for whom the social devastation of urban centres can seem somewhat distant. In addition, Ferejohn (1983) and Heclo (1986) argue that congressional politics militates against programs that redistribute income in a highly targeted fashion to the poor. The need to build fragile coalitions by spreading benefits widely over many districts militates against targeting programs on the areas of greatest need. In contrast, the concentrated power inherent in Canadian parliamentary institutions and cohesive political parties creates no such additional barriers to redistributive politics.

Federalism represents the only qualification to this general pattern of fewer institutional blockages in Canada. In the United States, federalism contributes to the larger system of checks and balances, but history records few major initiatives in social policy that were blocked primarily by constitutional limits on federal jurisdiction. Indeed, the dominant trend was the steady expansion of the federal role, a pattern that continued until the adoption of Supplementary Security Income (SSI) and the Earned Income Tax Credit (EITC) in 1974 (Pierson 1995). This is not to deny that federalism constrains social programs. For example, there is evidence that average AFDC benefits are depressed by economic competition among states (Peterson and Rom 1990; Marmor, Mashaw, and Harvey 1990). Moreover, the absence of any significant commitment to equalizing the fiscal capacity of the rich and poor states limits the scope for new initiatives at the state level, a constraint that may well loom larger in the future as retrenchment at the federal level and greater reliance on block funding enhances the role of state and local governments (Nathan and Doolittle 1987). Nevertheless, federalism still appears to be a secondary feature of the politics of social policy in the United States.

In Canada, federalism stood as a major barrier in the early history of the welfare state. In 1937 a judicial decision struck down social insurance programs as being beyond the constitutional powers of the federal government, and in 1946 a package of similar proposals foundered on the shoals of wider federal-provincial conflict. During the postwar decades, however, stronger political support for action overcame this barrier. In the field of health care, federalism actually facilitated expansion, as social democrats were able to capture power and introduce path-breaking legislation at the provincial level. Saskatchewan advanced the cause dramatically by introducing a health insurance program that became a model for the country, and then mounting a protracted campaign for national cost sharing of such programs (Gray 1991; Tuohy 1989). In other sectors, however, federalism did represent a constraint. For example, a complex system of federal and provincial vetoes over changes in contributory pensions has effectively insulated these programs from expansionist political pressures and has inclined the federal government to rely on other more limited instruments, such as the income-tested Guaranteed Income Supplement (Banting 1985). Overall, federalism has probably been a modestly conservative factor in the politics of the Canadian welfare state, although the sharpness of the contrast on this dimension with the United States that existed during the 1930s and 1940s has faded.

Thus, even when full weight is given to the complexities of Canadian federalism, the American combination of congressional government, federalism, and non-cohesive political parties diffuses power more thoroughly, amplifying resistance to expansive social programs and especially to redistributive efforts targeted on the poor.

The ideological complexion of the party systems in the two countries reinforces the pattern. Historically, the presence of a social democratic party in Canada added a forceful voice committed to both universal social programs and to targeted assistance for vulnerable groups. Until its serious electoral setback in 1993, the NDP – and its predecessor, the Co-operative Commonwealth Federation (CCF) – exercised an influence in national politics that was much greater than its third-party status might suggest. Not only did the NDP hold power at various times in four provinces, but it was an active participant in national debates in Parliament and the media, and a pressure on other parties, especially the Liberal Party, which borrowed ideas from the left at electorally strategic moments. NDP influence was considerably magnified during periods of minority Liberal governments, when the Liberal Party's hold on power depended on accommodating at least some parts of the left's agenda.

The combination of legislative and party structures in the two countries created distinctive patterns of policy innovation and expansion during the postwar period. As Weaver (1990) points out, reform in the United States came at times of great Democratic strength, whereas in Canada reform often came at times of Liberal weakness. The periods of Liberal weakness were more common than those of Democratic triumph. Large Democratic majorities were limited to brief periods in the 1930s and 1960s, when Social Security, Medicare, and other Great Society programs were passed. In contrast, Liberal vulnerability has been a recurring feature of Canadian politics. The first federal old age pensions were introduced by a minority Liberal government in 1927; Family Allowances were introduced in 1944 by a Liberal government that felt threatened by the sudden strength of the CCF in opinion polls; Medicare, contributory pensions, and the Canada Assistance Plan were all introduced by a minority Liberal government in the mid-1960s; and Family Allowances were tripled in value in 1973 by another minority Liberal government that was dependent on the NDP. These initiatives do not represent the entire history of the Canadian welfare state, but they do constitute one of its important themes.

Ideological and electoral coalitions in the two countries also differed in important ways during the conservative dominance in the 1980s and 1990s. The election of Ronald Reagan represented a realignment in presidential politics. The traditional New Deal coalition had been slowly eroding for over a decade, and the Republicans seized the opportunity to expand their support among southern whites, urban ethnics, white union members, and the fundamentalist religious movement (Wattenberg 1990; Carmines and Stimson 1989; Edsall 1991). The Republican approach to social issues reflected this political base. Changes made during the 1980s to social security – which remained well supported by the public, including Republican voters – reduced the expenditure level that would otherwise have prevailed in the early 1990s by only 8 per cent. Programs for the poor and inner cities fared less well; the comparable cut for AFDC was 36 per cent, and the figure was 54 per cent for programs covered by the social services block grant (U.S. Committee on Ways and Means 1991, 1515). In effect, the politics of retrenchment in the United States sharpened the traditional contrast between the two tiers of its welfare state by rolling back expansions of the lower tier that had crept in during the 1960s and early 1970s.

Canadian conservatism pushed in the opposite direction. Although the Liberal and Conservative parties tend to present broadly similar programs, their party activists lean in different directions. Surveys in the mid-1980s found Conservatives to be more concerned about welfare abuse, less supportive of enhanced funding for child care and the poor, and less sympathetic to universal programs such as Old Age Security (OAS) and Family Allowances (Perlin 1988). This last predisposition proved particularly important in government. Although some reductions implemented by the Mulroney government – such as the freezing of transfers to provincial governments for health care and postsecondary education – cut across the board, the Conservatives accelerated the trend towards greater selectivity. The universal OAS payments were clawed back from upper-income recipients through the tax system; the universal Family Allowances were replaced with an income-tested Child Benefit that eliminated support for middle- and upper-income families; reductions in Unemployment Insurance benefits continued to be much more dramatic in affluent regions than in poor ones; and a cap on the growth in federal support for provincial social assistance was applied only to the three richest provinces (Banting 1992a, 1995a).

Thus, ideological impulses embedded in the two countries' party systems differed, not only during the expansion of the welfare state but also in the period of conservative retrenchment. Cuts in the United States fell disproportionately on benefits for the poor, whereas Canadian cuts accelerated an historical trend of targeting benefits on such people.

The Sources of Distinctiveness: A Summary

The contrasts explored here might strike a distant observer as rather subtle, representing minor variations on the major themes of North American life. Cumulatively, however, these differences have provided a stronger base for the welfare state in Canada than in the United States. Historically, Canada's vulnerability to international economic pressures has contributed to a stronger tradition of collective responses to social needs, and core features of domestic life in the two countries reinforce this difference. Not only does organized labour represent a stronger presence in Canada, but social initiatives have been less constrained by racial and regional divisions than in the United States. Finally, political structures amplify these differences. Canadian political institutions provide fewer blocking opportunities to those resisting social programs in general and to income transfers to the poor in particular; and the ideological orientations embedded in the party systems have pushed the two social policy regimes in different directions at critical stages in their evolution.

THE SOCIAL POLICY REGIMES

The imprint of these economic, social, and political differences between Canada and the United States can be seen clearly in their social programs. This section examines health and income security programs in greater detail, paying particular attention to the three interrelated differences noted at the outset: comprehensiveness of support, especially for children and those of working age; the strength of selective programs targeted on the poor; and the redistributive impact of social policy on poverty and inequality.

Health Care

Health care traditionally has provided the most dramatic contrast between Canada and the United States. In Canada, Medicare covers basic hospital and medical services on a universal basis without deductibles, co-payments, or significant user fees. As a result, there is no parallel private sector in basic health care. Private health plans provide supplementary items not covered by the public program, such as semi-private accommodation in hospital, prescription drugs, the additional costs of out-of-country medical care, and dental care. Although the private sector has been growing incrementally as a result of some trimming in public coverage, private expenditures still represent less than 30 per cent of total health spending (OECD 1994c).

In contrast, public programs in the United States play a more limited role, covering only specific categories of the population. Medicare provides health insurance for the elderly, although those covered must still bear a proportion of the costs of basic care in the form of premiums, deductibles, and co-insurance payments, giving rise to private

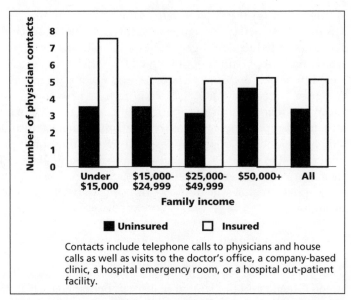

Figure 7.2   Average reported physician contacts, by income and insurance status, 1986
Source: U.S. Bipartisan Commission on Comprehensive Health Care 1990

"Medigap" policies for those who can afford them. Veterans Affairs provides health care for some elderly and disabled veterans. Finally, Medicaid, a means-tested program delivered by state governments, provides health care to less than half of the nation's poor, albeit with considerable variation among states. In 1995, for example, Nevada served 284 Medicaid beneficiaries for every 1,000 poor or near-poor individuals in the state, whereas Rhode Island served 913 per 1,000 (U.S. General Accounting Office 1995a). The rest of the American population must rely on the private sector. However, private coverage is seriously incomplete: approximately 16 per cent of the population – some 41 million people, primarily low-income workers and their families – were without coverage in 1992; and many more were seriously underinsured (Aaron 1996). The vast majority of these people must rely on the willingness of doctors and hospitals, especially public hospitals, to provide uncompensated care, largely through cross-subsidies from those who are fully insured. Otherwise, the uninsured must simply do without adequate medical care.[7]

Differences in coverage lead to differences in access. Given the universal coverage in Canada, differences in the utilization of health care among different social groups reflects other factors, such as geographic

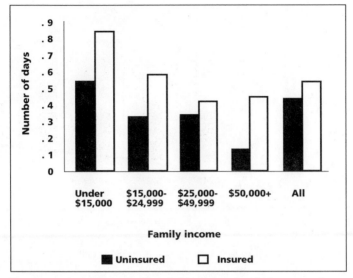

Figure 7.3   Average reported hospital in-patient days, by income and
insurance status, 1986
Source: U.S. Bipartisan Commission on Comprehensive Health Care 1990

location. In the United States, however, incomplete insurance coverage adds other inequalities. In 1986 a national survey found that uninsured Americans contacted a doctor two-thirds as often as the insured
population and used only three-quarters as many days in hospital (see
figures 7.2 and 7.3). The uninsured are more likely to delay seeking
care or to be turned away, leading eventually to more serious illnesses
and to hospital admissions that could have been avoided; and when
the uninsured do receive treatment for serious problems, they tend to
receive less extensive care than insured individuals with similar conditions. Sorting out the consequences for the actual health status of the
two groups is difficult, since health is also affected by related factors,
such as the poverty of many of the uninsured. Nevertheless, the uninsured are clearly less healthy. One study found that between 1982 and
1986 infants born to parents without health insurance were 30 per
cent more likely to become ill or die than those born to insured parents. In the words of a major commission, "Lack of health insurance
means diminished chances at the outset of life and more illness and
disability ahead" (U.S. Bipartisan Commission on Comprehensive
Health Care 1990, 35).

The contrast between the Canadian and American systems grew
sharper in the 1980s and 1990s. The intense pressure on health-care

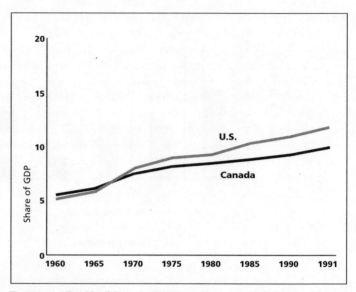

Figure 7.4   Total health expenditures as a proportion of GDP, Canada and the United States, 1960–1991
Source: OECD 1994c, table 2

costs has been a key political issue on both sides of the border, but the two countries have responded differently, as figure 7.4 attests. In Canada, concerns that extra billing by doctors and user fees in hospitals were beginning to undermine universal access led Parliament to adopt – with all-party support – the 1984 Canada Health Act, which imposed penalties on provinces that allowed such charges. This prohibition is not without its critics, and in the mid-1990s the federal government was locked in battles with a number of provincial governments – especially Alberta, which wished to expand the role of private clinics. Nevertheless, the 1984 Act has curbed the expansion of fees and user charges. Some provinces have narrowed the range of medical procedures covered by deinsuring such items as cosmetic surgery and newer reproductive technologies, and by refusing to pay the difference between domestic rates and the cost of medical care received by their citizens while visiting other countries (Tuohy 1988, 1994). In general, however, the burden of the substantial financial cuts imposed by provincial governments has fallen on the service providers. As the single payer responsible for financing health care within its jurisdiction, each provincial government is in a strong position to control costs – by setting budgets for hospitals, by supervising capital expenditures for new equipment and buildings, and by negotiating increases in physicians'

fees with medical associations. Critics of the Canadian model emphasize that this approach has resulted in a slower adoption of new technologies than in the United States and lengthy waiting lists for some
surgical procedures. In the early 1990s a favourite example of the
technological gap was the MRI scanner, the magnetic resonance imag-
ing device that represents a major advance in diagnostic science. In
1991 there were approximately fifteen MRIs in Canada but more than
two thousand in the United States – an immense gap even when the
size of the two countries is taken into consideration.[8] Moreover, Canadians seem to accept longer waits for some non-lifesaving operations,
such as knee replacements (Coyte et al. 1994). The Canadian version
of restraint is thus not without costs. So far, however, broad equality of
access has been preserved.

Health-care costs in the United States have not been controlled as
effectively, and this failure has further eroded equality of access. The
American health-care system is much more pluralistic, with private in-
surers, employers, and three levels of governments paying for health-
care services. As a result, no single unit is as well placed as Canadian
provincial governments to manage cost increases, and health expenditures continued their relentless climb throughout the 1980s (R. Evans
1986; R. Evans, Barer, and Hertzman 1991; U.S. General Accounting
Office 1991). In this context, employers have responded in two ways.
First, they have reduced their health commitments by transferring
more of the burden to both current and retired employees through reduced coverage and increased deductibles and co-payments; at the extreme, health insurance has collapsed completely in many small firms.
Second, private corporations have been turning to health-mainte-
nance organizations (HMOs) to deliver health care to their employees.
These agencies have the power to influence the pattern of care, access
to doctors, the salaries and fees paid to service providers, staffing levels
in hospitals, and other aspects of health care – all in the name of controlling costs. This transformation of health care in the United States is
occurring with breathtaking speed: most working-age, insured Americans are already receiving care through such plans, and the model is
expected to incorporate virtually all insured Americans within a few
years (Aaron 1996).

Medical coverage under public programs has also eroded in the
United States. Although the primary burden of the cuts in Medicare has
fallen on the service providers, the elderly have not escaped unscathed.
For example, out-of-pocket health spending increased from 7.8 per cent
of after-tax income in 1972 to 12.5 per cent in 1988 (U.S. Committee
on Ways and Means 1991, 250); and the 1988 Catastrophic Health Care
Act, which was designed to protect the elderly from the additional costs

of acute health problems, was repealed within a year of its passage. In the case of Medicaid, federal initiatives begun in 1986 did expand eligibility for low-income pregnant women and children, but sharp limits on reimbursement rates reduced the willingness of doctors and hospitals to accept large numbers of Medicaid patients.

The cumulative effect of all the changes is hardly surprising: the uninsured population rose from 24 million in 1980 to 41 million in 1994, and the number with inadequate coverage also continued to grow. In addition, much more stringent payment systems developed both by HMOs and by the public programs have been weakening the capacity of hospitals and others to provide uncompensated care to the growing uninsured population, thus drying up "the balm that has made socially tolerable the abrasive fact that one non-aged person in six is without insurance at any given time" (Aaron 1996, 35; see also U.S. Committee on Ways and Means 1994; and U.S. Bipartisan Commission on Comprehensive Health Care 1990).

Health care thus reflects two central differences between the welfare state in Canada and the United States. The public sector in Canada provides more comprehensive coverage and stronger redistribution of well-being between rich and poor, a contrast that has grown sharper during the 1980s and 1990s.

Income Security

Canada and the United States do not form such a sharp contrast in the world of income security. Nevertheless, the Canadian system does provide more comprehensive protection, especially for children and those of working age; it devotes more of its resources to selective programs; and its program structure has a larger redistributive impact. This pattern often comes as a surprise to those accustomed to thinking of Canada as more dedicated to the universal approach. Table 7.4 tracks expenditures on universal and selective transfer programs in the two countries between 1960 and 1992. Canada and the United States started in almost identical positions in the early 1960s. Since then, a growing proportion of Canadian income-security dollars have flowed through selective programs, whereas the American proportion remained stable until the 1980s and then declined. Initially, the Canadian trend reflected the introduction of income supplements, such as the Guaranteed Income Supplement (GIS) and the refundable Child Tax Credit (CTC). Since the 1980s, however, the pattern has also reflected the growth of social assistance programs and, more recently, the transformation of universal programs, such as Family Allowances and Old Age Security (OAS), into income-tested benefits. Moreover, table 7.4 probably understates the trend towards selective programs in Canada, since it does not reflect the

Table 7.4
Universal and selective expenditures as a proportion of total income security,
Canada and the United States, 1960–1992 (in percent)

	1960	1965	1970	1975	1980	1985	1990	1992
UNITED STATES[1]								
Universal	79.6	81.2	77.2	75.7	79.1	83.3	83.7	82.2
Selective	20.4	18.8	22.8	24.3	20.9	16.7	16.3	17.8
CANADA[2]								
Universal	79.2	72.4	69.2	70.7	62.6	64.5	52.5	48.0
Selective	20.8	27.6	30.8	29.3	37.4	35.5	47.5	52.0

Sources: Calculated from data in Health and Welfare Canada, Social Security Statistics: Canada and the Provinces (Ottawa, various years); U.S. Department of Health and Human Services 1994; and U.S. Office of Management and Budget 1995.

[1] Universal programs include OASDI, unemployment insurance, workers' compensation, plus public employee retirement benefits and railroad retirement and unemployment benefits not provided through social security. Selective programs include income-tested programs (earned income tax credit) and all means-tested income transfers.

[2] Universal benefits include demogrants and all social insurance income transfers. However, family allowances and old age security are considered to be increasingly selective due to the phasing in of the tax clawback of benefits from upper-income recipients. These expenditures are treated as 66% selective in 1990 and 100% selective in 1992. Selective programs include both income-tested programs (child benefit, guaranteed income supplement, spouses allowance, and refundable provincial tax credits) and means-tested benefits. Social assistance expenditures in Ontario, British Columbia, and Alberta in 1990 and 1992 are based on estimates.

fact that elements of income testing have also crept into Unemployment Insurance benefits.[9] In contrast, the fiscal dominance of Social Security has remained unchallenged in the United States. Despite the development of the Earned Income Tax Credit, which will be discussed more fully below, selective programs generally have declined as a proportion of income security expenditures. Clearly, the two systems have been travelling different pathways for decades.

Underlying this general pattern, however, is a more complex pattern of both convergence and divergence in different programs. A fuller appreciation of these contrasting trends requires a closer look at the core programs – pensions, unemployment insurance, child benefits, and social assistance – and at their redistributive impact.

Pensions

For the average senior citizen, the role of the state in providing retirement income is quite similar in Canada and the United States. Public programs provide comparable portions of the income of those aged

Table 7.5
Sources of income of the elderly, Canada and the United States, 1989[1]

Income source	Canada	United States
Public transfers	40.1	40.9
Private pensions	16.9	17.0
Investment income	26.2	27.5
Other	16.8	14.6

Sources: Canadian Institute of Actuaries 1993, 9; U.S. Committee on Ways and Means 1991, 1107.

[1] Canadian data are for couples in which both are aged 65 or over; U.S. data include both unattached individuals and couples in which both are aged over 65.

sixty-five and over on both sides of the border, as table 7.5 indicates; and similar benefits flow from the universal programs – the Canada and Quebec Pension Plans and the OAS in Canada, and in the United States the Old Age Security Income (OASI), which is a component of Social Security. The biggest difference lies in the more redistributive character of the benefit structure in Canada. During the late 1980s, close to half of the entire elderly population of the country, including many who had had average earning records before retirement and who held significant assets during retirement, received a GIS payment. In the United States, the Supplementary Security Income (SSI) is a means-tested benefit that has much more stringent income limits and requires individuals to exhaust most of their assets before they can qualify for it.[10] As a result, it reaches a tiny proportion of the elderly. In 1993, for example, only 6.7 per cent of elderly Americans received any benefit from the program (U.S. General Accounting Office 1995b, figure 1.3).

Table 7.6 compares replacement ratios, which measure retirement benefits as a proportion of preretirement earnings for new retirees. As can be seen, the general programs have comparable replacement capacity, but the GIS significantly enhances the position of low-income and average retirees in Canada. This table overstates the cross-national difference somewhat because it does not incorporate SSI in the calculations for the United States. It is difficult to include a means-tested benefit in replacement ratios, since assets constitute a major consideration in determining eligibility. Nevertheless, the general impression conveyed by the table is undoubtedly correct, since SSI reaches such a small portion of the elderly population. It is the power of their selective component that distinguishes Canadian retirement benefits from their counterparts south of the border.

The politics of the 1980s and 1990s accentuated this difference. Frontal assaults on major retirement benefits were initially repulsed on

Table 7.6
Replacement ratios: Public retirement benefits as a proportion of pre-retirement
earnings for new retirees, Canada and the United States, 1989

	Low earnings	Average earnings	High earnings
United States	57.9	41.7	24.1
Canada:			
without GIS	61.0	44.6	22.3
with GIS	86.5	50.7	22.3

Sources: Ratios for Canada calculated from benefit levels reported in National Council of Welfare 1990, tables 4 and 5; ratios for the United States from Committee on Ways and Means 1990, app. A, table 15.

both sides of the border, and only more limited adjustments survived the political process. Nevertheless, the burden of change fell differently in the two countries. Under changes in U.S. Social Security legislation, the pain was spread evenly, with the poorest and the richest recipients suffering approximately the same proportionate reduction in their replacement rates between 1981 and 1991 (U.S. Committee on Ways and Means 1994, table 1.7). In contrast, the Canadian system was made more redistributive: the GIS for low-income recipients was significantly enriched in the early 1980s, and the previously universal OAS payment was clawed back through the tax system from high-income recipients at the end of the decade. The 1996 federal budget announced the logical culmination of this process: beginning in the year 2001, the OAS and GIS will be replaced by an integrated, income-tested Seniors Benefit that will provide support to low- and middle-income Canadians only (Canada, Department of Finance 1996). Thus, the traditional differences have been accentuated by the politics of retrenchment in the two countries in the 1980s and 1990s.

Unemployment Insurance

If pensions have moved consistently in one direction, unemployment insurance has resembled a roller-coaster. The large historical difference between the two systems expanded dramatically during the 1980s, but it began to contract again during the 1990s.

In the United States, unemployment insurance is a federal-state program and is delivered by the state governments. The program is financed exclusively through a payroll tax on employers, with employees making no direct contributions. The federal government imposes a payroll tax on employers and then rebates the revenue to the state governments that operate a federally approved program. The state governments impose an additional payroll tax and can borrow from the federal Treasury if their programs are threatened with insolvency during periods of high unemployment. Federal legislation generally determines what employment is covered, but the states determine the qualification periods, as well as the level and duration of the regular state benefit programs. There is also a federal-state program of extended benefits, designed to be triggered on a state-by-state basis during recessions. In comparison, the Canadian program enjoys the simplicity of being an exclusively federal program, financed by contributions by employers and employees which were supplemented until 1991 from general federal revenues. The complexity of the Canadian program is found in the regional differentials that have been built into both the qualification periods and the duration of benefits, providing enriched support in areas of high unemployment.

After a major expansion in 1971, the Canadian program provided far greater protection to the unemployed than the program in the United States did. Although benefit levels were not dramatically higher, especially after they were trimmed in 1978, coverage in Canada was broader, work requirements were less restrictive, and benefit periods were longer. For example, maximum benefit periods were normally twenty-six weeks in the United States and fifty-two weeks in Canada. In addition, the Canadian program introduced elements, such as maternity and later paternity benefits, that are not covered in the United States. With this more liberal program structure, unemployment benefits represented a dramatically larger financial commitment for the public sector in Canada. For example, as recently as 1993 unemployment insurance benefits represented 2.6 per cent of GDP in Canada, but only 0.5 per cent in the United States, a gap far greater than the difference in unemployment rates (Osberg, Erksoy, and Phipps 1994).

The differences between the two programs grew strongly over the course of the 1980s. While the Canadian program suffered only marginal adjustments during the decade, the Reagan administration had a significant impact on unemployment insurance south of the border. Federal legislation virtually eliminated extended benefits, and it began to charge interest on state borrowing from the federal Treasury, which put pressure on the states to revise their programs. Given the weakness of organized labour in most state capitals, the revisions relied much more on benefit restrictions than on increased payroll taxes. According to Burtless, the result was a serious erosion of unemployment insurance that went "virtually unnoticed in the early 1980s at a time when far smaller proportional cutbacks in public assistance, disability insurance and social security caused loud public outcries" (Burtless

1991, 41; see also Hansen and Byers 1990). Whereas approximately 80 per cent of the unemployed received benefits during the recession of the mid-1970s, only 26 per cent of the unemployed were receiving benefits in 1987 (U.S. Committee on Ways and Means 1991, 483).

The divergence in the 1980s has given way to some convergence since then. Faced with major increases in spending on unemployment benefits during the recession of the early 1990s, Canadian governments of both Conservative and Liberal persuasion have taken slices from the program. In 1991 the federal government's financial contribution ended, shifting the full cost to employers and employees. In addition, the period of employment required to qualify for benefit was increased in 1990 and 1994, and was planned to rise again in 1996. The maximum length of time for which benefits can be received was reduced in 1990 and was to drop again in 1996. And benefits levels were reduced from 60 to 57 per cent of insurable earnings in 1993 and were cut further for most beneficiaries to 55 per cent in 1994. At the same time, the United States was temporarily repairing some of the damage to its program. After protracted political battles between president and Congress, benefits for victims of the current recession were extended in late 1991 and twice in 1992.

In summary, then, strong divergence in the 1980s has given way to convergence in the 1990s. Canada has withdrawn significant resources from its program in recent years, especially in the more affluent parts of the country. Nevertheless, it is important not to overstate the extent of convergence with the United States. As figure 7.5 suggests, the differences between the two programs in terms of coverage of the unemployed has remained significant.

Child Benefits

The strongest case of convergence is to be found in child benefits. In the mid-1970s the contrast between the two countries was clear. Canada had a universal program of Family Allowances, whereas the United States was the only major industrialized nation with no child-allowance program. Since then, the contrast has disappeared as both countries have experimented with the integration of the tax and transfer systems in order to provide more targeted support for low-income families. By the mid-1990s, the programs in the two countries differed only in their details.

The United States introduced its refundable Earned Income Tax Credit (EITC) for working-poor families with children as part of a wider tax-cut package in 1975. Coverage under the program is relatively narrow because, as a credit against earned income, it provides no

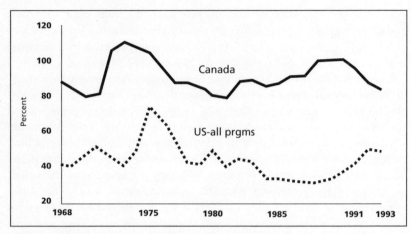

Figure 7.5   UI recipients as a proportion of unemployed workers, Canada and the United States, 1968–1993
Sources: Calculated from data in Committee on Ways and Means 1994 and from Statistics Canada 1994a and 1994b

support to welfare families who have few earnings. However, benefit levels were boosted significantly in 1986, 1990, and 1993. The final and biggest increase, in 1993, represented one of President Clinton's few victories in the domain of social policy. In 1994 the maximum annual benefits were $2,038 for a family with one child and $2,528 for larger families, and these levels were scheduled to rise to $2,094 and $3,370 by 1996.

Canada has moved in the same direction. The first major step came in 1978, when the federal government introduced the refundable Child Tax Credit (CTC), financed in part by a reduction in the universal Family Allowances. In the years that followed, child-related programs underwent a tortuous series of incremental changes, which culminated in the 1992 budget. The previously universal Family Allowance and the general tax exemption for children were replaced with a single, income-tested Child Benefit that was to be delivered through the tax system. Coverage under the Canadian program is broader than in the United States, since it goes to both the working poor and the welfare poor (although there is an additional supplement for the working poor). However, benefit levels are marginally lower in Canada for most families. In 1994 the maximum annual benefits were $1,020 per child, with a supplement of $213 for younger children and a supplement of up to $500 for families with employment earnings.

Thus, child benefits in the two countries have clearly converged over the last twenty years. The traditional contrast generated by the Canadian system of universal Family Allowances has given way to variations on a common theme of income-tested benefits delivered through the tax system. Nevertheless, the transition reflects the stronger shift in Canada towards redistribution to the poor. In abandoning its universal Family Allowances and the general tax exemption for dependent children, both of which provided benefits to middle- and upper-income earners in the mid-1970s, the reallocation of benefits towards low-income groups was marked. Moreover, the long-term prospects for targeted support to poor families seem better in Canada; for example, the 1996 federal budget announced a doubling of the supplement for working-poor families (Canada, Department of Finance 1996). In the United States, however, the bipartisan consensus that had sustained the expansion of the EITC had broken down by the mid-1990s, with congressional Republicans proposing significant cutbacks in the program (Weaver 1995; see also U.S. General Accounting Office 1995c).

Social Assistance

The pattern in social assistance resembles that in unemployment insurance, with significant divergence during the 1980s fading in the 1990s. Throughout all the turmoil, however, the underlying pattern of recent history has remained one of stronger redistribution towards poor people who live north of the border. Under the terms of the Canada Assistance Plan, which provided federal support to provincial welfare programs from 1965 to 1995, provinces were required to provide assistance to all persons in need. Although the level of support provided to single employable persons has not been overly generous in some provinces, support is provided to all categories of needy people. In contrast, coverage in the United States is much less complete. Traditionally, Aid to Families with Dependent Children (AFDC) has been restricted to single-parent families, with only some states extending partial support to the children in two-parent households when the principal wage earner is unemployed. Single persons and childless couples remain ineligible for AFDC in all states. Income support for these people is limited to Food Stamps (a federal program) and General Assistance (a purely state and local program which provides meagre benefits and does not exist at all in almost half of the states). In addition to differences in coverage, benefit levels have traditionally been higher in Canada. For example, Blank and Hanratty found that in 1986 "even in the least generous province in Canada, the [social assistance] benefit level for single-parent families exceeds the maximum low-income transfers (AFDC and Food Stamps) available in all states except Alaska" (Blank and Hanratty 1993, 197).

These differentials between the two countries grew in the 1980s and the first half of the 1990s. In the United States, AFDC benefit levels have undergone a long-term decline: between 1970 and 1994 the maximum AFDC benefits in the median state declined by 47 per cent in real terms, an erosion that has been only partially cushioned by the federal Food Stamps program (U.S. Committee on Ways and Means 1994, table 10.14). This trend reflects the failure to index benefits fully for inflation since the mid-1970s, plus explicit cutbacks in both eligibility and benefits during the last years of the Carter presidency and the early years of the Reagan administration. The pattern of decline accelerated again in the early 1990s. Unlike their Canadian counterparts, budget makers in the U.S. states could not rely on deficit financing. Forty-nine states are required by their constitutions or state law to balance their budgets, and the result was a wave of reductions in AFDC, and especially in General Assistance. In the recession year of 1991, for example, Michigan abolished General Assistance altogether; significant reductions in benefits took place in states as diverse as Massachusetts, California, Maryland, Ohio, Illinois, Maine, and the District of Columbia; and most other states froze benefit levels (Center on Budget and Policy Priorities and Center for the Study of the States, 1991).

Although comparable long-term data is unavailable in Canada, it is clear that the predominant pattern has been different. During the recession of the early 1980s, the three westernmost provinces did in fact reduce welfare rates, but most other provinces maintained their benefits in real terms (Banting 1987b). This record was repeated over the rest of the decade. Although benefits in several provinces declined in real terms, especially in Alberta, other provinces maintained or enriched the real value of their benefits, with particularly strong increases in the big provinces of Ontario, Quebec, and British Columbia. Indeed, Ontario increased its benefits in real terms by approximately 25 per cent between 1985 and 1990 (National Council of Welfare 1995). By the mid-1990s, the differential been Canada and the United States had never been greater.

This gap between the two systems seems to be narrowing again in the second half of the 1990s as Canadian governments struggle to reduce their deficits. In 1995 the federal government sharply reduced its transfers to provincial governments for social programs, and it rolled the Canada Assistance Plan into a broader block fund, which gives provinces more discretion in reforming welfare. In addition, the newly elected Conservative government in Ontario effectively eliminated most of the increases of the previous decade with a 21 per cent reduction in welfare benefits. Major changes in welfare were also being debated in the United States, including proposals to replace AFDC with a block fund to

Table 7.7
Social assistance benefits, Canada and the United States, 1994[1]

	Average benefit national $	Average benefit Cdn $
Canada:		
single parent/one child	13,487	13,487
couple/two children	18,289	18,289
United States:		
singe parent/two children	7,932	10,708

Sources: National Council of Welfare 1995, table 2; U.S. Committee on Ways and Means 1994, table 10.11

[1] Canadian figures represent the average provincial/territorial benefit, including social assistance, child benefits, and provincial refundable tax credits. U.S. figure represents AFDC and food stamps in the median state. The EITC is not paid to welfare families with no earnings and is not included.

state governments, similar to the Canadian initiative. However, divided government once again worked its magic. Early in 1996 President Clinton vetoed the Republican's welfare bill, ensuring that the issue would be swept up into the politics of the presidential race.

Despite this narrowing of the gap in the mid-1990s, it is important not to overstate the convergence between the systems. As in the case of unemployment insurance, the Canadian programs remain more generous than the American. Coverage is much more comprehensive, with single individuals, childless couples, and two-parent families eligible for support. Benefits also remain significantly higher. Table 7.7 demonstrates the differences in 1994, the most recent year for which data are available. Although the reductions in Ontario have undoubtedly reduced the Canadian average, the differences facing the poor on both sides of the border remain compelling. A comparison of the welfare program in Ontario at the time of the 1995 cuts, with that prevailing across the border in Michigan, concluded that "residents of Michigan may consider what Ontario is facing a walk in the park" (Gadd 1995).

Redistributive Impacts

In view of the more comprehensive coverage and the more targeted programs, it is hardly surprising that Canadian programs have a greater impact than the American on the distribution of income. Comparative studies of trends in both the rates of poverty and the extent of overall inequality confirm that Canadian programs have a stronger redistributive role and that the difference in the two systems grew during

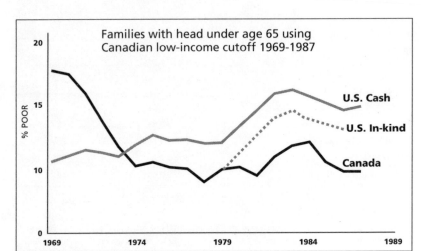

Figure 7.6   Canadian and U.S. poverty rates
Source: Hanratty and Blank 1992

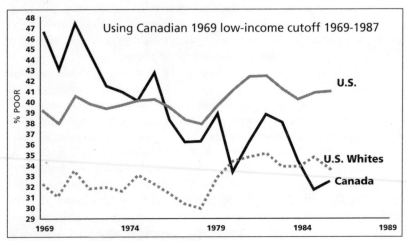

Figure 7.7   Female-headed family poverty rates, Canada and the United States, 1969–1987
Source: Hanratty and Blank 1992

the 1980s and early 1990s. Figure 7.6 tracks the poverty rates in Canada and the United States for families headed by an individual under sixty-five years of age during the period 1969–87, using the Canadian definition of poverty in both countries. Figure 7.7 supplements this basic data with evidence about one subgroup that is particularly vulnerable to poverty – female-headed families. Although the economic and demographic structure of the two countries is similar, the poverty rates

Table 7.8

Effect of taxes and transfers on levels of child poverty in Canada and the United States in the 1980s (% poor)[1]

	Canada		United States	
	1981	1987	1979	1986
Pre-tax and transfer	15.5	15.7	19.0	22.3
Post-tax and transfer	10.2	9.3	14.7	20.4
Reduction	5.3	6.4	4.3	1.9
% reduction	34.2	40.8	24.2	8.5

Source: Smeeding 1991

[1] Poverty is defined as 40 per cent of median disposable income in each country.

have followed different trajectories. Poverty in Canada declined rapidly over the course of the 1970s, from a rate considerably higher than that in the United States to one well below it. Although poverty increased in both countries during the recession of the early 1980s, the rate fell back in Canada but remained stubbornly above its pre-recession level in the United States.

An analysis by Hanratty and Blank (1992) demonstrates that the divergence in poverty rates during the 1980s did not flow from demographic or macroeconomic factors but from the different fate of income transfer programs in the two countries. The deterioration of social assistance, unemployment insurance, and other benefits in the United States had unmistakable consequences. Hanratty and Blank estimate that in 1979 Canadian social assistance, Family Allowances, and the Child Tax Credit provided an average combined benefit that was 14 per cent more generous than the comparable combination in the United States; by 1986 the gap had grown to 42 per cent. This pattern was reinforced by the growing gap in eligibility for, and duration of, unemployment insurance benefits. As a result, "virtually all of the divergence in poverty trends in the two countries may be explained by differences in the share of families who were moved out of poverty by transfers" (Hanratty and Blank 1992, 252). A separate simulation by the same authors concludes that if the United States adopted Canadian income-security programs, the poverty rate would drop significantly (Blank and Hanratty 1993).

The cross-national Luxembourg Income Study points to comparable conclusions for two vulnerable groups, children and the elderly. Table 7.8 examines child poverty. Although the definition of poverty in this analysis differs slightly from that in the studies just cited, the patterns are similar: the redistributive gap between the two countries grew

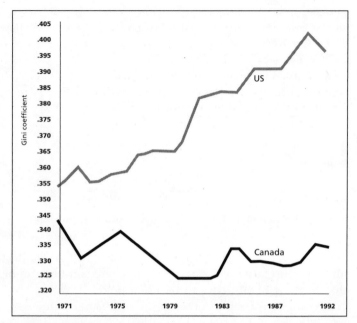

Figure 7.8   Changes in income inequality among families, Canada and the
United States, 1971–1992
Sources: Karoly 1993, fig. 2.1; Statistics Canada 1994d, 42

during the 1980s, primarily because of a weakening of the redistributive impulse in the United States. Using the same data set, Coder, Smeeding, and Torrey (1990) examined poverty among the elderly in Canada, the United States, and Australia in 1981 and 1987, and they concluded that changes in transfer programs reduced the number of Canadian elderly living in poverty more than elsewhere. The 1980s, they observed, "saw the low-income elderly in Canada as big winners."

Trends in inequality more generally in the two countries followed similar patterns. As chapter 2 discussed, the economic pressures of the decade generated greater inequality in the income that individuals and families derived from the market in both countries. The redistributive role of the state, however, was quite different. In the United States, a weakened redistributive impulse in both transfers and taxes could not compensate for the growing inequality in market incomes; no matter what indicator is used, the distribution of final income, incorporating both earnings and government transfers, became less equal throughout the 1980s and early 1990s (U.S. Committee on Ways and Means 1994, 1181–211). In contrast, across the border, the growing inequality in market earnings was offset by the expansion of transfer payments and changes in the tax system, producing a relatively stable distribution of final income (Blackburn and Bloom 1993). Figure 7.8 demonstrates this reality in statistical terms by tracking the Gini coefficients for the level of inequality in total family income from the early 1970s to the early 1990s. The higher the Gini coefficient, the greater is the degree of inequality. As the data reveal, inequality in family incomes rose sharply in the United States but stayed constant in Canada. The divergence in social life in the two countries could not be clearer.

CONVERGENCE AND DIVERGENCE IN A GLOBAL ECONOMY

As noted earlier, many advocates of an active social role for the state fear that global economic integration is undermining the effective sovereignty of the nation-state and constraining the ability of national governments to maintain distinctive social policy regimes. For Canadians, the issue is whether their distinctive social programs are compatible with even closer integration with the American economy; for Americans, attention focuses on the impact on labour and environmental regulation of NAFTA and economic integration with Mexico.

Although the evidence in this chapter cannot resolve this debate definitively, the patterns of the 1980s and 1990s are clearly relevant. As the preceding discussion has demonstrated, the evolution of social programs in Canada and the United States has created a complex pattern of convergence and divergence during the 1980s and the first half of the 1990s. Perhaps the broadest trend has been incremental divergence, with the traditional differences between the two countries growing more marked in certain areas – for example, in health care, in the broad balance between universal and selective income transfers, in the role of public pensions, and in the redistributive impact of the state. In part, this trend has resulted from program changes in Canada, but the divergence is largely the result of the more rapid erosion of coverage and benefits in the United States, especially during the Reagan-Bush years. Other programs, however, provide a counterpoint to this trend. In the case of social assistance, the strong divergence of the 1980s began to fade in the mid-1990s. Stronger patterns of convergence emerge in child benefits and unemployment insurance, with child benefits representing the most dramatic case of harmonization among the social programs surveyed here.

This complex pattern suggests two major conclusions. First, the persistence and indeed incremental accentuation of the traditional differences in many social programs is testimony to the enduring influence of domestic politics and cultures, even in a global economy, and to the ways in which the policy legacies from earlier generations structure the choices confronting policy makers in difficult times. The growing integration of economies, globally and continentally, still leaves important degrees of freedom for domestic choice.

Second, not all of the cases of convergence in Canadian and U.S. social programs flowed unambiguously from closer economic integration between the two countries. As was discussed in chapter 1, convergence in the programs of two countries can develop for a variety of reasons:

- *Convergence as a result of parallel domestic factors.* Convergence in policy regimes can emerge because two countries face similar problems and experience similar domestic political responses to them.[11] For example, the fiscal weakness of government has triggered similar political struggles over fiscal policy in the Canadian and American capitals, with powerful implications for social programs. Indeed, the higher levels of public debt in Canada presumably generate proportionately greater pressure on the role of the Canadian state and represent a pressure for narrowing traditional differences in expenditure levels.
- *Convergence as a product of emulation.* The policies of two countries can converge when one country adopts the other's policies not because it is pressured to do so but because it is attracted to that country's experience. For example, during the early stages of the recent health-care debate in the United States, the strengths and weaknesses of the Canadian model were debated by health-care experts, the media, and members of Congress. Similarly, the results of evaluations of experimental training and employment programs for displaced workers in the United States are scrutinized intently by policy specialists north of the border.
- *Convergence as a result of international constraints.* As critics of economic integration have emphasized, policies can also converge because of constraints inherent in the political and economic relations between and among countries, which limit the capacity for autonomous action by individual states. These constraints can arise from international treaties or from the mobility of factors of production, especially capital, in an increasingly globalized economy.

Separating these different dynamics in specific cases is not easy, even in the short term. In the longer term, the task becomes even more difficult because the categories can become conflated when secondary consequences come into play. For example, if close economic links between two countries eventually lead to greater cultural convergence, harmonizing the preferences that citizens bring to their politics, then a subsequent narrowing of policy differences that appears on the surface to reflect emulation or parallel domestic pressures may, in reality, reflect a deeper process of integration. Nevertheless, the distinctions between different sources of convergence do help when examining the recent evolution of social policy in Canada and the United States.

An examination of the two strongest cases of convergence in social policy – child benefits and unemployment insurance – is revealing. First, in both cases the narrowing of the gap between the countries stemmed in part from American decisions to develop the Earned Income Tax Credit and to extend unemployment benefits – and not even the most optimistic Canadian would attribute these changes to pressures inherent in the relationship between the two countries. Second, changes on the Canadian side that contributed to convergence in these policy areas were not driven by bilateral economic integration alone.

Convergence in child benefits has predominantly been a reflection of parallel domestic trends. The remaking of this sector has been a slow process of incremental change rooted initially in a common ideological debate about the nature of poverty and the interaction between tax and transfer systems, a debate which first emerged during the 1960s and 1970s in the form of proposals for a negative income tax. From the beginning, reform efforts on both sides of the border were also fuelled by economic issues, especially concerns about the perverse incentives facing those dependent on traditional welfare programs; in more recent years, these concerns have been reinforced by the impact of globalization and international trade on the prospects for low-skilled and displaced workers in developed nations generally. Nevertheless, parallel ideological development rather than economic integration between Canada and the United States seems to be the predominant factor in the convergence in child benefits. It could be argued that this pattern reflects a broader cultural integration of the two countries that flows with a lag from closer economic links, but such an argument would have to contend with the interest in similar ideas in Britain and other nations during the same period (Banting 1979; Lenkowsky 1986).

Unemployment insurance is more contentious. As noted earlier, changes in the 1990s in both Canada and the United States have narrowed the differences between the two countries. Although there is still a major difference between the two systems, the trend in the 1990s is towards convergence. Concern for economic competition and trade relations between the two countries may have been part of the calculus in Canada, but it was certainly not all-pervasive. In the 1991 changes, for example, the special benefit for fishermen, which has been a source of trade friction with the United States, was retained; regional differentials, which some analysts have argued will be undermined by economic integration with the United States, grew larger rather than smaller; and changes in financing increased rather than decreased employer costs (Smardon 1991). Changes in Canada since then have been driven by fiscal constraints, by a shift in support for the unemployed from income benefits to retraining, and by a desire to reverse some of the major increases in employers' contributions that were imposed earlier in the decade.

It seems more plausible to interpret the changes on the Canadian side as the joint product of domestic conservatism and pressures implicit in the global economy. Most of the cuts have been driven by the priority given by both Conservative and Liberal governments to reduction of the federal deficit; and decisions to cut passive income benefits and transfer the savings to retraining initiatives are consistent with a broader approach to employment programs in a period of rapid economic restructuring. This agenda is undoubtedly reinforced by an assessment of Canada's position both in North America and the world. However, these pressures go well beyond the immediate economic relationship with the United States; they reflect the Canadian version of a debate about labour markets, income support, and training programs that pervades OECD nations more generally.

In general, then, the record of the 1980s and the early 1990s offers only limited support for the proposition that closer economic integration of Canada and the United States will necessitate social policy convergence. Program structures changed, often dramatically, in those years, and in some cases significant damage was done to the social accomplishments of the postwar generation. The level of social protection provided to the average citizen was less generous in both countries in the mid-1990s than in the mid-1970s. Nevertheless, change was not driving both societies more firmly towards a single model of the welfare state. The pattern in many sectors is incremental divergence, and it is arguable that the Canadian and American welfare states are as different in the mid-1990s as they were in the late 1970s. Moreover, where convergence has taken place, it is difficult to establish a simple link to economic integration between the two countries.

FUTURE PROSPECTS

Nations are changing communities. The configuration of economic, social, and political factors that generated different approaches to the welfare state in Canada and the United States during the postwar period and sustained those differences in the 1980s is constantly evolving. There can be no guarantee that the patterns of today will persist into the future. Moreover, predictions in this sector are particularly hazardous, since the various factors that generated distinctive policy regimes during the postwar years are evolving along different trajectories and at different speeds. For example, the continued strength of organized labour in Canada hints at the possibility of even greater divergence in the future. Elsewhere, however, the trajectory of change points to the possibility of convergence. The full effects of economic globalization and closer integration within North America have yet to be felt. As noted earlier, the greater severity of the fiscal crisis facing governments in Canada could reverse the pattern of the 1980s, producing more rapid erosion of benefit levels in Canada than in the United States. And the social policy consequences of the increasingly multiracial nature of Canada, which is narrowing what was once a marked difference between the two societies, may yet generate political dynamics similar to those south of the border.

On the political level, the victory of President Clinton in the 1992 presidential election and that of the Liberal Party in the 1993 federal election in Canada did little to change the trajectories established in the 1980s. In the United States, reforms of health care and welfare represented the centrepoints of the domestic agenda of the Clinton presidency, but the weakness of the Democratic victory in 1992 precluded major change. Clinton won only 43 per cent of the popular vote, and the Democratic majorities in both houses of Congress remained weak. The expansion of the EITC in the first budget represented a marginal expansion in the redistributive role of government in the United States, but overall the direction of American social policy has not changed. Indeed, the subsequent shift in control of both houses of Congress to the Republican Party in the 1994 mid-term elections is likely to accentuate the trends established in the 1980s.

Similarly, the election of the Liberal government in Canada in 1993 did not change the overall direction of social policy established by the Conservatives. The priority accorded to deficit reduction is smothering any expansionist impulses that may still beat within the heart of the Liberal Party. The new government's first budget introduced significant reductions in Unemployment Insurance benefits; and the proposals for a broad restructuring of social programs introduced by the Minister of Human Resources Development in the fall of 1994 were largely swept aside by the 1995 budget, which sharply reduced federal transfers that support provincial programs in health, postsecondary education, and welfare, and which eased federal conditions on provincial social assistance programs (Banting 1995b).[12] The future will continue to be shaped by shifts in the partisan context of the federal government. The critical political pressures on the Liberals no longer come from the NDP, which was devastated in the election; instead, they come from two parties that are strongly opposed to an activist social role on the part of the federal government: the Bloc Québécois, the separatist party based in Quebec; and the Reform Party, which replaced the Conservatives on the right and is even more strongly opposed to social engineering on the part of the state. These political pressures, coupled with the depth of the fiscal crisis, are likely to continue to drive federal social policy towards restraint, more targeting of expenditures, and a greater emphasis on retraining rather than on simple income support.

Health care has represented the greatest contrast in the past, and in theory it presents the greatest scope for convergence in the future. However, the failure of the Clinton health plan and the 1994 victory of the Republicans in the congressional elections suggest that American initiatives are unlikely to narrow the widening gap between these two neighbours. If significant convergence is to occur, it is more likely to come from north of the border. In Canada, the fiscal pressures generated by rising health costs and large government deficits are putting serious pressure on the postwar model. The deinsurance of some minor medical procedures and the refusal of some provinces to cover additional health costs incurred when travelling outside of the country are already triggering an expansion of private health insurance, with "medigap-style" policies becoming more common for Canadians who can afford them (Tuohy 1994). The federal Liberal government seems determined to resist the growth of user fees, which is an issue in some provinces, particularly Alberta and British Columbia; however, how successful Ottawa can be as its own financial contribution to health care shrinks remains to be seen. The possibilities for some convergence with the American model are thus real. Yet they should not be overstated. The two health-care systems will remain profoundly different at their core. Whatever the incremental changes, health insurance in Canada will remain predominantly a public system; the death of health reform in the United States confirms that health care there will remain predominantly private.

In income security, the prospects for convergence seem more limited, partly because the contrast is already less marked. However, existing areas of convergence may well be accentuated. For example, differences between the two unemployment insurance systems may continue to narrow, although the tenacity of regional politics in Canada will undoubtedly prevent anything close to full harmonization. The reversal of the trend towards greater divergence in social assistance may also continue, although much depends on the outcome of the battles in Congress over welfare reform. In other income-security programs the prospects are for continued divergence, with Canada maintaining its trend towards a stronger targeting of transfers on low-income families and individuals. For example, the 1996 budget of the federal Liberal government pointed to the future with its announcement that the income-tested Seniors Benefit would be implemented in the year 2001. South of the border, the fate of the Bipartisan Commission on Entitlement and Tax Reform suggests that proposals to apply means tests to universal programs such as social security remain politically controversial. Formed to examine the fiscal pressures on entitlement programs, the commission could not agree on recommendations for action, and the modest proposals advanced personally by the senators who chaired the commission were widely criticized (U.S. Bipartisan Commission on Entitlement and Tax Reform 1994, 1995). The prospects for the late 1990s are thus for continued divergence between the two countries along these traditional lines.[13]

Overall, the record of the 1980s and early 1990s is helpful in warning against the assumption that convergence is necessarily a consequence of economic integration. Predictions of harmonization, whether in the context of the single European market or North American free trade, assume that future policy decisions will be shaped more by international economics than by domestic politics. Although international pressures on the state have clearly grown, narrowing the autonomy of national states in a palpable way, it is important to avoid determinist interpretations. Each nation must adjust to powerful pressures emanating from the global economy, but the global economy does not dictate the way in which each country responds. Policy is also shaped by domestic politics, and different countries respond to a changing world differently. As a result, the equilibrium point is unlikely to be harmonization on a standardized model.

During the postwar decades, Canada and the United States developed different versions of the liberal welfare state, reflecting important differences in the economic, social, and political structures of the two countries. During the last decade, they have been adjusting to a difficult global economy, and Canada has faced the added pressures emanating from the bilateral relationship between the two countries. The result has been a series of shifts in social programs that have altered the trajectory of development in the two welfare states. Many of these changes have done damage to the social protection that was painfully constructed in the postwar decades. But each country has adjusted to its economic context in its own way, subject to the rhythms of its domestic politics, and Canada and the United States continue to travel different paths in many parts of the welfare state. Despite a pervasive globalization of economic life, the nation-state retains important degrees of freedom in charting its course, and politics within the nation-state retains social importance.

8 The Judicialization of Politics: Rights and Public Policy in Canada and the United States

CHRISTOPHER MANFREDI

The purpose of this chapter is to examine the extent to which the conflicting pressures from global and domestic forces outlined in chapter 1 are reflected in the judicialization of politics in Canada and the United States. It argues that these two forces are responsible for convergence between Canada and the United States with respect to the degree to which organized social movements use litigation to seek policy outputs from government. However, the two countries are diverging with respect to the willingness of courts to respond positively to these new policy demands. Indeed, after a period of significant success from the mid-1950s to the early 1980s, U.S. social movements now face greater resistance from the courts, particularly the U.S. Supreme Court. By contrast, Canadian courts have been more willing to interfere with policy choices in a way that challenges the global trend towards government retrenchment. This chapter seeks to understand these contrasting developments and to assess the potential for future conflict between international and domestic constraints on policy development.

The chapter is divided into three parts. It begins with a general discussion of the global trend towards the judicialization of politics, in order to sketch out the relationship between judicialized politics and current domestic social and global economic change, and to provide a baseline for later analysis by examining the emergence and nature of judicialized politics in the United States. Then it proposes five indicators for measuring convergence in the judicialization of politics between two nations, and it uses them to compare Canada and the United States. Finally, the chapter examines two examples of social change through litigation in Canada and the United States – equality seeking and political representation – to determine the level of policy convergence or divergence produced by judicialized politics.

THE JUDICIALIZATION OF POLITICS

The judicialization of politics has become increasingly common in Western liberal democracies since 1945, for several reasons.[1] The United Nations' Universal Declaration of Human Rights, the European Convention on Human Rights, and the International Covenant on Civil and Political Rights have made the discourse of rights a global phenomenon and have provided practical instruments for the declaration and, in some cases, enforcement of rights. Moreover, as nations have become wealthier, the postwar generation has turned its attention away from purely material concerns to "post-material" values and a political agenda dominated by concerns such as the environment and sociopolitical marginalization.[2] This shift in values and political agenda has been accompanied by changing styles of political participation, including greater reliance on judicial institutions and rights-discourse to advance the post-material agenda (F.L. Morton and Knopff 1992).

The basic conflict between the post-materialist policy agenda and the capacity of traditional political institutions has been exacerbated by recent changes in global economic arrangements (Nevitte, Bakvis, and Gibbins 1989, 481). More specifically, international agreements such as the General Agreement on Tariffs and Trade (GATT) and the North American Free Trade Agreement (NAFTA), along with the unwillingness of global financial markets to tolerate large-scale government debt, have reduced the capacity of governments to respond to new policy demands. At the same time, the growing strength of domestic social movements dedicated to such issues as environmentalism and the welfare and political representation of marginalized groups has stepped up the demand for policies that are consistent with these values. The simultaneous decrease in the potential supply of policy outputs and increase in policy demands make it more difficult for social movements to extract favourable policies from traditional political institutions. This encourages these movements to seek a substitute for ordinary political activity. Rights-based litigation serves this function well because it drastically reduces the relevance of cost considerations in policy analysis. As Lorraine Weinrib has argued, policies based on constitutional rights "must receive a higher priority in the distribution of available government funds than policies or programmes that do not enjoy that status. A different preference for allocation of resources cannot justify encroachment on a right" (Weinrib 1988, 486).

This dynamic was clearly at work in the debate surrounding proposals for a social charter during Canada's most recent attempt at a large-scale formal amendment of its constitution. In response to federal "economic union" proposals, the NDP government of Ontario urged the adoption of constitutional provisions "that would entrench our commitment to social justice more explicitly, and would make governments more accountable, either in the courts or some other adjudicative body, for the obligations raised by that commitment" (Kymlicka and Norman 1992, 2). In its final form, the Ontario proposal provided that the "social charter should constitutionally entrench the positive obligations of governments to provide social programs and set national standards." Ontario also proposed to amend the Constitution Act, 1982, to provide specific protection for health care, social services and welfare, primary and secondary education, and the environment.

Ontario's idea was subsequently picked up by the committee charged with drafting new constitutional proposals, which added a "social covenant" component to the amendments designed to establish a tighter economic union.[3] The committee recommended that section 36 of the Constitution Act, 1982, be amended to underscore the federal and provincial commitment to providing comprehensive and universal public health care; reasonable access to housing, food, and other basic necessities; high-quality public education at all levels; protection for collective bargaining; and a clean environment. These commitments, the committee suggested, should be monitored and promoted by an intergovernmental review agency.

The value of an institutional alternative to Parliament for social policy formation was readily apparent to various social movements. Although the amendment proposals did not specify the structure of the review body, a proposal made on behalf of the National Anti-Poverty Organization envisioned the establishment of a social rights council and tribunal modelled on human rights tribunals (Bakan and Schneiderman 1992, 155–61). Like human rights tribunals, these institutions would not be disinterested participants in the process of defining and allocating social rights.[4] One of the qualifications for appointment to the council, for example, would be a "commitment to the objectives of the Social Charter." Similarly, one-third of the members of the tribunal were to be appointed from "non-governmental organizations representing vulnerable and disadvantaged groups," and the tribunal would "be made accessible to members of disadvantaged groups and their representative organizations by all reasonable means, including the provision of necessary funding by appropriate governments." The clear intent in these proposals was to create institutions that would presumptively support the interventionist and activist policies advocated by these social movements.

Although there was little support among either governments or social activists to make the document judiciable, the proposal provides a good example of an attempt to counter government retrenchment by transforming policy discussion into rights discourse. Indeed, the social charter emerged from the same sentiment underlying the judicialization of politics generally: a loss of faith in legislatures and the legislative process. This loss of faith is even more evident in the literature that argues that certain provisions of the Canadian Charter of Rights and Freedoms be used to protect welfare rights (Johnstone 1988; Howse 1995). In both cases, the judicialization of politics provides an opportunity to impose policies on governments that would have preferred to reduce their policy commitments in response to global economic pressures. Domestic rights instruments thus become a tool for pulling governments towards activism, a phenomenon that has its origins in the United States.

The Origins and Nature of Judicialized Politics:
The U.S. Experience

The judicialization of politics in Western Europe, Canada, and elsewhere represents global convergence towards what has been common practice in the United States since the early nineteenth century. As de Tocqueville remarked, "Scarcely any political question arises in the United States that is not resolved, sooner or later, into a judicial question" (1945, 1:290). The phenomenon that de Tocqueville observed has been particularly evident since the U.S. Supreme Court's decision in *Brown v. Board of Education* (1954).[5] Prior to *Brown*, judicial activism in the United States had a distinctly conservative and antiprogressive image. After establishing its power of judicial review in 1803, the U.S. Supreme Court refrained from nullifying any federal statutes until 1857, when it struck down Congress's attempt to prohibit the expansion of slavery into federally controlled territory.[6] The court's impact on racial equality was similarly negative throughout the era of post–Civil War reconstruction, when it exercised judicial review to undercut the Fourteenth Amendment's "privileges and immunities" clause, to deny Congress any power to apply the Fourteenth Amendment's "equal protection" clause to private discrimination, and to uphold the constitutionality of state-enforced segregation.[7] In the area of economic regulation, the court limited the power of both levels of government to set maximum working hours and minimum wages, and to regulate the working conditions of women and children.[8] Finally, the court mounted a counterattack against Franklin Roosevelt's New Deal legislation.[9] Decisions such as these left the distinct impression that the road to social progress did not go through the nation's courts.

Table 8.1
A comparison of litigation structures

Attribute	Traditional private litigation	Modern public litigation
Party structure	Bipolar	Amorphous
Fact type	Adjudicative (historical)	Legislative (social)
Remedial objective	Retrospective	Prospective

Brown represented a sharp departure from the conservatism of the past, and the court's nullification of a morally repugnant practice – racial segregation in public education – granted new legitimacy to the judicialization of American political life (Cover 1982). Indeed, as one Canadian commentator noted in 1982, *Brown* was "such a moral supernova in civil liberties adjudication that it almost singlehandedly justifies the exercise" (Gold 1982, 108). For political activists in the United States, *Brown* transformed judicial review from an impediment to social progress into an effective tool for implementing a progressive policy agenda that powerful state and federal legislators had resisted. Consequently, throughout the 1960s litigants took advantage of increased access to the courts and the willingness of judges to formulate novel remedies to persuade U.S. federal courts to participate actively in shaping and administering policy in areas such as zoning and land-use planning, housing, social welfare, transportation, education, and the operation of such complex institutions as prisons and mental health facilities (Yarborough 1985, 660).

Some idea of the increased level of judicial activism in the post-*Brown* era can be gained by comparing the change in the annual rate of Supreme Court decisions to overturn acts of Congress, state laws, and municipal ordinances. During the pre-*Brown* era (1789–1953); the Supreme Court overturned, on average, 0.47 acts of Congress, 3.26 state laws, and 0.39 municipal ordinances every year. Since *Brown*, these rates have increased approximately threefold to 1.80 acts of Congress, 10.60 state laws, and 0.97 municipal ordinances (O'Brien 1990, 60). The judicialization of politics evident in these data has been facilitated by the development of a distinctive litigation process that differs significantly from the traditional structure of adjudication in terms of party structure, the nature of the facts in dispute, and remedial objectives (Chayes 1976). Table 8.1 summarizes these differences.

The traditional model of adjudication views litigation as an essentially self-contained dispute between two distinct parties. By contrast, modern public law litigation has a structure much closer to that of a legislative committee hearing, with various interest groups aligning themselves with the nominal disputants in order to ensure that their views of the question at issue are considered by the court. Traditional adjudication is also designed to gather and evaluate historical or adjudicative facts that pertain to discrete events which occurred in the past between parties to a lawsuit. Public law litigation, however, must rely on social or legislative facts, which communicate information about causal relationships and the recurrent patterns of behaviour on which policy decisions are based (D. Horowitz 1977, 45). Finally, traditional adjudication relies on a model of "corrective justice" in which the sole remedial objective is to provide compensation for past wrongs by awarding damages; public law litigation relies on a model of "distributive justice" in which the remedial objective is to alter the structural conditions that are thought to produce systematic patterns of constitutional violation (Manfredi 1994, 440–1). In essence, public law litigation forces judges to act as political power brokers, a role to which the traditional structure of adjudication is not well suited (Diver 1979).

The U.S. experience clearly demonstrates that a crucial aspect of the judicialization of politics is interest-group litigation, designed to extract favourable legal rules from a key institution of the state.[10] These rules, which take the form of constitutional rights, common law rules, and statutory interpretations, constitute valuable resources that interest groups can deploy continually to modify the framework of procedural and substantive rules according to which social and political institutions operate (Tsebelis 1990, 92–118). The success of interest-group litigation depends on a number of strategic and tactical choices. The basic strategic choice is between direct sponsorship of test cases and indirect participation as *amicus curiae* (as interveners in litigation controlled by other parties). Although the direct sponsorship of test cases has the advantage of maximizing an interest group's control of litigation, it has the disadvantage of requiring the allocation of significant human and financial resources. *Amicus curiae* is less costly but provides far less control over the development of legal rules. In general, a complete litigation strategy will encompass both types of activity.

However, choosing to litigate test cases imposes additional strategic constraints. First, since social change through litigation usually proceeds incrementally, it is important that the cases be brought in the proper sequence. Second, the cases must be brought in favourable venues in order to increase the probability of success. Finally, a systematic litigation strategy requires centralized control in order to ensure that other strategic constraints are met and that counterproductive litigation does not occur in the target policy field. The strategic choices that interest groups make are closely related to the principal tactical choice they face: selecting specific cases and determining what arguments to make in those cases. The incremental character of judicial policy making (Manzer 1984, 588) means that the ultimate constitutional objectives of

a litigation campaign can only be achieved through the gradual development of discrete rules that will eventually form the basis of a new,
overarching constitutional doctrine. In practical terms, this means that
cases raising the easiest constitutional questions must be identified and
litigated first, before moving on to cases that raise more problematic
constitutional issues.

The principal legal instrument that interest groups seek through litigation is a remedial decree, which identifies the legal rules favourable
to the group and may contain a set of policy directives to other social
and political institutions. According to Philip J. Cooper, the process of
remedial decree litigation in which interest groups engage should be
viewed as having four key elements, which he describes as the trigger, liability, remedy, and post-decree phases of litigation (Cooper 1988, 16–
24). Although these phases correspond to the chronological progres-
sion of ordinary lawsuits, Cooper argues that they are also analytically
distinct categories, each of which exerts an independent influence on
the judicialization of politics. For example, the trigger phase encom-
passes both the general historical practices and the specific events that
have led to the initiation of a case. These practices and events are the
product of individual or group demands, local political forces, and
conditions in the broader political environment. During this phase, the
challenge facing litigants is to meet the threshold requirements necessary for continuing the lawsuit. At a minimum, this means gaining access to the courts. For parties directly involved in the dispute, the major
hurdle is to obtain *standing* to challenge the legislation or practices in
question. For groups with an indirect interest in the dispute, the major
hurdle is to obtain intervener, or *amicus curiae*, status. The fact that litigants must meet these threshold requirements before proceeding from
the trigger phase to the liability and remedy phases means that a significant degree of judicial choice is involved at the earliest stages of remedial decree litigation. Courts themselves, in other words, contribute to
the judicialization of politics through the doctrines they develop with
respect to these threshold issues.

The liability and remedy phases, in which new rules are defined, violations are determined, and remedies are formulated to correct these
violations, constitute the central components of remedial decree litigation. Interest-group litigants must carefully formulate their arguments
and liability claims to produce a strong and unequivocal judgment that
can survive appellate review, since weak liability judgments undermine
even the strongest remedial decrees. The remedies themselves can take
many forms, ranging from simple (and relatively weak) declarations of
rights to highly interventionist mandatory injunctions. At the interventionist end of the spectrum, mandatory injunctions may encompass
(1) process remedies, in which courts establish ongoing institutional

mechanisms to resolve disputes; (2) performance standards, in which courts set criteria for determining whether institutions are operating according to judicially defined rules; and (3) specified particular actions, in which courts identify detailed actions that must be taken immediately to comply with the new rules (Wood 1990, 36).

At the completion of the liability and remedy phases of remedial decree litigation, cases enter into a post-decree phase, during which remedies are implemented, evaluated, and refined. Three variables shape the degree of judicial supervision necessary to ensure proper implementation of any institutional reform remedy: the extent of the constitutional violation, the organizational capacity of the institution to change, and the surrounding political culture. Where the constitutional violations are narrow, the organizational capacity high, and the political culture supportive, it will usually be possible to formulate a process-oriented consent decree that requires relatively little judicial supervision. By contrast, if the constitutional violations are extensive, organizational capacity low, and the political culture hostile, it may be necessary to place the institution into court-supervised receivership (Wood 1990, 89–91).

The judicialization of politics thus entails more than the occasional use of litigation to settle intractable political disputes: it is a systematic strategy "to influence the course of judicial policy development to achieve a particular policy goal" (S. Lawrence 1990, 40). It is a process that is both complementary to, and serves as a substitute for, the ordinary politics of legislative and executive/bureaucratic decision making. Canadian convergence with U.S. practice thus has at least two meanings. First, it can refer to litigation as a strategy to achieve policy objectives. In this sense, convergence will be evident in changes to the rules governing the threshold, liability, remedy, and post-decree phases of litigation. Second, convergence can refer to the substantive outputs of judicial policy making. In this sense, convergence is evident in the narrowing of differences in the policies generated by litigation. The extent of convergence in this second sense is explored in the final part of this chapter. The next part examines the degree to which Canada is converging with the United States with respect to the strategic use of litigation as a process for policy development.

THE JUDICIALIZATION OF POLITICS: MEASURING CONVERGENCE BETWEEN CANADA AND THE UNITED STATES

In a recent article, Michael Howlett tested the Canada–United States convergence thesis by examining the judicialization of Canadian environmental policy. Howlett's principal concern was the extent to which

Table 8.2
Operational Indicators of Convergence

Indicator	Type	Description
Litigation activity	Quantitative	Level of rights-based litigation
Jurisprudential influence	Quantitative	Canadian use of U.S. jurisprudence
Threshold width	Qualitative	Liberalized standing rules and increased openness to intervenors
Liability risk	Qualitative	Liberalized justiciability rules and remedial powers
Remedial activism	Qualitative/Quantitative	Broad interpretation and use of remedial powers

the Canadian environmental policy style of closed, government-business bargaining was being replaced by a more open U.S.-style litigation model involving citizens and environmental groups. Howlett proposed three tests for measuring the convergence of Canadian environmental policy making with the legalistic U.S. policy style: increased levels of environmental litigation; liberalization of standing rules; and an expansion of judicial review powers. A legalized policy style exists, in other words, where environmental statutes generate significant levels of litigation and/or where judges are open to requests by citizens to review the actions of environmental regulators. In applying these measures, Howlett concluded that "there is no pattern of convergence in Canada–U.S. environmental policy in terms of an increased legalization or judicialization of Canadian environmental processes or policy style" (1994, 123).

Despite his negative conclusions on the particular question of environmental policy, Howlett's study does not preclude a more general Canada–U.S. convergence with respect to the judicialization of politics. Moreover, his approach to the question provides a good starting point for measuring convergence in a broader sense. Consequently, I offer five separate measures of convergence, which are inspired by Howlett's measures and have been modified to reflect the various phases of remedial decree litigation identifed by Cooper. These measures are summarized in table 8.2.

The most obvious measure is the quantity of litigation activity. How often are constitutionally entrenched rights mobilized to alter public policy? If Canada and the United States are converging, one would expect to observe the emergence of similar levels of rights-based litigation, with the Canadian level beginning to approach that of the United States. A second quantitative measure of convergence is jurisprudential influence. To what extent do Canadian courts rely on U.S. constitutional jurisprudence in formulating answers to rights-based claims? The easiest way of measuring this phenomenon is to examine the citation of U.S. cases by Canadian courts.

Three additional measures of convergence can be fashioned by considering Howlett's original measures in the light of Cooper's remedial decree litigation model. One such measure is threshold width, where the emergence of liberalized standing rules and increased openness to interveners signals greater judicialization of politics. To what extent, then, have Canadian rules on standing come closer to the U.S. pattern? Another measure is liability risk, where liberalized rules of justiciability (which include doctrines such as mootness and political questions) and judicial willingness to exercise substantive review indicate a more extensive judicialization of politics, making a wider range of policy decisions justiciable, increasing the liability risk of governments, and stimulating interest group litigation. Both threshold width and liability risk are qualitative indicators of convergence. Finally, the third of these measures, which has both quantitative and qualitative dimensions, is remedial activism, where the judicialization of politics is evident in judges' taking a broad view of their power to formulate novel and prescriptive remedies to enforce rights. Interest groups should be expected to adopt litigation strategies more frequently as the remedial payoffs increase. In summary, evidence for convergence will be found in the degree to which Canadian courts are moving towards less stringent threshold requirements, the imposition of broader liability risks on governments, and greater remedial activism.

Measure 1: Litigation Activity

Although the judicialization of politics includes litigation based on both statutes and common law principles, litigation involving constitutionally entrenched rights provides the greatest opportunity for advancing policy agendas through the adjudicative process. The reasons for this are twofold. First, the rules generated by constitutional litigation are more difficult to avoid or alter than rules generated by the interpretation of statutes or the common law. For example, although it is a relatively simple process to legislate around unwelcome interpretations of statutes or the common law, constitutional decisions can only be modified by formal amendment or by reliance on extraordinary (and controversial) provisions such as Canada's "notwithstanding" clause.[11] Second, rights-based litigation is more valuable to interest groups than constitutional litigation based on other grounds, because it provides a direct benefit. For example, federalism litigation provides interest groups only with the indirect benefits of a redistribution of legislative power between governments. For these reasons, the amount of rights-based constitutional litigation dealt with by a nation's highest court provides a reasonable measure of changes in the absolute level of the judicialization of political disputes. The relative level of judicialized politics in two nations can then be compared by constructing a "ratio of proportions" by simply dividing the proportion of rights-based litigation in one nation's highest court by the proportion in the other.

There is little doubt that constitutional litigation (and rights-based litigation in particular) has become more common in Canada over the past fifteen years.[12] For example, constitutional cases represented only 2.4 per cent of the Supreme Court's workload between 1962 and 1971, a proportion that doubled to a still small 5.5 per cent during the 1972–81 period. However, between 1982 and 1992, the proportion of constitutional cases in the court's workload quadrupled to 21.3 per cent. Most of this increase can be attributed to rights-based litigation under the Canadian Charter of Rights and Freedoms, which accounted for 82.6 per cent of the court's constitutional decisions during the 1982–92 period, or 195 of 236 constitutional decisions. Indeed, during the first decade of the Charter's existence, 18 per cent of the court's decisions (195/1,110) involved the Charter; and since 1987 the proportion of Charter cases among the court's workload has never fallen below 21 per cent. Moreover, since 1989, when the Supreme Court decided its first equality rights case, Charter decisions have constituted 27.7 per cent of all decisions.[13] The court has also displayed an increased willingness to nullify legislation on rights-based grounds: between 1960 and 1982, it nullified legislation only once on such grounds (under the 1960 Canadian Bill of Rights);[14] since 1982 it has nullified forty-one federal and provincial statutes.[15] To the extent that rights-based litigation activity indicates a judicialization of politics, therefore, there is little doubt that the trend in this direction is strong in Canada.

How does this recent Canadian experience compare with the level of rights-based litigation in the United States? Although the possibility of rights-based constitutional litigation has existed south of the border since 1791 (when the states ratified the U.S. Bill of Rights), it took some time for the litigation to become a significant element of the U.S. Supreme Court's workload. Indeed, during the pre-*Brown* era, Bill of Rights cases accounted for less than 10 per cent of the court's decided cases. However, since *Brown*, Bill of Rights cases have occupied just over 36 per cent of the court's workload (O'Brien 1990, 246). In overall terms, therefore, the proportion of rights-based decisions in the post-*Brown* U.S. court has been about twice as high as that in its Canadian counterpart during the post-Charter era (36.5 per cent to 18 per cent). This suggests that there is still a significant gap in the judicialization of politics in the two countries. But the gap is narrowing. For example, in 1984 the proportion of rights-based decisions among the U.S. court's workload was six times higher than the proportion in Canada, but by 1992 the ratio had decreased to less than two-to-one. Moreover, if the analysis is restricted to those years when the Supreme Court of Canada has had the full Charter to work with (i.e., after its first equality rights decision), the ratio is a fairly modest 1.3:1 (36.5 per cent to 27.7 per cent). A comparison of rights-based litigation activity in the Supreme Courts of the United States and Canada thus provides strong evidence of convergence with respect to the judicialization of politics.

Measure 2: Jurisprudential Influence[16]

The adoption of the Charter generated considerable debate among Canadian and American commentators about the potential impact of U.S. rights-based jurisprudence on Charter adjudication.[17] The Charter's drafters had laid the groundwork for this debate by consciously attempting to shape the Charter's language in a way that would allow for the incorporation of U.S. civil rights jurisprudence while avoiding some of the more problematic elements of the American experience (Manfredi 1993, 14–15). The justices of the Supreme Court then added substance to the debate by adopting a cautiously positive attitude towards the utility of U.S. jurisprudence in Charter adjudication and by increasingly citing U.S. cases in their Charter decisions (Manfredi 1992, 214).

The willingness of the Canadian court to be influenced by U.S. constitutional jurisprudence is both a strong indicator of convergence and a powerful engine for the convergence process. While jurisprudential influence can be measured in many ways, the most common method is to examine the frequency with which one court cites the decisions of another.[18] Although Canadian courts have always been willing to cite relevant U.S. authorities,[19] these citations played a negligible role in the development of Canadian jurisprudence until the Charter era. From 1949 to 1983, U.S. state and federal decisions constituted only 2.9 per cent of the Supreme Court of Canada's citations to authority. By contrast, during the first five years of Charter adjudication (1984–88) this proportion almost tripled, to 7.9 per cent; and in 1989 and 1990 the proportion of citations to authority drawn from U.S. sources rose to 8.6 per cent. Moreover, between 1984 and 1990 the Supreme

Court of Canada cited U.S. decisions in more than 40 per cent of its Charter decisions, with an average of about six U.S. citations per Charter decision. By contrast, the court averaged only slightly more than four Canadian provincial court citations per decision between 1984 and 1994 (Smithey 1995, table 4).

The relationship between jurisprudential influence and the judicialization of politics can be made clearer by examining the time period from which the U.S. citations in Charter cases are drawn. More than 70 per cent of the Canadian citations of U.S. Supreme Court decisions are taken from the post-*Brown* period – the very time when U.S. constitutional interpretation was taking on a distinctively legislative character (Wolfe 1981). The principal characteristic of modern judicial review is to look beyond the text of constitutions in order to "enforce norms that cannot be discovered within the four corners of the [constitutional] document" rather than to discover a constitution's fundamental meaning (Ely 1980, 1). The search for norms beyond the constitutional text energizes the judicialization of politics; and to the extent that the Canadian citation of U.S. jurisprudence encourages this form of judicial review, it promotes convergence.

Measure 3: Threshold Width

The threshold requirements that potential litigants must meet, such as acquiring standing and intervener status, are key elements in determining the degree to which politics can be judicialized. There is little doubt that Canadian practice with respect to these requirements is converging with that of the United States. For example, in 1975 the Supreme Court of Canada began to liberalize the rules of standing by holding that ordinary taxpayers could seek a declaration concerning the constitutional validity of a statute without showing that enforcement of the statute imposed any direct personal harm on them.[20] In reaching this conclusion, the court followed the example set by the U.S. Supreme Court in *Flast v. Cohen* (1968).[21] In *Flast*, which modified a much earlier decision, the U.S. court held that taxpayers could challenge congressional spending if it emanated directly from the taxing and spending powers of Congress, and if they could show a link between their status as taxpayers and a specific constitutional limitation on the spending power. By importing this significant U.S. jurisprudential development into Canada, the Supreme Court paved the way for even greater liberalization of standing rules. Thus, in 1981, the court declared that individuals could be granted standing to challenge legislation simply by showing that they have "a genuine interest in the validity of the legislation and that there is no other reasonable and effective manner in which the issue may be brought before the Court."[22] Canada has thus caught up with, and perhaps even surpassed, the United States in liberalizing standing rules for individuals. Nevertheless, there remains some reluctance by Canadian courts to grant standing to groups, a fact that makes the rules governing indirect third-party participation crucial to the development of interest-group litigation (Roach 1993, 173–4).

Third parties participate indirectly in U.S. Supreme Court litigation through *amicus curiae* briefs, which are partisan documents that may be filed with the consent of all parties to a case or on the court's own motion. The sole exception to this rule is that the solicitor general of the United States has an automatic right to participate as *amicus curiae* in any constitutional case. The principal consequence of these relatively liberal rules governing *amicus* participation is that controversial cases generate dozens of *amicus* briefs (O'Brien 1990, 248). By contrast, the Canadian rule (which remained unaltered from 1907 to 1982) provided for intervener status only by leave of, and according to rules set by, the court or one of its justices. Intervener status was thus difficult to acquire. However, in 1983 the Supreme Court articulated new rules that gave attorneys general an automatic right to intervene in constitutional cases, and gave parties that had intervened in the case at a lower court an automatic right to intervene in the Supreme Court. Although the Supreme Court later rescinded the second of these new rules, individual justices appear to have compensated by granting applications for leave to intervene more liberally. Thus, by 1990, approximately 80 per cent of all applications for leave to intervene in Charter cases were being granted, and interveners were appearing in half of all Charter cases (I. Brodie 1992; Welch 1985).

Thus, the threshold requirements that Canadian litigants must meet to establish standing or intervener status now resemble the relatively liberal requirements in the United States. There is one important exception to convergence along this dimension: class action suits. These suits serve an important function for interest advocacy through litigation by allowing an individual plaintiff to represent the claims of an entire class of persons. Canadian courts have thus far refused to allow class action suits, and only two provinces have established legislation to counter this judicial reluctance (Roach 1993, 174). This remains an important brake on the judicialization of politics in Canada.

Measure 4: Liability Risk

Rules governing the type of question that courts consider justiciable play an important role in determining the liability risk faced by governments.

One of the most common rules is the "political questions" doctrine, which holds that some disputes are simply beyond the competence of courts to resolve. In 1985, in reasons written by Justice Bertha Wilson, the Supreme Court of Canada rejected the application of this doctrine to Charter jurisprudence.[23] Although Wilson recognized that the doctrine constituted a "well established principle of American constitutional law," she found enough instances of the U.S. court's deciding politically contentious issues to declare that "courts should not be too eager to relinquish their judicial review function simply because they are called upon to exercise it in relation to weighty matters of State."[24] In reaching this conclusion, Wilson did not so much reject the American political questions doctrine as choose between two different interpretations of it. By adopting the doctrine's narrowest interpretation, Wilson rejected an interpretation that gives the legislatures and executives wide discretion in certain policy areas, and she chose instead the position most consistent with the judicialization of politics.

The Supreme Court has further broadened the liability risk of governments by embracing substantive judicial review and by holding that governments are liable for the unintended consequences of legislation. Substantive review, which examines the content of laws and policies rather than merely the manner in which they are administered, came to Charter adjudication in the British Columbia *Motor Vehicle Reference* (1985).[25] In this case, the court determined that the statute in question violated a substantive principle of fundamental justice by establishing an absolute liability offence, despite clear evidence that the Charter's framers had specifically selected language designed to foreclose the possibility of substantive review (Manfredi 1990a). Speaking on behalf of the court, Justice Antonio Lamer justified this departure from "framers' intent" on the grounds that adhering to it would cause the Charter's meaning to become "frozen in time to the moment of adoption with little or no possibility of growth, development and adjustment to changing social needs." In his view, the court's task was not to choose between substantive or procedural content per se, but to secure for persons "the full benefit of the Charter's protection."[26] If substantive review is necessary to secure these benefits, Lamer argued, then it is appropriate and legitimate.

The court extended the liability risk of governments further in *R. v. Big M Drug Mart* (1985), where Justice Wilson relied on the U.S. Supreme Court's decision in *Griggs v. Duke Power Co.* (1970) to assert that the Charter is "first and foremost an effects-oriented document."[27] Quoting Chief Justice Warren Burger's majority opinion, Wilson contended that the "starting point for any analysis of a civil rights violation is 'the *consequences* of the [discriminatory] practices, not simply

the motivation.' "[28] Wilson's approach, moreover, represented a significant extension of American doctrine, since the U.S. court has consistently refused to apply an "effects-oriented" test to determine the
constitutionality of government action because such a test would subject a vast array of legislation to constitutional challenge on systemic
discrimination grounds (Knopff 1989, 58). The Canadian court has
not shared this concern.[29]

By rejecting the political questions doctrine and embracing substantive, effects-oriented judicial review, the Canadian court has facilitated
the judicialization of politics by expanding the pool of justiciable disputes and the grounds on which policies can be challenged. Nevertheless, the court has resisted attempts to broaden liability risks even
further by refusing to expand the definition of "government action" to
include the activities of private and quasi-public institutions.[30] Consequently, groups hoping to use Charter litigation to advance their policy
preferences must show some nexus between the target of their efforts
and the actions of a legislative or executive body. Overall, however, the
liability risks that litigants can impose on Canadian governments are
consistent with a high level of judicialized politics.

Measure 5: Remedial Activism

The final indicator of convergence with respect to the judicialization
of politics is the willingness of Canadian courts to become more creative and active in their development of remedies for rights violations.
The textual opportunity for increased remedial activism is found in
section 24(1) of the Charter, which grants courts a broad power to
redress Charter infringements by crafting whatever remedies they
consider "appropriate and just in the circumstances." In contrast to
the proscriptive nature of the Charter's other remedial provisions,[31]
section 24(1) provides judges with an opportunity to shape and ad-
minister social policy directly through positive and prospective remedies. The judicialization of politics is facilitated to the extent that
litigants can persuade courts to deploy this broad remedial power.

Between 1982 and 1992, Canadian courts decided eighty-two cases in
which litigants sought relief exclusively under section 24(1). In general,
nothing about these decisions indicates an explosion of remedial activism (Manfredi 1994). For the most part, they tended to involve procedural matters and to result in the granting of traditional, relatively non-
intrusive remedies, such as declaratory judgments and various orders to
inferior tribunals. By contrast, the courts employed mandatory injunctions to impose positive obligations on governments in only five cases.
Indeed, in *Schacter v. The Queen* (1992),[32] the Supreme Court refused to

attach the broadest possible definition to the remedial powers granted
to courts under section 24(1). At issue in *Schacter* was whether courts
could remedy "underinclusive" benefit schemes by extending those
benefits to the excluded group. Both the trial and appellate divisions of
the Federal Court had held that section 24(1) empowers "a court to
extend benefits to groups aggrieved by an exclusion of benefits."[33]
However, the Supreme Court reversed these lower court decisions and
held that although courts have the power under section 52 of the Charter to read new provisions into legislation, this power cannot be used to
intrude so substantially into budgetary matters that "the nature of the
legislative scheme in question" is transformed.[34] With respect to
section 24(1), the court held that this remedy is only available to individuals when a violation of rights flows from unconstitutional government action under a statute that itself does not violate the Charter.[35]

One area in which remedial activism has been evident, however, is
minority-language education policy. For example, in 1986 an Ontario
court issued a mandatory injunction requiring that a school board establish appropriate facilities at its French-language secondary school
to provide industrial arts and shop programs that were equal to those
provided in the board's English-language schools.[36] Similarly, in 1988
a Nova Scotia court ordered a local school board to design a program
of French-language instruction, to establish the program in a school
"reasonably accessible" to minority-language students, and to conduct a special registration to determine the number of students who
would enrol in the facility.[37] Finally, in 1990 the Supreme Court held
that francophone parents in Edmonton must be guaranteed proportionate representation on local school boards and that minority-
language board members should have exclusive authority to make
decisions about various matters pertaining to minority-language education, including expenditures, appointments, instructional programs,
and service agreements.[38] Consequently, although Canadian courts
continue generally to adhere to a traditional view of their remedial
powers, there is a willingness to go further if warranted in certain policy areas.[39]

In summary, the evidence that can be marshalled from examining
litigation activity, jurisprudential influence, threshold width, liability
risk, and remedial activism broadly supports the conclusion that Canada is converging with the United States in terms of the judicialization of politics. The amount of rights-based litigation in the Supreme
Court of Canada has steadily increased since 1982 and is approaching
U.S. levels. The Canadian court has become more open to relying on
U.S. authorities in reaching its Charter decisions, and this both reflects and facilitates convergence. The court has liberalized threshold

rules and broadened the liability risk of governments by adopting US-style substantive review. The only area in which Canadian courts still lag significantly behind their U.S. counterparts is remedial activism. Nevertheless, the textual potential for such activism exists in section 24(1) of the Charter, and the Supreme Court of Canada has not entirely foreclosed the development of that potential.

THE SUBSTANCE OF JUDICIAL POLICY MAKING: CONVERGENCE OR DIVERGENCE?

The first part of this chapter argued that the rights-based litigation characteristic of the contemporary judicialization of politics is driven by a postmaterial, "new politics" agenda that is inconsistent with the constraints on government imposed by recent changes in the global economic environment.[40] This final part of the chapter examines the substantive convergence (or divergence) in the outputs of judicial policy making in Canada and the United States by analysing constitutional adjudication of disputes involving two crucial "new politics" issues: equality and political participation. I shall argue that the following dynamic has been at work in these areas: after a long period, during which the U.S. Supreme Court responded more positively than its Canadian counterpart to the claims of marginalized groups to equality and greater political participation, the Canadian court's responsiveness quickly converged with that of the post-*Brown* U.S. court. Furthermore, over the past five years, the Canadian court's responsiveness rate has continued to accelerate, while the U.S. court appears to have entered a period of retrenchment. Consequently, the substance of judicial policy making is now marked by divergence, with the Canadian court exhibiting a level of activism that its U.S. counterpart has abandoned.[41]

Equality

The principal textual source for judicial protection and promotion of equality in the United States is the equal protection clause of the Fourteenth Amendment to the U.S. Constitution. The principal jurisprudential source of modern equality rights adjudication, however, is a footnote found in an otherwise obscure New Deal decision: *United States v. Carolene Products* (1938).[42] In this footnote, Justice Harlan Fiske Stone suggested that legislation imposing burdens on religious, national, racial, or other "discrete and insular minorities" would be subject to "more searching judicial inquiry" than legislation regulating the economy. Stone's footnote led to the development of an approach to equality rights jurisprudence marked by "strict scrutiny." Under this standard, which applies to legislative distinctions affecting "fundamental rights" (e.g., voting) or "suspect classifications" (e.g., race) governments must show that a legislative distinction is *necessary* to achieve a *compelling* state interest. Described as "strict in principle, fatal in practice," this test is much more demanding than both the "minimal scrutiny" test, which applies to economic regulation and only requires that legislative distinctions have a rational basis, and the "intermediate scrutiny" standard, which requires that a "close fit" exist between legislative distinctions and "important" state interests (Gunther 1972).

The objective for U.S. social movements involved in equality rights litigation throughout the 1960s and 1970s was therefore to persuade the Supreme Court to apply the strict scrutiny standard to legislation and practices to which these movements objected. This could be accomplished either by convincing the court that the movement represented a discrete and insular minority that was the victim of a suspect classification or by showing that the legislation adversely affected a fundamental right. Consequently, social movements engaged in a concerted effort to expand the list of suspect classifications and fundamental rights.

The success of this effort with respect to both suspect classifications and fundamental rights was mixed. On the positive side, the Supreme Court held that legislation that distinguishes on the basis of citizenship and status as an alien in the United States is subject to strict scrutiny, and that legislation based on birth status (i.e., legitimate versus illegitimate birth), although not precisely suspect, should produce heightened judicial scrutiny. However, advocates for children's and women's rights, as well as for the poor, failed to raise age, gender, and indigency to the status of suspect classifications (Rossum and Tarr 1987). Indeed, one of the principal objectives of the ill-fated Equal Rights Amendment (ERA) was to overturn existing constitutional law by making gender-based classifications suspect. Unfortunately for these groups, the U.S. Supreme Court used the pending ratification of the ERA to justify, at least in part, its decision to leave intact its existing rule that gender classifications only require intermediate scrutiny.[43] Similarly, although the court extended the list of fundamental rights to include the exercise of the franchise and the right to travel,[44] it refused to include welfare or education within this category.[45]

The best place to observe changes in American equality rights adjudication is in the area of affirmative action through ameliorative racial preferences. These programs raise important constitutional issues, since by definition they involve the most suspect of classifications in U.S. constitutional jurisprudence: race. The basic question in this context is whether racial classifications that impose burdens on whites in order to compensate for past discrimination against African Americans or other racial minorities should be subject to strict scrutiny. In this case, advocates for equality-seeking groups sought to avoid strict scrutiny of affirmative action policies, and during the 1970s only two justices – Lewis Powell and Potter Stewart – took the position that strict scrutiny should apply.[46] In general, however, a majority of the court during this period took the view that ameliorative racial preferences should be subject to intermediate scrutiny and should be upheld if they served important governmental objectives and were substantially related to achieving those objectives. Consequently, even though it did so by narrow margins, the court upheld most affirmative action programs for racial minorities throughout the 1970s and early 1980s.

The tide began to turn in the mid-1980s as justices appointed by Ronald Reagan and George Bush began to constitute a majority of the U.S. Supreme Court, and as conservative interest groups began to recognize the strategic and tactical value of litigation (O'Connor and Epstein 1983). The Reagan administration's general approach to equality issues was based on preventing and remedying intentional acts of discrimination against specific individuals. It opposed group-based remedies such as affirmative action. This policy orientation eventually found its way into two important Supreme Court decisions in 1989: *City of Richmond v. J.A. Croson Co.* and *Ward's Cove v. Antonio.*[47] In *Croson*, the court invalidated a municipal program that guaranteed minority-owned businesses a proportion of city contracts. The court held that the plan should be analysed according to the strict scrutiny standard and that the city could demonstrate neither a compelling governmental interest in the plan nor that the plan constituted the least restrictive means of achieving its objectives. Consequently, the court held that the plan violated the equal protection clause because it discriminated against whites. Similarly, in *Ward's Cove* the court shifted the burden of proof in discrimination cases under the 1964 Civil Rights Act from employers to employees by invalidating the use of aggregate statistical evidence of disparate impact to prove discrimination. The principles of equality articulated in *Croson* and *Ward's Cove* were most recently affirmed by the court in *Adarand Constructors, Inc. v. Pena* (1995).[48] In this decision, a narrow five-to-four majority of the court held that the Fourteenth Amendment protects individuals rather than groups, that all racial classifications must be analysed under strict scrutiny, and that such classifications must serve a compelling governmental interest and be narrowly tailored to further that interest.

The current U.S. approach to equality represents a return to the doctrine of formal equality. This is precisely the doctrine that the Supreme Court of Canada has abandoned under the Charter. The Canadian court's pre-Charter approach to equality had its clearest articulation in two non-constitutional cases from the 1970s: *Lavell v. A.-G. Canada* and *Bliss v. A.-G. Canada.*[49] In *Lavell*, the court upheld a provision of the federal Indian Act which stipulated that Indian women (but not Indian men) who married non-Indians must surrender their Indian status. The court defined "equality before the law" as meaning "equality of treatment in the enforcement and application of the laws." Since the impugned provision applied equally to all Indian women, the court reasoned, it did not conflict with this definition of equality. At issue in *Bliss* was a provision of the Unemployment Insurance Act that denied regular benefits to women who interrupted their employment because of pregnancy. The court rejected Bliss's claim that the denial constituted discrimination on the basis of sex, and asserted that "any inequality between the sexes in this area is not created by legislation but by nature."[50]

Organized social movements in Canada, especially the feminist movement, used the *Lavell* and *Bliss* decisions to criticize the doctrine of formal equality on the grounds that its emphasis on equality of opportunity and neutral application of the law does nothing to compensate marginalized groups for the accumulated disadvantages of past exclusion. In order to be "truly" equal, these movements argued, the law must be sensitive to the substantive differences in the economic, social, and political status of various groups. This requires that courts adopt the doctrine of substantive equality, which prohibits facially neutral laws whose impact on marginalized groups is unfavourable and which protects (perhaps even mandates) differential treatment of individuals and groups where that treatment is part of a remedy for past disadvantage. In contrast to the doctrine of formal equality, substantive equality seeks to create equality of outcome through differential treatment.

The Supreme Court of Canada adopted the substantive equality approach in its first equality rights decision under the Charter: *Andrews v. Law Society of British Columbia.*[51] As Justice William McIntyre noted, commentators and lower courts had articulated three separate theories to guide judges in defining equality. According to a theory first proposed by constitutional scholar Peter Hogg, the best approach to the Charter's equality rights provision – section 15(1) – would be to consider all legislative distinctions as *prima facie* violations of the right to equality, thus requiring legislatures to provide a separate justification for each distinction under section 1 of the Charter.[52] A second theory, adopted by the British Columbia Court of Appeal in its consideration of *Andrews*, held that unequal treatment in itself does not constitute a *prima facie* violation of section 15(1) because that section's reference to "discrimination" means that the Charter prohibits only "unreasonable" or "unfair" legislative distinctions. A third theory, drawn from the judicial interpretation of human rights legislation, suggested that courts should focus primarily on legislative distinctions that disadvantage members of groups designated in the Charter or groups analogous to them, striking down these distinctions unless governments could justify them under section 1. Legislative distinctions that benefit these groups, or those that disadvantage groups who are neither enumerated nor analogous, would not usually violate section 15(1).[53] This was the theory urged upon the court by interveners representing Canadian feminists (Hausegger and Knopff 1994).

These interventions were successful. Justice McIntyre adopted a substantive, effects-oriented test under section 15 in which he defined discrimination as "a distinction, whether intentional or not but based on grounds relating to personal characteristics of the individual or group, which has the effect of imposing burdens, obligations, or disadvantages on such an individual or group not imposed upon others, or which withholds or limits access to opportunities, benefits, and advantages available to other members of society."[54] McIntyre went on to find that the "personal characteristics" that might give rise to discrimination extend beyond those enumerated in section 15 and include analogous characteristics, which he defined as those that relegate individuals and groups to the status of a "distinct and insular minority." As McIntyre's colleague Justice Bertha Wilson argued, this approach gave courts the flexibility necessary to "ensure the 'unremitting protection' of equality rights" in future cases by allowing judges to recognize novel grounds of discrimination.[55] Three months later, Justice Wilson would offer her own judgment that the discrete and insular minority category includes any group subject to "stereotyping, historical disadvantage or vulnerability to political and social prejudice."[56] In essence, *Andrews* defined three rules for analysing equality issues: (1) impact is as relevant as intent in evaluating legislation; (2) equality should be measured in substantive rather than formal terms; and (3) courts may, by analogy, extend equality rights protection to individuals and groups other than those enumerated in section 15.

The importance of this third rule is clearly evident in the court's 1995 decision in *Egan v. Canada*.[57] At issue in *Egan* was the constitutionality of a provision of the Old Age Security Act, which defines "spouse" as a person of the opposite sex. In considering this question, the court first had to determine whether discrimination on the basis of sexual orientation is prohibited by section 15 of the Charter. On this particular question the court was unanimous in finding that sexual orientation falls within the ambit of section 15 as being analogous to the enumerated grounds of discrimination. According to the court, sexual orientation merits protection because it is a relatively immutable characteristic of a deeply personal nature which is the source of discrimination and disadvantage. Although a majority of the court determined that the benefit scheme could be justified as a reasonable limit on the right to equality, the fact that it came within one vote of requiring that benefits be extended to same-sex couples demonstrates the court's willingness to use equality rights analysis to alter public policy.

The potential policy impact of the Canadian court's approach to equality is further evident in two recent decisions concerning the Income Tax Act (ITA): *Symes v. Canada* (1993) and *Thibaudeau v. Canada* (1995).[58] Although in neither case did the court accept the Charter claim presented to it, the decisions are noteworthy for the fact that the court unanimously agreed that the ITA, which probably contains more distinctions than any other piece of legislation in Canada, is subject to scrutiny under section 15. Moreover, a majority of the court agreed that the economic nature of the ITA does not justify a less stringent equality rights analysis.

At issue in *Symes* was whether professionals could deduct child-care expenses as business expenditures. Symes argued that the ITA's failure to permit the deduction of child-care expenses from business income violated section 15 because of its disproportionate impact on women. Writing on behalf of himself and six colleagues, Justice Iacobucci agreed with Symes that the ITA "is certainly not insulated against all forms of Charter review," that section 15 "guarantees more than formal equality," and that "adverse effects discrimination" is prohibited by section 15.[59] Although Iacobucci conceded that "women disproportionately bear the burden of *child care* in society," he averred that the relevant consideration for the question at issue was whether women "disproportionately *pay child care expenses.*"[60] In his view, Symes had not shown this and thus could not demonstrate that the impugned provision of the ITA created a distinction based on sex. Iacobucci left open the possibility, however, "that such a distinction might be proved in another case."[61]

Justices L'Heureux-Dubé and McLachlin, on the other hand, agreed with Symes, concluding that the ITA could be interpreted to allow for the business deduction of child-care expenses and that a contrary interpretation of the act would violate section 15. L'Heureux-Dubé began her judgment by noting that the ITA could serve as a "powerful tool" for preventing "the attainment of substantive equality for women."[62] After arguing that the ITA should be interpreted to reflect the changing social reality of increased female participation in the workforce, particularly in business and the professions, L'Heureux-Dubé stressed that the goal of section 15 with respect to gender "is the attainment of true substantive equality between men and women."[63] In her view, the majority's approach did not promote substantive equality because its interpretation of the ITA failed to compensate for the disproportionate child-care burden borne by women. A contextual approach to equality, L'Heureux-Dubé argued, leads to the conclusion that "s. 15 of the Charter demands that the experience of both women and men shape the definition of business expense."[64] To her, it was not the ITA itself that violated the Charter but the majority's traditional "male-centric" interpretation of it.

As in *Symes*, the court divided along gender lines in *Thibaudeau*. At issue was the constitutionality of another provision of the ITA, under which child support payments must be declared as income by the recipient custodial parent while being deducted from the income of the payer. The gravamen of the constitutional complaint was that the impugned provision of the ITA imposes a burden on separated and divorced custodial parents, and that this group constitutes an analogous ground of discrimination under section 15 because (1) it has historically been subject to disadvantageous treatment and (2) it is linked to an enumerated ground of prohibited discrimination (sex), because most custodial parents are women.

Although the court rejected Suzanne Thibaudeau's constitutional claim by a five-to-two margin, a majority actually endorsed an approach to equality rights analysis that was closer to the method proposed by counsel for the Canadian feminist movement than to the approach advanced by the government. At one end of the analytical spectrum were Justices La Forest, Sopinka, and Gonthier, all of whom took a relatively narrow approach to equality rights and subsequently found no inconsistency between this provision of the ITA and section 15. Writing on behalf of this group, Justice Gonthier focused his section 15 analysis on the relevance of the legislative distinction to the overall purpose and context of the legislative scheme.[65] At the other end of the spectrum were Justices L'Heureux-Dubé and McLachlin, who took a broader approach to equality rights and found a violation of section 15. L'Heureux-Dubé accused Gonthier of "watering down" the court's analysis of legislative distinctions,[66] and argued that any "distinction will be discriminatory within the meaning of s. 15 where it is capable of either promoting or perpetuating the view that the individual adversely affected by this distinction is less capable, or less worthy of recognition or value as a human being or as a member of Canadian society, equally deserving of concern, respect, and consideration."[67] Writing separately, Justice McLachlin also focused on the adverse impact of "irrelevant distinctions" on "human dignity," especially where the group affected "constitutes a discrete and insular minority" and where "the distinction is based on an immutable personal characteristic rather than on an individual's merit, capacities or circumstances."[68] Located between these two analyses were Justices Cory and Iacobucci, who embraced McLachlin's approach to equality rights but disagreed with her finding that the ITA imposes a burden on single custodial parents.[69]

What this brief comparison of Canadian and American equality rights jurisprudence tells us is that substantive judicial policy in this area has been diverging over the past five years. Organized social movements in Canada have successfully used the Charter to transform the Canadian Supreme Court from a conservative institution into one that is part of the vanguard of the movement towards substantive equality. Although this has not always translated into victory on specific issues, the foundation for future social reform has been laid in these decisions. At the same time, the politics of judicial appointment in the United States appears to have pushed that country's equality jurisprudence back towards its classical liberal roots. The objective is no longer to formulate group-based remedies for the disparate impact of public policies, but to provide individual relief for specific acts of intentional discrimination. This limited approach to the problem of discrimination is more consistent with the global movement towards more limited government than is the judicial social engineering implicit in the Canadian court's embrace of substantive equality. In this respect, Canadian social movements have successfully established a judicial counterweight to the global pressure for less government intervention. Whether this counterweight can be mobilized to practical effect remains an open question.

Political Participation

The constitutional jurisprudence regarding political participation in the United States has been closely intertwined with equality rights, focusing on issues such as barriers to voting and the dilution of voting strength. Since most barriers to voting (for example, racial and gender restrictions, literacy tests, and poll taxes) are now explicitly prohibited by the U.S. Constitution, most contemporary litigation involves practices that minimize or cancel out the voting strength of certain groups (Grofman 1992). The first cases, brought in the 1960s, attacked the constitutionality of large population discrepancies between electoral districts. The Supreme Court opened the door to this litigation in 1962, when it reversed a long-standing precedent and held that legislative apportionment is a justiciable issue.[70] Two years later, the Warren Court articulated its famous "one-man, one-vote" (*sic*) principle and declared that both houses of state legislatures must be strictly apportioned according to population.[71] The Warren Court held the states to a very strict standard throughout the 1960s, invalidating a Missouri re-apportionment plan, for example, in which the population discrepancy between the largest and smallest district was less than 6 per cent.[72] The Burger Court followed its predecessor in holding the federal government to an even more onerous standard: in 1983 it invalidated an apportionment plan for congressional districts in New Jersey in which the population discrepancy between the largest and smallest district was less than 1 per cent.[73] The Burger Court was somewhat more solicitous of the states, however, and allowed a 16.4 per cent deviation in the lower house of the Virginia legislature.[74] The result of this line of decisions is that vote dilution through malapportionment is controlled at the federal level by requiring that population discrepancies be as low as possible, and at the state level by generally prohibiting discrepancies above 10 per cent (Grofman 1992).

By the mid-1980s the rules governing population discrepancies between districts were so well defined and mechanically easy to apply that pure apportionment cases ceased to be a major part of U.S. constitutional litigation. Instead, the focus shifted to racial and partisan vote dilution through such devices as multimember districts and gerrymandering. In 1986 the Supreme Court established a three-pronged, effects-based test for determining whether racial vote dilution exists.[75] The first prong of the test requires that plaintiffs show that the minority population is large enough and geographically concentrated enough to constitute a majority in at least one single-member district. Second, plaintiffs must show that the minority community is cohesive and that voting is racially polarized. Finally, there must be evidence that minority candidates usually lose. Once these three conditions are met, a court may declare a constitutional violation that can be remedied by ordering the creation of one or more single-member districts in which the racial minority is a numerical majority. Going by the name of "affirmative gerrymandering," this measure can produce oddly shaped districts. In North Carolina, for example, affirmative gerrymandering produced a congressional district that included "parts of ten different counties and slices of 12 cities" (O'Rourke 1995, 37).

Ironically, the emergence of affirmative gerrymandering as a remedy for racial vote dilution occurred at precisely the same time when the U.S. Supreme Court was declaring that partisan gerrymandering is a justiciable issue.[76] Although no apportionment plan has been invalidated as an unconstitutional gerrymander for partisan purposes, the tension between judicial approval of affirmative gerrymandering and disapproval of partisan gerrymandering surfaced in *Shaw v. Reno* (1993).[77] In *Shaw*, a slim majority of the court (which included four of five Reagan appointees, as well as George Bush's sole appointee) raised questions about race-based reapportionments, as well as about the creation of electoral districts that violate unspecified geographical criteria. Led by Justice O'Connor, the majority accepted the legitimacy of race-conscious districting but held that these districts must still conform to traditional principles such as compactness and contiguity. Consequently, the court ruled that redistricting could only be used to enhance the representation of territorially concentrated minority groups. To some critics, the court's decision in *Shaw* suggested that no further gains in equality of political participation could be achieved within the context of a system of representation based predominantly on geography. The time had come, they argued, to reconsider the very concept of representation in the U.S. constitutional system (Guinier 1994, 119–56). Their proposals ranged from proportional representation to cumulative voting.

In many respects, the use of voting rights litigation to address the fundamental nature of political participation and representation – rather than merely their technical details – is precisely the point at which the Canadian court actually *started* its constitutional jurisprudence in this area. The court began its voting rights jurisprudence in *Reference re Saskatchewan Electoral Boundaries Act* (1991), in which it considered the constitutionality of legislation permitting constituency population deviations of 25 per cent.[78] Opponents of the legislation argued that it constituted an attack on the principle of "representation by population," and they asked the court to enshrine the principle of "one person, one vote" in the right to vote protected by section 3 of the Charter. Writing for a majority of the court, Justice Beverly McLachlin recognized the importance of equal voting power but argued that "deviations from absolute voter parity may be justified on the grounds of practical impossibility or the provision of more effective representation." In her view, a narrow focus on voter parity ignored "factors like geography, community history, community interests and minority representation" that "may need to be taken into account to ensure that our legislative assemblies effectively represent the diversity of our social mosaic."[79] McLachlin thus upheld the constitutionality of Saskatchewan's legislation.

Although some commentators have characterized the *Saskatchewan Electoral Boundaries* decision as narrow and deferential (Roach 1992), there are at least two reasons to question that characterization. First, while the decision might be deferential in a narrow, technical sense (since the court upheld the districting plan), it still contains elements of the broad and purposive interpretive method evident in the court's most activist decisions. Indeed, it is necessary to distinguish carefully between judicial deference and judicial restraint. Courts may defer to specific policy choices while simultaneously expanding their own political power. Second, Justice McLachlin's decision to define the "right to vote" as really meaning the right to "effective representation" is not a narrow interpretation of section 3. The narrowest interpretation of the right to vote would simply be the right to enter a voting booth every few years to mark an *X* on a piece of paper. Even this interpretation leaves ample room for judicial review, since existing limits on this right would have to be justified under section 1 of the Charter.[80]

By transforming the relatively straightforward word "vote" into the indeterminate phrase "effective representation," Justice McLachlin's judgment lays the groundwork for a powerful and continuing judicial role in supervising the electoral system. Although she conceded that one precondition for effective representation is "relative parity of voting power,"[81] she intimated that defining the right to vote in terms of absolute voter parity would actually be an overly restrictive interpretation of section 3. Implicit in her judgment is the view that the court has more important things to consider when addressing section 3 than simply guaranteeing adherence to the "one person, one vote" standard.

The open-ended nature of this recently declared collective right of various groups to "effective representation" opens the door to an abundance of constitutional litigation in the future. Indeed, the Saskatchewan decision opens up lines of inquiry that impose considerable burdens on the decision-making capacity of courts. For example, if the establishment of judicially manageable standards of a *quantitatively* defined right to effective representation is difficult, then this is doubly so for a *qualitatively* defined version of this right. Moreover, a qualitatively defined right to effective representation presents numerous remedial puzzles. For example, it is not inconceivable that the court could combine its equality rights jurisprudence with its political representation jurisprudence and find it necessary to order that legislative seats be reserved for groups whose historical exclusion from the political process has made them "discrete and insular minorities."

This combination of voting and equality rights jurisprudence surfaced in an action launched in 1995 against section 51(e) of the Canada Elections Act, which suspends the right to vote of inmates serving terms of two years or more in federal penitentiaries.[82] The plaintiffs in this action presented two equality rights arguments in addition to challenging the reasonableness of suspending inmates' right to vote. First, they argued that prisoners constitute a discrete and insular minority because as a group they have been historically subject to undue social, legal, and political disadvantages. These disadvantages, the plaintiffs averred, have been reflected in inhumane conditions of confinement, inadequate legal and political representation, and stigmatization, all of which are perpetuated in the suspension of the right to vote. Moreover, the plaintiffs argued that the criminal justice system is riddled with systemic discrimination because of the close association between criminal activity and pre-existing conditions of socio-economic deprivation. This point was further stressed in the second part of the equality rights argument, which concerned the disproportionate representation of Aboriginal Canadians in the federal inmate population. According to the plaintiffs, this fact alone invalidated section 51(e) on systemic discrimination grounds. In December 1995, the Federal Court did, in fact, strike down section 51(e) under section 3 of the Charter, illustrating the opportunity that social movements (in this case, the prisoners' rights movement) have to attack and alter public policy under the Charter.[83]

As in the equality rights field, a traditionally conservative Canadian judiciary appears willing to extend the boundaries of political participation jurisprudence much further than the U.S. Supreme Court is currently prepared to go. Indeed, with respect to apportionment, the Canadian court has entirely skipped the process of equalizing the numerical size of constituencies to open the door to more complex considerations of what constitutes "fair and effective representation." Moreover, by linking representation issues to substantive equality issues, the court has created a potentially powerful formula for restructuring the political process in order to provide for greater participation by those marginalized groups that are most affected by government retrenchment. Once again, Canadian social movements have succeeded in creating at least a potential domestic counterweight to global economic pressures.

CONCLUSION

There is little question that, over the past decade, Canada has converged with the United States with respect to the judicialization of politics. Although still at levels below that in the United States, rights-based litigation activity has increased dramatically since 1982. In adjudicating constitutional rights issues, the Supreme Court of Canada has exhibited an unprecedented receptivity towards American jurisprudential influences. The Canadian court has adopted new rules and doctrines governing threshold issues, liability risks, and remedies that bring its constitutional role closer to that of the U.S. Supreme Court. The most obvious explanation for this convergence is undoubtedly an important domestic change in Canada: the entrenchment of the Charter of Rights and Freedoms. However, while adoption of the Charter represents a necessary precondition for the judicialization of politics, it was not in itself sufficient to produce significant convergence along this dimension. Organized social movements needed incentives to pursue their policy agendas in the adjudicative arena, and I have suggested that global economic pressures to limit the policy outputs of governments enhanced those incentives. As global economic change makes governments less responsive to interventionist demands, social movements seek alternative means of achieving domestic sociopolitical change. A constitutionally entrenched declaration of rights makes the judicialization of politics an effective alternative to traditional political activity.

Convergence of process, however, has not meant convergence of policy. In many respects, the Canadian court has surpassed its U.S. counterpart in terms of responsiveness to constitutional claims in the areas of equality and political participation. While the U.S. court has returned to a formal, intent-based, individual-rights orientation towards equality rights issues, the Canadian court has embraced a substantive, effects-based, group-rights orientation. Similarly, the Canadian court appears uninterested in the U.S. court's formalistic concern with equalizing the population size of legislative districts, favouring instead an approach that permits a more searching analysis of the very concept of democratic representation. American judicial policy in these areas is thus more congruent with (although perhaps not caused by) recent developments in the global economic order, thereby dampening attempts by domestic social movements to establish an alternative basis for government intervention. In Canada, by contrast, judicial policy seems potentially more amenable to the demands of domestic social movements that wish to challenge government retrenchment.

What might explain this pattern of simultaneous convergence and divergence? The most obvious explanation for convergence is the adoption of the Charter, which provides the institutional framework for the judicialization of politics. The institutional framework is insufficient in itself, however, to generate the level of activism necessary to produce judicialized politics; there must also be judicial willingness to respond positively to demands for activism. The key reason for convergence in this respect has been the influence of American theories of constitutional interpretation, which led the Canadian court to establish early on in its Charter jurisprudence that constitutional interpretation now requires judicial creativity in defining the norms embedded in the Charter's specific provisions. Although justices have differed with respect to how creative they should be, there has never really been any dispute about the need to engage in "broad, purposive analysis, which interprets specific provisions of a constitutional document in the light of its larger objects."[84] Convergence, then, is due to similar perceptions of the nature of rights documents and the role of judges in interpreting those documents.

Policy divergence is the product of a more complicated set of cultural, textual, and political factors. In cultural terms, there is little doubt that the relatively greater emphasis on collective values in Canada influences rights discourse differently from the more individualistic American approach. This cultural difference is reflected in the text of the Charter, which protects the collective rights of linguistic minorities, Aboriginal peoples, and multicultural groups. It also contains an explicit limitations clause and a legislative check on the power of judicial review. Moreover, the Charter does not expressly protect private property rights, nor does it contain anything like the "takings" clause of the U.S. Fifth Amendment. The fact that the Charter allows for the pursuit of collective goals within its basic framework of individual rights protection is perhaps one reason why Canadian prime ministers have not used their political power of appointment to alter Supreme Court decision making to the extent that their American presidential counterparts have done. For all these reasons, the judicialization of politics has developed differently in policy terms in Canada and the United States during the 1980s and 1990s.

The last point about political differences raises an important issue. Canadian governments may find themselves in an increasingly difficult situation – pulled by global economic pressures towards retrenchment, while simultaneously being pushed by the litigation activities of domestic social forces towards greater intervention and activism. How Canadian governments manage this conflict, if it occurs, presents a crucial, unanswered question. However, one thing is clear from the American experience: political actors are unwilling to allow the judiciary to frustrate their policy preferences indefinitely.

9 Governing the Environment: Comparing Canada and the United States

GEORGE HOBERG

The field of environmental policy has been subject to the two dynamics emphasized throughout this volume. First, the rise of the modern environmental movement in the sixties and seventies is one of the most prominent examples of the increasing social diversity. By elevating concerns about the side effects of industrial activities, environmentalists have greatly complicated the governing tasks of policy makers. Frequently, there are harsh trade-offs between environmental protection and the economic activities that create environmental risks. Politically, this problem is aggravated by the nature of environmental policy itself, which requires the imposition of costs on relatively concentrated interests to benefit a broad, diffuse public.

Second, environmental policy has been strongly influenced by the globalization of environmental problems as well as of the economy more generally. Canada and the United States share a continental ecosystem, comprising among other things a shared air mass that promotes the flow of air pollution across national boundaries, and a remarkable system of large freshwater lakes, which have been subjected to massive infusions of industrial effluents and toxic chemicals from both countries. These problems can only be addressed through effective bilateral cooperation. Canada and the United States are also part of a global ecosystem, and as the problems of climate change become more important, the need for widespread multilateral collaboration increases. Moreover, as economic globalization has proceeded, national environmental standards have become increasingly scrutinized as threats to international competitiveness or hidden barriers to trade.

This chapter examines how Canada and the United States have tackled the environmental policy problem. The objective is to describe and explain both convergence and divergence in policy outcomes in the two countries. The chapter is divided into four sections. The first examines a number of potential determinants of environmental policy, ranging from science and technology to domestic pressures, to institutional structures, and finally to international influences. Each determinant is described in detail, and propositions are developed about how they would be expected to influence convergence or divergence in environmental policy. The second section compares actual policy outcomes in the two countries. Various policy indicators are compared, ranging from regulatory instruments and standards to changes in environmental quality and compliance costs. While the comparison reveals a complex pattern, it does highlight substantial convergence in environmental policy. The third section brings together the policy determinants to explain this pattern, arguing that the most important forces behind convergence are parallel domestic pressures and U.S. influence on Canada, particularly through emulation. Many Canadians have an impression of environmental superiority over Americans. Because of its larger population and industrial activity, the United States does contribute far more environmental contaminants to the shared environment; but in many areas, U.S. environmental policy has been quite aggressive, and as a result there are a significant number of cases in which the United States has had a positive influence on environmental protection policies in Canada, in this case, harmonizing up rather than down. The final section of the chapter draws together the broad conclusions and reflects on the prospects in this sector.

DETERMINANTS
OF ENVIRONMENTAL POLICY

Science, Technology, and the Nature of the Problem

Environmental policy makers face a multitude of conflicting pressures, some of which promote convergence among national policies while others promote divergence. First, the policy makers are constrained by the problems they confront. One of the benefits of cross-national policy comparisons is that they allow us to hold the problem constant so that we can measure the effects of other factors. While common problems tend to promote policy convergence, the presence of different problems can foster policy divergence, either because the need for policy is not as great or because the interests at stake can differ significantly. For instance, pulp mills that have similar technologies and are located in remote areas are likely to present fisheries with very similar environmental hazards. However, while there are many similarities between the environmental problems faced in the two countries, there are also some important differences.[1] The lower density of industry and population in Canada, for example, means that similar activities in the two countries may produce different levels of environmental problem.

The nature of environmental problems, and the solutions to them, are largely defined by the state of science and technology. Science provides evidence of the nature and magnitude of the problem, such as the effects of industrial pollutants on fish habitat, or the relationship between the depletion of the ozone layer and skin cancer. Scientific knowledge about environmental issues is shared by an international community of experts both in and out of government. When new information about the effects of a toxic chemical emerges, it is typically transmitted rapidly among specialists in the field and creates pressure for policy change.

The state of technology structures the options for addressing the problems, defining both the possible solutions to environmental problems and their costs. Science and technology tend to promote convergence, in that they are forces common to both Canada and the United States. However, the influence of science as a harmonizing pressure depends on the magnitude of uncertainty. Scientific uncertainties, which are endemic in the environmental area, weaken the extent to which science constrains policy makers. If the science is certain and the hazard clear, then science can be a powerful convergent force. However, if science is highly uncertain, its influence is much weaker. In this case, different scientific assumptions, value premises, economic interests, or political factors can play a larger role in the decision (K. Harrison and Hoberg 1994, ch. 9).

Societal Pressures: Public Opinion and Interest Groups

In addition to the characteristics of the problem and science, policy makers must be responsive to political forces – especially public opinion, which shapes the electoral incentives of politicians, and group pressures from those who support aggressive environmental policies and those who resist them. To understand the development of the environmental policy process in the two countries, it is important to understand the evolution of the environment as a political phenomenon. The environmental issue has gone through similar distinct phases in Canada and the United States, largely as a response to fluctuations in the business cycle (Hoberg 1993a; K. Harrison 1995a). The first major wave of environmentalism began to swell in the late 1960s and crested with the first Earth Day extravaganza in April 1970. As stagflation emerged in the early 1970s, however, environmental issues in North America declined in salience, and concerns about the economy eclipsed environmental issues on the political agenda (Inglehart 1981). While support for environmental protection among the public continued, the problem ceased to be viewed as a major political priority. By 1987 a second wave of environmentalism began forming and the salience of environmental issues surged, culminating with the second Earth Day in April 1990. This second wave crested shortly thereafter, and the environmental issue again dropped in salience as a result of economic anxieties in the two countries.

These waves can be tracked in opinion polls. During the first wave of environmentalism, the issue jumped to the top of public concern in both countries. In Canada, a 1970 opinion poll ranked pollution highest among the issues deserving more attention from the government.[2] In the United States, the need to reduce pollution jumped from ninth on the list of major domestic concerns in 1965 to second in 1970, just slightly below the need to reduce crime (Jones 1975, 152). The first wave also led to a dramatic rise in the number and resources of environmental groups in both countries. In the United States, the Natural Resources Defense Council, the Environmental Defense Fund, and Friends of the Earth were all formed in the late 1960s and early 1970s, while older conservation groups such as the Sierra Club and the National Audubon Society acquired new members and adopted a more activist approach to pressuring the government (Mitchell 1979; Ingram and Mann 1989). In Canada, Pollution Probe and the Society Promoting Environmental Conservation (SPEC) were formed in 1969, the Canadian Environmental Law Association was founded in 1970, and Greenpeace got its start in 1971 (Macdonald 1990, 96–9).

The subsequent slump in public concern was reflected in the polls. In the United States, the proportion of the public viewing pollution as one of the "two or three biggest problems facing people like yourself" dropped from 41 per cent in 1970 to 13 per cent in 1972 and to 6 per cent in 1976 (Dunlap 1989, 99). In Canada, by 1972 the environment had dropped below economic issues to rank around fourth or fifth, and by 1973 and 1974 only 3–4 per cent of the public ranked pollution as the top issue (Gallup poll, 13 April 1974; Macdonald 1990, 109–11).

During the late 1980s, interest in the environment surged in both countries. *Time* magazine declared Earth to be "Planet of the Year" in 1989. In salience polls, environmental issues ranked as high as economic issues and in some polls actually exceeded them. The *Maclean's-Decima* polls of 1989 and 1990 (displayed in table 9.1) show both

Table 9.1
Public opinion on the environment, Canada and the United States, 1990

1. In your opinion, what is the most important problem facing the United States/Canada today, the one that concerns you the most?

	Americans		Canadians	
	(1989)	(1990)	(1989)	(1990)
Pollution/environment	5	17	16	20
National unity/bilingualism	–	–	5	19
Economy/jobs/inflation	12	8	22	19
Government/deficit/debt	20	9	12	10
Drugs/alcohol problems	18	21	–	1
Other social/moral issues	25	24	17	6
Taxation (Canada GST)	4	3	4	15
World issues/war/peace	8	5	2	1
Foreign trade/investment	1	2	10	2
No problem/DK/NA	3	10	11	6

2. Would you describe the tap water in your home as not at all safe to drink, fairly safe, or very safe?

	Americans	Canadians
Not at all safe	11	11
Fairly safe	50	54
Very safe	38	34

3. Would you say the quality of air in the area you live in is very poor, poor, fair, good, or very good?

	Americans	Canadians
Very poor	4	4
Poor	9	8
Poor/very poor	13	12
Fair	28	25
Good/very good	59	63
Good	43	36
Very good	16	27

4. Do you believe you should have the right to drive an automobile anytime or anywhere you want as long as it is within existing laws, or do you feel driving an automobile should and can be restricted further to protect the environment and reduce congestion?

	Americans	Canadians
Drive anytime/anywhere	62	49
Restrict further	34	50

5. Would you oppose or favour shutting down a major company that provided many jobs in your community if it was polluting the environment?

	Americans		Canadians	
	(1989)	(1990)	(1989)	(1990)
Oppose	33	34	37	36
Favour	64	58	60	60
DK/NA	3	9	3	4

Source: Maclean's, 1990

countries ranking the environment quite high in 1990, although the issue was somewhat more salient in Canada than in the United States. As in the case of the earlier wave of environmental enthusiasm, salience declined precipitously in both countries shortly thereafter.[3]

Recent comparative surveys suggest substantial convergence on public opinion. As table 9.1 shows, the Canadian and U.S. public share very similar attitudes about the severity of water and air quality. More important, when asked if they would "favour shutting down a major company that provided many jobs in your community if it was polluting the environment," nearly identical sizable majorities in both countries answered yes. The one significant difference in attitude is that Americans are less likely to support restrictions on the use of automobiles to improve air quality (*Maclean's* 1990, 50–1, 69–70). A broader 1992 survey of public attitudes towards the environment, conducted in twenty-two nations, showed that Canada and the United States held similar attitudes on a broad range of questions. When asked how they would choose between environmental protection and economic growth, substantial majorities in both countries chose environmental protection, though larger majorities in Canada chose this option (68 per cent versus 59 per cent in the United States). In contrast, more Americans than Canadians (65 per cent to 61 per cent) were willing to pay higher prices to protect the environment (Dunlap, Gallup, and Gallup 1992).

Although there has been no systematic comparative analysis of the organized environmental movements in the two countries it is clear that they share two key features. In both countries, the movement is fragmented and diverse, lacking peak associations to concentrate pressure on government. In addition, environmental groups in both countries do not match the resources that are available to their business opponents (J. Wilson 1992).

Table 9.2 presents a survey of the membership and finances of several of the most influential organizations in the two countries. Although the sample is unscientific, the U.S. groups are clearly larger and wealthier. The five-group sample of U.S. groups consists of 9.650 million members and a budget of Cdn $222 million, whereas the five-group Canadian sample consists of 525,000 members and Cdn $20.5 million. On one hand, taking into account the fact that in terms of population and economic product the United States is approximately ten times larger than Canada, these figures show rough comparability in organizational capacities. On the other hand, there are substantial economies of scale associated with the larger U.S. groups. In particular, their greater size and wealth allow them to hire more professional staff, especially qualified scientists, and this strengthens the organizations' expertise and credibility.[4]

Table 9.2
Size of major environmental groups, 1993

	Members	Budget
UNITED STATES		
Environmental Defense Fund	200,000	$18 million
Greenpeace USA	2,000,000	$50 million
National Audubon Society	600,000	$44 million
National Wildlife Federation	6,200,000	$17 million
Sierra Club	650,000	$35 million
U.S. total	9,650,000	$164 million (U.S.) $222 million (Cdn)
CANADIAN GROUPS		
Friends of the Earth	15,000	$800,000
Greenpeace	300,000	$7 million
Canadian Nature Federation	20,000	$1.0 million
Canadian Wildlife Federation	150,000	$10 million
Pollution Probe	40,000	$1.7 million
Canadian total	525,000	$20.5 million (Cdn) $15.2 million (U.S.)

Sources: U.S. data from the 1994 *Encyclopedia of Associations*; Canadian data from personal contacts with individual groups. Friends of the Earth and Pollution Probe are for the 1992–93 year, others for the 1993–94 year.

The surge in environmental and other public interest groups that occurred around 1970 caught the business community in both Canada and the United States off guard. The lobbying apparatus of business had atrophied after years of cooperative relations with the government, resulting in a loss of control of both the public agenda and actual policy outcomes (Vogel 1989). American business did not remain docile in the wake of the increase in government regulation; it responded with a massive strengthening of its political capacities. First, it intensified its lobbying activities by expanding representation in Washington, emulating the successful political tactics of its opponents, and developing coalitions with its natural allies. Second, lobbying efforts were increasingly coordinated by new or enlarged peak associations. The Chamber of Commerce and the National Association of Manufacturing were revamped, and a new elite organization, the Business Roundtable, was created to represent the broader interests of the business community. Third, business launched an offensive in the ideological and intellectual spheres. Aided by the widespread heightened sensitivity to economic concerns induced by the stagflation of the mid-1970s, the corporate counteroffensive reclaimed some of the political clout for the business community (Edsall 1984; Vogel 1989).

Although the Canadian public interest movement was not as formidable as its American counterpart, the Canadian business community also felt threatened by the lack of adequate representation of its interests. Paralleling the changes south of the border, Canadian business began to take government relations more seriously (Stanbury 1986, ch. 5). In addition, a new association was formed, the Business Council on National Issues, modelled on the Business Roundtable, "to defend corporations against an increasing barrage of criticism from the public and from a growing level of government regulation and intervention" (Brooks and Stritch 1991, 211; Langille 1987).

Thus, in the case of environmental policy, domestic politics seem to have provided pressures for convergence, because the policy makers faced similar political pressures on both sides of the border. Public opinion has shown substantial convergence on support for aggressive environmental policies. Environmental interests have organized and been relatively successful at becoming institutionalized pressure groups in both countries, although the larger size of the U.S. movement gives it certain advantages. Business groups, caught off guard by the mobilization of environmental interests around 1970, strengthened their organizational capacities in response. These trends in interest representation occurred at about the same time in both countries. With the exception of the size of U.S. environmental groups (which can provide economies of scale that create greater effectiveness than the Canadian movement can achieve), overall domestic pressures have been a strong force for convergence in the two countries. Within this general pattern, however, there are particular cases where domestic pressures may promote divergence because of the different economic stakes of the producer groups in the two countries.

Institutional Structures and Policy Regimes

In Canada and the United States, environmental policy problems have been addressed within markedly different political systems. While there is some evidence that these differences are narrowing, they have been quite persistent.

Pluralist Legalism in the United States. In the United States, the first wave of environmentalism around 1970 was met with profound changes in the American "policy regime." This transformation, which was concentrated in the period 1969–72, had four fundamental aspects (Hoberg

1992). First, regulatory authority over the environment was dramatically expanded and centralized at the federal level. An array of new federal statutes was enacted,[5] and a new federal agency, the Environmental Protection Agency (EPA), was created to carry out these ambitious new programs. Prior to 1970, environmental regulation had largely been performed by state and local governments. The centralization of this new regulatory authority at the federal level was particularly important, because it eliminated competition between states or localities as a source of leverage for industry (Elliott et al. 1985).

Second, these new laws did not merely create more government authority over environmental matters; they also dramatically changed the form of that authority. Traditionally, when Congress made new laws, it did so by delegating vast amounts of authority to the executive branch (Lowi 1979). Through the use of specific goals and deadlines, these new environmental laws were written in such a way as to constrain the discretion of administrators far more carefully. The National Environmental Policy Act, for instance, required administrators to perform environmental impact assessments before they proceed with any major federal activities. The Clean Air Act, perhaps the most extreme version of these so-called action-forcing statutes, required that automobile emissions be reduced by 90 per cent within five years. Congress thus began to play a far more active role in controlling regulatory agencies and, as a result, in determining environmental policies (Ackerman and Hassler 1981; Melnick 1983).

Third, in addition to restructuring the relationship between Congress and the executive branch, these new laws transformed the relationship between citizens and the administrative state. Through changes in the doctrine of standing, citizen groups were given access to courts that they were previously denied. The specific goals and timetables in the new statutes, by creating nondiscretionary duties on behalf of administrators, gave these groups a "cause of action" to take to court.

Fourth, these changes would not have been possible without a fundamental shift in the role of the courts. In addition to opening their doors to environmentalists and other representatives of diffuse interests,[6] the courts became far more active in challenging administrative decisions. The judicial activism that began in the areas of civil rights and social policy in the 1950s was extended to the regulatory policy arena in the late 1960s (Stewart 1975). In the United States it is commonplace to refer to the relationship between regulatory authorities and the courts as a "partnership" (see, for example, Melnick 1985).

These changes in relations between citizens, Congress, the courts, and the administrative state reflected the emergence of a new doctrine of "pluralist legalism." This doctrine consisted of both a set of formal institutional relations and a guiding public philosophy. The notion of business's capture of regulatory agencies had become commonplace, and the perceived solution was to restrict agency discretion through more specific statutory mandates and to expand the representation of non-industry groups through the use of formal, legalistic procedures, monitored by the courts (McCann 1986; Harris and Milkis 1989a). This new doctrine signalled a marked departure from "interest group liberalism" – the term Lowi has used to describe the American policy process (Lowi 1979).

These changes have endured into the early 1990s. The regime weathered the storm of the early 1980s, when the Reagan administration sought to revert to the business-dominated system of the New Deal regime that had existed prior to 1970. The Reagan administration seriously underestimated the power of environmentalists – in Congress, the courts, the state governments, and public opinion – and by mid-1983 had abandoned its efforts to undermine pluralist legalism (Hoberg 1992; Harris and Milkis 1989a).

When U.S. institutions underwent their transformation around 1970, the system went directly from one of bipartite bargaining – what Americans refer to as the New Deal policy regime – to pluralist legalism. But in recent years, a new form of cooperative pluralism has been struggling to find its place in U.S. regulatory procedures.[7] "Regulatory negotiation" is based on the idea that cooperative discussions among relevant stakeholders produces better policy outcomes than the bewilderingly complex process of adversarial legalism. In 1983, EPA established its Regulatory Negotiation Project with great promise – it seemed an idea whose time had come. By May 1994, however, regulatory negotiation had barely made a dent in EPA's operations. The agency had completed only ten negotiations, an unspectacular rate of about one per year – an especially poor showing considering that the agency typically promulgates about one hundred major regulations every year. The Clinton-Gore administration has expressed great interest in increasing its reliance on negotiation,[8] but the limited success of the program thus far raises grave questions about the prospects for moving away from the adversarial, legalistic nature of U.S. environmental policy making.

Bargaining in Canada. In Canada, the first wave of environmentalism was not met with any comparable change in regulatory regime, though Canadian governments did respond with new policies and institutions. At the federal level, the Twenty-Sixth Parliament, which lasted from 1968 to 1972, enacted nine new environmental statutes, included the Clean Air Act, the Canada Water Act, and amendments to the Fisheries

Act. A new federal department, Environment Canada, was created in 1971. Provincial governments also responded with a wave of new statutes, agencies, and regulations. Ontario passed its Environmental Protection Act in 1971, and Quebec its Environmental Quality Act in 1972 (Woodrow 1974; Dwivedi 1974; Macdonald 1990, ch. 9). The Canadian Council of Resource Ministers was expanded to include the environment portfolio in 1971 and was renamed the Canadian Council of Resource and Environment Ministers.

But in contrast to the United States, the Canadian political system adapted to the new pressures without any major changes in structure or process. New bureaucracies were created and new policies enacted, but the governing arrangements for environmental policy marked no significant departure from either past patterns or the prevailing patterns in other policy domains. Environmental policy was not centralized to the same extent as it was in the United States. Provincial governments continued to be the dominant players in air and water pollution control (Harrison 1994; Lucas 1989; Dwivedi and Woodrow 1989). Policy making continued to be dominated by bipartite bargaining, conducted through closed, cooperative negotiations between government and industry. According to Andrew Thompson, "bargaining is the essence of the environmental regulatory process as it is practised in Canada" (Thompson 1980, 33; Schrecker 1984; Hoberg 1993a).

For the most part, environmentalists were excluded from this bargaining, because they lacked the organizational sophistication and political clout to inspire officials to invite them into the process, and they lacked the legal or procedural rights to pry the doors open. The ruling norm at the time was that environmental interests were to be represented in the policy process not by private interest groups as in the pluralist model, but by the relevant government agency, headed by the minister. To the extent that environmental interests were to be balanced against other societal concerns, this occurred behind closed doors either in cabinet or the bureaucracy, depending on the political sensitivity of the issue.

While a surge in public interest in the environment forced the Canadian government into some response, the rapid decline in salience of the issue in the early 1970s, and the limited clout of environmental groups, meant that limited, relatively symbolic responses were sufficient to maintain legitimacy for the system. As time went on, however, challenges to this system and its supporting norms escalated, and pressures for reform forced more fundamental institutional changes.

While the Canadian political system successfully coped with the first wave of environmentalism without significant changes in form, the second wave posed a greater threat to the system's adaptive capacity. The renewed salience of environmental issues challenged the legitimacy of the dominant policy regime (Howlett 1990). The system's ability to provide adequate levels of environmental protection was called into question, and much of the blame fell on the policy regime itself, particularly the mechanisms for representing environmental interests. After a decade and a half of experience, the idea that the state could adequately represent environmental interests was contested, and many now viewed the regulatory procedures as a cloak concealing a system dominated by business interests.

In consequence, two patterns of institutional response appear to be occurring. First, Canada has moved to expand the traditional bargaining processes to include representatives of environmental interests and others (labour, consumers, and so on) in what are referred to as "multistakeholder" consultations. As governments began to feel more pressure to produce new environmental policies, multistakeholder forums became a standard operating procedure of the policy process. They have been or are being used in virtually every policy initiative, the most prominent being the Canadian Environmental Protection Act of 1988, the Pesticide Registration Review of 1990, the federal pulp and paper effluent regulations, Ontario's overhaul of its water pollution control regime (the Municipal/Industrial Strategy for Abatement), and the federal government's showpiece Green Plan. Even the process of intergovernmental negotiations has been influenced by this new concept – the multistakeholder forums on urban smog and global warming were done under the auspices of the Canadian Council of Resource and Environment Ministers (Doern 1990b).

As a policy regime, both the policy network and legitimating philosophies of what we can call "multipartite bargaining" represent a departure from Canadian tradition. The traditional bipartite bargaining has been replaced by an expanded bargaining process that includes environmentalists and other groups. Significantly, the public philosophy underlying the policy process has also changed. The state is no longer trusted to represent environmental interests on its own – this task has devolved to organized environmental groups (Hoberg 1993a).

The second response to the loss of legitimacy of the bipartite bargaining of the Canadian past has been to take a page from the book of environmentalists south of the border and rely on the courts to pressure governments to change policy. Legalism emerged in Canadian environmental policy in disputes over environmental impact assessment. In 1989, in response to legal action by environmentalists, the courts intervened in several controversies involving the construction of dams, forcing the federal government to perform impact assessments. While such judicial decisions are standard fare in the United States, they were unprecedented in Canada, and they sent shock waves through the environmental policy community. In a series of decisions, the Federal Court of Canada responded to requests by environmental groups to block the construction of dams because the federal government had not complied with the guidlines order of the Environmental Assessment Review Process (EARP). These decisions transformed the guidelines order into a binding legal requirement and demonstrated the courts' willingness to force the government to comply with it.[9] After a period of considerable legal turmoil, the Supreme Court issued a landmark ruling on the issue in January 1992, upholding most of the Appeal Court's decision in the Oldman Dam case. The Supreme Court agreed with the lower court's interpretation that the EARP guidelines were binding, and it also agreed with the court's expansive interpretation of federal authority over the provinces. While the Supreme Court did not go as far as some of the earlier decisions, it nevertheless provided a solid endorsement of legalism in Canadian impact assessment.[10]

As a result of the uncertainty generated by these court cases, as well as strong public pressure for more rigorous environmental assessments, the federal government tabled legislation in June 1990 to incorporate environmental assessment into a statute through the Canadian Environmental Assessment Act.[11] Although it was originally an attempt by the government to remove the nondiscretionary duties which the courts had read into the guidelines order (Schrecker 1991), the act was later amended to restore a number of these duties. The bill passed the House of Commons in March 1992 but was not proclaimed until October 1994.

Efforts to judicialize Canadian environmental policy go beyond impact assessment. In British Columbia, the Sierra Legal Defence Fund launched a concerted effort to use the courts to reform B.C. forest practices. Thus far, however, its successes have been limited (Hoberg 1993b). A potentially more dramatic introduction of legalism was suggested by Ontario's commitment to the enactment of an "environmental bill of rights" when the New Democratic Party came to power in 1990. Proposals introduced by NDP members while in opposition, and urged by environmental lawyers in the Canadian Bar Association, would have produced a legalistic framework similar to that south of the border (Gertler, Muldoon, and Valiente 1990; Muldoon 1988). After a protracted period of consulation and negotiation, however, the environmental bill of rights that ultimately passed in Ontario did not go very far down the road to legalism. It did produce more formal regulatory procedures, similar to notice and comment rulemaking in the United States, but it did virtually nothing to impose substantive duties on the government or to grant substantive rights to environmentalists;

thus it is unlikely to cause a significant increase in the role of the courts (Estrin and Swaigen 1993, ch. 25). Efforts by British Columbia environmentalists to incorporate an environmental bill of rights into new comprehensive environmental legislation have also failed (Hillyer 1994).

While the combination of regulatory negotiation in the United States and creeping legalism in Canada may raise the prospect of some institutional convergence between the two countries, it seems unlikely that the profound differences between the countries will be significantly reduced.[12] There are significant macropolitical obstacles to any substantial departure from each country's dominant regulatory regime. Regulatory regimes are embedded in distinct national systems of political institutions and culture (Kelman 1981; Brickman, Jasanoff, and Ilgen 1985), and consequently significant changes in them are extremely difficult to achieve without simultaneous changes in the macropolitical system.

In the United States, institutional fragmentation and a culture of distrust militate against the emergence of cooperative bargaining. In Canada, the institutional structures militate against legalism. Legalism relies on restricting the autonomy of the executive, whether through specific statutes or a more general environmental right. In the American separation-of-powers system, Congress does not trust the executive, and it therefore writes highly specific statutes. In a parliamentary system such as Canada's the legislature and executive are fused. This fact – along with the presence of extremely tight party discipline in Canada – means that there are few institutional incentives to restrict regulatory discretion (Hoberg 1993a). It is this difference in the specificity of regulatory statutes that provides the principal explanation for the different role of the courts in environmental policy in the two countries – not rules of standing or judicial traditions, as claimed by Howlett (1994).

Thus, there remain substantial differences in Canadian and U.S. policy-making institutions and processes, both in terms of the degree of legalism and in the nature of fragmentation. First, legalism is far more pervasive in the United States, producing a more open, formal, and adversarial system, in which the autonomy of the regulators is carefully restricted by congressional statutes, interest-group demands, and court decisions. In Canada, environmental policy making is more closed, informal, and cooperative, and the regulators enjoy substantial autonomy. Second, the institutions in both countries are fragmented, but along different dimensions. In the United States, the separation of powers creates massive horizontal fragmentation. In Canada, there is considerable institutional concentration at each level of government but extensive vertical fragmentation in the form of a highly decentralized federalism.

How should we expect these institutional differences to influence environmental policy outcomes in the two countries? It would be too simplistic to state that they are a force for divergence. There is no simple, direct relationship between institutions and policy outcomes. While institutions may "load the dice" in favour of one type of outcome, their impact can vary from situation to situation, depending on a host of other factors (Weaver and Rockman 1993).

Perhaps the most important impact of legalism is that it gives environmentalists a great deal of control over the governmental agenda. Through petitioning regulatory agencies or court challenges, environmental groups can pressure reluctant agencies to act. Without as many legal tools, Canadian environmental groups are far more reliant on mobilizing public opinion to pressure the government. Lamenting the absence of legal recourse, one Canadian environmentalist despaired, "You can call a press conference, and that's about it" (quoted in Israelson 1990, 14). But legalism does not just grant tools to regulatory advocates; it also grants them to their opponents. The same doctrine of administrative law that can be used by the courts to force a reluctant agency to act can be used to overturn pro-environment agency decisions challenged by business interests. The policy implications of the legalistic constraints on agency discretion thus depends on the balance between the legal tools held by environmentalists and those held by business. There is no a priori basis to predict which of these two contraints is likely to be more powerful.

Canadian decision makers enjoy more autonomy from interest groups than their counterparts in the United States. On the one hand, they are more insulated from pressure by environmental groups, which may make them less sensitive to environmental concerns. But on the other hand, they are also more insulated from business pressures and may thus be free to represent environmental interests if they wish. Thus, in the Canadian system, the policy interests of the decision makers themselves are likely to be more important. Government officials may derive these interests from their ideas about good environmental policy, or they may respond to their perception of electoral incentives. If there is widespread public support for environmental protection, officials are likely to be motivated to provide policies aimed at protecting the environment, even if they are not being forced to do so through litigation.

As in the case of legalism, the policy implications of fragmentation are not straightforward. Indeed, under certain conditions, fragmented institutions can retard policy change, while under other conditions they can accelerate it. One of the most important impacts of fragmentation is that it disperses veto points, raising the level of consensus required before policy change can occur (Banting 1987a, 40–1). In the case of environmental policy, this would seem to thwart policy development, particularly given the powerful, concentrated business interests in opposition. However, a number of scholars have noted that under certain conditions, competition for political credit may result in a bidding-up process between different institutions, whether this occurs between different parties controlling Congress and the presidency in the United States, or between provinces and the federal government in Canada (Weaver and Rockman 1993; Weaver 1994; K. Harrison 1995a; Elliott et al. 1985). Thus, the impact of both legalism and fragmentation is unclear; further clarification will have to await the results of the policy comparison.

International Pressures

To date, the dominant force behind environmental policy has unquestionably been domestic pressure. Recently, however, pressures from the international arena have increased. Four types of international factors influence environmental policy, and they all tend to promote convergence: (1) the escalating importance of global environmental problems and the increased attempts at international collaboration to address these problems; (2) economic integration, including formal trade agreements such as the Canada–U.S. Free Trade Agreement (FTA), the North American Free Trade Agreement (NAFTA), and the General Agreement on Tariffs and Trade (GATT); (3) the cross-national transfer of ideas; and (4) cross-border lobbying. While these developments affect both the United States and Canada, the vulnerability to external forces is much greater in Canada because of its smaller size and more open economy. In addition, Canada faces the unique problem of its overwhelming dependence on the United States. As the following analysis will show, all four of these types of international influence can be expected to contribute to greater convergence in environmental policies in the two countries.

International pressures are, of course, not new to Canadian and U.S. environmental policy. The International Joint Commission was established to address shared environmental concerns in 1909, and the Migratory Birds Convention was forged to protect habitat in 1917. The most successful case of bilateral action between the two countries has been the Great Lakes Water Quality Agreement, signed in 1972. The greatest failure in collaboration is the case of transboundary air pollution. The United States stubbornly refused to enter into an agreement with Canada until 1991, after amendments to the U.S. Clean Air Act had been passed by Congress and signed into law in 1990 (R. Cohen 1992; Munton and Castle 1992).

In the late 1980s and early 1990s, mounting concern for global climate change and threats to biodiversity elevated international issues to the forefront of the environmental agenda. Agreement on the 1987 Montreal Protocol to reduce ozone-depleting substances represented a significant collaborative achievement. Much less progress has occurred on the higher-stakes issue of global warming, and neither Canada nor the United States has taken an aggressive role in promoting action. The United Nations Conference on Environment and Development in 1992 did much to elevate the profile of global environmental issues on the international agenda, but the progress on concrete measures was disappointing (Haas, Levy, and Parson 1992). While there has been limited progress thus far, both bilateral and multilateral efforts to address international environmental problems should encourage greater convergence in environmental policies.

The increasing importance of global environmental problems is not the only international pressure on domestic environmental policy. Economic globalization also has potentially profound implications, although the direction of its impact is not yet clear. First, pressure towards the harmonization of standards may occur as a result of the costs that environmental regulations impose on firms competing in international markets. In the case of "process standards," which control the way goods are produced (for example, effluent controls on a chemical plant), firms may suffer a competitive disadvantage if the costs of complying with environmental regulations exceed those of their competitors. Firms in such a situation are likely to lobby their governments to reduce regulatory burdens, creating the potential for a "race to the bottom" in which each nation attempts to create a competitive advantage for its firms by weakening environmental standards. Empirical studies show little evidence of such an effect, largely because environmental costs are relatively small compared to other factor costs. According to a U.S. government study, "compliance costs are not a major share of total costs for any industry, and are only one of many factors determining competitive advantage" (U.S. Office of Technology Assessment 1994; see also Olewiler 1994). Nonetheless, fears about the impact of environmental controls on competitiveness have been an important political phenomenon in recent years.

In the case of "product standards," which control the characteristics of the product itself (for example, by limiting the quantity of a particular chemical contained in a product), firms have an interest in the establishment of uniform regulations across nations so that they can take advantage of the economies involved in producing the same product for a larger market. In this case, however, it is more likely that firms will target their lobbying at international bodies rather than at their own governments.

Second, trade agreements may encourage the harmonization of environmental standards and may open a country's environmental policies to challenge by competitors on the grounds that they provide unfair subsidies or are a non-tariff barrier to trade (Esty 1994; U.S. Office of Technology Assessment 1992b; Zaehlke, Orbuch, and Houseman 1993). Many environmentalists in Canada were highly critical of the Canada–U.S. Free Trade Agreement (FTA) because they feared that it would lead to a weakening of Canadian environmental standards (Shrybman 1993; Swenarchuk 1993), and many American environmentalists expressed similar fears about NAFTA (Audley 1993).

Nothing in the three major international trade agreements explicitly requires harmonization of environmental standards. In fact, they all recognize the right of countries to have different standards. And although the environmental side agreement to NAFTA explicity addresses the issue, it focuses on the enforcement of each country's own laws and contains no requirement that these laws be changed.[13] There are some measures that are designed specifically to encourage harmonization. For instance, section 7 of the FTA established a binational working group to "work towards equivalence" in pesticide regulation. Canadian environmentalists have been very critical of this section because it adopts a risk-benefit standard instead of the risk-only standard that is permitted (though not required) by Canadian law. This criticism is misplaced, however, because Canadian practice already relies on a risk-benefit standard (Hoberg 1990, 1991b). Moreover, the harmonization efforts have not made much progress; serious discussion began only in late 1993, followed by several minor pilot projects. Whether or not Canadian concerns about a weakening of standards is valid depends on how U.S. and Canadian standards compare, a subject discussed in the policy comparisons below.

NAFTA's sections on "Sanitary and Phytosanitary Standards" and "Standards-Related Measures" contain provisions that encourage the adoption of international standards, but the measures are intended to promote upward harmonization. The parties to the agreement are urged to "pursue equivalence" and use international standards, but "without reducing the level of protection for the environment." The signatory countries are explicitly allowed to exceed international standards. It is true that if any of them believe that standards exceeding the international norm are a barrier to trade, they can challenge the standard under the agreement's dispute settlement measures, but the complaining party bears the burden of proof in demonstrating that the standard is not based on "scientific principles" (Charnovitz 1993).

These international trade agreements may constrain environmental policy in four ways. First, the principle of national treatment explicitly permits countries to adopt their own regulatory rules, but it also requires that the same rules apply to domestically produced and imported products. Second, policies that distort trade are subject to challenge or retaliation by competitors. Policies aimed at conservation and environmental protection are exempted from these challenges under article 20 of GATT, but whether or not the environmental justifications are legitimate is a matter of interpretation and is subject to the dispute resolution process (Esty 1994; Vogel 1994; U.S. Office of Technology Assessment 1992b, 32). Third, the ability of countries to use trade measures, such as import bans, on goods produced according to environmentally damaging processes is limited.[14] Finally, the NAFTA side agreement on the environment may make it more difficult for a country to engage in routine noncompliance with its own environmental standards, although the procedural hoops that a country must go through to impose sanctions on another country that fails to enforce its own laws are quite daunting (Charnovitz 1994).

Overall, economic globalization is a force for convergence, both in terms of economic integration and trade liberalization. But it is important not to overstate the magnitude of this factor. The trade agreements do impose some limits on national regulatory sovereignty, but they still provide a great deal of room for regulatory divergence. Much of their impact will depend on the manner in which they are interpreted by dispute resolution panels in the future.

Another potential force for convergence is emulation, where one country adopts another country's policy innovations (Heclo 1974; Bennett 1991a). In North American environmental policy, this phenomenon is pervasive and is virtually unidirectional – from the United States to Canada (Hoberg 1991a). Emulation usually occurs through one of two primary modes. The first is elite driven, when officials or policy specialists evaluating policy alternatives are attracted to the American experience. Officials may learn about U.S. policies through the media or specialized publications, or through participation in transnational policy communities. In many cases, formal meetings are scheduled between government officials in the two countries to share information and discuss common concerns.[15]

The second mode of emulation is activist driven, when political activists use the existence of an American program or standard to support their argument for policy change in Canada. In this case, activists try to "shame" the government into acting, with the logic that "if it is good enough for them, it is good enough for us." This dynamic is facilitated by the penetration of U.S. mass media into Canada. When an issue of importance emerges in the United States, it is often picked up by Canadian policy activists or by the media itself, forcing the government to respond.

The emulation dynamic goes beyond the bilateral influence of the United States on Canada. Much of the strategy of nascent international institutions relies not so much on making international rules that are binding on nation-states but on publicizing comparative information about the environmental policy performance of different nations. Although the Rio Conference in June 1992 did not yield much in the way of substantive agreements, it set in motion an institutional process whereby national governments submit reports to a new Sustainable Development Commission (Haas, Levy, and Parson 1992). Similarly, NAFTA requires reports to the new Commission for Environmental Cooperation. These reporting requirements create the possibility that exposing the performance of different national governments may "shame" laggards into improving their performance.

The fourth and final international influence on environmental policy is cross-border lobbying. Interest groups from one country increasingly engage in efforts to lobby the government of another country.[16] Cross-border lobbying has occurred in several areas of environmental policy in North America. The northward flow of lobbying is reflected in the efforts of U.S. environmentalists to block further hydroelectric developments in northern Quebec and to promote wilderness preservation in British Columbia; the southward flow, in the efforts of Canadian environmentalists to get Congress to adopt acid rain controls in the 1980s and in the attempt of Canadian industry to overturn the Environmental Protection Agency's ban on asbestos.

On balance, these policy determinants would seem to promote the convergence of environmental policies in the two countries. Similar environmental problems, common science and technology, common domestic pressures, and international forces all point towards convergence. The major exception is institutions, but their actual impact is highly contingent on other factors at work. We will later return to an analysis of how these forces work in concert to produce environmental policies, but first let us look at the policy indicators in the two countries.

POLICY RESPONSES

This section compares environmental policy outcomes in the two countries. This task is quite complex for a number of reasons. First, environmental policies are multitiered, ranging from broad statutory grants of authority to more specific regulatory requirements, to the enforcement of those standards at the level of the polluter. Second, policies may differ considerably within each country, making nation-wide generalizations difficult. Ultimately, we want to know what impact policies actually have on environmental quality. Unfortunately, much of the data to perform these sorts of analysis are not available, and even when they do exist they are difficult to compare across nations because of different measurement techniques. Nevertheless, this section marshals the available data to compare environmental policy in eight areas: policy discourse, regulatory authority, policy instruments, regulatory standards, protected areas, commitments to global agreements, enforcement, and impacts on business spending and environmental quality. Although the comparison is far from comprehensive, the patterns revealed are clearly suggestive.

Policy Discourse

There are interesting similarities and differences in environmental policy discourse in the two countries. As the earlier section showed, the environmental issue went through several phases of heightened concern in both countries at about the same time. During their peaks in 1970 and 1990, the media, the public, and politicians spent a great deal of time discussing environmental issues. While the timing has been quite similar, the nature of the discourse has differed somewhat. First, the Canadian discourse seems more focused on government spending on the environment, whereas the U.S. discourse seems more focused on the impact of regulation on business. This difference is perhaps best captured in comparing the discussion of each country's major environmental initiative of 1990: Canada's Green Plan and the U.S. Clean Air Act amendments. Debate over the Green Plan was almost exclusively focused on the government's budgetary commitment (Hoberg and Harrison 1994). In contrast, the debate over the U.S. Clean Air Act seemed virtually indifferent to the costs to government and was dominated by how stringent the regulations should be and what their impact would be on the economy (R. Cohen 1992; Bryner 1993). Of course, much of this difference is accounted for by the fact that the Clean Air Act contained a great deal more regulation than the Green Plan, but this emphasis in discourse seems to be more widespread. In general, it seems that American discourse is more preoccupied by regulation than Canadian discourse.

Second, since the late 1980s, Canadian environmental discourse has been dominated by the concept of "sustainable development," popularized by the report of the World Commission on Environment and Development (1987). However, the concept has had very little impact on discourse in the United States, particularly outside academia, although it does seem to be growing, one indicator being the Clinton-Gore administration's creation of a President's Council on Sustainable Development.[17] This difference may reflect a stronger belief in Canada in the compatibility of environmental and economic objectives, although it probably results from the differential timing of environmental policy development more than anything else. The environmental policy regime matured earlier in the United States, before the introduction of the concept. In Canada, the late 1980s was a time of significant environmental policy innovation, just as the concept of sustainable development was being introduced.

Regulatory Authority

In both countries, governments have responded to pressures for environmental policy with a complex array of statutes and administrative actions. As one would expect given the divergent policy regimes of the two countries, there are important differences in their regulatory frameworks. Two distinctions stand out. First, the Canadian system is significantly more decentralized, with most areas of environmental protection still being dominated by the provinces (K. Harrison 1995b; Dwivedi and Woodrow 1989). Second, even with the creeping legalism of late, the Canadian system is much more discretionary. In many cases, Canadian regulators are simply granted regulatory authority, whereas American statutes specify the rules themselves or explicitly require regulators to take particular actions. For example, Canadian auto emission standards are established by the minister of transport under a broad grant of authority by the Motor Vehicle Safety Act, while in the United States the standards are actually written into the legislation by Congress in the Clean Air Act. Similarly, Canadian provinces have the authority to protect endangered species, but the action-forcing nature of the U.S. Endangered Species Act, one of the world's most coercive environmental statutes, is the envy of Canadian environmentalists. Despite these differences in approach, however, the regulatory statutes in the two countries address the same subjects, and they provide regulators in both countries with similar policy instruments and authority. In no case do regulators in one country have statutory authority that is absent in the other country (Hoberg 1991b; Nemetz, Stanbury, and Thompson 1986).

Policy Instruments

There are various tools that governments can use to control behaviour affecting environmental quality, including spending, regulation, market-based incentives, and persuasion (Doern 1990a; Paehlke 1990). With some notable exceptions, there is a substantial amount of convergence on the use of policy instruments in Canada and the United States. Most importantly, despite two decades of cajoling and even ridicule from economists, both countries have relied almost exclusively on command-and-control regulation at the expense of market-based incentives. There are some significant recent exceptions, particularly in the United States. Regulators began experimenting with "bubble policies" in air pollution control in the 1980s, but the most important program to date has been the provision for emission trading in the acid rain provisions of the 1990 Clean Air Act amendments. The first significant market-based program in Canada was the one established to implement the Montreal Protocol on stratospheric ozone (D. Smith 1990). But these programs are the exception to the rule – regulation is unquestionably the dominant approach to environmental policy in both countries.

There are some differences in the use of subsidies to promote environmental protection. The Canadian government has funded more research and development on pollution control technology, and it has shown a greater historical willingness to subsidize private polluters to help with pollution abatement costs, most prominently in the pulp and paper and smelting industries. Overall, however, the patterns of government spending on the environment in the two countries are remarkably similar. As shown in table 9.3, if budgetary commitments to the environment in 1991 at both the federal and the state or provincial governments are included, U.S. environmental spending is approximately 0.82 per cent of total government spending, and Canadian environmental spending is about 0.77 per cent. Both governments increased environmental spending from 1986 by similar amounts.

The most significant divergence in the use of regulatory instruments concerns citizen access to information about environmental threats. The United States adopts a regulatory approach, relying far more on requirements for information disclosure than Canada does. The most prominent example is the "right to know" provisions of the 1986 amendments to the U.S. "Superfund" law. The law requires firms using or producing specified toxic chemicals to provide both EPA and state and local governments with information about the chemicals, including the quantities on site and, most importantly, their release into the environment. Any citizen has access to this information.

Table 9.3
Government spending on the environment (millions of dollars)

	Canada		United States	
	1986	*1991*	*1986*	*1991*
Federal environment budget				
Parks included	$520[1]	$863	$4,451[2]	$7,390
Parks excluded	231	442	3,446	6,004
Total federal budget	111,227	153,330	1,072,773	1,398,234
Per cent environment of total				
Parks included	0.46%	0.56%	0.41%	0.53%
Parks excluded	0.21%	0.29%	0.32%	0.43%
Subnational environment spending	699[3]	1,150	5,283[4]	9,334
Subnational total	78,513	106,856	361,897	630,676
Per cent environment of total	0.89%	1.08%	1.46%	1.48%
National environment total				
Parks included	1,219	2,013	9,734	16,724
Parks excluded	930	1,592	8,729	15,338
National budget total	189,740	260,186	1,434,670	2,028,910
Per cent environment of total				
Parks included[5]	0.64%	0.77%	0.68%	0.82%
Parks excluded[5]	0.49%	0.61%	0.61%	0.76%

[1] Canadian figures for total federal budget and Environment Canada budget are from *Public Accounts of Canada*, FY 85–6 and FY 90–1. The figure for Environment Canada excludes the Atmosphere Environment Service.
[2] Figures for EPA and total U.S. budget from Executive Office of the President, Office of Management and Budget, *Historical Tables – Budget of the U.S. Government: Fiscal Year 1988 and 1993*.
[3] Provincial spending on the environment includes the ministries of Environment in Ontario, Quebec, Alberta, and British Columbia. Figures derived from public accounts of the individual provinces.
[4] Spending by the states derived from council of State Governments, *Resource Guide to State Environmental Management* (Lexington, Ky: Council of State Governments, 1988, 1992).
[5] The amounts for parks include only federal spending on parks.

In February 1992, Environment Canada announced the creation of a similar National Pollutants Release Inventory, but this did not go into effect until 1994. This suggests that there has been considerable convergence, though after at least a seven-year lag. This lag is significant, because the effect of the program goes beyond providing information about toxic emissions to the public. As anticipated, many firms have responded to the disclosure requirements by reducing emissions of hazardous chemicals. Thus, in addition to giving citizens information which they can use to pressure governments to strengthen regulations, the right-to-know laws have directly reduced pollution (Hadden 1989, esp. 15, 149). According to one environmentalist, disclosure requirements "have had more impact than regulatory programs" (quoted in Holusha 1991).

While Canada lagged behind on right-to-know laws, it was ahead on "eco-labelling." The Canadian federal government has a program that certifies products as environmentally friendly by granting them a special seal. No such program exists in the United States. In addition, Canada was the first nation in the world to adopt an "ozone watch," which provides daily readings of ultraviolet radiation levels as part of the weather forecasts. The United States has yet to adopt such a program.

A related policy instrument is the attempt to change government behaviour by forcing agencies to perform certain types of analysis before making decisions. The classic example is environmental impact assessment, a process invented by the U.S. National Environmental Policy Act of 1970. This law requires that an environmental impact statement be performed for "every recommendation or report on proposals for legislation and other major Federal actions significantly affecting the quality of the human environment." Citizens have the right to sue the government to enforce compliance, and courts have rigorously enforced the requirement.

Until recently, Canadian impact assessment requirements were far less rigorous. In 1973 the federal cabinet established the Environmental Assessment and Review Process (EARP), but as a result of the recent spate of court decisions and new legislation discussed earlier, the environmental assessment process has been undergoing profound changes. When the Canadian Environmental Assessment Act went into effect in January 1995, Canadian impact assessment requirements became far more like those south of the border.

Comparing the two analytical systems is extremely difficult. It would seem that many more full-blown impact assessments are performed in the United States than in Canada, even when one takes into account the larger size of the United States. U.S. federal agencies perform approximately 440 formal environmental impact statements each year.[18] Between 1973 and August 1994, Canada completed a total of 44 panel reviews under the auspices of the Federal Environmental Assessment Review Office (FEARO).[19] While the impact on policy decisions of these different systems is uncertain, the American impact assessment requirements thus far have certainly been more rigorous and have generated more assessment activity.

Regulatory Standards

A more direct indicator of environmental policy can be found in the regulatory requirements imposed on particular environmentally damaging activities. Regulations will be compared in five areas: air pollution, water pollution, pesticides, toxic substances control, and forest practices.[20] In the case of air pollution, the standards are relatively similar, though the U.S. requirements are somewhat more stringent. The standards for the concentration of pollutants allowed in the ambient air in Canada differ from province to province, both in their levels and in their legal force. In general, the "maximum acceptable levels" of the Canadian federal guidelines (the standard most often used by the provinces) are slightly more stringent than the "primary level" National Ambient Air Quality Standards (NAAQS) in the United States (Federal-Provincial Advisory Committee on Air Quality 1988; Franson, Franson, and Lucas 1982, 115). However, the U.S. standards have more legal force. More importantly, the U.S. Prevention of Significant Deterioration program supplements NAAQS by imposing more stringent standards in clean air areas. Combined, the two U.S. programs produce more stringent air quality standards than those that exist in Canada.

Two of the most important air pollution problems in North America – acid rain and automobile emissions – reveal different patterns. With the 1990 amendments to the Clean Air Act in the United States, both governments have programs in place to reduce the emissions that cause acid rain by comparable amounts. However, the Canadian program was put in place five years earlier and required that the reductions be achieved by 1994, whereas the U.S. target date is 2000.

Automobile emission controls reveal a different pattern. Historically, U.S. standards have been far more stringent than those in Canada. Prior to 1988, Canadian standards were between three and seven times less stringent, depending on the pollutant in question (Nemetz 1986, 559). New standards that went into effect in 1988 made Canadian regulations equivalent to U.S. standards. However, the 1990 amendments to the U.S. Clean Air Act required much more stringent standards to be implemented between 1994 and 1996. In Canada, rather than producing new regulations, the federal government in 1992 entered into a "memorandum of understanding" with the auto industry that it would produce cars with the same auto emission requirements that exist in the United

States. While this agreement lacks the legal authority of regulations or statutes, it does represent Canadian convergence on U.S. standards. Significantly, auto emission standards in California are considerably more stringent than the 1990 Clean Air Act requirements, and twelve eastern states have now followed suit and adopted California standards (Wald 1994). As a result, 37 per cent of the U.S. population will be covered by standards significantly more stringent than those voluntarily agreed to by Canadian manufacturers. Thus, there has recently been a considerable amount of convergence in air pollution regulations, but U.S. standards are still somewhat more stringent.

U.S. regulations for water pollution are also more stringent than Canada's, though there are signs of recent convergence. The requirements for sewage treatment are very different. The U.S. Federal Water Pollution Control Act (1972) required virtually all municipalities to install "secondary" treatment of municipal wastes by 1977 (the deadline has been extended twice since then). No such requirement exists north of the border, although individual municipalities or provinces have installed secondary and even tertiary treatment. This difference has led to significant cross-border tensions on the West Coast, where residents and politicians from cities in Washington State have protested the fact that Victoria, B.C., continues to dump raw sewage into the marine waters shared by the two countries.[21] The different requirements also show up in aggregate statistics. In Canada, 63 per cent of the population was served by facilities with at least secondary treatment in 1985; in the United States the figure was 74 per cent (OECD 1993c, 57). Although more recent comparable statistics are not available, there is some indication that Canada has since narrowed the gap (Statistics Canada 1994c, 191).

In the Great Lakes area, the United States contributes far more water pollution than Canada, as a result of its larger population and industrial activity. But it has been significantly more aggressive in trying to control its effluents. For example, the states' limit for phosphorus in detergents, a major source of Great Lakes pollution, is more than four times more stringent than the comparable Canadian standard (Great Lakes Water Quality Board 1989, 19, 35). Pulp and paper mills are another major source of water pollution from both countries in the Great Lakes region. All pulp mills in the United States have been required to have secondary effluent treatment since the mid-1970s, whereas mills in Ontario were not required to do so until 1993. As a result, as of April 1989, only six of twenty-seven Ontario mills had secondary treatment (Ontario Ministry of the Environment 1989), compared with virtually all mills in the United States.[22] Despite a joint commitment of both countries to the "virtual elimination" of a number of persistent toxic chemicals in the region, the U.S. Environmental Protection Agency (EPA) announced its own initiative to decrease toxic discharges significantly (U.S. Environmental Protection Agency 1993a). The proposal, which went well beyond plans north of the border, was issued with little consultation with Canadian authorities. Interesting, while the Great Lakes Water Quality Agreement promotes cooperation between the two jurisdictions, it has not produced sweeping harmonization of standards in the region, nor has it led to the emergence of a powerful bilateral body that has the policy sovereignty of the two countries.

In the case of pesticides, there is a substantial amount of convergence on policy. A survey of ten high-profile pesticide controversies in the past two decades, including DDT, EDB, and alar, found that the two countries had taken similar action in eight cases (Hoberg 1991b). In the other two cases, Canada's action had been more stringent on one, and the U.S. action had been more stringent on the other. However, a slight edge can be granted to the United States because it acted first in seven cases, with Canada responding later. When evaluating the limits on the amount of pesticide residues in food, there is also a large amount of convergence, but in this case a definite edge for regulatory stringency goes to Canada. In 1991–92, 60 per cent of residue limits were identical, but Canadian tolerances were more stringent in 32 per cent of the cases, while American tolerances were more stringent in only 9 per cent. However, U.S. tolerances had been getting more stringent, and the gap was narrower than it had been five years earlier. In 1986 the number of residue limits that were identical had been the same 60 per cent, but the percentage of Canadian tolerances that were more stringent had been greater, at 38 per cent, while more stringent American tolerances had been even less common, comprising only 2 per cent of the cases.[23]

In the area of toxic substance control, there is a substantial amount of convergence, with the United States going further than Canada in some important cases. In the case of lead, both nations have banned the major source – its use as an additive in gasoline – although the United States acted earlier. In the case of PCBs, both countries have banned the manufacture and distribution of products containing PCBs, but the policies for storage and disposal have diverged significantly. The United States requires that PCBs be disposed of within one year of their removal from use, whereas Canada has no such requirement. Asbestos is also a case of divergence. Canada's policy of "controlled use" allows asbestos to be used under certain conditions, whereas the United States' EPA banned the substance. Parts of EPA's ban were struck down by a U.S. court in response to a lawsuit joined by the Canadian industry and government. Nonetheless, restrictions are still tighter in the United States than they are north of the border (K. Harrison and Hoberg 1994, ch. 7). Finally, both countries have developed new regulatory standards for dioxins, furans, and other chlorinated organics; but comparisons are difficult because of a complicated mix of federal and state/provincial standards. Canada developed formal regulations earlier than the United States, but existing U.S. water-quality regulations appear to provide at least as much protection as Canadian standards, and EPA's recent proposals promise to exceed Canadian federal standards and match the most stringent provincial standards (K. Harrison and Hoberg 1994, 51).

One final area of regulatory standards involves forest practices in the West. A comparison of a variety of forest practices – from limits on the size of clearcuts to the protection provided for fish habitat – reveals that the variation within the United States is greater than the difference between the United States and Canada. The regulations on U.S. federal forest lands are very stringent, but the rules on private forest lands (which are extensive) are significantly weaker. The regulations in British Columbia fall somewhere in between. B.C. forest practices are undergoing a significant tightening as a result of the new Forest Practices Code, but American rules on federal lands are also being tightened and are likely to remain more stringent than those north of the border. In addition, the United States has set aside more of the remaining old growth in the Pacific Northwest and Alaska than British Columbia has (Hoberg 1993b).

Protected Areas

Comparisons of protected wilderness areas are also very revealing. Currently, the United States has a larger amount of protected areas as a percentage of its entire land area. Protected areas make up 10.5 per cent of U.S. land area and 7.0 per cent of Canadian land area (OECD 1993c). However, Canada spends considerably more on parks than the United States does (see table 9.3). Parks spending in Canada is 38 per cent of the federal environmental budget; in the United States it is only 19 per cent. This may help explain the more pro-preservation orientation that Lowry found among parks officials north of the border (Lowry 1994). In addition, park expansion seems to be much higher on the Canadian agenda than it is in the United States. In the 1990 Green Plan, Canada committed itself to increasing the figure to 12 per cent. If achieved, this would push the Canadian protected areas well beyond the U.S. level.

Commitments to Global Agreements

As global environmental problems have become increasingly important on the environmental agenda, national responses to international initiatives have become a significant indicator of a nation's environmental commitment. In this area the record of both countries is mixed but very similar. Both countries, particularly the United States, were strong leaders in the international agreements to reduce chemicals that deplete stratospheric ozone (Haas 1992a; Doern 1993, 84).

The same cannot be said about global warming. Canada committed itself in 1990 to the goal of stabilizing greenhouse gas emissions at 1990 levels by the year 2000, but it has yet to develop an action plan to meet this objective. In the United States, despite its aggressive domestic clean air legislation, the Bush administration was openly hostile to any international agreement that involved specific targets or deadlines, and it emerged from the UNCED conference in 1992 with a reputation as an "environmental bad boy" (Reuters 1992). The Clinton administration reversed course in April 1993 and signed the international agreement, committing itself to the same stabilization objective that Canada had established three years earlier. The United States issued an action plan in October 1993, but there was a striking lack of any coercive measures; the plan relied on voluntary measures by industry. Within less than a year of its announcement, administration officials admitted that it would not succeed in achieving the stabilization objective (Cushman 1994). Thus, both countries have compiled similar records thus far on commitments to international agreements to protect the global atmosphere: strong on stratospheric ozone, weak on greenhouse gases.

Enforcement

Data on the enforcement of water pollution controls provide an opportunity to test one of the most common criticisms of American environmental programs. Analysts have repeatedly denounced the "implementation gap" in American regulation – the gap between regulatory requirements and the actions of polluters (Bardach and Kagan 1982; Hawkins 1984). However, the record suggest that this characterization is more myth than fact, at least when compared with Canada. In the Great Lakes area, U.S. compliance rates for both municipal and industrial sources are approximately 90 per cent. In contrast, Canadian municipal compliance rates are between 40 and 50 per cent, and industrial compliance rates are even worse – between 30 and 40 per cent. Differences in compliance definitions make only the most general comparisons possible with these aggregate figures. But when the Great Lakes Water Quality Board analysed an indicator for which there was consistent data – compliance with the agreement's phosphorus effluent benchmark – the same disparity emerged: 48 per cent of U.S. sources met the benchmark, compared with 29 per cent of Canadian sources (Great Lakes Water Quality Board 1989, 6–12). In a study of pulp and paper mill compliance in the two countries, Harrison shows significantly higher compliance rates in the United States. For biochemical oxygen demand (BOD) standards, 69 per cent of Canadian mills comply, compared with between 86 per cent and 98 per cent compliance in the United States, depending on the measure used. For total suspended solids (TSS) standards, 59 per cent of Canadian mills complied compared with 92 per cent of American mills (K. Harrison 1995b).

Impact

One way of measuring the consequences of regulation is through trends in air quality and emissions. Table 9.4 shows air quality trends for six major pollutants. In all cases but one (ozone), the trends are in the same direction. Both countries have made remarkably similar progress in reducing sulphur dioxide and lead. Canada has made more progress in reducing carbon dioxide, nitrogen dioxide, and particulates; the United States has been more successful in controlling ozone. When analysing the separate measure of emissions (the amount of pollution being released, rather than its concentration in the air) during the period 1980–92, it can be seen that Canada had more success in reducing emissions of sulphur dioxide, but the United States was slightly more successful in controlling nitrogen oxides. During the period 1985–92, the United States was slightly more successful than Canada in controlling volatile organic compounds.[24] Of the nine indicators, two were virtually the same, Canada made greater progress on four, and the United States made greater progress on three. The fact that Canada matched or slightly exceeded the U.S. performance overall is surprising given its less stringent air pollution regulations.

Another way to measure the impact of regulations is to analyse how much business has to spend to comply with them. While compliance costs are certainly not a direct measure of environmental quality, they do provide evidence of the extent of societal commitment to environmental protection. Indeed, if we think about policy as the allocation of costs and benefits (Wilson 1980), compliance costs can provide a useful indicator of the balance of power between environmental and business interests. Unfortunately, the data available to make such a comparison is of poor quality, and what is available gives conflicting

Table 9.4
North American air quality trends[1]

		Canada	United States
Sulphur dioxide (ppb)	1975	11	15.4
	1990	6	8.0
	% change	-45%	-48%
Carbon monoxide (ppm)	1975	1.9	11.96
	1990	0.8	5.89
	% change	-58%	-51%
Ozone (ppb)	1979	15	134
	1990	18	114
		+20%	-15%
Nitrogen dioxide (ppm)	1977	31	29
	1990	21	22
	% change	-32%	-24%
Total suspended particulates ($\mu g/m^3$)			
	1975	65.9	61.9
	1990	38.5	47.3
	% change	-42%	-24%
Lead ($\mu g/m^3$)	1975	0.55	1.04
	1990	0.02	0.07
	% change	-96%	-93%

Sources: Canada, Environment Canada 1990, 1994b, table J; U.S. Council on Environmental Quality 1992, table 40.

[1] Different measurement methods are used. All Canadian figures, and U.S. figures for nitrogen dioxide and sulphur dioxide, are annual arithmetic means. U.S. figures for carbon monoxide are based on the second highest readings for eight-hour periods; those for TSP are annual geometric means; ozone counts are the second highest daily one-hour maximums; and figures for lead are maximum quarterly averages.

impressions. Data collected by the OECD suggests the U.S. businesses spend more to comply with regulations than their counterparts north of the border. Spending on pollution abatement and control as a percentage of gross domestic product in 1989 was 1.1 per cent in Canada and 1.4 per cent in the United States. Investment by the business sector in pollution abatement and control, as a percentage of gross fixed capital formation in 1989, was 0.8 per cent in Canada, 1.3 per cent in the United States (OECD 1993c, 294–9).

A 1989 survey by Statistics Canada suggests a very different story. It showed pollution control spending in Canada to be 12.6 per cent of

new plant and equipment. Similar U.S. figures showed the U.S. share at
4.1 per cent in 1988, a factor of three lower than the Canadian level
(Rutledge and Stergioulas 1988; Olewiler 1994, 90–1). These result are
somewhat mysterious, because they are a factor of seven greater than a
survey conducted several years earlier (Statistics Canada 1989). If it is
more than an artifact of sampling, it suggests that there had been a dramatic intensification of Canadian regulation. But the new figures do not
necessarily demonstrate more stringent Canadian regulations, because
U.S. pollution control spending was considerably higher than Canada's
for some time. However, they certainly suggest that Canada is no longer
a laggard in pollution control spending. Olewiler speculates that the figures may be the result of the greater pollution intensity of Canadian industry, as well as "Canadian regulations catching up with or even
surpassing those in the United States" (Olewiler 1994, 90–1).

Convergence amidst U.S. Leadership

The results of the comparisons are complex and occasionally paradoxical. There are several areas of remarkable convergence: acid rain and
auto emission control, regulation of pesticide products, government
spending, the regulation of lead, and global initiatives. But there are
also some prominent cases of divergence. U.S. policies are stronger on
information requirements, environmental impact assessments, air quality standards, water pollution control, several toxic substances, and enforcement. Canadian policies are more stringent on limits on pesticide
residues in food, progress in reducing some air pollutants, eco-labelling,
and – if the new figures are to be believed – recent business spending.

It is hard to detect any strong pattern here, particularly since some
of the results seem paradoxical. Nevertheless, it is possible to conclude
that there is a substantial amount of convergence on environmental
policy. Certainly, it would be a dramatic overstatement to suggest any
kind of full-scale harmonization of policies. There are differences in
policy approaches and policy actions in a number of areas. But these
differences tend to be within relatively narrow bounds, and there is an
observable trend towards more common policies in many areas.

Overall, however, U.S. policies should be judged to be somewhat
more stringent for two reasons. First, in the areas of divergence de-
tected here, U.S. policies have more often been stronger than Canadian
policies. Second, the United States deserves a substantial amount of
credit for acting first.[25] In a significant number of convergent cases, it
acted before Canada – for example, automobile emissions, lead in gasoline, and seven of the ten pesticide cases. Even in the most notable case
of delay in U.S. actions, acid rain, the United States had more stringent

air pollution controls on its facilities than Canada did prior to explicit action on acid rain by either side.[26] Indeed, this suggests a more general phenomenon in this policy arena. In many areas the U.S. environmental policy regime was developed earlier than in Canada, and much of the convergence that has occurred results from Canada closing the gap. This fact is exceptionally important in the comparison. Given the pervasive phenomenon of emulation described in the next section, the Canadian environmental record is as strong as it is in many cases precisely because the American record is strong.

EXPLAINING POLICY OUTCOMES

How can we account for this pattern of policy outcomes? An earlier section examined a range of factors influencing environmental policy outcomes. This section analyses how those factors can be combined to explain the comparative outcomes just described. Clearly, the different forces described below do not operate independently of one another. We therefore conclude the chapter by attempting to draw the different explanatory forces together into a more integrated perspective.

Science, Technology, and the Nature of the Problem

Science and technology have contributed to common policy agendas and similar policy solutions. When new scientific information about the effects of a toxic chemical emerges, it is typically transmitted rapidly among specialists in the field, and this creates pressure for policy change; for instance, one of the reasons why the two countries take such similar actions on pesticides is that new data arose suggesting that a certain chemical was more dangerous than previously thought. Scientific consensus can also provide the basis for international collaboration, as it did in the case of the agreement to reduce ozone-depleting chemicals (Haas 1992).

Despite the fact that both countries share a common body of science about the extent of threats to health or the environment, science itself is rarely if ever a determining factor in policy change. In large part, this is due to the presence of widespread uncertainty in environmental and health sciences. A classic example of this phenomenon is the dispute between U.S. and Canadian government scientists throughout the 1980s on the causes and consequences of acid rain. The uncertainties in the assessment of risks from toxic chemicals are also notorious, permitting respectable scientists to form widely differing judgments about the magnitude of the hazards and thus the justification for regulation (Jasanoff 1990). For instance, estimates by the U.S. Environmental Protection Agency for an acceptable level of exposure to dioxin are

1,700 times lower than those made by Health and Welfare Canada (K. Harrison 1991).

When policy makers become concerned about a threat to health or the environment, their options for addressing the problem are largely constrained by the state of technology, in terms of the possible solutions to the problem as well as the costs of those solutions. For instance, much of U.S. pollution control law is based on the concept of "best available control technology" (BACT). While there are many different versions of these technology standards, and while their definition varies from program to program, the basic idea is that polluters are forced to install state-of-the-art technology as long as it is economically feasible.

While this concept has always had some influence in Canada, in recent years it has been adopted more explicitly. Both Ontario's major water pollution control initiative (the Municipal-Industrial Strategy for Abatement) and the federal-provincial smog control plan explicitly adopted technology-based standards. Because the same technology is available to both countries, it is extremely likely that greater convergence will result. This certainly occurred in the case of automobile emissions, as gradually improving control technologies were adopted as regulatory standards in the United States and then in Canada.

One force for divergence is that the two countries are not facing the same environmental problem. One of the major reasons why Canadian automobile emission standards have historically been weaker than those in the United States is that Canadians have not needed stringent standards to maintain an acceptable level of air quality. The presence of different problems also helps explain the apparent paradox in policy outcomes in air pollution. U.S. air pollution regulations have historically been more stringent, yet Canada has been more successful at reducing some kinds of air pollution. This outcome can be explained by the fact that Canada had a relatively small number of large, poorly controlled sources that could easily be targeted by regulators, and the government even offered financial assistance where necessary. In contrast, the greater population and industrial density south of the border has created extremely stubborn pollution control problems, and thus the marginal costs of achieving a given level of air quality are significantly higher (Hoberg 1991b).

Domestic Pressures

Both countries have experienced comparable domestic pressures for and against policy change on environmental issues. Public concern for the environment is equally strong in both countries. The relative priority given to environmental issues has fluctuated, but at nearly identical times in both countries. In general, these pressures have been a powerful force for convergence, providing pressure for policy expansion during periods of high policy salience. Two aspects of domestic pressure work against convergence, however. First, the economies of scale generated by the large size of the American environmental movement gives the U.S. environmental movement more power, which helps explain why the United States went further faster in many areas.

Second, in cases where each country confronts different economic or political interests in competition with environmental protection, domestic pressures can act as a source of divergence. Both countries may face different trade-offs between protecting the environment and the economic activities that cause the problem. The clearest examples of this phenomenon are acid rain and asbestos. Both countries produce acid rain and suffer environmental damage as a result. But in Canada, the ratio of societal costs from environmental damage to the economic benefits of the activities producing pollution is quite high. In the United States, because of the economic importance of the pollution-producing activities in the Ohio River Valley, the ratio is far lower, particularly since the United States exports a large fraction of its costs. As a result, Canadian policy makers acted on the problem earlier than the United States.

Asbestos provides a revealing counter-example. U.S. asbestos regulations are far more stringent than those in Canada, in large part because Canada is the largest producer of asbestos outside the Soviet Union. Asbestos presents the same hazard in the two countries, but the economic costs of controlling it are far higher in Canada.

Institutions

One of the most striking conclusions of this analysis is that the profound institutional differences between Canadian and U.S. environmental policy making do not have a larger impact on the result of the policy comparisons. In the attempt to sort out the effect of institutions, this section analyses the impact of the two most powerful institutional phenomena in Canadian and U.S. environmental policy: legalism and fragmentation. The most important institutional difference between the two countries is the dominance of legalism in the United States, the principal effect of which is that U.S. regulators have far less discretion than their Canadian counterparts. The impact of different degrees of discretion is a function of the relationship between the balance of pressures constraining the decision maker and the decision maker's own policy motivations.

One powerful impact of legalism is that it gives environmentalists a great deal of control over the governmental agenda, through action-forcing standards in legislation or through more general citizen-suit provisions. Legal pressures by U.S. environmental groups were instrumental in a number of the cases surveyed here, including bans on pesticides such as DDT and on toxic chemicals such as lead. The most dramatic case is probably the program to protect air quality in clean-air areas, the Prevention of Significant Deterioration program, which was created in the early 1970s as a result of a court decision in response to a legal challenge by the Sierra Club (Melnick 1983, ch. 4). Statutory provisions allowing citizen groups to sue polluters for violating their permits may also account for the fact that the United States gets much higher compliance with its water pollution regulations than Canada does. In general, legalism is one of the reasons why the United States went further faster than Canada in environmental regulation. But legalism also grants tools to the opponents of environmental regulation. For instance, various pro-business decisions by the courts slowed down the enforcement of the Clean Air Act in the 1970s (Melnick 1983, ch. 7); and the 1989 EPA decision to ban asbestos was struck down by an appeals court in late 1991.

The policy implications of the legalistic constraints on agency discretion thus depend on the balance between the legal tools held by environmentalists and those held by business. In U.S. environmental policy, this balance has tended to be to the advantage of environmental interests, largely because of the aggressive congressional statutes that provide environmental groups with a cause of action in court. The action-forcing nature of these statutes is extremely important, because it gives environmentalists powerful leverage over the implementation of statutory mandates. If regulators are insufficiently aggressive, environmentalists can use specific statutory standards or, more likely, deadlines to force agency action. Canadian decision makers enjoy more autonomy from interest groups, but during periods of high public salience of environmental issues, officials are likely to be motivated to provide policies to protect the environment even if they are not being forced to do so by litigation. This fact helps explain why, despite the absence of legalism, Canadian environmental policy is in many cases comparable to U.S. policy.

In addition to legalism, fragmentation is a pervasive institutional phenomenon in both countries. Two related questions must be addressed: (1) Which has been more powerful in environmental policy, the retarding or accelerating dynamic produced by fragmentation? (2) How do the different axes of fragmentation in the two countries – horizontal in the United States, vertical in Canada – matter for environmental policy? There are instances when fragmentation appears to have thwarted action to protect the environment. U.S. action on acid rain, for instance, was prevented during most of the

1980s because of the stubborn opposition of President Reagan, who would have vetoed any strict control law passed by Congress. In Canada, the decentralization of water pollution control has had a notably retarding influence on environmental progress, whereas in the United States there are both federal requirements and federal financial aid for sewage treatment.[27] Without this federal carrot and stick, Canadian municipalities and provinces have not provided as much water pollution control.

There are also examples of fragmentation that have accelerated policy development in each country. The stringency of U.S. air and water pollution control laws, born between 1970 and 1972, is in large part the result of a competition for environmental leadership between the incumbent president, Richard Nixon, and the Democratic challenger, Senator Edmund Muskie, who chaired the leading Senate subcommittee on environmental issues (Jones 1975). Two decades later, the same type of competition led President Bush to commit himself to strengthening the Clean Air Act, paving the way for the remarkably stringent 1990 amendments (R. Cohen 1992; Bryner 1993).

This same dynamic of policy escalation can occur between national and subnational governments. Harrison shows that the waves of public salience around 1970 and 1990 produced competition among federal and provincial governments in Canada to claim credit for environmental initiatives, creating an expansionist dynamic in environmental policy (K. Harrison 1995a, 1995b). A similar effect seems to have spurred the explosion of the U.S. regulatory state around 1970 (Elliott, Ackerman, and Millian 1985).

Aside from the acid rain case, there is little evidence that the separation of powers in the United States has produced less aggressive environmental policy than in Canada, and even in this case the divergence merely amounted to a five-year delay. Indeed, one of the most striking aspects of U.S. environmental policy is the scope and stringency of the regulatory statutes. The separation of powers gives Congress the incentive to write carefully detailed statutes, which in turn gives environmentalists the legal tools to ensure implementation of the statutory mandates. While the evidence presented here does not permit a definitive conclusion, Canadian federalism may prove to be a greater obstacle to environmental policy than the separation of powers in the United States. The disincentives which policy makers have to threaten business confidence by imposing more stringent regulations than other jurisdictions are powerful indeed (K. Harrison 1995a).

The different types of institutional fragmentation have contributed to one of the most important findings of the policy comparisons – the differential timing of the development of U.S. and Canadian environmental policy regimes. Politicians in both countries have tremendous incentives to respond to public demand for environmental protection at times of high issue salience, but they do so in different institutional environments. The horizontal fragmentation in the United States creates incentives for lawmakers to enshrine the distribution of power that exists at a given time into elaborate, specific statutes that constrain executive branch policy makers from deviating from them even when the public turn their attention to other issues. The laws, policies, and intergovernmental agreements that result from periods of Canadian environmental policy activism, because they are more discretionary, do not have the same enduring impact.

As a result of these differences, American environmentalists were able to build on the laws enacted in the early 1970s and beat back challenges to them in the early 1980s. There is no question that U.S. institutions helped thwart Reagan's efforts to relax environmental regulations in the early 1980s. His efforts to weaken statutes were defeated by Democrats in Congress, and many of his administration's attempts at administrative deregulation were successfully blocked by court challenges and environmental group opposition, which was channelled through the media, Congress, and state governments (Hoberg 1992; Harris and Milkis 1989a). Fragmentation has also been an ally for environmentalists in trying to fend off the more recent – and more sweeping – attacks on the U.S. regulatory state by the "Republican revolution" that swept through Congress after the 1994 elections. Republicans hold enough seats to push anti-environmental bills through the House, but not enough to overcome a filibuster in the Senate or a veto by President Clinton. As of February 1996, it appeared that the Republican assault on environmental statutes had been turned back, but the substantial budgetary cuts to environmental agencies threaten to weaken implementation and enforcement.

The greater autonomy of Canadian governments means that environmental interests are more vulnerable to retrenchment, as witnessed in the period 1972–87 (K. Harrison 1995a). The more recent period of policy expansion is Canada around 1990 has closed much of the gap in policy between the two countries. Whether Canadians can sustain the momentum in the wake of lagging salience seems doubtful given recent developments, as will be discussed in this chapter's conclusion.

International Influences

The earlier section identified four types of international influence, all promoting convergence: (1) the globalization of environmental problems; (2) economic integration; (3) emulation; and (4) cross-border lobbying. The increasing efforts of the international community to address global environmental problems has contributed to convergence in the two countries in controls on ozone-depleting chemicals and greenhouse gases. The bilateral initiatives on air and especially water have also contributed to convergence. But it is important not to overstate the internationalization of environmental policy making. National governments still dominate policy making even in the case of global or bilateral issues. In the case of acid rain, for instance, Canada was probably not irrelevant to U.S. decision making, but the 1991 air quality accord between the two countries merely sanctioned the outcomes of a ten-year domestic struggle within the United States. The Great Lakes agreement has had more influence, but there is still divergence in regulatory standards and enforcement across the border, and the administrative and regulatory capacities of the International Joint Commission pale in comparison to the national and state/provincial governments in the region.

Economic integration has also been a force for convergence, but it has limits as well. While this concern underlay much of the opposition to international trade agreements among Canadian environmentalists, it has not been much of a problem for Canadian policy makers, largely because regulations in the United States are at least as stringent as those in Canada. A prominent example is automobile emissions. The North American auto market is highly integrated and is dominated by the United States.[28] If Canada had sought to impose emission controls beyond those in force in the United States, it would have faced strong resistance from automakers, who would have had to produce a different product for a relatively small portion of the market. In fact, because the United States was far ahead of Canada in emission controls, it was much easier for Canada to harmonize its regulations once it decided to do so (Hoberg 1991a).

While strong U.S. standards have mitigated the downward pressures on Canadian policy, economic integration can actually pull environmental controls up rather than merely pushing them down. For instance, the Canadian forest products industry is being forced into more environmentally "friendly" practices as a result of market pressures from consumers outside the country. American states and municipalities are beginning to require newspapers to contain a certain percentage of recycled fibres, forcing Canadian exporters to increase their capacity to supply recycled newsprint. Demands from European governments and consumers for chlorine-free paper products and for more environmentally sensitive forest practices have encouraged the industry to adopt expensive controls to reduce emissions of dioxins and furans, and they have caused the province of British Columbia to overhaul its regulatory approach. Understanding these implications of globalization, Greenpeace and other Canadian environmental groups have been lobbying European governments with the goal of achieving environmental progress in Canada through global market pressures.

Being a small state does restrict the flexibility of Canadian regulators. For instance, when multinational chemical companies attempt to introduce a new pesticide, they typically apply for registration in the United States first because of its large market. If the product receives approval there, the large market allows relatively rapid recovery of product development and approval costs. Only after getting approval in the United States do manufacturers seek approval in smaller countries such as Canada. This situation constrains Canadian regulators in that the more "independent" they choose to be from the United States – for example, by requiring additional tests under Canadian field conditions – the more they drive up the costs of registering the product in Canada, thus potentially discouraging some manufacturers from applying. There are strong incentives simply to adopt the U.S. decision, especially since growers frequently place pressure on regulators to approve products that are in use in the United States so that they do not suffer a competitive disadvantage (Hoberg 1991a). From an environmental perspective, this small-state problem would be of much greater concern if the United States record on regulating pesticide products was not as strong as it is.

Trade agreements have had relatively little influence on environmental policy in the two countries so far.[29] One area of concern to Canadian environmentalists is the weakness of U.S. pesticide residue limits, given the provision in the Canada–U.S. Free Trade Agreement to "work towards equivalence" in pesticide regulation. If U.S. standards were used as the basis for harmonization, Canadian standards would be weakened. However, the trend seems to be in the opposite direction. The data presented earlier showed the United States moving towards greater stringency, not Canada relaxing its standards. The United States, recognizing that it is out of step with international norms and under pressure from its own environmental lobby, has proposed a revision to its process of setting residue limits that should result in a significant tightening of its standards (U.S. Office of Pesticide Programs 1994). This case shows how the threat that economic integration with the United States might pose for Canadian environmental policy is reduced by the strong U.S. environmental lobby.

The cross-border flow of ideas, or emulation, is also an important force for convergence. Elite-driven emulation of U.S. policy occurs frequently in Canada. A 1989 intergovernmental agreement to match the next stage of U.S. automobile emission limits resulted not from pressures from environmentalists but the fact that Jim Bradley, the Ontario environment minister, was informed about and impressed by the U.S. developments. The inspiration for the design of Ontario's water pollution control program came from the U.S. Federal Water Pollution Control Act, whose implementation an Ontario official had observed while visiting a regional office of the U.S. Environmental Protection Agency (Hoberg 1991a).

The phenomenon of activist-driven emulation is best illustrated by the case of alar, a growth regulator used primarily on apples. Amidst a media campaign by "Mothers and Others for Pesticide Limits" organized by the Natural Resources Defense Council and led by actress Meryl Streep, dozens of school systems, including New York, Los Angeles, and Chicago, stopped distributing apple products in response to concerns about contamination by an alar-related chemical. Market pressures and the threat of EPA action forced the manufacturer to withdraw the product voluntarily. This media extravaganza spilled over into Canada, where the media reported the stories with a Canadian angle. Environmentalists, consumer activists, and opposition critics in Parliament demanded swift action from the government. Despite public reassurances of the safety of the product, the Canadian subsidiary of the U.S. manufacturer announced that it was pulling the product off the market, one week after its parent company in the United States did so. At the request of the manufacturer, Canada cancelled its registration (K. Harrison and Hoberg 1994, ch. 4).

A final form of international influence is cross-border lobbying. While this is certainly the least powerful of the four international influences, it has nonetheless played a modest role and is likely to increase in importance in the future. Although Canadian environmental groups are far less influential than their southern counterparts, their lobbying on acid rain did provide a small contribution to the political pressures for action. Asbestos regulations are less divergent than they would otherwise have been because of the success of a lawsuit backed by the Canadian asbestos industry (with the organizational and financial support of the Canadian and Quebec governments). Forest practices in British Columbia are more environmentally sensitive than they would otherwise be as a result of cross-border lobbying by U.S. environmentalists, including Robert F. Kennedy, Jr, an attorney for the powerful Natural Resources Defense Fund.

These international forces all promote convergence. Because of the dominance of the United States, whether as a market or a model, much of the convergence involves Canada adopting U.S. policies. Fortunately for Canadian environmentalists, the historical leadership of

U.S. environmental regulation means that U.S. influence has tended to strengthen Canadian standards.

CONCLUSION

Given the variety of causal forces at work in environmental policy, it is not surprising that the pattern of environmental policy outcomes in Canada and the United States is complex. Nonetheless, the convergence between the two countries' environmental policies is striking. This final section of the chapter brings together the different explanatory factors, treated independently thus far, to explain the considerable convergence that has occurred, as well as the residual divergence.

While there are examples of convergence through agreement and constraint, the two most important pathways to convergence in environmental policy are parallel domestic pressures and emulation. Common problems and common science and technology contribute to convergence, but the extent of convergence observed cannot be explained by these factors alone. The degree to which science and technology constrains policy makers is variable, depending on the following factors: (1) the magnitude of the apparent hazard; (2) the relative amount of scientific certainty about the hazard; (3) the costs of controlling the hazard; and (4) the importance of societal interests in competition with hazard reduction.

When the scientific base is certain and the apparent hazard is great, then regulators are highly constrained. In this case, one would expect a significant amount of convergence among different nations. In extreme cases, where there are intense societal interests in competition with environmental protection, divergence may result even when there is a certain, significant environmental threat. If, however, there is a great deal of scientific uncertainty, regulators are less constrained, and this makes divergence more likely. In this case, different scientific assumptions about the magnitude of the problem are possible, and decision makers have more flexibility to respond to economic or political interests or to their own policy preferences. Uncertainty makes it easier for Canadian decision makers to respond to asbestos producers and for U.S. decision makers to respond to the coal-burning utilities that produce acid rain.

While there are instances of different political pressures in the two countries, in general domestic political pressures have tended to promote convergence. There are similar levels of public support for environmental policies in the two countries, and both countries have experienced significant fluctuations in environmental issue salience at comparable times. Organized environmental movements exist in both countries, although there is reason to believe that the larger size of the U.S. movement makes it a more formidable political presence.

The most striking difference in the two countries is their institutions and processes for environmental policy making. This analysis shows that these institutional differences did not have as substantial an impact on environmental policy outcomes as one might expect. The fragmented political institutions have not undermined U.S. environmental policy as much as they have other policy areas, and the distinctive legalistic policy style in the United States has actually helped U.S. environmentalists. Perhaps the most important effect of the divergent institutions is on the timing of environmental policy reforms in the two countries. The entrenchment of pluralist legalism in the United States in the early 1970s contributed to the fact that it went further faster in the environmental realm than Canada did.

International factors also serve to promote environmental policy convergence. First, international agreements have had a modestly convergent effect. Second, one of the most powerful forces promoting convergence is Canadian emulation of U.S. environmental policies. Whether U.S. policy innovations act as models for policy elites or as public relations devices for environmental groups, they have a powerful influence on Canadian policy making (Hoberg 1991a). The integration of North American economies, policy communities, and media culture provides a strong stimulus for convergence. Because of the expansiveness of the U.S. regulatory state, U.S. influence has served to prod rather than bridle Canadian environmental policy.

As in other policy areas, this integration has had markedly different consequences for the two countries. Canadian vulnerability to the United States is extreme, whereas the U.S. policy system operates with relative independence. In Pierre Trudeau's clever metaphor, the Canadian situation is like "sleeping with an elephant," but the U.S. elephant scarcely notices its bedmate. To the extent that U.S. policy makers are vulnerable to international forces on environmental policy, this is more likely to arise from European or even global concerns, rather than merely Canadian concerns.

Thus, as a result of policy integration through emulation, common science and technology, and shared values and politics, environmental policy in Canada and the United States has witnessed a substantial amount of convergence. Within these broad constraints, there is still room for other factors to operate – be they different interests or institutions, or some combination thereof – to produce different outcomes in certain circumstances. Looking towards the future, it is possible that this convergent trend will continue, but recent developments have created the possibility for renewed divergence. Since the second modern wave of environmental enthusiasm among the public peaked in 1990, it is important to look for signs of retrenchment. The U.S. institutional structures make retrenchment difficult, and there is not yet any evidence of backsliding on environmental policies. The election of the Democratic Clinton-Gore administration in 1992 increased the prospects for a new phase of environmental policy. Despite the strong environmentalism of Vice-President Albert Gore, however, the first two years of the Clinton administration were noteworthy for their failure to push a number of significant environmental bills through Congress. The 1994 congressional elections swept Republicans into the majority for the first time in forty years, and Republican legislators began an assault on the core statutes of the modern American regulatory state. Despite significant legislative action in the House of Representatives, by early 1996 it had become obvious that, like Ronald Reagan before them, the Republicans had mistaken their victory for a mandate to reverse decades of environmental policy. Their wholesale retreat from the attempt to rewrite environmental statutes is a clear indication of the persistence of widespread public support for environmental protection among the American public. But while core statutes have remained intact, the more furtive attack on the budgets of environmental agencies poses a considerable threat to the implementation and enforcement of existing statutory mandates.

In Canada, because of the discretionary nature of policy making, there is a greater risk of backsliding. The interjurisdictional competition for credit on environmental policy that characterized the period 1987–92 has ended. In fact, in recent years it appears to have been reversed (K. Harrison 1994). The federal government's 1990 showpiece environmental initiative, the Green Plan, was silently killed in the spring of 1995, and in early 1996 the trend was towards significant decentralization of environmental responsibilities away from the federal government. At the same time as responsibility for environmental policy was being devolved to the provinces, most provincial governments were engaging in massive budgetary cutbacks that would decrease their ability to carry out their environmental mandates. In addition, there appeared to be a distinct shift in mood away from regulation and towards more voluntary measures.

In the early 1990s, it was fair to conclude that while the momentum behind environmental policy had weakened, the trend in both countries was still towards stronger environmental policies. As we move into the last half-decade of the twentieth century, however, the momentum is clearly with the forces of retrenchment. In an ominous sign for environmentalists north of the border, Canadian institutions are less effective than American ones in thwarting policy reversals.

PART THREE

Conclusions

10 Globalization, Fragmentation, and the Social Contract

RICHARD SIMEON, GEORGE HOBERG, AND KEITH BANTING

Chapter 1 set out the fundamental questions that animate this book. First, what is the impact of two powerful forces of change, the globalization of the economy and diversification of society, that confront Canada and the United States? Second, to what extent have the responses of Canada and the United States produced convergence in the public policies and political processes of the two countries? Third, in a more evaluative mode, how effective have modern governments been in responding to major pressures for change and in establishing a new equilibrium between economy, society, and the state? This chapter summarizes our conclusions on these questions, explores some explanations for convergence and divergence, change and continuity, and offers some reflections on the future. Where are these two societies going? What are their common challenges, and what might be done to improve their capacity to make effective, democratic choices in a complex and constrained environment?

A broad framework has guided our analysis. As in times past, the modern state lies at the intersection of the domestic and international arenas and, like Janus, it must face two directions. It must respond to two different sets of incentives and constraints. To change the metaphor, government is in the position of the circus performer riding two horses at once – and often they pull in different directions. When they do, they reduce the capacity of the state to respond effectively. In the contemporary period, economic globalization and greater domestic diversity both generate profound challenges to governments. These pressures shape the policy agenda facing the two countries and affect the range of possible policy responses to it. Because in important respects these challenges point in different and contradictory directions, governments face difficult trade-offs. More importantly, globalization and social fragmentation both imply a diminution in the autonomy of the state – globalization by reducing its autonomy vis-à-vis international forces; social change by eroding its authority vis-à-vis domestic forces. By limiting state resources and capacities, they impose increasing constraints on what governments can achieve.

Moreover, both globalization and diversity represent sources of convergence in the political processes and public policies of the two countries. The competitive dynamics released by economic globalization have generated palpable pressures for greater harmonization of the regulatory and fiscal regimes of countries engaged in the world trading system. To the extent that heightened social pluralism takes similar forms in Canada and the United States, it represents a harbinger of more similar societies, a subtle source of convergence in the ways in which these two peoples live and the pressures that they bring to bear on their governments.

However, neither global forces nor domestic societal change translates automatically into preordained policy responses. Nations preserve important degrees of freedom in reacting to contemporary pressures, and core characteristics of each country mediate between the forces for change and public policy, conditioning the ways in which it adjusts. Enduring cultural patterns, political institutions and processes, and policy legacies tend to change slowly, and they constitute powerful elements of continuity in the affairs of nations. These elements of national tradition are counterweights to the pressures for convergence, and they carry forward the potential for distinctive national responses to the common policy agenda of the late twentieth century. Culture, institutions, and legacies are also important to how well each country addresses the need to re-establish a broad social contract, a new understanding of the relationship between citizens and governments.

A critical issue of the late twentieth century is thus whether the forces for convergence implicit in economic and social change increasingly outweigh these well-springs of national distinctiveness. The pattern revealed in the preceding chapters is mixed, as is so often the case when exploring complex comparative issues: convergence, yes, but significant continued difference; constraints that are obvious, but also significant degrees of freedom remaining for national choices. Which of these aspects one is more interested in – similarity or difference – is partly a matter of scholarly fashion. In the 1950s and 1960s, studies emphasizing harmonizing forces and convergent trends were in vogue (Kerr 1983); by the 1980s attention had shifted to the persistence of cross-national differences stemming from the historical and institutional legacies unique to each country;[1] the contemporary focus on globalization and technology has renewed interest in homogenizing forces (Hollingsworth, Schmitter, and Streeck 1994; Bennett 1991b, 1992). Our approach has allowed us to develop a more nuanced depiction of both dynamics and to identify more precisely the forces that underlie them.

CONVERGENCE AND DIVERGENCE

Let us briefly review the findings in the previous chapters. What patterns of convergence and divergence do we find in the discourse on policy, the substantive directions chosen, and the policy instruments deployed?

Macroeconomic policy demonstrates the most striking area of convergence. Chapter 5 showed that in general the two economies have followed similar trajectories, the major exceptions being that Canada managed to avoid the 1975 recession in the United States but suffered from diverging unemployment rates in the late 1980s. The discourse about macroeconomic policy has also been remarkably similar, as both countries struggled to balance the objectives of economic growth, employment, and price stability. Both became far more focused on fighting inflation than on tackling unemployment. The shift from Keynesian to monetarist economic thinking occurred at about the same time in the two countries, as did the recent powerful shift in economic discourse to a focus on debt and deficit reduction. Substantive policy has followed a similar track. Both countries have relied heavily on monetary policy as the primary tool of economic management, and chapter 5 traced the close parallels in the timing and direction of changes in interest rates. Knowledgeable Canadians purchasing their homes have become used to reading news speculation about the impending decisions of the U.S. Federal Reserve Board when they try to anticipate the interest rates they will face when renewing their mortgage. Fiscal policy has been characterized by sustained budget deficits in both countries since the 1970s, although the Canadian debt and deficit burden is much higher than the American, especially when the fiscal positions of state and provincial governments are taken into account.

Given the enormous degree of integration between the two countries, the striking parallels in macroeconomic policy are not surprising; nor, given the relative differences in size, is it surprising that Canadian policy follows the American lead. Nevertheless, it is important not to ignore the scope for independent choice even in this most integrated of policy sectors. In the late 1980s and early 1990s, Canada adopted even more stringent monetary policies than the United States – a divergence which carried a high cost in terms of reduced investment, increased costs of servicing the public debt, and a higher value for the Canadian dollar, which in turn made adjustment to the impact of the free trade agreement more difficult. On the fiscal side, aspects of tax policy provide similar examples. While Canada has followed the United States and other OECD nations in reducing reliance on corporate income taxes, Canadian governments have significantly increased overall taxation compared with the United States. In 1970, taxes as a fraction of GDP were similar – 31.3 per cent in Canada and 29.2 per cent in the United States. Twenty years later, the U.S. percentage was unchanged, but Canadian taxes had increased to 37.1 per cent (Perry 1993, 49). In addition, the Canadian federal government imposed the nationwide goods and services tax in 1991, an initiative with no counterpart in the United States.

The pattern is similar with *industrial policy*. In recent years both countries have made trade liberalization their primary instrument of industrial policy, as reflected in the FTA, NAFTA, and the completion of the Uruguay Round of the GATT. While these agreements constrain both countries, the United States retains considerably more capacity to engage in retaliatory trade policies than Canada does. Nevertheless, the broad reliance on trade liberalization, closely linked to globalization, significantly limits each country's ability to engage in more active industrial policies which target specific sectors. These constraints, which have been reinforced in the case of Canada by disenchantment with the results of previous industrial subsidies and regional development programs, have shifted the focus in both countries towards a new set of policy instruments. North and south of the border, the norm of international competitiveness is being brought to bear on framework policies, infrastructure, research and development, education and training, and labour market programs such as unemployment benefits. The current buzz-words of industrial policy are much the same in Ottawa and Washington. Within this broad strategy, differences of emphasis and strategy persist. Canadian governments spend considerably more on training than the United States does, thereby partly counteracting much greater private spending in the United States; American governments and the private sector spend more on research and development than Canadians do.

This shift to a more market-oriented industrial policy has constituted a larger change in traditional approaches in Canada than in the United States, representing a clear case of convergence. For example, Canada emerged from the postwar period with much higher levels of public ownership, but Canadian governments have recently been engaged in extensive privatization of Crown corporations such as Air Canada and Canadian National Railways. Similarly, the Canadian shift away from the activist subsidy programs that characterized the 1970s and early 1980s represents a movement towards the U.S. model.

If economic policies reveal a general convergence between the two countries, *social policy* offers some reassurance to those Canadians who are fearful of harmonization pressures as a consequence of free trade. One of the most striking findings in this book is the continuing differences in the two welfare states. At the level of policy discourse, Canadians tend to see their more generous social programs as a symbol of national identity, a key distinction between them and their neighbours to the south. Hence, there is much greater consensus among the public and elites over the basic contours of social policy. In the United States, middle-class entitlements have broad support, but anti-poverty programs have been under attack for years. These distinctive orientations sustain critical differences in policy. First, Canada provides far more comprehensive social support for its citizens than the United States does. This is most dramatically evident in health care. Second, Canadian income-security programs are more effectively targeted at the poor, with a greater emphasis on means- or income-tested programs, and benefits in these programs tend to be more generous than those in the United States. Third, as a result of these two features, Canadian policies are more effective at reducing the inequalities generated by the market economy.

These historic differences are not disappearing. In both Canada and the United States, economic restructuring and large public deficits have led to successive rounds of retrenchment and restructuring of social programs, many of which have been weakened as a result. But each country has responded in the light of its internal political dynamics. To be sure, there are cases of convergence, such as child benefits and – to a lesser extent – unemployment insurance. Nevertheless, the broader pattern has been one of incremental divergence, especially during the 1980s and the first half of the 1990s. Some of this enhanced distinctiveness may fade in the second half of the 1990s as Canadian governments focus more single-mindedly on deficit reduction. Nevertheless, in the mid-1990s, the two welfare states were as different as they were in the mid-1970s, the apogee of the postwar welfare state. Nor are there reasons to assume that future ways of restructuring the two systems will necessarily move them closer together. Despite the pressures generated by economic integration, social policy is not being driven towards a single, homogenized model.

In contrast, *environmental policy* reveals substantial convergence. At the level of discourse, Canadians have embraced the rhetoric of "sustainable development" more fully than Americans, resulting in somewhat greater optimism about the ability to reconcile economic growth and environmental health. But in substantive policy, the United States has tended to be the leader. It clearly led the first wave of environmental activism in the 1970s. In the second wave of the 1990s, Canada was more active, but this was in large measure a matter of catching up with the United States. Both countries have relied on a mix of regulatory and spending instruments, with the United States leaning more strongly towards regulation. But overall the message is convergence, especially on acid rain, automobile emissions, and the regulation of pesticides. Where there is divergence, American policies are usually more stringent.

Finally, policies with respect to *rights*, and the associated judicialization of politics represent another dramatic example of convergence in the policy domains surveyed here. This is largely a consequence of the adoption of the Charter of Rights and Freedoms in Canada, which, as Lipset notes, "probably goes further towards taking the country in an American direction than any other enacted change, including the Canada–U.S. Free Trade Agreement" (1990a, 116). The Charter's provisions for fundamental freedoms, democratic rights, and legal and equality rights closely correspond to similar provisions in the American Bill of Rights. The Charter both reflects and strongly reinforces an expanded "rights-consciousness" among Canadians and a tendency to debate policy issues in the language of rights. It has also dramatically enhanced the role of the courts in the policy process. But as chapter 8 notes, the broad convergence is tempered by greater Canadian emphasis on substantive, effects-based rights and by a greater willingness to depart from a strictly individualist point of view to support various group rights. As a result, as Manfredi concludes, Canadian Social Movements – the leading manifestations of greater pluralism – have been able to establish a more important judicial counterweight to economic pressures for less government intervention.

The overall pattern thus incorporates a powerful convergence in the policy agendas facing decision makers in the two countries, and a complex mix of convergence and divergence in policy responses, a mix that varies considerably from sector to sector.

EXPLAINING CHANGE AND CONVERGENCE

Given this complex pattern, the explanatory task is twofold: how to explain change and convergence in some areas, and how to account for continuity and divergence in others. The framework guiding this analysis looks to five possible sources of explanation. Two of them –

globalization and social pluralism – are linked primarily to convergence between the two countries. These are the factors that are most obviously in flux and that generally point in the same direction for each country. Three others – inherited policy legacies, political culture, and political institutions and processes – are more stable, enduring features, particular to each country. These factors are linked primarily to explanations of difference.

Economic Globalization

The first set of forces driving change are those arising from the fundamental economic forces explored in chapter 2 under the rubric of globalization. As the world economy becomes increasingly integrated and as goods, services, capital, and information become more mobile, domestic economies are increasingly vulnerable to developments beyond their borders. These developments in turn have fostered major change within both the Canadian and U.S. economies – increased volatility, economic restructuring, and increasing inequality in market incomes.

These forces affect the two societies in broadly similar ways. The decline in American economic hegemony in the global economy and Canada's continuing vulnerability to both global and U.S. economic shifts ensure that both countries must wrestle with the implications of international interdependence. These challenges push in different ways. On the one hand, they suggest the need for governments to focus on the "competitiveness" agenda, emphasizing policies that will foster adjustment and adaptation to the new economy and will ensure the capacity to compete effectively in an ever more open global setting. On the other hand, the disruptive effects of globalization increase pressures to find more effective ways of cushioning or protecting workers and citizens. Governments must simultaneously promote adjustment and manage the social consequences of economic change. This tension was evident in the anguished debates in Canada over the Canada–U.S. Free Trade Agreement (FTA) and the North American Free Trade Agreement (NAFTA), and was replicated with uncanny similarity in the United States debate over NAFTA. There is clearly a high degree of convergence in the economic policy agendas confronting the two countries.

There is also convergence in the repertoire of policy responses to globalization: a commitment by governments (Republican and Democratic, Conservative and Liberal) to the fundamental goal of freer global trade – despite widespread misgivings among many social groups; a suspicion of explicit industrial policies; an emphasis on policies to promote the development of human capital; and a stronger emphasis on reducing the size of government and its associated deficits and debts.

Thus, economic globalization has had major implications for the economic role of the state in both countries. Increasingly the state is the mediator between the domestic society and the global political economy, and governments in both countries have often found that this is not an easy role to play.

Globalization and the forces it sets in motion also constrain the political capacity of governments. Some of these are found in formal rules, the result of explicit limits set out in agreements such as NAFTA and the GATT. Others are economic, arising out of the mobility of capital and the fluidity of global capital markets, creating limits both on the revenue-raising capacity of the state, especially its ability to tax mobile capital and the wealthy, and on its regulatory reach. Mobile factors of production can respond more easily to such measures as stricter environmental regulation, higher minimum wages, or stronger health and safety regulations by exit rather than voice. In addition, globalization shifts the balance of power among societal interests, weakening labour, which is less mobile, and strengthening business, which is more mobile (I. Robinson 1993, 199–200). In both countries these constraints are real. No government can ignore the international ramifications of its actions – or inaction. And none can ignore the pervasive impact of globalization on its society and economy. Globalization clearly raises the costs associated with the use of some policy instruments, such as taxation and regulation, and renders others, such as monetary policy, less independent than they once were. International trade agreements diminish the availability of tariff policies, which were once the major industrial policy instrument in both countries.

While all these tendencies are common to both countries, there are some important differences in their impact. There is much truth underlying the historic Canadian concern with maintaining its identity and sovereignty in the face of American influence,[2] just as there is with the traditional American focus on its "exceptionalism." While international economic forces are a major factor promoting convergence, they operate more powerfully on Canada than on the United States. The latter remains far less dependent on foreign trade and foreign direct investment; in this sense Canada is much more vulnerable. This helps explain both Canada's historically more activist industrial policy (designed to build a Canadian economy north of the 49th parallel) and its more ample welfare state (designed to protect citizens against the vagaries of international markets).

The enormous size and dynamism of the U.S. economy, and its central role in the global system, mean that the United States is far more influential than Canada in writing the rules of the international trading system. Indeed, in some respects that system is the political and economic creation of the United States and American business interests. The United States remains much more capable of passing the burden of its adjustment to other actors in the global system. Canada lacks such powerful leverage outside its borders. In addition, economic globalization hits Canada in two ways: first as a general phenomenon, and secondly in the form of direct American influence on the Canadian economy. The tight embrace of the U.S. economy leaves less room for Canada to pursue an independent monetary policy or to impose corporate tax rates higher than American levels. Moreover, some characteristics of the Canadian economy, such as the salience of regional economic disparities and the linguistically bifurcated labour markets, mean that the Canadian adjustment to the new forces may have been more difficult.

Canadian exposure to international economic forces has been exacerbated by internal fiscal weakness represented by the level of public debt. Massive debt is a fundamental constraint in both countries. The causes of the debt are controversial, lying both in domestic politics and in the effects of international forces and restructuring. But the fact of the debt is real, and here again the Canadian state is more vulnerable, for two reasons. First, Canadian public debt is substantially larger as a proportion of GDP. Second, Canada relies more heavily on foreign borrowing.[3] Canada leads all other G7 countries in its reliance on foreign indebtedness by a considerable margin, making the country particularly sensitive to volatile global financial markets (Canada, Department of Finance 1994, 13). Foreign indebtedness has enfranchised international bond-rating agencies, making their pronouncements an important component of the country's fiscal politics. In the words of the federal Department of Finance, Canada has suffered "a tangible loss of economic sovereignty" (ibid., 78). Moreover, deeper fiscal weakness is becoming a powerful pressure for convergence in the two countries as Canadian governments face stronger pressure to reduce expenditures, thereby narrowing traditional policy differences between the two countries in a wide range of policy sectors.

Thus, Canada is both more influenced by and more constrained in responding to the economic forces explored here. Both countries have moved along a continuum from less to more constrained, but Canada started the modern period closer to the more constrained end. Thus, although the United States has also moved along the continuum, the distance between the two remains large. One result is that while U.S. citizens and policy makers have become much more sensitive to global influences than they once were, or needed to be, this awareness does not pervade the American political process nearly to the extent that it does in Canada.

The constraints facing contemporary policy makers as a result of economic globalization are real and important, but they do not constitute a strait-jacket. The challenges may be a given; the responses to them are not. International economic constraints are not so much a wall as a cost, which citizens and politicians may or may not be willing to pay. The stronger the constraints, the higher are the costs of policy divergence; the weaker they are, the lower are the costs associated with moving in distinctive directions. Moreover, the costs vary from policy area to policy area, depending primarily on the mobility of the factors of production that the policy is seeking to influence. The mobility of capital places strong constraints on Canadian economic policy, but even here there are some degrees of freedom. As noted earlier, Canadian monetary policy charted a separate course in the late 1980s and early 1990s; and with the exception of corporate income taxes, Canada has significantly increased the tax burden relative to the United States. Capital mobility can also constrain environmental policy, since companies can move to avoid the costs of stricter environmental regulation. Because such regulations generally constitute only a small fraction of the total costs, however, their impact is more limited. Moreover, in some cases, the need to placate consumers in foreign markets may involve pressures to harmonize "up" to more stringent standards.

Mobility, or the relative lack of it, also helps explain the continued differences in social policy. The mobility of the factor of production most crucial to social policy – individuals – is severely reduced by immigration laws. Except in the case of very wealthy persons and some professionals, Canada can impose higher taxes on citizens' incomes to finance its more generous welfare state without the fear of massive emigration to the United States. Nor need Canada worry unduly that its more generous social assistance will attract the poor from across the border. This situation reflects the fact that there is a lower level of economic integration in North America than in the European Union, which has gone much further in developing a common labour market. Moreover, the degrees of freedom for social policy generated by constraints on the mobility of labour are increased by other factors. On one hand, social programs that lower the costs of production, by socializing costs borne by employers in other countries, tend to enhance a country's competitive position; for example, universal health care strengthens the position of Canadian firms in the American market. On the other hand, social programs that raise the costs of production can be compensated for through adjustments in the exchange rate. As economists often argue, a flexible exchange rate provides considerable room for Canada to maintain more generous policies than the United States, along with higher taxes. The cost is a depreciation of the currency.[4]

Finally, in yet other policy areas, the impact of international economic factors is nonexistent. Policy regarding citizen rights, for example – while influenced by the international climate of ideas – is not driven by global economic competition.

Thus, globalization does increase the costs of distinctive policy choices in some crucial areas, but it does not eliminate them. Trade-offs may be more painful than they once were, but they are still there to be made, and domestic social and political factors continue to influence policy responses.

Societal Diversity

The second major determinant of policy outcomes is societal interests. This includes both diffuse, unorganized social forces, such as race, language, and region, and the organized interests that mobilize more focused concerns. Policy outcomes are also influenced by the balance of power among competing interests in domestic society. To the extent that the trend of social mobilization is similar in the two countries, we would expect increasingly similar policies; to the extent that societal developments diverge, so too should policy responses. Our examples suggest this is the case.

The similarities on the domestic side of the equation are striking: the emergence of new interests and identities and new forms of social diversity, which interact with older divisions such as language, race, and class. The image is of two societies increasingly fragmented and divided, pluralist in the most profound sense of the word. While there have been powerful cross-border influences in the development of feminism, environmentalism, and other social movements, the most powerful forces generating the new politics are domestic, the response of two peoples to parallel social and economic developments. Nevertheless, by multiplying the lines of social division and reducing the centrality of the historic cleavages that set Canada and the United States apart, such as race and language, the new social pluralism increases the similarities in the profiles of the two societies.

As chapter 2 demonstrated, these are powerful sources of convergence in terms of challenges to existing policy makers and the agendas with which they must grapple. The politics of diversity has challenged traditional conceptions of equality, democracy, and community in both countries. The repertoire of responses is also broadly similar: a more pluralistic and open political process, a greater judicial role in politics, a politics conducted in the discourse of rights and identity, an opening and broadening of policy networks, increased calls for a greater measure of direct democracy, and the tendency to institutionalize differences. As with the economy, social change has generated important new roles for the state – notably, the recognition and management of diversity, which plays out in immigration policy, in policies such as employment equity, and in debates concerning the representation of minorities in political institutions. Similarly, the rise of strong organized environmental movements in both countries has contributed to convergence in environmental policy, although chapter 9 also links the more aggressive U.S. environmental policy to the larger size and earlier development of the environmental movement in that country.

Here too, however, common patterns of social change do not tell the whole story. In part, this is because the balance of social forces and the alliances among them are different in the two countries. Historic differences continue; race plays a much greater role in the United States, language and regional divisions in Canada. The labour movement in Canada, while under some of the same pressures as that in the United States, is much stronger, sustaining a far broader coalition with other social movements in defence of a redistributive welfare state. More broadly, language, region, and class in Canada combine to provide a stronger base for social programs; in the United States, race and class interact in ways that undermine political support for the welfare state. Americans are also much more preoccupied with the crisis in the inner cities and with violent crime. The proximity of the United States to such countries as Cuba, Haiti, and Mexico, combined with the American political and economic presence in the Caribbean region, makes refugee and immigration policy far more difficult and contentious than it is in Canada. In the United States, in addition, the conservative Christian Right is a more influential political counterweight to the "new social movements," investing some issues, such as abortion, with much greater passion. This may be changing, however, for in both countries resistance to the political agendas of feminists and multicultural groups appears to be growing, and the burgeoning Reform Party in Canada gives voice to this resistance.

Despite these variations, the broad impact of both international economic and domestic social changes are parallel in Canada and the United States, and it is this parallelism that engenders the most powerful forces for convergence in policies and institutions. At the same time, there are important counterweights to these pressures for convergence. To some extent, variations in the detailed form that economic globalization and social diversity assume in each country help to explain the persistence of differences between Canada and the United States. However, the primary forces that contribute to distinctive national choices are rooted in the cultural and political traditions of the two countries.

EXPLAINING CONTINUITY
AND DIVERGENCE

Three sets of factors stand out in explaining continuity and divergence. The first are *policy legacies*. Policy change is seldom radical; most often in these societies it is incremental change woven around pre-existing patterns. Even when there is a clear shift in direction, the turn is more likely to be at the pace of an ocean liner than a jet ski, more easily discerned after the fact than at the time. For example, while there have been considerable moves towards privatization of Crown corporations in Canada in recent years – an element of convergence – public ownership remains much greater than in the United States because of the two countries' very different starting points. However, the effects of policy legacies often go even deeper, representing a form of path dependency, in which former choices tend to lock in a particular approach to policy, limiting subsequent adjustments to change in the prevailing model rather than making a clear transition to an entirely different model (Pierson 1994). When Canadians debate health-care reform, it is from the existing base of a universal, government-funded set of programs; when Americans debate health care, it is from a quite different base. Thus, much of the continuing difference we observe stems from the inertia exercised by different policy legacies inherited from the past and the policy networks that sustain them. This suggests, as well, that in newer policy areas, such as the environment, consumer protection, or child care, convergence is more likely, since there are fewer pre-existing differences to overcome.[5]

A second element often thought to be a source of stability is *political culture and values*. Almost by definition, political cultures change only slowly over time; this is what distinguishes them from the more short-run shifts in public opinion. But cultures are not static. Over time, newer attitudes may congeal into more settled values and beliefs, which themselves become resistant to change. In addition, cultures in diverse, complex societies such as the United States and Canada are not monolithic. Many streams – individualistic and collectivist, for example – co-exist. Different groups will draw on different elements in the cultural mix; changing events will evoke different cultural responses. Thus, in any culture, there are elements of both continuity and change, though again change is likely to be incremental rather than dramatic.

The analysis in chapter 3 underscores important similarities in the attitudes that Americans and Canadians bring to their political life. In both countries, economic anxieties dominate the preoccupations of the electorate; the public is resistant both to tax increases and to significant benefit reductions in the name of deficit control; and there is a pervasive mistrust of political leaders. Similarly, citizens in both countries show little confidence in the government's ability to intervene effectively in the economy, a similarity that helps explain the failure of either country to engage in an activist industrial policy. On both sides of the border, then, governments confront popular constraints on their room for manoeuvre as they grapple with contemporary agendas.

Within this broad pattern, however, lie important differences that contribute to continuity and divergence in policy responses. Canadians still manifest greater faith in the role of government generally. Although even here the differences may be narrowing, they help explain the commitment to a more expansive welfare state north of the border. Other significant differences reflect the nature of the two countries and their place in the world: Americans are more concerned about domestic crime and international issues; Canadians are more concerned with national unity.

Again we have to decide whether the glass is half full or half empty – whether to be impressed with the broad similarities or to focus on the importance of specific differences. In Canada, it is widely understood that the advent of the Charter of Rights and Freedoms in 1982 both reflected and strongly contributed to significant change in the political culture, in the direction of a greater emphasis on rights, legalization, and less deference to elites, suggesting a very strong convergence with the United States. Support for populist elements of direct democracy has also grown; it is hard today to characterize Canadians as deferential to their elites. Yet in other areas the historic differences which Lipset and others (Lipset 1990a; Horowitz 1966) describe remain, although the evidence in chapter 3 suggests that they may be more prevalent at the elite level and in institutional arrangements than they are in popular attitudes. While Canadian distrust of politics and politicians has grown, it does not appear to have proceeded as far as the profound antipolitical mood evident in recent American election campaigns. Thus, persisting if diminishing differences in political culture continue to have an effect. Once again, they are more likely to sustain difference in older rather than newer policy areas.

Political institutions represent a third source of continuity and difference. Institutions establish the rules of the game and associated procedures, allocate resources among agencies and actors, and create incentives and disincentives for alternative strategies. They can influence effectiveness by shaping the capacity to set priorities, target resources, and impose costs. Institutional design does much to determine the autonomy of governing elites, on one hand, and the openness of the system to societal interests on the other. Institutions are highly resistant to change; almost by definition they represent the crystallization of earlier political ideas and divisions. An observer surveying the two economies and societies after an absence of twenty-five years would likely marvel at the pace and extent of change; but an observer viewing Congress, Parliament, or the bureaucracies of the two countries would probably feel right at home. Thus, as chapter 4 outlined, although there are some important elements of convergence in the political process, the core institutions of parliamentary government and congressional government remain fundamentally different, with critical implications for other elements of politics, such as the party system and the electoral process.

Institutions help explain policy differences. One reason why government ownership of business has been higher in Canada is because the Canadian institutional structure makes it easier to establish government corporations and then control them (Weaver 1985). Chapter 7 argued that the structure of political institutions and party ideologies contributed to the different welfare states that emerged in the two countries. Historically, the greater fragmentation of power in the congressional system gave conservative political interests more opportunities to delay, dilute, or defeat new social programs than were available to their Canadian counterparts; and more recent experience confirms that the constant need to build coalitions in the U.S. system makes it harder to target benefits on the poor. Others have argued in a similar vein that the numerous veto points make it easier in the U.S. system to block tax increases (Steinmo 1989). In addition, the presence in Canada of a social democratic party, which has exercised considerable influence at critical historical junctures, and more recently the different attitudes of Canadian and American conservative parties towards the poor, also contributed to the different trajectories that social policy has followed on the two sides of the border.

However, the striking contrast between social and environmental policy in the two countries raises serious questions about any simple association of active, effective government with the concentration of authority in the parliamentary system, or of policy immobilism with the fragmentation of authority in the U.S. system. For while Canada stands out as the more expansive welfare state, the United States is a more powerful environmental state. In part, this difference seems to stem from institutional factors. In Canada, executive power helped overcome resistance to the welfare state. In the United States, it was the existence of very strict standards in environmental statutes, combined with a judiciary willing to enforce them, that empowered environmentalists and resulted in a number of policy gains. The U.S. courts had no such powerful standards to apply in social policy. But this is by no means the whole story. A major part of the explanation for the difference is the level of public support for the two programs. American environmental laws were passed with widespread public support, backed by influential and well-organized interest groups. Policies seeking to ameliorate conditions for the poor lack such approval; but U.S. social programs that do enjoy mass support, such as social security, are more generous and are closer to the Canadian model. So politics and public opinion appear to be more important determinants of policy than institutions.

Although institutions influence the potential for concerted action, they cannot guarantee it. The concentration of authority in the cabinet did not ensure that the government of Prime Minister Mulroney controlled the Canadian deficit any better than U.S. administrations handle their deficit. Indeed, the Canadian record in that period was significantly worse than the American on this score, perhaps reflecting Weaver's observation that an additional effect of parliamentary systems is that they concentrate accountability and blame, making governments highly reluctant to impose costs (Weaver and Rockman 1993, 15–16). But this argument fails to account for dramatic executive action in the teeth of formidable opposition in other cases; for instance, with the imposition of a national goods and services tax or the recent moves to attack deficits both in Ottawa and in a number of the provinces. The point is that cabinet government may provide the opportunity for more decisive action, but it will only be realized when the political will or economic necessity exists as well.

In addition, institutions at a more micro-level may also have an impact. Despite their broad constitutional differences, Canada and the United States are alike in insulating their central banks from the play of normal politics, allowing a small community of specialists to set very similar policies, with few constraints. Similarly, despite the enormous convergence implied by the Canadian Charter of Rights and Freedoms, as chapter 8 points out, many of the remaining differences in judicial decisions are best explained by differences in the documents which the judges are called on to interpret.

Institutions, then, seldom shape policies on their own; their impact can only be understood as they interact with other political forces. Moreover, institutions are more likely to affect the style and process of policy making and the availability of different kinds of policy instruments than the outcomes themselves.

This analysis underlines the need to distinguish the explanatory factors that can be adduced to explain similarity from those that account for difference; and to distinguish those that account for change and innovation from those that explain stability and continuity. We have found strong forces pressing for change, which tend to operate in the same direction in the two countries, resulting in many elements of convergence, both in policy and in the political process. But there are many sources of historical continuity. These are so powerful that despite the pressures generated by global and domestic changes, Canada and the United States are not being driven inexorably towards a single, homogenized model of social and economic life. Although the constraints on state activity have strengthened in palpable ways, there is still room for domestic choice, and policies continue to be shaped by the rhythms of domestic culture and politics. As a result, national politics in Canada and the United States remain important to the future of the citizens of these two countries. It still matters whether one lives in Vancouver or Seattle, Toronto or Chicago, Montreal or Philadelphia, Ottawa or Washington.

CONVERGENCE: CONSTRAINT AND CHOICE

The analysis in this book reveals considerable convergence, but it is necessary to bear in mind that convergence does not always flow from tightening constraints; it often reflects domestic choices. Chapter 1 identified three potential pathways to convergence. The first was *parallel domestic pressure*. If governments face similar sets of problems or challenges and if they have similar changes in their underlying economic or social structure, they are likely to face similar policy agendas and to have a similar repertoire of possible responses to them. There need be no interaction between the countries for them to respond in similar ways. Differences in institutions, styles of political discourse, and the like may abound, but the policy results will not be very different. Because the processes of social and economic change have been very similar in Canada and the United States – and, indeed, in most other Western industrial countries – one would expect to see convergence between them in many areas even if they were thousands of kilometres apart.

A second path does imply interaction. This is *emulation*, resulting from international example and international learning. It can operate either at a societal level – as ideas and movements such as feminism and environmentalism wash across open borders – or at a governmental level, as public officials routinely explore alternatives that are being pursued by their counterparts elsewhere. No coercion or pressure is involved (Rose 1993). Undoubtedly, there has been an enormous increase in emulation at both levels, both internationally and bilaterally, as global communications have increased and institutions like the OECD and G7 bring governing elites together. This study has highlighted many examples: the enormous impact of the American rights tradition on Canada's Charter, the rise of populist feeling, the preoccupation with deficits, the impact of a common scientific and research community on environmental policies, and so on.[6] However, the practices of others must always be accommodated to domestic tradition, and we have found few if any examples of direct borrowing of whole policy strategies.

Given the size and dynamism of the United States and the pervasiveness of its media in Canada, it seems clear that most of the emulation – whether this be the growth of neoconservatism or the growth of environmentalism – involves influences flowing from south to north. But there is a trickle the other way, for example, the attention paid in the United States to Canadian health insurance during the U.S. health-care debate. This imbalance, of course, is a matter of great concern to many Canadians, who fear the erosion of a distinctive Canadian culture and values. Yet it remains fundamentally a matter of choice, and in many policy areas – from the death penalty and gun control to health care and social policy – Canadians have explicitly chosen an alternative path, and indeed have used the American example as a negative one to be avoided.

More problematic is the third path to convergence: tightening *international constraints* on policy. Here the freedom to choose a distinct policy set is restricted by external forces. One such form of constraint – the international mobility of capital – has already been discussed at some length. Overt political pressure, such as the extraterritorial application of American law to the subsidiaries of U.S. firms operating in Canada, or the threat of trade sanctions, may also constrain policy. Once again, the American influence on Canada far outweighs the reverse. The terms of international treaties, such as the FTA and NAFTA, often directly limit the policy instruments available to governments. Here too, however, there is an element of choice. These are agreements that were voluntarily entered into – indeed, Canada took the initiative on the FTA – presumably on the assumption that the benefits outweighed the constraints they imposed (Keohane 1993). Although, again, the dominant forces flow south to north, such treaties may give the smaller country some power to fend off threatening policies imposed by the larger; for example, the dispute-resolution mechanism embedded in NAFTA gives Canada additional opportunities to challenge American trade policies that affect it.

Overall, we conclude that parallel domestic pressures and emulation constitute the most common pathways to convergence; international constraints, while powerful, operate over a narrower range of issues – strongest on trade and macroeconomic policy, and least strong on matters of cultural concern. Indeed, it is interesting to note that one of the most striking examples of convergence – the judicialization of politics and the growth of rights discourse – is in an area that is least subject to international economic pressures.

STATE CAPACITIES AND THE SOCIAL CONTRACT

The discrepancy between dramatic social and economic change and the innate conservatism of institutions and processes raises profound questions about the future of both countries. The preceding chapters have suggested the enormous difficulty and complexity of the policy agendas they face. Moreover, these agendas and the related prescriptions for future policy development are in some ways deeply at odds with each other. In particular, the "economic agenda," focused on the need to reduce the size of government, increase productivity, rein in the welfare state, and tame deficits, is at odds with a "social agenda" that places greater weight on promoting equity and equality, preserving the environment, and maintaining – even expanding – the social safety net. From this perspective, the volatility associated with economic restructuring increases rather than decreases the need to have a strong social policy, in order to cushion and protect against the effects of change.

Linked to the competing policy agendas are competing images of the political process. While the economic or competitiveness agenda seeks to shift the balance from public to private, it also seeks, at least implicitly, to increase the authority of governments to act decisively, to impose costs, and to make hard decisions. From the competitiveness perspective, the problem is not a matter of having too much government authority but of having too little – in Huntington's terms, an "excess of democracy," a "democratic distemper" (1976). This suggests that the concept of state "autonomy," or strong and weak states, has a double meaning in the present context. If international economic forces undermine state autonomy vis-à-vis the outside world, the state needs to be strong, relatively insulated, and autonomous from mass pressures if it is to respond to the external challenge. This was dramatically evident in the extent to which Prime Minister Mulroney and President Clinton used all the resources at their disposal to ensure passage of the FTA and NAFTA, respectively.

Associated with the "progressive" agenda, on the other hand, is the desire to increase citizen participation, disperse authority, broaden the representation of diverse social groups throughout political institutions, and so on. The problem here is not too much democracy but too little. This suggests that the attenuation of state autonomy vis-à-vis external forces at the same time diminishes its capacity to be responsive to societal pressures.

This conflict between the state's need to respond to the disciplines of the external market and its need to respond to a politicized society is perhaps best manifested in the difficulties both countries face in managing their debts and deficits. It is a tension that is particularly acute for Canada, given its commitment to maintain a more expansive welfare state in the face of higher external vulnerability.

These tensions are linked to a high degree of disaffection from the political system in both countries, as was seen in chapters 3 and 4. This lack of trust and confidence in leaders and institutions shows up in many ways in both countries – in public attitudes, in the rise of protest parties and movements (for example, Ross Perot and the Reform Party), and in institutional deadlock, whether between president and Congress or between federal and provincial governments. This disaffection appears to be both a result and a cause of government failure. It is a result in the sense that in the face of global and domestic challenges, governments often seem unable to act effectively. And governments that cannot deliver on citizen expectations are unlikely to sustain support; perceived policy failure generates pervasive hostility against those seen to be responsible. On the other hand, the disaffection is a cause of government failure in that it undermines the authority of governments and inhibits their ability to build consent for major policy change. Again, debt and deficits exacerbate this tension. They make the trade-offs among policies and interests much more visible, painful, and conflictual. Such a trade-off was made explicit in the 1990 U.S. Budget Enforcement Act, which requires that any proposed spending increase be accompanied by explicit spending cuts or tax increases of the same amount (Thurber and Durst 1993). Such legislation, like proposed constitutional caps on deficit spending, constitutes attempts by politicians to protect themselves from the temptations of politics, and it underlines the constrained environment in which politicians now operate. Moreover, the cost of debt servicing is a powerful source of citizen disaffection. When one-third of the taxes that citizens pay (in Canada), or one-sixth (in the United States), is consumed by debt-service costs, there is inevitably an enormous shortfall between what citizens pay for and what they receive in government services.

The sense of failure and political malaise in the two countries suggests that the causes are to be found well beyond the most frequently cited culprits – the excessive demands of citizens, the venality or incompetence of politicians, the sclerosis of institutions, the incompetence and power seeking of bureaucracies, or scandal mongering by the press. A number of scholars have suggested that the malaise lies at a deeper level. They see the periods of political and policy stability as being characterized by settled understandings that embody more or less coherent relationships between economic and social conditions, political alignments, and public philosophies (Beer 1978; Bowles and Gintis 1982; Piore and Sabel 1984; Greenberg 1994; Simeon 1994). Lawrence C. Dodd (1994) argues that periods of political stability, widespread consensus, faith in the legitimacy of leaders and institutions, and policy coherence occur when the prevailing political values and practices are consistent with the economic and social realities that confront the society. When they diverge, however, consensus is likely to break down, social conflict to increase, self-interested forms of behaviour to proliferate, alternative ideological prescriptions to multiply, the sense of community to break down, faith and trust in government to decline, institutions to appear cumbersome and unresponsive, and policy to be incoherent and ineffective.

Dodd argues that American political history is characterized by a dynamic relationship between these two levels of reality. In each era, a broad consensus or settled set of premises and understandings is established. This can be seen as a more or less explicit social contract, which embodies a number of related elements: a clear policy blueprint or project; a political accommodation among the dominant social groups of the period; a balance among competing social and political values such as equity and efficiency; and a reasonably stable pattern of governance (Simeon 1994).

Such a contract is sustained by the underlying social and economic conditions. Once established, however, the fit or congruence between them typically begins to break down. This is partly a result of internal contradictions within the world view and in its associated policy and practices. But more profoundly, it is because the economic and social conditions underlying the world view change. The greater the divergence, the greater is the ensuing sense of political crisis, and the more urgent is the search for a new "strategy of action," a new world view or "public philosophy," one that can resolve the contradictions and restructure the political world in order to respond better to the underlying dynamics of the society and the economy. Thus, cyclical theorists such as Dodd (1994), Arthur Schlesinger, Jr (1986), Walter Dean Burnham (1994) and Albert Hirschman (1982) see American history in terms of broad cycles, in which world views are created, become progressively more rigid, inflexible, and out of tune with social and economic realities, consequently break down, and are then – more or less successfully – reconstituted. These analysts distinguish the founding era, the Civil War and Reconstruction, the late-nineteenth-century period of the growth of capitalist industrialism, and the New Deal period that grew out of depression and war. A parallel Canadian periodization could distinguish the Confederation era, the turn-of-the-century westward expansion and industrialism, and the postwar construction of the Keynesian welfare state. Each of these eras, it could be argued, was characterized by a broad, settled understanding that was widely spread across the society.

The New Deal or Keynesian welfare state era embodied these elements, although it is easy to exaggerate the degree of consensus associated with it and the clarity with which its creators understood what they were doing. Nor should the political struggles in developing and implementing the model be ignored. Nevertheless, in both countries, a broad social contract was developed. The policy blueprint involved a commitment to freer international trade, to strengthening the rights of labour, to broad-scale economic management through fiscal and monetary policy, and to a stronger social safety net. It involved a political accommodation between management, labour, and government. It embodied a "virtuous circle" between economic equality and economic growth: a strong social safety net would ensure business the skilled, healthy labour it required while socializing the costs of providing for those outside the workforce; a strong, profitable business sector would generate the revenues to finance the welfare state. Politically, it embodied, in both countries, a stable party system and relatively cooperative relations between legislative and executive branches, between central and state/provincial governments, and among governments, bureaucracies, and interest groups. There were, of course, major exceptions to this pattern: the exclusion of African Americans, leading to the civil rights movement in the United States; and the hostility of Quebec governments to the new agenda in Canada. Nevertheless, in broad outline this model did reflect a congruence between the patterns of governance and the economic, social, and geopolitical conditions of the time. It was underpinned by – and, arguably, contributed to – the unprecedented era of postwar economic growth, which lasted until the end of the 1960s.

Just as it took a lengthy period to build the postwar model, so was it slow to unravel. Unravel, however, it did. In the first stages, this may be seen as a reaction against the internal contradictions within the model. One of its necessary consequences was a massive expansion of the size of government and of the bureaucracy. Reactions to this took two forms, both of which emerged with greater force in the United States: on the one hand, the emergence of the new left; on the other, the growth of neoconservatism. The former reacted against the growth of institutional power, public and private, and the concentration of authority; the latter, against the expansion of the public sector, the costs and power of bureaucracy, and the "revolution of rising entitlements."

More fundamentally, the economic and social conditions underpinning the postwar model shifted dramatically. At the economic level, this took the form of the major transformations we described in chapter 2: the end of steady economic growth; shifts in global markets; technological change; and changes in the organization of business. Similarly, the social shifts tracked in chapter 2 include transformations in the relations between men and women, the emergence of new identities and interests, and profound demographic changes. These developments undermined the postwar social contract at every level. The policy blueprint no longer seemed to work; growth and equity came to be seen as a vicious rather than a virtuous circle; and new issues outside the traditional blueprint emerged, as did new social groups not included in the original contract. The established political relationships broke down; on both left and right "government," in different ways, came to be seen as part of the problem rather than part of the solution. The result was the disarray we have described, along with the broad range of "solutions" debated in both countries, and with sharply competing reform agendas, which often speak past each other.

Hence, the challenge: How can we develop new understandings and practices that can sustain enduring values while adapting institutions and practices to new conditions? The broad outlines of the challenge are similar in the two countries, but there are very significant differences in detail – in part because of the way the new challenges interact with historical legacies, and in part because of the differences in institutional structure. Both countries, it might be argued, are ill-equipped to undertake such a reconstruction – the search for a new politics, more attuned to contemporary realities.

It is useful, therefore, to ask whether they have the political or institutional capacity to meet the contemporary agendas effectively. Political capacity is an elusive concept. Institutions, processes, and policy outcomes can be assessed from several vantage points: an assessment predicated on democratic values may be very different from one based on policy competence or on the capacity to manage social conflict. Judgments are difficult to separate from the observer's preferences. For example, both countries have been engaged in debate over reform of the welfare system in the mid-1990s, but some would assess the results in terms of how much they reduced the total cost of these programs, while others would judge reform in terms of its effectiveness in reducing poverty levels. Weaver and Rockman have attempted to develop a more value-free set of criteria for weighing state capacities. These can be judged in terms of their ability to set and maintain priorities; target resources; innovate; coordinate conflicting objectives; impose losses; represent diffuse, unorganized interests; ensure effective policy implementation; ensure policy stability; make and maintain international commitments; and manage political cleavages or conflicts (1993, ch. 1).

As Weaver and Rockman point out, many commentators argue that parliamentary regimes are more likely to be effective on most of these dimensions than the congressional regime. The fusion of legislature and executive, combined with disciplined parties, allows governments to develop and promote a coherent program and then gives them the authority and autonomy to enact it. In principle, this should permit parliamentary regimes to set priorities and objectives, coordinate activities, and ensure effective implementation more effectively. It should give them greater ability to resist the importuning of special interest groups, and to give greater weight to unorganized or diffused interests. On the other hand, the fragmentation of power in the American system, with a candidate-centred electoral system, the prevalence of organized interest groups, undisciplined parties, and divided government, is said to be more able to veto change than to innovate, to be hostage to organized interests, and so on. These ideas were reviewed in chapter 4.

Such hypotheses imply that Canada should have greater capacity to address the profound challenges we have described. But no such broad conclusion can be drawn from the preceding analyses. At the level of macroeconomic policy, for example, Canadian slowness in grappling with deficits has generated a much higher level of accumulated debt. Neither country can be seen as having particularly coherent or effective industrial policies. Canada has maintained a stronger, more redistributive social safety net and has provided more comprehensive health care at a lower cost than the United States. In environmental policy, however, the United States has been the pacesetter more often than not. Canada has moved further in formal recognition of multiculturalism; the United States has continued to give greater weight to individual rights. Both countries have made some progress in securing greater representation for women and minorities, but the differences are not large. While judgments will vary from case to case and while assessments of policy success must also take into account the scale of the challenge to be met, it is difficult to sustain the argument of a systematic difference in governmental capacity along the dimensions Weaver and Rockman cite.

Why is this so? In part the answer may be institutional. That is, some characteristics of Canadian institutions may counterbalance the alleged virtues of the parliamentary system. For example, as Weaver and Rockman point out (1993), if that system focuses authority, it also focuses accountability. The easier it is for citizens to assign blame and exact punishment, the more political will it requires to impose costs or ignore interest groups. Second, the more decentralized federalism in Canada in some respects mirrors the American phenomenon of divided government.

However, this is only part of the story. Governmental capacity is not only a function of institutional structures, important as they are; it is equally a function of the society and of the ways the society interacts with institutions. Congressional and parliamentary government are long-standing institutional landmarks in each country. Checks and balances are not new: they are an essential part of the institutional design of the American constitution. The pathologies of gridlock and immobilism that we focus on today are, in a sense, built into the structure of American government. But the crucial point is that in some periods it seems to function relatively effectively, while at others it does not. Similarly, parliamentary government is the historic Canadian model, but it too has performed differently at different times.

So attention must turn to developments in the society – to changes in economic structures and the cleavages and tensions these engender. These in turn affect the resources available to governments, the mobilization of social groups, and changes in the "technology" of politics. Deep social tensions and powerfully mobilized groups can render even governments with the potential authority of the Canadian model ineffective and indecisive; similarly, they can exacerbate the fragmentation already implicit in the American model.

Hence, these countries may bring significantly different strengths and weaknesses to the task of political restructuring. Canada may be stronger at the institutional level to provide decisive, coherent policy, to act autonomously of social forces, and to develop effective leadership. A strong, committed government does indeed have at least the potential to act, despite the constraints of federalism and the loss of legitimacy of elites that we described. The rub is whether there is the will to act. Preoccupied with Quebec, with the need to balance regional interests, and with fiscal crisis, Canadian governments have until recently been unable or unwilling to exercise the potential authority with which they are endowed. This suggests that the major barrier to political restructuring in Canada lies in its civil society rather than in its institutions. What makes this perspective surprising is that in recent years, neo-institutionalist explanations of Canadian politics, especially Canadian federalism, have been particularly dominant and influential (Cairns 1977; Smiley 1987; Gibbins 1982).

Our sense is that civil society in both countries is highly fragmented and divided, and that these divisions, along with an increasingly fragmented media, do indeed make the forging of consensus extremely difficult. But the United States may have some important strengths in this regard, which Canada lacks. These include, first, a stronger sense of nationhood which transcends many divisions, along with a powerful set of founding myths. In seeking new forms of community, Americans can appeal to strong continuities in historical values; by contrast, Canada lacks a founding myth and instead embraces competing conceptions of nationhood. In Peter Russell's term (1993), Canada has yet to constitute itself as a "sovereign people." Moreover Canadian history embraces many elements which in the current era are divisive rather than unifying; in some respects, unifying ideas today must reject rather than build on the Canadian historical experience. This idea is captured in a recent comment on Canadian immigration policy. The solution, suggested Rick Salutin, "is not fewer immigrants, but more Canada when they get here" (*Globe and Mail*, 22 July 1994).

Second, the close presence of U.S. society and culture has enormous effects on Canadians' capacity to conduct an autonomous debate centred on "Canadian" issues and ideas. Canada's openness, and its ability to borrow ideas and values, constitutes one of its most important resources. But for present purposes, it means that American culture, and with it American perceptions of values, ideas, and policy agendas, tends to dominate the Canadian landscape. For example, while Robert Reich and others suggest that the American business community has in some sense become more global than American, it is even more the case that with high levels of foreign ownership and investment, Canada has had an even less autonomous "Canadian" business community. Similarly, the media may be becoming more fragmented in the United States, but the central fact for Canada is the predominance of American television, American films, and American magazines, both at the mass and elite levels. There are no Canadian equivalents of *Harper's* or the *Atlantic Monthly*; and it is these journals, together with the *Economist* from Britain, that are most likely to be found on the desks of Canadian decision makers. The point here is not that Canadians are victims of American cultural, economic, and political imperialism (though many Canadian scholars and commentators have made this argument). Nor is it that there are not enduring Canadian political values – some Canadian policies are defended precisely because they distinguish Canadians from Americans. Rather, it is that despite the fragmentation decried by so many American commentators, and despite its much greater size, American civil society – at least at elite levels – may be more capable than Canada of coming to a settled or "considered" judgment (Yankelovich 1991) on a public philosophy.

This relative optimism about the United States must be tempered by a recognition that it rests in part on a disconcerting capacity of the American system to evade its most explosive and system-threatening challenge: the enduring multiple crises of urban decay, poverty, crime, and racial conflict. The Los Angeles riots of 1992 were a stark reminder of the threat these problems pose to the American system. But the apparent ease with which American society put the incident aside, without any serious policy response, is an indication of the capacity of the political order to absorb periodic eruptions without systemic crisis or change. However, the embers are smouldering and the tinder remains dry. Nor can the enormous costs of the fragmentation of authority in Washington be underestimated.

The task of rethinking the political order may be more pressing in Canada for two reasons: first, because of its greater vulnerability to international economic forces, and the tension between these forces and the broader Canadian commitment to expansive government and to a stronger welfare state than that of the United States; second, because of the looming crisis of national unity, which Canadians have failed to resolve in successive rounds of constitutional negotiation – culminating in the rejection of the Meech Lake and Charlottetown accords, and the breathtakingly narrow loss of the Yes forces in the Quebec referendum on sovereignty in 1995. This issue can overwhelm the capacity to address the other elements on the political, economic, and social agendas. The "national question" will continue to dominate Canadian politics.

CONCLUSION

We have painted a picture of two societies, each increasingly diverse and fragmented along multiple lines, and of two polities, each divided by dispersed power and institutional rivalries. This is unpromising ground, one might argue, for formulating a project for the twenty-first century equivalent to the postwar model. The fundamental requirement for achieving some degree of coherence of common purpose across the institutions of American government, or for achieving coherent policy and intergovernmental cooperation in Canada, is an integrating "public philosophy" or world view. It must both be attuned to the new social and economic realities and be consistent with the enduring values of liberal democracy, which is the philosophical bedrock of political life in both countries.

This is not an easy task. Indeed, the best prediction may well be one of continued muddling through – the sense of crisis varying with the state of the economy, the value of the dollar, or the dramatic evidence of social discord, such as the riots in Los Angeles or the election of a separatist party in Quebec. Or the situation may be one in which the problem is not the lack of blueprints but a "blooming, buzzing confusion" of them, none able to bridge the social divides or to reconcile equity and growth. Or possibly, in the Canadian case, an acute fiscal crisis may force radical change at the insistence of international financial institutions.

Yet each of these countries faces these challenges with enormous reservoirs of strength: a civic rather than ethnic sense of political community; a deep commitment to liberal, democratic, pluralist political values, however much these may be contested in detail; a commitment to economic markets with a human face; and functioning, if creaky, political institutions. The challenges they face in common; the responses will be shaped by their historic and continuing differences.

Notes

CHAPTER ONE

1 Most of the existing literature comparing Canada and the United States emphasizes the differences between the two countries, as suggested by the titles of Lipset's *Continental Divide* (1990) and D. Thomas's *Differences that Count* (1993). More recent writings, however, have tended to qualify or challenge this emphasis, as evidenced by Card and Freeman's *Small Differences that Matter* (1993) and Reitz and Breton's *The Illusion of Difference* (1994).

2 For a survey of this literature, see Kerr 1983.

3 The literature on globalization is now immense. See, for example, Anderson and Blackhurst 1993; Courchene 1991, 1992; Gill and Law 1988; Omhae 1990; Porter 1990, 1991; Reich 1991; Stubbs and Underhill 1994; Walters and Blake 1992; Zysman 1988; and Zysman and Tyson 1983.

4 For discussions of the concept and nature of convergence, see Bennett 1991b; Goldthorpe 1984; Hollingsworth, Schmitter, and Streeck 1994; Kerr 1983; Moon 1987; and J. O'Connor 1988.

CHAPTER TWO

1 For a discussion of the various forms of Laurier's assertion, see Colombo 1974, 331–4. Henry Luce is quoted in Graham 1992, 7.

2 It is important not to overstate this pattern. As Harris notes, "Fordism is not dead – there are a large number of industries that still use mass production systems, and economics of scale are significant" (1993, 22).

3 For a sceptical view from the OECD on U.S. productivity trends, see French and Jarret 1993. For conflicting views of the Canadian data, see Denny and Wilson 1993; Fortin 1994.

4 A substantial literature on polarization has emerged in recent years. In addition to a special issue of the *Quarterly Journal of Economics* (1992, 107), see Beach and Slotsve 1994; Danziger and Gottschalk 1993; B. Harrison and Bluestone 1988; Krugman 1990; Levy and Murnane 1992; K. Phillips 1993; R. Lawrence 1984; Morrisette, Myles, and Picot 1995; and Myles, Picot, and Wannell 1988.

5 The most direct comparative analysis of greater inequality in earnings in the two countries concluded that the biggest contributor to the increase in earnings variation in the United States from 1979 to 1987 was education. In contrast, the education effect was not important in Canada (Blackburn and Bloom 1993).

6 The Economic Council (1991a) concluded that for all other immigrant groups there was no wage discrimination. For an opposing view, see Reitz and Breton 1994.

7 Crime statistics are notoriously open to varying measures and interpretations. In the United States, for example, violent crime as measured by police statistics almost doubled from 1973 to 1992; measured by the National Crime Victimisation Survey, which tracks reported experience of crime, the rate is unchanged in the same period. The politics of crime is probably driven less by overall crime rates than by the visibility of crime in particular settings, such as schools, and by broader concerns over social change and disruption (*Economist* 1994, 22).

CHAPTER THREE

1 Two examples are the adoption by Liberal leader Jean Chrétien, in his speeches leading up to the 1993 election, of Bill Clinton's message of "hope" from the 1992 American campaign and the way in which the major parties in Canada felt constrained to respond to the populist thrust of the "town hall" model of campaigning used by Clinton and Ross Perot in 1992. Perot's infomercials had large audiences in Canada.

2 Most of the comparative studies that have been done have been limited in one way or another. For example, two studies specifically concerned with political values (Arnold and Barnes 1979; Nevitte and Gibbins 1990) both used samples of university students. Another, the World Values Studies in 1980 and 1990 (Nevitte, Inglehart, and Basanez 1991), used samples of the general population but asked few questions about public policy and was focused in its concern about values on issues reflecting a concern with the development of new "post-materialist" values. Three studies that compare opinions about policy – surveys by Decima Research for *Maclean's* magazine

in 1989 and 1990 and the Reid Group's Canada and the World survey in 1992 (Reid and Burns 1992) – while they all contain useful questions, are very limited in their range and depth of coverage.

3 The data from the *Decima Quarterly Report* used here were originally collected by Decima Research and made available by the Centre for the Study of Public Opinion, Queen's University, Kingston, where Decima has deposited the database from the *Quarterly*.

4 Data on the representation of African Americans in national samples are not routinely provided. Since lower-status groups are less likely to respond to requests for interviews, it is likely that many surveys undersample African Americans.

5 There is one feature in the pattern of American references to the drug issue that requires separate comment. From May 1989 to April 1990 the number of people mentioning this issue rose dramatically. This shift is probably explained by the fact that it coincides with heightened media attention created by President Bush's war on drugs.

6 In the *Globe and Mail*–CBC poll in October 1989, 13 per cent of respondents named "taxes," the GST, or "over-taxation" as the most important issue.

7 Interestingly, when a very similar question was asked of Canadians in the Charter Project survey in 1987, the number of both anglophones and francophones who supported the use of emergency powers was higher, but the difference between francophone and anglophone groups was approximately the same.

8 In Canada, the failure of fundamentalist Protestants to secure support for their agenda within the Progressive Conservative Party contributed to the establishment of the Christian Heritage Party, which managed to win less than 1 per cent of the popular vote when it ran candidates in the 1988 federal election.

9 These attitudes are best documented on the public record in polls done by the CBC and the Toronto *Globe and Mail* and reported in the *Globe* at the end of June 1990, in October 1990, April 1991, and October 1991. Note that although issues of national unity did get on the public's issue agenda, never more than 30 per cent of Canadians in the CBC-*Globe* polls and in the Decima polls reported earlier were prepared to recognize the primacy of these issues.

CHAPTER FOUR

1 Intrastate federalism focuses on the ways in which state/provincial interests are given formal expression within the institutions of the national government – for example, by a Senate designed to reflect these interests. It contrasts with interstate federalism, defined by the division of powers between levels or orders of government and by the relations between them. For a summary of the literature, see Smiley and Watts 1986.

2 The process of face-to-face interactions between senior officials and cabinet ministers, the characteristic mode of intergovernmental relations in Canada.

3 For a good review of new social movements in Canadian politics, see S. Phillips 1994.

4 The Republicans have pledged to reduce the size of congressional and committee staffs significantly in order to produce a less bloated structure.

5 Alan Ehrenhalt (1991) has labelled this the "politics of ambition."

6 These observations were, of course, made by conservatives objecting to the Democratic Congress's ability to block the initiatives of Republican presidents. After the 1994 congressional elections, the positions were reversed, and the new GOP Congress embraced "imperialist" ambitions with a vengeance.

7 In some cases, when Congress is confident that administration decisions will meet its objectives or when it wishes to minimize its openness to political pressure, Congress has continued to delegate. Examples are the "fast-track" negotiating procedures for trade agreements and delegating to a commission the thankless task of closing military bases.

8 Indeed, soon after the 1993 election, and despite the Liberals' overwhelming majority, traditional forms of discipline were being wielded against party dissidents.

9 The issues discussed in this section are developed further in chapter 8.

10 Which allows provinces to exempt provisions of their legislatures from certain sections of the Charter for a (renewable) five-year period.

11 This paradox is nicely captured in the ideology of Ralph Nader and his supporters. It is significant that when a colleague sought to establish a Nader-type group in Canada, one of his first questions was whether it might be possible to find public funding – something that was anathema to Nader himself. See Michael McCann (1986) for a brilliant analysis.

12 There is a paradox here: the same voters who have supported term limits by two-to-one margins have continued to re-elect incumbents. U.S. voters appear to dislike Congress but to like their individual representatives.

13 In recent elections., voters in Saskatchewan and British Columbia voted for statutory limits on deficits, but in neither case has the requisite legislation been enacted. As another way to restrain government, some of the advocates of the Canada–U.S. Free Trade Agreement and NAFTA argued that one of the "benefits" would be that governments would be more constrained from making politically advantageous but economically "foolish" decisions.

14 Charles Jones (1994) makes this argument forcefully for the American separated system.

CHAPTER FIVE

1 Purvis (1977, 1985) stressed such policy dependence in the context of the policy response in Canada in the early 1970s and in Canada and Europe in the early 1980s to developments in the United States; more recently, John Floyd (1992) has discussed the same phenomena in terms of "acquiescent policy."

2 Data sources are listed in the appendix to this chapter. Data for 1992 are provisional estimates. All growth rates are measured from fourth quarter to fourth quarter.

3 Trend output is estimated using a simple linear regression on time.

4 See Card and Riddell 1993; Milbourne, Purvis, and Scoones 1991; and Green and Riddell 1992.

5 M1 is defined as currency and (non-interest-bearing) demand deposits – for example, "true" chequing accounts. M2 includes M1 as well as some (interest-bearing) notice and personal savings accounts. It is sometimes argued that because its demand is more sensitive to changes in interest rates, M1 is less useful as a policy instrument than M2.

6 Both on a national accounts basis.

7 An alternative explanation is related to the rise of commodity prices in the late 1980s and their subsequent collapse. If commodity price increases were more positive for Canada than the for the United States, appropriate monetary conditions would diverge. The subsequent collapse in commodity prices would in turn lead to a more severe recession in Canada than in the United States.

8 For an excellent account of the U.S. experience through much of the 1970s, see Blinder 1979.

9 In 1971, in an attempt to stimulate the economy without sparking an inflationary rise in prices, the president had introduced a package of wage and price guidelines to contain prices.

10 This and the ensuing discussion draws heavily on Courchene 1976. See also Purvis 1977.

11 The uncertainty about the desired direction of policy makes judging it *ex post* as difficult as formulating it *ex ante*; whatever the outcome, some success in terms of one goal will occur and will be offset by some failure in terms of the other.

12 The latter caused outlays to grow rapidly because many federal transfer payments such as old age pensions were indexed to inflation. Tax revenues also rose due to inflation, although not as quickly as they would have had the income tax system not been indexed. The lack of indexation of the U.S. tax system may have contributed to the difference in the fiscal responses.

13 Whether by accident or design, the two policies made a coherent package. The monetary policy was meant to reduce the speed with which demand

was growing, while wage and price controls were meant to reduce the speed with which costs were growing. If the two forces could be contained at the same rate, the inflation rate could be reduced without having to endure stagflation.

14 See Boothe and Poloz 1988 for evidence on this shift in money demand.

15 Indeed, if the central banks had paid more attention to the interest rate – which had been discredited as an intermediate target – they would have realized that monetary policy was not restrictive. Several times during this period the real interest rate (the money rate corrected for the rate for inflation) was negative. Research by Longworth and Poloz (1986) suggests that targeting a less interest-sensitive monetary aggregate such as M2 might have been better, though it would have been harder since the degree of control exerted by the central bank is reduced as broader definitions of money are considered.

16 Our discussion of U.S. monetary policy in the early Reagan years relies heavily on Niskanen 1988, ch. 5.

17 Note that this was the opposite of the shift that disrupted Canadian monetary policy in the 1970s.

18 Real interest rates did not fall as much, if indeed they fell at all, as inflation fell to an equal or greater extent than nominal interest rates.

19 In addition to Niskanen 1988 cited earlier, good accounts of the economic policies of the Reagan years are found in Cagan 1986; and Hulten and Sawhill 1984.

20 See Niskanen 1988, 64–7.

21 See Boadway and Bruce 1992; R. Gordon 1992.

22 This concern was mitigated to some extent, however, by the collapse in oil prices in 1986.

23 The ability of the central bank to control the money supply precisely should not be overstated. Operationally, the key policy issue is how quickly interest rates should be allowed to adjust to lower inflation.

24 The period was dominated by the dramatic fall in the value of the U.S. dollar in terms of the Japanese yen and the major European currencies. In late 1985 and early 1986 the Canadian dollar fell in terms of the U.S. dollar; during a brief period in January 1986 speculative pressures – apparently motivated by concern over Canada's large government budget deficit – drove the Canadian dollar below 70 cents U.S. The Bank of Canada took strong measures to counter the speculative attacks and kept to its medium-term goal of stabilizing the inflation rate. In late 1986 and early 1987 the market acknowledged its faith in these policies, and the Canadian dollar strengthened considerably in terms of the U.S. dollar, rising to around 74 cents U.S. This mitigated the depreciation experienced in terms of the overseas currencies, and the Canadian dollar stayed almost constant in terms of a trade-weighted average of all currencies.

25 In 1974, when inflation rose to the "unprecedented peak" of 4 per cent, it was considered a national emergency and led to the introduction of wage and price controls in the United States and their serious consideration in Canada!

26 Prospects for the U.S. economy in the 1990s are discussed in Krugman 1990.

CHAPTER SIX

1 The G7 nations are the United States, Japan, Germany, France, the United Kingdom, Italy, and Canada.

2 See article 19, the "safeguards" provision of the GATT, which is parallelled by analogous though rather differently structured provisions in the FTA and NAFTA.

3 Government-funded research and development as a percentage of GDP in 1984 was 0.76 per cent in Canada but 1.29 per cent in the United States (Ontario 1988, 189).

4 See, for example, Canada, Royal Commission on the Econonomic Union and Development Prospects for Canada 1985; also Canada, Commission of Inquiry on Unemployment Insurance 1986.

5 For one of many examples, see Ontario 1988, 3:122–5.

CHAPTER SEVEN

1 Wilensky (1975) argued that defence spending undercut welfare expenditures in the United States during the 1950s and 1960s, but subsequent analyses have found less support for the proposition (Russett 1982; Domke, Eichenberg, and Kelleher 1983; Mintz 1989).

2 Canada's relationship with the international system has been central to virtually every interpretation of the scope of state activity in the country. For a useful summary of this literature, see Laux and Molot 1988, chs. 2 and 3.

3 For the flavour of the debate, see Crispo 1988; Drover 1988; Economic Council of Canada 1988a; Gold and Leyton-Brown 1988; Manga 1988; and Warnock 1988.

4 For a useful survey of this literature, see Shalev 1983. More recent developments in this literature emphasize the nature of coalitions among different classes at critical junctures in this history of the welfare state (Esping-Andersen 1990; P. Baldwin 1990; Gourevitch 1986).

5 The *Globe and Mail* reported that blacks made up 26 per cent of families receiving services from the Metro Toronto Children's Aid in 1990 even though they represented only about 7 per cent of the population; in Montreal, black children make up 23 per cent of those receiving services from

the anglophone child-welfare agency, despite making up only 4 per cent of the city's anglophone population (*Globe and Mail*, 6 August 1991).

6 Unemployment insurance generates much more substantial interregional transfers in Canada than in the United States not only because of the size of the Canadian program but because of key features of its design. First, the Canadian system has an explicit system of regional differentials both in qualification requirements and in maximum benefit periods, creating a more generous program in regions with high unemployment. Second, the absence of experience rating in the formula determining contributions to the program generates a significant transfer from industries with comparatively stable patterns of employment to industries with highly seasonal employment, which are disproportionately located in the poorer regions. In the United States, state payroll taxes for unemployment insurance vary with the unemployment history of the industry.

7 For a survey of the contemporary patterns of health care in the United States, see the U.S. Bipartisan Commission on Comprehensive Health Care (the Pepper Commission) 1990. For a recent reformist analysis, see Marmor 1994. For a useful comparative survey of the Canadian and U.S. systems, see the U.S. General Accounting Office 1991.

8 An example of the American focus on waiting lists for surgical procedures and the technological gap can be found in a feature-length analysis of the Canadian system in the *New York Times*, 30 April 1991. For a more systematic analysis, see U.S. General Accounting Office 1991.

9 Under changes to unemployment insurance announced in 1995, low-income beneficiaries with children are entitled to special family supplements. In addition, individuals who collect unemployment benefits for part of the year but still have an above-average income for the year as a whole face a "clawback" of their benefit through the tax system; this clawback can reach 100 per cent (Canada, Human Resources Development 1995).

10 In determining assets, a number of items such as the individual's home and some personal effects are not included.

11 For example, Overbye 1994 argues that there has been a long-term convergence in pension outcomes among Western nations during the twentieth century, which has been driven by the spread of industrialization and democratic politics.

12 The initial federal proposals for social policy reform, which were released in the fall of 1994 and launched a cross-Canada consultative process, were set out in Canada, Human Resources Development 1994; for commentaries on the proposals, see Banting and Battle 1994.

13 For an alternative view of the significance of the Bipartisan Commission and the prospects for means-testing entitlements in the United States, see Myles 1995.

CHAPTER EIGHT

1 Vallinder 1994. This issue of the *International Political Science Review* contains articles on the judicialization of politics in the United States, Germany, the United Kingdom, France, the Netherlands, Sweden, Canada, Israel, and the Philippines and Southeast Asia. See also, Shapiro and Stone 1994; and Stone 1992.

2 Nevitte, Bakvis, and Gibbins 1989. For a broader discussion of post-materialism, see Inglehart 1971 and 1977.

3 Canada, Special Joint Committee on a Renewed Canada 1992.

4 Bias in human rights tribunals is discussed in Flanagan, Knopff, and Archer 1988.

5 347 US 483 (1954).

6 *Dred Scott v. Sandford*, 60 US 393 (1857).

7 *The Slaughterhouse Cases*, 83 US 36 (1873); *Civil Rights Cases*, 109 US 3 (1883); *Plessy v. Ferguson*, 163 US 537 (1896).

8 See, for example, *Lochner v. New York*, 198 US 45 (1905); *Hammer v. Dagenhart*, 247 US 251 (1918); *Adkins v. Children's Hospital*, 262 US 525 (1923).

9 *Shecter Poultry Corp. v. United States*, 295 US 495 (1935); *United States v. Butler*, 297 US 1 (1936); *Carter v. Carter Coal Co.*, 298 US 238 (1936).

10 The literature on interest-group litigation is extensive. See Vose 1958; Galanter 1974; K. O'Connor 1980; K. O'Connor and Epstein 1983; Wasby 1985; Olson 1990; and Scheppele and Walker 1991.

11 Section 33 of the Canadian Charter of Rights and Freedoms provides that the federal and provincial governments may declare that legislation "shall operate notwithstanding" the Charter's provisions concerning fundamental freedoms, legal rights, and/or equality rights.

12 See Monahan 1987, 21; Morton, Russell, and Riddell 1994, 3.

13 The equality rights section of the Charter (s. 15) did not become enforceable until 1985, in order to give governments time to adjust legislation to the new requirement. Consequently, the first case concerning s. 15 did not reach the Supreme Court until 1989.

14 *R. v. Drybones*, [1970] SCR 282.

15 Figures cited in this paragraph are from Morton, Russell, and Riddell 1994, 3–4, 19.

16 I have explored this issue in detail in two previous publications: Manfredi 1990b and 1992.

17 See, for example, Stone and Walpole 1983; Tarnopolsky 1983; Bender 1983; Days 1984; Rosenberg 1986; and Spitz 1986.

18 See Friedman, Kagan, Cartwright, and Wheeler 1981; Caldeira 1988; and Smithey 1995.

19 See MacIntyre 1964–66; Bushnell 1986.

20 *Thorson v. A.-G. Canada,* [1975] 1 SCR 138.

21 392 US 83 (1968). Cited by Laskin, CJC, at [1975] 1 SCR 138, 159.

22 *Minister of Justice (Canada) v. Borowski,* [1981] 2 SCR 575, 598.

23 *Operation Dismantle v. The Queen* (1985), 18 DLR (4th) 481, 500–5.

24 Ibid., 503.

25 *Reference re s. 94(2) of the Motor Vehicle Act* (1985), 24 DLR (4th) 536.

26 24 DLR (4th) at 546, 554.

27 *R. v. Big M Drug Mart* (1985) 18 DLR (4th) 321, 371–2; *Griggs v. Duke Power Co.,* 401 US 424 (1970).

28 18 DLR 321, 371 (citing 401 US 424, 432).

29 See *Law Society of British Columbia v. Andrews,* [1989] 1 SCR 143, 170–1.

30 *R.W.D.S.U (Local 580) v. Dolphin Delivery* (1986), 33 DLR (4th) 174; *McKinney v. University of Guelph* (1990), 76 DLR (4th) 545.

31 These provisions are s. 52(1), which provides for judicial nullification of statutes, and s. 24(2), which provides for the exclusion of evidence.

32 (1992) 93 DLR (4th) 1.

33 *Schacter v. The Queen* (1990), 66 DLR (4th) 635, 652 (FCA).

34 93 DLR (4th) at 21. "Reading in" is a technique that courts can use to make legislation conform with the constitution in lieu of nullifying it.

35 Ibid., 29.

36 *Marchand v. Simcoe Board of Education* (1986), 29 DLR (4th) 596, 621 (Ont. HCJ).

37 *Lavoie v. Nova Scotia* (1988), 47 DLR (4th) 586, 593 (NSSCTD). An appellate court subsequently ruled that the fifty students identified by the registration were sufficient to require the provision of minority-language instruction: (1989) 58 DLR (4th) 293 (NSSCAD).

38 *Mahé v. Aberta* (1990), 68 DLR (4th) 69, 107–8 (SCC).

39 See, for example, *Reference re Public Schools Act (Manitoba), ss. 79 (3), (4), (7),* [1993] 1 SCR 839. In this decision the court held that francophone parents in Manitoba have a right to a separate school board, and it ordered the province to enact legislation to that effect.

40 For an analysis of the relationship between rights-based litigation and the "new politics" agenda, see I. Brodie and Nevitte 1993.

41 This is true even in the area of criminal procedure, where some analysts have noted that the Canadian court has taken the American "due process revolution" further than the Warren Court; See Harvie and Foster 1990. I have elected not to discuss this aspect of the judicialization of politics because it is less strongly associated with post-material social movements.

42 *United States v. Carolene Products,* 304 US 144, 152–3 n. 4 (1938).

43 *Frontiero v. Richardson,* 411 US 167 (1973).

44 *Reynolds v. Sims,* 377 US 533 (1964) (franchise); *Shapiro v. Thompson,* 394 US 618 (1969) (right to travel).

45 *Dandridge v. Williams*, 397 US 471 (1970) (welfare); *San Antonio Independent School District v. Rodriguez*, 411 US 1 (1973) (education).

46 *Regents of the University of California v. Bakke*, 438 US 265 (1978); *Fullilove v. Klutznick*, 448 US 448 (1980). See generally, Rossum and Tarr 1987, 549–50. Powell upheld affirmative action on the grounds that such racial classifications meet the "compelling state interest" standard.

47 *City of Richmond v. J.A. Croson Co.*, 109 S. Ct. 706 (1989); *Ward's Cove v. Antonio*, 109 S. Ct. 2115 (1989).

48 *Adarand Constructor's Inc. v. Pena, Secretary of Transportation*, Case no. 93–1841, 12 June 1995.

49 *Lavell v. A.-G. Canada*, [1974] SCR 1349; *Bliss v. A.-G. Canada*, [1979] 1 SCR 183. These cases were decided under the 1960 Canadian Bill of Rights, which is a federal statute without constitutional status.

50 [1979] 1 SCR 183, 190.

51 *Andrews v. Law Society of British Columbia*, [1989] 1 SCR 143.

52 Hogg 1985, 800–1. Section 1 of the Charter provides that rights may be subject to "reasonable limitations."

53 [1989] 1 SCR at 178–81.; *Andrews v. Law Society of British Columbia* (1985), 22 DLR (4th) 600, at 610 (*per* McLachlin, JA); *Smith, Kline and French Laboratories Ltd. v. Canada (Attorney General)*, [1987] 2 FC 359, at 367–9 (*per* Hugessen, JA).

54 *Andrews*, 56 DLR (4th) 1 at 18.

55 *Andrews*, [1989] 1 SCR 143 at 152–3.

56 *R. v. Turpin*, [1989] 1 SCR 1296 at 1332.

57 *Egan v. Canada*, file no. 23636, Supreme Court of Canada, 25 May 1995.

58 *Symes v. Canada* (1993), 110 DLR (4th) 470; *Thibaudeau v. Canada*, file no. 24154, Supreme Court of Canada, 25 May 1995.

59 110 D.L.R. (4th) at 551–2. (*per* Iacobucci, J).

60 Ibid., 558 (emphasis in original).

61 Ibid., 559.

62 Ibid., 482 (*per* L'Heureux-Dubé, J).

63 Ibid., 506.

64 Ibid., 511.

65 *Thibaudeau v. Canada*, pars. 103–119 (*per* Gonthier, J).

66 Ibid., par. 6 (*per* L'Heureux-Dubé, J).

67 Ibid., par. 42 (*per* L'Heureux-Dubé, J).

68 Ibid., par. 205 (*per* McLachlin, J).

69 Ibid., pars. 156–7 (*per* Cory and Iacobucci, JJ).

70 *Baker v. Carr*, 369 US 186 (1962).

71 *Reynolds v. Sims*, 377 US 533 (1964).

72 *Kirkpatrick v. Preisler*, 394 US 526 (1969).

73 *Karcher v. Daggett*, 462 US 725 (1983).

74 *Mahan v. Howell,* 410 US 315 (1973).
75 *Thornburg v. Gingles,* 478 US 30 (1986); Grofman 1992, 160.
76 *Bandemer v. Davis,* 478 US 109 (1986).
77 *Shaw v. Reno,* 113 S. Ct. 2816 (1993).
78 *Reference re Saskatchewan Electoral Boundaries Act* (1991), 81 DLR (4th) 16 (SCC).
79 Ibid., 35–6.
80 The most litigated limit on the right to vote has been the exclusion of convicted criminals from the franchise. For an overview, see Knopff and Morton 1992, 292–331.
81 81 DLR (4th) at 35.
82 *McCorrister et al. v. A.-G. Canada; Sauvé v. A.-G. Canada et al.,* file no. T-1084–94, Federal Court of Canada, Trial Division.
83 *McCorrister et al. v. A.-G. Canada; Sauvé v. A.-G. Canada et al.* File no. T-1084-94, Federal Court of Canada, Trial Division.
84 *Hunter v. Southam* (1984), 11 DLR (4th) 641, 650. See Manfredi (1993, 52–60).

CHAPTER NINE

1 Even the pulp mill example can be used to illustrate this fact. The effect of a mill on a fishery will depend on the type of water body at stake, the species of fish that inhabit it, and the number of other sources of pollution on the same water body.
2 Sixty-five per cent of the public ranked it first, above unemployment (second with 62 per cent) and poverty (third at 35 per cent); see Gallup poll, 2 December 1970.
3 Gallup polls in Canada show that the percentage of respondents listing the environment as the nation's most important problem declined from a peak of 16.5 per cent in mid-1989 to 3.8 per cent at the end of 1990 and to less than 1.0 per cent by the beginning of 1994 (K. Harrison 1994).
4 On the importance of expertise and credibility as an organizational resources, see Schlozman and Tierney 1986; ch. 5.
5 These included the National Environmental Policy Act (1969), Clean Air Act (1970), Federal Water Pollution Control Act (1972), Federal Insecticide, Fungicide, and Rodenticide Act (1972), and the Endangered Species Act (1973).
6 Congress helped expand standing through the novel device of "citizen suits," first introduced by the Clean Air Act in 1970 and subsequently included in virtually every environmental statute (Boyer and Meidinger 1985). But the courts had already begun opening the doors to public interest groups through their changing interpretations of the Administrative Procedures Act (Stewart 1975).

7 An extensive collection of analyses of regulatory negotiation is contained in Administrative Conference of the United States 1990. For the most insightful political analysis of the phenomenon, see Fiorino 1988, 1990.

8 Gore's National Performance Review contained strong recommendations to increase the use of "consensus-based rulemaking" (U.S. National Performance Review 1993, 29–33).

9 In the case involving the Rafferty and Alameda dams in Saskatchewan, the court ruled that the EARP guidelines order was legally binding, that "it is not a mere description of a policy or programme; it may create rights which may be enforceable by way of *mandamus.*" Because the dam was on an international river, the federal government had jurisdiction over the project and therefore was required to perform an impact assessment; see *Canadian Wildlife Federation v Canada (Minister of the Environment)* 3, CELR (NS) 287. The case was upheld on appeal: *Canadian Wildlife Federation v. Canada (Minister of the Environment)*, 4 CELR (N.S.) 1. The other major case involved the Oldman dam in Alberta: *Friends of the Oldman River Society v. Canada (Minister of Transport)*, action no. A-395–89, Federal Court of Appeal, 13 March 1990.

10 The Supreme Court did narrow the scope of the Oldman Dam decision. The Federal Court of Appeal ruled that both the Minister of Transport and the Minister of Fisheries and Oceans had to perform assessments. The Supreme Court ruled that Transport had to comply because it was required to issue a permit in this case, but that Fisheries and Oceans did not have to comply because it did not have any "affirmative regulatory duty," even though it has authority to protect inland fisheries; see *Friends of the Oldman River Society v. Canada (Minister of Transport)*, Supreme Court of Canada, file no. 21890, 23 January 1991.

11 Canada, House of Commons, Bill C-78, An Act to Establish a Federal Environmental Assessment Process, first reading, 18 June 1990. As a result of both provincial and environmental opposition, the original version of the bill died on the order paper in May 1991. When the next session of Parliament convened, the government reintroduced the legislation, this time labelled Bill C-13.

12 A survey of court cases in the two countries up through 1989 – before the judicialization of impact assessment in Canada – found little evidence of convergence in judicial roles in environmental policy in the two countries (Howlett 1994).

13 A prominent expert on trade and the environment denounces this provision as retrogressive: "An international obligation based on each government's own standard is the weakest conceivable form of international agreement … The three governments resorted to an atavistic, uninspiring approach aimed at the wrong target" (Charnovitz 1994, 22).

14 In a landmark 1991 case, a GATT dispute resolution panel ruled that the United States could not impose a ban on tuna imported from Mexico because of fishing practices that threatened dolphins (Esty 1994, 27–32).

15 These transnational policy communities extend beyond government officials. There are strong bilateral organizational links among some environmental groups, and industry officials in the two countries frequently interact, either because Canadian firms are subsidiaries of American parent companies or through participation in related trade organizations. Policy analysts in Canadian and U.S. think-tanks also often share ideas.

16 The category of international influence is also intended to include the activity of interest groups such as Greenpeace that have effectively become international.

17 Several empirical observations support this claim. According to the Oxford University Press, *Our Common Future*, the report of the World Commission on Environment and Development, has sold 43,000 copies in Canada but only 34,000 in the United States, despite the market being ten times larger south of the border. A Lexis-Nexus search of two available newspaper databases shows that the term "sustainable development" occurred 580 times in Canadian Press wire stories over the period 1989 to August 1994, but only 84 times in the *New York Times*. A report by a prestigious U.S. commission that advocated adopting the language and ethic of sustainable development received remarkably little attention (National Commission on the Environment 1993).

18 The five-year average from 1987 to 1991 is 438 (U.S. Council of Environmental Quality 1992).

19 Many more "initial environmental assessments" are performed by individual agencies in Canada, but they are typically not nearly as elaborate and formal as NEPA statements. Recent court decisions have intensified Canadian assessment activity: the average number of reviews completed each year doubled from 1.9 before the first court decision to 3.8 since then (Grady 1994).

20 This analysis has been updated and expanded beyond that contained in Hoberg 1991b.

21 For an environmental criticism of Canada's performance on sewage treatment, see Sierra Legal Defence Fund 1994. A binational panel of scientists largely vindicated Victoria's argument that sewage treatment would have little environmental benefit. But this does not change the fact that U.S. cities across the Strait of Juan de Fuca, which face essentially the same environmental problem, have been required to install expensive treatment facilities.

22 The figure for all Canadian mills that had secondary treatment in 1987 was 28 per cent (Sinclair 1990, 166).

23 Compare the U.S. Code of Federal Regulations, volume 40, section 180, with the Canadian Food and Drug Regulations, division 15, table 2, for 1986. The more recent figures are for 1991 in Canada and 1992 in the United States. Note that these figures compare only those tolerances that the two countries have in common. There are many more legal applications of pesticides in the United States, largely because of the greater variation in crops and growing conditions.

24 From 1980 to 1992, the United States reduced its emissions of sulphur dioxide by 13 per cent; Canada by 36 per cent. Over the same period, U.S. emissions of nitrogen oxides decreased by 2 per cent; Canadian emissions increased 5 per cent. Over the period 1985–92, the United States reduced its emissions of volatile organic compounds by 9 per cent; Canada's remained unchanged (data for the United States from U.S. Environmental Protection Agency 1993b; for Canada from Environment Canada 1994a).

25 On the other hand, the United States deserves blame for exporting so much of its air and water pollution to Canada (Hoberg 1991b).

26 For instance, the United States had more than one hundred scrubbers – a technology that substantially reduces sulphur dioxide emissions – in place in 1984, while Canada had none. This fact was used to pressure the Canadian government into action: "One cannot go to the United States and demand that costly pollution controls be implemented when Canada's record is obviously deficient in a number of important areas" (Canada, House of Commons 1984, 41).

27 To encourage compliance with federal sewage treatment requirement, Congress created an $18 billion construction grant program that would pay for 75 per cent of the costs of constructing new sewage-treatment facilities. The construction grant program has become America's second largest public works program behind the highway system (Rosenbaum 1985, 167–73).

28 The United States accounts for about 90 per cent of the market for cars produced in North America. Approximately 80 per cent of the cars manufactured in Canada are exported to the United States; while 75 per cent of the vehicles sold in Canada are manufactured in the United States (Canada, Canadian House of Commons 1984, 16).

29 In addition to the GATT "tuna-dolphin" decision referred to in note 14 above, in January 1996 the recently created World Trade Organization ruled against a provision of the U.S. Clean Air Act on the grounds that it discriminated against foreign competitors (Sanger 1996).

CHAPTER TEN

1 For example, the opening chapter of a widely cited volume on comparative public policy was entitled "The End of Convergence" (Goldthorpe 1984). See also S. Berger 1981.

2 The most powerful recent manifestation of this concern was of course the soul-searching national debate on the Canada–United States Free Trade Agreement, a debate that went far beyond the narrowly trade-oriented terms of the agreement itself. The literature on this opposition is vast. See, for example, Bowker 1988; D. Cameron 1988; D. Cameron and Watkins 1993; and L. Martin 1993.

3 At the end of 1993, just under 15 per cent of the U.S. federal public debt was held by foreigners. In Canada, the figure for federal public debt was 26 per cent, with an even higher portion of the growing provincial debt held outside the country (Bank of Canada 1994, table G-5; Federal Reserve System 1994, A-30; Mendelson 1993).

4 As with virtually all important issues, there is not complete agreement on this point. For a view that is less optimistic about the ability of exchange rates to operate in this manner, see Harris 1993, 46–7.

5 For an interesting discussion of parallels in the approach to child care, see Teghtsoonian 1993.

6 With respect to rethinking the role of government, two U.S. publications – Osborne and Gaebler's *Reinventing Government* (1993) and the Gore report to President Clinton (U.S. National Performance Review 1993) – have become required reading for Canadian policy makers.

Bibliography

Aaron, H. 1996. "End of an Era: The New Debate over Health Care Financing." *Brookings Review* 13:35–7.

Aaron, H., B. Bosworth, and G. Burtless. 1989. *Can America Afford to Grow Old? Paying for Social Security.* Washington, DC: The Brookings Institution.

Aberbach, J.D. 1990. *Keeping a Watchful Eye: The Politics of Congressional Oversight.* Washington, DC: The Brookings Institution.

Abowitz, D.A. 1986. "Data Indicate the Feminization of Poverty in Canada Too." *Sociology and Social Research* 70:209–13.

Ackerman, B., and W. Hassler. 1981. *Clean Coal/Dirty Air.* New Haven: Yale University Press.

Adams, M. 1988. "Canadian and American Attitudes toward the Quality of Life." Paper presented at the annual meeting of the World Association for Public Opinion Research, Toronto.

– 1993a. "The Post-Modern Canadian." *Globe and Mail,* 12 August.

– 1993b. Personal communication. Results from the 3SC Social Values Monitor.

Adams, O. 1990. "Divorce Rates in Canada." In *Canadian Social Trends,* ed. C. McKie and K. Thompson. Toronto: Thompson Publishing.

Adams, O., and D. Nagnur. 1990. "Marrying and Divorcing: A Status Report for Canada." In *Canadian Social Trends,* ed. C. McKie and K. Thompson. Toronto: Thompson Publishing.

Adams, R. 1988. "North American Industrial Relations: Divergent Trends in Canada and the United States." Working Paper 307. Hamilton, Ont.: Faculty of Business, McMaster University.

Administrative Conference of the United States. 1990. *Negotiated Rulemaking Sourcebook.* Washington, DC: Government Printing Office.

Advisory Council on Adjustment. 1989. *Adjusting to Win.* Ottawa: Supply and Services Canada.

Agnew, J. 1987. *The United States in the World Economy: A Regional Geography.* New York: Cambridge University Press.

Ahlstrom, S.E. 1988. "National Trauma and Changing Religious Values." *Daedalus* 107:13–29.

Aitken, H. 1961. *American Capital and Canadian Resources.* Cambridge, Mass.: Harvard University Press.

Anderson, B. 1983. *Imagined Communities: Reflections on the Origin and Spread of Nationalism.* London: Verso.

Anderson, K., and R. Blackhurst, eds. 1993. *Regional Integration and the Global Trading System.* London: Harvester Wheatsheaf.

Andrew, C., and J. Morrison. 1995. "Canada Infrastructure Works: Between 'Pick and Shovels' and the Information Superhighway." In *How Ottawa Spends 1995–1996*, ed. S. Phillips. Ottawa: Carleton University Press.

Angus Reid Inc. 1991. *Multiculturalism and Canadians: Attitude Study 1991.* Ottawa: Multiculturalism and Citizenship Canada.

Archer, K., and F. Ellis. 1994. "Opinion Structure of Party Activists." *Canadian Journal of Political Science* 27 (June): 277–308.

Arnold, S.J., and J.G. Barnes. 1979. "Canadian and American National Characteristics as a Basis for Market Segmentation." In *Research in Marketing*, Vol. 2, ed. J. Sheth. Greenwich, Conn.: JAI Press.

Ashenfelter, O., and D. Card. 1986. "Why Have Unemployment Rates in Canada and the United States Diverged?" *Economica* 53 (supplement): S171–96.

Atkinson, M., ed. 1993. *Governing Canada: Institutions and Public Policy.* Toronto: Harcourt Brace Jovanovich.

Atkinson, M., and W. Coleman. 1989. *The State, Business, and Industrial Change in Canada.* Toronto: University of Toronto Press.

Aucoin, P. 1994. "Prime Minister and Cabinet." In *Canadian Politics*, ed. J.P. Bickerton and A.-G. Gagnon. Peterborough, Ont.: Broadview Press.

Audley, J. 1993. "Why Environmentalists are Angry about the North American Free Trade Agreement." In *Trade and the Environment*, ed. D. Zaehlke, P. Orbuch, and R. Houseman. Washington, DC: Island Press.

Bach, R.L. 1986. "Immigration: Issues of Ethnicity, Class and Public Policy." *Annals* 485:139–52.

Backhouse, C., and D.H. Flaherty, eds. 1992. *Challenging Times: The Women's Movement in Canada and the United States.* Montreal: McGill-Queen's University Press.

Badets, J. 1990. "Canada's Immigrant Population." In *Canadian Social Trends*, ed. C. McKie and K. Thompson. Toronto: Thompson Publishing.

Baer, D., E. Grabb, and W. Johnston. 1990. "Reassesing Difference in Canadian and American Values." In *Images of Canada, the Sociological Tradition*, ed. J. Curtis and L. Tepperman. Scarborough, Ont.: Prentice-Hall Canada Inc.

Bakan, J., and D. Schneiderman, eds. 1992. *Social Justice and the Constitution: Perspectives on a Social Union for Canada*. Ottawa: Carleton University Press.

Bakvis, H., ed. 1991. *Representation, Integration and Political Parties in Canada*. Research Studies of the Royal Commission on Electoral Reform and Party Financing, vol. 14. Toronto: Dundurn Press.

Bakvis, H., and D. Macdonald. 1993. "The Canadian Cabinet: Organization, Decision-Rules and Policy Impact." In *Governing Canada: Institutions and Public Policy*, ed. M. Atkinson. Toronto: Harcourt Brace Jovanovich.

Baldwin, J.R., and P.K. Gorecki. 1990. *Structural Change and the Adjustment Process: Perspectives on Firm Growth and Worker Turnover*. Ottawa: Statistics Canada and the Economic Council of Canada.

Baldwin, P. 1990. *The Politics of Social Solidarity: Class Bases of the European Welfare State, 1875–1975*. Cambridge: Cambridge University Press.

Bank of Canada. 1994. *Bank of Canada Review*. Summer. Ottawa: Bank of Canada.

Banting, K.G. 1979. *Poverty, Politics and Policy: Britain in the 1960s*. London: Macmillan.

– 1985. "Institutional Conservatism: Federalism and Pension Reform." In *Canadian Social Welfare Policy: Federal and Provincial Dimensions*, ed. J.S. Ismael. Montreal: McGill-Queen's University Press.

– 1987a. *The Welfare State and Canadian Federalism*. 2d ed. Montreal: McGill-Queen's University Press.

– 1987b. "The Welfare State and Inequality in the 1980s." *Canadian Review of Sociology and Anthropology* 24:309–38.

– 1992a. "Neoconservatism in an Open Economy: The Social Role of the Canadian State." *International Political Science Review* 13:149–70.

– 1992b. "Economic Integration and Policy Harmonization: Convergence and Divergence in Social Policy in Canada and the United States." In *Social Policy in the Global Economy*, ed. T. Hunsley. Kingston: School of Policy Studies, Queen's University.

– 1995a. "The Welfare State as Statecraft: Territorial Politics and Canadian Social Policy." In *European Social Policy: Between Fragmentation and Integration*, ed. S. Liebfried and P. Pierson. Washington, DC: The Brookings Institution.

– 1995b. "The Social Security Review: Policy-Making in a Semi-Sovereign State." *Canadian Public Administration* 38:283–90.

Banting, K.G., and K. Battle. 1994. *A New Social Vision for Canada? Perspectives on the Federal Discussion Paper on Social Security Reform*. Kingston: School of Policy Studies, Queen's University.

Banting, K., T.J. Courchene, and D.M. Brown, eds. 1994. *The Future of Fiscal Federalism*. Kingston: School of Policy Studies, Queen's University.

Bardach, E., and R. Kagan. 1982. *Going by the Book: The Problem of Regulatory Unreasonableness*. Philadelphia, Pa.: Temple University Press.

Barnet, R.J. 1993. "The End of Jobs." *Harper's*, September, 47–52.

Bashevkin, S. 1993. "Building a Political Voice: Women's Participation and Policy Influence in Canada." In *Women and Politics Worldwide*, ed. B. Nelson and N. Chowdhury. New Haven: Yale University Press.

Battle, K. 1992. "Critique of the 1992 Budget's New Child Tax Benefit." Ottawa: Caledon Institute for Social Policy.

Beach, C., and G. Slotsve. 1994. "Polarization of Earnings in the Canadian Labour Market." In *Stabilization, Growth and Distribution: Linkages in the Knowledge Era*, ed. T.J. Courchene. Kingston: John Deutsch Institute, Queen's University.

Beaujot, R. 1988. "The Family in Crisis?" *Canadian Journal of Sociology* 13:305–11.

– 1990. "The Family and Demographic Change in Canada: Economic and Cultural Interpretations and Solutions." *Journal of Comparative Family Studies* 21:25–38.

Beer, S. 1973. "The Modernization of American Federalism." *Publius* 3:49–96.

– 1978. "In Search of a New Public Philosophy." In *The New American Political System*, ed. A. King. Washington, DC: American Enterprise Institute.

– 1993. *To Make a Nation: The Rediscovery of American Federalism*. Cambridge, Mass.: Belknap Press.

Bellah, R., et al. 1985. *Habits of the Heart: Individualism and Commitment in American Life*. New York: Harper and Row.

Bence, J.-F., and M.G. Smith. 1989. "Subsidies and the Trade Laws: The Canada-U.S. Dimension." *International Economic Issues*, April–May, 67–71.

Bender, P. 1983. "The Canadian Charter of Rights and Freedoms and the United States Bill of Rights: A Comparison." *McGill Law Journal* 28:811–66.

Bennett, C. 1991a. "How States Utilize Foreign Evidence." *Journal of Public Policy* 11:31–54.

– 1991b. "Review Article: What is Policy Convergence and What Causes It?" *British Journal of Political Science* 21:215–33

– 1992. *Regulating Privacy: Data Protection and Public Policy in the United States*. Ithaca, NY: Cornell University Press.

Berger, R. 1977. *Government by Judiciary: The Transformation of the Fourteenth Amendment*. Cambridge, Mass.: Harvard University Press.

Berger, S., ed. 1981. *Organizing Interests in Western Europe: Pluralism, Corporatism and the Transformation of Politics*. New York: Cambridge University Press.

Bergmann, B.R. 1988. "A Workable Family Policy: Child Care, Income Supports, Jobs." *Dissent* 35:88–93.

Berry, J.M. 1984. *The Interest Group Society*. 2d ed. Glenview, Ill.: Scott Foresman.

– 1989. "Subgovernments, Issues, Networks and Political Conflict." In *Remaking American Politics*, ed. R.M. Harris and S.M. Milkis. Boulder: Westview Press.

Bibby, R. 1990. *Mosaic Madness: The Poverty and Potential of Life in Canada*. Toronto: Stoddart Publishing Co.

Bickerton, J.P., and A.-G. Gagnon, eds. 1994. *Canadian Politics.* 2d ed. Peterborough, Ont.: Broadview Press.

Bissoondath, N. 1994. *Selling Illusions: The Cult of Multiculturalism in Canada.* Toronto: Penguin Books.

Black, N. 1992. "Ripples in the Second Wave: Comparing the Contemporary Women's Movement in Canada and the United States." In *Challenging Times: The Women's Movement in Canada and the United States,* ed. C. Backhouse and D.H. Flaherty. Montreal: McGill-Queen's University Press.

Blackburn, M., and D. Bloom. 1993. "The Distribution of Family Income: Measuring and Explaining Changes in the 1980s for Canada and the United States." In *Small Differences that Matter: Labour Markets and Income Maintenance, in Canada and the United States,* ed. D. Card and R. Freeman. Chicago: University of Chicago Press.

Blais, A. 1986. "The Political Economy of Public Subsidies." *Comparative Political Studies* 19:201–16.

Blais, A., P. Faucher, and R. Young. 1986. "La dynamique de l'aide financière directe du gouvernement fédéral à l'industrie manufacturière du Canada." *Canadian Journal of Political Science* 19:29–52.

Blank, R., and M. Hanratty. 1993. "Responding to Need: A Comparison of Social Safety Nets in the United States and Canada." In *Small Differences that Matter: Labour Markets and Income Maintenance in Canada and the United States,* ed. D. Card and R. Freeman. Chicago: University of Chicago Press.

Blinder, A. 1979. *Economic Policy and the Great Stagflation.* New York: Academic Press.

Bliss, M. 1991. "Do No Harm." In *Essays on Canadian Public Policy,* ed. T.J. Courchene and A. Stewart. Kingston: School of Policy Studies, Queen's University.

Bluestone, B. 1992. *The Deindustrialization of America: Plant Clearings, Community Abandonment and the Dismantling of Basic Industries.* 2d ed. New York: Basic Books.

Boadway, R., and N. Bruce. 1992. "Pressures for the Harmonization of Income Taxation between Canada and the United States." In *Canada-U.S. Tax Comparisons,* ed. J. Shoven and J. Whalley. Chicago: University of Chicago Press.

Boddez, T., and M.J. Trebilcock. 1993. *Unfinished Business: Reforming Trade Remedy Laws in North America.* Toronto: C.D. Howe Institute.

Boone, K.C. 1989. *The Bible Tells Them So: The Discourse of Protestant Fundamentalism.* Albany, NY: State University of New York Press.

Boothe, P. 1991. "Interest Parity, Cointegration and the Term Structure in Canada and the United States." *Canadian Journal of Economics* 24:595–603.

Boothe, P., and S. Poloz. 1988. "Unstable Money Demand and the Monetary Model of the Exchange Rate." *Canadian Journal of Economics* 21:785–98.

Boothe, P., K. Clinton, A. Cote, and D. Longworth. 1986. *International Asset Substitutability: Theory and Evidence for Canada.* Ottawa: Bank of Canada.

Borins, S.F., and L. Brown. 1986. *Investments in Failure: Five Government Enterprises that Cost the Canadian Taxpayer Billions.* Toronto: Methuen.

Bovard, J. 1991. *The Fair Trade Fraud: How Congress Pillages the Consumer and Decimates American Competitiveness.* New York: St Martin's.

Bowker, M.M. 1988. *On Guard for Thee: An Independent Analysis Based on the Actual Text of the Free Trade Agreement.* Hull, Que.: Voyageur Publishing.

Bowles, S., and H. Gintis. 1982. "The Crisis of Liberal Democratic Capitalism: The Case of the United States." *Politics and Society* 11:51–93.

Boyer, B., and E. Meidinger. 1985. "Privatizing Regulatory Enforcement: A Preliminary Assessment of Citizen Suits under Federal Environmental Laws." *Buffalo Law Review* 34:833–964.

Brand, D.R. 1989. "Reformers of the 1960s and 1970s: Modern Anti-Federalists?" In *Remaking American Politics,* ed. R. Harris and S. Milkis. Boulder: Westview Press.

Bratt, H.A. 1982. "Issues in Worker Certification and Questions of Future Direction in the Trade Adjustment Assistance Program." *Law and Policy in International Business* 14:819–58.

Braudo, R. 1995. "Global Competition in the Technology Sector: Sematech and the Case for Competitive Industrial Policy." Paper prepared for the Conference on Competitive Industrial Development: The Role of Cooperation in the Technology Sector. Toronto: University of Toronto, Faculty of Law. 19 May.

Breton, R. 1988. "From Ethnic to Civic Nationalism: English Canada and Quebec." *Ethnic and Racial Studies* 11:85–102.

– 1992. *Why Meech Failed: Lessons for Canadian Constitution-Making.* Toronto: C.D. Howe Institute.

Brickman, R., S. Jasanoff, and T. Ilgen. 1985. *Controlling Chemicals: The Politics of Regulation in Europe and the United States.* Ithaca, NY: Cornell University Press.

Brock, K. 1993. "The Issue of Self-Government: Canadian and American Aboriginal Policy Compared." In *Canada and the United States: Differences that Count,* ed. D. Thomas. Peterborough, Ont.: Broadview Press.

Broder, D. 1971. *The Party's Over: The Failure of Politics in America.* New York: Harper and Row.

Brodie, I. 1992. *Interest Groups and the Charter of Rights and Freedoms: Interveners at the Supreme Court of Canada.* MA thesis, Department of Political Science, University of Calgary.

Brodie, I., and N. Nevitte. 1993. "Evaluating the Citizens' Constitution Theory." *Canadian Journal of Political Science* 26:235–59.

Brodie, J., with the assistance of Celia Chandler. 1991. "Women and the Electoral process in Canada." In *Women in Canadian Politics: Toward Equity in Representation,* ed. K. Megyery. Research Studies of the Royal Commission on Electoral Reform and Party Financing, vol. 6. Toronto: Dundurn Press.

Brooks, S., and A. Stritch. 1991. *Business and Government in Canada*. Scarborough, Ont.: Prentice-Hall Canada.

Bruce, P. 1989. "Political Parties and Labour Legislation in Canada and the United States." *Industrial Relations* 28:115–41.

Bryner, G. 1993. *Blue Skies, Green Politics: The Clean Air Act of 1990*. Washington, DC: CQ Press.

Burge, R. 1993. "A Question of Confidence: Revisited." Paper presented at the annual meeting of the Canadian Political Science Association, Ottawa.

Burnham, W.D. 1994. "Pattern Recognition and 'Doing' American Political History: Art, Science, or 'Bootless' Enterprise?" In *The Dynamics of American Politics: Approaches and Interpretation*, ed. L.C. Dodd and C. Jillson. Boulder: Westview Press.

Burns, J.M. 1984. *The Power to Lead: The Crisis of the American Presidency*. New York: Simon and Schuster.

Burt, S. 1986. "Women's Issues and the Women's Movement in Canada since 1970." In *The Politics of Gender, Ethnicity and Language in Canada*, ed. A. Cairns and C. Williams. Toronto: University of Toronto Press.

– 1990. "The Second Wave of the Canadian Women's Movement." In *Canadian Politics: An Introduction to the Discipline*, ed. A.-G. Gagnon and J. Bickerton. Peterborough, Ont.: Broadview Press.

Burt, S., L. Code, and L. Dorney, eds. 1988. *Changing Patterns: Women in Canada*. Toronto: McClelland & Stewart.

Burtless, G. 1991. "The Tattered Safety Net." *Brookings Review* 9:38–41.

Bushnell, S.I. 1986. "The Use of American Cases." *University of New Brunswick Law Journal* 35:157–81.

Caesar, J.W. 1990. "Political Parties: Declining, Stabilizing or Resurging?" In *The New American Political System*, 2d ed., ed. A. King. Washington, DC: American Enterprise Institute.

Caesar, J.W., and A. Busch. 1993. *Upside Down and Inside Out: The 1992 Elections and American Politics*. Lanham, Md: Rowman and Littlefield.

Cagan, P., ed. 1986. *The Impact of the Reagan Program*. Washington, DC: American Enterprise Institute.

Cairns, A.C. 1977. "The Governments and Societies of Canadian Federalism." *Canadian Journal of Political Science* 10:695–725.

– 1986. "The Embedded State: State-Society Relations in Canada." In *State and Society: Canada in Comparative Perspective*, ed. K.G. Banting. Toronto: University of Toronto Press.

– 1991. *Disruptions: Constitutional Struggles from the Charter to Meech Lake*. Toronto: McClelland & Stewart.

Cairns A.C., and C. Williams. 1986. *The Politics of Gender, Ethnicity and Language in Canada*. Research Studies of the Royal Commission on the Economic Union and Development Prospects for Canada, vol. 34. Toronto: University of Toronto Press.

Caldeira, G.A. 1988. "Legal Precedents: Structures of Communication between State Supreme Courts." *Social Networks* 10:29–55.

Cameron, D., ed. 1988. *The Free Trade Deal.* Toronto: James Lorimer.

– 1993. "Introduction." In *Canada under Free Trade,* ed. D. Cameron and M. Watkins. Toronto: James Lorimer.

Cameron, D., and M. Watkins. 1993. *Canada under Free Trade.* Toronto: James Lorimer.

Cameron, D.R. 1978. "The Expansion of the Public Economy: A Comparative Analysis." *American Political Science Review* 72:1243–61.

– 1986. "The Growth of Government Spending: The Canadian Experience in Comparative Perspective." In *State and Society: Canada in Comparative Perspective,* ed. K.G. Banting. Toronto: University of Toronto Press.

Canada. Advisory Council on Adjustment. 1989. *Adjusting to Win.* Ottawa: Minister of Supply and Services Canada.

– Canadian Panel on Violence against Women. 1993. *Final Report.* Ottawa: Minister of Supply and Services Canada.

– Citizens' Forum on Canada's Future (Spicer Commission). 1991. *Report.* Ottawa: Minister of Supply and Services Canada.

– Commission of Inquiry on Unemployment Insurance. 1986. *Report.* Ottawa: Minister of Supply and Services Canada.

– Department of Finance. 1994. *A New Framework for Economic Policy.* Ottawa: Department of Finance.

– Department of Finance. 1995. *Budget Plan: Including Supplementary Information and Notices of Ways and Means Motions.* Ottawa: Department of Finance.

– Department of Finance. 1996. *Budget Plan: Including Supplementary Information and Notices of Ways and Means Motion.* Ottawa: Department of Finance.

– Employment and Immigration Canada (Strategic Policy and Planning). 1992. *Program Evaluation Report, Canadian Jobs Strategy Evaluation Outcomes: Lessons Learned.* Ottawa. Unpublished.

– Environment Canada. 1990. *National Urban Air Quality Trends, 1978–1987.* EPS: 7/UP/3. May. Ottawa: Minister of Supply and Services Canada.

– Environment Canada. 1994a. Pollution Data Analysis Division, Personal Communication, 22 July 1994.

– Environment Canada. 1994b. *National Urban Air Quality Trends, 1981–1990.* EPS 7/UP/4. Ottawa: Minister of Supply and Services Canada.

– Health and Welfare Canada. 1987. *1986–87 Estimates, Part III, Expenditure Plan.* Ottawa: Minister of Supply and Services Canada.

– Health and Welfare Canada. 1989. *Social Security Statistics: Canada and the Provinces: 1963–64 to 1987–88.* Ottawa: Minister of Supply and Services Canada.

– Health and Welfare Canada. 1990. *National Health Expenditures in Canada, 1975–1987.* Ottawa: Minister of Supply and Services Canada.

– House of Commons. Standing Committee on Labour, Employment and Immigration. 1988. *A Review of the Canadian Jobs Strategy.* Ottawa: Minister of Supply and Services Canada.
– House of Commons. Subcommittee on Acid Rain. 1984. *Time Lost: A Demand for Action on Acid Rain.* Ottawa: Minister of Supply and Services Canada.
– Human Resources Development Canada. 1994. *Improving Social Security in Canada.* Ottawa: Minister of Supply and Services Canada.
– Human Resources Development Canada. 1995. *A 21st Century Employment System for Canada.* Ottawa: Minister of Supply of Services Canada.
– Industry Canada. 1994. *Building a More Innovative Economy.* Ottawa: Minister of Supply and Services Canada.
– Industry, Science and Technology Canada. 1991. *Selected Science and Technology Statistics.* Ottawa: Minister of Supply and Services Canada.
– Labour Canada. Bureau of Labour Information. 1995. *Directory of Labour Organizations in Canada 1994–1995.* Ottawa: Canadian Government Publishing Centre.
– Royal Commission on Aboriginal Peoples. 1993. *Partners in Confederation: Aboriginal Peoples, Self-Government and the Constitution.* Ottawa: Minister of Supply and Services Canada.
– Royal Commission on the Economic Union and Development Prospects for Canada (Macdonald Commission). 1985. *Report.* Ottawa: Minister of Supply and Services Canada.
– Royal Commission on Electoral Reform. 1991. *Report.* Ottawa: Minister of Supply and Services Canada.
– Royal Commission on Employment Equity. 1982. *Report.* Ottawa: Minister of Supply and Services Canada.
– Royal Commission on the Status of Women. 1973. *Report.* Ottawa: Minister of Supply and Services Canada.
– Special Joint Committee on a Renewed Canada. 1992. Ottawa: Minister of Supply and Services Canada.
Canada 21 Council. 1994. *Canada and Common Security in the Twenty-First Century.* Toronto: Centre for International Studies.
Canadian Institute of Actuaries. 1993. *Canadian Retirement Income Social Security Programs.* Toronto: Canadian Istitute of Actuaries.
Caplow, T., et al. 1991. *Recent Social Trends in the United States, 1960–1990.* Montreal: McGill-Queen's University Press.
Card, D., and R. Freeman, eds. 1993. *Small Differences that Matter: Labour Markets and Income Maintenance in Canada and the United States.* Chicago: University of Chicago Press.
Card, D., and C. Riddell. 1993. "A Comparative Analysis of Unemployment in Canada and the United States." In *Small Differences that Matter: Labour Markets and Income Maintenance in Canada and the United States,* ed. D. Card and R. Freeman. Chicago: University of Chicago Press.

Carmines, E., and J. Stimson. 1989. *Issue Evolution: Race and the Transformation of American Politics*. Princeton, NJ: Princeton University Press.

Center on Budget and Policy Priorities and Center for the Study of the States. 1991. *The States and the Poor: How Budget Decisions in 1991 Affected Low Income People*. Washington, DC.

Chaison, G.N., and J.B. Rose. 1988. "Continental Divide: The Direction and Fate of North American Unions." Working Paper 309. Hamilton, Ont.: Faculty of Business, McMaster University.

Charnovitz, S. 1993. "NAFTA: An Analysis of Its Environmental Provisions." *Environment Law Reporter* 23:10067–73.

– 1994. "The NAFTA Environmental Side Agreement and Its Implications for Environmental Cooperation, Trade Policy, and American Treatymaking." *Temple International and Comparative Law Journal* 8:257–314.

Chayes, A. 1976. "The Role of the Judge in Public Law Litigation." *Harvard Law Review* 89:1281–316.

Chiswick, B., ed. 1992. *Immigration, Language and Ethnicity: Canada and the United States*. Washington, DC: American Enterprise Institute.

Chubb, J.E., and P. Peterson, eds. 1989. *Can the Government Govern?* Washington, DC: The Brookings Institution.

Citrin, J. 1974. "Comment: The Political Relevance of Trust in Government." *American Political Science Review* 68:973–88.

Clarke, H.D., J. Jenson, L. LeDuc, and J. Pammett. 1991. *Absent Mandate: Interpreting Change in Canadian Elections*. 2d ed. Toronto: Gage.

Clarke, H.D., E.W. Elliott, W. Mishler, M.C. Stewart, P.F. Whiteley, and G. Zuk. 1992. *Controversies in Political Economy: Canada, Great Britain and the United States*. Boulder: Westview Press.

Clarkson, S. 1985. *Canada and the Reagan Challenge: Crisis and Adjustment, 1981–85*. Toronto: James Lorimer.

Coder, J., T. Smeeding, and B. Torrey. 1990. "The Change in the Economic Status of the Low-Income Elderly in Three Industrial Countries: Circa 1977–1986." Paper for the annual research conference of the Bureau of the Census, Washington, DC.

Cohen, L., and R. Noll, eds. 1991. *The Technology Pork Barrel*. Washington, DC: The Brookings Institution.

Cohen, M.G. 1992. "The Canadian Women's Movement and Its Efforts to Influence the Canadian Economy." In *Challenging Times: The Women's Movement in Canada and the United States*, ed. C. Backhouse and D.H. Flaherty. Montreal: McGill-Queen's University Press.

Cohen, R. 1992. *Washington at Work: Back Rooms and Clean Air*. New York: Macmillan.

Coleman, J.S. 1988. "Social Capital in the Creation of Human Capital." *American Journal of Sociology (supplement)* 94:S95–S120.

– 1990. *The Foundations of Social Theory.* Cambridge, Mass.: Harvard University Press.

Coleman, W.D. 1989. "Monetary Policy in Canada and the United States: An Examination of Policy Networks." Paper presented at a Conference on Policy Networks, Max Planck Institute. December. Mimeo.

– 1991. "Fencing Off: Central Banks and Networks in Canada and the United States." In *Policy Networks: Empirical Evidence and Theoretical Considerations*, ed. B. Marin and R. Mayntz. Boulder: Westview Press.

Coleman, W.D., and G. Skogstad, eds. 1990a. *Organized Interests and Public Policy.* Toronto: Copp Clark Pitman.

– eds. 1990b. *Policy Communities and Public Policy in Canada.* Toronto: Copp Clark Pitman.

Colombo, J. 1974. *Colombo's Canadian Quotations.* Edmonton: Hurtig.

Compas Inc. 1995. *The Business Agenda.* Ottawa: Compas Inc.

Competitiveness Policy Council. 1993. *A Comprehensive Strategy for America: Second Report to the President and Congress.* Washington, DC: U.S. Government Printing Office.

Conlan, T. 1988. *New Federalism: Intergovernmental Reform from Nixon to Reagan.* Washington, DC: The Brookings Institution.

Converse, P.E. 1964. "The Nature of Belief Systems in Mass Publics." In *Ideology and Discontent*, ed. D.E. Apter. New York: The Free Press.

Cooper, P.J. 1988. *Hard Judicial Choices: Federal District Court Judges and State and Local Officials.* New York: Oxford University Press.

Council of Economic Advisors. 1992. *Economic Report of the President 1992.* Washington, DC: U.S. Government Printing Office.

– 1994. *Economic Report of the President 1994.* Washington, DC: U.S. Government Printing Office.

Council on Competitiveness. 1989. *Governing America: A Competitiveness Policy Agenda for the New Administration.* Washington, DC: U.S. Government Printing Office.

– 1991. *Gaining New Ground.* Washington, DC: U.S. Government Printing Office.

Courchene, T.J. 1976. *Money, Inflation and the Bank of Canada: An Analysis of Canadian Monetary Policy from 1970 to Early 1975.* Toronto: C.D. Howe Institute.

– 1983. *No Place to Stand? Abandoning Monetary Targets: An Evaluation.* Toronto: C.D. Howe Institute.

– 1991. *Rearrangements.* Oakville, Ont.: Mosaic Press.

– 1992. "Mon pays, c'est l'hiver: Reflections of a Market Populist." *Canadian Journal of Economics* 25:759–91.

– 1994. *Social Canada in the Millennium.* Toronto: C.D. Howe Institute.

Courchene, T.J., and A. Stewart, eds. 1991. *Essays on Canadian Public Policy.* Kingston: School of Policy Studies, Queen's University.

Cover, R.M. 1982. "The Origins of Judicial Activism in the Protection of Minorities." *Yale Law Journal* 91:1287–316.

Cox, G., and S. Kernell, eds. 1991. *The Politics of Divided Government*. Boulder: Westview Press.

Coyne, D. 1993. *Seven Fateful Challenges for Canada: A Viable and Dynamic Canada in an Interdependant World.* Montreal: Robert Davies.

Coyte, P., et al. 1994. "Waiting Times for Knee-Replacement Surgery in the United States and Ontario." *New England Journal of Medicine* 331:1068–71.

Crane, D. 1992. *The Next Canadian Century: Building a Competitive Economy.* Toronto: Stoddart.

Crispo, J., ed. 1988. *Free Trade: The Real Story.* Toronto: Gage.

Cronin, T.E. 1989. *Direct Democracy: The Politics of Initiative, Referendum and Recall.* Cambridge, Mass.: Harvard University Press.

Crotty, W.J. 1984. *American Parties in Decline.* 2d ed. Boston: Little Brown.

Crovitz, G., and J. Rabkin, eds. 1989. *The Fettered Presidency: Legal Constraints on the Executive Branch.* Washington, DC: American Enterprise Institute.

Cuomo Commission on Trade and Competitiveness. 1988. *The Cuomo Commission Report: A New American Formula for a Strong Economy.* New York: Simon & Schuster.

Cushman, J. 1994. "Clinton Seeks Tougher Treaty on Clean Air." *New York Times,* 16 August.

Dalton, R.J. 1988. *Citizen Politics in Western Democracies: Public Opinion and Political Parties in the United States, Great Britain, West Germany and France.* Chatham, NJ: Chatham House.

Daniels, R.J., and R. Morck. 1995. "Canadian Corporate Governance: The Challenge." In *Corporate Decision-Making in Canada,* ed. R.J. Daniels and R. Morck. Calgary: University of Calgary Press.

Danziger, S., and P. Gottschalk, eds. 1993. *Uneven Tides: Rising Inequality in America.* New York: Russell Sage Foundation.

Davidson, R., ed. 1992. *The Postreform Congress.* New York: St Martin's Press.

Davis, L. 1991. "Technology Intensity of U.S., Canadian, and Japanese Manufactures' Output and Exports." In *Technology and National Competitiveness: Oligopoly, Technological Innovation and International Competition,* ed. J. Nioso. Montreal: McGill-Queen's University Press.

Days, D.S., III. 1984. "Civil Rights in Canada: An American Perspective." *American Journal of Comparative Law* 32:307–38.

Decima Research. 1993. *Report on Attitudes towards Race and Ethnic Relations in Canada.* Toronto: Canadian Council of Christians and Jews.

Denny, M., and T. Wilson. 1993. "Productivity and Growth: Canada's Competitive Position." In *Productivity, Growth and Canada's International Competitiveness,* ed. T.J. Courchene and D.D. Purvis. Kingston: John Deutsch Institute, Queen's University.

Derthick, M. 1979. *Policymaking for Social Security.* Washington, DC: The Brookings Institution.

De Seve, M. 1992. "The Perspectives of Quebec Feminists." In *Challenging Times: The Women's Movement in Canada and the United States,* ed. C. Backhouse and D.H. Flaherty. Montreal: McGill-Queen's University Press.

DeSilva, A. 1992. *Earnings of Immigrants: A Comparative Analysis.* Ottawa: Economic Council of Canada/Supply and Services Canada.

de Tocqueville, A. 1945. *Democracy in America,* trans. Henry Reeve, ed. Phillips Bradley. New York: Vintage Books.

Deutsch, K. 1963. *The Nerves of Government: Models of Political Communication and Control.* New York: Free Press.

Devereaux, M.S. 1990. "Changes in Living Arrangements" and "Marital Status." In *Canadian Social Trends,* ed. C. McKie and K. Thompson. Toronto: Thompson Publishing.

Dewitt, D., and J. Kirton. 1983. *Canada as a Principal Power: A study in Foreign Policy and International Relations.* Toronto: Wiley & Sons Canada.

Diamond, S. 1994. *Spiritual Warfare.* Boston: South End Press.

Dion, S. 1992. "Explaining Quebec Nationalism." In *The Collapse of Canada?,* ed. R.K. Weaver. Washington, DC: The Brookings Institution.

– 1993. "La secession du Quebec: Evaluation des probabilités après les élections fédérales du 25 Octobre, 1993." Paper presented at a colloquium, Centre for Research on North America, Autonomous National University of Mexico.

Diver, C.S. 1979. "The Judge as Political Powerbroker: Superintending Structural Change in Public Institutions." *Virginia Law Review* 65:43–106.

Dodd, L.C. 1994. "Political Learning and Political Change: Understanding Development across Time." In *The Dynamics of American Politics: Approaches and Interpretation,* ed. L.C. Dodd and C. Jillson. Boulder: Westview Press.

Dodd, L.C., and B.I. Oppenheimer, eds. 1989. *Congress Reconsidered.* 4th ed. Washington, DC: Congressional quarterly.

Doern, G.B. 1987. "The Political Administration of Government Reorganization: The Merger of DREE and ITC." *Canadian Public Administration* 30:34–56.

– ed. 1990a. *Getting It Green: Case Studies in Canadian Environmental Regulation.* Toronto: C.D. Howe Institute.

– 1990b. "Regulations and Incentives: The NOX-VOCs Case." In *Getting It Green: Case Studies in Canadian Environmental Regulation,* ed. G. Bruce Doern. Toronto: C.D. Howe Institute.

– 1993. *Green Diplomacy: How Environmental Policy Decisions Are Made.* Policy Study 16. Toronto: C.D. Howe Institute.

Doern, G.B., and B.W. Tomlin. 1995. "The Internationalization of Canadian Trade and Industrial Policy." Paper presented to the Conference on the

Internationalization of Canadian Public Policy, School of Public Administration and School of International Affairs. Ottawa: Carleton University.

Domke, W., R. Eichenberg, and C. Kelleher. 1983. "The Illusion of Choice: Defense and Welfare in Advanced Industrial Democracies, 1948–1978." *American Political Science Review* 77:19–35.

Drover, G., ed. 1988. *Free Trade and Social Policy.* Ottawa: Canadian Council on Social Development.

Dunlap, R. 1989. "Public Opinion and Environmental Policy." In *Environmental Politics and Policy: Theories and Evidence,* ed. J.P. Lester. Durham, NC: Duke University Press.

Dunlap, R., G. Gallup, Jr, and A. Gallup. 1992. *The Health of the Planet Survey.* Princeton, NJ: The George H. Gallup International Institute.

Dwivedi, O.P. 1974. "Canadian Governmental Response to Environmental Concern." In *Protecting the Environment: Issues and Choices, Canadian Perspectives,* ed. O.P. Dwivedi. Vancouver: Copp Clark.

Dwivedi, O.P., and R.B. Woodrow. 1989. "Environmental Policy-Making and Administration in a Federal State: The Impact of Overlapping Jurisdiction in Canada." In *Challenges to Federalism: Policy-Making in Canada and the Federal Republic of Germany,* ed. W. Chandler and C. Zollner. Kingston: Institute of Intergovernmental Relations, Queen's University.

Economic Council of Canada. 1988a. *Adjustment Policies for Trade-Sensitive Industries.* Ottawa: Minister of Supply and Services Canada.

– 1988b. *Back to Basics: Twenty-Fifth Annual Review.* Ottawa: Minister of Supply and Services Canada.

– 1988c. *Venturing Forth: An Assessment of the Canada-U.S. Trade Agreement.* Ottawa: Minister of Supply and Services Canada.

– 1989a. *Legacies: Twenty-Sixth Annual Review.* Ottawa: Minister of Supply and Services Canada.

– 1989b. *A New Frontier: Globalization and Canada's Financial Markets.* Ottawa: Minister of Supply and Services Canada.

– 1990. *Good Jobs, Bad Jobs: Employment in the Service Economy.* Ottawa: Minister of Supply and Services Canada.

– 1991a. *New Faces in the Crowd: Economic and Social Aspects of Immigration.* Ottawa: Minister of Supply and Services Canada.

– 1991b. *Economic and Social Impacts of Immigration.* Research Report. Ottawa: Minister of Supply and Services Canada.

– 1992. *Pulling Together: Productivity, Innovation and Trade.* Ottawa: Minister of Supply and Services Canada.

Economist, The. 1991. "Survey of America." 26 October.

– 1992. "The Godly Right Gears Up." 5 December, 25–6.

– 1994. "Measuring Crime." 15 October, 21–4.

Edsall, T.B. 1984. *The New Politics of Inequality.* New York: W.W. Norton.

Edsall, T.B., with M. Edsall. 1991. *Chain Reaction: The Impact of Race, Rights and Taxes on American Politics.* New York: W.W. Norton.

Eggleton, A. 1995. "Infrastructure in Canada." *Policy Options* 16:12–15.

Ehrenhalt, A. 1991. *The United States of Ambition: Politics, Power and the Pursuit of Office.* New York: Times Books.

Eichler, M. 1990. "Dilemmas in Matching Policies to Changing Families: Canada and the United States of America." Paper prepared for the Joint Center for Political and Economic Studies. Washington, DC.

Elliott, J.L., and A. Fleras. 1990. "Immigration and the Canadian Ethnic Mosaic." In *Race and Ethnic Relations in Canada,* ed. P.S. Li. Toronto: Oxford University Press.

Elliott, E.D., B. Ackerman, and J. Millian. 1985. "Toward a Theory of Statutory Evolution: The Federalization of Environmental Law." *Journal of Law, Economics, and Organization* 1:313–40.

Ely, J.H. 1980. *Democracy and Distrust: A Theory of Judicial Review.* Cambridge, Mass.: Harvard University Press.

Esping-Andersen, G. 1990. *The Three Worlds of Welfare Capitalism.* Princeton, NJ: Princeton University Press.

Esping-Anderson, G., and W. Korpi. 1984. "Social Policy as Class Politics in Post-War Capitalism: Scandinavia, Austria, and Germany." In *Order and Conflict in Contemporary Capitalism,* ed. J.H. Goldthorpe. Oxford: Oxford University Press.

Estrin, D., and J. Swaigen. 1993. *Environment on Trial: A Guide to Ontario Environmental Law and Policy.* 3d ed. Toronto: Edmond Montgomery Publications Ltd.

Esty, D.C. 1994. *Greening the GATT: Trade, Environment, and the Future.* Washington, DC: Institute for International Economics.

Evans, P., D. Rueschemeyer, and T. Skocpol, eds. 1985. *Bringing the State Back In.* Cambridge, Mass.: Harvard University Press.

Evans, P., H. Jacobson, and R. Putnam. 1993. *Double-Edged Diplomacy: International Bargaining and Domestic Politics.* Berkeley: University of California Press.

Evans, R. 1986. "Finding the Levers, Finding the Courage: Lessons from Cost Containment in North America." *Journal of Health Politics, Policy and Law* 11:585–615.

Evans., R., M. Barer, and C. Hertzman. 1991. "The 20-year Experiment: Accounting for Explaining and Evaluating Health Care Costs in Canada and the United States." *Annual Review of Public Health* 12:481–518.

Evans, S.M. 1992. "The Women's Movement in the United States in the 1960s." In *Challenging Times: The Women's Movement in Canada and the United States,* ed. C. Backhouse and D. Flaherty. Montreal: McGill-Queen's University Press.

Fausold, M., and A. Shank, eds. 1991. *The Constitution and the American Presidency.* Albany, NY: State University of New York Press.

Federal-Provincial Advisory Committee on Air Quality. 1988. *Discussion Paper on Air Quality Management Strategies Based on National Air Quality Objectives.* Saint John, NB, May.

Federal Reserve System. 1994. *Federal Reserve Bulletin.* Washington, DC: Federal Reserve System. September.

Feigenbaum, H., R. Samuels, and R.K. Weaver. 1993. "Innovation, Coordination, and Implementation in Energy Policy." In *Do Institutions Matter? Government Capabilities in the United States and Abroad,* ed. R.K. Weaver and B. Rockman. Washington, DC: The Brookings Institution.

Ferejohn, J. 1983. "Congress and Redistribution." In *Making Economic Policy in Congress,* ed. A. Schick. Washington, DC: American Enterprise Institute.

Fiorina, M. 1991. "Divided Government in the States." In *The Politics of Divided Government,* ed. G. Cox and S. Kernell. Boulder: Westview Press.

Fiorino, D. 1988. "Regulatory Negotiation as a Policy Process." *Public Administration Review* 48:764–72.

– 1990. "Dimensions of Negotiated Rule-Making: Practical Constraints and Theoretical Implications." In *Conflict Resolution and Public Policy,* ed. M.K. Mills. New York: Greenwood Press.

Firebaugh, G., and K. Davis. 1988. "Trends in Anti-Black Prejudice: Region and Cohort Effects." *American Journal of Sociology* 94:251–72.

Fisher, L.K. 1991. "The Constitution and Presidential Budget Powers: The Modern Era." In *The Constitution and the American Presidency,* ed. M. Fausold and A. Shank. Albany, NY: State University of New York Press.

Fishlow, A., and S. Haggard. 1992. *The United States and the Regionalisation of the World Economy.* Paris: Organization for Economic Cooperation and Development.

Flanagan, T., R. Knopff, and K. Archer. 1988. "Selection Bias in Human Rights Tribunals: An Exploratory Study." *Canadian Public Administration* 31:483–500.

Floyd, J. 1992. "Stochastic Interdependence of National Monetary Policy: Theory, Evidence and Implications." Mimeo.

Forbes, H.D. 1978. "Hartz-Horowitz at Twenty: Nationalism, Toryism and Socialism in Canada and the United States," *Canadian Journal of Political Science.* 20:287–315.

Fortin, P. 1994. "Slow Growth, Unemployment and Debt: What Happened? What Can We Do?" In *Stabilization, Growth and Distribution: Linkages in the Knowledge Era,* ed. T.J. Courchene. Kingston: John Deutsch Institute, Queen's University.

Fortin, P., and K. Newton. 1982. "Labour Market Tightness and Wage Inflation in Canada." In *Workers, Jobs and Inflation,* ed. M.N. Bailey. Washington, DC: The Brookings Institution.

Fosler, R.S. 1988. *The New Economic Role of American States: Strategies in a Competitive World Economy.* New York and Oxford: Oxford University Press.

– 1989. "State Economic Policy." *Business and the Contemporary World*, Summer, 94–101.

Fox, B.J., and J. Fox. 1987. "Occupational Gender Segregation in the Canadian Labour Force, 1931–1981." *Canadian Review of Sociology and Anthropology* 24:374–97.

Franks, C.E.S. 1987. *The Parliament of Canada.* Toronto: University of Toronto Press.

– 1991. "Decision Processes and Decision Rules: Canada's Problem?" Paper presented to the Western Social Science Association, Reno, Nev.

Franson, M.A.H., R.T. Franson, and A.R. Lucas. 1982. *Environmental Standards.* ECA83-SP/1. Edmonton: Environment Council of Alberta.

Freedman, C. 1983. "Financial Innovation in Canada: Causes and Consequences." *American Economic Review* 73:101–6.

French, M., and P. Jarrett. 1993. "The United States: Restoring Productivity Growth," *OECD Observer* 185:46–48.

Frideres, J. 1990. "Policies on Indian People in Canada." In *Race and Ethnic Relations in Canada*, ed. P.S. Li. Toronto: Oxford University Press.

Friedman, L., R. Kagan, B. Cartwright, and S. Wheeler. 1981. "State Supreme Courts: A Century of Style and Citation." *Stanford Law Review* 33:773–818.

Friedman, M. 1980. "Religion and Politics in an Age of Pluralism, 1845–1976: An Ethno-cultural View." *Publius* 10:45–75.

Fry, E. 1990a. *Subsidies and International Trade: The Provincial and State Dimensions.* Halifax: Institute for Research on Public Policy.

– 1990b. "Trade and Investment Promotion in the United States: New Frontiers." In *Canadian Federalism: Meeting Global Challenges?*, ed. D.M. Brown and M. Smith. Kingston: Institute of Intergovernmental Relations, Queen's University.

Furstenberg, F. 1990. "Divorce and the American Family." *Annual Review of Sociology* 16:379–403.

Gadd, J. 1995. "Ontario, Michigan Welfare Standards Show Bold Contrast." *Globe and Mail,* 4 November.

Gagnon, A.-G., and J. Bickerton. 1990. *Canadian Politics: An Introduction to the Discipline.* Peterborough, Ont.: Broadview Press.

Galanter, M. 1974. "Why the 'Haves' Come Out Ahead: Speculations on the Limits of Legal Change." *Law and Society Review* 9:95–160.

Gates, H.L. 1992. "Black Demagogues and Pseudo-Scholars." *New York Times,* 20 July.

Gertler, F., P. Muldoon, and M. Valiente. 1990. "Public Access to Environmental Justice." In *Report of the Canadian Bar Association Committee on Sustainable Development in Canada: Options for Law Reform*, ed. Canadian Bar Association. Ottawa: CBA.

Gertler, M.S. 1991. "Canada in a High-Tech World: Options for Industrial Policy." In *The New Era of Global Competition: State Policy and Market Power*, ed. D. Drache and M.S. Gertler. Montreal: McGill-Queen's University Press.

Gestrin, M., and A.M. Rugman. 1993. *The NAFTA's Impact on the North American Investment Regime.* C.D. Howe Institute Commentary no. 42. Toronto: C.D. Howe Institute.

Gibbins, R. 1982. *Regionalism: Territorial Politics in Canada and the United States.* Toronto: Butterworths.

Gill, S., and D. Law. 1988. *The Global Political Economy: Perspectives, Problems and Policies.* Baltimore: Johns Hopkins University Press.

Gillespie, E., and B. Schellhas, eds. 1994. *Contract with America.* New York: Random House, Times Books.

Gillroy, J.M., and R.Y. Shapiro. 1986. "The Polls: Environmental Protection." *Public Opinion Quarterly* 50:270–9.

Gilpin, R. 1987. *The Political Economy of International Relations.* Princeton, NJ: Princeton University Press.

Glendon, M.A. 1991. *Rights Talk: The Impoverishment of Political Discourse in the United States.* New York: The Free Press.

Glenn, N. 1987. "Continuity versus Change: Sanguineness versus Concern: Views of the American Family in the Late 1980s." *Journal of Family Issues* 8:348–54.

Glick, P.C. 1990. "American Families: As They Are and Were." *Sociology and Social Research* 74:139–45.

Gold, A.D. 1982. "The Legal Rights Provisions – A New Vision or Déjà Vu." *Supreme Court Law Review* 4:107–30.

Gold, M., and D. Leyton-Brown. 1988. *Trade-Offs on Free Trade: The Canada-U.S. Free Trade Agreement.* Toronto: Carswell.

Goldfarb, M. 1992. "Blacks, Other Minorities Need Employment Equity." *Toronto Star,* 24 June.

Goldstein, J., and R.O. Keohane. 1993. *Ideas and Foreign Policy: Beliefs, Institutions, and Political Change.* Ithaca: Cornell University Press.

Goldthorpe, J.H. 1984. "The End of Convergence: Corporatist and Dualist Tendencies in Modern Western Societies." In *Order and Conflict in Contemporary Capitalism,* ed. J.H. Goldthorpe. Oxford: University of Oxford Press.

Gordon, M.M. 1981. "Models of Pluralism: The New American Dilemma." *Annals* 454:178–88.

Gordon, R. 1992. "Canada-U.S. Free Trade and Pressures for Tax Coordination." In *Canada-U.S. Tax Comparisons,* ed. J. Shoven and J. Whalley. Chicago: University of Chicago Press.

Gough, I. 1980. *The Political Economy of the Welfare State.* London: Macmillan.

Gould, S., and J. Palmer. 1988. "Outcomes, Interpretations and Policy Implications." In *The Vulnerable,* ed. J. Palmer, T. Smeeding, and B. Torrey. Washington, DC: Urban Institute Press.

Gourevitch, P. 1978. "The Second Image Reversed: The International Sources of Domestic Politics." *International Organization* 32:881–911.

- 1986. *Politics in Hard Times: Comparative Responses to International Economic Crises*. Ithaca: Cornell University Press.

Grady, K. 1994. Federal Environmental Assessment Review Office. Personal communication, 8 August.

Graham, E., and M. Ebert. 1991. "Foreign Direct Investment and U.S. National Security in Fixing Exon Files." *World Economy in Perspective: Essays on International Trade and European Integration.*

Graham, O., Jr. 1992. *Losing Time: The Industrial Policy Debate*. Cambridge, Mass.: Harvard University Press.

Granatstein, J.L., and N. Hillmer. 1991. *For Better or for Worse: Canada and the United States to the 1990s*. Toronto: Copp Clark Pitman.

Grant, G. 1965. *Lament for a Nation: The Defeat of Canadian Nationalism*. Toronto: McClelland & Stewart.

Grant, W. 1989. *Government and Industry: A Comparative Analysis of the U.S., Canada, and the UK.* Aldershot: Edward Elgar.

Gray, G. 1991. *Federalism and Health Policy: The Development of Health Care Systems in Canada and Australia*. Toronto: University of Toronto Press.

Great Lakes Water Quality Board. 1989. *1989 Report on Great Lakes Water Quality.* Report to the International Joint Commission, presented at Hamilton, Ont., October.

Green, D., and C. Riddell. 1992. "The Economic Effects of Unemployment Insurance: An Empirical Analysis of UI Disentitlement." UBC Discussion Paper 92–15. Vancouver: Department of Economics, University of British Columbia.

Greenberg, E.S. 1994. "Macroeconomic Change and Political Transformation in the United States." In *The Dynamics of American Politics: Approaches and Interpretations*, ed. L.C. Dodd and C. Jillson. Boulder: Westview Press.

Gregg, A., and M. Posner. 1990. *The Big Picture: What Canadians Think about Almost Everything*. Toronto: Macfarlane, Walter, and Ross.

Grofman, B. 1992. "What Happens After One Person-One Vote? Implications of the United States Experience for Canada." In *Drawing Boundaries: Legislatures, Courts, and Electoral Values*, ed. J.C. Courtney, P. MacKinnon, and D.E. Smith. Saskatoon: Fifth House Publishers.

Guillateri, R. 1994. "Science Policy and Basic Research in Canada." In *How Ottawa Spends 1994–95: Making Change*, ed. S. Phillips. Ottawa: Carleton University Press.

Guinier, L. 1991. "No Two Seats: The Elusive Quest for Political Equality." *Virginia Law Review* 77:1413–514.

- 1994. *The Tyranny of the Majority: Fundamental Fairness in Representative Democracy*. New York: The Free Press.

Gunther, G. 1972. "The Supreme Court, 1971 Term-Forward: In Search of Evolving Doctrine on a Changing Court: A Model for Newer Equal Protection." *Harvard Law Review* 86:1–48.

Gusella, M. 1992. "Institutional Change in the 1990s: Public Administration Challenges." Presentation at the Canadian Centre for Management Development, 26 November.

Haas, P. 1992. "Banning Chlorofluorocarbons: Epistemic Community Efforts to Protect Stratospheric Ozone." *International Organization* 46:187–224.

Haas, P., M. Levy, and E. Parson. 1992. "Appraising the Earth Summit: How Should We Judge UNCED's Success?" *Environment* 34:6–11, 26–33.

Hacker, A. 1992. *Two Nations: Black and White, Separate, Hostile and Unequal.* New York: Charles Scribners and Sons.

Hadden, S. 1989. *A Citizen's Right to Know: Risk Communication and Public Policy.* Boulder: Westview Press.

Hadden, J.K., and A. Shupe. 1988. *Televangelism: Power and Politics on God's Frontier.* New York: Henry Holt and Co.

Haddow, R. 1991. "The Canadian Labour Congress and the Welfare State Debate." Paper presented to the Canadian Political Science Association meetings, Kingston.

– 1995. "Canada's Experiment with Labour Market Neocorporatism." In *Labour Market Polarization and Social Policy Reform,* ed. K. Banting and C. Beach. Kingston: School of Policy Studies, Queen's University.

Halberstam, D. 1993. *The Fifties.* New York: Villard Books.

Hall, P. 1986. *Governing the Economy: The Politics of State Intervention in Britain and France.* New York: Oxford University Press.

– ed. 1989. *The Power of Economic Ideas: Keynesianism across Nations.* Princeton, NJ: Princeton University Press.

– 1993. "Policy Paradigms, Social Learning, and the State: The Case of Economic Policymaking in Britain." *Comparative Politics,* April, 275–96.

Hamilton, R., and M. Barrett. 1986. *The Politics of Diversity: Feminism, Marxism and Nationalism.* London: Verso.

Hanratty, M., and R. Blank. 1992. "Down and Out in North America: Recent Trends in Poverty Rates in the U.S. and Canada." *Quarterly Journal of Economics* 58:233–54.

Hansen, L., and J. Byers, eds. 1990. *Unemployment Insurance: The Second Half-Century.* Madison, Wis.: University of Wisconsin Press.

Harrington, M. 1984. *The New American Poverty.* New York: Holt, Rienhart, and Winston.

Harris, R. 1985. *Trade, Industrial Policy and International Competition.* Toronto: University of Toronto Press.

– 1993. *Trade, Money and Wealth in the Canadian Economy.* Toronto: C.D. Howe Institute.

Harris, R., and S. Milkis. 1989a. *The Politics of Regulatory Change: A Tale of Two Agencies.* New York: Oxford University Press.

– eds. 1989b. *Remaking American Politics.* Boulder: Westview Press.

Harris, R., and W. Watson. 1993. "Three Visions of Competitiveness: Porter, Reich and Thurow on Economic Growth and Policy." In *Productivity, Growth and Canada's International Competitiveness*, ed. T.J. Courchene and D.D. Purvis. Kingston: John Deutsch Institute, Queen's University.

Harrison, B., and B. Bluestone. 1988. *The Great U-Turn: Corporate Restructuring and the Polarizing of America*. New York: Basic Books.

Harrison, K. 1991. "Between Science and Politics: Assessing the Risks of Dioxins in Canada and the United States." *Policy Sciences* 24:367–88.

- 1994. "Prospects for Intergovernmental Harmonization in Environmental Policy." In *Canada: The State of the Federation 1994*, ed. D.M. Brown and J. Hiebert. Kingston: Institute of Intergovernmental Relations, Queen's University.

- 1995a. "Federalism, Environmental Protection, and Blame Avoidance." In *New Trends in Canadian Federalism*, ed. M. Smith and F. Rocher. Peterborough, Ont.: Broadview Press.

- 1995b. "Is Cooperation the Answer? Canadian Environmental Enforcement in Comparative Context." *Journal of Policy Analysis and Management* 14:221–44.

Harrison, K., and G. Hoberg. 1994. *Risk, Science, and Politics: Regulating Toxic Substances in Canada and the United States.* Montreal: McGill-Queen's University Press.

Hart, J.A. 1992. *Rival Capitalists: International Competitiveness in the United States, Japan and Western Europe.* Ithaca: Cornell University Press.

Hart, S. 1987. "Privatization in American Religion and Society." *Sociological Analysis* 47:319–34.

Harvie, R., and H. Foster. 1990. "Ties That Bind? The Supreme Court of Canada, American Jurisprudence, and the Revision of Canadian Criminal Law under the Charter." *Osgoode Hall Law Journal* 28:729–88.

- 1991. "Different Drummers, Different Drums: The Supreme Court of Canada, American Jurisprudence, and the Continuing Revision of Criminal Law under the Charter." *Ottawa Law Review* 24:39–115.

Hatzichronoglou, T. 1991. "Indicators of Industrial Competitiveness: Results and Limitations." In *Technology and National Competitiveness: Oligopoly, Technological Innovation and International Competition*, ed. J. Niosi. Montreal: McGill-Queen's University Press.

Hausegger, L., And R. Knopff. 1994. "The Effectiveness of Interest-Group Litigation: An Assessment of LEAF's Participation in Supreme Court Cases." Paper presented to the annual meeting of the Canadian Political Science Association.

Hawkins, K. 1984. *Environment and Enforcement.* Oxford: Oxford University Press.

Hawthorne, M.R. 1991. "High Technology Economic Policy: Some Thoughts on Sematech and Political Efforts to Develop High Technology Policies in the U.S." Paper presented to the annual meeting of the American Political Association, Washington, DC.

Heatherly, C.L. 1989. "The Politics of Presidential Leadership." In *Mandate for Leadership: Policy Strategies for the 1990s*, ed. C.L. Heatherly and B.Y. Pines. Washington, DC: The Heritage Foundation.

Heclo, H. 1974. *Modern Social Policies in Britain and Sweden: From Relief to Income Maintenance.* New Haven: Yale University Press.

– 1986. "The Political Foundations of Antipoverty Policy." In *Fighting Poverty: What Works and What Doesn't*, ed. S. Danziger and D. Weinberg. Cambridge, Mass.: Harvard University Press.

– 1989. "The Emerging Regime." In *Remaking American Politics*, ed. R. Harris and S. Milkis. Boulder: Westview Press.

Helliwell, J. 1994a. "What's Left for Macroeconomic and Growth Policies?" In *Stabilization, Growth and Distribution: Linkages in the Knowledge Era*, ed. T.J. Courchene. Kingston: John Deutsch Institute, Queen's University.

– 1994b. "What Can Governments Do?" *Policy Options* 15:22–6.

Herring, C. 1989. "Convergence, Polarization or What? Racially Based Changes in Attitudes and Outlooks." *Sociological Quarterly* 30:267–81.

Hiebert, J. 1991. "Interest Groups and Canadian Federal Elections." In *Interest Groups and Elections in Canada*, ed. F.L. Seidle. Toronto: Dundurn Press.

Hillmer, N. 1989. *Partners Nevertheless: Canadian-American Relations in the Twentieth Century.* Toronto: Copp Clark Pitman.

Hillyer, A. 1994. "Province Shelves Environmental Bill of Rights." *West Coast Environmental Law Foundation Newsletter* 18 (October): 1.

Hirschman, Albert O. 1982. *Shifting Involvements: Private Interest and Public Action.* Princeton, NJ: Princeton University Press.

Hoberg, G. 1990. "Risk, Science, and Politics: Alachlor Regulation in Canada and the United States." *Canadian Journal of Political Science* 23:257–78.

– 1991a. "Sleeping with an Elephant: The American Influence on Canadian Environmental Regulation." *Journal of Public Policy* 11:107–31.

– 1991b. "Comparing Canadian Performance in Environmental Policy." In *Canadian Environmental Policy: Ecosystems, Politics, and Process*, ed. R. Boardman. Toronto: Oxford University Press.

– 1992. *Pluralism by Design: Environmental Policy and the American Regulatory State.* New York: Praeger.

– 1993a. "Environmental Policy: Alternative Styles." In *Governing Canada: State Institutions and Public Policy*, ed. M. Atkinson. Toronto: Harcourt Brace Jovanovich.

– 1993b. "Regulating Forestry: Comparing Institutions and Policies in British Columbia and the American Pacific Northwest." Working Paper 185. Vancouver: Forest Economics and Policy Analysis Unit, University of British Columbia.

Hoberg, G., and K. Harrison. 1994. "It's Not Easy Being Green: The Politics of Canada's Green Plan." *Canadian Public Policy–Analyse de Politiques* 20:119–37.

Hogg, P. 1985. *Constitutional Law of Canada.* 2d ed. Toronto, Ont.: Carswell.

Hollingsworth, J.R., P.C. Schmitter, and W. Streeck. 1994. *Governing Capitalist Economies: Performance and Control of Economic Sectors.* New York: Oxford University Press.

Holusha, J. 1991. "The Nation's Polluters: Who Emits What, and Where." *New York Times,* 13 October.

Horowitz, D. 1977. *The Courts and Social Policy.* Washington, DC: the Brookings Institution.

Horowitz, G. 1966. "Conservatism, Liberalism, and Socialism in Canada: An Interpretation." *Canadian Journal of Economics and Political Science* 32:143–71.

– 1968. *Canadian Labour in Politics.* Toronto: University of Toronto Press.

Howitt, P. 1986. *Monetary Policy in Transition: A Study of Bank of Canada Policy, 1982–85.* Toronto: C.D. Howe Institute.

Howlett, M. 1990. "The Round Table Experience: Representation and Legitimacy in Canadian Environmental Policy-Making." *Queen's Quarterly* 97:580–601.

– 1994. "The Judicialization of Canadian Environmental Policy, 1980–1990: A Test of the Canada–United States Convergence Thesis." *Canadian Journal of Political Science* 27:99–127.

Howse, R. 1992. *Economic Union, Social Justice and Constitutional Reform: Towards a High but Level Playing Field.* North York, Ont.: York University Centre for Public Law and Public Policy.

– 1995. "Another Rights Revolution? The Charter and the Reform of Social Regulation in Canada." In *Redefining Social Security,* ed. P. Grady, R. Howse, and J. Maxwell. Kingston: School of Policy Studies, Queen's University.

Howse, R., and M.J. Trebilcock. 1993. "Protecting the Employment Bargain." *University of Toronto Law Journal* 43:751–96.

Hughes, R. 1993. *Culture of Complaint: The Fraying of America.* New York: Oxford University Press.

Hulten, C., and I. Sawhill. 1984. *The Legacy of Reaganomics: Prospects for Long-Term Growth.* Washington, DC: The Urban Institute Press.

Hunter, J.D. 1991. *Culture Wars: The Struggle to Define America.* New York: Basic Books.

Huntington, S. 1975. "The United States." In *The Crisis of Democracy,* ed. S. Huntington et al. New York: New York University Press.

– 1976. "The Democratic Distemper." In *The Public Interest: The New American Commonwealth.* New York: Basic Books.

Inglehart, R. 1971. "The Silent Revolution in Europe: Intergenerational Change in Post-Industrial Studies." *American Political Science Review* 65:991–1017.

– 1977. *The Silent Revolution: Changing Values and Political Styles among American Publics.* Princeton, NJ: Princeton University Press.

– 1981. "Post-Materialism in an Environment of Insecurity." *American Political Science Review* 75:880–900.

– 1990. *Culture Shift in Advanced Industrial Society.* Princeton, NJ: Princeton University Press.

– 1994. "The Impact of Culture on Economic Development." Unpublished manuscript.

Inglehart, R., N. Nevitte, and M. Basanez. 1991. "Convergence in North America, Closer Economic, Political and Cultural Ties between the United States, Canada and Mexico." Unpublished manuscript.

Ingram, H., and D. Mann. 1989. "Interest Groups and Environmental Policy." In *Environmental Politics and Policy: Theories and Evidence,* ed. J.P. Lester. Durham, NC: Duke University Press.

Insight Canada Research. 1993. *Aspirations Project: Qualitative Research Report.* Toronto: Premier's Council on Health, Well-Being and Social Justice, Government of Ontario.

International Monetary Fund. 1988. *Issues and Developments in International Trade Policy.* Washington, DC: IMF.

– 1994. *International Financial Statistics Yearbook.* Washington, DC: IMF.

– 1995. *International Financial Statistics Yearbook.* Washington, DC: IMF.

Ip, I. 1991. *Big Spenders: Provincial Government Finances in Canada.* Toronto: C.D. Howe Institute.

Israelson, D. 1990. *Silent Earth: The Politics of our Survival.* Markham, Ont.: Viking.

Jacobson, G.C. 1990. *The Electoral Origins of Divided Government: Competition in U.S. House Elections, 1946–1988.* Boulder: Westview Press.

– 1993. "Congress: Unusual Year, Unusual Elections." In *The Elections of 1992,* ed. M. Nelson. Washington, DC: Congressional Quarterly Press.

Jarvenpa, R. 1985. "The Political Economy and Political Ethnicity of American Indian Adaptations and Identities." *Ethnic and Racial Studies* 8:29–48.

Jarvis, S.R. 1992. "Brown and the Afrocentric Curriculum." *Yale Law Journal* 101:1285–304.

Jasanoff, S. 1990. *The Fifth Branch: Science Advisers as Policymakers.* Cambridge, Mass.: Harvard University Press.

Jencks, C. 1991. "Is the American Underclass Growing?" In *The Urban Underclass,* ed. C. Jencks and P.E. Peterson. Washington, DC: The Brookings Institution.

Jencks, C., and P.E. Peterson, eds. 1991. *The Urban Underclass.* Washington, DC: The Brookings Institution.

Jenson, J. 1992. "Citizenship and Equity: Variations across Time and Space." In *Political Ethics: A Canadian Perspective,* ed. J. Hiebert. Toronto: Dundurn Press.

Johnson, C., L. Tyson, and J. Zysman. 1989. *Politics and Productivity: How Japan's Development Strategy Works.* New York: Harper.

Johnston, R. 1985. *Public Opinion and Public Policy in Canada: Questions of Confidence.* Toronto: University of Toronto Press.

Johnston, R., A. Blais, H. Brady, and J. Crete. 1992. *Letting the People Decide: Dynamics of a Canadian Election*. Montreal: McGill-Queen's University Press.

Johnstone, I. 1988. "Section 7 of the Charter and Constitutionally Protected Welfare." *University of Toronto Faculty of Law Review* 46:1–47.

Jones, C.O. 1975. *Clean Air*. Pittsburgh, Pa: Pittsburgh University Press.

– 1990. "The Separated Presidency: Making It Work in Contemporary Politics." In *The New American Political System*, 2d ed, ed. A. King. Washington, DC: American Enterprise Institute.

– 1994. *The Separated Presidency*. Washington, DC: The Brookings Institution.

Kalbach, W. 1990. "A Demographic Overview of Racial and Ethnic Groups in Canada." In *Race and Ethnic Relations in Canada*, ed. P.S. Li. Toronto: Oxford University Press.

Kallen, E. 1990. "Ethnicity and Human Rights in Canada: Constitutionalizing a Hierarchy of Minority Rights." In *Race and Ethnic Relations in Canada*, ed. P.S. Li. Toronto: Oxford University Press.

Karoly, L.A. 1993. "The Trend in Inequality among Families: Individuals, and Workers in the United States: A Twenty-Five-Year Perspective." In *Uneven Tides: Rising Inequality in America*, ed. S. Danziger and P. Gottschalk. New York: Russell Sage Foundation.

Kasse, M., and K. Newton. 1995. *Beliefs in Government*. Oxford: Oxford University Press.

Katzenstein, P., ed. 1978. *Between Power and Plenty: Foreign Economic Policies of Advanced Industrial States*. Madison, Wis.: Wisconsin University Press.

– 1984. "The Small European States in the International Economy: Economic Dependence and Corporatist Politics." In *The Antimonies of Interdependence: National Welfare and the International Division of Labour*, ed. J. Ruggie. New York: Columbia University Press.

– 1985. *Small States in World Markets: Industrial Policy in Europe*. Ithaca: Cornell University Press.

Katzenstein, P., M. Fainsod, and C.M. Mueller, eds. 1987. *The Women's Movements of the United States and Western Europe*. Philadelphia, Pa: Temple University Press.

Kaufman, L. 1994. "Life beyond God." *New York Times Magazine*, 16 October, 46–50, 60, 70, 73.

Kelman, S. 1981. *Regulating America, Regulating Sweden: A Comparative Study of Occupational Safety and Health Policy*. Cambridge, Mass.: MIT Press.

Kennedy, P.M. 1987. *The Rise and Fall of the Great Powers: Economic Change and Military Conflict from 1500–2000*. New York: Random House.

Kent, T. 1989. *Getting Ready for 1999: Ideas for Canada's Politics and Government*. Halifax: Institute for Research on Public Policy.

Keohane, R.O. 1984. "The World Political Economy and the Crisis of Embedded Liberalism." In *Order and Conflict in Contemporary Capitalism*, ed. J.H. Goldthorpe. Oxford: Oxford University Press.

– 1993. "Sovereignty, Interdependence, and International Institutions." In *Ideas and Ideals: Essays on Politics in Honor of Stanley Hoffman*, ed. L.B. Miller and M.J. Smith. Boulder: Westview Press.

Kerr, C. 1983. *The Future of Industrial Societies: Convergence or Continuing Diversity?* Cambridge, Mass.: Harvard University Press.

Kesselman, J.R. 1992. "Income Security via the Tax System: Canadian and American Reforms." In *Canada–U.S. Tax Comparisons*, ed. J.B. Shoven and J. Whalley. Chicago: Chicago University Press.

Kettering Foundation, the Harwood Group. 1991. *Citizens and Politics: The View from Mainstream America.* Washington, DC: The Kettering Foundation.

King, A., ed. 1990. *The New American Political System.* 2d ed. Washington, DC: American Enterprise Institute.

Kitchen, H. 1995. "The Infrastructure Works Program: Some Economic Concerns." *Policy Options* 16:16–18.

Knopff, R. 1989. *Human Rights and Social Technology: The New War on Discrimination.* Ottawa: Carleton University Press.

Knopff, R., and F.L. Morton. 1992. *Charter Politics.* Scarborough, Ont.: Nelson Canada.

Knubley, J., L. Krause, and S. Sadeque. 1991. "Canadian Acquisitions Abroad: Patterns and Motivations." In *Corporate Globalization through Mergers and Acquisitions*, ed. L. Waverman. Calgary: University of Calgary Press.

Kochan, T., ed. 1985. *Challenges and Choices Facing American Labor.* Cambridge, Mass.: MIT Press.

Koenig, L.W. 1991. "The Modern Presidency and the Constitution: Foreign Policy." In *The Constitution and the Modern Presidency*, ed. M. Faushold and A. Shank. Albany, NY: State University of New York Press.

Kornberg, A., and H.D. Clarke. 1992. *Citizens and Community: Political Support in a Representative Democracy.* New York: Cambridge University Press.

Krasner, S. 1978. *Defending the National Interest: Raw Material Investments and U.S. Foreign Policy.* Princeton, NJ: Princeton University Press.

Krauss, E., and J. Pierre. 1993. "Targeting Resources for Industrial Change." In *Do Institutions Matter? Government Capabilities in the United States and Abroad*, ed. R.K. Weaver and B. Rockman. Washington, DC: The Brookings Institution.

Krugman, P. 1990. *The Age of Diminished Expectations: U.S. Economic Policy in the 1990s.* Cambridge, Mass.: MIT Press.

– 1993. "The Current Case for Industrial Policy." In *Protectionism and World Welfare*, ed. D. Salvatore. New York: Cambridge University Press.

– 1994. "Competitiveness: A Dangerous Obsession." *Foreign Affairs* 73:28–44.

Krugman, P., and M. Obstfeld. 1991. *International Economics: Theory and Practice.* 2d ed. New York: HarperCollins.

Kumar, P. 1993. *From Uniformity to Divergence: Industrial Relations in Canada and the United States.* Kingston: Industrial Relations Centre Press, Queen's University.

Kumar, P., and J. Holmes. 1993. "Change, but in What Direction? Divergent Union Responses to Work Restructuring in the Integrated North American Auto Industry." Working Paper Series. Kingston: Industrial Relations Centre, Queen's University.

Kuttner, R. 1991. *The End of Laissez-Faire: National Purpose and the Global Economy after the Cold War.* New York: Knopf.

Kymlicka, W. 1992. "Recent Work in Citizenship Theory." Report prepared for Multiculturalism and Citizenship Canada, Ottawa. Mimeo.

Kymlicka, W., and W.J. Norman. 1992. "The Social Charter Debate: Should Social Justice Be Constitutionalized?" Ottawa: Network on the Constitution.

Labour Market Research Group. 1991. *Building a Training System for the 1990s: A Shared Responsibility.* Ontario: Minister of Skills Development.

Ladd, E.C. 1982. *Where Have All the Voters Gone? The Fracturing of America's Political Parties.* 2d ed. New York: W.W. Norton.

Langille, D. 1987. "The Business Council on National Issues and the Canadian State." *Studies in Political Economy* 24:41–85.

– 1991. "Canadian Labour Law Reform and Free Trade." *Ottawa Law Review* 23:581–622.

Lauber, V. 1986. "The Political Economy of Industrial Policy in Western Europe." In *Economics and Politics of Industrial Policy: The United States and Western Europe,* ed. S. Shull and J. Cohen. New York: Praeger.

Laux, J., and M. Molot. 1988. *State Capitalism: Public Enterprise in Canada.* Ithaca, NY: Cornell University Press.

Lawrence, M. 1993. *Pledge of Allegiance: The Americanization of Canada in the Mulroney Years.* Toronto: McClelland & Stewart.

Lawrence, R. 1984. "Sectoral Shifts and the Size of the Middle Class." *Brookings Review,* Fall.

Lawrence, R., and R. Litan. 1986. *Saving Free Trade: A Pragmatic Approach.* Washington, DC: The Brookings Institution.

– 1990. "The World Trading System after the Uruguay Round." *Boston University International Law Journal* 8:247–50.

Lawrence, S. 1990. *The Poor in Court: The Legal Services Program and Supreme Court Decision-Making.* Princeton, NJ: Princeton University Press.

Lazar, H. 1990. "Global Competition and Canadian Federalism: The Financial Sector." Paper presented at Conference on Global Competition and Canadian Federalism, University of Toronto.

Laycock, D. 1994. "Reforming Canadian Democracy? Institutions and Ideology in the Reform Party Project." *Canadian Journal of Political Science* 27:213–48.

Leana, C.R., and D.C. Feldman. 1992. *Coping with Job Loss: How Individuals, Organizations and Corporations Respond to Layoffs.* New York: Lexington Books.

Lenkowsky, L. 1986. *Politics, Economics and Welfare Reform: The Failure of the Negative Income Tax in Britain and the United States.* Lanham, Md: University Press of America.

Leslie, P.M., et al. 1993. *A Partnership in Trouble: Renegotiating Fiscal Federalism.* Toronto: C.D. Howe Institute.

Levitt, K. 1970. *Silent Surrender: The Multinational Corporation in Canada.* Toronto: Macmillan.

Levy, F. 1987. *Dollars and Dreams: The Changing American Income Distribution.* New York: Russell Sage Foundation.

Levy, F., and R. Murnane. 1992. "U.S. Earning Levels and Earnings Inequality: A Review of Recent Trends and Proposed Explanations." *Journal of Economic Literature* 30:1333–81.

Lewis, D. 1995. "Infrastructure and Economic Growth." In *Infrastructure and Competitiveness*, ed. J. Mintz. Kingston: John Deutsch Institute, Queen's University.

Lewis, S. 1992. "Dear Bob." Report to Premier Bob Rae on Race Relations in Ontario. Toronto. Mimeo.

Li, P.S., ed. 1990. *Race and Ethnic Relations in Canada.* Toronto: Oxford University Press.

Liberal Party of Canada. 1993. *Creating Opportunity: The Liberal Plan for Canada.* Ottawa: Liberal Party of Canada.

Lindberg, L. 1985. "Models of the Inflation-Disinflation Process." In *The Politics of Inflation and Economic Stagnation: Theoretical Approaches and International Case Studies*, ed. L. Lindberg and C. Maier. Washington, DC: The Brookings Institution.

Lipset, S.M. 1990a. *Continental Divide: The Values and Institutions of the United States and Canada.* New York: Routledge.

– 1990b. *North American Cultures: Values and Institutions in Canada and the United States.* Orono, Maine: Borderlands Project.

Lipset, S.M., and W. Schneider. 1983. *The Confidence Gap: Business, Labor and Government and the Public Mind.* New York: The Free Press.

Lipsey, R. 1987. "Sovereignty and a Canadian-American Free Trade Agreement." In *Assessing the Canada-U.S. Free Trade Agreement*, ed. M.G. Smith and F. Stone. Halifax: Institute for Research on Public Policy.

Lodge, G.C. 1987. "The United States: The Costs of Ambivalence." In *Ideology and National Competitiveness*, ed. G.C. Lodge and E.F. Vogel. Cambridge, Mass.: Harvard Business School Press.

Longworth, D., and S. Poloz. 1986. "A Comparison of Alternative Monetary Policy Regimes in a Small, Dynamic, Open-Economy Simulation Model." Bank of Canada Technical Report 42. Ottawa: Bank of Canada.

Lowi, T. 1979. *The End of Liberalism: The Second Republic of the United States.* 2d ed. New York: W.W. Norton.

– 1985. *The Personal President: Power Invested, Promise Unfulfilled.* Ithaca: Cornell University Press.

– 1988. "The Theory of the Underclass: A Review." *Policy Studies Review* 7:852–8.

– 1991. "Presidential Power and the Ideological Struggle over Its Interpretation." In *The Constitution and the American Presidency*, ed. M. Fausold and A. Shank. Albany, NY: State University of New York Press.

– 1992. "The Party Crasher." *New York Times Magazine, 23 August, 28–33.*

Lowi, T., and B. Ginsberg. 1992. *American Government: Freedom and Power.* 2d ed. New York: W.W. Norton.

Lowry, W. 1994. *The Capacity for Wonder: Preserving National Parks.* Washington, DC: The Brookings Institution.

Lucas, A. 1989. "The New Environmental Law." In *Canada: State of the Federation, 1989,* ed. R.L. Watts and D.M. Brown. Kingston: Institute for Intergovernmental Relations, Queen's University.

Lumsden, I., ed. 1970. *Close the 49th Parallel etc: The Americanization of Canada.* Toronto: University of Toronto Press.

McCann, M. 1986. *Taking Reform Seriously: Perspectives on Public Interest Liberalism.* Ithaca: Cornell University Press.

McClosky, H.W., and A. Brill. 1983. *Dimensions of Tolerance: What Americans Believe about Civil Liberties.* New York: Russel Sage Foundation.

McClosky, H.W., and J. Zaller. 1984. *The American Ethos: Public Attitudes toward Capitalism and Democracy.* Cambridge, Mass. Harvard University Press.

Macdonald, D. 1990. *The Politics of Pollution.* Toronto: McClelland & Stewart.

McDonald, F. 1991. "Foreword." In *The Constitution and the American Presidency,* ed. M. Fausold and A. Shank. Albany, NY: State University of New York Press.

McFetridge, D.G. 1985. "Commercial and Political Efficiency: A Comparison of Government, Mixed and Private Enterprises." In *Canadian Industrial Policy in Action,* ed. D.G. McFetridge. Toronto: University of Toronto Press.

– 1995. "Competition Policy and Cooperative Innovation." Paper prepared for the Conference on Competitive Industrial Development: The Role of Cooperation in the Technology Sector. Toronto: University of Toronto, Faculty of Law.

MacIntyre, J.M. 1964–1966. "The Use of American Cases in Canadian Courts." *University of British Columbia Law Review* 2:478–90.

McKay, D. 1987. *Politics and Power in the USA.* London: Penguin.

McKie, C., and K. Thompson, eds. 1990. *Canadian Social Tends.* Toronto: Thompson Publishing.

Macklem, P. 1993. "Distributing Sovereignty: Indian Nations and Equality of Peoples." *Stanford Law Review* 45:1311–67.

Maclean's. 1990. "Special Report: Portrait of Two Nations." 25 June, 50–1.

McRoberts, K. 1988. *Quebec: Social Change and Political Crisis.* Toronto. McClelland & Stewart.

Madison, J., A. Hamilton, and J. Jay. 1987. *The Federalist Papers,* ed. I. Kramnick. Middlesex: Penguin Books.

Magnusson, W. 1990. "Critical Social Movements: De-Centring the State." In *Canadian Politics: An Introduction to the Discipline,* ed. A.-G. Gagnon and J. Bickerton. Peterborough, Ont.: Broadview Press.

Mahon, R. 1990. "Adjusting to Win? The New Tory Training Initiative." In *How Ottawa Spends: 1990–91,* ed. K.A. Graham. Ottawa: Carleton University Press.

Mahood, H.R. 1990. *Interest Group Politics in America: A New Intensity.* Englewood Cliffs, NJ: Prentice-Hall.

Maisel, S., ed. 1990. *The Parties Respond: Changes in the American Party System.* Boulder: Westview Press.

Mandel, M. 1989. *The Charter of Rights and the Legalization of Politics in Canada.* Toronto: Wall and Thompson.

Manfredi, C. 1990a. "Fundamental Justice in the Supreme Court of Canada: Decisions under s.7 of the *Charter of Rights and Freedoms.*" *American Journal of Comparative Law* 38:658–59.

– 1990b. "The Use of United States Decisions by the Supreme Court of Canada under the *Charter of Rights and Freedoms.*" *Canadian Journal of Political Science* 23:499–518.

– 1992. "The Canadian Supreme Court and American Judicial Review: United States Constitutional Jurisprudence and the Canadian Charter of Rights and Freedoms." *American Journal of Comparative Law* 40:213–35.

– 1993. *Judicial Power and the Charter: Canada and the Paradox of Liberal Constitutionalism.* Toronto: McClelland & Stewart.

– 1994. "Appropriate and Just in the Circumstances: Public Policy and the Enforcement of Rights under the Canadian Charter of Rights and Freedoms." *Canadian Journal of Political Science* 27:435–63.

Manga, P. 1988. "The Canada–U.S. Free Trade Agreement: Possible Implications on Canada's Health Care System." Discussion Paper no. 348. Ottawa: Economic Council of Canada.

Mann, T.E. 1990. "Breaking the Political Impasse." In *Setting National Priorities: Policy for the Nineties.* Washington, DC: The Brookings Institution.

Manzer, R. 1984. "Public Policy-Making as Practical Reasoning." *Canadian Journal of Political Science* 17:577–94.

– 1985. *Public Policies and Political Development in Canada.* Toronto: University of Toronto Press.

March, J., and J. Olsen. 1989. *Rediscovering Institutions: The Organizational Basis of Politics.* New York: Free Press.

Markusen, A., P. Hall, S. Campbell, and S. Deitrick. 1991. *The Rise of the Gunbelt: The Military Remapping of Industrial America.* New York and Oxford: Oxford University Press.

Marmor, T.R. 1994. *Understanding Health Care Reform.* New Haven: Yale University Press.

Marmor, T.R., J.L. Mashaw, and P.L. Harvey. 1990. *America's Misunderstood Welfare State: Persistent Myths, Enduring Realities.* New York: Basic Books.

Marshall, K. 1990. "Women in Professional Occupations: Progress in the 1980s," and "Women in Male Dominated Professions." In *Canadian Social Trends,* ed. C. McKie and K. Thompson. Toronto: Thompson Publishing.

Martin, A. 1986. "The Politics of Employment and Welfare: National Policies and International Interdependence." In *The State and Economic Interests,* ed. K.G. Banting. Toronto: University of Toronto Press.

Martin, L. 1993. *Pledge of Allegiance: The Americanization of Canada in the Mulroney Years.* Toronto: McClelland & Stewart.

Massey, D.S., and M.L. Eggers. 1990. "The Ecology of Inequality: Minorities and the Concentration of Poverty, 1970–1980." *American Journal of Sociology* 95:1153–88.

Massicotte, L. 1994. "Parliament: The Show Goes On but the Public Seems Bored." In *Canadian Politics: An Introduction to the Discipline*, ed. A.-G. Gagnon and J. Bickerton. Peterborough, Ont.: Broadview Press.

Mayhew, D.R. 1991. *Divided We Govern: Party Control, Lawmaking and Investigations, 1946–1990.* New Haven: Yale University Press.

Megyery, K., ed. 1991. *Ethno-Cultural Groups and Visible Minorities in Canadian Politics: The Question of Access.* Research Studies of the Royal Commission on Electoral Reform and Party Financing, vol. 7. Toronto: Dundurn Press.

Meisel, J. 1991. "Decline of Party in Canada." In *Party Politics in Canada*, 6th ed., ed. H.G. Thorburn. Scarborough: Prentice-Hall.

Melnick, R.S. 1983. *Regulation and the Courts: The Case of the Clean Air Act.* Washington, DC: The Brookings Institution.

– 1985. "The Politics of Partnership." *Public Administration Review* 45:653–60.

– 1989. "The Courts, Congress and Programmatic Rights." In *Remaking American Politics*, ed. R.A. Harris and S.M. Milkis. Boulder: Westview Press.

– 1994. *Between the Lines: Interpreting Welfare Rights.* Washington, DC: The Brookings Institution.

Meltz, N. 1993. "Manufacturing Sector Unionism: Canada–U.S. Comparisons." Working Paper Series. Kingston: Industrial Relations Press, Queen's University.

Mendelson, M. 1993. "Fundamental Reform of Fiscal Federalism." In *Fiscal Federalism for the 21st Century*, ed. S. Torjman. Ottawa: The Caledon Institute.

Mezey, M.L. 1989. *Congress, the President and Public Policy.* Boulder: Westview Press.

Milbourne, R., D. Purvis, and D. Scoones. 1991. "Unemployment Insurance and Unemployment Dynamics." *Canadian Journal of Economics* 24:804–26.

Miller, A.H. 1974. "Political Issues and Trust in Government: 1964–1970." *American Political Science Review* 68:951–72.

Miller, A.H., and S.A. Borelli. 1991. "Confidence in Government during the 1980s." *American Politics Quarterly* 19:147–73.

Mintz, A. 1989. "Guns versus Butter: A Disaggregated Analysis." *American Political Science Review* 83:1285–93.

Mitchell, R.C. 1979. "National Environmental Lobbies and the Apparent Illogic of Collective Action." In *Collective Decision Making: Applications from Public Choice Theory*, ed. C. Russell. Baltimore, Md: Johns Hopkins University Press.

Monahan, P. 1987. *Politics and the Constitution: The Charter, Federalism and the Supreme Court of Canada.* Toronto: Carswell.

Moodley, K.A. 1984. "The Predicament of Racial Affirmative Action: A Critical Review of Equality Now." *Queen's Quarterly* 91:795–806.

Moon, J. 1987. "Convergence/Divergence Hypotheses of Governments' Activities: Some Methodological Considerations." *Politics* 22:36–45

Mori, G.A. 1990. "Religious Affiliation in Canada." In *Canadian Social Trends,* ed. C. McKie and K. Thompson. Toronto: Thompson Publishing.

Morrisette, R., J. Myles, and G. Picot. 1995. "What Is Happening to Earnings Inequality in Canada?" In *Labour Market Polarization and Social Policy Reform,* ed. K.G. Banting and C. Beach. Kingston: School of Policy Studies, Queen's University.

Morton, F.L., and R. Knopff. 1992. "The Supreme Court as the Vanguard of the Intelligentsia: The Charter Movement as Post Materialist Politics." In *Canadian Constitutionalism, 1781–1991,* ed. Janet Ajzenstat. Ottawa: Canadian Study of Parliament Group.

Morton, F.L., P.H. Russell, and T. Riddell. 1994. "The *Canadian Charter of Rights and Freedoms*: A Descriptive Analysis of the First Decade, 1982–1992." *National Journal of Constitutional Law* 5:1–60.

Morton, W.L. 1981. "The Historical Phenomenon of Minorities: The Canadian Experience." *Canadian Ethnic Studies* 13:1–39.

Mossman, M.J., and M. MacLean. 1986. "Family Law and Social Welfare: Towards a New Equality." *Canadian Journal of Family Law* 5:79–110.

Mukherjee, A. 1992. "Women of Colour and American Feminist Theory." In *Challenging Times: The Women's Movement in Canada and the United States,* ed. C. Backhouse and D.H. Flaherty. Montreal: McGill-Queen's University Press.

Muldoon, P. 1988. "The Fight for an Environmental Bill of Rights." *Alternatives* 15:33–9.

Munton, D., and G. Castle. 1992. "Air, Water, and Political Fire: Building a North American Environmental Regime." In *Canadian Foreign Policy and International Economic Regimes,* ed. A.C. Cutler and M.W. Zacher. Vancouver: University of British Columbia Press.

Murray, C. 1984. *Losing Ground: American Social Policy, 1950–1980.* New York: Basic Books.

Murray, C., and R. Herrnstein. 1994. *The Bell Curve: Intelligence and Class Structure in American Life.* New York: The Free Press.

Myles, J. 1991. "Social Structures and Welfare Policies: Perspectives for Canada and the United States." Working Paper 91–8. Ottawa: Department of Sociology and Anthropology, Carleton University.

– 1995. "Where Markets Fail: Social Welfare in Canada and the United States." Geneva: United Nations Research Institute for Social Development. Discussion Paper Series DP-68.

Myles, J., G. Picot, and T. Wannell. 1988a. "The Changing Wage Distribution of Jobs, 1981–1986." *Canadian Economic Observer,* November.

– 1988b. "Wages and Jobs in the 1980s: Youth Wages and the Declining Middle." Research Paper 17. Ottawa: Statistics Canada.

Nathan, R.P. 1990. "Federalism: The Great Composition." In *The New American Political System*, 2d ed, ed. A. King. Washington, DC: American Enterprise Institute.

Nathan, R.P., and F. Doolittle. 1987. *Reagan and the States.* Princeton, NJ: Princeton University Press.

National Commission on Children. 1991. *Beyond Rhetoric: A New American Agenda for Children and Families.* Washington, DC: National Commission on Children.

National Commission on the Environment. 1993. *Choosing a Sustainable Future.* Washington, DC: Island Press.

National Council of Welfare. 1990. *Pensions Reform.* Ottawa: Minister of Supply and Services Canada.

– 1991. *Welfare Incomes 1990.* Ottawa: Minister of Supply and Services Canada.

– 1994. *Welfare Incomes 1993.* Ottawa: Minister of Supply and Services Canada.

– 1995. *Welfare Incomes 1994.* Ottawa: Minister of Supply and Services Canada.

Nau, H. 1990. *The Myth of America's Decline: Leading the World into the 1990s.* New York: Oxford University Press.

Nedelsky, J. 1991. *Private Property and the Limits of American Constitutionalism: The Madisonian Framework and Its Legacy.* Chicago: University of Chicago Press.

Nelson, B., and N. Chowdhury, eds. 1994. *Women and Politics Worldwide.* New Haven: Yale University Press.

Nemetz, P. 1986. "Federal Environmental Regulation in Canada: An Overview and Comparison with the American Model." *Natural Resources Journal* 26:552–608.

Nemetz, P., W.T. Stanbury, and F. Thompson. 1986. "Social Regulation in Canada." *Policy Studies Journal* 14:580–603.

Nevitte, N. 1991a. "North American Continental Integration and Value Change: Cross-National Evidence." Paper presented to the American Political Science Association.

– 1991b. "New Politics, the Charter and Political Participation." In *Representation, Integration and Political Parties in Canada*, ed. H. Bakvis. Toronto: Dundurn Press.

Nevitte, N., and R. Gibbins. 1990. *New Elites in Old States: Ideologies in the Anglo-American Democracies.* Toronto: Oxford University Press.

Nevitte, N., H. Bakvis, and R. Gibbins. 1989. "The Ideological Contours of 'New Politics' in Canada: Policy, Mobilization and Partisan Support." *Canadian Journal of Political Science* 22:481.

Nevitte, N., R. Irglehart, and J. Basanez. 1991. "World Values Studies." Unpublished manuscript.

Niemi, R.G., J. Mueller, and T.W. Smith. 1989. *Trends in Public Opinion: A Compendium of Survey Data.* New York: Greenwood.

Niosi, J. 1985. *Canadian Multinationals.* Toronto: Between the Lines.

Niskanen, W. 1988. *Reagonomics.* New York: Oxford University Press.

Nordlinger, E. 1981. *On the Autonomy of the Democratic State.* Cambridge, Mass.: Harvard University Press.

O'Barr, J.F. 1992. "Exclusions and the Process of Empowerment: The Case of Feminist Scholarship." In *Challenging Times: The Women's Movement in Canada and the United States,* ed. C. Backhouse and D.H. Flaherty. Montreal: McGill-Queen's University Press.

O'Brien, D.M. 1990. *Storm Center: The Supreme Court in American Politics.* 2d ed. New York: W.W. Norton.

O'Connor, J. 1988. "Convergence or Divergence?: Change in Welfare Effort in OECD Countries 1960–1980." *European Journal of Political Research* 16:277–99.

O'Connor, K. 1980. *Women's Organizations' Use of the Courts.* Lexington, Mass.: Lexington Books.

O'Connor, K., and L. Epstein. 1983. "The Rise of Conservative Interest Group Litigation." *Journal of Politics* 45:479–89.

O'Hara, S.T. 1983. "Worker Adjustment Assistance: The Failure and the Future." *Northwestern Journal of International Law and Business* 5:394–431.

O'Hare, W.P. 1987. "Black Demographic Trends in the 1980s," *Milbank Quarterly* 65, supplement, 1:35–55.

Olewiler, N. 1994. "The Impact of Environmental Regulations on Investment Decisions." In *Getting the Green Light: Environmental Regulation and Investment in Canada,* ed. J. Benidickson, G.B. Doern, and N. Olewiler. Toronto: C.D. Howe Institute.

Olson, S. 1990. "Interest Group Litigation in Federal District Courts: Beyond the Political Disadvantage Theory." *Journal of Politics* 52:854–82.

Omhae, K. 1990. *The Borderless World: Power and Strategy in the Interlinked Economy.* New York: Harper's.

Ontario. 1988. *Report of the Premier's Council: Industrial Policy Studies.* Vol. 3 Toronto: Queen's Printer for Ontario.

Ontario Law Reform Commission. 1991. *Appointing Judges: Philosophy, Politics and Practice.* Toronto: Ministry of the Attorney General.

– 1993. *Report on the Rights and Responsibilities of Cohabitants under the Family Law Act.* Toronto: Ontario Law Reform Commission.

Ontario Ministry of the Environment. 1989. *Interim Pollution Reduction Strategy for Ontario Kraft Mills.* Toronto: Ministry of the Environment.

Orchard, D. 1993. *The Fight for Canada: Four Centuries of Resistance to American Expansionism.* DonMills: Stoddart.

Organization for Economic Cooperation and Development. 1985. "The Role of the Public Sector: Causes and Consequences of the Growth of Government." *OECD Economic Studies* no. 4. Paris: OECD.

– 1987. *Structural Adjustment and Economic Performance.* Paris: OECD.

– 1989. *OECD in Figures: Statistics on the Member Countries, 1989 Edition.* Supplement to *the OECD Observer* no. 158. Paris: OECD.

– 1990a. *Economic Outlook.* Paris: OECD.

– 1990b. *Investment Incentives and Disincentives: Effects on International Direct Investment.* Paris: OECD.

– 1991a. *OECD Declaration and Decisions on International Investment and Multinational Enterprises: 1991 Review.* Paris: OECD.

– 1991b. *Economic Outlook: Historical Statistics, 1960–1990.* Paris: OECD.

– 1991c. *Economic Survey: United States (1991–1992).* Paris: OECD.

– 1992. *Monthly Statistics of Foreign Trade.* Paris: OECD.

– 1993a. *OECD Observer* no. 180. Paris: OECD.

– 1993b. *Main Economic Indicators: Historical Statistics: Prices, Labour and Wages, 1962–1991.* Paris: OECD.

– 1993c. *OECD Environmental Data: Compendium 1993.* Paris: OECD.

– 1994a. *The OECD Jobs Study: Facts, Analysis, Strategies.* Paris: OECD.

– 1994b. *The OECD Jobs Study: Evidence and Explanations.* Part 1 *Labour Market Trends and Underlying Forces of Change.* Paris: OECD.

– 1994c. *New Orientations for Social Policy.* OECD Social Policy Studies 12. Paris: OECD.

– 1995. *Historical Statistics 1960–1993.* Paris. OECD.

– 1996. *Main Economic Indicators: Historical Statistics: Prices, Labour and Wages.* Paris. OECD.

Orloff, A.S. 1988. "The Political Origins of America's Belated Welfare State." In *The Politics of Social Policy in the United States*, ed. M. Weir, A.S. Orloff, and T. Skocpol. Princeton, NJ: Princeton University Press.

– 1991. "The American Social Policy Agenda: Constraints on Reform." In *Policy Choices: Political Agendas in Canada and the United States*, ed. K. Banting, M. Hawes, R. Simeon, and E. Willis. Kingston: School of Policy Studies, Queen's University.

O'Rourke, T.G. 1995. "*Shaw v. Reno* and the Hunt for Double Cross-Overs." *PS: Political Science and Politics* 28:36–41.

Osberg, L., S. Erksoy, and S. Phipps. 1994. "Labour Market Impacts of the Canadian and U.S. Unemployment Insurance Systems." Discussion Paper Series 94–12. Halifax, NS: Department of Economics, Dalhousie University.

Osborne, D. 1988. *Laboratories of Democracy: A New Breed of Governor Creates Models for National Growth.* Cambridge, Mass.: Harvard Business School Press.

Osborne, D., and T. Gaebler. 1993. *Reinventing Government: How the Entrepreneurial Spirit Is Transforming the Public Sector.* New York: Plume.

Overbye, E. 1994. "Convergence in Policy Outcomes: Social Security Systems in Perspective." *Journal of Public Policy* 14:147–74.

Packer, A.H. 1991. "The Demographic and Economic Imperatives." In *Human Capital and America's Future: An Economic Strategy for the Nineties*, ed. D.W. Hornbeck and L.M. Salamon. Baltimore, Md: Johns Hopkins University Press.

Paehlke, R. 1990. "Regulatory and Non-Regulatory Approaches to Environmental Protection." *Canadian Public Administration* 33:17–36.

Page, B.I., and R. Shapiro. 1992. *The Rational Choice.* Chicago: University of Chicago.

Pal, L. 1988. *State, Class and Bureaucracy: Canadian Unemployment Insurance and Public Policy.* Montreal: McGill-Queen's University Press.

– 1993. *Interests of State: The Politics of Language, Multiculturalism and Feminism in Canada.* Montreal: McGill-Queen's University Press.

Pammett, J. 1990. "Elections." In *Canadian Politics in the 1990s,* ed. M.S. Whittington and G. Williams. 3d ed. Scarborough, Ont.: Nelson Canada.

Panitch, L., ed. 1977. *The Canadian State: Political Economy and Political Power.* Toronto: University of Toronto Press.

Paquet, G., and J. Roy. 1995. "Prosperity through Networks: The Bottom-Up Strategy that Might Have Been." In *How Ottawa Spends 1995–96: Mid-Life Crisis,* ed. S. Phillips. Ottawa: Carleton University Press.

Parliament, J.B. 1990. "Women Employed Outside the Home." In *Canadian Social Trends,* ed. C. McKie and K. Thompson. Toronto: Thompson Publishing.

Peele, G., et al. 1992. *Developments in American Politics.* London: Macmillan.

Perlin, G., ed. 1988. *Party Democracy in Canada: The Politics of National Party Conventions.* Toronto: Prentice-Hall.

Perry, D. 1993. "What Price Canadians? Taxation and Debt Compared." In *Canada and the United States: Differences that Count,* ed. D. Thomas. Peterborough, Ont.: Broadview Press.

Pesticide Registration Review. 1990. *Recommendations for a Revised Federal Pest Management Regulatory System.* Final Report. Ottawa. December.

Peterson, P.E. 1991. "The Urban Underclass and the Poverty Paradox." In *The Urban Underclass,* ed. C. Jencks and P.E. Peterson. Washington, DC: The Brookings Institution.

Peterson, P.E., and M. Rom. 1990. *Welfare Magnets: A New Case for a National Standard.* Washington, DC: The Brookings Institution.

Peterson, P.E., B.G. Rabe, and K. Wong. 1986. *When Federalism Works.* Washington, DC: The Brookings Institution.

Petracca, M., ed. 1992. *The Politics of Interests: Interest Groups Transformed.* Boulder: Westview Press.

Phillips, K. 1993. *Boiling Point: Republicans, Democrats and the Decline of Middle-Class Prosperity.* New York: Random House.

Phillips, S. 1994. "New Social Movements in Canadian Politics: On Starting and Fighting Fires." In *Canadian Politics,* 2d ed, ed. J. Bickerton and A.-G. Gagnon. Peterborough, Ont.: Broadview Press.

Pierson. P. 1994. *Dismantling the Welfare State? Reagan, Thatcher and the Politics of Retrenchment.* Cambridge: Cambridge University Press.

– 1995. "The Creeping Nationalization of Income Transfers in the United States, 1935–94." In *European Social Policy: Between Fragmentation and Integration,* ed. S. Leibfried and P. Pierson. Washington, DC: The Brookings Institution.

Pierson, P., and R.K. Weaver. 1993. "Imposing Losses in Pension Policy." In *Do Institutions Matter? Government Capabilities in the United States and Abroad*, ed. R.K. Weaver and B. Rockman. Washington, DC: The Brookings Institution.

Pines, M., and A. Carnevale. 1991. "Employment and Training." In *Human Capital and America's Future*, ed. D.W. Hornbeck and L.M. Salamon. Baltimore, Md: Johns Hopkins University Press.

Piore, M., and C. Sabel. 1984. *The Second Industrial Divide: Possibilities for Prosperity.* New York: Basic Books.

Polsby, N. 1990. "Political Change and the Character of the American Congress." In *The New American Political System*, 2d ed, ed. A. King. Washington, DC: American Enterprise Institute.

Porter, M.E. 1990. *The Competitive Advantage of Nations.* New York: The Free Press.

Porter, M.E., and the Monitor Company. 1991. *Canada at the Crossroads: The Reality of a New Competitive Environment.* Ottawa: Business Council on National Issues/Supply and Services Canada.

Premier's Council. 1988. *Report: Industrial Policy Studies*. Vol. 3. Toronto: Queen's Printer for Ontario.

Prestowitz, C.V., Jr. 1988. *Trading Places: How We Allowed Japan to Take the Lead.* New York: Basic Books.

Price, D.E. 1989. "The House of Representatives: A Report from the Field." In *Congress Reconsidered*, 4th ed, ed. L.C. Dodd and B.I. Oppenheimer. Washington, DC: Congressional Quarterly.

– 1992. *The Congressional Experience: A View from the Hill.* Boulder: Westview Press.

Pross, P. 1986. *Group Politics and Public Policy.* Toronto: Oxford University Press.

– 1990. "Pressure Groups: Talking Chameleons." In *Canadian Politics in the 1990s*, 3d ed, ed. M.S. Whittington and G. Williams. Scarborough, Ont.: Nelson Canada.

Purvis, D.D. 1977. "The Exchange Rate Regime and Economic Policy in Theory and Practice." *Canadian Public Policy – Analyse de politiques* 5: 205–18.

– 1985. "Public Sector Deficits, International Capital Mobility, and the Domestic Economy: The Medium-Term Is the Message." The 1985 Harold Innis Memorial Lecture. *Canadian Journal of Economics* 18:423–57.

Putnam, R. 1988. "Diplomacy and Domestic Politics: The Logic of Two Level Games." *International Organization* 42:427–60.

– 1993a. "The Prosperous Community: Social Capital and Public Life." *American Prospect* 13:35–45.

– 1993b. *Making Democracy Work: Civic Traditions in Modern Italy.* Princeton, NJ: Princeton University Press.

– 1994. "Bowling Alone: Democracy in America at the End of the Twentieth Century." Unpublished paper.

Quadagno, J. 1988. *The Transformation of Old Age Security: Class Politics in the American Welfare State.* Chicago: University of Chicago Press.

– 1990. "Race, Class and Gender in the United States Welfare State: Nixon's Failed Family Assistance Plan." *American Sociological Review* 55:11–28.

Quarterly Labour Market and Productivity Review. 1992. "The Role of Business-Labour Sectoral Initiatives in Economic Restructuring."

Rabkin, J. 1989. *Judicial Compulsions: How Public Law Distorts Public Policy.* New York: Basic Books.

Ranney, A. 1975. *Curing the Mischiefs of Faction: Party Reform in America.* Berkeley: University of California Press.

– 1990. "Broadcasting, Narrowcasting and Politics." In *The New American Political System,* 2d ed., ed. A. King. Washington, DC: American Enterprise Institute.

Rao, S., and T. Lemprière. 1992. *Canada's Productivity Performance.* Ottawa: Canada Communication Group.

Rashid, A. 1993. "Seven Decades of Wage Changes." *Perspectives on Labour and Income* no. 5. Ottawa: Statistics Canada.

Reich, R.B. 1992. *The Work of Nations: Preparing Ourselves for 21st-Century Capitalism.* New York: Alfred A. Knopf.

Reid, A., and M.M. Burns. 1992. *Canada and the World: An International Perspective on Canada and Canadians.* Winnipeg: Angus Reid Group.

Reimers, D.M., and H. Troper. 1992. "Canadian and American Immigration Policy since 1985." In *Immigration, Language and Ethnicity: Canada and the United States,* ed. B. Chiswick. Washington, DC: American Enterprise Institute.

Reitz J., and R. Breton. 1994. *The Illusion of Difference: Realities of Ethnicity in Canada and the United States.* Toronto: C.D. Howe Institute.

Reporters of the *New York Times.* 1996. *The Downsizing of America: A Special Report.* New York: New York Times.

Reuters. 1992. "U.S. Unanimous Choice as Environmental Bad Boy." *Globe and Mail,* 9 June.

Richards, J. 1993. "A Tangled Tale: Unions in Canada and the United States." In *Canada and the United States: Differences that Count,* ed. D. Thomas. Peterborough, Ont.: Broadview Press.

Riddell, C. 1993. "Unionization in Canada and the United States: A Tale of Two Countries." In *Small Differences that Matter: Labour Markets and Income Maintenance in Canada and the United States,* ed. D. Card and R. Freeman. Chicago: University of Chicago Press.

Rivlin, A. 1992. *Reviving the American Dream: The Economy, the States and the Federal Government.* Washington, DC: The Brookings Institution.

Roach, K. 1992. "Chartering the Electoral Map into the Future." In *Drawing Boundaries: Legislatures, Courts and Electoral Values,* ed. J.C. Courtney, P. MacKinnon, and D.E. Smith. Saskatoon: Fifth House Publishers.

– 1993. "The Role of Litigation and the Charter in Interest Advocacy." In *Equity and Community: The Charter, Interest Advocacy and Representation,* ed. F. Leslie Seidle. Montreal: Institute for Research on Public Policy.

Robbins, T., and A. Dick. 1979. "The Sociology of Contemporary Religious Movements." *Annual Review of Sociology* 5:75–89.

Robinson, D.L. 1990. *Reforming American Government: The Bicentennial Papers of the Commission on the Constitutional System.* Boulder: Westview Press.

– 1991. "The Presidency and the Future of Constitutional Government." In *The Constitution and the American Presidency,* ed. M. Fausold and A. Shank. Albany, NY: State University of New York Press.

Robinson, I. 1990. "Organizing Labour: Explaining the Canada–U.S. Union Density Divergence in the Post-War Period." PH D dissertation, Yale University.

– 1993. "The NAFTA, the Side-Deals, and Canadian Federalism: Constitutional Reform by Other Means?" In *Canada: The State of the Federation 1993,* ed. R.L. Watts and D.M. Brown. Kingston: Institute of Intergovernmental Relations, Queen's University.

Rohde, D. 1991. *Parties and Leaders in the Post-Reform Congress.* Chicago: University of Chicago Press.

Roof, W.C. 1982. "America's Voluntary Establishment: Mainline Religion in Transition." *Daedalus* 111:165–84.

Rose, R. 1993. *Lesson-Drawing in Public Policy: A Guide to Learning across Time and Space.* Chatham, NJ: Chatham House.

Rosen, C., and K. Young, eds. 1991. *Understanding Employee Ownership.* Ithaca: Cornell University Press.

Rosenbaum, W. 1985. *Environmental Politics and Policy.* Washington, DC: CQ Press.

Rosenberg, D. 1986. "Litigating Civil Rights and Liberties in the United States: A Vital but Flawed Enterprise." In *Litigating the Values of a Nation: The Canadian Charter of Rights and Freedoms,* ed. J.M. Weiler and R.M. Elliot. Toronto: Carswell.

Rossum, R.A., and G.A. Tarr. 1987. *American Constitutional Law: Cases and Interpretation.* 2d ed. New York: St Martin's Press.

Rotstein, A., and G. Lax, eds. 1974. *Getting It Back: A Program for Canadian Independence.* Toronto: Clarke, Irwin and Co.

Ruggie, J. 1982. "International Regimes, Transactions and Change: Embedded Liberalism in the Postwar Order." *International Organization* 36:379–415.

– 1994. "Trade Protectionism and the Future of Welfare Capitalism." *Journal of International Affairs* 48:1–11.

Rugman, A. 1990. *Multinationals and Canada–United States Free Trade.* Columbia: University of South Carolina Press.

Rugman, A., and J.R. De Cruz. 1992. *New Compacts for Canadian Competitiveness.* Toronto: Kodak Canada.

Russell, P. 1987. *The Judiciary in Canada: The Third Branch of Government.* Toronto: McGraw-Hill Ryerson.

– 1993. *Constitutional Odyssey: Can Canadians Become a Sovereign People?* 2d ed. Toronto: University of Toronto Press.

– 1994. "The Three Dimensions of Charter Politics." In *Canadian Politics: An Introduction to the Discipline,* ed. A.-G. Gagnon and J. Bickerton. Peterborough, Ont.: Broadview Press.

Russett, B. 1982. "Defense Expenditures and National Well-Being." *American Political Science Review* 76:767–77.

Rutledge, G., and N. Stergioulas. 1988. "Plant and Equipment Expenditures by Business for Pollution Abatement, 1987 and Planned 1988." *Survey of Current Business*, November, 26–9.

Sabato, L. 1988. *The Party's Just Begun: Shaping Political Parties for America's Future*. Glenview, Ill.: Scott Foresman.

Salamon, L.M. 1991. "Overview: Why Human Capital? Why Now?" In *Human Capital and America's Future*, ed. D.W. Hornbeck and L.M. Salamon. Baltimore, Md: Johns Hopkins University Press.

Salisbury, R.H. 1990. "The Paradox of Interest Groups in Washington: More Groups, Less Clout." In *The New American Political System*, 2d ed., ed. A. King. Washington, DC: American Enterprise Institute.

Sanger, D. 1996. "World Trade Group Orders U.S. to Alter Clean Air Act." *New York Times*, 18 January.

Sargent, T.C. 1995. *An Index of Unemployment Insurance Disincentives*. Working Paper no. 95-10. Ottawa: Department of Finance.

Scanzoni, J. 1989. "Alternative Images for Public Policy: Family Structure versus Families Struggling." *Policy Studies Review* 8:599–609.

Schaefer, R.T. 1986. "Racial Prejudice in a Capitalist State." *Phylon* 47:192–8.

Schattschneider, E.E. 1942. *Party Government*. New York: Holt Rinehart.

Schepple, K.L., and J.L. Walker. 1991. "The Litigation Strategies of Interest Groups." In *Mobilizing Interest Groups in America: Patrons, Professions and Social Movements*, ed. J.L. Walker, Jr. Ann Arbor, Mich.: University of Michigan.

Schick, A. 1993. "Governments versus Budget Deficits." In *Do Institutions Matter?* ed. R.K. Weaver and B. Rockman. Washington, DC: The Brookings Institution.

Schlesinger, A.M., Jr. 1986. *The Cycles of American History*. Boston: Houghton Mifflin.

– 1992. *The Disuniting of America: Reflections on a Multicultural Society*. New York: W.W. Norton.

Schlozman, K.L., and J.T. Tierney. 1986. *Organized Interests and American Democracy*. New York: Harper and Row.

Schneider, A., and H. Ingram. 1993. "Social Constructions of Target Populations: Implications for Politics and Policy." *American Political Science Review* 87:334–47.

Schrecker, T. 1984. *The Political Economy of Environmental Hazards*. Ottawa: Law Reform Commission.

– 1991. "The Canadian Environmental Assessment Act: Tremulous Step Forward or Retreat into Smoke and Mirrors?" *Canadian Environmental Law Reports* 5:192–246.

Schultz, R., and A. Alexandroff. 1985. *Economic Regulation and the Federal System*. Toronto: University of Toronto Press.

Schwartz, H., ed. 1987. *The Burger Years: Rights and Wrongs in the Supreme Court, 1969–1986.* New York: Viking.

Sears, D., and J. Citrin. 1982. *Tax Revolt: Something for Nothing in California.* Cambridge, Mass.: Harvard University Press.

Seidle, F.L., ed. 1991. *Comparative Issues in Party and Election Finance.* Toronto: Dundurn Press.

Selier, T.P. 1993. "Melting Pot and Mosaic: Images and Realities." In *Canada and the United States: Differences that Count,* ed. D. Thomas. Peterborough, Ont.: Broadview Press.

Shalev, M. 1983. "The Social Democratic Model and Beyond: Two 'Generations' of Comparative Research on the Welfare State." *Comparative Social Research* 6:315–51.

Shapiro, M. 1990. "The Supreme Court from Earl Burger to Early Rehnquist." In *The New American Political System,* 2d ed., ed. A. King. Washington, DC: American Enterprise Institute.

Shapiro, M., and A. Stone. 1994. "The New Constitutional Politics of Europe." *Comparative Political Studies* 26:393–420.

Shoven, J.B., and J. Whalley, eds. 1992. *Canada–U.S. Tax Comparisons.* Chicago: Chicago University Press.

Shrybman, S. 1993. "Trading Away the Environment." In *The Political Economy of North American Free Trade,* ed. R. Grinspun and M. Cameron. Montreal: McGill-Queen's University Press.

Sierra Legal Defence Fund. 1994. *The National Sewage Report Card.* Vancouver: Sierra Legal Defence Fund.

Sigurdson, R. 1994. "Preston Manning and the Politics of Postmodernism in Canada." *Canadian Journal of Political Science* 27:249–76.

Simard, C., et al. 1991. "Visible Minorities and the Canadian Political System." In *Ethno-Cultural Groups and Visible Minorities in Canadian Politics: The Question of Access,* ed. K. Megyery. Toronto: Dundurn Press.

Simeon, R. 1972. *Federal-Provincial Diplomacy: The Masking of Recent Policy in Canada.* Toronto: University of Toronto Press.

– 1994. *In Search of a Social Contract: Can We Make Hard Decisions as if Democracy Matters?* Toronto: C.D. Howe Institute.

– 1995. "Federalism in Canada and the United States." In *Rethinking Federalism: Citizens, Politics and Markets,* ed. K. Knop, S. Ostry, R. Simeon, and K. Swinton. Vancouver: UBC Press.

Simeon, R., and I. Robinson. 1990. *State, Society and the Development of Canadian Federalism.* Toronto: University of Toronto Press.

Sinclair, W.F. 1990. *Controlling Pollution from Canadian Pulp and Paper Manufacturers: A Canadian Perspective.* Ottawa: Minister of Supply and Services Canada.

Skocpol, T. 1979. *States and Social Revolutions.* Cambridge: Cambridge University Press.

– 1991. "Targeting within Universalism: Politically Viable Policies to Combat Poverty in the United States." In *The Urban Underclass*, ed. C. Jencks and P. Peterson. Washington, DC: The Brookings Institution.

Slessarev, H. 1988. "Racial Tensions and Institutional Support: Social Programs during a Period of Retrenchment." In *The Politics of Social Policy in the United States*, ed. M. Weir, A.S. Orloff, and T. Skocpol. Princeton, NJ: Princeton University Press.

Smardon, B. 1991. "The Federal Welfare State and the Politics of Retrenchment in Canada." *Journal of Canadian Studies* 26:123–41.

Smeeding, T.M. 1991. "Cross-National Perspectives on Trends in Child Poverty and the Effectiveness of Government Policies in Preventing Poverty among Families with Children in the 1980s: The First Evidence from LIS." Unpublished manuscript.

Smiley, D.V. 1970. *Constitutional Adaptation and Canadian Federalism since 1945*. Ottawa: Queen's Printer.

– 1987. *The Federal Condition in Canada*. Toronto: McGraw-Hill Ryerson.

Smiley, D.V., and R.L. Watts. 1986. *Intrastate Federalism in Canada*. Toronto: University of Toronto Press.

Smith, A. 1994. *Canada: An American Nation? Essays on Continentalism, Identity, and the Canadian Frame of Mind*. Montreal: McGill-Queen's University Press.

Smith, D. 1990. "The Implementation of Canadian Policies to Protect the Ozone Layer." In *Getting It Green: Case Studies in Canadian Environmental Regulation*, ed. G.B. Doern. Toronto: C.D. Howe Institute.

Smith, M.G. 1990. "Overview of Provincial and State Subsidies: Their Implications for Canada–U.S. Trade." *International Economic Issues*, April. Halifax: Institute for Research on Public Policy.

Smith, T. 1987. "That Which We Call Welfare by Any Other Name Would Smell Sweeter: An Analysis of the Impact of Question Wording on Response Patterns." *Public Opinion Quarterly* 51:75–83.

Smithey, S.I. 1995. "Judicialization and Its Effects on Federal and Regional Tensions in Canada." Paper presented to the annual meeting of the Canadian Political Science Association.

Sniderman, P.M., J.F. Fletcher, P.H. Russell, and P.E. Tetlock. 1988. "Liberty, Authority, and Community: Civil Liberties and the Canadian Political Culture." Paper presented to the annual meeting of the Canadian Political Science Association.

Sorrentino, C.C. 1990. "The Changing Family in International Perspective." *Monthly Labour Review*, March, 41–58.

Southam News/Angus Reid. 1996. "Change Tears at Canadian Fabric." *Medicine Hat News*, 29 June.

Spitz, S.L. 1986. "Litigation Strategy in Equality Rights: The American Experience." In *Litigating the Values of a Nation: The Canadian Charter of Rights and Freedoms*, ed. J.M. Weiler and R.M. Elliot. Toronto: Carswell.

Stairs, D. 1988. "The Impact on Public Policy: A Leap of Faith." In *Trade-Offs on Free Trade: The Canada–U.S. Free Trade Agreement*, ed. M. Gold and D. Leyton-Brown. Toronto: Carswell.

Stanbury, W.T. 1986. *Business-Government Relations in Canada: Grappling with Leviathan*. Toronto: Methuen.

Stasiulis, D. 1990. "Theorizing Connections: Gender, Race, Ethnicity and Class." In *Race and Ethnic Relations in Canada*, ed. P.S. Li. Toronto: Oxford University Press.

Stasiulis, D., and Y. Abu-Laban. 1990. "Ethnic Minorities and the Politics of Limited Inclusion in Canada." In *Canadian Politics: An Introduction to the Discipline*, ed. A.-G. Gagnon and J. Bickerton. Peterborough, Ont.: Broadview Press.

– 1991. "The House that Parties Built: (Re)constructing Ethnic Representation in Canadian Politics." In *Ethno-Cultural Groups and Visible Minorities in Canadian Politics*, ed. K. Megyery. Toronto: Dundurn Press.

Statistics Canada. 1989. *Analysis of the Categories of Capital Investment, 1985 to 1987*. Discussion Paper. November.

– 1993. *Income Distributions by Size in Canada: 1992*. Cat. no. 13-207. Ottawa: Minister of Supply and Services Canada.

– 1994a. *Canadian Economic Observer: Historical Statistical Supplement, 1993/94*. Ottawa: Minister of Supply and Services Canada.

– 1994b. *Unemployment Insurance Statistics* 53, no. 7 (July). Ottawa: Minister of Supply and Services Canada.

– 1994c. *Human Activity and the Environment 1994*. Ottawa: Minister of Supply and Services Canada.

– 1994d. *Income after Tax: Distributions by Size in Canada*. Ottawa: Minister of Supply and Services Canada.

– 1995. *Income Distributions by Size in Canada. 1994*. Ottawa: Minister of Industry.

Steinbruner, J. 1974. *The Cybernetic Theory of Decision-Making*. Princeton, NJ: Princeton University Press.

Steinmo, S. 1989. "Political Institutions and Tax Policy in the United States, Sweden, and Britain." *World Politics* 41:500–35.

Stern, R., P. Tresize, and J. Whalley, eds. 1988. *Perspectives on a U.S.–Canada Free Trade Agreement*. Ottawa and Washington, DC: Institute for Research in Public Policy/The Brookings Institution.

Stewart, R. 1975. "The Reformation of American Administrative Law." *Harvard Law Review* 88:1667–813.

Stone, A. 1992. *The Birth of Judicial Politics in France*. Princeton, NJ: Princeton University Press.

Stone, D., and F.K. Walpole. 1983. "The Canadian Constitution Act and the Constitution of the United States: A Comparative Analysis." *Canadian-American Law Journal* 2:1–36.

Stone, K.V.W. 1988. "Labor and the Corporate Structure: Changing Conceptions and Emerging Possibilities." *University of Chicago Law Review* 55:73–173.

Strange, S. 1988. *States and Markets.* London: Pinter.

Stubbs, R., and G. Underhill, eds. 1994. *Political Economy and the Changing Global Order.* Toronto: McClelland & Stewart.

Sullivan, T.A. 1992. "The Changing Demographic Characteristics and Impact of Immigrants in Canada." In *Immigration, Language and Ethnicity: Canada and the United States*, ed. B. Chiswick. Washington, DC: American Enterprise Institute.

Sundquist, J.L. 1986. *Constitutional Reform and Effective Government.* 1st ed. Washington, DC: The Brookings Institution.

– 1992. *Constitutional Reform and Effective Government.* 2d ed. Washington, DC: The Brookings Institution.

Swenarchuk, M. 1993. "Environment." In *Canada under Free Trade*, ed. D. Cameron and M. Watkins. Toronto: James Lorimer.

Tanguay, A.B., and B.J. Kay. 1991. "Political Activity of Local Interest Groups." In *Interest Groups and Elections in Canada*, ed. F.L. Seidle. Toronto: Dundurn Press.

Tarnopolsky, W.S. 1983. "The New Canadian Charter of Rights and Freedoms as Compared and Contrasted with the American Bill of Rights." *Human Rights Quarterly* 5:227–74.

Taylor, C. 1991. "Shared and Divergent Values." In *Options for a New Canada*, ed. R.L. Watts and D.M. Brown. Toronto: University of Toronto Press.

Taylor, D.W. 1991. *Business and Government Relations: Partners in the 1990s.* Toronto: Gage.

Teghtsoonian, K. 1993. "Neo-Conservative Ideology and Opposition to Federal Regulation of Child Care Services in the United States and Canada." *Canadian Journal of Political Science* 26:97–121.

Teixeira, R.A. 1992. *The Disappearing American Voter.* Washington, DC: The Brookings Institution.

Terkel, S. 1992. *Race: How Blacks and Whites Think and Feel about the American Obsession.* New York: The New Press.

Theodore L. 1992. "The Party Crasher." *New York Times Magazine*, 23 August, 28–33.

Thirsk, W. 1993. "Fiscal Sovereignty and Tax Competition." Government and Competitiveness Project Discussion Paper 93–08. Kingston: School of Policy Studies, Queen's University.

Thomas, D. 1993. *Canada and the United States: Differences that Count.* Peterborough, Ont.: Broadview Press.

Thomas, G. 1989. "Discerning the Posture of American Race Relations in the 1980s: Competitive vs. Paternalistic?" *Sociological Spectrum* 9:1–21.

Thompson, A. 1980. *Environmental Regulation in Canada: An Assessment of Regulatory Regimes.* Study prepared for the Economic Council of Canada by the Westwater Research Centre. Vancouver: University of British Columbia.

Thompson Educational Publishing. 1994. *Canadian Social Trends*. Vol. 2. Toronto: Thompson Publishing.

Thurber, J., and S. Durst. 1993. "The 1990 Budget Enforcement Act: The Decline of Congressional Accountability." In *Congress Reconsidered*, 5th ed., ed. L. Dodd and B. Oppenheimer. Washington, DC: CQ Press.

Thurow, L. 1992. *Head to Head: The Coming Economic Battle among Japan, Europe and America*. New York: Morrow.

Tilly, C., B. Bluestone, and B. Harrison. 1987. "What Is Making American Wages More Unequal?" In *Proceedings of the 39th Annual Meeting*, Industrial Relations Research Association Series. Madison, Wis.: University of Wisconsin.

Trebilcock, M.J., and R. Howse. 1994. *The Regulation of International Trade*. London: Routledge.

– 1995. "Reforming the Canadian Standards System." Paper prepared for the Canadian Standards Association.

Trebilcock, M.J., M. Chandler, and R. Howse. 1990. *Trade and Transitions: A Comparative Analysis of Adjustment Policies*. New York: Routledge.

Tsebelis, G. 1990. *Nested Games: Rational Choice in Comparative Politics*. Berkeley: University of California Press.

Tsiganou, O.H. 1991. *Workers' Participative Schemes: The Experience of Capitalist and Plan-Based Societies*. New York: Greenwood Press.

Tuohy, C. 1988. "Medicine and the State in Canada: The Extra-Billing Issue in Perspective." *Canadian Journal of Political Science* 21:267–96.

– 1989. "Federalism and Canadian Health Policy." In *Challenges to Federalism: Policy-Making in Canada and the Federal Republic of Germany*, ed. W. Chandler and C. Zöllner. Kingston: Institute of Intergovernmental Relations, Queen's University.

– 1994. "Health Policy and Fiscal Federalism." In *The Future of Fiscal Federalism*, ed. K.G. Banting, D.M. Brown, and T.J. Courchene. Kingston: School of Policy Studies, Queen's University.

Tupper, A. 1982. *Public Money in the Private Sector: Industrial Assistance Policy and Canadian Federalism*. Kingston: Institute for Intergovernmental Relations, Queen's University.

– 1986. "Federalism and the Politics of Industrial Policy." In *Industrial Policy*, ed. A. Blais. Toronto: University of Toronto Press.

Turcotte, P. 1990. "Common Law Unions." In *Canadian Social Trends*, ed. C. McKie and K. Thompson. Toronto: Thompson Publishing.

Tyson, L. 1993. *Who's Bashing Whom: Trade Conflict in High-Technology Industries*. Washington, DC: Institute for International Economics.

United Nations Centre on Transnational Corporations. 1988. *Transnational Corporations in World Development: Trends and Prospects*. New York: United Nations.

– 1995. *World Investment Report 1995: Transnational Corporations and Competitiveness*. New York and Geneva: United Nations.

United States. Bipartisan Commission on Comprehensive Health Care (Pepper Commission). 1990. *A Call to Action: Final Report.* Washington, DC: Government Printing Office.

– Bipartisan Commission on Entitlements and Tax Reform. 1994. *Interim Report to the President.* Washington, DC: Superintendent of Documents.

– Bipartisan Commission on Entitlements and Tax Reform. 1995. *Final Report to the President.* Washington, DC: Superintendent of Documents.

– Bureau of the Census. 1992. "Money Income of Households, Families and Persons in the United States, 1991." *Current Population Reports,* series P-60, no. 180. Washington, DC: Government Printing Office.

– Bureau of the Census. 1994. *Statistical Abstract of the United States: 1994.* Washington, DC: Government Printing Office.

– Bureau of the Census. 1996. *The Official Statistics.* HTTP://www.census.gov/.

– Committee on Ways and Means. 1990. *Overview of Entitlement Programs: 1990 Green Book.* Washington, DC: Government Printing Office.

– Committee on Ways and Means. 1991. *Overview of Entitlement Programs: 1991 Green Book.* Washington, DC: Government Printing Office.

– Committee on Ways and Means. 1993. *Overview of Entitlement Programs: 1993 Green Book.* Washington, DC: Government Printing Office.

– Committee on Ways and Means. 1994. *Overview of Entitlement Programs: 1994 Green Book.* Washington, DC: Government Printing Office.

– Council of Environmental Quality. 1992. *Environmental Quality, 1992.* Washington, DC: Government Printing Office.

– Department of Commerce. 1991. "Trends in Relative Income: 1964 to 1989." *Current Population Reports.* Washington, DC: Government Printing Office.

– Department of Health and Human Services. 1994. *Social Security Bulletin: Annual Statistical Supplement, 1994.* Washington, DC: Government Printing Office.

– Department of Labour. 1996. Bureau of Labour Statistics. *Employment and Earnings.* Washington, DC: Government Printing Office.

– Environmental Protection Agency. 1993a. "Proposed EPA Water Quality Guidance for Great Lakes System." 58 *Federal Register* 20801, 16 April.

– Environmental Protection Agency. 1993b. *National Air Pollutant Emission Estimates, 1980–1992.* October.

– General Accounting Office. 1991. *Canadian Health Insurance: Lessons for the United States.* Washington, DC: U.S. General Accounting Office.

– General Accounting Office. 1995a. *Medicaid: Spending Pressures Drive States Towards Program Prevention.* Washington, DC: Government Printing Office.

– General Accounting Office. 1995b. *Supplementary Security Income: Growth and Changes in Recipient Population Call for Reexamining Program.* Washington, DC: Government Printing Office.

– General Accounting Office. 1995c. *Earned Income Credit: Targeting to the Working Poor.* Washington, DC: Government Printing Office.

– National Performance Review. 1993. *From Red Tape to Results: Creating a Government that Works Better and Costs Less.* Washington, DC: Government Printing Office. Also published as *The Gore Report on Reinventing Government.* New York: Random House, Times Books.

– Office of Management and Budget. 1995. *Historical Tables, Budget of the U.S. Government-Fiscal Year 1995.* Washington, DC: Government Printing Office.

– Office of Pesticide Programs. 1994. *Reinventing the Tolerance System: A Proposal under Consideration for Better Protecting the Safety of the Food Supply.* Washington, DC: Environmental Protection Agency.

– Office of the President. 1993. *Technology for America's Economic Growth: A New Direction to Build Economic Strength.* Washington, DC: Government Printing Office.

– Office of Technology Assessment. 1992a. NAFTA *Study.* Washington, DC: Government Printing Office.

– Office of Technology Assessment. 1992b. *Trade and Environment: Conflicts and Opportunities.* Washington, DC: Government Printing Office.

– Office of Technology Assessment. 1994. *Industry, Technology, and the Environment: Competitive Challenges and Business Opportunities.* Washington, DC: Government Printing Office.

Vaillancourt, F. 1992. "An Economic Perspective on Language and Public Policy in Canada and the United States." In *Immigration, Language and Ethnicity: Canada and the United States,* ed. B. Chiswick. Washington, DC: American Enterprise Institute.

Vallinder, T. 1994. "The Judicialization of Politics – A World-wide Phenomenon: Introduction." *International Political Science Review* 15:91–99.

Valverde, M. 1992. "Racism and Anti-Racism in Feminist Teaching and Research." In *Challenging Times: The Women's Movement in Canada and the United States,* ed. C. Backhouse and D. Flaherty. Montreal: McGill-Queen's University Press.

Vanier Institute of the Family. 1994. *Profiling Canada's Families.* Ottawa: Vanier Institute of the Family.

Varat, J. 1990. "Economic Integration and Interregional Migration in the United States Federal System." In *Comparative Constitutional Federalism: Europe and America,* ed. M. Tushnet. New York: Greenwood Publishers.

Vickers, G. 1965. *The Art of Judgment.* London: Chapman and Hall.

Vickers, J. 1992. "The Intellectual Origin of the Women's Movement in Canada." In *Challenging Times: The Women's Movement in Canada and the United States,* ed. C. Backhouse and D. Flaherty. Montreal: McGill-Queen's University Press.

Vogel, D. 1989. *Fluctuating Fortunes: The Political Power of Business in America.* New York: Basic Books.

– 1994. *The GATT: Non-Tariff Barriers and Environmental Regulation.* Paper for the annual meeting of the American Political Science Association, New York.

Vose, C. 1958. "Litigation as a Form of Pressure Group Activity." *Annals of the American Academy of Political and Social Science* 319:20–31.

Wald, M. 1994. "Tougher Car Emission Rules Requested by Eastern States." *New York Times*, 2 February.

Walker, D. 1985. "The Contemporary Condition of American Pluralism: A Comparative and Chronological Assessment." Washington, DC: Advisory Commission on Intergovernmental Relations. Mimeo.

Walters, R., and D. Blake. 1992. *The Politics of Global Economic Relations.* Englewood Cliffs, NJ: Prentice-Hall.

Waltman, J., and D. Studlar, eds. 1987. *Political Economy: Public Policies in the United States and Britain.* Jackson, Miss.: University Press of Mississippi Press.

Warnock, J.W. 1988. *Free Trade and the New Right Agenda.* Vancouver: New Star Books.

Wasby, S.L. 1985. "Civil Rights Litigation by Organizations: Constraints and Choices." *Judicature* 68:337–52.

Wattenberg, M. 1990. "From a Partisan to a Candidate-Centered Electorate." In *The New American Political System*, 2d ed, ed. A. King. Washington, DC: American Enterprise Institute.

– 1991a. *The Rise of Candidate-Centered Politics: Presidential Elections of the 1980s.* Cambridge, Mass.: Harvard University Press.

– 1991b. "The Republican Presidential Advantage in the Age of Party Disunity." In *The Politics of Divided Government*, ed. G.W. Cox and S. Kernell. Boulder: Westview Press.

Watts, R. 1989. "Centralization, Decentralization and Noncentralization in Canada and the United States." Paper presented to Conference on Comparative Federalism, Dartmouth College.

Weaver, R.K. 1985. *The Politics of Industrial Change: Railway Policy in North America.* Washington, DC: The Brookings Institution.

– 1990. "The State and Welfare State in the United States and Canada." Paper for Conference on the New Institutionalism, Boulder, Colo.

– ed. 1992. *The Collapse of Canada?* Washington, DC: The Brookings Institution.

– 1994. "Federalism and Activist Government." Paper presented at the annual meeting of the American Political Science Association, New York.

– 1995. "Policy-making for Low-Income Families in the Clinton/Gingrich Era." Paper presented to the 1995 annual research conference of the Association for Policy Analysis and Management, Washington, DC.

Weaver, R.K., and B.A. Rockman. 1993. "Assessing the Effects of Institutions." In *Do Institutions Matter? Government Capabilities in the United States and Abroad*, ed. R.K. Weaver and B.A. Rockman. Washington, DC: The Brookings Institution.

Weiler, P. 1990. *Governing the Workplace: The Future of Labor and Employment Law.* Cambridge, Mass.: Harvard University Press.

Wein, F. 1991. *The Role of Social Policy in Economic Restructuring.* Halifax: Institute for Research in Public Policy.

Weinrib, L.E. 1988. "The Supreme Court of Canada and Section One of the Charter." *Supreme Court Law Review* 10:469–513.

Weir, M., A. Orloff, and T. Skocpol, eds. 1988. *The Politics of Social Policy in the United States.* Princeton, NJ: Princeton University Press.

Weisband, E., ed. 1989. *Poverty amidst Plenty: World Political Economy and Distributive Justice.* Boulder: Westview Press.

Welch, J. 1985. "No Room at the Top: Interest Group Intervenors and Charter Litigation in the Supreme Court of Canada." *University of Toronto Faculty of Law Review* 43:204–31.

Whalley, J., and I. Trela. 1986. *Regional Aspects of Confederation.* Toronto: University of Toronto Press.

Wharton, A.S. 1989. "Gender Segregation in Private Sector, Public Sector and Self-Employment Occupations." *Social Science Quarterly* 70:923–40.

White, P.M. 1990. "Ethnic Origins of the Canadian Population." In *Canadian Social Trends*, ed. C. McKie and K. Thompson. Toronto: Thompson Publishing.

Wildavsky, A. 1990. "A World of Difference: The Public Philosophies and Political Behaviour of Rival American Cultures." In *The New American Political System*, 2d ed., ed. A. King. Washington, DC: American Enterprise Institute.

Wilensky, H. 1975. *The Welfare State and Equality: Structural and Ideological Roots of Public Expenditures.* Berkeley: University of California Press.

Wills, G. 1990. *Under God: Religion and American Politics.* New York: Touchstone/Simon & Schuster.

Wilson, J. 1992. "Green Lobbies: Pressure Groups and Environmental Policy." In *Canadian Environmental Policy*, ed. R. Boardman. Toronto: Oxford University Press.

Wilson, J.Q., ed. 1980. *The Politics of Regulation.* New York: Basic Books.

Wilson, W.J. 1980. *The Declining Significance of Race: Blacks and Changing American Institutions.* Chicago: University of Chicago Press.

– 1987. *The Truly Disadvantaged: The Inner City, the Underclass and Public Policy.* Chicago: University of Chicago Press.

– 1991. "Public Policy Research and the Truly Disadvantaged." In *The Urban Underclass*, ed. C. Jencks and P.E. Peterson. Washington, DC: The Brookings Institution.

Wise, L.R. 1989. *Labor Market Policies and Employment Patterns in the United States.* Boulder: Westview Press.

Wolfe, C. 1981. "A Theory of U.S. Constitutional History." *Journal of Politics* 43:292–316.

Wolfe, D. 1995. "The Role of Cooperative Industrial Policy." Unpublished manuscript.

Wonnacott, R. 1993. *Hemispheric Trade Liberalization: Is the NAFTA on the Right Track?* C.D. Howe Institute Commentary no. 49, The NAFTA Papers. Toronto: C.D. Howe Institute.

Wonnacott, R.J., and R. Hill. 1987. *Canadian and U.S. Adjustment Policies in a Bilateral Trade Agreement.* Toronto and Washington: C.D. Howe Institute/National Planning Association.

Wood, R.C., ed. 1990. *Remedial Law: When Courts Become Administrators.* Amherst, Mass.: University of Massachusetts Press.

Woodrow, R.B. 1974. "Resources and Environmental Policy-Making at the National Level: The Search for Focus." In *Resources and the Environment: Policy Perspectives for Canada,* ed. O.P. Dwivedi. Toronto: McClelland & Stewart.

World Commission on Environment and Development. 1987. *Our Common Future.* Oxford: Oxford University Press.

World Trade Organization. 1995a. *International Trade: Trends and Statistics.* Geneva: WTO.

– 1995b. *Regionalism and the World Trading System.* Geneva: WTO.

Wyckoff, A. 1993. "The International Expansion of Productive Networks." *OECD Observer* 180:8–11.

Yankelovich, D. 1991. "A Missing Concept." *Kettering Review,* Fall, 54–66.

Yarborough, T.E. 1985. "The Political World of Federal Judges as Managers." *Public Administration Review* 45:660–6.

Yates, C. 1995. "Job Ready, I Ready: Job Creation and Labour Market Reform in Canada." In *How Ottawa Spends, 1995–96: Mid-Life Crises,* ed. S. Phillips. Ottawa: Carleton University Press.

Zaehlke, D., P. Orbuch, and R. Houseman, eds. 1993. *Trade and the Environment.* Washington, DC: Island Press.

Zolberg, A.R. 1992. "Response to Crisis: Refugee Policy in the United States and Canada." In *Immigration, Language and Ethnicity: Canada and the United States,* ed. B. Chiswick. Washington, DC: American Enterprise Institute.

Zysman, J. 1988. *Dynamics of Trade and Employment.* Cambridge, Mass.: Ballinger.

Zysman, J., and L. Tyson. 1983. *American Industry in International Competition: Government Policies and Corporate Strategies.* Ithaca: Cornell University Press.

Contributors

KEITH BANTING is Stauffer-Dunning Professor of Policy Studies and director of the School of Policy Studies at Queen's University.

PAUL BOOTHE is a professor in the Department of Economics at the University of Alberta.

MARSHA CHANDLER is Dean of Arts and Science at the University of Toronto.

GEORGE HOBERG is an associate professor in the Department of Political Science at the University of British Columbia.

ROBERT HOWSE is an associate professor in the Faculty of Law at the University of Toronto.

CHRISTOPHER MANFREDI is director of Graduate Studies and an associate professor in the Department of Political Science at McGill University.

GEORGE PERLIN is a professor in the Department of Political Studies at Queen's University.

DOUGLAS PURVIS was, before his untimely death, head of the Department of Economics at Queen's University.

RICHARD SIMEON is a professor in the Department of Political Science and the Faculty of Law at the University of Toronto.

ELAINE WILLIS is a consultant in Kingston, Ontario.

Index